West Germany under Construction

Social History, Popular Culture, and Politics in Germany
Geoff Eley, Series Editor

A History of Foreign Labor in Germany, 1880–1980: Seasonal Workers/Forced Laborers/Guest Workers
Ulrich Herbert, translated by William Templer

Reshaping the German Right: Radical Nationalism and Political Change after Bismarck
Geoff Eley

The Stigma of Names: Antisemitism in German Daily Life, 1812–1933
Dietz Bering

Forbidden Laughter: Popular Humor and the Limits of Repression in Nineteenth-Century Prussia
Mary Lee Townsend

From Bundesrepublik *to* Deutschland: *German Politics after Unification*
Michael G. Huelshoff, Andrei S. Markovits, and Simon Reich, editors

The People Speak! Anti-Semitism and Emancipation in Nineteenth-Century Bavaria
James F. Harris

The Origins of the Authoritarian Welfare State in Prussia: Conservatives, Bureaucracy, and the Social Question, 1815–70
Hermann Beck

Technological Democracy: Bureaucracy and Citizenry in the German Energy Debate
Carol J. Hager

Society, Culture, and the State in Germany, 1870–1930
Geoff Eley, editor

Paradoxes of Peace: German Peace Movements since 1945
Alice Holmes Cooper

Jews, Germans, Memory: Reconstruction of Jewish Life in Germany
Y. Michal Bodemann, editor

Exclusive Revolutionaries: Liberal Politics, Social Experience, and National Identity in the Austrian Empire, 1848–1914
Pieter M. Judson

Feminine Frequencies: Gender, German Radio, and the Public Sphere, 1923–1945
Kate Lacey

How German Is She? Postwar West German Reconstruction and the Consuming Woman
Erica Carter

West Germany under Construction: Politics, Society, and Culture in Germany in the Adenauer Era
Robert G. Moeller, editor

West Germany under Construction

Politics, Society, and Culture in the Adenauer Era

Robert G. Moeller, Editor

Ann Arbor

THE UNIVERSITY OF MICHIGAN PRESS

Copyright © by the University of Michigan 1997
All rights reserved
Published in the United States of America by
The University of Michigan Press
Manufactured in the United States of America
♾ Printed on acid-free paper

2000   1999   1998   1997   4 3 2 1

A CIP catalog record for this book is available from the British Library.

Library of Congress Cataloging-in-Publication Data

West Germany under construction: politics, society, and culture in
   the Adenauer era / Robert G. Moeller, editor.
      p.   cm. — (Social history, popular culture, and politics in
Germany)
   Includes bibliographical references and index.
   ISBN 0-472-09648-6 (alk. paper). — ISBN 0-472-06648-X (pbk. :
alk. paper)
   1. Reconstruction (1939–1951)—Germany.   2. Military government—
Germany.   3. Jews—Germany.   4. Denazification.   5. Germany—
Economic conditions—1945–1990.   I. Moeller, Robert G.
II. Series
DD259.2.W475   1997   96-38008
                                                         CIP

Contents

Acknowledgments

I wish to thank the Center for German and European Studies at the University of California, Berkeley, which provided a publication subsidy for this book. I would also like to express my gratitude to Geoff Eley, who supported the project from the start, and to Susan Whitlock of the University of Michigan Press, whose enthusiasm for the project was enormously important.

My commitment to compiling and editing this book came from my own frustrating experiences in attempting to find high-quality English-language readings for seminars and lecture courses on the history of Germany after 1945. This reader is intended to take students beyond survey texts; it serves as an introduction to the growing body of scholarly work on the history of the Federal Republic of Germany.

The introduction appears here for the first time. Citation and style form of republished articles conforms with that used in the original place of publication. Original publication information is as follows:

Atina Grossmann, "A Question of Silence: The Rape of German Women by Occupation Soldiers," *October* no. 72 (1995): 43–63. Copyright © 1995 by October Magazine, Ltd. and Massachusetts Institute of Technology. It is reprinted with permission of the publisher.

Rainer Schulze, "Growing Discontent: Relations between Native and Refugee Populations in a Rural District in Western Germany after the Second World War," *German History* 7 (1989): 332–49. It is reprinted with permission of Oxford University Press.

Josef Foschepoth, "German Reaction to Defeat and Occupation," first appeared as "Zur deutschen Reaktion auf Niederlage und Besatzung," in *Westdeutschland 1945–1955: Unterwerfung, Kontrolle, Integration,* ed. Ludolf Herbst (Munich: R. Oldenbourg, 1986), 151–65. It is reprinted with permission of the publisher.

James M. Diehl, "Change and Continuity in the Treatment of German *Kriegsopfer,*" *Central European History* 18 (1985): 170–87. It is reprinted with permission of the author.

Robert G. Moeller, "Reconstructing the Family in Reconstruction Germany: Women and Social Policy in the Federal Republic, 1949–1955," *Feminist Studies* 15 (1989): 137–69. It is reprinted with permission of the publisher, Feminist Studies, Inc., c/o Women's Studies Program, University of Maryland, College Park, MD 20742.

Curt Garner, "Public Service Personnel in West Germany in the 1950s: Controversial Policy Decisions and Their Effects on Social Composition, Gender Structure, and the Role of Former Nazis," *Journal of Social History* 29 (1995): 25–80. It is reprinted with permission of the editor.

Frank Stern, "The Historic Triangle: Occupiers, Germans and Jews in Postwar Germany," *Tel Aviver Jahrbuch für deutsche Geschichte* 19 (1990): 47–76. It is reprinted with permission of the editor.

Constantin Goschler, "The Attitude towards Jews in Bavaria after the Second World War," *Leo Baeck Institute Yearbook* 36 (1991): 443–58. It is reprinted with permission of the editor.

Robert G. Moeller, "The Homosexual Man Is a 'Man,' the Homosexual Woman Is a 'Woman': Sex, Society, and the Law in Postwar West Germany," *Journal of the History of Sexuality* 4 (1994): 395–429. Copyright © 1994 by The University of Chicago Press. It is reprinted with permission of the publisher.

Mark Roseman, "The Organic Society and the 'Massenmenschen': Integration of Young Labour in the Ruhr Mines, 1945–58," *German History* 8 (1990): 163–94. It is reprinted with permission of Oxford University Press.

Heide Fehrenbach, "The Fight for the 'Christian West': German Film Control, the Churches, and the Reconstruction of Civil Society in the Early Bonn Republic," *German Studies Review* 14 (1991): 39–63. It is reprinted with permission of the editor.

Erica Carter, "Alice in the Consumer Wonderland: West German Case Studies in Gender and Consumer Culture," in *Gender and Generation,* ed. Angela McRobbie and Mica Nava (London: MacMillan, 1984), 185–214. It is reprinted with permission of the publisher.

Uta G. Poiger, "Rock 'n' Roll, Female Sexuality, and the Cold War Battle over German Identities," *Journal of Modern History* 68 (September 1996): 577–616. Copyright © 1996, The University of Chicago Press. It is reprinted with permission of the publisher.

Axel Schildt and Arnold Sywottek, "'Reconstruction' and 'Modernization': West German Social History during the 1950s," first appeared as "'Wiederaufbau' und 'Modernisierung': Zur westdeutschen Gesellschaftsgeschichte in den fünfziger Jahre," *Aus Politik und Zeitgeschichte* B 6–7 (1989): 18–32. It is reprinted with permission of the authors.

Introduction: Writing the History of West Germany

Robert G. Moeller

West Germany is history. Even as the Federal Republic of Germany celebrated its fortieth birthday in 1989, many forces converged to make that birthday its last. The collapse of communism in eastern Europe and the East German decision to open the border to the west suddenly created circumstances under which the unification of the two German states was a real possibility; remembrances of the past were eclipsed by predictions about the future. Since *die Wende,* the dramatic "turn" of late 1989–90 that led to unification, many assessments have stressed that for Germans the postwar era is finally at an end; free markets and parliamentary politics have triumphed over communist experiments. A united Germany can finally be a "normal" nation, moving decisively beyond the Third Reich and post–World War II division between east and west.

From the perspective of the 1990s, it is possible to see the road to the Bonn Republic and West Germany's "social market economy" as the "correct" postwar German path to democratic politics and the unqualified blessings of a capitalist economy.[1] However, a unified Germany continues to confront enormous problems of social inequality among classes, between women and men, and between "Wessies" and "Ossies." It is marred by the continued presence of racism and aggression toward foreigners and a widespread resistance to the acceptance of a truly multicultural society. And Germans still share a unified past that ties any strains of a revitalized nationalism to memories of the Third Reich.

The attempt to analyze and understand these problems in the present can be illuminated by the critical exploration of how West Germans confronted—

My thanks to Geoff Eley, Alice Fahs, Lynn Mally, Josef Mooser, Omer Bartov, and Uta G. Poiger. Their critical responses to earlier drafts of this introduction were invaluable.

1. Tending in this direction, for example, is A. J. Nicholls, *Freedom with Responsibility: The Social Market Economy in Germany, 1918–1963* (Oxford: Clarendon Press, 1994).

or failed to confront—similar problems in the early history of the Federal Republic. In the 1990s, Germans are once again involved in a process of reconstruction in the wake of a war, though this time no armistice was signed and the conflict was one in which ideology was the dominant weapon. A clearer understanding of how West Germans defined political identities, articulated common values, and crafted social, economic, and political institutions in the wake of the Second World War can offer a perspective on how unified Germans are redefining themselves in the wake of the Cold War.

This reader seeks to contribute to such a critical reexamination of the Federal Republic's early history by bringing together some of the most important recent work by British, North American, Israeli, and German historians. Moving beyond a historiography long dominated by accounts of high politics and international relations, the articles focus in particular on the points of intersection between the "politics of daily life" (*Alltagspolitik*) and the politics of the nation-state, and the fluid boundaries between political, economic, social, and cultural history.

At a methodological level, *West Germany under Construction* emphasizes the ways in which postwar West German political identities and the priorities of the state shaped and in turn took shape in ostensibly apolitical and depoliticized realms. The authors acknowledge that the Federal Republic was created by a postwar settlement that subjected West Germans to geopolitical forces beyond their control and located West Germany at the center of the Cold War split between east and west, but they also insist that in the 1950s, West Germans made their own history and created themselves.

The work of many of the contributors builds on the methodological approaches of women's history, social history, and cultural studies, which have combined to transform the concept of *political culture* by outlining a range of contexts outside the arena of parliamentary electoral politics and formal associational life where political consciousness emerges and in turn influences politics at the national level. Thus, the volume emphasizes that the process of defining West Germany in the 1950s took place not only in the geopolitical arena of the Cold War and the halls of parliament but also in dance halls and at the movies, in worker-training programs, and in patterns of consumption. By expanding the arena in which they investigate the formation of political identities, many of the authors also indicate that the politics of daily life in the early history of the Federal Republic included discussions of sexuality, ethnicity, and gender; thus, topics that are largely absent even from more recent social hitorical accounts of the West German past are effectively illuminated and firmly placed on the agenda for future research. The volume thus not only expands our understanding of the early formation of West German society, it also outlines ways to continue the excavation of that past.

Outlines of West German Historiography

Until the early 1980s, historical treatments of the Federal Republic still largely concentrated on foreign relations and political institutions, narrowly defined, and devoted particular attention to West Germany's geopolitical position in a post–1945 world dominated by the Cold War. The forces driving West Germany into the western alliance, the rapidly diminishing possibilities for German reunification, West German rearmament, and the Federal Republic's entry into the North Atlantic Treaty Organization (NATO) were important areas of historical research. In exploring these developments, the attention of historians and political scientists remained riveted at the top; an understanding of the "German Question" was sought in accounts of the clash of great leaders and great nation-states. The primary actors were West Germany's first chancellor, Konrad Adenauer, and U.S., French, British, and Soviet leaders and foreign ministers, for whom Germany became a central battlefield in the Cold War. Postwar West German history took place as much in London and Geneva as in Bonn, let alone Bochum or Bielefeld.[2]

Much of this scholarship was based on the premise that politics were of little interest to most Germans in the immediate postwar period. Rather, West Germans, politically alienated after the experience of National Socialism, retreated into the ostensibly nonpolitical worlds of family, workplace, and community, although these worlds—the preserve of the social historian—were never subjected to systematic historical investigation. The history of politics paid little attention to the history of society.

---

2. A useful introduction to this literature can be found in Anselm Doering-Manteuffel, *Die Bundesrepublik Deutschland: Aussenpolitik und innere Entwicklung 1949–1963* (Darmstadt: Wissenschaftliche Buchgesellschaft, 1983); Josef Foschepoth, ed., *Adenauer und die deutsche Frage* (Göttingen: Vandenhoeck & Ruprecht, 1988); idem, ed., *Kalter Krieg und deutsche Frage: Deutschland im Widerstreit der Mächte, 1945–1952* (Göttingen: Vandenhoeck & Ruprecht, 1985); and Rudolf Morsey, *Die Bundesrepublik Deutschland: Entstehung und Entwicklung bis 1969* (Munich: R. Oldenbourg, 1987). In general, for good introductions to postwar historiography, see Diethelm Prowe, "The New *Nachkriegsgeschichte* (1945–1949): West Germans in Search of Their Historical Origins," *Central European History* 10 (1977): 312–28; Wolfgang Benz, "Deutsche Geschichte nach dem Zweiten Weltkrieg: Probleme and Tendenzen zeitgeschichtlicher Forschung in der Bundesrepublik," *Tel Aviver Jahrbuch für deutsche Geschichte* 16 (1987): 398–420, which provides extensive references to many of the documentary collections that appeared in the 1980s; and most recently, Anselm Doering-Manteuffel, "Deutsche Zeitgeschichte nach 1945: Entwicklung und Problemlagen der historischen Forschung zur Nachkriegszeit," *Vierteljahrshefte für Zeitgeschichte* 41 (1993): 1–29; Axel Schildt, "Nachkriegszeit: Möglichkeiten und Probleme einer Periodisierung der westdeutschen Geschichte nach dem Zweiten Weltkrieg und ihrer Einordnung in die deutsche Geschichte des 20. Jahrhunderts," *Geschichte in Wissenschaft und Unterricht* 44 (1993): 567–84; and Paul Erker, "Zeitgeschichte als Sozialgeschichte: Forschungsstand und Forschungsdefizite," *Geschichte und Gesellschaft* 19 (1993): 202–38.

Historians also argued that West Germans had finally moved beyond the class conflicts that had defined society and politics in the 1920s. Echoing Helmut Schelsky, a sociologist who proclaimed in the 1950s that West Germany had become a "leveled-out petit bourgeois–*mittelständische* society" (*nivellierte kleinbügerlich-mittelständische Gesellschaft*), Hans-Peter Schwarz, author of a massive volume on the history of the years 1949–57, described a West German society in which class differences still existed, but in which an expansive middle class was dominant.[3] Class, the central category of analysis for social historians, seemed to be of little relevance for illuminating the political history of the 1950s.

Amid a sea of articles and monographs that focused on the place of West Germany in a world divided between west and east, there were also important historical analyses of postwar denazification, the domestic policies of Allied occupation in the areas controlled by the Americans, British, and French immediately following the war, and the reformulation of West German legal structures and political institutions, leading to the founding of the Federal Republic in 1949. The outlines of an economic history of the Federal Republic also clearly emerged.[4]

---

3. See Hans-Peter Schwarz, *Die Ära Adenauer: Gründerjahre der Republik 1949–1957* (Deutsche Verlags-Anstalt: Stuttgart, 1981), 395–402; Hans Braun, "Helmut Schelskys Konzept der 'nivellierten Mittelstandsgesellschaft' und die Bundesrepublik der 50er Jahre," *Archiv für Sozialgeschichte* 29 (1985): 199–223; Robert G. Moeller, *Protecting Motherhood: Women and the Family in the Politics of Postwar West Germany* (Berkeley and Los Angeles: University of California Press, 1993), 119–20; and the contribution by Axel Schildt and Arnold Sywottek in this volume.

4. This literature is described at length in the review essays cited above in note 2. Particularly important was Lutz Niethammer, *Entnazifizierung in Bayern* (Frankfurt am Main: S. Fischer, 1973). Doering-Manteuffel, *Aussenpolitik*, and Morsey, *Entstehung*, provide good overviews and extensive references to monographic literature. Other recent contributions to this literature include Rebecca L. Boehling, "German Municipal Self-Government and Local U.S. Military Government," *Archiv für Sozialgeschichte* 25 (1985): 333–83; Klaus-Dietmar Henke, *Die amerikanische Besetzung Deutschlands* (Munich: R. Oldenbourg, 1995); Hermann-Josef Rupieper, *Der besetzte Verbündete: Die amerikanische Deutschlandpolitik 1949–1955* (Opladen: Westdeutscher Verlag, 1991); Ian D. Turner, ed., *Reconstruction in Post-War Germany: British Occupation Policy and the Western Zones, 1945–55* (Oxford: Berg, 1989); Thomas Alan Schwartz, *America's Germany: John J. McCloy and the Federal Republic of Germany* (Cambridge: Harvard University Press, 1991); and several of the contributions in Jeffry M. Diefendorf, Axel Frohn, and Hermann-Josef Rupieper, eds., *American Policy and the Reconstruction of West Germany, 1945–1955* (Cambridge: Cambridge University Press, 1993). For a good introduction to the economic history of the Federal Republic, see Werner Abelshauser, *Die langen fünfziger Jahre: Wirtschaft und Gesellschaft der Bundesrepublik Deutschland, 1949–1966* (Schwann: Düsseldorf, 1987); idem, *Wirtschaftsgeschichte der Bundesrepublik Deutschland (1945–1980)* (Frankfurt am Main: Suhrkamp, 1983). Essential for illuminating postwar U.S. influence on West German economic development and for describing the generational shift in the entrepreneurial elite is Volker R. Berghahn, *The Americanisation of West German Industry, 1945–1973* (Leamington Spa: Berg, 1986). And for a very positive assessment of West German economic policy, see Nicholls, *Freedom with Responsibility*.

In addition, in the late 1960s and 1970s a left-wing revisionist historiography revived debates of the immediate postwar period in which some critical voices had expressed the fear that in the 1950s West Germany was headed toward a conservative restoration that embodied elements of the National Socialist past and a fascist potential. In these accounts, the United States and Britain played a crucial role in foiling German plans to establish a socialist alternative in the west. However, formulations such as "blocked new order" and "enforced capitalism" tended to oversimplify the complex motives of the occupation powers and domestic resistance to radical experiments, and even this critical scholarship remained methodologically within the fairly narrow confines of a traditional political history.[5]

By the early 1980s, the scholarship on the postwar period and the early history of the Federal Republic was substantial enough to allow synthesis; a massive five-volume history of the Federal Republic devoted ample space to the postwar years and the "Adenauer era," and other overviews effectively demonstrated that West Germans had gained enough distance from their beginnings to see them in historical perspective. But largely absent from all these accounts was a history that extended much beyond formal institutions and the processes of political policy-making.[6] Thus, a social history of West Germany had yet to be written at a time when social history reigned supreme at some of the most important West German universities and leading historians of modern Germany declared traditional political and diplomatic history woefully inadequate. West German, British, and North American historians had done much to illuminate the social history of politics and the politics of daily life, popular culture, relations of gender and generation, class formation, and the history of

---

5. See, for example, Ute Schmidt and Tilman Fichter, *Der erzwungene Kapitalismus: Klassenkämpfe in den Westzonen 1945–48* (Berlin: Verlag Klaus Wagenbach, 1971); Theo Pirker, *Die verordnete Demokratie: Grundlagen und Erscheinungen der Restauration* (Berlin: Olle und Wolter, 1977); Ernst-Ulrich Huster et al., *Determinanten der westdeutschen Restauration 1945–1949* (Frankfurt am Main: Suhrkamp, 1972); and Eberhard Schmidt, *Die verhinderte Neuordnung 1945–1952* (Frankfurt am Main: Europäische Verlagsanstalt, 1970).

6. See Theodor Eschenburg, *Jahre der Besatzung, 1945–1949* (Stuttgart: Deutsche Verlags-Anstalt, 1983); and Schwarz, *Die Ära Adenauer*, the first two contributions to a five-volume *Geschichte der Bundesrepublik Deutschland*, edited by Karl Dietrich Bracher, Theodor Eschenburg, Joachim C. Fest, and Eberhard Jäckel. Important exceptions to this rule are offered by Christoph Klessmann, *Die doppelte Staatsgründung: Deutsche Geschichte 1945–1955* (Göttingen: Vandenhoeck & Ruprecht, 1982); the multivolume history of the Federal Republic, first issued in 1983 and reissued in 1989 on the eve of West Germany's fortieth anniversary: Wolfgang Benz, ed., *Die Geschichte der Bundesrepublik Deutschland*, 4 vols. (Frankfurt am Main: Fischer Taschenbuch Verlag, 1989); and with a particular emphasis on cultural and intellectual history, Dieter Bänsch, ed., *Die fünfziger Jahre: Beiträge zu Politik und Kultur* (Tübingen: Gunter Narr, 1985). Another good survey of the state of research in the mid-1980s is provided in Ludolf Herbst, ed., *Westdeutschland 1945–1955: Unterwerfung, Kontrolle, Integration* (Munich: R. Oldenbourg, 1986), which includes Josef Foschepoth's contribution to this volume.

the family in the imperial period (1871–1918), World War I (1914–18), the Weimar Republic (1919–33), and the National Socialist years (1933–45), but very few social historians had ventured onto the terrain of the Federal Republic's past. A history of the German empire, Weimar, and National Socialism that began by asking rhetorically, "Is it a mistake to begin with Bismarck?" might be viewed as the defensive response of an old-fashioned political approach, but a history of the Federal Republic that began with Adenauer was the rule, not the exception.[7]

To be sure, a major impediment to the kinds of investigations from the bottom up or to analyses that emphasized the points of intersection of politics, society, and culture, which were being written about other periods in modern German history, was the restriction on the use of archival sources for the years after 1945. Provisions barring access to all archival materials in state and national archives less than thirty years old prohibited use of sources that could be employed to make West Germans more central to the narrative of West German history.[8] The farther away from 1945 historians moved, the greater was their access to archival sources.

In addition, forty years after the end of the war it was easier for historians to see the early years of the Federal Republic as part of longer-term continuities in modern German history, not as an extended postlude to World War II and the postwar settlement.[9] The "historians' conflict" (*Historikerstreit*), a scholarly controversy over the place and significance of National Socialism and the Holocaust in modern German history, was one clear indication that by the mid-1980s historians of modern Germany were pondering the relationship between history and national identity. Increasing interest among historians in the early history of the Federal Republic was another.[10]

Once serious social historical investigation of the postwar period began, it had implications that challenged the established view of the Federal Republic's early years. Common to most accounts in place in the early 1980s was an em-

7. Gordon A. Craig, *Germany, 1866–1945* (New York: Oxford University Press, 1978), 1. And for a review of social historical approaches to the Kaiserreich, see Robert G. Moeller, "The Kaiserreich Recast? Continuity and Change in Modern German Historiography," *Journal of Social History* 17 (1984): 655–83.

8. Erker, "Zeitgeschichte als Sozialgeschichte," 212.

9. In general, see Lutz Niethammer, "Zum Wandel der Kontinuitätsdiskussion," in Herbst, *Westdeutschland*, 65–83.

10. For introductions to the *Historikerstreit*, see Geoff Eley, "Nazism, Politics and Public Memory: Thoughts on the West German *Historikerstreit* 1986–1987," *Past & Present* no. 121 (November 1988): 171–208; Charles S. Maier, *The Unmasterable Past: History, Holocaust, and German National Identity* (Cambridge: Harvard University Press, 1988); and Peter Baldwin, ed., *Reworking the Past: Hitler, the Holocaust, and the Historians' Debate* (Boston: Beacon Press, 1990). See also Christoph Klessmann, "Ein stolzes Schiff und krächzende Möwen: Die Geschichte der Bundesrepublik und ihre Kritiker," *Geschichte und Gesellschaft* 11 (1985): 476.

phasis on the *Stunde Null,* or "zero hour." May 1945 and the war's end represented a completely new beginning. In some versions of this story, the "National Socialist revolution of modernity" had leveled the "traditional basis of German society in family and religion and all other spheres,"[11] but it was the unintended consequences of Hitler's war—the leveling of German cities and the postwar dismemberment and division of the Reich—that even more dramatically wiped clean the slate on which West Germans could write economic modernization and democratic values.

The view of the war's end as a dramatic rupture was also implicitly underscored by the vast literature on the Kaiserreich and Weimar that emphasized a German *Sonderweg,* a "peculiar path" of German history that stretched from an authoritarian Kaiserreich to an authoritarian Third Reich.[12] For those who subscribed to the theory of a *Sonderweg* leading from Bismarck to Hitler, it was possible to argue that the path did not extend beyond the Thousand Year Reich; once key parts of the *Sonderweg* had been obliterated by the defeat of National Socialism and the postwar division of Germany, once the Prussian state had vanished, the military elite was out of work, and the conservative, aristocratic, estate-owning agrarian ruling class east of the Elbe was expropriated, its property transformed into the collective farms of the German Democratic Republic, it was possible for West Germans to shed entirely the authoritarian legacies of the Kaiserreich and the Third Reich. A capitalist economy remained in place after 1945, but West German society represented a dramatically new and unprecedented construction in modern German history, a "normal" nation, comparable to other liberal-democratic regimes.[13]

In a 1983 volume, advertised as a *Sozialgeschichte der Bundesrepublik Deutschland* (Social history of the Federal Republic of Germany), Werner

---

11. Ralf Dahrendorf, *Society and Democracy in Germany* (Garden City, NY: Doubleday, 1967), quotations from 390, 384; and most recently, in another variant, Michael Geyer, "The Stigma of Violence, Nationalism, and War in Twentieth-Century Germany," *German Studies Review* Special Issue (winter 1993): 97–103; also the general discussion in Ian Kershaw, *The Nazi Dictatorship: Problems and Perspectives of Interpretation,* 3d ed. (London: Edward Arnold, 1993), 131–49; and David F. Crew, introduction to *Nazism and German Society, 1933–1945,* ed. idem (London: Routledge, 1994), 23–27.

12. For a critical summary of this literature, see David Blackbourn and Geoff Eley, *The Peculiarities of German History: Bourgeois Society and Politics in Nineteenth-Century Germany* (Oxford: Oxford University Press, 1984).

13. Jürgen Kocka, "1945: Neubeginn oder Restauration?" in *Wendepunkte deutscher Geschichte, 1848–1945,* ed. Carola Stern and Heinrich August Winkler (Frankfurt am Main: Fischer, 1979), 141–68, quotation from 167 (a new edition of this book was published in 1994); and more recently, Jürgen Kocka, "Revolution und Nation: Zur historischen Einordnung der gegenwärtigen Ereignisse," *Tel Aviver Jahrbuch für deutsche Geschichte* 19 (1990): 495–96. For a range of assessments of the significance of 1945 as a radical break, see also the important recent collection, Hans-Erich Volkmann, ed., *Ende des Dritten Reiches—Ende des Zweiten Weltkriegs: Eine perspektivistische Rückschau* (Munich: Piper, 1995).

Conze, one of the leading advocates of social historical method among postwar West German historians, and M. Rainer Lepsius, a historical sociologist, gave notice that the vision of 1945 as a radical break obscured the extent to which some characteristics of the Federal Republic were firmly grounded in the history of a unified German Reich. The product of seminars organized by Conze over the years 1976-79, the volume carried the subtitle *Beiträge zum Kontinuitätsproblem* (Contributions to the continuity problem), an explicit announcement that assuming discontinuity was in fact the problem; it was time to see the Federal Republic as part of a German history that had not begun with the signing of the armistice in May 1945. Contributors to the volume did not seek continuities in facile conceptions of "restoration," but they did insist that a complete understanding of the foundations of West German social institutions, economic trends, political attitudes, and social stratification required locating West Germany in the continuum of German history, stretching back all the way to the Kaiserreich. The essays in the volume also argued forcefully that key questions that had largely been excluded from historical investigations of the Federal Republic—demographic patterns, class structure, the development of the welfare state, the intersection of politics and religion—belonged on the agenda.[14]

Rethinking rupture and continuity was also central to a major project that explored the history of working people in the Ruhr over the long period from 1930 to 1960. Lutz Niethammer and a talented team of coinvestigators confirmed that for many Germans, 1945 had not defined a completely new beginning. If historians took seriously the importance of the cultural and political socialization that Germans brought with them from the 1920s and 1930s, it became meaningless to see 1945 as a *Stunde Null;* there was already far too much time on the clock.

Niethammer's credentials as a postwar historian were solidly established with his pathbreaking study of denazification,[15] but in the Ruhr project, he turned from a careful study of documentary sources to the techniques of the oral historian. Life histories, Niethammer argued, defined outlines that did not neatly parallel the economic and political structures that framed many accounts of the war and postwar years. An emphasis on political discontinuities had obscured and submerged the "social-cultural continuity of the people," and oral histories were the method best suited to rescue these "fragments of memory of

---

14. Werner Conze and M. Rainer Lepsius, eds., *Sozialgeschichte der Bundesrepublik Deutschland: Beiträge zum Kontinuitätsproblem* (Stuttgart: Ernst Klett, 1983). Among the contri-butors to this volume, particularly noteworthy is Josef Mooser, whose essay, "Abschied von der 'Proletarität': Sozialstruktur und Lage der Arbeiterschaft in der Bundesrepublik in histori-scher Perspektive," was expanded into a pathbreaking monograph, *Arbeiterleben in Deutschland, 1900–1970: Klassenlagen, Kultur und Politik* (Frankfurt am Main: Suhrkamp, 1984), that superbly outlines a framework for the study of the postwar West German working class.

15. Niethammer, *Entnazifizierung in Bayern.*

another re-education" in the transition from Third Reich to Bonn Republic.

The participants in the Ruhr oral history project not only indicated that it was essential to consider continuities across the great divide of 1945, but they also challenged a socio-historical approach, well established in the Federal Republic, that emphasized the primacy of social structures and economic development in shaping human experience and questioned the reliability and significance of first-person accounts and interview techniques for advancing historical understanding. Explicitly rejecting a structural approach, Niethammer insisted that an adequate account of modern German history must grant the "right to speak" (*Mitspracherecht*) to those "who otherwise are all too often neglected in historical accounts."[16]

The interviews collected for the Ruhr oral history project also underscored that men's and women's experience often diverged; gender was an important category of analysis for understanding German history in the 1930s, 1940s, and 1950s. Testimonies collected by Sibylle Meyer, Eva Schulze, and other feminist historians in the late 1970s and early 1980s made the same point; placing women's experience at the center, feminist historians confirmed that the dates that defined chapter divisions in standard histories did not make sense of most German women's lives.[17]

The events that punctuated the life histories collected by Niethammer and

---

16. Lutz Niethammer, ed., *"Die Jahre weiss man nicht, wo man die heute hinsetzen soll": Faschismus-Erfahrungen im Ruhrgebiet* (Berlin: J. H. W. Dietz Nachf., 1983); idem, ed., *"Hinterher merkt man, dass es richtig war, dass es schiefgegangen ist": Nachkriegs-Erfahrungen im Ruhrgebiet* (Berlin: J. H. W. Dietz Nachf., 1983); and Lutz Niethammer and Alexander von Plato, *"Wir kriegen jetzt andere Zeiten": Auf der Suche nach der Erfahrung des Volkes in nachfaschistischen Ländern* (Berlin: J. H. W. Dietz Nachf., 1985). For a good overview of the project, see Ulrich Herbert, "Zur Entwicklung der Ruhrarbeiterschaft 1930 bis 1960 aus erfahrungsgeschichtlicher Perspektive," in *"Wir kriegen jetzt andere Zeiten"*, ed. Niethammer and Plato, 19–52; and for a good illustration of the ways in which oral testimonies can be blended with contemporary sociological accounts and other published sources, see Lutz Niethammer, "Privat-Wirtschaft: Erinnerungsfragmente einer anderen Umerziehung," in *"Hinterher merkt man, dass es richtig war, dass es schiefgegangen ist"*, ed. Niethammer, 17–106. See also Beatrix Hochstein, *Die Ideologie des Überlebens: Zur Geschichte der politischen Apathie in Deutschland* (Frankfurt: Campus Verlag, 1984). For a first-rate review of the directions in modern German social history in the 1980s, see Geoff Eley, "Labor History, Social History, *Alltagsgeschichte*: Experience, Culture, and the Politics of the Everyday—A New Direction for German Social History?" *Journal of Modern History* 61 (1989): 297–43.

17. Sibylle Meyer and Eva Schulze, *Wie wir das alles geschafft haben: Alleinstehende Frauen berichten über ihr Leben nach 1945* (Munich: C. H. Beck, 1985); idem, *Von Liebe sprach damals keiner: Familienalltag in der Nachkriegszeit* (Munich: C. H. Beck, 1985); idem, *Auswirkungen des II. Weltkriegs auf Familien: Zum Wandel der Familie in Deutschland* (Berlin: Gerhard Weinert, 1989). The same point was made by Edgar Reitz's *Heimat*, the saga of one German town from the end of World War I until the early 1980s, aired on West German television in eleven episodes in 1984. For a good introduction to the extensive debate around this series, see Anton Kaes, *From Hitler to Heimat: The Return of History as Film* (Cambridge: Harvard University Press, 1989), 163–92.

others were not January 1933, the Nazi seizure of power; September 1939, the German invasion of Poland and the start of World War II; or May 1945, German defeat and surrender. Rather, time was marked by the intensification of Allied bombing in 1943, blurring the line between war at the front and war at home; the shock of defeat at Stalingrad and the increasing number of German military casualties; the phenomenon of mass rapes of German women by Allied and particularly Red Army soldiers as the eastern front moved relentlessly westward in the winter and spring of 1944–45; after May 1945, the deprivations of the postwar period that often meant the exchange of one form of misery for another once there were "no more bomb attacks . . . but nothing more to eat"; the return of soldiers from prisoner-of-war camps; and the currency reform of 1948 that ended postwar shortages and miraculously filled shop windows overnight, as West Germans moved from an economy of barter to a market where money once again had meaning.[18]

In many ways, these oral histories paralleled the testimonies collected immediately after the war by sociologists, concerned with the crisis of the family and the "mass fate" of Germans who saw themselves as victims of a war that Hitler had started but all Germans had lost—those bombed or driven out of their homes; the "war-damaged"; women who now confronted life as single parents; returning veterans, particularly those who had spent time in Soviet prisoner-of-war camps; and "expellees" who fled or were driven out of eastern Germany and eastern Europe and for whom May 8, 1945, meant "liberation" not from National Socialism but from their homes, loved ones, and property. The willingness of West Germans in the late 1970s and 1980s to speak of their experience in the 1940s echoed the compulsive drive to record eyewitness testimonies and memoirs immediately after the war.[19]

In the accounts of the immediate postwar years and in oral histories col-

---

18. In addition to the work of Meyer and Schulze, see also Annette Kuhn, "Power and Powerlessness: Women after 1945, or the Continuity of the Ideology of Femininity," *German History* 7 (1989):35–46; Annemarie Tröger, "Between Rape and Prostitution: Survival Strategies and Chances of Emancipation for Berlin Women after World War II," in *Women in Culture and Politics: A Century of Change,* ed. Judith Friedlander et al. (Bloomington: Indiana University Press, 1986), 97–117; and idem, "German Women's Memories of World War II," in *Behind the Lines: Gender and the Two World Wars,* ed. Margaret R. Higonnet et al. (New Haven: Yale University Press, 1987). See also Gabriele Rosenthal, ed., with the assistance of Christiane Grote, *"Als der Krieg kam, hatte ich mit Hitler nichts mehr zu tun": Zur Gegenwärtigkeit des "Dritten Reiches" in Biographien* (Opladen: Leske + Budrich, 1990).

19. See Susanne zur Nieden, *Alltag im Ausnahmezustand: Frauentagebücher im zerstörten Deutschland 1943 bis 1945* (Berlin: Orlanda Frauenverlag, 1993); idem, "Chronistinnen des Krieges: Frauentagebücher im Zweiten Weltkrieg," in Volkmann, ed., *Ende des Dritten Reiches— Ende des Zweiten Weltkriegs,* 835–60; Helmut Peitsch, *"Deutschlands Gedächtnis an seine dunkelste Zeit": Zur Funktion der Autobiographik in den Westzonen Deutschlands und den Westsektoren von Berlin 1945 bis 1949* (Berlin: Edition Sigma, 1990); idem, "Autobiographical Writing as *Vergangenheitsbewältigung* (Mastering the Past)," *German History* 7 (1989): 47–70;

lected over thirty years after the war's end, "war and postwar years" (*Kriegs-und Nachkriegszeit*) were fused into a strangely depoliticized episode in which the culprits were bomb attacks, extreme shortages, fears of starvation, and a victor's peace that dismantled the German state and economy. Contemporary accounts and oral histories that emphasized the sociocultural continuity of the people put Germans—not the Allied forces of occupation or diplomatic machinations of the Cold War—at the center of the story of the war years and the early history of the Federal Republic.

Accounts based on oral histories offered an alternative vision of a war that began not in 1939 but with intensified Allied bomb attacks and German defeat at Stalingrad in 1943 and ended not in May 1945 but only with the introduction of a new currency and the de facto division of Germany by the Allies in 1948. The same periodization registered clearly in another important collection of essays, edited by Martin Broszat and others at the Institute for Contemporary History in Munich. In their introduction to the volume, *Von Stalingrad zur Währungsreform* (From Stalingrad to currency reform), the editors agreed that the collapse of the Third Reich marked a dramatic rupture in modern German history, but they located the origins of the break in the last two years of the war. The editors also emphasized that by 1943, increasing numbers of Germans were able to discern the gap between Goebbels's propaganda and the reality of the Third Reich; amidst falling bombs and destroyed cities, they argued, it was possible to see a new Germany emerging. The sense of self-reliance fostered by the adverse conditions of the war's end created the bases for a liberal democratic renewal and the headlong charge into capitalist reconstruction after 1945. Thus, it was not only the forces of Allied occupation that had transformed and democratized postwar West Germany; that process of transformation had already begun from within before the shooting stopped.[20]

---

and for an introduction to the sociological literature on the "crisis of the family," Dieter Wirth, "Die Familie in der Nachkriegszeit: Desorganisation oder Stabilität?" in *Vorgeschichte der Bundesrepublik Deutschland: Zwischen Kapitulation und Grundgesetz,* ed. Josef Becker, Theo Stammen, and Peter Waldmann (Munich: Wilhelm Fink Verlag, 1979). Extensive references to this literature can also be found in Moeller, *Protecting Motherhood,* 18–34.

20. Martin Broszat, Klaus-Dietmar Henke, and Hans Woller, ed., *Von Stalingrad zur Währungsreform: Zur Sozialgeschichte des Umbruchs in Deutschland* (Munich: R. Oldenbourg, 1988); and Hans Woller, "Germany in Transition from Stalingrad (1943) to Currency Reform (1948)," in *America and the Shaping of German Society, 1945–1955,* ed. Michael Ermarth (Providence: Berg, 1993), 23–34. The Munich Institut für Zeitgeschichte (Institute of Contemporary History), headed by Broszat, was a leader in sponsoring research into the immediate postwar period, and beginning in the 1980s its journal, *Vierteljahrshefte für Zeitgeschichte,* devoted increasing space to the history of the Federal Republic. The journal's annual bibliography is an invaluable source for all research into the history of the Federal Republic.

Introducing *West Germany under Construction*

The essays in *West Germany under Construction* develop many of the themes that emerged in these early social historical investigations of the Federal Republic's history. However, they depart from analyses that focused primarily *either* on the structural continuities—economic, political, demographic—that crossed the divide of May 1945 *or* on a history from the bottom up, based largely on oral histories, which gave primacy to the sociocultural continuity of the people. Rejecting any clear distinction between politics at the bottom and the top, the essays in this book illuminate crucial points where these two realms intersect.

Central to the essays in the first part, "Confronting the Consequences of Defeat," is the direct interrogation of the usefulness of the concept of a zero hour, May 1945 as a radical break in the transition from war to peace. The contributions of Atina Grossmann, Rainer Schulze, and Josef Foschepoth stress the long-term continuities tying the Bonn Republic to Weimar and the Third Reich, and they emphasize that attempts to define a West German future were always parts of a dialogue with a German past. In her essay, "A Question of Silence: The Rape of German Women by Occupation Soldiers," Atina Grossmann describes the experience of German women in Berlin at the end of the war and details how for many, the end of the war was marked by memories of violation, not liberation. Analyzing women's responses to rape, Grossmann also emphasizes the longer-term continuities that shaped popular reactions to the war's end; women's demands for abortions in the wake of rape by Red Army soldiers drew not only on a rhetoric of Nazi racialism that depicted Soviet soldiers as subhuman "Mongols," but also on a Weimar discourse of sexual reform in which social necessity was recognized as a legitimate ground to seek the termination of an unwanted pregnancy.[21] Grossmann's work makes clear that the conceptual distinction between the politics of the nation-state and the politics of daily life can obscure more than it illuminates for analyzing perceptions of Soviet occupation policies that first registered for many Germans—women and men—in the literal occupation of German women's bodies.

For expellees from eastern Europe and from the parts of the former Reich that were incorporated into postwar Poland, the war also did not end in 1945. The expulsion of some twelve million Germans from eastern Europe—two-thirds of whom resided in the Federal Republic by 1950—received con-

---

21. No one has done more than Grossmann to illuminate that Weimar discourse. See Atina Grossmann, *Reforming Sex: The German Movement for Birth Control and Abortion Reform 1920 to 1950* (New York: Oxford University Press, 1995).

siderable attention from anthropologists and sociologists in the 1950s, and even historians, for the most part uninterested in analyzing the *Zeitgeschichte* ("contemporary history") of the Federal Republic, found this an important topic. A massive project headed by Theodor Schieder, Hans Rothfels, and Werner Conze, some of the most eminent postwar West German historians, sought to collect eyewitness accounts of the "expulsion from the East" in an effort to understand this part of the German "collapse" and to depict the ways in which Soviet crimes at the war's end equaled German crimes during the war. Beginning in the late 1970s and 1980s, the expellees again emerged as a major focus of historical research, and an explosion of studies made it possible to learn about their experience in many parts of West Germany.[22] As Rainer Schulze's important work in this volume indicates, the self-congratulatory accounts of the rapid success at integrating expellees that dominated public discourse by the late 1950s—and that reemerged in some of the studies of the 1980s—did not capture the tensions that existed between the indigenous population and "new citizens" (*Neubürger*) who had fled or were driven in front of the Red Army at the war's end. Schulze's essay, "Growing Discontent: Relations between Native and Refugee Populations in a Rural District in Western Germany after the Second World War," is also an excellent example of how the careful examination of the Federal Republic's past can potentially illuminate contemporary German problems; there are obvious parallels between the "Growing Discontent" that complicates relations between "old" and

---

22. For a good introduction to this literature, see Rainer Schulze, Doris von der Brelie-Lewien, and Helga Grebing, eds., *Flüchtlinge und Vertriebene in der westdeutschen Nachkriegsgeschichte: Bilanzierung der Forschung und Perspektiven für die künftige Forschungsarbeit* (Hildesheim: August Lax, 1987); and Wolfgang Benz, ed., *Die Vertreibung der Deutschen aus dem Osten: Ursache, Ereignisse, Folgen* (Frankfurt am Main: Fischer, 1985); and Albrecht Lehmann, *Im Fremden ungewollt zuhaus: Flüchtlinge und Vertriebene in Westdeutschland* (Munich: C. H. Beck, 1991). On the precedents for this scholarly preoccupation in the 1950s, see Eugen Lemberg and Friedrich Edding, eds., *Die Vertriebenen in Westdeutschland,* 3 vols. (Kiel: Ferdinand Hirt, 1959). The expulsion from the east was also a major focus for some of the most important West German historians in the first postwar decade. See Theodor Schieder et al., eds., *Dokumentation der Vertreibung der Deutschen aus Ost-Mitteleuropa,* 5 vols. (Munich: Deutscher Taschenbuch Verlag, 1984), a reissue of a massive collection of first-person testimonies, framed by scholarly introductions, that appeared between 1954 and 1961. Useful as an introduction to the older literature is the annotated bibliography in Marion Frantzioch, *Die Vertriebenen: Hemmnisse, Antriebskräfte und Wege ihrer Integration in der Bundesrepublik Deutschland* (Berlin: Dietrich Reimer, 1987). See also the survey in Johannes-Dieter Steinert, "Die grosse Flucht und die Jahre danach: Flüchtlinge und Vertriebene in den vier Besatzungszonen," in Volkmann, ed., *Ende des Dritten Reiches—Ende des Weltkriegs,* 555–79. And on the ways in which the experiences of expellees were incorporated into the "contemporary history" of the Federal Republic in the early 1950s, see Robert G. Moeller, "Driven into 'Contemporary History': The Expulsion from the East in the Public Memory of the Federal Republic," working paper 5.30, Center for German and European Studies, University of California, Berkeley, 1995.

"new" citizens of the Federal Republic today and the tensions between "old" and "new" citizens in West Germany's early history.[23]

In discussions of the expulsion of Germans from eastern Europe, West Germans frequently laid blame for this massive population transfer at the feet of the Western Allies who were taken to task for realizing only too late the dangers of communism and hastily abandoning eastern Europe behind a rapidly sinking "iron curtain." Soviet barbarism was manifest in the expulsion of Germans from eastern Europe, but it was the passivity of the Western Allies at Yalta that delivered eastern Europe and eastern Germany to Stalin. Contemporaries maintained that by accepting the mandatory removal of all ethnic Germans from areas seized by the Red Army, the Western Allies joined the Soviets in responding to the National Socialist regime with brutal methods worthy of the Nazis. How thoroughly the Allies misunderstood Germans was apparent, many Germans maintained, in the victors' initial schemes to dismember Germany completely, attempts to dismantle German industry, and particularly in the immediate postwar years, the tendency to justify German suffering by invoking a misinformed conception of "collective guilt." In his essay, "German Reaction to Defeat and Occupation," Josef Foschepoth analyzes the ways in which many Germans held the Western Allies responsible not only for Germany's postwar fate, but also for the triumph of Hitler. This opinion spanned the political spectrum, and it was Kurt Schumacher, head of the postwar West German Social Democratic party, who claimed that if the Allies had treated Hitler the way they treated postwar Germans, "Hitler never would have become a danger to the world." In such accounts of the war's end, 1945 represented a rupture, but for many West Germans, it also represented the exchange of one form of oppression for another. Germans, first victimized by demonic Nazis, were now victimized by the Western Allies who were shortsighted, inefficient, and incompetent at best and deliberately vengeful at worst.[24]

In the late 1940s and early 1950s, telling stories of absent fathers, widowed mothers, shattered veterans, and those left to cope in severely damaged cities, driven permanently from their homes in eastern Europe, or unjustly stigmatized by Allied notions of collective guilt outlined a picture of the war and the transition from war to peace in which Germans too were victims. A second group of essays in *West Germany under Construction* focuses on the ways in which these key elements in the sociocultural continuity of the people and the politics of daily life also registered in politics at the national level, as West Germans negotiated the transition reflected in the title of part 2, "From Warfare State to

---

23. See also Alexander von Plato, "Fremde Heimat: Zur Integration von Flüchtlingen und Einheimischen in die Neue Zeit," in Niethammer and Plato, *"Wir kriegen jetzt andere Zeiten,"* 172–219.

24. See also Barbara Marshall, "German Attitudes to British Military Government 1945–1947," *Journal of Contemporary History* 15 (1980): 655–84.

Welfare State"; particularly in key areas of social policy, West Germans' emphasis on their own status as victims of the war structured the priorities of the state, and state policy in turn reinforced certain memories of the war and its legacy.[25]

James M. Diehl's analysis of measures aimed at meeting the needs of veterans, my work on policies affecting the family, and Curt Garner's exploration of the restoration of the civil service indicate that stories of German suffering were not just the stuff of private memories; they also constituted some of the crucial founding myths of the Federal Republic, clearly repeated with endless variation not only by victim groups but by politicians and policymakers of all ideological persuasions. The essays in part 2 suggest the ways in which addressing the just claims and rights to entitlement of those who had suffered most during the war and the moral obligations of others who had escaped relatively unscathed emerged as a central part of the project of establishing the bases for social solidarity in West Germany; the terrorist, belligerent, destructive, aberrant Germany of the Third Reich was succeeded by the Bonn Republic, a nation of victims, ruled by a state that could justly meet victims' needs. All major political parties could agree on the version of the past that was embodied in parliamentary discussions of the German victims of the war because it was ostensibly outside the realm of party-political wrangling. The deep divisions between Social Democrats and the coalition of the Christian Democratic Union (CDU) and Christian Social Union (CSU) were at least momentarily bridged by a shared commitment to overcoming this legacy of the war. In the realm of foreign policy, Adenauer's government sought to move a new Germany from a past as pariah to a present as a sovereign state, able to act in the international community with "equal rights." In the realm of domestic policy, meeting the needs of the "war-damaged" was part of West Germans' transformation from passive victims, the objects of "fate," into agents, shapers of their own destiny, capable of providing for the common welfare.[26]

In Diehl's study of the Federal Republic's treatment of veterans of World War II,[27] parts of which are summarized in his essay in this volume, "Change and Continuity in the Treatment of German *Kriegsopfer*," he argues that the West German state defused the potential radicalism of veterans by aggressively

---

25. See the useful summary in Hans Günter Hockerts, "Integration der Gesellschaft: Gründungskrise und Sozialpolitik in der frühen Bundesrepublik," *Zeitschrift für Sozialreform* 32 (1986): 25–41.

26. See the insightful analysis of Michael L. Hughes, "Restitution and Democracy in Germany after Two World Wars," *Contemporary European History* 4 (1994): 1–18; and on the *Lastenausgleich*, the complex system of transfer payments to "equalize the burdens" of the war, Reinhold Schillinger, *Der Entscheidungsprozess beim Lastenausgleich 1945–1952* (St. Katharinen: Scripta-Mercaturae, 1985).

27. James M. Diehl, *The Thanks of the Fatherland: German Veterans after the Second World War* (Chapel Hill: University of North Carolina Press, 1993).

representing and addressing their interests and successfully involving veterans in the formulation of programs to integrate them into postwar society. Although soldiers who had fought in World War II never received everything they demanded, the West German parliament quickly took action to introduce and implement a range of policies that assisted veterans and returning prisoners of war. Diehl argues that West German measures were self-consciously formulated in response to the harsh actions taken by the Allies to dismantle programs aiding veterans, part of their efforts to demilitarize and denazify Germany and, in the immediate postwar period, to hold all Germans collectively responsible for National Socialism. Built on the foundations of Weimar social welfare legislation, measures to meet the needs of German victims of the war at the front found widespread support in parliament. They indicated West Germans' willingness to learn from the best of their own history and served to justify the claims of Adenauer's government to promote "social justice" and run its own affairs without Allied oversight.

In "Reconstructing the Family in Reconstruction Germany," I describe the parliamentary debates around the introduction of *Kindergeld* ("money-for-children"), the West German system of family allowances. I explore how the project of constructing a beneficent welfare state, capable of "protecting motherhood," took on particular significance in the early 1950s. For politicians and policymakers, the family—with the German woman at its center—was a social institution that had been seriously threatened by the invasion of National Socialist ideology, the war on the home front, and the privations of the postwar years; it commanded particular attention as the storehouse of specifically German values that had not been permanently tainted by the Thousand Year Reich. Reconstructing the family was central to reconstructing Germany; the social contract in a new West Germany included a reformulated sexual contract. For wives and mothers, political citizenship was primarily defined by their responsibility to create a new generation of West Germans, and in the nuclear age of the Cold War, nuclear families were the first line of defense against the communist menace. My article also offers another example of the ways in which social policies put in place during the Federal Republic's first decade continue to structure policy discussions over four decades later. Public concerns over low birthrates, fears that Germany is "dying out," and debates over how much the state should intervene to provide families with economic assistance in a unified Germany in the 1990s have a striking resonance with similar discussions in the 1950s.[28]

In his study of the postwar civil service ("Public Personnel in West Germany in the 1950s"), Curt Garner analyzes the experience of other "victims" of May 8, 1945—state employees whose jobs with the Reich or the Prussian state no longer existed; professional soldiers; and public employees who had

---

28. These arguments are made at greater length in Moeller, *Protecting Motherhood*.

been fired in the process of Allied denazification. Garner's emphasis on the continuities in patterns of recruitment for civil servants and the rapid rehabilitation of many who had loyally served the Nazi regime, in many cases joining the National Socialist German Workers' Party (NSDAP), points to strong lines of continuity from Third Reich to Bonn Republic. He provides a detailed description of the law passed in 1951 with virtually unanimous support in the parliament that amounted to a program of affirmative action for those who had lost their jobs at the end of the war, including many former Nazis. Far-reaching measures called for the reinstatement of dismissed male civil servants. In contrast, women, employed in growing numbers during the war, found themselves unwanted as state employees after 1945, and forceful attacks on "double earners" exhorted married women in particular to do one job, not two.

Garner's work suggests the ways in which postwar Germans distinguished between *real* Nazis and those who ostensibly had joined the NSDAP for opportunistic reasons and whose lapses were easily forgiven. His study of civil service reform also illuminates how the state led the way in seeking to restore a sexual order in which women's most important work was in the home. However, his emphasis on the long-term decline in the size and influence of the civil service and the evidence that by the mid-1950s a full-employment economy led to recruiting more women than ever before into state service indicate the ways in which categories like "restoration" become oversimplifications when confronted with careful, nuanced historical analysis.[29]

The postwar West German landscape was populated not only by self-identified German victims, but also by the victims of Germans. How West Germans faced the "most recent past" (*jüngste Vergangenheit*) in which they were not victims but perpetrators is the subject of the essays in part 3, "Coming to Terms with the Past." Frank Stern and Constantin Goschler offer analyses of Germans' responses to Jews after 1945, and I examine the ways in which male homosexuals, another group systematically persecuted by the Nazis, were denied victim status altogether in the Federal Republic.

Studies of how Germans understood—or misunderstood—the past of the crimes of Germans against others, particularly the systematic attempt to eliminate European Jewry, are plentiful, but these studies are for the most part excellent examples of how historical accounts of the 1950s have tended

---

29. See also Curt Garner, "Schlussfolgerungen aus der Vergangenheit? Die Auseinandersetzungen um die Zukunft des deutschen Berufsbeamtentums nach dem Ende des Zweiten Weltkrieges," in Volkmann, ed., *Ende des Dritten Reiches—Ende des Zweiten Weltkriegs*, 607–74; and for a closer look at the special case of foreign ministry officials, see Gottfried Niedhardt, "Aussenpolitik in der Ära Adenauer," in *Modernisierung im Wiederaufbau: Die westdeutsche Gesellschaft der 50er Jahre*, ed. Axel Schildt and Arnold Sywottek (Bonn: J. H. W. Dietz Nachf., 1993), 806–8; and on the reinstatement of veterans, see Diehl, *Thanks of the Fatherland*, 141–62.

to focus on the politics of the state. Examinations of Adenauer's attempts to pave a West German "path to Israel" have thus concentrated on the realm of foreign relations and the chancellor's efforts to rehabilitate West Germany as a "moral nation" in a geopolitical context.[30] Analyses of popular attitudes have emphasized that in the 1950s, West Germans exhibited a singular "inability to mourn" the victims of National Socialism or to acknowledge their own responsibility for the Third Reich, rushing instead into economic reconstruction, and along the way building a path to the future, creating a highly selective memory of the past without pausing to unearth the ruins of their own complicity in the Third Reich.[31] As the essays by Stern and Goschler in this book make clear, however, the negotiations surrounding the West German–Israeli reparations treaty by no means defined the only arena in which the German Question and the Jewish Question were explicitly linked after 1945, nor did West Germans uniformly deny, forget, or repress National Socialist crimes against the Jews; German-Jewish relations were also part of the politics of daily life in the Federal Republic. Read together, these two essays also point to the necessity of capturing Jewish voices in the postwar period; in the oral histories collected by Niethammer and others, those who testified spoke German and were not Jewish, and subjective stories of other

---

30. See, for example, Lily Gardner Feldman, *The Special Relationship between West Germany and Israel* (Boston: George Allen & Unwin, 1984), 32–86; also Kai von Jena, "Versöhnung mit Israel? Die deutschisraelischen Verhandlungen bis zum Wiedergutmachungsabkommen von 1952," *Vierteljahrshefte für Zeitgeschichte* 34 (1986): 457–80; Yeshayahu A. Jelinek, "Political Acumen, Altruism, Foreign Pressure or Moral Debt: Konrad Adenauer and the 'Shilumim,'" *Tel Aviver Jahrbuch für deutsche Geschichte* 19 (1990): 77–102; and for illuminating the Israeli side of negotiations, Tom Segev, *The Seventh Million: The Israelis and the Holocaust,* translated by Haim Watzman (New York: Hill and Wang, 1994), 189–252.

31. The classic statement of this view can be found in Alexander Mitscherlich and Margarete Mitscherlich, *Die Unfähigkeit zu trauern: Grundlagen kollektiven Verhaltens* (Munich: R. Piper & Co., 1967). Although the Mitscherlichs employed techniques of Freudian analysis in their exploration of the German "inability to mourn," many studies that have not followed them methodologically have adopted their formulation. See the lucid discussion in Eric L. Santner, *Stranded Objects: Mourning, Memory, and Film in Postwar Germany* (Ithaca, N.Y.: Cornell University Press, 1990), 1–6. See also Theodor W. Adorno, "What Does Coming to Terms with the Past Mean?" in *Bitburg in Moral and Political Perspective,* ed. Geoffrey Hartmann (Bloomington: Indiana University Press, 1986), 114–29. And for recent critical perspectives on this position, Hermann Graml, "Die verdrändgte Auseinandersetzung mit dem Nationalsozialismus," in *Zäsuren nach 1945: Essays zur Periodisierung der deutschen Nachkriegsgeschichte,* ed. Martin Broszat (Munich: R. Oldenbourg, 1990), 169–83; Manfred Kittel, *Die Legende von der "zweiten Schuld": Vergangenheitsbewältigung in der Ära Adenauer* (Frankfurt am Main: Ullstein, 1993); Christa Hoffmann, *Stunden Null? Vergangenheitsbewältigung in Deutschland 1945 bis 1989* (Bonn: Bouvier, 1992); Udo Wengst, "Geschichtswissenschaft und 'Vergangenheitsbewältigung' in Deutschland nach 1945 und nach 1989/90," *Geschichte in Wissenschaft und Unterricht* 46 (1995):189–205; Norbert Frei, *Vergangenheitspolitik: Die Anfänge der Bundesrepublik und die NS-Vergangenheit* (Munich: C. H. Beck, 1996); Ulrich Brochhagen, *Nach Nürnberg: Vergangenheitsbewältigung und Westintegration in der Ära Adenauer* (Hamburg: Junius, 1994); and Robert G. Moeller, "War Stories: The Search for a Usable Past in the Federal Republic of Germany,"

victims of the war remained largely untold.[32] And finally, Goschler and Stern emphasize that the concept of the *Stunde Null* has different meanings for, on the one hand, victims of Nazi persecution and, on the other, German victims of the war both at the front and at home. For understanding the experience of those persecuted by the Nazis, a recent assessment that "the catchphrase *Zero Hour* has completely gone out of fashion" is too global; for the victims Goschler and Stern describe, May 1945 marked a decidedly new beginning.[33]

The title of the German-language edition of the book that Stern's essay summarizes insists that "In the beginning was Auschwitz" (*Im Anfang war Auschwitz*), a clear challenge to accounts of the Federal Republic's early history that maintained that "in the beginning was Adenauer."[34] His pathbreaking work reveals the extent to which wartime Allied carpet bombing and postwar reeducation programs failed to destroy the deep-seated prejudice of many Germans toward Jews. In "The Historic Triangle: Occupiers, Germans and Jews in Postwar Germany," he analyzes the shortcomings of Allied occupation policy and the anti-semitism of postwar West Germans that combined to isolate and stigmatize Jews who remained in Germany.

The author of a superb analysis of the politics of *Wiedergutmachung,*

American Historical Review 101 (1996): 1008–48.

32. An exception is Juliane Wetzel, "'Mir szeinen doh': München und Umgebung als Zuflucht von Überlebenden des Holocaust 1945–1948," in Broszat, Henke, Woller, *Von Stalingrad zur Währungsreform,* 327–64; see also idem, *Juden in München 1945–1951: Durchgangsstation oder Wiederaufbau?* (Munich: Kommissionverlag Uni-Druck, 1987); idem, "Trauma und Tabu: Jüdisches Leben in Deutschland nach dem Holocaust," in Volkmann, ed., *Ende des Dritten Reiches—Ende des Zweiten Weltkriegs,* 419–56; Michael Brenner, *Nach dem Holocaust: Juden in Deutschland, 1945–1950* (Munich: C. H. Beck, 1995); Frank Stern, "Antagonistic Memories: The Post-War Survival and Alienation of Jews and Germans," *International Yearbook of Oral History and Life Stories,* vol. 1, *Memory and Totalitarianism,* ed. Luisa Passerini (Oxford: Oxford University Press, 1992), 21–43; and in general, on the "DPs," Wolfgang Jacobmeyer, *Vom Zwangsarbeiter zum heimatlosen Ausländer: Die Displaced Persons in Westdeutschland 1945–1951* (Göttingen: Vandenhoeck & Ruprecht, 1985); Abraham J. Peck, "Liberated But Not Free: Jewish Displaced Persons in Germany after 1945," *November 1938: From "Reichskristallnacht" to Genocide,* ed. Walter H. Pehle (New York: Berg, 1991), 222–35; and Angelika Königseder and Juliane Wetzel, *Lebensmut im Wartesaal: Die jüdischen DPs (Displaced Persons) im Nachkriegsdeutschland* (Frankfurt am Main: Fischer Taschenbuch Verlag, 1994). Also useful on postwar anti-semitism is Werner Bergmann and Rainer Erb, eds., *Antisemitismus in der politi-schen Kultur nach 1945* (Opladen: Westdeutscher Verlag, 1990); and the important work of Harold Marcuse, "Nazi Crimes and Identity in West Germany: Collective Memories of the Dachau Concentration Camp, 1945–1990" (Ph.D. diss., University of Michigan, 1992).

33. Woller, "Germany in Transition," 24. See also the reflections on periodization, drawn from the Ruhr oral history project, in Ulrich Herbert, "'Die guten und die schlechten Zeiten': Überlegungen zur diachronen Analyse lebensgeschichtlicher Interviews," in Niethammer, ed., *"Die Jahre weiss man nicht,"* 67–96.

34. See Frank Stern, *Im Anfang war Auschwitz: Antisemitismus und Philosemitismus im deutschen Nachkrieg* (Gerlingen: Bleicher Verlag, 1991); and Arnulf Baring, *Aussenpolitik in Ade-*

the measures taken in the early history of the Federal Republic to "make good" the losses of the victims of National Socialism, Goschler offers in his essay, "The Attitude towards Jews in Bavaria after the Second World War," a careful analysis of postwar Bavaria, moving from Stern's broad outlines to a case study of a region that by 1946 became home to eighty thousand Jewish "displaced persons" ("DPs"), mostly from Poland, who awaited the opportunity to emigrate to Palestine or the United States. Germans might claim that they knew nothing of the past of Jewish persecution and mass extermination, but as Goschler shows, when confronted with the survivors of Nazi extermination policies, they frequently responded not with generosity and compassion but with open hostility and aggression.[35]

In my assessment of the criminal prosecution of male homosexuality in the 1950s, "The Homosexual Man is a 'Man,' the Homosexual Woman is a 'Woman,'" I focus on a case brought before the West German Federal Constitutional Court in which two gay men charged that Paragraph 175 of the Criminal Code, the sanction against male homosexuality, was a legacy of National Socialism, which had no place in a new West Germany. In rejecting the appeal, the court did not avoid, forget, or repress the history of the Nazi regime's persecution of gay men; it did not show an inability to mourn their fate, rather, it *chose* not to mourn them, arguing instead that Nazi policies aimed at male homosexuals were completely consistent with a "democratic political order." West Germans explicitly accepted the Nazis' dramatic expansion of the bases for the persecution of gay men as part of a past that required neither rationalization nor rejection, that should be accepted and endorsed, not overcome. Describing homosexuality in pathological terms was also the essential counterpart to the celebration of normative heterosexuality that took place in policies addressing women and the family. Thus, "reconstructing the family" involved criminalizing, marginalizing, and psychoanalyzing homosexuality.

My treatment of West German attitudes toward homosexuality and the articles by Stern and Goschler also indicate that in the early 1950s, most West Germans collapsed the crimes of National Socialism into the attempt to exterminate European Jewry; "National Socialist racial teachings" were not understood to include other forms of racial discrimination, sexism, and homophobia, or the tacit acceptance of the marginalization of those not meeting the Nazis' racial, political, sexual, and religious criteria in the 1930s, which had

nauers *Kanzlerdemokratie: Bonns Beitrag zur Europäischen Verteidigungsgemeinschaft* (Munich: R. Oldenbourg Verlag, 1969). The English-language version of Stern's book is *The Whitewashing of the Yellow Badge: Antisemitism and Philosemitism in Postwar Germany,* translated by William Templer (Oxford: Pergamon Press, 1992).

35. See Constantin Goschler, *Wiedergutmachung: Westdeutschland und die Verfolgten des Nationalsozialismus (1945–1954)* (Munich: R. Oldenbourg, 1992); idem, "Nachkriegsdeutschland und die Verfolgten des Nationalsozialismus," in Volkmann, ed., *Ende des Dritten Reiches—Endes des Zweiten Weltkriegs,* 317–42; and Ludolf Herbst and Constantin Goschler, eds., *Wiedergutmachung in der Bundesrepublik* (Munich: R. Oldenbourg, 1989).

paved the way to mass extermination in the early 1940s.[36] Read together with the essays by Garner and Diehl, these contributions reveal that in the early 1950s, West Germans did not avoid discussing the National Socialist past; rather, they "came to terms with" that past by narrowly defining it, focusing on their own woes, applauding at least some of what the Nazis had accomplished—programs to support families and veterans, the intensification of criminal penalties for male homosexuality—and understanding many of the Third Reich's excesses as responses to the exigencies of war.

The essays in Part 4, "Ideology and Political Identities in the 'Economic Miracle,'" explicitly address the ways in which West German political identities in the 1950s were shaped in patterns of work, popular culture, and consumption. The political scientist Benedict Anderson calls the "deep horizontal comradeship" that defines the bases for social and political solidarity an "imagined community."[37] Unlike the Southeast Asian cases of greatest interest to Anderson, where an "imagined community" was largely shaped through an ideology of nationalism, the problem for Germans after 1945 was not how to create a conception of the nation, but rather how to establish a sense of collectivity that did not draw on a nationalist rhetoric contaminated by its association with Nazism and that could allow West Germans to claim a national identity without abandoning hopes of reunification with the east.[38] The essays by Mark Roseman and Heide Fehrenbach outline some of the conservative strategies for defining an imagined community that could articulate conceptions of "Germanness" without being explicitly nationalist.

Roseman's study of apprenticeship programs for young miners in the Ruhr, "The Organic Society and the 'Massenmenschen,'" examines the ways in which transforming young men into skilled workers involved much more than technical training. For employers, state officials, academics, and the church, worker socialization also included lectures on "German music or jazz" and "healthy and unhealthy female beauty"—in short, exposure to a "valid German aesthetic" and proper moral values. In Roseman's analysis, apprenticeship programs, an ostensibly apolitical arena, where young men should learn to be good workers, emerge as a profoundly politicized space in which

---

36. In general, see Goschler, *Wiedergutmachung;* some of the essays in Herbst and Goschler, *Wiedergutmachung in der Bundesrepublik;* and Michael Berenbaum, ed., *A Mosaic of Victims: Non-Jews Persecuted and Murdered by the Nazis* (New York: New York University Press, 1990).

37. Benedict Anderson, *Imagined Communities: Reflections on the Origin and Spread of Nationalism,* rev. ed. (London: Verso, 1991), 7.

38. For introductions to the postwar German discussions, see, for example, Peter Alter, "Nationalism and German Politics after 1945," in *The State of Germany: The National Idea in the Making, Unmaking and Remaking of a Modern Nation-State,* ed. John Breuilly (London: Longman, 1992), 154–76; Heinrich August Winkler, "Nationalismus, Nationalstaat und nationale Frage in Deutschland seit 1945," in *Nationalismus-Nationalitäten-Supranationalität,* ed. Heinrich August Winkler and Hartmut Kaelble (Stuttgart: Klett-Cotta, 1993), 12–16; and the suggestive comments of Wolfgang Kaschuba, "Volk und Nation: Ethnozentrismus in Geschichte und Gegenwart," in

the end result should be good Germans, fully equipped to withstand the dangers of materialism and the mass age.[39] A modern postwar work force was to be rooted in the values of a distant past that was German but not National Socialist, though, as Roseman shows, the discussion of worker-training programs involved not avoiding the "most recent past" but rather rejecting explicitly the tenets of Nazi ideology that had sought to obliterate individuals by subordinating them completely to the priorities of the *Volk*. These attempts to submerge the individual in the collective were not, however, uniquely German in origin; they were characteristic of all modern mass societies. In this discourse, National Socialism and its horrifying excesses could be euphemistically subsumed under the category of the "problems of the modern age."

Fehrenbach's essay, "The Fight for the 'Christian West,'" based on the research for her study of postwar West German cinema,[40] reveals the ways in which struggles over film policy constituted another context where political identities were debated and described. Fehrenbach draws on older studies of the postwar film industry,[41] but unlike these other works that address film as part of a discrete cultural realm, Fehrenbach's research reveals that defining political culture was at the heart of cultural politics.[42] When a leading Catholic film expert asked "Does film . . . assist in the reconstruction of the Christian West?" he already knew the answer. Mass demonstrations to protest the screening of movies like *Die Sünderin* (The [female] Sinner), the tale of a woman who falls into prostitution and whose redemption through love does not prevent her from taking both her lover's and her own life, had a political as well as an ethical thrust, part of a conservative agenda for the social and political reconstruction of postwar West Germany. Fehrenbach's subtle discussion of *Heimatfilme,* wildly popular movies that evoked a carefree rural idyll, as a mode for representing an invented German past that rescued German traditions and authorized one version of nationalism, untouched by National Socialism,

Winkler and Kaelble, eds., *Nationalismus-Nationalitäten-Supranationalität*, 56–81.

39. For a fuller treatment of these themes, see Mark Roseman, *Recasting the Ruhr, 1945–1958: Manpower, Economic Recovery and Labour Relations* (New York: Berg, 1992).

40. Heide Fehrenbach, *Cinema in Democratizing Germany: Reconstructing National Identity after Hitler* (Chapel Hill: University of North Carolina Press, 1995).

41. E.g., Willi Höfig, *Der deutsche Heimatfilm, 1947–1962* (Stuttgart: Ferdinand Enke Verlag, 1973); and Martin Osterland, *Gesellschaftsbilder in Filmen: Eine soziologische Untersuchung des Filmangebots der Jahre 1949 bis 1963* (Stuttgart: Ferdinand Enke Verlag, 1970).

42. Useful overviews that attempt to locate cultural trends in a larger political context include Jost Hermand, *Kultur im Wiederaufbau: Die Bundesrepublik Deutschland, 1945–1965* (Munich: Nymphenburger, 1986); and Hermann Glaser, *Kulturgeschichte der Bundesrepublik Deutschland*, vol 1., *Zwischen Kapitulation und Währungsreform, 1945–1948* (Munich: Carl Hanser, 1985), vol. 2, *Zwischen Grundgesetz und Grosser Koalition 1949–1967* (Munich: Carl Hanser, 1986). The first volume of Glaser's history is available in English translation as *The Rubble Years: The Cultural Roots of Postwar Germany, 1945–1948*, trans. Franz Feige and Patricia Gleason (New York: Paragon House, 1986). See also Bernhard Schulz, ed., *Grauzonen/Farbwelten: Kunst*

also points in the direction of a postwar cultural history that recognizes the intersection of culture and politics. Like Roseman, she illustrates that West Germans came to terms with the past in many different ways.

The essays by Erica Carter and Uta Poiger demonstrate the ways in which gender figured not only on the silver screen but also in the marketplace. Carter and Poiger also make clear that the communities imagined by conservative Catholic film review boards and Ruhr businessmen were not the only visions of a new Germany that circulated in the 1950s. As Carter shows in "Alice in the Consumer Wonderland," a postwar rhetoric of "consumer democracy" and the insistence of Adenauer's economics minister, Ludwig Erhard, that the Federal Republic would ensure the "basic democratic right of consumer freedom" shifted the boundaries between public and private, crucially linking notions of female political citizenship to what Erhard called the "will to consume." Carter pays particular attention to the ways in which the postwar economy made specific appeals to young women as consumers, transforming "whole new areas of their lives . . . [into] the 'public' property of marketing institutions." Yet in her highly original interpretation, young women did not become the hapless victims of capitalist consumer culture; rather, the market provided them with symbols of political self-definition, allowing them to don the nylon stockings and scarlet lipstick that represented a forceful disavowal of Nazi conceptions of unadorned female beauty. Patterns of consumption also defined an important site of generational conflict as allegiance to a consumer culture based on the built-in obsolescence of synthetic silk nylons became a mode for rejecting an older generation's counsel of moderation in all things.[43]

The Americanization of youth culture, one of several themes in Carter's wide-ranging essay, is at the center of Uta Poiger's analysis of rock 'n' roll in the mid-1950s ("Rock 'n' Roll, Female Sexuality, and the Cold War Battle over German Identities"). Poiger's work draws on her superb study of youth culture in the two Germanies,[44] and in that respect, it also outlines an agenda for future research in which East Germany will serve historians of the Federal Republic not as a referent, viewed through the lens of the anticommunism that pervaded

und Zeitbilder, 1945–1955 (Berlin: Medusa Verlagsgesellschaft, 1983).

43. Although Carter's essay first appeared over a decade ago, there have been surprisingly few attempts to view the emergence of consumer society in the 1950s as a complex arena in which political, social, and sexual identities were negotiated. An exception to this rule is the important recent work of Michael Wildt, "Privater Konsum in Westdeutschland in den 50er Jahren," in Schildt and Sywottek, *Modernisierung im Wiederaufbau,* 275–89; idem, "Plurality of Taste: Food and Consumption in West Germany during the 1950s," *History Workshop Journal* no. 39 (1995):24–41; idem, *Am Beginn der Konsumgesellschaft: Mangelerfahrung, Lebenshaltung, Wohlstashoffnung in Westdeutschland in den fünfziger Jahren* (Hamburg: Ergebnisse, 1994); and Axel Schildt, *Moderne Zeiten: Freizeit, Massenmedien und "Zeitgeist" in der Bundesrepublik 50er Jahre* (Hamburg: Christians, 1995).

44. Uta G. Poiger, American Culture, German Identities: Cold War Battles over Gender,

West German society, but as a key part of truly comparative investigations.

Poiger provides a compelling analysis of how German discussions of the Americanization of youth culture were always discussions about race and sexuality as well. The potential for young women to succumb to "orgiastic hysteria" at the sight of Elvis Presley challenged not only conventional conceptions of female sexual propriety but also racial boundaries, because American rock music was invariably associated with black culture and negative stereotypes of "blackness," and black culture was always defined as sexual. Discussions of rock 'n' roll were thus also discussions of proper "Germanness"; when West Germans talked about Americans, they were talking about themselves. In the east, the state condemned rock 'n' roll as an expression of "American cultural barbarism" and "decadence," a form of capitalist seduction that threatened to undermine the values of socialism and to make "youth ripe for atomic war." No less than in the west, notions of "Germanness" were at stake when communist leaders attacked cultural forms that transgressed racial and sexual boundaries. For young women in both East and West Germany, adopting American culture became a form of political expression, subversive behavior that directly challenged gender, sexual, and racial conceptions of an older generation. Like Carter's work, Poiger's essay also is a radical revision of much of the research on postwar youth culture that has marginalized the experience of young women, focusing instead on male leather-clad motorcycle riders and "hooligans" (*Halbstarken*) and equating youth rebellion with male experience.[45]

Part 5 is entitled "'Conservative Modernization' in the Adenauer Era?" In the final essay in the volume, Axel Schildt and Arnold Sywottek ask whether the 1950s should be seen as a period of "'Reconstruction' and 'Modernization.'" They offer a balance sheet of much recent work on the early history of the Federal Republic, and they also demonstrate how much can be learned from a careful look at sociological studies and public opinion surveys conducted by contemporaries. Analyzing trends in economic development, geographic mobility, consumption, and by the late 1950s, reductions in working hours and the expansion of "leisure," Schildt and Sywottek conclude that the Adenauer era was characterized by some qualities of "social modernity," but that it was, borrowing Christoph Klessmann's formulation, a "modernization under a conservative guardianship" (*Modernisierung unter konservativer Auspizien*).[46]

Race, and Nation, 1949–1962 (forthcoming, University of California Press).

45. See, for example, Kaspar Maase, *BRAVO Amerika: Erkundungen zur Jugendkultur der Bundesrepublik in den fünfziger Jahren* (Hamburg: Junius Verlag, 1992); and the nuanced treatment of Uta G. Poiger, "Rebels with a Cause? American Popular Culture, the 1956 Youth Riots, and the New Conception of Masculinity in East and West Germany," in *The American Impact on Postwar Germany*, ed. Reiner Pommerin (Providence, R.I.: Berghahn Books, 1995), 93–124.

46. The formulation is taken from Christoph Klessmann, "Ein stolzes Schiff," 485. Schildt

As Schildt and Sywottek suggest—and as the essays in this volume by Fehrenbach, Poiger, and Carter indicate as well—adopting aspects of "Westerniza-
tion" and "modernization" did not mean forsaking "Germanness" or embracing
all aspects of "Americanization."

Toward a History of Society in the Federal Republic

Although the history of West German society in the 1950s has come of age, it
is not yet ready for early retirement, and in some senses the questions still to be
asked outnumber the answers that are presently in place. This volume thus
offers outlines of a social and cultural history of West Germany, but it also indicates what parts of that story remain to be told.

As Poiger's contribution announces, in the future much work on German
history in the 1950s will be comparative history,[47] but many topics in the history of the Federal Republic continue to demand far more attention in their
own right. For example, the political history of the 1950s remains dominated
by party histories in which programmatic statements and leaders take center
stage; a social history of politics remains to be written.[48]

The same holds for treatments of organized religion, and as Fehrenbach's
study indicates, there is still much to be said about how the church and its asso-

---

and Sywottek's essay framed a major research initiative, sponsored by the Volkswagen Founda-
tion and the University of Hamburg, on "'Modernity' and 'Modernization' in the Federal
Republic of Germany of the 1950s." The first results of the project appeared in Schildt and
Sywottek, *Modernisierung in Wiederaufbau.*

47. And students of the Federal Republic will also be able to draw on the studies
of the German Democratic Republic, likely to pour into the academic marketplace in the next few
years. For previews, see Hartmut Kaelble, Jürgen Kocka, and Hartmut Zwahr, eds.,
Sozialgeschichte der DDR (Stuttgart: Klett Cotta, 1994); Jürgen Kocka, ed., *Historische-DDR
Forschung: Aufsätze und Studien* (Berlin: Akademie Verlag, 1993); and Jürgen Kocka and Martin
Sabrow, eds., *Die DDR als Geschichte: Fragen-Hypothesen-Perspektiven* (Berlin: Akademie
Verlag, 1994). Also useful is the collection of documents in Christoph Klessmann and Georg
Wagner, *Das gespaltene Land: Leben in Deutschland 1945–1990: Texte und Dokumente
zur Sozialgeschichte* (Munich: C. H. Beck, 1993).

48. An invaluable resource for all explorations of party history is Richard Stöss,
ed., *Parteien-Handbuch: Die Parteien der Bundesrepublik Deutschland 1945–1980,* 2 vols.
(Opladen: Westdeutscher Verlag, 1983–84); for a summary of the literature that existed
by the late 1980s, Doering-Manteuffel, *Aussenpolitik,* 30–31, 136–72; on recent studies of
the CDU, Udo Wengst, "Die Partei Adenauers: Neuerscheinungen zur Geschichte der Union,"
Archiv für Sozialgeschichte 32 (1992): 510–22. See also the interesting local study of Everhard
Holtmann, *Politik und Nichtpolitik: Lokale Erscheinungsformen politischer Kultur im frühen
Nachkriegsdeutschland. Das Beispiel Unna und Kamen* (Opladen: Westdeutscher Verlag, 1989);
and Marie-Luise Recker, "'Bonn ist nicht Weimar': Zur Struktur und Charakter des poli-
tischen Systems der Bundesrepublik Deutschland in der Ära Adenauer," *Geschichte in Wissenschaft
und Unterricht* 44 (1993): 287–307. Useful on the immediate postwar period is also Daniel E.
Rogers, "Transforming the German Party System: The United States and the
Origins of Political Moderation, 1945–1949," *Journal of Modern History* 65 (1993): 512–41;
and idem, *Politics after Hitler: The Western Allies and the German Party System* (New York:
New York University, 1995).

ciated lay organizations served as a vital institutional framework for defining and championing conservative political, social, and moral values.[49] Diehl's work provides important insights into the political battles of organized veterans after the war, and a literature exists on the rehabilitation of the German military and the transformation of West Germans into "citizens in uniform"—a rearmed West Germany with an exclusively defensive military, firmly under civilian control—but we know little about how the soldiers and officers who were not active in interest groups experienced their transition from "Stalingrad to currency reform," from the war at the front to the competitive battlefields of the "economic miracle."[50]

Traditional preoccupations of social historians—community, class formation, the determinants of social inequality, working-class culture, the educational system as an arena of social control, generational conflict, and social mobility—remain largely unexplored for the 1950s. Informed by methodologies that insist on the centrality of gender for understanding class and the necessity to study class formation both at and away from the wage workplace, historians can provide more satisfying accounts of the 1950s than those that were written about the German empire, Weimar, and National Socialism in the 1970s and early 1980s.[51]

---

49. See, for example, Werner K. Blessing, "'Deutschland in Not, wir im Glauben . . .': Kirche und Kirchenvolk in einer katholischen Region, 1933–1949," in Broszat, Henke, and Woller, *Von Stalingrad zur Währungsreform*, 3–111.

50. See, for example, Georg Meyer, "Soldaten ohne Armee: Berufssoldaten im Kampf um Standesehre und Versorgung," in Broszat, Henke, and Woller, *Von Stalingrad zur Währungsreform*, 682–750; Detlef Bald, "'Bürger in Uniform': Tradition und Neuanfang des Militärs in Westdeutschland," in Schildt und Sywottek, *Modernisierung im Wiederaufbau*, 392–402; Donald Abenheim, *Reforging the Iron Cross: The Search for Tradition in the West German Armed Forces* (Princeton: Princeton University Press, 1988); David Clay Large, "Reckoning without the Past: The HIAG of the Waffen-SS and the Politics of Rehabilitation in the Bonn Republic, 1950–1961," *Journal of Modern History* 59 (1987): 79–113; idem, *Germans to the Front: West German Rearmament in the Adenauer Era* (Chapel Hill: University of North Carolina Press, 1996); and Albrecht Lehmann, *Gefangenschaft und Heimkehr: Deutsche Kriegsgefangene in der Sowjetunion* (Munich: C. H. Beck, 1986). One of the most fascinating studies of the political attitudes of veterans, returned from prisoner-of-war camps, remains the study of the Institut für Sozialforschung, *Zum politischen Bewusstsein ehemaliger Kriegsgefangener: Eine soziologische Untersuchung im Verband der Heimkehr: Forschungsbericht* (Frankfurt am Main: n.p., 1957).

51. See, for instance, the suggestive thoughts of Josef Mooser, "Arbeiter, Angestellte und Frauen in der 'nivellierten Mittelstandsgesellschaft': Thesen," in Schildt and Sywottek, *Modernisierung im Wiederaufbau*, 362–76. Mooser's perceptive challenge to visions of a "classless society" or a "levelled-out petit bourgeois middle-class society" in the postwar Federal Republic, the formulation of the sociologist Helmut Schelsky, remains unsurpassed and offers an invaluable framework for the study of postwar class formation in the context of the longer-term continuities in twentieth-century German history. He also demonstrates how much can be learned from the extensive sociological literature on the working class, which was produced in the 1950s. See Mooser, *Arbeiterleben in Deutschland*. For outlines of a history of the bourgeoisie in the postwar period, see Hannes Siegrist, "Ende der Bürgerlichkeit? Die Kategorien 'Bürgertum' und 'Bürgerlicht-

Several of the essays in this volume also point the way toward understanding gender both as the lived historical experience of women and men and as part of a symbolic order, informing state policy and political ideology, locating the divide between public and private, and shaping identities. Exploring the process by which postwar West Germans renegotiated boundaries between women and men remains an extremely lively area of research. In addition to the articles included in this volume, a number of other important recent studies indicate how much remains to be said about the redefinition of *man* and *woman,* as West Germans moved from an obsession with the postwar "surplus of women" (*Frauenüberschuss*) and fears of "women standing alone" (*alleinstehende Frauen*)—perceived as lasting legacies of the high rate of adult male death during the war—to a status quo defined by the celebration of "complete" heterosexual families and "marriages of partners."[52]

As Poiger, Carter, and Fehrenbach expertly demonstrate, the study of the social and political history of the early Federal Republic will increasingly be influenced by approaches borrowed from the field of cultural studies and the understanding that the boundaries between "society," "culture," and "politics" are typically far clearer in the minds of historians than in the lives of the people we study. From this perspective, novels, movies, theater, the mass media, and popular music appear not as ephemera, but as crucial sources for exploring politics and society.[53] As the articles in this volume also indicate, historical explorations of popular culture can yield important insights into how West Germans came to terms with the past of National Socialism and constructed competing visions of an imagined community in the 1950s.

---

keit' in der westdeutschen Gesellschaft und Geschichtswissenschaft der Nachkriegsperiode," *Geschichte und Gesellschaft* 20 (1994): 549–83.

52. See, for example, Maria Höhn, "Frau im Haus, Girl in *Spiegel:* Discourse on Women in the Interregnum Period of 1945–1949 and the Question of German Identity," *Central European History* 26 (1993): 57–90; Donna Harsch, "Public Continuity and Private Change? Women's Consciousness and Activity in Frankfurt, 1945–1955," *Journal of Social History* 27 (1993): 29–59; Klaus-Jörg Ruhl, *Veordnete Unterordnung: Berufstätige Frauen zwischen Wirtschaftswachstum und konservativer Ideologie* (Munich: C. H. Beck, 1994); Merith Niehuss, "Kontinuität und Wandel der Familie in den 50er Jahren," in Schildt and Sywottek, *Modernisierung im Wiederaufbau,* 316–34; Katherine Pence, "The 'Fräuleins' meet the 'Amis': Americanization of German Women in the Reconstruction of the West German State," *Michigan Feminist Studies* 7 (1992–93): 83–108; Elizabeth Heineman, "'Standing Alone': Single Women from Nazi Germany to the Federal Republic" (Ph.D. diss., University of North Carolina, 1993); idem, "The Hour of the Woman: Memories of Germany's 'Crisis Years' and West German National Identity," *American Historical Review* 101 (1996): 354–95; idem, "Complete Families, Half Families, No Families at All: Female-Headed Households and the Reconstruction of the Family in the Early Federal Republic," *Central European History* 29 (1996): 29–60; and Katharina C. Tumpek-Kjellmark, "From Hitler's Widows to Adenauer's Brides: Towards a Construction of Gender and Memory in Postwar West Germany, 1938–1963" (Ph.D. diss., Cornell University, 1994).

53. In addition to Fehrenbach, see Poiger, "Rebels with a Cause?"; and Margit Szöllösi-

Poiger also points to the necessity for much more systematic exploration of racialist attitudes in the aftermath of fascism; students of modernization and Americanization would do well to follow her lead, examining the ways in which discussions of modernity are invariably discussions of race and sexuality. Her work also indicates the importance of analyzing the various ways in which America figured in the political culture of the Federal Republic—as symbol of modernity, as economic power, and as a political and cultural presence. U.S.-West German relations played themselves out not only at the conferences of heads of state, but also in communities near U.S. bases where American GIs crossed paths with West Germans daily, at the cosmetics counter, in movie theaters, and in teenagers' bedrooms, where the American Forces Network offered new languages of sexual expression and foreign relations that became decidedly domestic. Serious research into these subjects has only just begun.[54]

Discussion of the usefulness of the concept of modernization to describe the 1950s, suggested by the title of Schildt and Sywottek's contribution, must also include more careful consideration of the dark side of modernity, illuminated so clearly in Detlev Peukert's pathbreaking study of the Weimar Republic.[55] German defeat and the postwar settlement may have destroyed some institutions that predisposed Germans toward authoritarian solutions, and the economic stability of the 1950s provided far firmer bases for democratic political institutions than the crisis-ridden 1920s. However, these powerful forces could not eradicate the tensions inherent in modern industrial societies—between rapid growth and social inequality; between old and young; between women and men; between those included and those excluded by the provisions of the welfare state; between a national culture created by mass media and the survival of distinct cultural forms at the local and regional level; between the blessings of economic prosperity and the long-term environmental consequences of unregulated growth;[56] between consumer desires and counsels of moderation; between aesthetic forms that represented a break with the past and deep-seated pressures to maintain cultural traditions.

Janze, "'Aussuchen und abschiessen': Der Heimatfilm der fünfziger Jahre als historische Quelle," *Geschichte in Wissenschaft und Unterricht* 44 (1993): 308–21.

54. See, for example, the important dissertation of Maria Höhn, "GIs, Veronikas, and Lucky Strikes: German Reactions to the American Military Presence in the Rhineland-Palatinate during the 1950s" (Ph.D. diss., University of Pennsylvania, 1995). In addition, Heide Fehrenbach is now completing a research project entitled "'Mixed Blood': Discourses of Race, Sex, and Nation in American-Occupied Germany."

55. Detlev J. K. Peukert, *The Weimar Republic: The Crisis of Classical Modernity,* trans. by Richard Deveson (New York: Hill and Wang, 1992).

56. See, for example, Dietmar Klenke, "Bundesdeutsche Verkehrspolitik und Umwelt: Von der Motorisierungseuphorie zur ökologischen Katerstimmung," in *Umweltgeschichte:*

The 1950s also saw no complete disappearance of political ideologies that borrowed from a language of social hygiene and scientific racism to justify the marginalization, exclusion, and in some cases, criminal prosecution of those who violated the "healthy sensibility of the people."[57] *Bonn ist nicht Weimar*, announced the title of Fritz Renée Allemann's 1956 book, and there is no question that the Federal Republic was allowed to negotiate the "crises of modernity" under far more propitious circumstances than the democratic experiment of the 1920s. Still, historians have yet to begin systematic study of how the "tensions generated by the impact of modernization on society, culture, and the political system"[58] articulated themselves in the first decade of the Federal Republic's history. Bonn's stability allowed Germans to establish institutions of democratic governance, but it also forcefully shut down the spaces in which some of what made Weimar distinctive—artistic experimentation and the explicit intersection of culture and politics, a vibrant gay and lesbian culture, a wide-ranging sex reform debate, Social Democratic and communist conceptions of social and economic reform that drew on the Marxist tradition—had flourished.

Looking east as well as west, it will be important to examine the ways in which the merger of anti-Soviet, anti-Slav, and anti-Asian attitudes in the rhetoric of postwar anticommunism allowed for the survival of other forms of pre-1945 racism that reinforced fears of the "monstrous power of Asia"; the "east" became a racial, geographic, and political designation that could be expanded from the border with East Germany to the Gulf of Shanghai and that could be kept at bay only by an "economically and spiritually healthy western Europe." A political rhetoric of *Abendland* ("occident"), always Christian, trumpeted particularly by Catholic politicians within the Christian Democratic Union, gave a particular cast to Cold War ideology in the Federal Republic, and pointed—explicitly or implicitly—to an east that might not be godless but worshiped the wrong god.[59] Tracing out these ideological legacies in the 1950s can potentially shed light on the postwar history of prejudice against Turks and others from a non-Christian "east" in Germany today.[60]

The essays by Schildt and Sywottek, Carter, and Poiger also look ahead to the late 1950s, away from the rubble of the immediate postwar years to an "economic miracle" that was becoming not just promise, but reality; they indi-

---

Umweltverträgliches Wirtschaften in historischer Perspektive, ed. Werner Abelshauser (Göttingen: Vandenhoeck & Ruprecht, 1994), 163–90.

57. The language of *"gesundes Empfinden des Volkes,"* employed by the Nazis, was also used as a justification for the criminal prosecution of male homosexuality in the 1950s. See Moeller, "The Homosexual Man Is a 'Man,'" in this volume.

58. Peukert, *Weimar Republic*, 83.

59. On the significance of the rhetoric of *Abendland* immediately after the war, see the insightful work of Maria Mitchell, "Materialism and Secularism: CDU Politicians and National Socialism, 1945–1949," *Journal of Modern History* 67 (1995): 278–308.

60. For the contemporary discussion, see Sabine von Dirke, "Multikulti: The German

cate that the more we know about the 1950s, the more important it becomes to disaggregate this decade, differentiating between those trends and developments that constituted part of postwar reconstruction and those that led ahead to a distinctly different Germany, marked by changing patterns of consumption, work, leisure, and the coming of age of a generation that had experienced the war neither at the front nor in Hitler youth organizations, but in diapers.[61] As Poiger suggests, a new intellectual elite, a group she calls "cold war liberals," was also assuming positions of social and political power, registering a change of guard from the Weimar establishment that had still dominated the early 1950s. From this perspective, the standard of measurement for postwar continuity and change becomes not 1933 or 1945, but the 1960s, 1970s, and 1980s.[62] The dimensions of the "continuity problem" (*Kontinutitätsproblem*) and the place of the 1950s in the history of the Federal Republic are thus bound to shift as we know more not only of the history of society in the first postwar decade, but in the decades that followed as well.

This list of areas for future research is meant to be suggestive, not exhaustive. It is offered to indicate that this volume should be understood as an introduction to a discussion, not the last word, an invitation to response, challenge, and revision. Perhaps most importantly, the volume underscores the need for continued work on the early history of the Federal Republic. Since unification, the post–World War II German history that has most interested historians is the history of the failed communist experiment in the east; locating the past of the German Democratic Republic in the context of comparative studies of twentieth-century dictatorships, historians have insisted that after 1989, there were two pasts, not just one, to be overcome in a unified German state. Still preoccupied with the "long shadow of Hitler" and the history of a fascist dictatorship, they have also begun to examine the long shadows of a past dominated by a state security system of truly astonishing proportions, of Otto Grotewohl, Walter Ulbricht, and Erich Honnecker, East German communist leaders.[63] The essays brought together in this volume, however, are a forceful reminder that West Germany's first chancellor, Konrad Adenauer, also continues to cast a long shadow; there remains yet another past that a unified Germany should critically confront.

Debate on Multiculturalism," *German Studies Review* 17 (1994): 519–20.

61. An important contribution toward filling in these dimensions is offered by Axel Schildt, *Moderne Zeiten;* also, idem, "'Mach mal Pause!': Freie Zeit, Freizeitverhalten und FreizeitDiskurse in der westdeutschen Wiederaufbau-Gesellschaft der 1950er Jahre," *Archiv für Sozialgeschichte* 33 (1993): 357–406.

62. See Mooser, "Abschied von der 'Proletarität,'" 186; Erker, "Zeitgeschichte als Sozial geschichte," 215–16; Berghahn, *Americanisation of West German Industry,* 295–97; and in general, Schildt, "Nachkriegszeit."

63. In addition to Kocka, *Historische DDR-Forschung;* and Kaelble, Kocka, and Zwahr, *Sozialgeschichte der DDR;* see *Totalitäre Herrschaft-totalitäres Erbe, German Studies Review* Special Issue (fall 1994).

Part 1.
Confronting the
Consequences of Defeat

A Question of Silence:
The Rape of German Women
by Occupation Soldiers

Atina Grossmann

> Until that time I had lived so happily with my husband and the children. I had four children; the youngest I had to bury on May 18; it was 4 months old. Now I am in a desperate condition and do not want to have this child under any circumstances.[1]

Prologue

This statement submitted to the Health Office of Berlin's working-class Neukölln district on December 16, 1945, by a woman requesting a medical abortion on grounds of rape by a Soviet soldier, encapsulates the extraordinaily convoluted nature of my topic. I came to it unintentionally, quite unwillingly but irresistibly, through my research on the politics of abortion and birth control in postwar Germany. Finding this affidavit among the 995 cases approved for abortion on the grounds of rape recorded in the Neukölln district office (*Bezirk-samt*) files on "Termination of pregnancy" between June 7, 1945, and June 17, 1946,[2] I was both moved (despite myself) by the poignancy and desperation of a woman's and mother's statement, and horrified (despite all I know) at the notion that anyone could describe herself as having lived happily—and normally—in Germany until the defeat of the Third Reich and the arrival of the Red Army.

An earlier version of this essay appeared in German in *Frauen und Film* 54/55 (April 1994).

1. December 16, 1945, Landesarchiv Berlin (LAB) Rep. 214/2814/221/2 (Gesundheitsamt Neukölln).

2. The interruption-of-pregnancy records are from the Landesarchiv Berlin, Gesundheits-amt Neukölln, Rep. 214. Neukölln seems to be the district that has the most completely preserved Gesundheitsamt records, so it is difficult to judge—at this point at least—whether the number of applications and near universal approval rate was similar in other Berlin districts.

The question of rape of German women by occupation, mostly Red Army, soldiers during and after World War II is intricate as well as richly and perilously overdetermined. It partakes of two highly developed discourses that continually intersect and threaten to block each other—so much so that the silence referred to in the title of this chapter is at least as much that of the historian trying to figure out how to tell the story as about the events discussed.

On the one hand, the feminist discourse on rape, its representation and construction, while not trusting every single story, validates and publicizes the voices of women who speak of sexual violation and tries to integrate rape into its analysis of "normal" heterosexual relations. On the other hand, the historical discourse on Germany's confrontation with its Nazi past (*Vergangen heitsbewältigung*) tends to distrust any narrative that might support postwar Germans' self-perception as victims insofar as it might participate in a dangerous revival of German nationalism, whitewash the Nazi past, and normalize a genocidal war. This fear became dramatically clear in the *Historikerstreit* of the mid-1980s and continues to haunt current historical and political debates in Germany, as well as among observers abroad.[3] It is compounded by the renewed nationalism and xenophobia in a reunited Germany which seeks, among other things, to claim Wehrmacht soldiers as heroic and beleaguered fighters on the eastern front holding back the Stalinist Slavic onslaught. Indeed, just announcing apparent "facts" about the massive incidence of rape perpetrated by soldiers of the Red Army which smashed the Nazi war machine is enough to provoke enormous anxiety and resistance among many who are otherwise not averse to documenting the widespread existence of male violence against women. Historical analysis becomes even more difficult in the current context of anguish and confusion about the proper analysis of, and response to, the rapes in former Yugoslavia and especially in Bosnia.[4]

The ironically titled documentary film *BeFreier und Befreite*, on precisely this topic, made by the noted West German feminist filmmaker Helke Sander, highlights my dilemmas—as the child of German-Jewish refugees working as a feminist historian of modern Germany. Much as I respect Sander's efforts to document a complicated and important history and to create a public space for its discussion, I find her approach deeply problematic, at times wildly self-righteous and historically disingenuous. Sander claims finally to be breaking

---

3. See, among many other considerations, Geoff Eley, "Nazism, Politics, and Public Memory: Thoughts on the West German *Historikerstreit* 1986–1987," *Past and Present* 121 (November 1988), pp. 171–208; Charles S. Maier, *The Unmasterable Past: History, the Holocaust, and German National Identity* (Cambridge: Harvard University Press, 1988); and the special issue of New German Critique 44 (Spring/Summer 1988).

4. See, for example, the uproar about Catherine MacKinnon's analysis of the connections between rape and pornography in former Yugoslavia in *MS* cover story (July/August 1993), pp. 24–30. See Erika Munk's critique, *Women's Review of Books* (January 1994).

the silence on a story long subject to taboo and ignored either as exaggerated anti-Communist propaganda or as the "normal" by-product of a vicious war, a story sacrificed on the altar of the "myth of antifascism" or of East-West rapprochement. But in many ways, the criticism Sander hurled at Gertrud Koch's negative review—*"Du machst es Dir viel zu einfach"* (You make it much too easy for yourself)[5]—needs rather to be applied to the film. Oblivious to historians' analyses of the ways in which the stubborn (and noncontextualized) search for "real information" can distort far more than illuminate, Sander insists that she just wants to present the "hard facts."[6] These are represented for her by numbers and in a quite peculiar manner, indeed, one that borders on parody, for the pencil and blackboard wielded by her demographic expert, Dr. Reichling, hardly seem the instruments of modern statistical analysis.

But, hard—or even soft—facts are hard to come by and unreliable. It has been suggested that perhaps one out of every three of about one and a half million women in Berlin at the end of the war were raped—many but certainly not all during the notorious days of "mass rapes," from April 24 to May 5, 1945, as the Soviets finally secured Berlin. The numbers cited for Berlin vary wildly; from 20,000 to 100,000, to almost one million, with the actual number of rapes higher because many women were attacked repeatedly. Sander and her collaborator, Barbara Johr, speak, perhaps conservatively, of about 110,000 women raped, many more than once, of whom up to 10,000 died in the aftermath.[7] At the same time—and despite their virtual fetishization of statistical clarity—they announce on the basis of *Hochrechnungen* (projections or estimations) that 1.9 million German women altogether were raped at the end of the war by Red Army soldiers.[8] This may be a horrifically accurate estimate, but one wonders whether or not the focus on numbers has something to do with precisely a competitiveness about the status of victim (*"ein Verbrechen mit dem anderen aufgerechnet"*), so sensitive in the context of World War II, that Sander claims to resist in her work; it even suggests a lust for generally portraying women as victims that seems central to her particular historical and feminist agenda.[9]

---

5. Helke Sander, "Du machst es Dir viel zu einfach," *Frankfurter Rundschau* (November 26, 1992).

6. Helke Sander and Barbara Johr, eds., *BeFreier und Befreite: Krieg, Vergewaltigungen, Kinder* (Munich: Verlag Antje Kunstmann, 1992), p. 11. See Joan Scott, "The Evidence of Experience," *Critical Inquiry* 17 (Summer 1991), pp. 773–97; see also the exchange between Laura Lee Downs and Joan Scott in *Comparative Studies in Society and History* 35 (April 1993).

7. Barbara Johr, "Die Ereignisse in Zahlen," in Sander and Johr, *BeFreier und Befreite*, pp. 48, 54–55. See also Erich Kuby, Die Russen in Berlin 1945 (Bern/Munich: Scherz, 1965), pp. 312–13.

8. Ibid., pp. 48, 54–55, 59.

9. See Helke Sander, "Du machst es Dir viel zu einfach," *Frankfurter Rundschau* (November 26, 1992). The insistence on the critical importance of precise figures seems especially ironic given that Sander in a notorious short story (which refers to the "exterminatory will" of the five

When telling this important and tangled story, the point cannot be to argue about numbers or to gather "just the facts." As the historian Norman Naimark concludes in his careful history of the Soviet zone, "It is highly unlikely that historians will ever know how many German women were raped by Soviet soldiers in the months before and years after the capitulation."[10] At the same time, however, he demonstrates that, despite all necessary caveats about similar episodes of violence and indiscipline on the part of other occupation troops,

> rape became a part of the social history of the Soviet zone in ways un-known to the Western zones. . . . It is important to establish the fact that women in the Eastern zone—both refugees from further East and inhabi-tants of the towns, villages, and cities of the Soviet zone—shared an ex-perience for the most part unknown in the West, the ubiquitous threat and the reality of rape, over a prolonged period of time.[11]

Sander's film opens with a familiar still frame of shattered Berlin 1945, women searching through the ruins and Red Army soldiers swaggering down the street. The voice-over, however, comes as a provocation. "Just like in Kuwait, just like in Yugoslavia," the narrator intones, as we see newsreel footage of soldiers grabbing bicycles from women or posing with newly ac-quired loot. This is the film's essential (and essentialist) message; even as it deals with a particular historical moment, it posits the horrific universality of rape. The universal soldier, whether in the Red Army or the SS, in the U.S. Army or the French Foreign Legion, the Iraqi Army or the Serb irregulars, rapes and pillages innocent women; women as universal victim are the booty of every war, the unrecognized and uncompensated targets of war crimes.

However, as the African-American literary critic Hazel Carby has pointed out, "Rape itself should not be regarded as a transhistorical mechanism of women's oppression but as one that acquires specific political or economic meanings at different moments in history."[12] In other words, even as we strug-gle to name sexual violence and to create community among women in order

---

books of Moses and the "literally murderous patriarchy" of the Old Testament) is so contemptu-ous of the focus on numbers in discussion of the Final Solution. See "Telefongespräch mit einem Freund" in *Die Geschichten der drei Damen K.* (Munich: Weissmann Verlag, 1987), pp. 140–41. (Translated by Helen Petzold as "A Telephone Conversation with a Friend" in *The Three Women K.* [London: Serpent's Tail, 1991], pp. 118–30.) Inevitably, once one enters the realm of millions, one enters the terrain of Holocaust and of women's claim to equal or similar status with Jews as victims—a hallmark of some German feminist writing.

10. Norman M. Naimark, *The Russians in Germany: A History of the Soviet Zone of Occu-pation, 1945–1949* (Cambridge: Harvard University Press, 1995), pp. 132–33.

11. Ibid., pp. 106–7.

12. Hazel Carby, *Reconstructing Womanhood: The Emergence of the Afro-American Woman Novelist* (New York: Oxford University Press, 1987), p. 18. See also Kathryn Gravdal, "Chretien de Troyes, Gratian, and the Medieval Romance of Sexual Violence," *Signs* 17 (Spring 1992), pp. 558–85.

to combat it, we must understand it as both an intensely personal and a public, politically and historically constructed event. In one particularly gruesome moment in the film, the camera darts back and forth between grainy shots of women's disheveled, disemboweled bodies while a female voice repeats, "German women, Russian women, German women, Russian women," all united by one vicious male orgy of transhistorical, transpolitical patriarchal violence. But these are not any (or all) women: what the film does not make clear is that these pictures intended to represent the "equality" of male violence affecting women are in fact taken from the *Deutsche Wochenschau,* the Nazi war propaganda newsreels, and were used to demonstrate the "bestial" and "animalistic" actions of the Red Army "horde" against *German* women. Ironically, the very image Sander uses to establish that she is not limiting her critique to Russians is lifted from a Nazi film showing German victims.[13]

In this particular case, then, on the most mundane (and melodramatic) level, the problem is that this is not (yet another) "universal" story of women being raped by men, as Helke Sander would have it, but of German women being abused and violated by an army that fought Nazi Germany and liberated death camps. Mass rapes of civilian women also signaled the defeat of Nazi Germany—a historical event I learned to call *Befreiung* (liberation) but which Germans usually described as *Zusammenbruch* (collapse). Therefore, beyond arguments about the veracity of women's reports or pseudostatistical investigations (although I do think that much conventional historical research remains to be done), I am interested in "de-essentializing" and historicizing the rapes Sander addresses in her film; these events cannot, I think, be usefully understood by quick comparison to Kuwait or Yugoslavia, nor can they gain macabre comic relief by editing in clips of U.S. Army anti–venereal disease films.

In particular, I want to examine two points that seem to me important when thinking about German history and how feminists might approach the place of these events in German history. First, the massive experience of rape, the fear of rape, and the incessantly repeated stories of rape—both at the time and years later—need to be solidly located within a pervasive German self-perception and memory of victimization so strong and enduring that it continues to surprise many Americans, and especially Jews, as it repeatedly pops up. Second, I want to read the language of the various rape narratives quoted here as offering clues to the continuing impact within the immediate postwar period of both Weimar and National Socialist population and social welfare policy, and the links and differences between the two.

We need to ask how the (eventually privately transmitted and publicly silenced) collective experience of rape of German women in the absence of (protective) German men insinuated itself into postwar Germans' view of

---

13. See *Deutsche Wochenschau* nos. 755/10/1945, 754/9/1945, and 739/46/1944. Filmarchiv BArch(Koblenz).

themselves as primarily "victims" and not "agents" of National Socialism and war. The mass rapes of 1945 inscribed indelibly in many German women's memory a sullen conviction of their own victimization and their superiority over the vanquisher who came to liberate them. Mass rapes confirmed Germans' identity—both the women who were assaulted and the men (dead, wounded, maimed, or in prisoner-of-war camps) who could not/would not protect them—as victims of *Missbrauch* (abuse). The term was ubiquitous when used by women to circumscribe their experience but was also deployed more generally to suggest all the ways in which the German Volk as a whole had been woefully abused—by the Nazis, by Hitler, who reneged on his promises of national renewal and led them into a war that could not be won, by the losses on the front and the Allied bombing raids, and then by defeat, occupation, and a de-Nazification that was generally perceived as arbitrary and unfair.

Let me be clear: I am not suggesting that raped German women were not victims (as long as we are stuck with this somewhat insufficient vocabulary); there must be no doubt that they were. The problem is that Sander's eagerness to integrate German women into the international transhistorical sisterhood of victims of male violence leads to a problematic historical slippage and displacement in which German women seem to become the victims primarily of National Socialism and the war, rather than of the failure of National Socialism and defeat in the war. It both leads to, and is symptomatic of, the exasperating insistence of some German feminists that women as a group were only victims (and not also agents, collaborators, or beneficiaries) of National Socialism.[14] Sander's own deliberately innocent narrative style (she is the righteous and beleaguered investigator who just wants to know the truth) undergirds this slippage. It is critical, however, to remember that in the case of mass rape of German women, it was not the Third Reich but rather its collapse (*Zusammenbruch*) that led to women's violation.

Given the current preoccupation (especially in Germany) with "tabooand silence-breaking" in discussions of World War II and genocide and the relative crimes of Nazis and Soviets—and Sander's film is a significant contribution to this growing genre—it is also important to clarify that these were not, initially at least, rapes that had been silenced. They became an official problem located in the public sphere because they had social health and population political consequences that required medical intervention: venereal disease and pregnancy. They were immediately coded as public issues, not as an experience of violent sexual assault, but as a social and medical problem

---

14. This debate about whether German women should be studied primarily as *Opfer* (victims) or *Täter* (perpetrators) has now been played out in many forums, notably the bitter arguments between Gisela Bock and Claudia Koonz over the latter's book *Mothers in the Fatherland: Women, the Family and Nazi Politics* (New York: St. Martin's Press, 1987). See my review essay "Feminist Debates about Women and National Socialism," *Gender and History* 3 (Autumn 1991), pp. 350–58.

that needed to be resolved. And it was in that context that women received at least some help—medical treatment and abortions—and that some of the documents cited in this chapter were produced.

Nor were these rapes silenced among the women themselves, again at least initially; as I looked at the literature of the postwar years—diaries, memoirs, and novels—I found rape stories everywhere, told matter-of-factly, told as tragedy, told with ironic humor and bravado.[15] Women told their stories to authorities from whom they expected specific forms of redress, and they also obsessively retold their stories to each other and to their daughters. They lived, interpreted, and represented their rapes in a particular historical context which they participated in creating. We need to understand how the experience of, the reaction to, and the memory of these rapes were framed by the specific historically toxic conjuncture in which they took place.

The Expectation of Rape

It is crucial to note how massively these rapes had been prefigured in Nazi propaganda. Women living in self-styled "cellar tribes" in ravaged Berlin were already transfixed by intense fear of rape as the Red Army advanced. Horrific images of invading Mongol barbarians raping German women were a vital part of the Nazi war machine's feverish (and successful) efforts to bolster morale on the eastern front and keep the home front intact. Nazi propaganda had been relentless in characterizing the Russians as subhuman and animalistic (*"das viehisches Treiben dieser Untermenschen"*). The threat of a surging Asian flood and marauding Red Beast tearing through what was supposedly still a pacific, ordinary German land was used to incite desperate resistance even long after it was clear that the war was fundamentally lost. By the end of the war most German women had already seen graphic newsreel footage of the bodies of "violated women, battered old people, and murdered children" (geschändete Frauen, erschlagene Greise, und ermordete Kinder) left behind as the Red Army pounded westward. Indeed the very last newsreel released in 1945 showed a white fence with the desperate message scrawled on it, "Protect our women and children from the Red Beast."[16]

Moreover, Germans knew enough of *Wehrmacht* and SS crimes in the East to have reason to believe that vengeful Russians would commit atrocities and to make the oft-repeated (but never proven) account of the Jewish-Russian

---

15. For further references see the (different) German language version of this article, "Eine Frage des Schweigens: Die Vergewaltigung deutscher Frauen durch Besatzungssoldaten. Zum historischen Hintergrund von Helke Sanders Film *BeFreier und Befreite*," *Frauen und Film* 54/55 (April 1994), pp. 15–28.

16. *Deutsche Wochenschau* no. 755/10/1945. Sander's film uses clips from this newsreel of a radio reporter interviewing German women about rapes committed by Soviet "bestial hordes." See also nos. 754/9/1945 and 739/46/1944.

writer Ilya Ehrenburg's infamous call for Soviet soldiers to seek retribution by raping "blond" German women plausible.[17] Whatever the level of ordinary Germans' detailed knowledge of the systematic extermination of European Jewry, it was no secret that *Wehrmacht* actions on the eastern front (in contrast to the western front) went well beyond the standards of ordinary brutal warfare. German soldiers had been explicitly commanded to liquidate all putative "Bolsheviks," and during their "scorched earth" retreat, as a matter of policy, not of indiscipline, they laid waste to huge territories of civilian population and massacred entire villages. Again and again in German recollections of what Russian occupiers told them, the vengeful memory summoned was not a parallel violation by a German raping a Russian woman, but of a horror on a different order: it was the image of a German soldier swinging a baby, torn from its mothers arms, against a wall—the mother screams, the baby's brains splatter against the wall, the soldier laughs.[18]

The embittered defense by the retreating *Wehrmacht* forced exhausted and in part disbelieving Soviet commanders to continue hard fighting right into the center of devastated Berlin. By February, they were only thirty-five miles east of Berlin, and still the Germans would not surrender as they tried to carve out escape routes for themselves to the west and north. Fortified by huge caches of alcohol conveniently left behind by the retreating Germans, reinforced by brutalized Soviet prisoners of war liberated along the way, and enraged by the street-to-street, house-to-house German defense, loyally carried out by young boys and old men as well as regular soldiers, the Red Army pushed through East Prussia toward Berlin in what the military historian John Erickson has called "a veritable passion of destructiveness."[19] In a remarkably infelicitous sentence, Erickson concluded: "The fighting drained both sides, though Russian lustiness won through."[20]

---

17. See Susan Brownmiller's discussion in *Against Our Will: Men, Women and Rape* (New York: Simon and Schuster, 1975), pp. 70–71.

18. This terrifying image obviously has a long lineage not limited to memories of World War II. For a specific reference in this context, see Ingrid Strobl's response to Sander's film, "Wann begann das Grauen?" *Konkret* (September 1992), p. 55. There is no reliable comparative data on rapes committed by the *Wehrmacht* because, while rape by German soldiers on the western front was generally severely punished, "In the Soviet Union, however, we no longer hear of soldiers being tried, let alone executed, for acts of violence and plunder against Soviet citizens." See Omer Bartov, *Hitler's Army: Soldiers, Nazis, and War in the Third Reich* (New York: Oxford University Press, 1991), p. 70. See also the recent film *Mein Krieg*, in which German veterans talk about their experiences on the eastern front.

19. See (among many sources) John Erickson, *The Road to Berlin: Stalin's War with Germany*, vol. 2 (London: Weidenfeld and Nicolson, 1983), p. 512; Omer Bartov, *The Eastern Front 1941–45: German Troops and the Barbarisation of Warfare* (New York: St. Martin's Press, 1986); and Richard Evans, *In Hitler's Shadow: West German Historians and the Attempt to Escape from the Nazi Past* (New York: Pantheon, 1989), chap. 2.

20. Erickson, *Road to Berlin*, p. 603.

Official Soviet policy, reflecting Stalin's pronouncement that "the Hitlers come and go but the German *Volk* remains," obstinately refused to acknowledge that the Red Army would engage in atrocities on anything more than the level of "isolated excesses." Ilya Ehrenburg himself (whose line of "we shall be severe but just" was in any case being pushed aside by Stalin's new interest in mollifying the *Volk*) insisted that "The Soviet soldier will not molest a German woman. . . . It is not for booty, not for loot, not for women that he has come to Germany."[21]

In this instance however, Goebbels' propaganda—for once—turned out to be correct. So much so that many women reported feeling that they were re-enacting a scene in a film they had already seen when the drama they were expecting actually unfolded: soldiers with heavy boots, unfamiliar faces (invariably coded as Mongol), and shining flashlights entered a darkened cellar, searched for weapons and watches, and then, revolver in hand, commanded the proverbial *"Frau, Komm."*

Even the public policy response to the rapes—the unofficial but generally accepted suspension of Paragraph 218 which had criminalized all nonmedical or noneugenic abortions—had already been set into motion by the Nazis. The other side of harsh wartime regulations limiting abortion and access to contraceptives were secret directives permitting—or coercing—abortions on female foreign workers and women defined as prostitutes and non-"Aryans," as well as on the growing number of German women who became pregnant, via consensual sex or rape, by foreign workers or prisoners of war. Already in 1940, the Minister of the Interior had issued a secret memo instructing local health offices to consider "voluntary" extralegal abortions not provided for in the 1935 amendment to the 1933 Sterilization Law (which sanctioned eugenic abortions prior to sterilization), in "urgent, proven" cases of rape or undesirable racial combinations (with someone "racially alien," *artfremd*).[22]

By the beginning of 1945, the encroaching Red Army had advanced to such a point that the possibility of mass "violations" of German women by Soviet troops was acknowledged and indeed widely publicized. Since rapes were already supposedly resulting in many pregnancies, the Ministry of

---

21. Ilya Ehrenburg, *The War: 1941–1945. Volume 5. Of Men, Years—Life* (Cleveland: The World Publishing Company, 1964), trans. Tatiana Shenunina in collaboration with Yvonne Kapp, p. 175. See also Erika M. Hoerning, "Frauen als Kriegsbeute. Der Zwei-Fronten Krieg. Beispiele aus Berlin," in *"Wir kriegen jetzt andere Zeiten." Auf der Suche nach der Erfahrung des Volkes in antifaschistischen Ländern. Lebensgeschichte und Sozialkultur im Ruhrgebiet 1930 bis 1960*, vol. 3, ed. Lutz Niethammer and Alexander von Plato (Berlin: Verlag J. H. W. Dietz Nachf., 1985), pp. 327–46.

22. Sterilization was recommended as a follow-up. BArch(Koblenz), Schumacher collection 399, RMI, September 19, 1940, secret memo to health offices and local governments. I am grateful to Gabriele Czarnowski for sending me copies of these materials.

Interior even suggested the establishment "in large cities [of] special wards for the care of such women."[23]

The Experience of Rape

For German women in 1945—certainly in Berlin and to its east—rape was experienced as a collective event in a situation of general crisis. While frightful and horrific, it seemed to provoke no guilt; if anything it confirmed their expectations and reinforced preexisting convictions of cultural superiority. Rape came as just one more (sometimes the worst, but sometimes not) in a series of horrible deprivations and humiliations of war and defeat: losing your home, becoming a refugee, having your menfolk killed, maimed, or taken prisoner, your children die or sicken of disease and malnutrition. It is not even clear to me that rape claimed a particularly privileged status in the long litany of miseries women confronted. The story of rape was told as part of the narrative of survival in ruined Germany. As one observer noted, "rape had become routine."[24] Margaret Boveri, a German journalist who published in 1968 what she presented as her "Survival Diary" of the Battle of Berlin, laconically noted for May 8, 1945:

> Rode [on her bicycle] a ways with a nice bedraggled girl . . . imprisoned by Russians for 14 days, had been raped but well fed. . . . May 8, 1945. The usual rapes—a neighbor who resisted was shot. . . . Mrs. Krauss was not raped. She insists that Russians don't touch women who wear glasses. Like to know if that is true . . . the troops were pretty drunk but did distinguish between old and young, which is already progress.[25]

If many German women felt confirmed as well as violated, Jews and antifascists who emerged from hiding to welcome the liberators only to have to flee again from the threat of rape felt betrayed, or simply grimly accepting. Inge Deutschkron, in hiding with her mother, remembered her growing joy and relief as she heard the rumble of Russian tanks approaching Berlin. But one of the soldiers she welcomed with a happy smile grabbed at her clothes muttering the already classic phrase, *"Komm, Frau, Komm."* At first uncomprehending, she ran to her mother, who sighed, "So it is true after all," and added hopefully, "we must show them our Jewish identity cards"—they had been hidden in the goat shed for just this occasion—"they will understand." But Deutschkron

---

23. RMI to RMJ, express letter, Berlin, Feb. 26, 1945, in BArch(Koblenz) R22/5008.

24. Michael Wieck, *Zeugnis vom Untergang Königsbergs. Ein "Geltungsjude" berichtet* (Heidelberg: Heidelberger Verlagsanstalt und Druckerei, 1990), p. 261.

25. Margaret Boveri, *Tage des Überlebens. Berlin 1945* (Munich: Piper, 1985, first published 1968), pp. 121–22, 126.

adds, "they understood nothing. They couldn't even read the identity cards." Another kind of chase began: flight and hiding not from deportation to the death camps but from sexual violation. Eventually the shooting was over, the Nazis gone, and a semblance of order restored, but Deutschkron noted, "I could no longer be really happy."[26]

Anne-Marie Durand-Wever, an anti-Nazi physician, emerged from "gruesome" nights in her cellar in bombed-out Berlin and returned to work in a first-aid station; she hastened to test women and girls for venereal disease and to ferret out gynecological instruments since, as she reported in her diary, "I guess we'll have to do abortions." Durand-Wever was sure that "our" soldiers had comported themselves no differently, but on May 23 she made a sad note about her own daughter: "This afternoon Annemie was here with her child. Four Russians. Swab inconclusive. In any case sulfa medication (Albucid). For this one tends one's child!" Still in February 1946, she portrayed a "loathsome" situation of continuing rapes, venereal disease, unwanted pregnancies, and mass abortions.[27]

But in this situation of wartime and occupation, women were not only victims but also agents; as caretakers and providers they scrounged and bartered for food and shelter, and negotiated protection for their children and themselves with occupation soldiers. They also reported extremely diverse experiences of what they variously named as rape, coercion, violation, prostitution, or abuse. Some women and young girls were brutally gang-raped in public with a line of soldiers waiting for their turn. In some cases, women's bodies were slit open from stomach to anus, or they were killed afterward. Others were forced to have sex alone in a room with a lonely young soldier for whom they occasionally even developed ambivalent feelings of hate, pity, and warmth; still others consciously offered themselves in exchange for protection of a daughter; some made deliberate decisions to take up with an occupier—preferably an officer with power—to shield themselves from others and to garner privileges. And of course there were also moments of genuine affection and desire. Women recorded brutality, but also, at times, their own sense of confusion about the fine lines between rape, prostitution, and consensual (albeit generally instrumental) sex. In a recurring trope in memoirs and diaries, women are gathered at water pumps in bombed-out streets, exchanging "war stories" with a certain bravado and *"Berliner Schnauze"* (sarcastic humor). Almost gleefully they revealed their stratagems to trick Russians as gullible as they were brutal: masquerading as men or ugly old women disguised by layers of clothing or faces smeared with dirt and ash, pretending to

---

26. Inge Deutschkron, *Ich trug den gelben Stern* (Munich: Deutscher Taschenbuch Verlag, 1987), pp. 179–81.

27. Anne-Marie Durand-Wever, *Als die Russen kamen. Tagebuch einer Berliner Ärztin,* unpublished diary, with kind permission of Dr. Madeleine Durand-Noll.

have typhus or venereal disease. But they also marveled at soldiers' apparently indiscriminate "taste" in women, the fact that they seemed to prefer fat ladies, or their astounding sexual prowess even when utterly inebriated.

The anonymous narrator of *A Woman in Berlin,* a compelling diary—albeit of unclear provenance and authenticity—to which Sander accords a prominent place in her film, explained her reaction after a series of brutal rapes during the first chaotic week of April–May 1945:

> Then I say loudly, "Damn it!" and make a decision. It is perfectly clear. I need a wolf who will keep the wolves away from me. An officer, as high as possible, Kommandant, General, whatever I can get. For what do I have my spirit and my little knowledge of foreign languages? As soon as I could walk again I took my pail and crept onto the street. Wandered up and down . . . practiced the sentences with which I could approach an officer; wondered if I didn't look too green and wretched to be attractive. Felt physically better again now that I was doing something, planning and wanting, no longer just dumb booty.[28]

The Consequences of Rape

Women's rape stories were framed in incredibly complicated ways, shaped by their audience and the motives behind their telling. Their experiences were ordered and given meaning within a complex grid of multiple images and discourses. Most immediately, there was the political fact that doctors in Berlin, driven by a complicated set of health, eugenic, racist, and humanitarian motives, and with the support of the Protestant bishop, quickly decided to suspend Paragraph 218 prohibiting most abortions and to perform abortions on raped women who wanted them. And as Durand-Wever later reported, "they all wanted them."[29] The ad hoc decision was quickly institutionalized by a highly organized medical and social hygiene system which had never really broken down, at least in the cities. Throughout most of the first year after May 1945, a medical commission composed of three or four physicians attached to district health offices approved medical abortions—almost up until the last month of pregnancy—on any woman who certified that she had been raped by a for-

---

28. Anonymous, *Eine Frau in Berlin. Tagebuchaufzeichnungen* (Geneva and Frankfurt: Helmut Kossodo Verlag, 1959), p. 78; in English, *A Woman in Berlin,* with an introduction by C. W. Ceram, trans. James Stern (New York: Harcourt Brace, 1954). Uncertainty about authorship and authenticity notwithstanding, the language used and the experiences reported are consistent with other reports.

29. Dr. Anne-Marie Durand-Wever, "Mit den Augen einer Ärztin. Zur Kontroverse zwischen Prof. Nachtsheim und Dr. Volbracht," *Berliner Ärzteblatt* 83 (1970), offprint, n.p.n.

eigner, usually but not always a member of the Red Army. (There were also abortions granted to women who reported being raped by American and French military, or foreign workers; I found no reports of rape by a German.) All these applications were carefully recorded with name, marital status, address, month of pregnancy, date of request, date of approval by the medical commission.[30] With dubious legality but with virtually full knowledge and tolerance by all relevant—both German and occupation—authorities, indeed with the consent of the Protestant—although not the Catholic—church, abortions were, it would appear, performed on a fast assembly line in the immediate postwar period.[31] Rapes were immediately medicalized and their consequences eliminated (*beseitigt*). The plans already in place for setting up abortion wards to eliminate unwanted Mongol and Slav offspring were in fact instituted after the Nazis had been defeated. In the summer of 1945 a young German army surgeon just released from an American POW camp in France and ordered to work for no pay in a Berlin hospital noted in his diary:

> There is much medical work on the gynecological ward. On orders of the British and American authorities all pregnancies which can be proven to have resulted from rape (mostly by Russians) are to be terminated. There are also many illegal abortions by quacks which are then admitted infected into the hospital.[32]

Abortions were performed in public hospitals at public cost. The physician in charge of the Neukölln district health office, Dr. Brandt, was an antifascist who had been newly appointed by the occupation authorities; however, at least some of the doctors on the commissions approving the abortions and probably many of those performing them in hospitals were former committed Nazi Party members who had been (temporarily) suspended from private prac-

---

30. For example, from November 8, 1945, until February 1, 1946, seven to nine months after the height of sexual violence in April/May 1945, of the 253 pregnancies approved for termination 4 were in the first to second month, 34 in the second month, 26 in the second to third month, 87 in the third month, 15 in the third to fourth month, 38 in the fourth month, 4 in the fourth to fifth month, 22 in the fifth month, 3 in the fifth to sixth month, 15 in the sixth month, 1 in the sixth to seventh month, 6 in the seventh month, 1 in the seventh to eighth month! LAB Rep. 214/2814/220 (Bezirksamt Neukölln). See also Rep. 214/2814/221/1–2, 2740/156.

31. See (Probst) Heinrich Gruber, *Erinnerungen nach sieben Jarhzehnten* (Cologne: Kiepenheuer and Witsch, 1971). The alacrity with which German and occupation officials turned to abortion as an obvious remedy contrasts sharply, for example, with the French response to reports of rape by German soldiers in the First World War. See the excellent article by Ruth Harris, "The 'Child of the Barbarian': Rape, Race and Nationalism in France During the First World War," *Past and Present* 141 (November 1993), pp. 170–206.

32. Unpublished diary, Dr. Franz Vollnhals. By kind permission of Mrs. Itta Vollnhals.

tice and forced to serve in public positions as part of their de-Nazification proceedings. It seems likely that the techniques used to abort women at extremely
late stages of pregnancy had previously been tested on wartime foreign female
forced laborers.[33]

This background has led some historians to characterize these postwar
abortions as a continuation of Nazi race policy.[34] But the picture is more complicated and overdetermined, the discontinuities at least as dramatic as the
continuities. All women applying for medical abortions were required to submit certified statements detailing the events that had led to their unwanted
pregnancy. The individual letters are all different, but somehow also the same;
among the approximately one thousand that I read, certain narrative codes do
emerge (on the other hand, the pattern of events described are no different from
those reported in memoirs or diaries). The affidavits are in women's voices.
But they are framed by the necessity of appealing to political and medical authority and by certain preexisting available languages.

In interpreting the rape experience to officials and also to themselves and
their friends or family, and in making their case for abortion in the affidavits
submitted to health offices, women (and the medical authorities approving the
abortions) relied on a mixed legacy of Weimar and National Socialist population policy discourses, as well as current occupation policy. They repeatedly
referred to both the social and racial/eugenic grounds on which their abortion
should be sanctioned—despite the presumably compelling and popularly
known fact that neither of those indications but only rape by an occupation soldier was recognized as justifying an *"interruptio."*[35]

Thus, women utilized rhetoric that was helpful in avoiding guilt and
managing recourse. First, they hearkened back in narrative terms to the social
hygiene, Sex Reform, and maternalist discourses of the Weimar welfare
state—which predated Nazi racialist formulations and would outlast them—
and couched the abortion issue in terms of medical, social, and eugenic
indications. Women matter-of-factly and pragmatically asserted their right to
terminate pregnancies that were not socially, economically, or medically
viable—in the name of saving the family or preventing the birth of unwanted
or unfit children. Within this framework of social necessity, the problem was
not a moral one of bearing a child resulting from an act of violence and terror,
nor even necessarily a racial one of bearing inferior offspring, but quite directly
social and economic—the problem of any unwillingly pregnant woman who

33. See Michael Burleigh and Wolfgang Wippermann, *The Racial State: Germany
1933–1945* (Cambridge: Cambridge University Press, 1991), p. 263.

34. See especially Ingrid Schmidt-Harzbach, "Eine Woche im April. Berlin 1945. Vergewaltigung als Massenschicksal," *Feministische Studien* 5 (1984), pp. 51–62, and Hoerning,
"Frauen als Kriegsbeute."

35. All depositions quoted from LAB Rep. 214/2814/220.

could not care for a child or another child. Invoking this discourse of social (not moral or racial) emergency, one woman wrote to the Neukölln health office: "I am pregnant due to rape by a Russian on April 27, 1945. I request removal of the fetus since I already have an illegitimate child and live with my parents who themselves still have small children."

After April and early May when women had mainly been raped in their cellars, public spaces became sites of danger as women ventured out to look for food, fuel, or water, scrounge through ruins, try to locate relatives or recuperate belongings. A woman who had been robbed of her bicycle and raped while on her way to the suburb of Potsdam wrote on November 9, 1945: "Since I am single, my mother dead for fifteen years, my father a half-Jew from whom I have had no sign of life for six years, it is impossible for me to set a child into the world under these conditions."

Another letter dated August 6, 1945: "I have three children aged five to eleven years. My husband, a former soldier, is not yet back. I have been bombed out twice, fled here in January from West Prussia, and now request most cordially that I be helped in preventing this latest disaster for me and my family."

Secondly—and importantly—women also drew upon the Nazi racial hygiene discourse which banned "alien" (*artfremd*) offspring (indeed, when rapes by other occupation forces were certified, the perpetrator was frequently identified as Negro if American or North African if French). They availed themselves of the rich repertory of Nazi racial imagery of the barbarian from the East, especially the Mongol from the Far East, associated with the cruel frenzy of Genghis Khan. A letter from July 24, 1945: "I hereby certify that at the end of April this year during the Russian march into Berlin I was raped in a loathsome way by two Red Army soldiers of Mongol/Asiatic type." Even Inge Deutschkron, who had initially been so happy to greet the Soviets, described her first "Russian" as small, with crooked legs and "a typical mongolian face with almond eyes and high cheekbones, clad in a dirty uniform with his cap perched lopsided on his head."[36]

In the (successful) affidavits presented to health offices, multiple and overlapping voices all talked at once, often in the same document. In an interesting indication of the dissimultaneity of social welfare understandings in the immediate postwar period, many statements freely mixed the social necessity discourse familiar from the Weimar debates over abortion reform and the racial stereotypes popularized by the Nazis, with threats of suicide or descriptions of serious physical ailments that might have legitimated a medical indication under any regime. A letter from August 20, 1945:

---

36. Inge Deutschkron, *Ich trug den gelben Stern*, p. 178.

On the way to work on the second Easter holiday I was raped by a Mongol. The abuse can be seen on my body. Despite strong resistance, my strength failed me, and I had to let everything evil come over me. Now I am pregnant by this person, can think of this only with disgust and ask for help. Since I would not even consider carrying this child to term, both my children would lose their mother. With kind greetings.[37]

In a matter-of-fact but also desperate manner, women mobilized existing discourses, entangled them, and deployed them to tell their own stories for their own purposes.

Although such remarkably similar tropes are evident in virtually all the recorded rape stories, whether official depositions requesting abortions or diaries and memoirs, the image of the *Russe* was also complicated and multifaceted. The Russian was split into good and bad on many levels. Inevitably, there was the drunken, primitive Mongol who demanded watches, bicycles, and women and did not even know that a flush toilet was not a sink. He was generally counterposed, however, to the cultivated officer who spoke German, had memorized Dostoyevsky and Tolstoy, deplored the excesses of his comrades, and could be relied on for protection even as he sought to educate his captives about German war crimes. (Incidentally, such "cultivated" status was rarely achieved by American occupiers, who were persistently categorized as primitive and vulgar, even if not so dangerous, since they could supposedly achieve their conquests with nylons and chocolate rather than by rape. As Durand-Wever recalled, there were those who quipped, "The difference is that the American and the British ask the girls to dinner and then go to bed with them, while the Russians do it the other way round.")[38]

But even the "primitive" Soviets were cast in a dual if ultimately consistent mold: the ignorant peasant soldier with the peculiar racial features associated with Slavs or Mongols (finally anyone who did not look German was identified as Mongol) could be cruel but also a child- or perhaps puppy-like character, easily distracted by a playful baby or even dominated by the proper amount of authoritative response on the part of women who ordered him about as they might a child or a pet animal. Invariably there was mention of Russians' pleasure in small children and their tenderness toward babies (in explicit contrast to the stories the Red Army soldiers told of German behavior in the East). But this positive characteristic was, of course, only another aspect of their underdevelopment. And in an indication of the highly variable nature of Soviet occupation, some officers were even known to shoot an offending sol-

---

37. LAB Rep. 214/2814.

38. Durand-Wever in *Proceedings of the International Congress on Population and World Resources in Relation to the Family, August 1948. Cheltenham, England* (London: H. K. Lewis and Co., n.d.), p. 103.

dier on the spot—although this display of "justice" often served only to confirm Germans' sense of Russians as uncivilized. Strikingly—and disturbingly—the former Soviet soldiers Sander found to interview for her film conform to such stereotypes and resemble, in quite uncanny fashion, the grotesque "primitive" figures of Soviet prisoners of war the Nazis paraded in their *Wochenschauen*. Sander further reinforces these prejudices with her filmic stance: a more respectable-looking former soldier is interviewed with his back to her; the toothless Russian with a crooked grin holding forth about male sex drives is filmed head-on.

German women at the end of the war did not, however, reserve their contempt for Soviet men alone. Indeed, some narratives favorably compared Russian officers with contemptible, defeated German men who were now pathetic parodies of the manly Teutonic genus valorized by the SS; even if not dead, wounded, or detained in Soviet POW camps, they were unable and unwilling to defend the women for whose safety they had supposedly been fighting. Preoccupied only with saving their own skins, they were not above pressuring women to go with Russian soldiers, in order not to endanger themselves— rape, after all, was a less horrific fate than Siberia or getting shot.

Thus, women's negative and prejudiced image of the Russians helped them to distance the horror of their own experience. The narrative of the Russian primitive or exotic curiously absolved him of guilt, as it also absolved women themselves. Such child-like, primitive, animal-like creatures could not be expected to control themselves—especially when tanked up with alcohol— or adhere to rules of civilized behavior. Nor could women be expected to defend themselves against such an elemental force, backed up in many cases, of course, by rifle or revolver. In the end, German women lost their honor, but they also preserved it. They managed to maintain the conviction of their own superiority, not only against the former enemy but also against their own men, who either abetted their humiliation or sought to punish them for it. Speaking of the major she has finally cornered into her bed, hoping that he will fend off rivals, the anonymous narrator of *A Woman in Berlin* wrote (not untypically but in an analytical style somewhat improbable for a diary composed at the time):

> On the other hand, I do like the Major, I like him the more as a person, the less he wants from me as a man. And he won't want a lot, I can feel that. His face is pale, his wounded knee gives him trouble. Probably he is searching for human, womanly companionship more than the purely sexual. And that I give him freely, even gladly. Because among all the male creatures of the last several days he is the most tolerable man and human being.[39]

---

39. *Eine Frau in Berlin*, p. 138.

For the most part however, Russians might be terrifying or sometimes amusing, but certainly not on the same level as Germans. To Germans in the spring of 1945, after all that had happened, it was clear who had more *Kultur.*

The Aftermath of the Rapes

After the rubble was cleaned up, and the men were home, the pregnancies aborted (at least 90 percent apparently were, especially in Berlin), and the VD treated, the initial explosion of speech about the rapes was muted, at least in public. This was certainly the case in the East, where the Soviet Military Administration stymied all efforts by German Communists to broach the subject as a potential block to public support for the occupation and above all to the electoral chances of the Communist Party against the Social Democrats (SPD) in Berlin's first open elections in 1946. (The Communists lost, certainly in part because a majority female electorate had not forgotten what the Soviet "friends" had done.)[40]

Not even in the West where, presumably, such tales might have served as a useful Cold War propaganda tool did the public discussion continue. With the return of prisoners of war and the "remasculinization"[41] of German society, the topic was suppressed, not as too shameful for women to discuss, but as too humiliating for German men and too risky for women who feared (with much justification, given the reports of estrangement and even murder) the reactions of their menfolk.

German women, especially in the East and among refugees from the East in the West, were left with memories that had not been worked through, that had no easy access to public space even as they were, whether directly or indirectly, constantly invoked or alluded to. There were no rituals of guilt and expiation as in commemorations of persecutions of Jews and the Holocaust, no structures of compensation and memory as in veterans' organizations and benefits.[42] And this, of course, provides the resonance for Sander's claim to breaking the silence. In their privatized but pervasive discourse, women remembered and passed on to their daughters their experiences: of bombing raids and flight with

---

40. See Wolfgang Leonhardt, *Child of the Revolution* (Chicago: H. Regnery Co., 1958); Naimark, *The Russians in Germany,* 120–21; Schmidt-Harzbach, "Eine Woche im April," 51–65.

41. I borrow the term *remasculinization* from Robert Moeller; he refers to Susan Jeffords, *The Remasculinization of America: Gender and the Vietnam War* (Bloomington: Indiana University Press, 1989).

42. Rape victims were not completely ignored by the Federal Republic. In the 1950s, some women in the West were minimally compensated, not for rapes, but in the form of support payments for any living children that had resulted. See BArch(Koblenz) 189 (Federal Ministry for Family and Social Welfare) 6858 and especially 6863 for records of children of rape.

women and old people from the advancing Red Army, rapes and fear of rape, and also pictures of sturdy *Trümmerfrauen* tidying up the ruins of the bombed-out cities. In an analogue to their heroic and pathetic brothers, fathers, husbands, lovers, and sons on the eastern front—who also felt no shame or guilt because they perceived themselves as having had no choice—women too invented themselves as both victims and heroines. They expressed little shame or guilt even though many of their menfolk expected it of them—a circumstance that left its depressing traces in postwar gender relations.

The memories, if suppressed, remained raw and distorted but hardly, as Sander's film would claim, completely silenced. Their abundant traces can be found in postwar literature, film, and government documentation.[43] Women felt victimized, violated, humiliated, but finally not guilty or responsible—a sentiment feminists laud when confronted by survivors of sexual assault but historians deem highly problematic in the context of the general German unwillingness to acknowledge responsibility for the misery they endured and the crimes that they perpetrated. In the postwar period, women's stories were combined with men's more openly validated tribulations on the eastern front and as prisoners of war, to construct a new national community of suffering that served not only to avoid confrontation with Nazi crimes, but also, of course, as a strategy for reauthorizing and reestablishing the unity of the *Volk,* providing the basis for a "sick" Germany to "recover" once again (a metaphor much used by postwar women's groups from all political camps).

At the beginning of the recent upsurge of research and discussion about guilt and complicity, German women's historians and feminists felt themselves especially exempt from charges of this kind and sought assiduously to document and certify women's status as victims of a patriarchal regime. Now, in a curious kind of way, they are perhaps particularly faced with the task of confronting and working through the problem of acknowledging their agency during and after the Third Reich and as contributors to the reworking of national identity in both West and East Germany.

We are now, after unification, hearing women's war stories again, some for the first time since the 1950s, and beginning to record and study them. I think that the care with which we tell those stories, in each historical case, matters, and may help us to find a usable language to talk about rape—so universal and so specific—as well as German history. It is finally this responsibility

---

43. See, among many sources, the massive documentation of Soviet crimes (prominently including rape) against Germans, gathered in the 1950s by the West German Ministry for the Displaced and Refugees (*Vertriebene und Flüchtlinge*), *Ostdokumentation,* BArch(Koblenz). American references include James Burke, *The Big Rape* (Frankfurt a. M.: Friedrich Rudl Verlegr Union, 1951) and Cornelius Ryan, *The Last Battle* (London: Collins, 1966); even for the GDR see Konrad Wolf's DEFA film, *Ich war neunzehn* (1968).

to address a particular, complicated historical legacy that Helke Sander has evaded, as a filmmaker, as documentarian or historian, as a feminist, and as a German.

Growing Discontent:
Relations between Native and Refugee Populations in a Rural District in Western Germany after the Second World War

Rainer Schulze

The influx [of people] from the East has created in Western Germany a propertyless class whose members, embittered by dispossession and by the misery of months spent in the transit camps and emergency accommodation, are obliged to exist on standards which they cannot willingly accept and which are noticeably lower than those of the native Western Germans. The latter, for their part, dislike the immigrants as outsiders who have brought filth and disease with them and as intruders into already cramped accommodation. The misery of the immigrants brings out all the latent impulses of the German character to persecute the underdog and though the treatment of refugees is not everywhere uniform, they remain in most places, and particularly in the areas of closest concentration, a class apart bearing a stigma which only the passage of time combined with a marked improvement in their physical conditions can hope to efface. The dangers for the future of German society of the continued existence of this large and underprivileged proletarian group can hardly be exaggerated.

The origins of this chapter lie in my contribution to the discussion of Ian Connor's paper 'The Effects of the Currency Reform of June 1948 on Refugees and Expellees in the Western Zones of Germany' at the 1987 Regional Conference of the German History Society on 'British Occupation and the Reconstruction of West Germany, 1945–1955' (see *German History* 5 (Autumn 1987), 68). The organizers of this conference encouraged me to develop my comments into a coherent article. A shorter version of the chapter, and one with a slightly different emphasis, was given at the German History Society's seminar on 'The Re-Integration of Refugees and "Heimkehrer" into Postwar German Society, 1945–50: Comparisons East and West', on 28 April 1988 (see *German History* 6, no. 2 (1988), 176–7, and 6: 3 (1988), 298–9.)

Brian Robertson, the Military Governor of the British Zone of occupied Germany, made these comments in February 1949 as part of a memorandum to his Foreign Secretary, Ernest Bevin. Robertson was describing the 'psychological consequences' which in his view had resulted from the mixing of native and refugee populations in the Western Zones.[1]

As the Nazi regime collapsed, millions of Germans had left their original homes in central, eastern and south-eastern Europe. Some of them had fled from the Red Army alongside the retreating German troops at the onset of the great Soviet offensive, whilst the majority had been expelled after the end of the war, or compulsorily 're-settled' under the provisions of Article 13 of the Potsdam Agreement. From 1945/46, moreover, further large numbers of people escaped from the Soviet Zone into the Western Zones; they included a significant number of people who had already fled or been expelled from the eastern territories and had initially settled in this part of Germany. Reliable calculations indicate that around 11 to 13 million people were affected by this (compulsory) transfer of population from east to west.[2] According to British estimates on the basis of the census of 29 October 1946, there were already more than 7 million refugees and expellees in the three Western Zones (almost 16 percent of the population) by that date. No fewer than 3.6 million of them were in the British Zone. The British Zonal Statistical Office defined a *refugee* as someone 'who was dwelling in areas east of the British Zone on 1st September 1939, or who is a member of a family unit which was so dwelling on the same date'; the definition thus specifically included the refugees from the Soviet Zone.[3] The numbers continued to rise during the following years. The census of 13 September 1950 revealed that 9.6 million people (around 20 percent of the total population) had only arrived in the territory of the Federal Republic of Germany during, or after the end of, the Second World War.[4]

The distribution of the refugees to the reception areas in the west was initially determined by the spontaneous and largely undirected flight of the

---

1. 'The Refugees and the Demographic Problem Presented by Western Germany', 26 Feb. 1949, Public Record Office Kew (PRO) FO 1030/119. Still indispensable for a study of this subject is Bundesministerium für Vertriebene, Flüchtlinge und Kriegssachgeschädigte (ed.), *Dokumentation der Vertreibung der Deutschen aus Ost-Mitteleuropa* (5 vols. and 3 supplements; Bonn, 1953–63, reprinted Munich, 1984); E. Lemberg and F. Edding (eds.), *Die Vertriebenen in Westdeutschland* (3 vols.; Kiel, 1959); for a first general survey see W. Benz (ed.), *Die Vertreibung der Deutschen aus dem Osten* (Frankfurt a.M., 1984); also R. Schulze et al. (eds.), *Flüchtlinge und Vertriebene in der westdeutschen Nachkriegsgeschichte* (Hildesheim, 1987).

2. See for example G. Reichling, 'Flucht und Vertreibung der Deutschen', in Schulze et al., *Flüchtlinge und Vertriebene*, 46–50.

3. Definition given in Public Opinion Research Office of Control Commission for Germany (British Element): CCG(BE), Special Report No. 278, 14 Feb. 1949, PRO FO 1005/1869; figures given in 'The Refugees and the Demographic Problem', Appendix D, PRO FO 1030/119.

4. See W. Nellner, 'Grundlagen und Hauptergebnisse der Statistik', in Lemberg and Edding, *Die Vertriebenen in Westdeutschland*, 83.

refugees ahead of the advancing Soviet troops. After the end of the war the Allies attempted to manage the distribution by negotiating specific 'contingents' for the various occupation Zones. However, this plan had only a limited degree of success. The French did not regard themselves as bound by the Potsdam Agreement and kept their Zone largely closed to the stream of refugees; moreover, it soon became apparent that many refugees regarded the Soviet Zone as an 'intermediate stop' at best and were determined to escape over the 'green border' into the western occupation Zones as quickly as possible.

Consequently, the main burden of the flood of refugees was borne by the British and American Zones. Even within these two regions, the immigration was distributed very unequally; as a result of massive war damage in the major cities and industrial conurbations, the majority of refugees were directed into rural areas. In absolute terms Bavaria (1,937,000) and Lower Saxony (1,851,000) took in the highest number of refugees. However, as a percentage of the total population the highest proportion was taken by Schleswig-Holstein (33 percent), followed by Lower Saxony (27.2 percent) and Bavaria (21.2 percent). Acceptance of refugees into the city-states of Hamburg (7.2 percent) and Bremen (8.6 percent), as well as into North Rhine-Westphalia (10.1 percent), was well below the average.[5] These huge differences were only gradually levelled out to some extent during the 1950s by means of internal immigration, sometimes unorganized and sometimes directed by the state.

What conditions awaited the refugees and expellees in the Western Zones? It is fair to say that the circumstances in which they were forced to start a new life were, initially, extremely unfavourable. First and foremost, their material and economic situation was very difficult. The war had caused enormous devastation: approximately 45 percent of houses had been destroyed or severely damaged; around 40 percent of the road network had been put out of use; the loss of the eastern territories meant the loss of those areas of the German Reich which had produced a surplus of basic foodstuffs such as grain, vegetables, and meat; industrial production, measured against pre-war levels, had fallen by more than half. Of course, these shortages and bottlenecks affected the whole population in the Western Zones, but the refugees and expellees suffered most of all. As latecomers, they had to be content with what was left over or allocated to them, more or less voluntarily, by the native inhabitants. Unlike many native inhabitants of the region, they could not improve their living standards by using their savings or by selling or bartering valuable possessions, since most of them had been forced to abandon all their belongings before their flight or had lost them during it.

---

5. Ibid. 87. These figures are taken from the census of September 1950. It should be noted that, by this time, there was already a small degree of migration by refugees within the Federal Republic.

In addition to these material problems there were also social and psychological difficulties to be faced. In the vast majority of cases, the refugees were not able to settle in established groups with their social network still intact. Many of the old village communities or neighbourhoods had been torn apart during the flight itself, whilst those that had managed to remain intact were broken up by deliberate Allied policies of redistribution, which were designed to prevent the development of revisionist movements. In consequence, individual refugees lost the social and emotional support of the communities in which they had grown up. Their sense of isolation was intensified by a dispersal and intermingling of the religious denominations: Protestant refugees were frequently settled in predominantly Catholic districts, and Catholics in areas which had previously been exclusively Protestant. Traditional ties and ways of life, as well as a sense of identity, were thus destroyed in a manner which was little short of traumatic for many refugees.

Despite these general statements, recent research has shown that it is essential to make clear distinctions between the various regions in the Western Zones. An excellent example is provided by an oral history project covering the *Ruhrgebiet*, based on 165 interviews and life histories and including twenty-three life histories of refugees from the Soviet Zone, the territories east of the Oder and Neisse rivers, and the Sudetenland. The project revealed that the native inhabitants and the immigrant population of the Ruhr shared many experiences and feelings in the wake of the Second World War, particularly the sense of being uprooted and foreign. Though the refugees were indeed 'homeless foreigners' in the *Ruhrgebiet*, the native inhabitants also had to live in a 'home which had become foreign' in 1945. The preliminary result of this study therefore states:

> In the *Ruhrgebiet*, expellees and refugees certainly had to integrate themselves into a new *area*, but at the same time *everyone*—established inhabitants and newcomers alike—had to integrate themselves into a new *time* with new demands and norms, with political re-evaluations and with new social spheres. In this sense, the integration of the refugees and expellees is an extreme case of a general development.[6]

However, the observation of fundamental similarities in the experience of immigrants and native population depends very much on the nature of the region under discussion. The conclusions relate mainly—and ultimately exclusively—to major urban and industrial regions such as the *Ruhrgebiet*

---

6. A. von Plato, 'Fremde Heimat. Zur Integration von Flüchtlingen und Einheimischen in die Neue Zeit', in L. Niethammer and A. von Plato (eds.), *'Wir kriegen jetzt andere Zeiten'* (Berlin/Bonn, 1985), 210, 213 (italicization in original source).

which had been severely affected by Allied military action. In rural areas which had been little disturbed by the actual events of the war, but were then forced to accept the greatest influx of refugees, the situation was very different. A good example of this is provided by the *Landkreis* Celle.

This *Landkreis,* on the southern edge of the Lüneberg Heath in today's Federal German *Land* of Lower Saxony, had suffered almost no direct war damage; until the entry of the Allied troops in April 1945 the war itself had left little trace.[7] In 1939, Celle had 53,397 inhabitants. Because the *Landkreis* was so remote from the war, many city-dwellers—especially from Hamburg and Hanover and from the Ruhr—fled or were evacuated to this region when Allied air raids increased after 1943. By the end of 1944 the evacuee population in Celle numbered between 8,000 and 10,000 people and was already causing some anxiety and unease among the native population.[8] Then from summer and autumn 1944, and in increasing numbers from the beginning of 1945, refugees from the eastern territories began to enter the *Landkreis.* After the end of the war and the establishment of the Allied control machinery in Germany in April–May 1945, this migration ceased for a time, but it began again during the summer. The British Military government at Celle estimated in August 1945 that the population was now almost 70 percent higher than the pre-war level.[9] A census of 1 October 1945 confirmed this assessment, showing a native population of 58,721 people and a refugee and evacuee community of 31,944.[10] The highest proportion of newcomers was to be found in communities with 200–300 inhabitants; here the ratio between native and refugee population was

---

7. It has sometimes been suggested that *Landkreis* Celle may have been an exceptional case because it suffered so little war damage. In fact, however, most rural areas in western Germany were not greatly affected either by Allied air raids, which were concentrated on the large cities and industrial areas, or by infantry combat and the 'scorched earth' strategy, which caused most damage in the east. In this sense, *Landkreis* Celle can actually be regarded as typical of rural areas in western Germany. See for example C. Klessmann, *Die doppelte Staatsgründung* (Göttingen, 1982), 44–6, and the sources quoted there.

8. See Landesplanungsgemeinschaft Hannover-Braunschweig in Lüneburg, 'Umquartierungsplan für den Gau Ost-Hannover' (Stichtag 25 Dez. 1944), Niedersächsisches Hauptstaatsarchiv Hannover (NHStA-H) Nds. 120 Lüneburg, acc. 50/79, Nr. 218; see also description of *Landkreis* Celle for the British Military Authorities, *Landrat* Celle to RAF Security Service, 27 Nov. 1945, Kreisarchiv Celle (KrA-C) 021-07-2 (Fach 98, Nr. 2). Moreover, thousands of foreign (slave) labourers had come into the district since the end of the 1930s; in 1944–5 they numbered about 10,000. See 'Die Ergebnisse der Ausländererhebung vom 30 Sept. 1944' in Der General-bevollmächtigte für den Arbeitseinsatz (ed.), *Der Arbeitseinsatz im Grossdeutschen Reich,* No. 11/12 (30 Dec. 1944), 10–12; 914 Mil. Gov. Det. R/B Lüneburg, Monthly Labour Report for January 1946, Employment and Labour Supply, PRO FO 1010/119.

9. 912 Mil. Gov. Det. (Landkreis Celle), Report for Fortnight ending 9 Aug. 1945, Appendix D, PRO WO 171/8101.

10. 'Verzeichnis über den Bevölkerungsstand des Landkreises Celle nach dem Stande vom 1 Okt. 1945' KrA-C 022-13 Bd. 1 (Fach 5, Nr. 7).

100:86.4. Nine of the 93 communities within *Landkreis* Celle actually had more newcomers than natives. At the beginning of October 1945, the school supervisor of the *Landkreis* informed the Military government that there were 10,041 native children and 6,113 refugee children of school age in the *Kreis*; typically, he referred to the native children as 'own children'.[11] *Landrat* Erich Wentker commented on the situation in a report to the RAF Security Service on 27 November 1945: '*Kreis* and communities are facing exceptionally difficult tasks as a consequence of the overcrowding with evacuees and refugees . . . The coexistence of so many people in a confined space naturally creates dissatisfaction on one side as on the other, particularly if good will is lacking on one or even on both sides.'[12] And a report of 14 February 1946 to the police commandant of *Regierungsbezirk* Lüneberg, to which *Landkreis* Celle belonged, contained the following statement: 'As a result of the great crowding of dwellings with refugees some dissatisfaction is emerging, mostly when the farmers do not show the necessary understanding for the emergency situation of the refugees. On the other hand the refugees believe that they can have the right to take wherever an opportunity presents itself.'[13]

Fortunately, there is precise evidence of the nature of the discontent among native inhabitants and refugees and of the tensions created between the two population groups. It is provided by a collection of around 350 personal accounts taken from the *Landkreis* Celle, which is unique in the Federal Republic.[14] The accounts were collected by Hanna Fuess (1886–1972), a pastor's daughter from Altencelle who was a friend of Hermann Löns and later became a vernacular poet as well as a reporter for the *Cellesche Zeitung*. On the directions and with the support of the Celle farmers' association, whose director between 1945 and 1947 was Edmund Rehwinkel (later the President of the Lower Saxony *Landvolk* and the German Farmers' Organization), Fuess travelled round the *Landkreis* in the years 1946–9 and questioned native inhabitants and refugees about their experiences in the immediate post-war period. The accounts collected give a clear and unfiltered picture of the way the people in this

---

11. 912/513 Mil. Gov. Det., Monthly Report for October 1945, Appendix E, PRO WO 171/8101.

12. Landrat Celle to RAF Security Service, 27 Nov. 1945, KrA-C 021-07-2 (Fach 98, Nr. 2).

13. Polizei Kreis Celle to Polizeikommandeur im Regierungsbezirk Lüneburg, 14 Feb. 1946, KrA-C 035-10 (Fach 18, Nr. 5).

14. The accounts, part of the 'Sammlung Hanna Fuess', are deposited at the Kreisarchiv Celle: 331-01-4 (Fach 281, Nr. 1 and 2); another copy is located at the Niedersächsisches Hauptstaatsarchiv Hannover: ZGS 1, Nr. 361–623; 61 of these reports, with a detailed introduction, have been published: R. Schulze (ed.), *Unruhige Zeiten. Erlebnisberichte aus dem Landkreis Celle 1945–9* (Munich, 1989). All the following quotations are taken from the accounts in the 'Sammlung Hanna Fuess'. It has not been thought necessary to provide an individual reference for each quotation. To protect individual identities, initials have been provided rather than proper names.

rural area lived, the problems they faced, and the methods they used to deal with them. Almost all the accounts contain references to the refugee issue.

Among the old-established population, negative judgments of the unwanted refugees predominate. Thus, for example, a farmer's wife from Burg commented in May 1948:

> We all find the refugees hard to take. We don't quarrel with any of them, but over the years we've seen through them, that they don't like us and the farm. None of them ever lends a hand, however much it is needed. Frau F. just helps with the potato lifting, but only because she wants potatoes. At first, when we killed a goose I gave them one too, and the same with chickens. They have some of our beds and bedlinen. But how things have been messed up! Instead of taking the trouble to change their dirty linen they sleep on the ticking. I wrote the things off as a loss long ago . . . It isn't right when we are crammed so full with foreign people, our houses are not equipped for it. Despite this I bought a second bathtub for my refugees and provided a cauldron for heating the water. But that's too much bother for them. They only use my equipment and when that's broken then I get: 'Frau M., can I have another broom (or whatever else it is)?'

There was general agreement that the refugees were dirty and untidy: 'From whether it's clean outside the front door you can see what sort of person lives there. I could not manage to make my refugees keep any order in front of the house, now I do it myself every Saturday, but have locked up the garden . . . But the refugees smirk and say: "It's not my property after all!"' The native inhabitants were also convinced that the refugees were unable to distinguish between 'Mine and Thine', in the words of a farmer from Boye. The pastor of another community argued: 'The refugees are not liked because there is continual thieving. This is according to the saying: "If it isn't given, then we'll take it ourselves!"' As late as August 1949, an old-established farmer from a neighbouring community was claiming categorically:

> They all do thieving! That's not regarded as bad, and as I've heard them say themselves, where they come from it's quite usual. There a neighbour takes the crates from his neighbour's field . . . I've got 24 refugees, but among them I only trust the Pomeranians, not those from the Warthegau. I have reproached them for their infringements: 'Folks, we don't go for this here!' On the other hand they are sweet as sugar when they want something. But if a man from the Warthegau goes out to the fields, he's sure to bring something back with him stuffed into his jacket, even it it's only a cabbage or a swede that he's picked in passing. It must be in the

tribe. They have explained it to me themselves: 'We're not so particular about it!'

Many native inhabitants complained that the refugees were not ready to help on the farms and in felling trees. This attitude, it was claimed, went hand in hand with an excessively demanding approach:

> Most refugees don't do anything, but they all want to eat. It makes one bitter when one has so much to do and nobody lends a hand. Every day they get a litre of milk, the families on our farm put out their pot and get it back full. Now, after two years, I wanted them to pay from 1 April [1947], but now I'm not worth anything any more. I pay for the electricity too. We don't cook with electricity, but the refugees all have hotplates, they don't touch a stick of wood all summer. They iron with electricity as well. Beds, bedlinen, and all their furniture are from us. Every refugee family is allocated 4 cubic metres of wood from the communal woodland, brought to them cut. I have also given them 4 cubic metres each from my own stock so they don't need to steal, but there is no question of any service in return, they prefer to eat with us at our table and do nothing.

Most of all, the refugees were reproached for being less grateful than the natives thought they ought to be. Instead, according to the complaints, they only made more demands: 'In many cases in refugee circles they take the view that: "We have nothing so it's your duty to give us something!"' A local clergyman claimed: 'When the refugees grumble that they lack the basic essentials, one has to make them realize the kind of sacrifice our poor people have made and that not everything can be replaced'. And the teacher of another community made an implied threat:

> Many refugees ask and demand. But we can only raise them gradually to a better position as regards their equipment. However, if they carry this kind of demand too far they can discover how hard Lower Saxon heads are, and how hard their fists. It isn't just angels who came over the border, there are a lot of black sheep among them too.

And in any case: 'In the first instance we have to look after our home, since if we have nothing left then the refugees have nothing either'.

There were distinct undercurrents in these accounts which were made explicit in other reports. The attitude they revealed involved a fundamental rejection of all foreigners simply because they were foreign and therefore posed a latent threat to the world of the native inhabitants, to everything that was established and unquestioned. Thus one estate owner commented in 1947:

Every farm is completely undermined by the ferment of refugees,[15] this foreign element actually undermines every enterprise. They are hostile to family and to work and these spiritual and mental imponderables permanently shatter the uniform character of village and farm. Every farm is an organism, it does not have a healthy effect when one part works and gets up at 5 a.m. whilst the other part sleeps till 10 and then goes for a walk. Such elements are unpleasant and not to be digested.

The danger of 'infiltration with foreign elements' by means of the refugees was particularly emphasized by pastors and teachers:

The occupation itself is not dangerous, the refugee business is much more dangerous for the people. One must be careful not to do them an injustice. The refugees are not worse then we are, they only have different ways. They know no free peasantry . . . The great question is whether we become completely infiltrated with foreign elements or whether it is good for us to receive fresh blood through the refugees. Whether this blood is pure is very much the question. The influx . . . carries the danger that the original character of our *Volkstum* will lose its authenticity through mixing with a character alien to its land and ways. The decline of the Low German speech is showing this already . . . One may say without exaggeration that life in our Heath villages was the healthiest and happiest conceivable in its religious and cultural, its economic and social relations, [but] now the axe seems to have been taken to the roots of the old tree.

Another pastor expressed the same anxiety and also feared that the native population of *Landkreis* Celle would not resist this threatened 'infiltration with foreign elements' strongly enough:

The foreign element which has now penetrated by way of the refugees is proving itself stronger, people are going along with it, for the peasant does not like to be seen as outdated and so he easily exchanges the inferior for the valuable . . . The Lower Saxons allow themselves to be blown over easily, we saw that with Nazism,[16] and now they are letting themselves be blown over by the refugees as regards their own ways . . . The peasants

---

15. Jeder Hof ist völlig zersetzt durch das Ferment der Flüchtlinge.

16. At the Reichstag elections of July 1932, the NSDAP received 53% of the vote in the *Landkreis* Celle, 16.5% more than the national average. In the neighbouring *Landkreise* of Fallingbostel, Soltau, Rotenburg (Wümme), and Bremervörde the NSDAP actually scored 60% and above. For more details see J. Noakes, *The Nazi Party in Lower Saxony 1921–1933* (London, 1971); J. Bohmbach, 'Die Endphase der Weimarer Republik in Niedersachsen', *Niedersächsisches Jahrbuch für Landesgeschichte*, 54 (1982), 65–94.

only defend themselves against the refugees economically. But they do not defend the native spirit of the village. The young generation has been completely materialized, the old peasants are perhaps suffering under the advance of foreign influence. Our villages will never assimilate the refugees, they will never be incorporated by us.

The native inhabitants were anxious to restrict the influence of the refugees in the village wherever possible. Even in November 1948 it was said that: 'The refugees have no influence on village life . . . The natives remain in authority.' Above all, the aim was to exclude refugees from important offices; in one community, when the post of village burgomaster fell vacant, a local man who did not want the job 'in any circumstances' was 'talked round' and persuaded to take it: 'It is better for the community than if a foreign refugee took it, at least we still have a proper farmer.' The refugees could not be excluded from teaching posts so easily because of the general shortage of teachers and the large increase in the number of schoolchildren as a result of the refugee influx. As a result, there were many complaints from natives that there were too many refugee teachers. Thus, the *Gemeindedirektor* and the mayor of one locality complained that seven out of ten teachers there were refugees: 'Herein lies the difficulty, that they speak their native dialect and our children here don't learn any pure German.' The pastor of another parish made it clear why there was so much resistance to refugee teachers:

Before, there was an hour of instruction in Low German every week, but now there is only one Lower Saxon teacher out of five. The others have no more ties with their home and cannot teach the children links with their native soil. The teacher shapes the image of the village. He moulds the picture of the village, gives the community its model, the pastor cannot do it but the teacher has the children—the future village—in his hands for five hours every day.

Amid this general hostility, there were clear differences of approach based on the origins of the refugees: 'With the Pomeranians you can get along better, they have learned more than the East Prussians, are Protestants, one can explain things to the Pomeranians better. Those from the Warthegau cannot find their place here, it is difficult to deal with them, there is Polish blood there and they are hot-tempered.' The Silesians were not well-regarded either, and of the Black Sea Germans who arrived in *Landkreis* Celle it was said that in them there was 'no culture to be found, they preferred to crawl into bed together and simply didn't know about bedlinen at all. All the love given to these people fell on stony ground . . . For German *Volkstum* they were completely ruined, they were lazy and stole with a deftness which was remarkable. They were so spoiled by their good soil.'

The farmers of Celle generally regarded the 'Ostbauern' with grave mistrust:

> The *Ostbauern* acted the gentleman in their homeland and did not contribute to the work. Here, if they help at all, they don't persist at the work. There is an otherwise very decent and reasonable farmer who cannot even plough a straight furrow. He might otherwise be fine, but he is no man of the soil. It's terrible! In general the *Ostbauern* are not decent farmers, they haven't achieved much. They had most of their work done by the Poles.

A local pastor added that there were continuing difficulties because 'the refugees from the east mostly had quite different farming relationships. They . . . don't understand the drudgery of our peasant wives.'

Refugees from the cities often encountered even greater antipathy, however. As the same pastor remarked: 'They arrived almost totally without religion and bring big city assumptions with them to the countryside as well as the unwillingness to help. The worst in this way are the Berliners, who in any case get very little sympathy from our Guelfish population.' Another pastor commented simply: 'These refugees have no understanding of the work of the peasants.' One farmer described a refugee woman billeted with him as follows: 'But she was a big city woman, and that says it all.' Native attitudes were summarized with great precision in one simple comment: 'The Heath-man is simply another breed from the East Elbian. In addition, the Heath is too quiet for big city people in the long run.'

However, most negative opinions about the immigrant population were expressed in a sweeping and generalized way when the subject was the refugees as a whole. When the talk was of refugees taken in by the speaker, refugees who helped on the farm, who had possibly managed to bring some possessions and who showed themselves willing to adopt traditional ways of life, then the assessment was usually more balanced and often much less hostile: 'In my house we are four families with 26 people altogether, among them one single lady, we ourselves are 10 people. We are certainly rather cramped by the refugees, the furniture is pushed together somewhat, but we manage.' Yet this same farmer added that 'a proper relationship of trust does not emerge'.

It was generally considered impossible for the refugees to stay permanently. This view was taken even by natives who had stated that they personally got on relatively well with the refugees: 'There will be no more tranquillity until they have all gone and have got their own soil again . . . The peace between natives and refugees is only on the surface.' Here, fears about property mingled with the traditional hostility to everything foreign:

> The struggle for the assets of the village has been brought to the most extreme pitch by the influx of refugees and by intermingling with them.

Somehow the Lower Saxon peasant is in retreat in this encounter; no one knows how this development will turn out. There is only one solution that can help the peasantry: that the area in the east be given back again, that the refugees be told: there is your only chance, we simply cannot get on in the long run, in terms of space and economically.

A philologist who had fled from Dresden to relatives in Celle had some understanding for the reaction of the natives:

> The excessive number of refugees streaming into the Western Zones in practice placed such an over-large demand on the charitable will of the natives, which does undoubtedly exist, that they often found themselves under pressure because of the severe shortage of space. Such experiences naturally turned the best will into bitterness among many natives. If, on the other side, the refugee insists without sympathetic understanding on demands or rights which have already been granted, this in itself widens the notorious gulf between natives and refugees. Courteous ways and an honest desire to reach a settlement will at all times build a bridge over the gulf. But this bridge-building does not succeed everywhere. Both sides must work to eliminate harsh behaviour, brusque unkindness. This seems to me to be the most serious social problem of the overcrowded West Zone.

The comments of the other refugees are almost all dominated by disappointment and even bitterness, caused by the feeling of being rejected by the native inhabitants, of being unwanted, and of failing to find the remotest understanding of their difficulties:

> I am so very disappointed by the Lower Saxon farmers, especially the Wathlingen people.[17] We Silesians are accustomed to a generous hospitality. We are border dwellers and German welcomes German with a particular warmth . . . But here we have found no kindness at all . . . If I had not been three years in Russia and got to know communism there, I would certainly be a communist now. But now I can't be . . . The most unjust thing is the distribution of foodstuffs. It is high time that these local farmers, too, learned what it means to be forced to beg. This injustice is terrible.

Only those refugees who managed to establish themselves relatively quickly, and had thus ceased to be dependent on the kindheartedness of the natives, were more positive about their new life. This young peasant woman from

---

17. Wathlingen is a community in the *Landkreis* Celle.

the Stettin area had married the son of an old-established farming family in *Landkreis* Celle in December 1945, though she too spoke of considerable problems of acclimatization:

> The Lower Saxon farmers were so foreign to me at first. With us there is house and stable separate from each other. But the method of housekeeping is fairly similar. At home we always spoke Low German too. But it's a different Low German. Otherwise the Pomeranian peasant has a lot in common with the one here, in ways of cooking as well. But I still hadn't heard about 'Heaven and Earth'.[18]

Yet despite her marriage into a local family, this woman still felt that she had not been fully accepted by the native population: 'The peasant women pay no attention to me here, I am a refugee and so there is a barrier between us though otherwise they are friendly.' On the other hand, although she should have sympathized with the plight of the refugees, this woman adopted the attitude of the locals toward immigrant groups: 'Here on the farm we have a refugee family of four people, but we don't speak with them.'

One refugee farming family from Mecklenburg had quickly succeeded in obtaining a tenancy of their own, not least because the wife's father, a long-established tenant-farmer in Rotenburg/Wümme, had recommended them. This family was relatively content with their new situation and became keen to succeed there: 'My husband feels very happy here, and I wouldn't go back to Mecklenburg, either. We must now see how we can get round the problem of not being accepted. We shall have to show that we weren't chosen from among 100 applicants without good cause.'

This desire to remain in *Landkreis* Celle was very much the exception, however. Otherwise, almost all the refugees and expellees expressed both tremendous homesickness for their lost homeland and the desire to return there as soon as possible: 'Things are good for us here, and we've even got a little vegetable patch. But we are always homesick for our lovely East Prussia with its broad, fertile plains. At first we simply couldn't imagine that anything could grow here.' And a farmer's wife from Köslin reported:

> I much prefer to get outside, for working makes you forget to brood because you can't just neglect your livelihood . . . But one day we'll return to our own land. We all firmly believe that. Until then we don't let ourselves get down-hearted—there's no point in that, it won't help . . . Even our dentist has come with us to the British Zone; although he's living in

---

18. 'Himmel und Erde' (Heaven and Earth) is a Lower Saxon dish consisting of apples ('heaven') and potatoes ('earth').

Flensburg, he's over here! And I'll be going there soon! I certainly couldn't get used to anyone else.

In the same breath, however, this woman also said: 'It's very beautiful here, with the fields and meadows scattered with trees. And here we don't have to live in fear, that's the great thing.'

The refugee spokesman in Winsen, himself an estate owner who had fled from the Wartheland, commented in June 1946:

> The spiritual attitude of the refugees is that they are suffering more from homelessness than from the loss of their material property. They can only be at home here when they are no longer regarded by the natives as foreigners or intruders, when they are allowed to help to rebuild in all areas . . . The refugees have to have equal rights in public life and in the administration. The worst thing is that, as a refugee, one is unable to offer anyone even a plate of food. Mostly one finds understanding only when they [the natives] have suffered the same fate or have had similar difficult experiences. People who have been spared cannot put themselves in the refugees' place.

A balanced assessment of the situation, unusual because of its attempt to understand both sides, came from a former director of the AEG company who had fled from Vienna. It must be noted, however, that his wife's family lived in *Landkreis* Celle and that he had already spent holidays there previously. In consequence, he can hardly be described as a real newcomer and was himself acting as something of a bridge between natives and refugees. In summer 1948, he gave his assessment of the situation:

> As far as the refugees are concerned, most of them bear their heavy lot bravely and have maintained an astonishing cheerfulness. Only in individual cases does one find bitterness and resignation, although life is often not made easy for them . . . The native inhabitants of E. did not suffer any damage,[19] or at most some theft at the start of the occupation, but some of them believe that they have suffered ever so much. You can hear claims (though only from a few): 'I have lost almost everything'. These are people who still possess their entire farm and had only a couple of pieces of clothing and jewellery stolen and a couple of bits of furniture broken. Naturally, these few people do not show the slightest understanding for refugees who literally lost everything down to the clothes on their back. In their self-pity they regard their suffering as equal to that. Such types can be found everywhere [but as] isolated cases.

---

19. E. is Eldingen, a community in the *Landkreis* Celle.

As a further illustration, he continued:

> There are also cases where the native inhabitants say that people must
> show consideration for each other. Perhaps the refugee shows it in this
> case, but not the native; he thinks that he is doing everything. The Heath-
> dweller still has things too easy. He has not had any bomb damage, has
> not suffered through occupation; here in the village they have not expe-
> rienced great distress on a personal level. They have no yardstick for
> judging what it would be like for them to be in the kind of situation that
> the refugees are in . . . But it is also bad when the refugees, out of igno-
> rance, are careless with things entrusted to them.

These accounts from the *Landkreis* Celle reveal that the native inhabitants
and the refugees in this rural area did not share common feelings of being uprooted, as was the case in the Ruhr. In Celle, by contrast, the two groups tended
to form two hostile camps; bridges between them could be constructed only
with difficulty. The situation was aggravated by the fact that several worlds
were clashing, rather than two alone: the old-established and the uprooted,
the haves and the have-nots, village and city-dwellers, farmers and manual or
clerical workers, Protestants and Catholics, Guelfs and Prussians. Different
standards and ways of life, temperaments and casts of mind, political traditions
and established customs had a more damaging effect on the prospects for coexistence than was the case in urban industrial areas which had always encouraged a higher degree of social mobility and had acted as a melting-pot.
Moreover, in rural areas there was a much greater increase in population as a
result of the refugee influx; in many communities the number of inhabitants
actually doubled. The classic differences and antagonisms between town and
country continued to exist in the refugee problem and were, for a time, even intensified.

The native rural population still had almost everything: homeland, housing, possessions, an established occupation and employment, their own land to
provide food, and, above all, an accepted social status and a secure identity. All
this had now to be shared with the refugees who had lost so much, and in some
cases everything. As the area round Celle had been largely spared the direct effects of war, its inhabitants had little empathy for the position of the refugees,
even though they might be capable of understanding it on a rational level. The
refugees had disrupted a world which had previously remained intact and isolated, and had brought with them other ways of life, models, and standards. In
consequence, the native inhabitants grew to regard them as a threat to their
own existence, both material and philosophical. Undoubtedly, the refugees
were initially accepted and treated in a spirit of hospitality and charity, but
misgivings quickly developed when it became clear that these 'guests' (unlike
groups of outsiders during the war, such as foreign prisoners of war, forced

labourers, and evacuees from German cities) were staying for a longer period. As the refugees began to claim equal rights, rivalry and fears about property rights grew and the gulf between the population groups increased. Hostility towards the newcomers, and sometimes even hatred of them, became apparent. The following remark by a native inhabitant typified the attitude of many: 'Friction arose only later, as a result of living together over a longer period. The people were happy just to have somewhere to live at first; the demands didn't arise until later.' Generally, the natives did not distinguish greatly between the evacuees from the large towns and the refugees from the east; both groups were referred to as 'refugees' and treated as foreigners who did not belong in Celle. Only a few of the newcomers were judged in a more balanced and often less hostile way: those from a similar background who were ready to help on the farms, who had perhaps managed to bring some belongings with them, and who showed themselves willing to adjust to the traditions of the local community.

It seems clear that the antagonism between natives and refugees in rural areas existed, at least in essence, from the outset. Developments after the end of the war only served to increase its immediacy and intensity. As in post-war German history as a whole, the years 1947–8 were particularly significant in this respect. The position of the refugees became clearer as a result of general political developments, particularly the meetings of the Council of the Four Allied Foreign Ministers in Moscow (March–April 1947) and London (November–December 1947), the Communist takeover in Czechoslovakia, the signing of the fifty-year defence pact uniting Great Britain, France, the Netherlands, Belgium, and Luxembourg (a forerunner of the North Atlantic Treaty of 4 April 1949), and the breakup of the Allied Control Council in spring 1948. These developments showed beyond doubt that the return of the refugees and expellees to their homes in the east was impossible for the foreseeable future. At the same time, the return of large numbers of German POWs from Allied captivity led to a further deterioration in the employment prospects of refugee groups and exacerbated the problem of refugee unemployment. On the other hand, the Western Allies *de facto* ended their ban on separate refugee organizations from spring 1948; in March of that year the Aufbaugemeinschaft der Kriegsgeschädigten was established in the British Zone as a direct successor to the Notgemeinschaft der Flüchtlinge, which had been banned two years earlier. However, a separate refugee political party was created only in spring 1950. The personal accounts from *Landkreis* Celle reveal that it was at about this time that the native population came to regard the refugees, who had arrived as 'guests', more and more as 'permanent residents'.

At the conclusion of these developments came the Currency Reform of June 1948 in the Western Zones. This brought about a further deterioration in the economic position of the refugees and heightened the antagonism between native and immigrant groups. Yet in the end it only served to emphasize, once again and in a very drastic way, the need for a system of compensation for damage suffered in the course of the Second World War, a *Lastenausgleich*, which refugee groups had long been demanding. In the words of Ian Connor: 'The Currency Reform highlighted the formidable economic problems associated with the influx of the refugees and expellees into the Western Zones of Germany after the Second World War, problems which had in some respects been concealed by the inflationary conditions prevailing up until the middle of 1948.'[20] This factor is confirmed by contemporary British investigations and surveys, which commented that the refugees

> stress the fact that after currency-reform regulations allowed the 'Black Marketeers' and 'leading circles' to fill their pockets they are no longer willing to help the others. Refugees in towns bitterly comment on the native authorities' tendency to hinder the refugees in trying to build up their existence. It is said that all officials, i.e. Trade Chambers etc., make it extremely difficult for refugees to open shops etc. Refugees in rural districts are disturbed because they see native inhabitants building houses, shops etc. while the same people always claim their lack of money when asked to help the refugees. 'This goes to prove', so the refugees say, 'that with a bit of good will on the part of officials there will, in spite of all complaints from natives, be a lot of money collected for the "Lastenausgleich"'.[21]

In this situation, it seemed highly likely that the refugees would prove susceptible to political radicalism of right or left. A development of this kind was actually forecast by both German and British observers of the contemporary scene. Hence the British Military governor, Brian Robertson, argued in his memorandum to Foreign Secretary Bevin:

> The loss of self-respect which these people [the refugees] have undergone and the discontent which their mode of life engenders lay them open to the temptations of nationalist agitation and provides ready made material for the first unscrupulous leader that comes to power. Paradoxically enough, though the refugees as a class owe their miseries in large measure to the policy of the Soviet Union in Germany and Eastern Europe, the

---

20. I. Connor, 'The Effects of the Currency Reform of June 1948 on Refugees and Expellees in the Western Zones of Germany', paper for the 1987 Regional Conference of the German Historical Society, p. 16.

21. Public Opinion Research Office at HQ 229 CCG(BE) Hanover, Morale Report for Lower Saxony (24 June–8 July 1949), PRO FO 1005/1857.

conditions in which they live make them an easy prey to communist blandishments.[22]

Yet apart from a few local exceptions, political radicalization of this kind either failed to materialize or was limited to a verbal radicalism. Despite some spectacular electoral successes for the Bund der Heimatvertriebenen und Entrechteten (BHE) and the Sozialistische Reichspartei (SRP) at the beginning of the 1950s, especially in areas with a high concentration of refugees, the majority of refugees remained immune to right-wing, and, even more so, to left-wing extremism. This fact is perhaps the true West German 'miracle' of the post-war period.

One important element preventing the rise of political extremism was the fact that the urgent economic problems facing the refugees began to be addressed during the 1950s. Mention need only be made here of the general economic recovery in the wake of the Korean War and the positive effects of the Immediate Aid Law (*Soforthilfegesetz*) of August 1949 and the *Lastenausgleichsgesetz* of August 1952,[23] among other official measures. Although the living standards of the refugees and expellees usually remained lower than those of the native inhabitants, their most extreme distress was alleviated relatively quickly; compared with their situation at the end of the Second World War, they shared significantly in the general prosperity enjoyed by West Germans. Another important factor preventing refugee radicalism was the ideology of anti-communism which permeated the new Federal Republic of Germany and prevailed in almost all sections of the population, native and refugee alike. Since the refugees could share this ideology whilst maintaining their own identity, it had an important integrative effect within society. However, many social and emotional problems were not so easily or quickly resolved. Until well into the 1970s, refugees and their children had inferior career and promotion prospects to those of the native population; some of the discrimination and stigmatization which they suffered has yet to be forgotten or overcome.[24] All these are fields where further investigation and research is required.

The gradual acceptance of the refugees and expellees into West German society is largely a 'normal' process of the integration of an underclass, of the type revealed in all the migration processes of the nineteenth and twentieth

---

22. 'The Refugees and the Demographic Problem Presented by Western Germany', 26 Feb. 1949, PRO FO 1030/119.

23. For details see W. Abelshauser, 'Der Lastenausgleich und die Eingliederung der Vertriebenen und Flüchtlinge', in Schulze et al., *Flüchtlinge und Vertriebene*, 229–38.

24. See, for example, F. Dettmer, 'Konflikte zwischen Flüchtlingen und Einheimischen nach Ende des Zweiten Weltkrieges', *Jahrbuch für ostdeutsche Volkskunde*, 26 (1983), 311–34; K. Kluth, 'Die Verarbeitung der Identitäts- und Integrationsprobleme der deutschen Heimatvertriebenen in der II. Generation', *Jahrbuch für ostdeutsche Volkskunde*, 28 (1985), 289–317.

centuries.[25] However, this integration did not require adjustment and change on the part of the refugees alone; it also made demands on the native population, especially in those rural areas which had until then been relatively isolated from the outside world. The structure and character of the rural areas underwent a substantial change because of the influx of the refugees and expellees. In many places, agricultural acreage was increased, and new settlements were added to the existing villages. But even more importantly, industrial and business enterprises came to many rural districts: Refugee entrepreneurs often resumed their businesses here rather than move to urban and industrial regions, and above all, enterprises founded and owned by natives were newly established.[26] The interpenetration and mixture of different ways of life and traditions, which had already set in during the pre-war years and continued during the war years, thus increased considerably in the post-war years. The experiences of *Landkreis* Celle clearly reveal the truth of this analysis. A history of a village written in 1952 points to the long-term changes caused by the Second World War and its consequences, not least among them the influx of refugees:

> It was not only the outer picture of the village which was altered, but the way in which its people lived together was greatly influenced by the war and its consequences. Its remote position and one-sided rural character had lent village life its own special features before the war, to which the inhabitants consciously adhered. These special features lost their rigidity during the war period. Those who returned home had learned in the field to understand people with other views and now adopted a critical approach to many old customs in their native village . . . Life with the refugees also contributed much towards this change in the behaviour and thinking of the village inhabitants. Initially, mutual distress bridged much hostility between them and the natives. Then the children from the east

---

25. See R. Mackensen, 'Offene Fragen und Thesen zu den sozialen und demographischen Auswirkungen der deutschen Zuwanderung um 1945 und danach', in Schulze et al., *Flüchtlinge und Vertriebene*, 305–7; also K. Bade, 'Sozialhistorische Migrationsforschung und "Flüchtlingsintegration"', in Schulze et al., *Flüchtlinge und Vertriebene*, 126–62.

26. These measures were followed and/or supported from an early stage by the authorities in Bavaria, in particular. For details, see M. Kornrumpf, *In Bayern angekommen. Die Eingliederung der Vertriebenen* (Munich, 1979), 290–316; F. J. Bauer, *Flüchtlinge und Flüchtlingspolitik in Bayern* (Stuttgart, 1982), 322–39; F. Prinz (ed.), *Integration und Neubeginn. Dokumentation über die Leistung des Freistaates Bayern und des Bundes zur Eingliederung der Wirtschaftsbetriebe der Vertriebenen und Flüchtlinge und deren Beitrag zur wirtschaftlichen Entwicklung des Landes* (2 vols., Munich, 1984). For Lower Saxony and for the *Landkreis* Celle in particular, see H. J. Malecki, 'Die wirtschaftliche Eingliederung der Flüchtlinge in Niedersachsen', *Flüchtlinge in Niedersachsen*, iii (Hanover, 1951); H. Pröve et al., (eds.), *Heimatchronik der Stadt und des Landkreises Celle* (Oldenburg, 1966), 192–3, 246–51, 305–9.

grew up here and formed friendships with their peers from the village, and through the children the parents came together more and more. Outwardly the influence of the refugees is perceptible in the fact that the schoolchildren today speak High German almost exclusively. Even many parents who speak Low German to each other get their children used to High German speech in the pre-school years.[27]

The influx of refugees and expellees contributed significantly to a structural change of rural regions in Western Germany, even though this change hardly ever came about as smoothly and harmoniously as this village history would like us to believe, but instead it led first to a growing discontent between native and refugee populations. Considering this, the flight and expulsion of the refugees had still other effects, perhaps ones more crucial to the development of the Federal Republic of Germany than the economic and material dimensions which have until recently always been at the centre of investigation.

---

27. Gisela Meyer (Bonstorf), 'Unser Dorf im Krieg und in der Nachkriegszeit', KrA-C 331-01-4 (Fach 281, No. 1). This chronicle was written by a native, as is obvious on reading it. The difficulties of coexistence with the refugees are somewhat obscured in order to make the process of mutual adjustment appear a little more harmonious than was actually the case. For this last section see also Helga Grebing, 'Zum Begriff Integration', in Schulze et al., *Flüchtlinge und Vertriebene*, 302–4.

German Reaction to Defeat and Occupation

Josef Foschepoth

Whoever does not lie and is not blind cannot dispute that the postwar German mood of 1918 lives on in the postwar mood of today. We have a "national" resistance movement. The emotional aversion to being conquered and occupied, the instinctive alliance against non-Germans; the exasperated criticism when something does not take place as it perhaps should according to promises or regulations; the thoughtless protest, "That was better under the Nazis"; the disillusioned cry during shortages, "Is this democracy?" at every restriction of some liberty; a hostile and vainglorious recital of each endured hardship and the snotty comment, "And you think you're better"; the complacent narration of stories in which one "boldly spoke one's mind"; the disparagement of admissions of guilt, reducing them to "dust and ashes"; the refusal, when something German is taken away from Germany, to reflect upon losses others incurred at German hands; the refusal to listen to the outrage that overcomes others who suffered from the brutal injustice of assault; the stupid "I don't believe it" when confronted with evidence of atrocities committed by German soldiers and officers; the erection of walls to shield oneself against the gruesome crimes against Poles, Jews, and prisoners; the stupidly arrogant ingratitude for the gift of foodstuffs received from America and England; the naive reproach that others contributed to Hitler's rise by entering into pacts with him; the falsely understood "national solidarity" that will not form an alliance with the truly different Germany—this misdirected or positively egotistical German resistance to considerations of justice and moral principle pervades all political parties.[1]

(The translation was prepared by the editor with the assistance of Corinne Antezana-Pernet and Rita B. Bashaw. Bracketed words or phrases are those of the editor.)

The question of the German response to defeat and occupation has not been systematically investigated. A first, suggestive attempt to analyze the discussion of German guilt in the early postwar years is provided by Barbro Eberan, *Luther? Friedrich "der Grosse"? Wagner? Nietzsche?. . . ?. . . ? Wer war an Hitler schuld? Die Debatte um die Schuldfrage 1945–1949* (Munich, 1983).

1. *Berliner Tagesspiegel*, January 23, 1947, quoted in Michael Balfour, *Vier-Mächte-Kontrolle in Deutschland 1945–1946* (Düsseldorf, 1959), 343.

In occupied Germany, such sentiments were the exception, not the rule, in the mixed chorus of publicly articulated opinions. Self-criticism, the admission of partial responsibility for what happened under the Nazis, or even the acknowledgment of personal or collective guilt was rare. For example, the Protestant Church's admission of guilt was the work of a limited number of individuals and long remained controversial within regional branch churches. The Catholic Church basked in its resistance to National Socialism and rejected any sense of collective responsibility or even partial guilt. Statements such as those by Bishop Sproll von Rottenburg were exceptions; he declared that every Christian should at least recognize his or her responsibility and suffer the consequences to the same degree that he had personally favored National Socialism's victory.[2] More typical of the German episcopate was Cardinal Josef Frings's view, according to which the "current regime is scarcely different from a totalitarian state."[3] Given such comparisons, it is not surprising that West Germans would not doubt the legitimacy—indeed, the necessity—of resolute resistance against the occupation government. Trade unionists and politicians, regardless of political creed, hardly viewed the matter differently. The more reflective among them, such as Karl Arnold or Max Brauer, repeatedly pointed out that Germans should not forget that the actual cause of postwar misery had been the politics and policies of the Third Reich.[4] Yet not even they offered any admissions of personal or collective responsibility, nor did any other politician who aspired to a new office or position. This omission is understandable if we consider that according to a survey conducted by the British military government, Germans expected a "good" German politician to prove himself or herself "upright, courageous, and responsible" and above all to advocate the interests of the German people and resist "Allied policies directed toward the destruction of Germany."[5]

How was it possible that the Germans, so soon after their unconditional surrender and the greatest defeat that they had ever suffered as a nation, were for the most part convinced that not they, but rather the occupation forces, were the true cause of the difficulties inflicted upon Germans after the end of the war? What consequences did this view have for the attitudes of Germans toward the Allies, the occupied toward the occupiers? Is it possible to de-

---

2.   This analysis is based on available published reports and a number of unpublished materials, including monthly and weekly reports, public opinion surveys, and other analyses of conditions in the British zone of occupation and in the rest of Germany that are in the Public Record Office in London (hereafter PRO). Quotations from the pastoral letter of Bishop Sproll are in PRO, FO 371/64389/C 3957.

3.   PRO, FO 371/70617/C 3509; Frings in an interview with the Associated Press, February 1948.

4.   PRO, FO 371/64391/C 8878 and 64392/C 11983.

5.   PRO, FO 371/64516/C 6951; German Reaction Report of April 1947.

scribe a type of "national resistance"? If so, how did it express itself? What purpose did it serve? What were its consequences for the development of postwar Germany?

It is not easy to cope with defeat, and it was certainly not easy for Germans who for twelve years had been so loyally devoted to Adolf Hitler and who together with their Führer were committed to total victory. "Germany will be a world power or it will cease to exist"[6]—this was the dictator's maxim. Only victory could be sweet; defeat would be horrifying. The more desperate the German Reich's situation became during the war, the more intensely Propaganda Minister Joseph Goebbels hammered these alternatives into the minds of the German people. Indeed, fully portraying the horrors of imminent defeat became part of the propagandistic exhortation to prepare for the final struggle that would bring victory. The worst that could be imagined was the victory of Bolshevism, whether Bolshevism triumphed on its own or in league with the Western Allies; in either case, Bolshevik victory would result from inadequate German preparedness and resistance. Repeated, extreme propagandistic exertions were aimed at prohibiting this outcome: "A nation that is resolved to defend its country by the bravest and most daring means is utterly invincible. It can continue fighting indefinitely."[7]

The end was predictable. Defeat was as total as the victory that had been promised. On May 8, 1945, the German Reich surrendered unconditionally. What had made possible defeat, war, National Socialism, and, last but not least, the German chancellor and Führer Adolf Hitler? Outside Germany, these sorts of questions had already been posed during the war. The answers the victors had provided before 1945 determined their attitudes toward the Germans after Nazism's defeat. The Soviets had pointed to structural causes as the root of fascism and thus saw structural changes as the only way to overcome fascism. In contrast, the theme of German collective guilt was widely accepted among the Western Allies. According to the thesis of collective guilt, it was not possible to differentiate between good and bad Germans, Nazis, collaborators, and opponents of the National Socialist regime. As late as 1950, British Foreign Secretary Ernest Bevin declared in a foreign policy debate in the House of Commons that "Hitler's revolution did not alter the German character, rather, it was the full expression of that character."[8] Not Hitler, nor the Nazis, nor any other individuals bore exclusive blame for World War II; rather, it was the responsibility of the entire German nation.

---

6.   Adolf Hitler, *Mein Kampf*, 12th ed. (Munich, 1933), 742.
7.   Goebbels, February 1945, in the "Reich," cited in Helmut Heiber, *Joseph Goebbels* (Munich, 1974), 332.
8.   PRO, FO 371/85001/C 2520.

From this perspective, without complete reeducation, the aggressive German character could not be altered, and the negative trajectory of German history from Luther to Hitler could not be reversed.[9]

Because Germany bore responsibility for the chaos and unspeakable suffering that it had visited upon Europe and the world, the Americans wanted "not to liberate Germany, but to occupy it as a conquered and hostile nation."[10] The goal of U.S. occupation policy was to ensure that Germany would not pose a threat to world peace for a third time in the twentieth century. British Field Marshal Bernard Law Montgomery expressed similar sentiments when he affirmed that the German people were to blame for the outbreak of World War II. Montgomery also demanded that Germans assume responsibility for the atrocities they had committed, even when their acts were carried out under orders. "This nation is responsible for its leaders [Führer]."[11]

Once the war ended and victors became aware of the full extent of the Nazis' reign of terror, it is understandable that they were inclined to hold all Germans responsible for what had happened. However, the thesis of the collective guilt of all Germans was never elevated to official doctrine. On June 5, 1945, the Four Powers stated their position on German defeat, declaring that Germany "[carried] responsibility for the war."[12] The principles adopted in Potsdam, outlining the treatment of Germany during the first phase of Allied occupation, likewise spoke only of the unavoidable "responsibility" of Germans for the things they had done.[13] And on November 21, 1945, at the opening of the Nuremburg trials, American chief prosecutor Robert Jackson stated that in no way was it his intention "to accuse the entire German nation."[14]

The more circumspect the occupation forces became in their use of the words *collective guilt* and the more distinctly they distinguished between guilt and responsibility, the more popular the term seemed to become among Germans themselves. To be sure, they did not accept the concept of collective German guilt; rather, they fiercely attacked it. They resolutely contested the unity of *Volk* and Führer, underscored by National Socialist ideology and em-

---

9. A particularly lasting influence on the Allies' image of Germany was exerted in Britain by Lord Vansittart, former undersecretary of the Office of Foreign Affairs. See, for example, Hermann Fromm, *Deutschland in der öffentlichen Kriegszieldiskussion Großbrittaniens 1939–1945* (Frankfurt, 1982), 69–84.

10. From the renowned directive of the U.S. Joint Chiefs of Staff, April 1945 (JCS 1067), quoted in Beate Ruhm von Oppen, *Documents on Germany under Occupation 1945–1954* (London, 1955), 13–27; here, 16.

11. Cited in Eberan, *Die Debatte um die Schuldfrage*, 22.

12. Von Oppen, *Documents*, 29.

13. Ibid., 43.

14. Cited in Eberan, *Die Debatte um die Schuldfrage*, 23.

phasized by the proponents of the collective guilt thesis as well. The Führer, the Nazis—yes, they were to blame, but not the German nation as a whole. According to public opinion polls in the American zone, in the early postwar years typically more than 70 percent of those polled rejected the notion that Germans bore total responsibility [*Gesamtverantwortung*] for the war.[15] To be sure, what the overwhelming majority rejected was not collective guilt for every single crime perpetrated by Germans, but rather the responsibility for the war and its consequences. In other words, the attack on the thesis of collective guilt—a thesis blown out of proportion by the Germans themselves—aimed to absolve Germans not only from guilt for starting the war, but also of all responsibility for the war's consequences.

This argument was based upon the distinction between those who were and were not Nazis, between bad and good Germans, between a minority of seducers and a majority of those who had been seduced. Of course, it was necessary to explain that a minority among the Germans was capable of aggression on a truly monstrous scale. That was accomplished on the one hand by a "demonization" of Hitler, a continuity of the "myth of the Führer in reverse,"[16] and on the other by going on the attack against foreign countries, particularly Great Britain, claiming that the West had strongly contributed to the establishment and stability of the National Socialist regime. Thus, other nations should "be congratulated that God spared them such a demon as he visited upon us. That was their good luck, not anything they deserved."[17] The minister-president of Schleswig-Holstein explained this line of argument quite clearly in an interview in *Die Zeit* [a weekly newspaper that appealed to a liberal, middle-class readership] in December 1946; the British would have deserved their good fortune, if they had not finalized the German-British naval agreement of 1935, or if Chamberlain and Daladier had never traveled to Munich.[18] Kurt Schumacher [head of the postwar German Social Democratic party (SPD)] shared this opinion. If the Allies had treated Hitler the way they were now treating Germany, "Hitler never would have become a danger to the world."[19] From here it was but a small step to argue that Germans were the first victims, not the perpetrators, of National Socialist crimes. Rather than asking how Germans were capable of such acts of violence, they should ask how "Hitler was capable of violating the German nation [*Volk*]." The nations that

15. See Anna J. Merritt and Richard L. Merritt, eds., *Public Opinion in Occupied Germany: The OMGUS Surveys, 1945–1949* (Urbana, 1970), 36.

16. Eberan, *Die Debatte um die Schuldfrage*, 206.

17. Ibid., 67.

18. PRO, FO 371/64389/C 266.

19. PRO, FO 371/64390/C 5389; Schumacher at a Berlin rally, end of March–beginning of April 1947.

now summoned Germany before the tribunal of justice were thus offered the unequivocal recommendation that they should start by asking themselves "to what degree they had contributed to Hitler and his ability to plunge the whole world into such misery."[20]

If National Socialism was primarily the result of a series of external factors such as the Versailles treaty, the world economic depression, or the appeasement policies of the 1930s—for which the victorious powers, not just the Germans, were also accountable—then, from the German point of view, the occupation government considerably depleted its supply of political and moral legitimacy. German critics also deployed a host of other arguments, generally culminating in invocations of timeless transcultural norms and values and international law, to pose fundamental questions about the rule of the victors over the vanquished. Konrad Adenauer [the leader of the Christian Democratic Union who would become the Federal Republic's first chancellor in 1949] opined that German capitulation was of a purely military nature. For this reason, he contested the right of the occupation forces to implement far-reaching political measures such as the socialization of Ruhr industry, territorial losses in the east of Germany, or even the administrative reorganization of the Reich; such steps could not be taken without the explicit consent of the German people. Ultimately, a purely military capitulation did not invalidate rights accorded defeated nations under the tenets of the Hague convention.[21]

The Atlantic Charter was also invoked as another set of principles that should set limits to Allied occupation policy. Those who protested the expulsion of Germans from eastern Europe, the reduction of daily caloric intake standards, the continuation of dismantling programs, and more also claimed to base their case on "international law," though they never specified which international laws they had in mind. Ultimately, these protests were unsuccessful, but Germans maintained that their "powerlessness" increasingly resulted in their "lawlessness," according to a lead article in *Die Zeit*. As the article explained, this development was a "bitter and depressing experience for those of us who retained our beliefs in moral values during the entire Hitler period."[22]

What took place in the public consciousness of Germans during the first two years after the war's end was above all a complete inversion of values; the standards of moral and immoral conduct were completely reversed. Those who had wished for a restoration of law and morality and had thus entered the war to fight against Germany were criticized after Germany's defeat for pursuing policies that were little different from those they had only recently opposed. Cardinal Frings was not alone in believing that it was impossible to identify any difference between present and past. Germans so repressed their own guilt

20. PRO, FO 371/64390/C 7106; *Niederdeutsche Zeitung*, April 24, 1947.
21. PRO, FO 371/64389/C 602; Adenauer on January 9, 1947.
22. PRO, FO 371/64389/C 266, *Die Zeit*, mid-January 1947.

and so emphasized the failings of the Allies that it was necessary to ask who had actually begun the war. Guardians of law, political morality, and even democracy were no longer to be found on the side of the victors; rather, they were on the side of vanquished. Adenauer believed the occupation forces had to be taught that some laws were writ in stone, "binding on all powers, including the victors; these laws cannot be transgressed without punishment."[23]

Apparently hoping that law and morality would indeed triumph in the long run, Richard Tüngel, license holder [*Lizenzträger*] and chief columnist for *Die Zeit*, exhorted his readers to come together in a "community of law" [*Rechtsgemeinschaft*] against the Allies. If the Allies did not accord Germans the protection of the law, reasoned Tüngel, then "we have an even greater obligation in our dealings with one another to place nothing higher than the law."[24] FDP politician and future vice chancellor Franz Blücher threatened that the occupation forces would one day be held accountable. "It will be our task to point out candidly where the laws of the Allies have transgressed the boundaries of German law."[25] Schumacher went even further in September 1949, when he spoke of democracy's legitimacy crisis and then continued; "We are democrats, even if the occupation forces do not let us have democracy. We must defend democracy, even if it means opposing the occupation forces."[26]

The tendency to attribute the misery of the postwar years exclusively to the Allies paralleled the refusal to accept responsibility for the National Socialist dictatorship and the outbreak and consequences of World War II. Many Germans believed that if only they could take their fate back into their own hands, everything would improve significantly in no time at all. There was little evidence of a capacity to distinguish between cause and effect and to assess the situation objectively. Instead, many Germans believed that they found themselves in the worst of all possible worlds; in contrast, the Nazi period was frequently portrayed in rosy hues. Should democracy, so highly praised, be the only alternative to National Socialism? Such completely unrealistic assessments, appearing in published and unpublished opinion polls, were shocking.

Germans expected nothing good from the Russians, and evidence that their expectations were fulfilled was delivered by the great stream of refugees from eastern Europe; in contrast, they had high hopes for better treatment by the British and Americans. In a letter to the British prime minister, a German farmer who had been "forcibly evacuated" explained that "Eastern nations, mostly uncultured and uncivilized, have settled in our once prosperous farms, villages, and cities," leading him to hope "that our beloved homeland province, 'Silesia,'

23. PRO, FO 371/55879/C 6697; Adenauer, June 6, 1947.

24. PRO, FO 371/64389/C 266; *Die Zeit*, mid-January 1947.

25. PRO, FO 371/64390/C 4733, German Press Service, March 3, 1947.

26. PRO, FO 1030/229.

would in future be governed by the Anglo-Americans."[27] It was anticipated that the British and Americans would not simply enter the country as conquerors; rather, they were also greeted as liberators. However, the corollary of this view was the expectation that life in the British and American zones of occupation would soon return to normal and that Anglo-American forces sought nothing more than to put Germany back on its own feet as quickly as possible. In contrast to the Soviet occupation zone, where at least in the first year of occupation policies were not as bad as expected, the British and Americans soon demonstrated that they were there as occupying powers, not as mere liberators. From the start, the United States and Great Britain disappointed the high hopes of many Germans. Topping the list of German complaints were the process of denazification, the lack of economic progress, insufficient provision of foodstuffs and housing, and administrative failures. In a public opinion poll carried out in the British zone in December 1946, 60 percent of those surveyed indicated they had expected better policies under British military rule.[28]

Faith in the Western occupation forces continued to decline. According to American polls taken in September 1946, 43 percent believed that the Allies favored German reconstruction; by January 1948, only 30 percent still expressed this opinion. Of those, 10 percent remained convinced that the Allies would cooperate to achieve German reconstruction.[29] In early January 1947, a CDU member of the Hamburg municipal council declared that Germans had already been asking themselves for quite a long time whether their difficult situation was a product of a lack of vision and inefficiency or simply ill will on the part of the Allies. Moreover, he claimed that he could perceive a renewed interest on the part of the occupation forces "to pull the noose even tighter around the neck of those Germans who refuse to do what they are ordered to do."[30]

On January 4, 1948, at a function sponsored by the Christian Social Union (CSU) in Erlangen, Director Semler of the Economics Office for the Bizone [*Zweizonenamt für Wirtschaft*] also offered particularly harsh judgments of Allied and especially British economic policies. "The existence of black and gray markets," he said, "is not the result of the 'wickedness' of the Germans; rather it is solely a symptom of a disease that cannot be traced back to German failure . . . The mistakes of Allied economic policies are immediately apparent even to lay people." Above all, he opined that three years after the end of the war it was high time to convince the British to give up their habit of "plundering the German economy."[31]

---

27. PRO, FO 371/64359.
28. PRO, FO 371/64516/C 1681.
29. See Merritt and Merritt, *OMGUS Surveys*, 211.
30. PRO, FO 371/64389/C 1430.
31. PRO, FO 371/70616/C 426.

Germans experienced no immediate improvement in their circumstances after capitulation; indeed, at first, matters grew worse. Today we know that these deteriorating conditions were not the fault of destructive Allied policies. In fact, the Allies introduced significant measures to ease the greatest suffering of the Germans as quickly as possible. Still, the Germans believed that their situation was not only particularly grim but highly unjust. The lasting effects of Germans' inability to understand their responsibility for the war registered in the view that if occupation rule had any purpose at all, it could only consist in helping the Germans stand on their own feet as soon as possible. The absence of any clear improvement in general conditions or individual circumstances became, for many, an indication that in the postwar period, Germans were suffering the effects of incompetent or destructive forces worse than what they had suffered during the war. Germans could only expect relief once they controlled their own destiny. Measured by their willingness to work, organizational talent, and ingenuity—abilities and qualities that were important for overcoming difficult situations—Germans believed themselves to be superior to the occupation forces.[32]

Across the German political spectrum, there was a tendency to depoliticize occupation rule somewhat by judging it—or condemning it—according to its ability to solve technical problems. An interview in *Die Zeit* with Theodor Steltzer makes this tendency especially clear. Pointing to the difficulties of adequately provisioning the British zone with foodstuffs, he questioned whether the occupation government was capable of coming to grips with any pressing problems. Although he conceded that many Germans would have starved had the British not imported large quantities of foodstuffs into their zone, he nevertheless added that the policies pursued by the victorious powers since Germany's capitulation were the sole cause of the current critical situation. "If the eastern territories were returned to Germany, if the export of coal from Germany was stopped, then Germany would be in a far better condition than it is now, even in the absence of foodstuffs from elsewhere." He paid absolutely no attention to data released by London, indicating that British taxpayers were paying 80 million pounds a year [to cover the expenses of occupation], because he thought that the revenues from German exports, the liquidation of German foreign assets, and various reparations payments would more than balance out the expenditures. Steltzer concluded that the catastrophic

---

32. This phenomenon is impressively substantiated in a study by Barbara Marshall, in which she states: "The collapse of 1945 and the shortcomings of the subsequent occupation served in a perverted sense to prove to the Germans yet again that they were more efficient, harder working, and, in a phrase, much superior to the British and everyone else." See Barbara Marshall, "German Attitudes toward British Military Government 1945–1947," *Journal of Contemporary History* 15 (1980): 655–84; here, 668.

situation could only be overcome if "the German authorities alone [were charged] with long-term planning."[33]

Steltzer's statements revealed a characteristic inability to offer accurate assessments of the political connection between defeat and occupation. The Allies' decision to cede the German territories beyond the Oder-Neisse [to Poland] was a consequence of a war that Germany had provoked. Defeat in this war meant that reparations were due; at the very least, those reparations should make partial restitution for the destruction wrought by Germany, and in no way could reparations be calculated as payments for imported foodstuffs. According to the logic of Steltzer's argument, it was the Allies' task to pull out of Germany as soon as possible after the defeat of National Socialism, leaving everything as they had found it. If the Allies had treated Germany as if nothing had really happened, the Germans would not have gone hungry, they would govern themselves and administer their own affairs, and they would not have been a burden for the taxpayers of other countries.

Other politicians followed similar lines of argumentation. In a speech delivered in Bonn in February 1947, Adenauer claimed,

> We will have to come to terms with the fact that we will remain under the control of the Allies for some time to come. But let me say again: Under Allied control, not under Allied administration. [Allied administration] represents an intolerable state for a nation such as ours. Even the best and most intelligent nation cannot rule a nation so differentiated and highly developed as the German nation (*Volk*). No other nation has at its disposal the personnel that would be necessary for such a task. Not even England can do that. That is simply impossible. (Bravo!) There have been many blunders and much harm done, because in taking over the administration of the British-occupied zone, England assumed a task that neither it nor any other country could possibly have mastered.[34]

The vice chair of the SPD, Erich Ollenhauer, delivered a similar declaration that paralleled Adenauer's, right down to the choice of words.[35] Naturally, Blücher also believed that the occupation forces were not in a position to rule Germany; rather, they were exclusively to blame for everything—at least everything bad—that had happened since capitulation. With bold black-and-white strokes he contrasted the Allies' measures with the achievements of the German nation, referring not only to significant German accomplishments since the end of the war, but also to things that Germany had achieved before

---

33. PRO, FO 371/64389/C 266.
34. Adenauer, *Briefe 1945–1947* (Rhöndorfer edition) (n.p., n.d.), 455.
35. PRO, FO 371/64389/C 3957.

the war was over. "There is no reason for a nation, capable of such accomplishments during the war, to suffer from an inferiority complex. In the same manner, it can be proud of what it has accomplished since 1945."[36]

The classic conditions for fomenting a decisive resistance to an unjust regime, particularly one of foreign origin, include judging existing circumstances to be unfair, knowing the law to be on one's side, and being convinced of one's own superiority. Were Germans ready to resist Allied occupation after 1945? If so, what were the cause, the purpose,and the consequence of this resistance?

In many respects, 1947 marked a turning point in postwar history and in Germany's relationship to the occupation forces. Conditions in Germany still had not improved, and the Allies had made no tangible progress in their deliberations on Germany; this situation led to growing irritation with and public opposition to the occupation forces. A strike wave swept over the country, particularly affecting the British zone. Food rations, rather than increasing, diminished. A worldwide scarcity of foodstuffs, a hard winter, exhausted soil, and problems with the distribution system all combined to make conditions even worse. None of these circumstances, however, could in any way be attributed to the sheer incompetence or vindictiveness of the occupation forces.[37]

At this critical juncture, the announcement of an American plan to reconstruct Europe unleashed hopes that strengthened the Germans' desire for reconstruction and their resolve to dispense with those impediments that blocked the swift economic development of their country. The tendency, even among Western occupation forces, to differentiate between the good and bad, the well-meaning and the destructive, intensified. Ever since the Americans let it be known that they were willing to reverse their policies toward Germany, the anger of the Germans was increasingly directed toward the British. When asked if differences existed between American and British occupation policies for the economic reconstruction of Germany, more than 70 percent of those Germans surveyed responded in the affirmative. Of these, 92.4 percent were of the opinion that American policies were better for the Western zones; only 5.8 percent favored British over American policies.[38]

German criticism of the British was devastatingly harsh. In additional polls conducted in October and December 1947,[39] exactly half of those surveyed said the primary goal of the British occupation policies was to ruin the

---

36. Ibid. See also PRO, FO 371/64390/C 4733.

37. See John E. Farquharson, "Landwirtschaft und Ernährung in der Politik der Alliierten 1945–1948," in *Kalter Krieg und Deutsche Frage: Deutschland im Widerstreit der Mächte 1945–1948*, ed. Josef Foschepoth (Göttingen, 1985), 147–74.

38. PRO, FO 371/64516/C 9307; poll from June 1947.

39. PRO, FO 371/70617/C 2576.

German economy. The majority also agreed that this goal would be achieved by dismantling German industry. Analyses of Britain's motives reached the conclusion that the British sought to take advantage of Germany's weakened condition and dispense once and for all with a traditional competitor. Writing in 1982, Hanns D. Ahrens recalled the battle over the dismantling program and still maintained that the British "feared that the Germans—hardly a lazy or unimaginative people—would once again become active on world markets."[40]

By now research has adequately documented that the positive effects of the Marshall Plan and the currency reform have frequently been exaggerated, while the negative claims about the impact of policies to dismantle German industry were also overstated. Compared with figures for 1936, estimates of how much German industrial capacity decreased as a result of dismantling range from 4 to 5 percent. A more detailed picture of the effects of the dismantling program emerges when one considers that in the postwar years, factories and machinery were underutilized and capital stock was generally of higher quality than before the war. Measuring the expansion of the capital stock after 1948 also requires recognizing that at that point, existing levels were already higher than they had been before the war. The dismantling of industry was thus of little significance for the actual economic development of West Germany after World War II.[41]

Economists in the countries that received dismantled German industries understood this. The "white book" of the British government that assessed the years of occupation asserted "that the total worth of dismantled facilities is less than the amount of reparations demanded by Bismarck from France after the war of 1870–1871; the British portion of these reparations represents only approximately 2 percent of the amount British taxpayers paid for the restoration of Germany and its industry."[42]

If both sides recognized the limited economic value of dismantling and acknowledged that in the final analysis it neither benefited the occupiers nor disadvantaged Germans, why did the policy of dismantling become "a question of life and death for the German nation," as Adenauer claimed?[43] On October 16, 1947, the final list of plants to be dismantled was made public. Only 682 of the 1,636 firms originally targeted remained on the list. Of these 682, 302 were armaments factories and another 63 had already been dismantled. Nonetheless, the German members of the zonal council in the British zone took the opportunity to disrupt negotiations with the occupation forces. "This

---

40. Hanns D. Ahrens, *Demontage: Nachkriegspolitik der Alliierten* (Munich, 1982), 69.

41. See Heiner R. Adamsen, "Faktoren und Daten der wirtschaftlichen Entwicklung in der Frühphase der Bundesrepublik Deutschland 1948–1954," *Archiv für Sozialgeschichte* 28 (1978): 217–44; here, 233.

42. PRO, FO 371/109759/CW 10116/5, 54.

43. Adenauer, *Briefe 1945–1947*, 454.

is a matter of life and death for our people. At stake is the existence or extinction of our industry, and with it our entire economy," opined Lehr, a CDU politician. Speaking for the members of his party, he expressed the desire "to resume immediately discussions with our political allies in order to make them fully aware of the significance of this list."[44]

Dismantling had become a call to arms. It is revealing that *reparations*, a word that conveys a less destructive tone than *dismantling* and does not carry overtones of destruction, was virtually never used by German politicians. Dismantling became a universally accepted symbol of policies directed against Germany. Every demolition and every removal of industrial plant and machinery symbolized Germany's continued state of powerlessness and dependence on the victorious Allies, not the equality that Germany sought. Germans failed to perceive their moral and political responsibility to make restitution, and they were unable to understand the security goals of West European countries, which were concerned lest Germany rapidly return to a position of strength. As a consequence, Germans saw the policy of dismantling as a measure dictated by hate and a sense of revenge, aimed at holding the German people hostage. Germans thus saw the fight against the dismantling of industry as a moral and patriotic act.

The dismantling issue provided an ideal opportunity for many German politicians to make a name for themselves in their struggle against the occupation forces; using this issue, they could achieve recognition at the national level and assert their claims to be good Germans who acted in the national interest. This was true both of Adenauer and Schumacher. "If he [Adenauer] had been *persona grata* with the Allies in the days of great hunger and the dismantling of industry," wrote the earl of Longford, Lord Pakenham, former minister for German affairs in the British cabinet, "he might well never have succeeded in rallying the people behind his leadership."[45] When it came to criticizing the occupation forces, the head of the SPD was fully the equal of his counterpart in the CDU. Indeed, Schumacher was resolved not to allow anyone to outdo him in his relentlessly harsh attitude toward the Allies. Ultimately, that was an advantage for Adenauer; despite his criticism of the Allies, he emerged as a more approachable negotiating partner than Schumacher.[46] Nevertheless, both politicians were quite intent on avoiding any impression that they were the servants

---

44. Bundesarchiv und Institut für Zeitgeschichte, ed., *Akten zur Vorgeschichte der Bundesrepublik Deutschland 1945–1949*, vol. 3 (Munich, 1982), 675.

45. Earl of Longford, "Erfahrungen mit Adenauer als Minister für die britische Besatzungszone," in *Konrad Adenauer und seine Zeit: Politik und Persönlichkeit des ersten Bundeskanzlers: Beiträge von Weg- und Zeitgenossen*, ed. Dieter Blumenwitz et al. (Stuttgart, 1976), 415–20; here, 416.

46. See, for example, Karl Günther von Hase, "Adenauer und Großbritannien," in Blumenwitz et al., *Konrad Adenauer und seine Zeit*, 636.

of one or another foreign power. It is well known that neither missed any opportunity to accuse the other of close ties to the Allies. From Adenauer came charges that the SPD found particular favor with the Labour-backed British government because it was dependent on the British. Schumacher countered that Adenauer was the "Chancellor of the Allies."[47]

To be sure, the dismantling of industry did not top the list of the West German population's worries.[48] Nonetheless, this issue was particularly well suited as a vehicle for expressing criticism of the occupation forces. On the one hand, whoever expressed this critique could be sure that all Germans would agree with him or her. On the other, all major problems of the postwar period, ranging from the lack of foodstuffs and housing to low work-force morale and rising unemployment, could be traced with ease back to the question of dismantling. Since the spring of 1947, the growing gulf between Washington and London on the reparations question made it easier for the Germans to perfect their attacks on British policies in particular, drawing increasingly on a traditional store of resentment against the British. The perception that even as the Cold War reached a climax, Great Britain continued to act like a victorious power, not a genuine partner, led Ernst Friedländer to ask in *Die Zeit* why "British policies were eternally 'behind the times' . . . , always limping along behind history." Since he could not imagine that a "law of inertia" was to blame, he surmised that what motivated British policy was "fear of competition, eternal hostility, a war that continued even into peace."[49] These were familiar themes in the German critique of British occupation policy.

There is a tradition of anti-British sentiment in Germany, stemming from the Anglo-German antagonism of the nineteenth century; it embodies a mixture of envy and admiration for a competitor and rival viewed to be equal or even slightly superior to the Germans themselves. Even the triumph of the British over the Germans twice in the twentieth century did little to alter these sentiments. Rather, the view was widespread that although Great Britain might have won the war in a formal sense, it actually had lost, because Britain did not possess the capabilities and qualities of a true victor; it should be the victor's primary task, indeed moral duty, as rapidly as possible to help rebuild a conquered nation that had suffered for twelve years under the "foreign" rule of National Socialism, particularly now that new, even greater threats came from the east. However, under the given circumstances, Germans could anticipate

---

47. Calls for limitations on the occupation powers played a special role in the election campaign of 1949. See, for example, PRO, FO 371/76678/C 4433.

48. A survey conducted in August 1949 to determine the most important problems that confronted the West German government revealed that ten other issues were mentioned more frequently than dismantling. See PRO, FO 1036/771.

49. Norbert Frei and Franziska Friedländer, eds., *Ernst Friedländer: Klärung für Deutschland: Leitartikel in der Zeit 1946–1950* (Munich, 1982), 129f.

that only the United States or perhaps France, but certainly not Great Britain, would act as a proper victor.

Lack of vision, inefficiency, a desire for revenge, hypocrisy, malevolence, and economic competitiveness—the verdict was harsh. It also influenced academic assessments of the occupation years. Only recently has research begun to depart from this German perspective that focused on unsuccessful and destructive British policies and that characterized British policy as hypocritical and myopic, even though British policy was quite insignificant, given the dominant position of the United States.[50] After the German defeat, the decisive issue for London was to identify foreign and domestic political mechanisms that would eliminate Germany as a security threat in the long term but would have no negative repercussions for Europe's economic and political development. The formula for achieving these objectives was a cautious balance of external security, economic reconstruction, and the internal democratization of Germany. It is characteristic of British policy that despite all the changes in the general climate of foreign affairs following World War II, the British sought to balance their policies on the basis of these principles.

After Yalta, the British did not want to set a fixed sum for reparations; at Potsdam, they repeatedly presented the potential dangers of destroying Germany's economic and political unity; and in the spring of 1946 in the deliberations of the Allied Control Council, they advocated significantly higher production levels for German industry in strong opposition to the other occupation forces. To be sure, once the Americans had reversed their policies toward Germany, the British were not ready to sacrifice their security interests to a boundless euphoria for reconstruction together with all of its political consequences. For this reason, reparations policies that had already been negotiated were maintained beyond 1947; in addition, dismantling that had already begun was continued, and dismantled industries were delivered to those countries entitled to reparations, including the Soviet Union.[51]

However, even if the execution of occupation policies by the British left much to be desired, German criticism of those policies was exaggerated; it said more about the critics than it did about those at whom criticism was directed. Although there was no national resistance movement against the policies of dismantling, there were certainly attempts to express a national will to resist not only dismantling, but more generally the entire burden of the past, the

---

50. For examples, see Claus Scharf and Hans-Jürgen Schröder, eds., *Die Deutschlandpolitik Großbritanniens und die britische Zone 1945–1949* (Wiesbaden, 1979); Dietmar Petzina and Walter Euchner, eds., *Wirtschaftspolitik im britischen Besatzungsgebiet 1945–1949* (Düsseldorf, 1984); Josef Foschepoth and Rolf Steiniger, eds., *Die britische Deutschland- und Besatzungspolitik 1945–1949* (Paderborn, 1985).

51. See, for instance, Josef Foschepoth, "Konflikte in der Reparationspolitik der Alliierten," in Foschepoth, *Kalter Krieg und Deutsche Frage*, 175–97.

acknowledgment of individual guilt, and the feeling of being subject to superior powers. That led to the notorious German struggle for equal rights, the desire to stand on the same level with the victors and to remain an actor, involved in making history. Not only Adenauer and other politicians expressed these sentiments; they were generally held by the majority of the German population. In the summer of 1948, as if nothing had happened in the recent past and as if dismantling was simply an economic problem, North Rhine-Westphalian Minister Erik Nölting threatened to stop cooperating with the German-Allied dismantling committee. In his words: "One still has the impression that victors are confronting the vanquished; we still have not entered the realm of economic rationality."[52]

In conclusion, we can see that discontent with the "Fourth Reich" and the criticism of the occupying powers that grew out of it served three purposes: First, criticism of Allied occupation served to repress individual German guilt for dictatorship and war; second, it exonerated Germans from responsibility for the misery of postwar years; and third, it justified Germany's desire to terminate the statute of occupation with appeals to the genuine sense of the superiority of the German people. The diagnosis of the postwar disaster was that it was the consequence of the lack of vision, inefficiency, and destructive intentions of the occupying forces. This diagnosis repressed questions of the actual source of the disaster and German responsibility for what had occurred; indeed, it made it possible to believe that things had been better under the Nazis. In contrast to the post–World War I settlement, after World War II authority lay exclusively in Allied hands, which made it easy for Germans to blame the Allies for everything that went wrong while claiming responsibility for everything that succeeded. The same tendency is even apparent in a historiography that has painted all developments preceding currency reform in dark colors, while portraying everything that occurred after 1948 in brightly colored hues. An occupying power that failed to eliminate suffering quickly, the primary task of any occupying power, lost moral legitimacy. The German demand to be allowed once again to control Germany's own fate thus appeared all the more justified.

In general, consistently intensifying criticism, documented here with the example of German reaction to occupation policy, aimed at creating self-confidence or, better yet, reviving and validating an *old* German sense of self-assurance that had been battered by defeat and occupation. It contrasted German virtues of superior inventiveness, efficiency, and economic competence with British lack of vision, inefficiency, and dishonest economic methods. Thus, the economic collapse of 1945 seemed to prove once more that Germans were indeed more efficient, industrious, better at planning and orga-

---

52. PRO, FO 1036/18.

nization, and could work harder than the victorious powers—at least the European ones—in short, that Germans were superior. The Germans became acceptable for the rest of western Europe only once Germany was definitively divided between east and west, West Germany was fully integrated into the Western alliance, and the German superiority complex could be focused on communism and their own "brothers and sisters in the zone."

Montgomery said it would take ten years to change "the German heart and the German way of life." He was wrong. More than twenty years would pass before the "inability to mourn"[53] would give way to a willingness to begin the active work of grieving.

---

53. See the book of the same title by Alexander and Margarete Mitscherlich, *Die Unfähigkeit zu trauern: Grundlagen kollektiven Verhaltens* (Munich, 1967). The publication date may well be indicative of the Federal Republic's spiritual and political development.

Part 2.
From Warfare State
to Welfare State

Change and Continuity in the Treatment of German *Kriegsopfer*

James M. Diehl

The immediate postwar period in Germany has often been referred to as *Stunde Null*, zero hour. Although at first an expression of exhaustion and despair, the term gradually took on a more positive connotation, namely that of a decisive and welcome break with an oppressive past. *Stunde Null* came to signify both an end and a beginning: the end of a troubled, authoritarian phase of German history and the beginning of what was hoped would be a brighter, democratic phase in which Germany, reformed, would join the comity of western democratic nations.

No one was more convinced that 1945 could and should be a *tabula rasa* than the occupying powers, who were determined that their mission entailed not only the defeat of Nazi Germany, but the rooting out of pernicious, antidemocratic elements in German society and the introduction of democracy through reform and reeducation. The subsequent emergence of a successful parliamentary democracy in western Germany helped to lend credence to the idea that 1945 had indeed been a *Stunde Null* and a decisive watershed in German history.

Today, we know that 1945 did not in fact represent so decisive a change as has been popularly accepted. Neither the fears of those who opposed nor the hopes of those who supported root and branch reform were realized. Instead, historians can easily make the case that there was as much continuity as discontinuity after 1945. Indeed, a considerable literature has emerged criticizing the degree of continuity and the lack of substantive reform in German institutions and society. Much of the blame for the failure of reform is placed on the western Allies, who, it is charged, either never really supported decisive change or else, under the impact of the Cold War, quickly lost whatever enthusiasm they may have had for reform.[1] The treatment of disabled veterans after the Second World

---

1. On the problem of reform versus restoration and the relevant literature, see Hans-Jürgen Rautenberg, "Zur Standortbestimmung für künftige deutsche Streitkräfte 1945–1956," in Roland

War provides an interesting example of the problem of continuity and discontinuity in German history, as well as a different look at the respective roles of the
occupiers and occupied in promoting or resisting reform. In order to contrast
what happened after 1945, however, it is necessary to examine the treatment of
disabled veterans in the 1920s and 1930s.

Like the other belligerent nations, Germany entered World War I with a
war-disability system that was geared to an era of short, decisive wars with
limited casualties. The system was administered by the army. Disabled soldiers
received pensions scaled to the severity of their wounds, but little was provided
for their families or for the next-of-kin of soldiers who were killed. The volun-
taristic schemes designed to supplement the meagre official pension system soon collapsed under the weight of the unprecedented carnage of the First
World War. During the war public pressure for the reform and expansion of the
outdated and inadequate war-disability system became increasingly intense.[2] In
spite of several stopgap improvements, however, the government resisted such
pressure, hoping to postpone the enormously expensive problem until after the
war when, it was hoped, indemnities would help to ease the financial burden of
caring for the *Kriegsopfer*. With the collapse of the Empire it fell to the beleaguered Weimar Republic to provide for the victims of a war that had resulted in
large part from the irresponsible actions of its predecessor—a situation that was
to be echoed in 1950, when the Federal Republic was forced to assume responsibility for the victims of the war unleashed by the wanton policies of the Third
Reich.

Although drafted hurriedly and in many regards imperfect, the
Reichsversorgungsgesetz (RVG) of May 1920 represented a significant improvement over the previous war-disability system in Germany and, on
balance, it was one of the most progressive of its day.[3] Animated by social
welfare, rather than military principles, the new system was put under the jurisdiction of the newly created Labor Ministry, which was also responsible for
the administration of the old age and industrial accident disability programs.
The war-disability system was a separate entity, however, with its own administrative structure.

G. Foerster, et al., *Anfänge westdeutscher Sicherheitspolitik*, vol. 1, *Von der Kapitulation bis zum
Pleven Plan* (Munich, 1982), 765ff.

2. On the treatment of disabled veterans during and after the First World War, see Robert
W. Whalen, *Bitter Wounds: German Victims of the Great War, 1914–1939* (Ithaca, 1984).

3. For details of the RVG, see ibid., chaps. 9–10, and Helmut Rühland, "Entwicklung,
heutige Gestaltung und Problematik der Kriegsopferversorgung in der Bundesrepublik Deutschland" (Inauguraldissertation, Universität Köln, 1957), 24–61. For a comparative perspective, see
Michael Geyer, "Ein Vorbote des Wohlfahrtsstaates: Die Kriegsopferversorgung in Frankreich,
Deutschland und Grossbritannien nach dem Ersten Weltkrieg," *Geschichte und Gesellschaft* 9,
no. 2 (1983).

Under the RVG earlier distinctions between professional and nonprofessional soldiers as well as pension differentials based on military rank were abolished. The main thrust of the new system was not simple monetary compensation for injury, but physical and vocational rehabilitation and the reintegration of disabled veterans into society as productive citizens. The first component of the RVG was therefore the guarantee and provision of free medical care to cure or alleviate the suffering associated with war-related injuries. Provisions were also made for vocational rehabilitation and retraining. An elaborate system of pensions was established for those who were permanently disabled and the survivors of those killed in the war. As the most tangible and expensive component of the RVG, these pensions were also the most controversial component of the new law. The pensions were computed in a complex and multileveled manner. A base allowance was calculated according to the disabled person's decrease in earning capacity as determined by a doctor who took into account, among other things, the victim's education, social standing, and prewar occupation. Pensions began with a disability of 20 percent. Men with a disability of 50 percent or more received a severe disability allowance in addition to the base allowance. A further supplement, the equalization allowance, compensated those who had had, or—barring wartime injury—could reasonably have been expected to attain, positions of special responsibility. The base allowance plus the severe disability and equalization allowances comprised the full pension or *Vollrent*. The *Vollrent* could be increased further through additional allowances which were geared to family status, place of residence, and the need for in-home medical care. Widows' pensions were calculated at 30 percent of the husband's *Vollrent* or at 50 percent if the widow was over fifty years of age, herself disabled, or had children to support. During the 1920s several amendments to the *Reichsversorgungsgesetz* were passed but its basic structure remained the same throughout the Weimar Republic.

With the onset of the Depression, pensions for war victims were cut in several areas as a result of the austerity measures introduced by the Brüning government. Predictably, this created anxiety and anger among pensioners.[4] Their discontent was adroitly seized upon by the Nazis. In the fall of 1930, shortly after the Brüning government's first *Notverordnung* and just before the Reichstag elections in which the NSDAP was to score its great breakthrough, Nazi propaganda for the first time began seriously to concern itself with the plight of the war victims. From 1930 until 1933 the National Socialists pursued a two-track strategy with regard to the war disabled: on the one hand, they

---

4. On these cuts and the response to them, see, for example, "Die Rückläufigkeit der Versorgung und Fürsorge für die Kriegsopfer im Zeichen der Notverordnungen," distributed in 1932 to members of the Reichstag and the government by the Reichsbund der Kriegsbeschädigten, Kriegsteilnehmer und Kriegshinterbliebenen.

ruthlessly attacked the Republican government and the existing disabled veterans' organizations, claiming that the cuts in pensions demonstrated the Republic's lack of concern for veterans and the inability of the existing war victims' organizations, the largest of which was Social Democratic, to represent the interests of their members; on the other hand, they criticized the "Marxist" RVG for creating a "pension psychosis" that made disabled veterans think of themselves as welfare recipients rather than as the military heroes they were.[5]

Once in power, the National Socialist regime consolidated the existing disabled veterans' organizations into the *Nationalsozialistische Kriegsopferversorgung* (NSKOV), headed by Hanns Oberlindober, an old crony of Hitler's from the early Bavarian *Kampfzeit*.[6] In spite of an intensive propaganda campaign heralding a massive reform of the RVG, little substantive change took place in the treatment of the victims of the Great War. Some of the cuts introduced by the Brüning government were rescinded and in July 1934 a new supplemental allowance was introduced for soldiers wounded at the front; the latter was accompanied by other, largely cosmetic, measures designed to restore the honor of disabled soldiers, whose position in society presumably had been denigrated by the Republic and debased by the social welfare emphasis of the RVG. While largely symbolic, the changes of 1934 foreshadowed a general National Socialist policy of emphasizing the disabled veteran's role as a former soldier, rather than as a crippled victim of war.

Following the reimposition of universal conscription, a new military welfare system that hewed more closely to National Socialist precepts was introduced to cover members of the enlarged Wehrmacht. Inaugurated in 1938 and early 1939, the new system restored some of the principles connected with the old Imperial system and reflected the Nazi desire to emphasize military service while deemphasizing the costly social welfare aspects of the RVG, which remained in effect for veterans of the First World War. The *Wehrmachtsfürsorge- und Versorgungsgesetz* (WFVG) of 1938[7] provided pensions for service-related disabilities computed on the following basis: whereas the guiding principle of the RVG was the degree of the victim's loss of earning power as a civilian, the new system was based on the severity of the wound, of which there were four categories. The payment of a flat sum based on the type of disability marked a return to the type of pension scale employed by the Imperial army. The next step in the calculation of a disabled soldier's pension hinged on the concept of *Arbeitsverwendungsfähigkeit* or *Arbeitsverwendungsunfähig-*

5. For examples of the National Socialist arguments, see the publications of the N.S.-Kriesopferversorgung in the Bundesarchiv, Koblenz (hereafter cited as BAK), Bestand NSD/54.

6. For a history of the NSKOV and details on the treatment of war victims in the Third Reich, see my "Victors or Victims? Disabled Veterans in the Third Reich," *Journal of Modern History* 59 (December 1987).

7. For details, see Rühland, 66–85, and Max Wenzel, "50 Jahre Kriegsopferversorgung,"

keit. Only soldiers deemed incapable of working received the so-called AVU pension, which in turn was geared to the recipient's family status, place of residence, and military rank. The introduction of the latter factor in the calculation of pensions represented another reversion to the Imperial system.

The WFVG, which was designed for a peacetime army, and which incidentally included generous provisions for civil service appointments for retired professional soldiers, especially non-commissioned officers, was supplemented in 1939, on the eve of the Second World War, by the *Einsatz-Wehrmachtsfürsorge- und Versorgungsgesetz* (EWFVG), which retained the basic structure of the 1938 law but increased and expanded the benefits accorded to soldiers injured in active combat, as opposed to peacetime or rear echelon duty.

A comparison of the war-disability systems of the Weimar Republic and the Third Reich reveals a definite militarization under the National Socialists. Civilian points of reference in determining pensions were downgraded in favor of military ones. The type of wound and the circumstances from which it resulted, rather than the decline in civilian earning power, became the primary point of reference. In addition, military rank and the length and type of military service became determining factors. In short, the system of 1938/39 emphasized the individual's role in society as a soldier, rather than as a civilian. This militarization was also reflected institutionally: a separate administrative structure for the WFVG/EWFVG was created that was subordinated to the War Ministry instead of the Labor Ministry.

Both the Weimar and the National Socialist war-disability systems had as their goal the reintegration of the disabled soldier into the economic marketplace, but whereas the RVG stressed rehabilitation and forms of social and economic assistance that were designed to ease the transition, the legislation of the Third Reich relied more heavily on financial exigency to force disabled soldiers to reenter the labor market.[8] The structure of the 1938/39 laws, in which increased retirement benefits and opportunities for professional soldiers[9] were combined with reduced benefits for disabled conscript soldiers, provides an indirect but convincing confirmation (or corollary) of Hitler's Blitzkrieg strategy, which envisioned short wars, limited casualties, and territorial gains that would open up new civilian administrative positions for former soldiers.

At the outbreak of the Second World War, then, there existed two separate systems for the care of the war-disabled in Germany: that of the 1920 *Reichsversorgungsgesetz*, under the direction of the Labor Ministry, which cared for the victims of the First World War, and the WFVG/EWFVG system of 1938/39, which covered the disabled veterans of the new war. Immediately

---

    8. Wenzel, 24, 29–30.
    9. On Wehrmacht benefits, see Rudolf Absolon, *Die Wehrmacht im Dritten Reich* (Boppard,

following the war's outbreak, on 8 September 1939, the overall direction of both systems was transferred to the High Command of the Wehrmacht (OKW).

Once German casualties began to rise, the inadequacies of the new legislation became apparent. Men who suffered the same wounds as their fathers had in the First World War found that their benefits were less; widows of soldiers killed in the Second World War found that their benefits were less than those received by their counterparts from the First World War.[10] As discontent mounted, the leaders of the Third Reich, concerned about morale on both the fighting and the home fronts, responded with an avalanche of ad hoc measures designed to bring the procedures and benefits of the 1938/39 laws into line with those of the RVG, whose benefits were also expanded. The result was administrative and fiscal chaos.[11] In October 1943 the overall administration of the two programs was transferred from the OKW to the Labor Ministry, and efforts were begun to unify the two systems. By the war's end this still had not been accomplished, however, and as a result of structural deficiencies and the overextension of benefits, the system was bankrupt.[12]

1971), vol. 2, chap. 6 and vol. 4, chap. 7.

10. Wenzel, 28. One expert even claimed that benefits had been better under the Kaiserreich. Ibid., 29.

11. Ibid., 23–34. Also see "Die Versorgung der Kriegsbeschädigten und ihrer Hinterbliebenen in Deutschland," esp. 3, 15, National Archives and Records Service, Washington, D.C. (hereafter NARS), Office of Military Government, United States, Record Group 260, Box 56, Folder 13. Materials from this collection will hereafter be cited as OMGUS 260, followed by box and folder number.

12. The bankruptcy of the war-disability system reflected the bankruptcy of the Third Reich as a whole. In the six wartime budget years the Reich spent 685 billion Reichsmarks, of which nearly three-quarters (some 510 billion Reichsmarks) went for the war and armaments proper (Gustav Stolper, et al., *The German Economy 1870 to the Present* [New York, 1967], 165). The expenditures for disabled veterans and survivors naturally increased dramatically, especially after 1942. In August 1938, 1.6 million Germans were eligible for pensions under the RVG and WFVG. Expenditures for the two systems totalled 937 million Reichsmarks, with 99% going to beneficiaries of the RVG. In 1944 expenditures for the war disabled and survivors had increased to 3,491 million Reichsmarks, of which 62% was being paid to victims of the Second World War (*Die Versorgung der Kriegsopfer in der Bundesrepublik Deutschland*, hrsg. von Presse- und Informationsamt der Bundesregierung, Stand 30.9.52, 15–16). An additional source of war-related social expenditure was the generous pensions paid to military dependents in order to shore up morale and maintain support for the war (on this, see Hedwig Wachenheim, "Allowances for Dependents of Mobilised Men in Germany," *International Labour Review*, Mar. 1940). Only a very small part of the skyrocketing costs of the war effort was covered by taxes. Instead, the regime employed a system of so-called "noiseless" war financing which consisted of borrowing (i.e., forcing loans) from public corporations, social security funds, and various party agencies, the exploitation of conquered foreign assets and, above all, as in the First World War, deficit financing. As a result, the Reich debt, which had been about 30 billion Reichsmarks at the outset of the war, had risen to nearly 400 billion Reichsmarks by the war's end (Stolper, 147–49, 164–66; Karl Hardach, *The Political Economy of Germany in the Twentieth Century* [Berkeley, 1980], 85). The inflationary consequences of National Socialist financial practices were largely hidden through rigid wage and

The National Socialist militarization of the war-disability system proved to be a double disservice to German war victims. Not only had it in many cases reduced benefits, but, in addition, it helped prompt the Allies to dismantle the system as part of their overall demilitarization program, an action that further increased the misery of Germany's war victims. If the victors agreed on little else, they were united in their determination to root out Nazism and militarism in Germany. According to JCS 1067, which laid down the basic guidelines for occupation policy, this included the prohibition of the payment of "all military pensions, or other emoluments or benefits, except compensation for physical disability limiting the recipient's ability to work, at rates which are no higher than the lowest of those for comparable physical disability arising from non-military causes." In a series of decrees culminating in Control Law Number 34 of 20 August 1946, which repealed all German laws concerning the legal status and privileges of military and ex-military personnel and their families, the Allies systematically dismantled the German system of war-disability benefits.[13] Pension payments were stopped, *Versorgungsämter* were closed and dissolved. Disabled veterans were forced to rely on pension benefits accrued in other pension plans or, lacking these, to turn to public welfare. No comprehensive, unified system was created to replace the one that was dismantled. From 1945 to 1950 the treatment of disabled veterans was a zonal matter that varied from one occupation zone to another.

In the Soviet zone, all pension payments were stopped and the offices of the corresponding administrative authorities were disbanded. Benefits were limited to those who qualified for general welfare. In the fall of 1945 a unified social insurance system was erected that united the previous old age, industrial disability, and miners' compensation systems. Payments under these programs were resumed in the spring of 1946. War-disability pensions as such were not resumed. Instead, state social insurance agencies were empowered to pay pensions to disabled persons who were not members of the established social insurance programs if they were unable to work. Pensions for war-disabled veterans as such were only authorized in July 1948 and then were limited to

price controls, but with the collapse of the Third Reich, the fiscal sleight-of-hand could no longer be continued or concealed. The long-established social insurance systems, such as old age, sickness, and industrial disability, which had access to independent and continuing sources of fiscal support, e.g., pension funds (insofar as they had not been totally depleted by government raids) and member contributions, were able, though with considerable difficulty, to reestablish themselves after the war (see n. 20, below). Programs dependent solely on public funds, such as those for war victims and military dependents, whose spiraling costs had been covered primarily by the printing press, were, however, like the Third Reich, bankrupt.

13. All veterans' organizations, including those concerned solely with the rights of disabled veterans, were also prohibited. On the genesis of JCS 1067 and its implementation, see John Gimbel, *The American Occupation of Germany: Politics and the Military, 1945–1949* (Stanford, 1968), and Earl F. Ziemke, *The U.S. Army and the Occupation of Germany, 1944–46* (Washington,

persons who were two-thirds disabled, i.e., those whose vocational ability had been reduced by two-thirds as a result of their wounds. Pensions for the survivors of soldiers killed in the war were equally narrowly defined and limited.[14] Although improvements were later made in the amounts paid, the basic structure of the war-disability system in the eastern zone remained the same after the creation of the DDR. Thus, in eastern Germany one can speak of a fundamental and permanent discontinuity in the treatment of war-disabled veterans. In the west, things were more complicated.

In the western zones the course of events initially was similar to that in the Soviet zone.[15] War-disability pensions were stopped, the associated administrative offices were dissolved, and benefits were essentially limited to those who qualified for general welfare. Later, the payment of pensions to disabled veterans and the next-of-kin of soldiers killed in the war was taken over by traditional social security programs. In the British zone war-disability pensions were brought under the jurisdiction of the old-age disability program. In the U.S. zone the care of the war-disabled was placed under the jurisdiction of the industrial accident disability program. In the French zone, no unified system was established. Instead, each state developed its own. Baden continued to apply the principles of the old RVG, although considerable cuts and limitations were introduced; Württemberg-Hohenzollern introduced a system similar to that in the U.S. zone; and in the Rhineland-Pfalz a system eventually emerged that was a mixture of those in the other two states.

No matter which principles were used by the occupying powers, the extent of care and the level of pension payments were less than they had been before 1945. This was a deliberate policy. The Allies' dismantling of the old war-disability system was motivated by their desire to extirpate militarism from German society. They believed that the generous pensions and the favored (i.e., separate or *gehoben*) treatment of the victims of war in Germany had served to encourage pro-military sentiment and to shield Germans from fully comprehending and experiencing the horrible consequences of war. In their view, the treatment of the war-disabled as a favored group only worked to perpetuate the German tradition of glorifying the military and war—including its victims—a practice that had allowed the military to retain its position as a privileged and arrogant caste. As a report of the U.S. Military Government put it: "The objective of abolishing war pensions is to discredit the military class in

---

D.C., 1975).

14. On the treatment of war victims in the Soviet zone and the DDR, see Rühland, 98–103, 191–99, and "Tatsachen hinter dem eisernen Vorhang," *Ostinformationsdienst der Bundespresse-stelle des DGB*, no. 9 (19 Dec. 1963).

15. On the treatment of war victims in the western zones, see Rühland, 88–98, 103–19, *Die Versorgung der Kriegsopfer in der Bundesrepublik Deutschland*, 18–19, and Leonhard Trometer, "Die Kriegsopferversorgung nach 1945," *Sozialpolitik nach 1945*, ed. Reinhart Bartholomäi et al.

Germany, to reduce their influence in society and to impress upon the public that a military career bears neither honor, profit or security."[16] In addition to this political and unmistakably punitive goal, the occupiers were also motivated by the desire to rationalize and cut the costs of German social services, which, in a period of social dislocation and economic stagnation, presented a tremendous fiscal burden.[17]

Impelled by the dual imperatives of ideological conviction and financial necessity, the Allies effectively demolished the German war-disability system. As a consequence hundreds of thousands of disabled veterans, their families, and the next-of-kin of soldiers killed in the war were reduced to poverty and made dependent on the already overburdened general welfare services. The material desperation of the war victims was matched by an equally great sense of injustice and degradation. Convinced of the rightness—and righteousness—of their cause, the occupying powers seemed either oblivious or indifferent to the effects of their actions. German officials who had been put in charge of implementing the policies could not remain indifferent to the plight of the war victims, however, especially since the latter's sense of moral outrage over their treatment was shared by the German public at large.[18] Moved by humanitarian sympathy, as well as concern over the potentially explosive social and political consequences of further inaction, German officials urged the military governments to change their policies and began to draft alternate ones that would alleviate the suffering of the war victims while remaining within the guidelines established by the occupying powers.

Gradually, military government officials responsible for the formulation of social policy, at least those in the U.S. and British zones, began to realize that their policies had produced genuine hardship for a class of citizens that was innocent and that in their zeal to root out militarism they had created conditions that were producing political consequences exactly the opposite of those

---

(Bonn, 1977), 192–93.

16. "War Pensions in Connection with Demilitarization," AC 019 (MD), 8 Jan. 1947, OMGUS 260, 56/10.

17. According to one estimate, between 25 and 30% of the population in the three western zones needed monetary assistance. Franz Blücher, "Financial Situation and Currency Reform in Germany," *The Annals* 260 (Nov. 1948): 64.

18. In a public opinion survey conducted in the American zone in April 1946 to sample German opinion regarding support for the claims of various categories of war victims, the war-disabled were placed at the head of the list of those deserving support (84% favoring aid), followed by those who had been bombed out (75%), expellees (70%), refugees (65%), dependents of war victims (61%), Jews (47%), victims of political persecution (47%), and DPs (39%). Information Control Intelligence Summary No. 45, 8 June 1946, NARS, Record Group 319, Records of Army "I" Staff, Intelligence (G-2) Library, Box 699. Another poll taken later in the year produced similar results, with 63% placing war casualties at the top of the list of those deserving aid. Ann J. and Richard L. Merritt, *Public Opinion in Occupied Germany: The OMGUS Surveys, 1945–1949*

intended. Whereas the old system of war-disability pensions had been scrapped out of fear of fostering an arrogant pro-military (and, thus, by definition, anti-democratic) group within German society, concern now began to grow that the new policies might create a large, bitter, and resentful social group that would remain alienated and become a significant obstacle to the growth of democracy. This change of viewpoint, which began to manifest itself in early 1946, was summed up in an OMGUS report of January 1947:

> The objective of abolishing war pensions is to discredit the military class in Germany. . . . At the same time to leave a large category of disabled, aged, and survivors without any means to care for their needs [other] than public relief, especially when large numbers were unwilling draftees, would run the danger of creating a revengeful, self-conscious, under-privileged class detrimental to successful democratic development in Germany. The problem is therefore to cut off all privileges heretofore ac-corded for military service without creating a resentful class dangerous to democracy and without promoting obvious injustice.[19]

With such considerations in mind, Anglo-American authorities acted to introduce systems of war-disability benefits in their zones that conformed to their principles of reform. During the course of 1946 the British constructed a system of war-disability payments that was administered under the old-age disability insurance program. In early 1947, after nearly a year of negotiations with German officials, the U.S. Military Government approved a war-disability system that was subordinated to the industrial accident disability insurance program.

Although logical and justifiable in theory, the incorporation of the war-disabled into the traditional social security programs raised some problems. The financial situation of these systems already had been made precarious as a result of the combined effects of the war, Germany's collapse, and the general eco-nomic chaos of the immediate postwar years. The inclusion of large numbers of pensioners who, due to their youth, had made no or only limited contributions to the social insurance programs' funds threatened to overburden them. Those entitled to pensions under the programs feared that their pensions might be cut to pay benefits to those who had contributed nothing to the programs;[20] at the

---

(Urbana, 1970), 121.

19. "War Pensions in Connection with Demilitarization," AC 019 (MD) 8 Jan. 1947, OMGUS 260, 56/10.

20. In order to prevent such fears from becoming reality, the military governments decreed that the additional costs incurred by the social insurance programs as a result of their taking over war-disability payments were to be covered by general tax revenues, not pension funds. Moreover, to keep the additional costs as low as possible eligibility requirements for war-disability pensions

same time, the war-disabled and survivors were angered because they received fewer benefits under the new systems than they had under the old.

While the new programs represented an improvement in the lot of the war victims, they were still far from generous and, at least in the eyes of the Germans, in serious need of further reform. Of the two plans, the British was the most seriously flawed. Like the Soviets, the British limited war-disability pensions to those who were at least two-thirds disabled. Moreover, the incorporation of the war-disability system into the old-age disability program, regulated according to the principles of the *Reichsversicherungsordnung* (RVO), was beset with structural problems that worked to the disadvantage of the war-disabled.[21] For example, the methods of determining the percentage of disability under the RVO were different—and, in effect, more stringent—than those used under the old RVG, so that many veterans who would have been certified as two-thirds disabled under the latter were given a lower rating under the new law and, therefore, did not qualify for a pension. In addition, the health care and, above all, the vocational rehabilitation programs of the old-age disability system were structured to meet the needs of a clientele (aged pensioners) whose needs were radically different from those of the majority of disabled veterans and their families.

Many of the problems of the British system were overcome in the U.S. zone by placing the war-disabled under the industrial accident disability program, whose structure, especially in the areas of health care and vocational rehabilitation, more closely resembled that of the old RVG and, therefore, better met the needs of disabled veterans. Moreover, disability payments in the U.S. zone started with a disability of 40 percent, as determined by criteria similar to those of the RVG. Nonetheless, pension rates were low, largely because pensions, especially those for younger veterans, were calculated on the basis of a fictive annual income that was considerably lower than the recipient was likely to have been receiving had he been employed as a civilian instead of serving in the armed forces.[22] Finally, in the U.S. zone, as in the others, pensions for survivors, widows, children, and dependent parents were substantially less than they had been under the old war-disability system.

---

were more stringent in many areas than those employed by the general program, e.g., for regular members of the industrial accident insurance program disability payments began with a disability of 25%, whereas disabled veterans only began to receive pensions with a disability of more than 40%. For a contemporary account of the difficulties confronting the various social insurance systems in postwar Germany, see Rudolf Wissel, "Social Insurance in Germany," *The Annals* 260 (Nov. 1948), esp. 128–30. A recent, comprehensive account of the rebuilding of German social insurance after the war is provided by Hans Günter Hockerts, *Sozialpolitische Entscheidungen im Nachkriegsdeutschland: Alliierte und deutsche Sozialversicherungspolitik 1945 bis 1957* (Stuttgart, 1980).

    21. The following is based on Rühland, 103–10.

    22. For details and examples, see ibid., 111–19.

There is a natural tendency to see the period of military occupation in Germany as one in which the military governments simply dictated policy to the defeated, powerless Germans. The actual situation was much more complex. As the desire for revenge gave way to concern for overcoming the chaotic conditions in defeated Germany and the occupying powers became increasingly dependent upon German personnel for the implementation of their policies, a dialogue emerged between the victors and the vanquished.[23] To be sure, it was never a dialogue of equals, but the vanquished were not voiceless. Thus, although the occupying powers generally imposed their will, German officials were able to wage determined (if not always successful) opposition against unpopular policies, occasionally undertook important initiatives of their own, and frequently played a not insignificant role in shaping legislation implemented during the occupation.[24]

The history of the treatment of the war-disabled from 1945 to 1950 reflects such a dialogue. German officials helped to convince representatives of the military governments that the latter's treatment of war victims was unduly harsh and was not only producing dangerous discontent among those directly affected, but could have more general, politically deleterious consequences as well.[25] At the same time the occupying powers were unyielding in their insistence that the previous system of separate—and, in their eyes, privileged—treatment of war victims must be scrapped, that military and civilian casualties be treated equally, and that the best way to achieve this was to incorporate the treatment of war victims into existing civilian disability programs. Attempts by German officials to circumvent these guidelines, either wittingly or unwittingly, were to no avail.[26] Similarly, early efforts to liberalize the new legislation af-

---

23. That the formulation and implementation of occupation policy was not simply a one-way street and involved considerable give and take in other areas as well is confirmed by the recent studies of James Tent and Edward Peterson: James F. Tent, *Mission on the Rhine: Reeducation and Denazification in American-Occupied Germany* (Chicago, 1982); Edward N. Peterson, *The American Occupation of Germany: Retreat to Victory* (Detroit, 1978).

24. The degree of "Mitbestimmung" in the treatment of war victims, as in other matters, varied from zone to zone. It was greatest in the American zone, where an independent German position was reinforced by the *Länderrat*, whose competence was greater than that of the analagous institutions in the other zones, e.g., the *Zonenbeirat* of the British zone. In the French, and, especially, the Soviet zones the opportunities for—and extent of—indigenous German input were considerably less than in the American and British zones.

25. *Länderrat Unterausschuss Sozialversicherung: Sitzung am 10.4.1946*, 3–4 and *Sitzung am 9. und 10.10.1946*, 15, OMGUS 260, 107/8; "Estimates of Expenditures Arising for Pensions for War Wounded, Widows, and Orphans of Deceased Soldiers," 16 May 1946, 4–5, OMGUS 260, 56/12; "War Pensions and Social Insurance," 9 Aug. 1946, 2, "Amendment of Military Government Regulations," 9 Aug. 1946, TAB C, OMGUS 260, 56/16.

26. The ongoing dialogue between German and U.S. Military Government officials can be traced in the protocols of the *Länderrat* subcommittee on Social Insurance, OMGUS 260, Boxes 102 and 107 and the OMGUS Manpower Division policy papers in ibid., Boxes 51, 52, and 56. The extent to which OMGUS officials were willing to go in order to root out all vestiges of past, osten-

fecting war victims were resisted on fiscal grounds and the fear, at least on the part of some, that liberalization would benefit "militarists."[27] Occupation officials were not totally deaf to criticism, however. The meagre pensions of survivors, which had been a constant source of German complaint, were gradually improved and in 1947, following the creation of Bizonia, the British reorganized their war-disability system along the lines employed in the U.S. zone, transferring the care of the war-disabled from the old-age disability system to the industrial accident disability program, which experience had shown was better suited to the needs of the war-disabled.[28] Also, in the wake of the currency reform of June 1948, which further exacerbated the precarious economic situation of German war victims, the occupying powers approved improved benefits. Yet, in spite of the persistent efforts of German officials on behalf of further reforms and the introduction of a unified system, the care of German war victims remained uneven and limited as the period of rule by military government drew to a close.[29] On the eve of the founding of the Federal Republic the suffering of the *Kriegsopfer* constituted a pressing social problem that threatened to become a political problem of major proportions.

The government of the new Federal Republic was well aware that its legitimacy, as well as future support for the Republic, was dependent on its ability to meet the social needs of its citizens. This was an enormous task, since virtually every German family had suffered as a result of the war. The multiplicity of constituencies demanding recompense was staggering, including, in addition to the war-disabled, the victims of Nazi persecution, those whose homes had been bombed out, returning POWs, and the millions of expellees and refugees from Germany's former eastern territories. The demands of all of

---

sibly militaristic, practices is shown by their response to the *Länderrat*'s final draft of the new law in which they demanded that the term *Versorgung* be replaced by another, since it "has been used in the past to mean the war pensions and special assistance to war veterans which are now prohibited by Military Government Regulations" and their opposition to a war victims' organization using the terms *Schwerkriegsbeschädigten* and *Kriegshinterbliebenen*. "OMGUS Action on Länderrat Proposals," 27 Nov. 1946 and "Use of Terminology Distinguishing between War Disabled or War Survivors on the one hand and Civilian Disabled or Survivors on the other," 28 May 1947, OMGUS 260, 56/16 and 56/11.

27. During a discussion of the *Länderrat* committee on social policy concerning a law for the employment of the disabled it was noted that the U.S. military government had expressed concern over the plans to set aside 12% of work force places for the seriously disabled, since it could lead to a "Hineinströmung von Militaristen" into public administrations and factories. *Länderrat: Sozialpolitischer Ausschuss, 17.9.46*, OMGUS 260, 102/7.

28. "Liberalization of Benefits to Widows of War-Killed," 4 Apr. 1947, OMGUS 260, 51/2; Rühland, 91, 94–95.

29. *Akten zur Vorgeschichte der Bundesrepublik Deutschland*, vol. 5, bearbeitet von Hans-Dieter Kreikamp (Munich, 1981): 33, 604, 652; Rühland, 92–93. For a systematic and comprehensive overview and comparison of the benefits in the three western zones, see *Rechtsvergleichende Darstellung über Leistungen an Kriegsopfer in den Ländern der Bundesrepublik Deutschland*, BAK, B136/388.

these groups were compelling, but it was universally recognized that the needs of the war-disabled should be placed at the top of the social agenda.[30] In his inaugural address the new chancellor, Konrad Adenauer, stated specifically that legislation providing for the welfare of the war-disabled and the families of those killed in the war was needed, and subsequent actions demonstrated the high priority the government assigned to the question. Immediately after convening, the Bundestag created a special committee to deal with the problems of the war-disabled, and in March 1950 a provisional law was passed that standardized and raised existing pensions for the war-disabled and survivors.[31] At the same time, officials began to draft a comprehensive new law. As in the Weimar Republic, the Labor Ministry was made responsible for the drafting and administration of the new law. Also, as in the case of the 1920 *Reichsversorgungsgesetz*, representatives of the war-disabled were given input into the legislative process through the creation of a special advisory committee. Both the officials responsible for the new law and those who would be affected by it agreed that it should be patterned after the former RVG and that the schemes introduced by the occupation governments, which had subordinated the treatment of war victims to other social insurance programs, should be scrapped.[32]

As a consequence, the *Bundesversorgungsgesetz* (BVG), enacted in October 1950, closely resembled the RVG. What differences there were reflected changed circumstances and, in particular, the difficult financial situation of the Federal Republic, rather than fundamental differences in principle.[33] Like its predecessor, the BVG's main goal was the physical and vocational rehabilitation of the victim; in cases where this was not, or was only partially, possible, social welfare assistance was provided to facilitate reintegration into society. The pension structure of the BVG was closely modeled on that of the former RVG. All disabled persons received a base allowance calculated on the basis of the percentage decrease of their potential civilian earning capacity. For financial reasons these base allowances had to be kept low; however, those unable to subsist on the base allowance qualified for a second allowance (*Aus-*

---

30. See n. 18 above. The war victims were the first social group to receive assistance in the Federal Republic. *Die Versorgung der Kriegsopfer in der Bundesrepublik Deutschland*, 6.

31. Trometer, 193–94; Rühland, 120–22.

32. See, for example, the *Vorläufiger Referentenentwurf*, BAK, B136/389–2 and the proposals presented by the organizations of the war-disabled to the *26. Bundestag Ausschuss*, Bundestag-Archiv, Bonn, I/87, Band B.

33. One difference was that the BVG, unlike the RVG, covered civilians who had suffered disabilities as a result of the war. In this case, the Allied powers' insistence that military and civilian victims of the war should be treated under the same system was honored; the grounds for this were not ideological or political, however, but practical, since the nature of warfare in the Second World War, in particular the use of strategic bombing, had effectively obliterated the earlier distinction between the home and fighting fronts.

gleichsrente), that was tailored to the economic status of the individual.[34] The two-part division of the pension was opposed by many of the war-disabled, who wanted higher base allowances, but the government resisted attempts to change the law on the ground that financial considerations made it impossible to abandon the two-tiered system. In later years, when the *Wirtschaftswunder* generated greater state revenues, the levels of the BVG's pensions were raised and, in retrospect, the *Bundesversorgungsgesetz* has proved to be a durable and progressive piece of legislation.[35]

If one traces the history of the treatment of the war-disabled in twentieth-century Germany, both continuity and discontinuity are evident. As with a sine wave, there is a certain alternating pattern of symmetry. Under the Kaiserreich and the Third Reich, regimes that emphasized military virtues, the treatment of the war-disabled tended to be regulated by military rather than civilian considerations and, on the whole, was not generous; under the two German Republics, which inherited the casualties produced by the war policies of the militaristic regimes, treatment of the war-disabled was governed by civilian social welfare principles and, on the whole, was generous.

In the specific context of post-1945 development and the questions of continuity versus discontinuity and reform versus restoration, the problem of the treatment of the war-disabled presents a picture that diverges from a simple dichotomous model. While not a fundamental issue for the occupying powers, the restructuring and reform of the German war-disability system was considered to be necessary and important. Accordingly, the system was reformed and—at least in the eyes of the victors—made more democratic. Although some changes were made at the end of the occupation period, the military occupation governments steadfastly clung to the principle of merging the war-disability system into existing social security programs and resisted German efforts to restore a system modeled on the *Reichsversorgungsgesetz* of 1920. Once the heavy hand of the occupation authorities was removed, however, the Germans quickly moved to discard the presumably more democratic systems and replaced them with one similar to that which had been prohibited as being too militaristic. In the area of the treatment of war victims, therefore, one cannot speak of *Weichenstellungen* or *Vorentscheidungen* during the occupation period that predetermined or irrevocably shaped the later policies of the Federal Republic.[36] The passage of the BVG established legislative and

---

34. On the structure and provisions of the BVG, see *Die Versorgung der Kriegsopfer in der Bundesrepublik Deutschland*, Rühland, 123ff. and Trometer, 193ff.

35. On the expansion of benefits, see Trometer, 196ff.

36. For examples of such decisions, which were unquestionably made in the economic and political spheres, see *Politische Weichenstellungen im Nachkriegsdeutschland 1945–1953*, ed. Heinrich August Winkler (Göttingen, 1979), and the introductory sections of the volumes in the series *Akten zur Vorgeschichte der Bundesrepublik Deutschland 1945–1949*.

institutional continuity with the past.[37] It was clearly restorative, but to argue that this act of restoration represented a rejection of democratic reform and a reversion to undemocratic forms would be absurd.

Indeed, I would argue that in this case restoration represented both an affirmation and a strengthening of the democratic process in the Federal Republic. The reforms in the war-disability system introduced by the Allies were rejected by the overwhelming majority of the German people. During the occupation the efforts of German officials to change the new system, although in vain, nonetheless helped to establish their legitimacy as representatives of the interest of the German people.[38] Similarly, the passage of the BVG helped to establish the Federal Republic's legitimacy in at least two ways. First, it demonstrated the Republic's willingness and ability to provide social services that were considered indispensable. Second, by overturning unpopular legislation imposed by the occupying powers it demonstrated its growing sovereignty. In the area of war-disability legislation, therefore, restoration did not signify a relapse into authoritarian ways but a step on the path to democracy.

---

37. The *Kriegsopferverbände*, whose role I explore in *The Thanks of the Fatherland: German Veterans After the Second World War* (Chapel Hill, N.C., 1993), provide another, related example of continuity with the past, although here there are significant discontinuities as well.

38. This was also true in the case of the fight for the restoration of retirement pensions for professional soldiers, which also were abrogated by occupation officials. The nonpartisan support for and eventual restoration of these pensions helped to establish the legitimacy of German officials and politicians in the eyes of many former *Berufssoldaten* and helped to reconcile them to the Republic.

Reconstructing the Family in Reconstruction Germany: Women and Social Policy in the Federal Republic, 1949–1955

Robert G. Moeller

The rebuilding of West Germany after the Second World War included the political reconstruction of the family. In debates over social policies, concerns over relations between women and men, the future of the family, and women's social and political status were at center stage; these debates provide insights into the ways in which West Germans sought to reconstitute the social order after the shock and trauma of National Socialism and defeat in war. It was most explicitly in this arena—borrowing from Joan Wallach Scott—that "politics construct[ed] gender and gender construct[ed] politics."[1] An analysis of social policy can illuminate the extent to which postwar West Germans viewed a careful evaluation of gender relations and a distinct break with the ideology of *Kinder, Küche, Kirche* as essential parts of a general commitment to change in the aftermath of fascism. Tim Mason, writing of Nazi policies toward women, argues that these were "in fact policies towards the family, policies towards the

Research for this article was funded by the German Marshall Fund of the United States, the German Academic Exchange Service (Deutscher Akademischer Austauschdienst), and a summer stipend from the National Endowment for the Humanities. An earlier version was presented to a conference on Gender and German History, held at Rutgers University in April 1986. My appreciation to the members of the New York German Women's History Study Group, who organized the conference, and to all other discussants, particularly Ute Frevert. Thanks go also to Jane Caplan, Geoff Field, Temma Kaplan, Susan Pedersen, Rosalind Petchesky, Ioannis Sinanoglou, Carroll Smith-Rosenberg, Marilyn Young, Linda Zerilli, and especially Lynn Mally, who commented on additional drafts and did much to help me clarify my argument. I have attempted to keep references to a minimum.

1. Joan Wallach Scott, "Women in History: The Modern Period," *Past and Present*, no. 101 (1983): 156.

whole population."[2] In this chapter, I will turn this formulation around to argue that in the late 1940s and 1950s, policies that ostensibly protected the family were in fact policies that defined the social and political status of women.

The study of state policies affecting women and the family in the past can provide a useful perspective on the problems of defining a feminist social policy in the present. The interpretation of the West German experience offered here is a reminder that the welfare state can be both "friend and foe" for women.[3] Measures intended to "protect" women are often responses to genuine social needs, but once in place, they may limit the ways certain problems are perceived and the areas where solutions are sought and obscure alternative perceptions and other potential solutions.[4] In the case of post–World War II West Germany, laws aimed at protecting the family ultimately protected and preserved much else—patriarchal authority; women's economic dependence on men; the ideological elevation of motherhood; pronatalist sentiments; and the normative conception of the "family" as an ahistorical social unit transcending class divisions. The historical study of family policy and the state's attempts to construct definitions of gender difference can thus alert us to the ways in which the identification of women's needs can all too easily lead to the ideological limitation of women's rights.

This chapter examines one part of a larger post-1945 West German policy discussion that extended to the reform of family law, the nature of paternal authority over wives and children, the economic value of women's unpaid labor, protective legislation for working women, comparable worth, "latchkey children" and "working mothers," and ways for women to manage the double burden. It focuses on the introduction of *Kindergeld,* literally "children-money," the West German system of family allowances that was initiated in 1954.

Although historians of West Germany have paid scant attention to the ways in which post–World War II reconstruction involved gender relations, the salience of gender as a political concern was not lost on contemporaries.[5] Writing in 1946, Agnes von Zahn-Harnack summarized the obvious.

---

2. Tim Mason, "Women in Germany, 1925–1940: Family, Welfare, and Work," pt. 1, *History Workshop Journal,* no. 1 (1976): 87.

3. Jane Jenson, "Both Friend and Foe: Women and State Welfare," in *Becoming Visible: Women in European History,* 2d ed., ed. Renate Bridenthal, Claudia Koonz, and Susan Stuard (Boston: Houghton Mifflin, 1987), 535–56.

4. This point eludes Sylvia Ann Hewlett in her invocation of West European examples to highlight her critique of the inadequacy of state support for families in the United States. See Hewlett's *A Lesser Life: The Myth of Women's Liberation in America* (New York: Warner Books, 1986).

5. For recent attempts to rectify this situation, see in particular, Lutz Niethammer, ed., *"Hinterher merkt man, dass es richtig war, dass es schiefgegangen ist": Nachkriegs-Erfahrungen*

Hardly any other question will be so important for the future shaping of internal German life, for German culture and morals, and for [Germany's] reintegration into world culture as the question of the relation of the sexes to each other. [This question] will be raised in the arena of politics as well as economics, and in the specifically sexual arena as well. Every war and postwar period brings serious devastation and crisis, but defeated peoples are doubly endangered. They must fear the internal dissolution of many bonds that the victor can maintain more easily. The defeated party runs the risk of self-hate that allows it to throw away even that which might be maintained.[6]

Zahn-Harnack's credentials as the last president of the League of German Women's Associations (*Bund deutscher Frauenvereine*), the national umbrella organization that brought together various strands of the bourgeois women's movement before its dissolution in 1933, doubtless qualified her as a keen observer of sexual politics. But it did not take such credentials to realize that a reassessment of gender relations would be a crucial part of rebuilding Germany after 1945.

On the most basic level, Germany was a society with far more adult women than men. Over 3 million men who had left to fight the war never returned. Even in 1950, when many men had come back from prisoner-of-war camps, there were 1,400 women for every 1,000 men in the age group twenty-five to thirty-nine. When fathers and sons did return, they were often physically or psychologically scarred, unwilling or unable to work, or disqualified from some jobs because of their National Socialist loyalties. Within families, the severe shortages of the postwar years meant that conflicts were often of the most fundamental sort—over who would have enough to eat.[7] The strains on marriages caused by long separations and difficult reunions registered in a divorce rate that continued to climb until the early fifties. Together with war widows and the growing number of unmarried mothers, this development resulted in a huge increase in the number of households headed by women.

---

im Ruhrgebiet (Bonn: J.H.W. Dietz Nachf., 1983); Doris Schubert, *Frauen in der deutschen Nachkriegszeit* (vol. 1: *Frauenarbeit, 1945–1949, Quellen und Materialien*) (Düsseldorf: Schwann, 1984); Annette Kuhn, ed., *Frauen in der deutschen Nachkriegszeit* (vol. 2: *Frauenpolitik, 1945–1949, Quellen und Materialien*) (Düsseldorf: Schwann, 1986); Anna-Elisabeth Freier and Annette Kuhn, eds., *"Das Schicksal Deutschlands liegt in der Hand seiner Frauen"—Frauen in der deutschen Nachkriegsgeschichte* (Düsseldorf: Schwann, 1984); Sibylle Meyer and Eva Schulze, *Wie wir das alles geschafft haben: Alleinstehende Frauen berichten über ihr Leben nach 1945* (Munich: C.H. Beck, 1985); Meyer and Schulze, *Von Liebe sprach damals keiner: Familienalltag in der Nachkriegszeit* (Munich: C.H. Beck, 1985).

6. Agnes von Zahn-Harnack, "Um die Ehe (1946)," in *Agnes von Zahn-Harnack: Schriften und Reden, 1914 bis 1950*, ed. Marga Anders and Ilse Reiche (Tübingen: Hopfer Verlag, 1964), 49.

7. Vivid descriptions are provided in Meyer and Schulze's *Von Liebe*.

Indeed, in 1950 after most prisoners of war had returned, nearly one-third of the slightly more than 15 million German households were headed by divorced women or widows. The problems of women who had fled westward ahead of the Soviet forces of occupation in the last years of the war, and in even greater numbers after 1945, were even more serious as these women attempted to establish themselves in new surroundings under extremely adverse circumstances.[8]

The distinction between economic and sociopsychological reconstruction became blurred in a language that described an "over-supply of women" (*Frauenüberschuss*) and a "scarcity of men" (*Männermangel*). There were no obvious ways to regulate this abnormal market situation. As the Western Allied forces of occupation quickly learned, their plans to mobilize the "silent reserve" of women into the wage labor force to compensate for the shortage of adult males met with resistance; women knew that a paycheck bought little on the black market, which flourished until currency reform in 1948. In the immediate postwar period, it was women's unpaid labor—as scroungers and black marketers; as negotiators with Allied and German officials over ration cards, medical care, and access to housing; as "fraternizers," able to win favors from soldiers of the occupying forces; as psychological providers for returning men—that was more important than their wage work.[9]

Women's status and the future of the family—issues placed firmly on the political agenda by the particular circumstances of the immediate postwar period—remained important domestic political concerns in the late 1940s and early 1950s. Conflicting visions of women's needs and social status—drawn from the social reality of the postwar period—were locked into place, not reconciled by the West German Basic Law (*Grundgesetz*), adopted in 1949 by the Parliamentary Council of the French, United States, and British zones of occupation. On the one hand, this constitutional basis for a new democratic state acknowledged that women's equality with men had been proven by their ability to replace absent men in many jobs during the war and by their contributions to postwar reconstruction; on the other hand, the drafters of the *Grundgesetz* underscored the need to "protect" women and to restore the family as the realm where women might best exercise their equality.

The *Grundgesetz* explicitly guaranteed that "men and women have the same rights," language that represented an important step beyond the Weimar constitution's promise that equality was "fundamentally" guaranteed. In the 1920s, this loophole had left room for restricting equality by ascribing specific

8. These are figures on war losses for *all* parts of occupied Germany. See Adelheid zu Castell, "Die demographischen Konsequenzen des Ersten und Zweiten Weltkriegs für das Deutsche Reich, die Deutsche Demokratische Republik und die Bundesrepublik Deutschland," in *Zweiter Weltkrieg und sozialer Wandel*, ed. Waclaw Dtugoborski (Göttingen: Vandenhoeck & Ruprecht, 1981), 119–21.

9. See Schubert, 32–70.

obligations and capacities to one sex or the other. Thus, the promise of equal rights in the *Grundgesetz* was a victory, won against Christian Democratic (CDU) and Christian Social (CSU) opposition by the Social Democratic (SPD) legal expert, Elisabeth Selbert, and by the intense pressure from socialist and middle-class women's organizations. It represented a clear reaction against women's political exclusion under the Nazis and a recognition of women's experience during the war and after 1945. As Frau D. Groener-Geyer, an outspoken petitioner to the Parliamentary Council put it:

> After Stalingrad, there is no aspect of life in which the actions of German men have protected German women from want, misery, and poverty. After our men fell victim to the obsession of a man and followed him from Berlin via Paris to Stalingrad and then back again, and did not have the energy to contain the delusions of power of that obsessed individual, thus gambling away the sovereignty of our state, leaving our cities in ruins, destroying our homes, and leaving millions homeless and with no basis for their existence, the equality of women has been accomplished de facto. Nothing human or inhuman is foreign to her any longer; she has been spared no terror.[10]

Although the members of the Parliamentary Council did not endorse this particular formulation or accept its logic, they did draw the same conclusions—it was essential to create the legal foundations for women's equality in the postwar world.[11]

The *Grundgesetz*'s promise that marriage and the family required special protection was another reflection of the desire to bring legislative prescription into line with perceptions of social reality. Unanswered was the question of how best to reconcile the elevation of the family as the fundamental social unit with the guarantee of individual equality and rights to personal fulfillment. Could women achieve equality *within* families as well as civil equality before the law and in the workplace? Any response required a thoroughgoing revision of the 1900 civil code (*Bürgerliches Gesetzbuch*), which had explicitly underwritten a patriarchal family form. Although it acknowledged that this task lay ahead, the Parliamentary Council postponed any final action until 1953. Ultimately, the major overhaul of the family law was not completed until 1957.[12]

---

10. D. Groener-Geyer to Parliamentary Council, 2 Jan. 1949, Bundesarchiv, Koblenz (hereafter cited as BA), Z5/111.

11. Anna Späth, "Vielfältige Forderungen nach Gleichberechtigung und 'nur' ein Ergebnis: Artikel 3 Abstaz 2 GG," in *"Das Schicksal Deutschlands,"* 112–69; and Ines Reich-Hilweg, *Männer und Frauen sind gleichberechtigt* (Frankfurt: Europäische Verlagsanstalt, 1979).

12. Christoph Sachsse and Florian Tennstedt, "Familienpolitik durch Gesetzgebung: Die juristische Regulierung der Familie," in *Staatliche Sozialpolitik und Familie*, ed. Franz-Xaver Kaufmann (Munich: R. Oldenbourg, 1982), 87–100.

Women's social status and the family's structure were also central to the reformulation of social policy in a new Germany. Perhaps even more clearly than in the abstract, legalistic debates around the revised civil code and court battles over the meaning of equality, social policy discussions served as an excellent vehicle for identifying salient conceptions of relations between women and men and the boundaries of women's proper place. What sort of family needed protection? What were women's responsibilities as wives and mothers, and how should they shape women's perceptions of the possibilities for individual fulfillment? These were central political questions in the 1950s; the agenda outlined by Zahn-Harnack in 1946 was still being hotly debated a decade later.

The *Grundgesetz* had placed the family under the state's particular protection, but it had not specified which family was to be protected nor what form that protection should take. These open questions were addressed explicitly in the debates around "money for children." There were precedents for supplementary payments to families in Nazi social legislation. The artillery in the National Socialist "battle for births" consisted of a wide range of family policies, including marriage loans and direct supplements to families with four children or more. Women's reproductive labors could pay off the marriage loans; each birth reduced the principal by one-fourth.[13] The Allies had suspended these measures at the end of the war as part of a Nazi past in which the prime objective was population expansion according to racialist criteria.[14]

Domestic political pressure for the reintroduction of state-financed payments to families intensified in 1948 when currency stabilization ended the postwar inflation. Rising price levels brought demands from trade unionists to consider the needs of families with inadequate earnings and incomes that left them with less money than families on welfare. Trade unionists rejected any notion that wage supplements be left to the discretion of individual employers, because this might lead to discriminatory hiring and disadvantages for "fathers of families." Instead, they sought a state-financed and state-administered system that would entitle all parents with incomes below a certain level to receive payments according to family size.[15]

A commission appointed by the Federal Council (*Bundesrat*) and including representatives from business, the trade unions, social welfare agencies,

---

13. See Mason, 95–103; and most recently, Claudia Koonz, *Mothers in the Fatherland: Women, the Family, and Nazi Politics* (New York: St. Martin's Press, 1987), 185–89.

14. Jutta Akrami-Göhren, "Die Familienpolitik im Rahmen der Sozialpolitik mit besonderer Berücksichtigung der Vorstellungen und der praktischen Tätigkeit der CDU" (Ph.D. diss., Bonn University, 1974), 260.

15. Memo of 29 June 1946 from Ministerialrat Goldschmidt, Labor Ministry, BA, B153/733.

and the academic community began discussing specific measures in 1949. A draft proposal prepared by Gerhard van Heukelum, head of the Office of Labor and Welfare in Bremen, called for immediate action and the introduction of state-administered supplements. Heukelum linked family assistance to economic recovery and argued: "it is high time that we give careful consideration to the importance of people as factors of production." To ignore the significance of the "individual as the agent of work" was to risk a "danger of dismantling" a site of production—the family—that would be less easily replaced than the factories dismantled by the Allies. The problems of large families could not be addressed adequately through existing welfare measures. Far better precedents could be found in National Socialist policies; devoid of their racialist content, they offered a model that had much in common with family allowance schemes introduced in many other advanced industrial countries.[16]

However, Heukelum's hope that his recommendations would initiate immediate action by the newly elected West German parliament (*Bundestag*) faltered as it became obvious that a widely held commitment to assisting the family did not unambiguously translate into practical measures. In parliamentary discussions, there was consensus on a number of issues. Across the political spectrum, all agreed that the war had placed particularly great strains on the family and that "more than any other societal institution, the family had fallen into the whirlpool created by the collapse." This made the "family the central problem of the postwar era."[17] Unanimity broke down quickly, however, over very basic questions—just what constituted a family, and what system could best meet its needs?

For the conservative CDU/CSU coalition, the "family" did not include the large numbers of single women—whether never married, widowed, or divorced—who headed households and carried responsibility for children or dependent adults. The coalition emphasized the threats to the family posed by a mother's decision to enter wage work, implying that in a family, there was also a wage-earning father. Support for families was essential in order to achieve a "higher ethical estimation in particular of the mother and child."[18] However, this goal would not be achieved by a system of across-the-board

16. "Niederschrift über die vom Unterausschuss Kinderbeihilfen des Ausschusses für Arbeit und Sozialpolitik des Bundesrates einberufene Konferenz am 21.12.49," Nordrhein-Westfälisches Hauptstaatsarchiv, NW42/547.

17. The quotations are from Bernhard Winkelheide, *Verhandlungen des deutschen Bundestags* (Bonn: Universitäts-Buchdruckerei Gebr. Scheur, 1950) (hereafter cited as *VdBT*), [1.] Deutscher Bundestag, 162. Sitzung, 13 Sept. 1951, 6569; and Winkelheide, "Warum Familienausgleichskassen?" *Soziale Arbeit* 1 (December 1951): 100. For a summary of the SPD position, see Louise Schroeder, "Kinderbeihilfe," *Soziale Arbeit* 1 (December 1951): 97–100.

18. Winkelheide, *VdBT*, [1.] Deutscher Bundestag, 1949, 60. Sitzung, 28 Apr. 1950, 2202.

payments to all children, because a male "wage [determined by] achievement" in the marketplace, the *Leistungslohn*, should support at least a non-wage-earning wife and two children. In fact, it was a fundamental right of the male "provider" to found a family, and basic wage levels should guarantee that right. Men, not women, "founded families," and it was the male *Leistungslohn* that should be the basis for this construction. Even those who considered the particular needs of single mothers identified these "fatherless," "half," or "incomplete" families as deviations from the norm of a male breadwinner and a wife who stayed at home with at least two children. This position was forcefully seconded by officials within the Finance Ministry, who added that the fledgling republic's fiscal condition would permit no scheme providing payments for all children, particularly at a time when the government was confronting the potentially massive costs of rearmament.[19]

According to CDU/CSU proposals, determination of the *Leistungslohn* was the business of the "social partners"—capital and labor. For larger families this wage might not suffice, and supplementary payments to the male wage would insure that mothers of large families—those with more than two children—would not be forced out to work. The state should not be allowed to regulate this system of family allowances; moves in this direction represented a return to the institutional forms of National Socialism and a dangerous expansion of the state's authority over private relations. Rather, self-regulation by the private sector was the only acceptable administrative solution. Proposed was a system of employer contributions that would be redistributed to families with more than two children through the existing framework of occupational insurance providers. These principles embodied the CDU/CSU commitment to the "social market economy" (*soziale Marktwirtschaft*) proclaimed by Ludwig Erhard, economics minister in Konrad Adenauer's first postwar government. Although it must not lose its social conscience, the German economy must be reconstructed according to the competitive laws of the market with as little state intervention as possible; "what we need," Erhard emphasized, "is not *more* government, but rather *less*."[20]

Doubtful that capitalism and less government would guarantee just solutions, critics from within the ranks of the opposition SPD argued that although wages *should* support a family, they might well not. In addition, excluding those with only one or two children from benefits would particularly disadvantage widows and divorced women whose needs were the same as those of the low-income family father. A policy of equal payments to all children and the elimination of the highly regressive system of tax deductions for dependents—

19. See the discussions in *VdBT*, [1.] Deutscher Bundestag, 1949, 60. Sitzung, 28 Apr. 1950, 2197–2206; also ibid., 162. Sitzung, 13 Sept. 1951, 6569–78.

20. Ludwig Erhard, quoted in *Dritter Parteitag der Christlich-Demokratischen Union Deutschlands, Berlin, 17.–19. Oktober 1952* (Cologne: Kölnische Verlagsdruckerei, n.d.), 202.

a Nazi legacy—would permit all mothers to stay at home and would not limit the "higher ethical estimation . . . of the mother and child" to certain groups. Fears that the costs of this alternative would be prohibitive were met with claims that increased wages would translate immediately into increased consumption. The SPD proposed a system of state administration, financed through a tax on the gross income of all wage earners, and argued for the elimination of all other deductions for minor dependents.[21] This alternative won approval as well from some middle-class women's organizations, which also emphasized that payments should be made directly to mothers, not as a supplement to the male wage.[22]

By mid-1953, these conflicting views were still unresolved. A leading expert from within the Labor Ministry temporized that "a law that is so complicated and that has implications for so many other established legal measures cannot be rushed; rather it requires the most careful planning."[23] In the interim, the continued debate around family allowances created an opportunity for academic sociologists and social theorists to leave the ivory tower and to set the political discussion of family allowances in an explicitly theoretical framework. Their writings were particularly important because their views were incorporated into the political discussion of policy alternatives and because their theoretical formulations made explicit key elements underlying the parliamentary debates over family policy.

Helmut Schelsky, who in 1948 had become the director of the newly founded Academy for Communal Economics in Hamburg, played an important role in reshaping German sociology after 1945. He was a leading exponent of an empirical sociological method that claimed to be more concerned with problem solving than with grandiose theories.[24] The author of a major study of families who had fled to West Germany from the east after the war, Schelsky argued forcefully that the family's stability in the face of a general societal collapse justified its elevation to the central focus of social policy. The postwar years had created an extraordinary situation in which the "family association" had borne many of the social pressures normally assumed by the state welfare system. In the 1950s, the question for policymakers was whether they could build on these

---

21. See the comments of SPD representatives in "Kurzprotokoll der 148. Sitzung des Ausschusses für Sozialpolitik (of the Bundestag) am Freitag, den 12. September 1952," 16–20 (copy in Parlamentsarchiv [hereafter cited as PA], Bonn).

22. Edith Hinze, "Was denken die Frauen über Familienausgleichskassen?" *Bundesarbeitsblatt* (1952): 263–65.

23. Wilhelm Herschel of the Labor Ministry, as reported in a memo from Jüngst, 29 June 1953, BA, B153/738.

24. M. Rainer Lepsius, "Die Entwicklung der Soziologie nach dem zweiten Weltkrieg," in *Deutsche Soziologie seit 1945: Entwicklungsrichtungen und Praxisbezug,* ed. Günther Lüschen (Cologne: Westdeutscher Verlag, 1979), 38.

developments to make the family the focus of state welfare policy.

According to Schelsky, social policy had been tied to a "strata or class-bound" perspective for too long. Outdated measures had aimed at increasing the chances for social mobility by encouraging the collective advancement of the working class. These policies had achieved the upward mobility of some members of the working class. In postwar West Germany, however, the downward mobility of many other Germans, caused by the crisis of the war and postwar years, had significantly reduced the distance between social classes. All West Germans were now part of a "levelled-out petit-bourgeois *mittelständish* society" (*nivellierte kleinbürgerlichmittelständische Gesellschaft*).[25] Schelsky's use of the category, *Mittelstand*, the nineteenth-century term for describing shopkeepers, independent craftsmen, and small-scale entrepreneurs, and the "new *Mittelstand*" of white-collar workers, invoked an image of a society in which class differences were less extreme. Indeed, according to Schelsky's analysis, in postwar West Germany class lines were blurred or totally dissolved. Under these altered circumstances, the family, not social class, became the agent of upward social mobility and the appropriate object of state social policy. It was not the family that should be forced to adjust to the demands of advanced industrial society; rather, society should capitalize on its most important asset and make every effort to support and maintain the family.

In Schelsky's analysis, it was the "motherly care for the life of future generations" that had contributed significantly to holding families together after the war. Precisely because they had proved their indispensability in the postwar years, women's authority within families was greatly enhanced. Their expanded responsibilities should not, however, be confused with the individualist equality championed by the bourgeois women's movement in the Kaiserreich and Weimar. The emancipation of women in the war and the postwar years was an "emancipation out of necessity." Equality of rights in industrial societies was a dubious gain when it resulted in burdens like compulsory work in wars. The involvement of women in work outside the home threatened to pull them into the contradictions between "primary and abstract social relationships" that already dominated men's lives.[26] "How many working women," Schelsky asked rhetorically in 1952, "would resign their jobs,

---

25. Helmut Schelsky, "Die Wandlungen der deutschen Familie in der Gegenwart und ihr Einfluss auf die Grundanschauungen der Sozialpolitik," *Sozialer Fortschritt* 1 (December 1952): 284, 287.

26. Helmut Schelsky, "Die gegenwärtige Problemlage der Familiensoziologie," in *Soziologische Forschung in unserer Zeit*, ed. Karl Gustav Specht (Cologne: Westdeutscher Verlag, 1951), 293–94. In his *Wandlungen der deutschen Familie in der Gegenwart*, 4th ed. (Stuttgart: Ferdinand Enke Verlag, 1960), probably the most influential sociological analysis of the family in this period, Schelsky fully develops his position. Schelsky was part of a "scientific advisory board," which counseled the Ministry of Family Affairs on social policies affecting the family.

if they could pursue their wishes; for them work does not mean acquisition of property and personal economic independence, but rather an uncertain income, competition, monotonous labor in order to insure the most basic provision for themselves and for those others for whom they must care." Self-proclaimed emancipatory movements—whether the bourgeois women's movement or the Frankfurt School—had always attacked patriarchal authority; but their efforts promoted not liberation but greater subordination to the "rule of bureaucratic power and abstract authority."[27] For Schelsky, this negative example could be found across West Germany's eastern border, where the protection of mothers served not the interests of families but those of the state.

The family was thus society's bedrock, but if left without adequate support, it could not properly perform its essential functions. This was also the theme of those who defended family allowances with the scientific elaboration of fears about the declining birthrate—the dwindling supply of human factors of production. Friedrich Burgdörfer, a demographer whose pronatalist past dated from the 1920s and whose credentials included loyal service to the National Socialists, found that he could still find work as an expert on questions of family allowances. In a lengthy analysis commissioned by the Bavarian Free Democratic party, Burgdörfer warned that at present, *"We are on the way to a two-child system"* that threatened not only *"population growth but also . . . the maintenance of the very bases of the population."* He rejected as outdated the argument popular in Free Democratic circles that the state should in no way interfere in the private sphere of marriage. It was the state's responsibility to insure the preconditions for growth and prosperity, which included policies to "surmount the socio-biological climate that was inimical to families and the new generation." Burgdörfer pointed approvingly to the renewed increase in the birthrate in the years 1930 through 1940 "that delivered irrefutable evidence that our people (*Volk*) was biologically healthy and . . . was prepared to respond to population policies." At issue was the preservation of *"that living human capital, that works for our economy and that is certainly no less important for our national income than money capital."* Supplementary payments should not be restricted to low-income groups, because this would contribute to a *"negative selection"* that was already under way.[28]

Reformulating the description of a "classless" society and fears of population decline in the context of a general postwar social policy, Gerhard Mackenroth addressed the Association for Social Reform (*Verein für Sozial-*

27. Schelsky, "Die Gleichberechtigung der Frau und die Gesellschaftsordnung," *Sozialer Fortschritt* 1 (June 1952): 131.

28. A typescript of Friedrich Burgdörfer's remarks is in Archiv der liberalen Demokratie, Gummersbach (Niedersessmar), DA/1161 (= Nachlass Dehler); on Burgdörfer's career under the Nazis, see Mason, 85–86.

politik) in 1952. His proposals represented a major addition to the theoretical debate around the reformulation of social policy in the 1950s. Mackenroth, who had specialized in questions of social policy and demographic theory as a professor for national economy in Kiel from 1934 to 1941, took over the chair for sociology, social science, and statistics in Kiel in 1948.[29] With Schelsky, Mackenroth argued that the collapse of German social policy after 1945 had cleared the ground for the construction of something new. The "classical conception" of a working class no longer had meaning, and the differences among working people were as important as those characteristics unifying them. The family should replace class as the object of social policy. In the wake of industrialization, the family's functions had changed. Children no longer contributed to family income, nor were they a guarantee of old-age security; social security was now a function of the state. This did not make children any less important. They were the future labor force of a prosperous economy, and they would pay into social insurance funds from which pensioners lived. However, although children's economic contributions were now redistributed through collective institutions, the costs of raising children were still borne by individual families. This inequitable situation resulted in social divisions not along the class lines separating "poor and rich" but between those "poor" and "rich in children" (*kinderarm* and *kinderreich*). According to Mackenroth, a policy of "distributing the burdens of families" (*Familienlastenausgleich*) was essential, and redistribution should take place, not among income groups, but within income groups among families.[30]

In yet another important variant of this general discussion, Ferdinand Oeter located the debate around family allowances within the context of a theory of economic growth. Oeter had served as an expert witness for the parliamentary subcommittee that debated legislative proposals for *Kindergeld*, and he had been particularly influential in one draft of thoroughgoing tax reform according to principles of family size. Only the family, he argued, could deliver the "human material" that would fuel economic growth and guarantee the future social security of an aging German population. However, Oeter pointed out, in a modern industrial economy, "the family . . . was no longer in a position to harvest the fruits of its labor itself." Declining birthrates were a clear reaction against the expenses of raising the next season's crop. A married couple's cost of living increased by 12 to 15 percent with each child, Oeter reckoned. Increased accumulation among those who did not bear these additional expenses would skew economic demand in favor of luxury goods and away from basic necessities. The long-term consequences in a market economy were a dwindling labor supply, a crippled social security system, and an economy capable of producing

---

29. Lepsius, 33.

30. Gerhard Mackenroth, "Die Reform der Sozialpolitik durch einen deutschen Sozialplan," in *Schriften des Vereins für Sozialpolitik*, n.s., 4 (1952): 39–75.

televisions and motorcycles but not a decent loaf of bread. Capital should be understood as accumulated labor. "Why," asked Oeter rhetorically, "should this capital be treated better than the human capital represented in the labor of families?" A system of income redistribution to help families would mean that economically "the capitalized value of human labor power would also have the same rank as capital more narrowly understood."[31] The family was the "Cinderella" of a competitive market economy. By strengthening it, the state would permit it to do its job. This was far wiser than strengthening the collective—"the way . . . that leads directly to the east."[32]

Although this brief survey in no way exhausts the sociological treatment of family policy in the early 1950s, it does identify certain of its central themes. The discussion acknowledged that the work of reproduction was clearly on a par with the work of production, once human capital accumulation was equated with other forms of created value. Indeed, the emphasis on the family as the vehicle for upward social mobility suggested that women's work in the home had intensified since the war. According to sociological investigations of women's unpaid labor, what time women gained from advances in the rationalization of housework and the transfer of some services from the home to the economy was now spent checking over children's school assignments and caring for their psychological as well as their physical needs. Mothers were also accountable for children's proper moral education and for preparing children to enter society as responsible individuals. The home was no "haven in a heartless world"; it was the site of important work, essential to economic prosperity and the foundation for any future system of social security.

Social theorists agreed that women who toiled for wages outside the home were working a double shift. In the long-term, the results would be either human factory rejects or, even worse, reproduction slowdowns—a declining birthrate. Family allowances could not compensate women fully for their work, nor should they; love was work, but at the same time, women's care for their families was motivated by instincts that could not be measured in money terms alone. As commentators from left to right agreed, the home "should not be a hotel in miniature," and the "warmth of the nest," not the furnace's hot blast, was the atmosphere that the mother should achieve in her domestic workshop.[33] Still, at least supplementary benefits could create the possibility for mothers to reject wage work, and the literature unanimously assumed that given the option, mothers would choose to stay at home. Family policy should

---

31. Ferdinand Oeter, cited in "Protokoll über die 149. Sitzung des Ausschusses für Sozialpolitik (of the Bundestag) am Freitag, den 19. September 1952," 8–10 (copy in PA). Oeter was also brought into a "scientific advisory board" that counseled the Ministry of Family Affairs.

32. Ferdinand Oeter, "Ausgleich der Familienlasten—Eine notwendige Klärung," *Bundesarbeitsblatt* (1952): 308.

33. Marta Gieselmann, "Gedanken über die Hausarbeit," *Gleichheit* 15, no. 8 (1952): 244–45. See the theoretical discussion by Gisela Bock and Barbara Duden, "Arbeit aus Liebe—

help to achieve this goal in contrast to the measures introduced in East Germany, the "Soviet Zone of Occupation." There the state sought to drive women into wage labor at the expense of their health, their reproductive capacities, and family life. "Money for children" represented society's acknowledgment of the importance of women's work in the home and the need to elevate the value of this nonwage labor. However, this acknowledgment was to take the form of a supplement to a male wage.

By late 1953 when a newly elected Bundestag resumed discussions of family allowance proposals, the initial emphasis on the postwar recovery of disadvantaged groups had given way to a focus on the reproductive work of the family in an expanding economy. As Chancellor Adenauer stated in his opening remarks to the new parliament, technological advance might slow down the corrosive effects of a declining birthrate, but it could not completely reverse a process that threatened to "destroy our entire population in the course of a few generations." A constant birthrate, not machines, was the best guarantee of prosperity and future social security. "Only one thing can help: strengthening the family and thereby strengthening the will for children (*Willen zum Kind*)."[34]

A further indication that questions of family policy would remain of interest to the ruling coalition was the creation of a new post in Adenauer's second cabinet. The Ministry for Family Questions made clear the importance of this aspect of social policy for the Bonn government, and the man named to head it, Franz-Josef Wuermeling, quickly distinguished himself as the outspoken proponent of a conservative Catholic worldview. Wuermeling lauded the family's "natural," sacramental quality and invoked the Scriptures to justify women's permanent relegation to the domestic sphere and subordination to men. His staff was small and his ministry had little power to initiate legislation; it was intended as an advocate for the family's concerns with other cabinet offices that held responsibility for shaping and guiding legislation through the parliamentary process. But the ministry's existence guaranteed that Wuermeling would be heard on every important social policy issue affecting women and the family, and it lent his reactionary views a cabinet-level legitimacy. With the strong backing of extremely conservative religiously affiliated family organizations and with close ties to leading church officials, he proudly declared himself to be the "Protective Patron of the Family."[35]

The CDU/CSU wasted no time in initiating renewed discussions of "money for children"; *Kindergeld* would help to strengthen the *Willen zum*

Liebe als Arbeit: Zur Entstehung der Hausarbeit im Kapitalismus," in *Frauen und Wissenschaft: Beiträge zur Berliner Sommeruniversität für Frauen, July 1976* (Berlin: Courage, 1977), 118–99.

34. *VdBT*, 2. Deutscher Bundestag, 3. Sitzung, 20 Oct. 1953, 18.

35. "Des Papstes Garde," *Der Spiegel* 8, no. 38 (1954): 8–15; and Akrami-Göhren, 89–91.

Kind. The debate resumed under decidedly altered political circumstances, and Adenauer had returned to power with an overwhelming mandate that registered a noticeable shift in the parliamentary balance of power. The CDU/CSU coalition had enjoyed only an eight-vote edge over the SPD after the 1949 election. In the second Bundestag, its margin soared to ninety-two; with 243 representatives, it controlled as many votes as all other political parties combined. Assured the forty-eight votes of the Free Democratic party on most questions of family policy, the Adenauer government was in a strong position.

The SPD continued to propose state-administered payments to *all* children and contended that the "normal family" of two adults and two children living from a male wage did not fully capture the social reality of postwar Germany in which female-headed households were anything but abnormal. But it was this "normal family" that remained at the core of proposals drafted by the Labor Ministry and backed by the CDU/CSU coalition. The plight of never-married, widowed, or divorced mothers, and other low-income families was dismissed as a legacy of the war that would pass. "Incomplete" or "half families"—those without fathers—were extraordinary developments of extraordinary times, which would cease to be a problem with continued economic growth and the disappearance of the "surplus of women."[36] The ruling coalition also continued to reject state-administered schemes as attempts to make the family a "pensioner of the collectivity," the recipient of "alms from the state." Wuermeling emphasized that family allowances represented not a "welfare measure for needy families, but a matter of state policy to achieve social justice for all large families." Not state subsidies but the male wage should be the family's foundation; supplements to the large family should be supplements to that wage paid through funds collected by the private sector and redistributed by individual employers.[37] Proposals that payments go directly to mothers were not even discussed.

From its powerful position in parliament, the CDU/CSU coalition could insure that controversy would not lead to stalemate as it had two years earlier. Fearing that further delays would create the space for the more forceful presentation of SPD alternatives, the coalition railroaded through a law in 1954 that provided monthly payments of 25 marks to wage earners with three or more children. The amount did not cover the estimated cost of feeding and clothing an infant and represented less than one-half of what was needed to support a school-aged child.[38] Although, in theory, single women in wage work were eligible for these payments, few had three or more children, and the nor-

---

36. *VdBT*, 2. Deutscher Bundestag, 21. Sitzung, 4 Apr. 1954, 735–37.

37. See Wuermeling's comments, *VdBT*, 2. Deutscher Bundestag, 44. Sitzung, 23. Sept. 1954, 2118–19.

38. CDU/CSU-Fraktion des Deutschen Bundestages, "Kurzprotokoll über die Sit-

mative conception underlying the law was of a male breadwinner and a non-wage-earning wife. In cases where both parents worked, payments went to the husband. Excluded were all those not in wage work—the unemployed, those on welfare and pensions—and all those with only one or two children.[39]

Family allowances helped few people. A year after the passage of the initial legislation, benefits were extended to the unemployed and to recipients of welfare assistance, but the restriction of payments to families with at least three children guaranteed the exclusion of most Germans. A 1957 survey recorded that 57.7 percent of all married couples with children had only one or two. Only 20.3 percent had more than three. Sixty-nine percent of divorced and widowed mothers had too few children to qualify for *Kindergeld*, and only 13 percent could receive more than 25 marks monthly. It was these female heads of "incomplete families" who remained overrepresented among those living below the poverty level. Moreover, there were many indications that family size increased with income; thus, those likely to be entitled to *Kindergeld* were in higher income groups and received substantial benefits from tax deductions for dependents as well. There was certainly no evidence that the system of family allowances had triggered a baby boom. On the contrary, statistics for the late 1950s suggested that the pattern within the working class was to limit family size according to income, and this practice was in no way altered by family allowances. There were indications that many women ceased full-time work outside the home once children arrived, but this reflected the adequacy of income from other sources and/or the lack of alternatives more than options created by the nominal payments provided by the 1954 legislation.[40]

Once the basic outlines of the system were in place, there were few efforts to change its dimensions. Social Democrats and trade unionists concentrated on increasing benefits within the existing framework; they fully accepted and endorsed the argument that mothers of preschool and school-aged children should not have to work outside the home. Outspoken in their claims that "socialism

---

zung des Unterausschusses Familienausgleichkassen [*sic*] vom 4.3.1954," Archiv für christlich-demokratische Politik, Sankt Augustin bei Bonn (hereafter cited as ACDP), VIII-005–059/2; and Arnd Jessen, "Der Aufwand für Kinder in der Bundesrepublik im Jahre 1954," in *Familie und Sozialreform* (= Jahresversammlung der Gesellschaft für Sozialen Fortschritt e.V.) (Berlin: Duncker & Humblot, 1955), 107–11.

39. Payments were increased to 30 marks monthly in 1957 and to 40 marks monthly in 1959. In 1961, payments were introduced for the second child in low-income families. By 1963, the CDU/CSU coalition finally dropped its objections to a system financed out of tax revenues and administered by a state agency, arguing that *Kindergeld* was the responsibility of the entire society, not just employers and employees. See Akrami-Göhren, 151–53, 277–90.

40. "Kinder und Jugendliche in Familien," *Wirtschaft und Statistik*, n.s., 12 (1960): 215; Statistisches Bundesamt, *Bevölkerung und Kultur, Reihe 2: Natürliche Bevölkerungsbewegung, Sonderbeitrag: Kinderzahl der Ehen, Oktober 1962* (Stuttgart: W. Kohlhammer, 1966), 19–21.

protects the family," they rejected the attacks of CDU/CSU critics, who invoked the "Marxist specter" to charge that the SPD sought to destroy, not defend, the nuclear family. With intensifying volume, Social Democrats emphasized that "state and society must protect, strengthen, and promote the family." For women, this meant guaranteeing them the right "to be housewife and mother, [which] is not only a woman's natural obligation but of great social significance."[41] Nor were they any less critical than the ruling coalition of family policy in the "Soviet Zone of Occupation," which, charged *Gleichheit*, the SPD women's monthly, was intended only to "increase the human reserve, which can be economically exploited."[42] Social democratic demands for increased benefits confronted the continued resistance of the Finance and Economics ministries, which opposed any impediments to the competitive wage structure, but left socialists agreeing with Wuermeling and ultraconservative family organizations.[43] Champions of the family on the Right and Left insisted that increased benefits would achieve a vital objective—allowing all mothers to stay at home. For children, the mother was irreplaceable and indispensable. The fight for a male *Leistungslohn* that was adequate to support a family and the battle for extending the coverage of family allowances were two related means to achieve the same objective. Both strategies left no doubt about women's proper place.

The legislation regulating *Kindergeld* centered on a nuclear family headed by a male wage earner. From a historical perspective, we know that "normal families" seldom existed in the Kaiserreich or Weimar; few families could be economically supported by a single wage, and households headed by single women were no unique product of the post-1945 years. At least for the working class, the "normal family" of family policy in the 1950s could not be reestablished, because it had never existed.[44] However, this was of little concern to

---

41. The quotations are from Herta Gotthelf in *Protokoll der Verhandlungen des Parteitages der Sozialdemokratischen Partei Deutschlands vom 20. bis 24. Juli 1954 in Berlin* (Berlin-Grunewald: Graphische Gesellschaft Grunewald, n.d.), 235; the Fundamental Program (*Grundsatzprogramm*), proclaimed in 1959, *Protokoll der Verhandlungen des ausserordentlichen Parteitages der Sozialdemokratischen Partei Deutschlands vom 13.–15. November 1959 in Bad Godesberg* (Hannover: Neuer Vorwärts-Verlag, Nau & Co., n.d.), 23, 257–58; and "SPD-Frauenprogramm," *Gleichheit* 20, no. 8 (1957): 293.

42. "Objekt Frau," *Gleichheit* 14, no. 4 (1951): 110.

43. See "Der Familienlastenausgleich: Erwägungen zur Gesetzgeberischen Verwirklichung—Eine Denkschrift des Bundesministers für Familienfrage," November 1955, PA, II/201 A; "Kurzprotokoll der 66. Sitzung des Ausschusses für Sozialpolitik [of the Bundestag] am Freitag, den 18. November 1955" (copy in PA); and *VdBT*, 2. Deutscher Bundestag, 120. Sitzung, 15 Dec. 1955, 6378–6403.

44. See the survey in Heidi Rosenbaum, *Formen der Familie: Untersuchungen zum*

policymakers who invoked a past that, according to their accounts, had withstood the invasion of National Socialism and the postwar crisis to prove itself as the basis for a new social order. The advocates of family allowances consistently argued that women's most important work was raising children. Women's work outside the home might be necessary at certain stages of their lives, but their contributions to the family were far more essential to the future of economic growth and social security. The mother of two children was best protected by a male wage. The "normal family" did not need state support. Families that deviated from this norm by overfulfilling their responsibilities to accumulate human capital deserved social recognition. They had earned extra compensation because of their special contribution to the welfare of society.

Perhaps the emphasis of social policy on women's dependent status within nuclear families deserves no lengthy explanation. After 1945, it was not only West Germans who were involved in what Juliet Mitchell has called the "political reconstruction of the family."[45] To be sure, German social policy in the 1950s addressed this agenda, which was prevalent throughout Europe after the Second World War. However, a closer look at the debates over "money for children" indicates that West Germans pursued restoration along a peculiarly German path. Of course, *how* peculiar the Germans were is a question that ultimately will require systematic comparative analysis. The thoughts that follow are offered as a basis for such a comparative discussion. They also serve as a vehicle to bring us from the details of family policy debates back to the larger dimensions of post-1945 West German history.

In the Federal Republic's first decade, it is difficult to discover anyone criticizing the idea of the "normal family." Conservatives encouraged it to produce more than two children; socialists argued that only increases in male wages could support it properly. But no one examined it as an arena of conflict and power relations between genders and generations, and no one questioned its fundamental stability. To be sure, in the immediate postwar years there were proposals for "Mother Families" and alternatives to marriage for women confronted by the "scarcity of men."[46] But by the early 1950s, the particular problems of single women—with or without children—did not count as the problems of families.

Alternative conceptual bases for social policy were not entirely lacking in other western European countries. For example, in the Swedish discussion of family allowances that intensified in the 1930s, the needs of children without

Zusammenhang von Familienverhältnissen, Sozialstruktur und sozialem Wandel in der deutschen Gesellschaft des 19. Jahrhunderts (Frankfurt: Suhrkamp, 1982).

45. Juliet Mitchell, *Psychoanalysis and Feminism* (New York: Vintage, 1974), 231.

46. Angela Seeler, "Ehe, Familie und andere Lebensformen in den Nachkriegs jahren im Spiegel der Frauenzeitschriften," in *"Das Schicksal Deutschlands,"* 90–111.

fathers and of single mothers had been at the center of policy formulation from the beginning, not pushed to the margins or treated as anomalous. Not the "family," but the "citizen," was the focus of social policy. From this starting point, it was possible to develop programs of income maintenance based on the assumption that all adults would work outside the home and that single women with children needed particular assistance so that their children's standard of living would not fall below that of families with two incomes.[47]

Like the Swedish discussion, the move toward a comprehensive family policy in Germany had also been advanced in the 1930s by fears of population decline, although, obviously, Nazi policies were based on very different conceptions of "family" and "citizenship." Although the National Socialist desire for an expanding birthrate had justified a tolerance for unmarried motherhood, this was still an exception to the rule of legal marriage. Zahn-Harnack observed that solutions to certain problems in the postwar world were more difficult for defeated nations. This was doubtless true, but in the case of defining the needs of single women responsible for the care of children and adult dependents, defeat, the massive loss of adult male life, and the consequent "surplus of women" made it easier to label these as "incomplete" or "half families" that had been created by the war and would disappear as normal times made possible "normal families." Once deemed to be exceptional, the problems of these groups required only short-term solutions; the needs of "normal families," in contrast, were there to stay, constants in an advanced industrial society.

The demographic legacy of the war also gave new life to intense fears of a reduced birthrate. Socialists, liberals, and the conservative CDU/CSU coalition shared conceptions of economic growth that were predicated on an expanding German population. They feared that declining family size would set limits to economic recovery, despite the fact that West German gains from postwar immigration from the east had more than canceled out war losses. Indeed, between 1939 and 1950 the population of those areas constituting the Federal Republic grew in population by over 7,600,000, an increase of 18.2 percent.[48] Nonetheless, Germans remained obsessed by the specter of population decline, and these fears translated unambiguously into pronatalist sentiments. To be sure, it was no longer the Führer and the Reich that demanded population growth, but the needs of the economy and the social security system delivered new justifications for familiar rhetoric. Although Wuermeling—and with him

---

47. Rita Liljeström, "Sweden," in *Family Policy: Government and Families in Fourteen Countries*, ed. Sheila B. Kamerman and Alfred J. Kahn (New York: Columbia University Press, 1978), 19–48; and Mary Ruggie, *The State and Working Women: A Comparative Study of Britain and Sweden* (Princeton: Princeton University Press, 1984).

48. Castell, 130.

those who warned that Germany would soon die out—insisted that *family* policy should not be confused with National Socialist or communist *population* policy, he typically protested far too much.[49]

In West Germany, an emphasis on pronatalism and motherhood did not register in a dramatically rising birthrate, nor did it prompt women to stay at home. The demands of an expanding economy meant that by the mid 1950s, employers were once again eager to mobilize the "silent reserve." The levels of female labor force participation increased more rapidly than those of men, and the number of married women in wage work rose as well, from one in four in 1950 to one in three a decade later.[50] Still, despite clear evidence that for many women wage work was a lifelong economic necessity, not a stage, social policy continued to focus on ways for women to manage the double burden, or even better, to eliminate it altogether by staying at home. There was little serious discussion of programs that would allow women to be mothers *and* wage earners—for example, in the form of expanded daycare services or tax credits for childcare.[51] Instead, policies focused on the male wage; the possibilities for expanding part-time work for women; and by the late 1950s, the availability of foreign workers to fill the demands of continued economic growth.

The Nazis' war had thus created a *Frauenüberschuss* and generated the problems of "incomplete" families. It had also diminished the possibilities for any post-1945 critique of the *complete* "normal" family by driving into exile those most accomplished at delivering a critical perspective on the family in the 1920s. Ideas by themselves cannot restructure human relations, but theoretical frameworks can provide categories for the analysis of needs and ways of meeting them. The Institute of Social Research, including Max Horkheimer, Herbert Marcuse, and Erich Fromm, left Frankfurt in 1934, first for Geneva, then New York. The institute's major collective project of the 1930s, *Studien über Autorität und Familie* (Studies of authority and the family), was a massive investigation of the political consequences of familial socialization; it appeared in 1936 not in Berlin or Frankfurt, but in Paris. The sociological analyses that most influenced the discussion of the family in the 1950s were the

---

49. See Wuermeling, "Der Sinn der Familienpolitik," *Bulletin des Presse- und Informationsamtes der Bundesregierung*, no. 211 (1954): 1911–12.

50. Angelika Willms, "Segregation auf Dauer? Zur Entwicklung des Verhältnisses von Frauenarbeit und Männerarbeit in Deutschland, 1882–1980," in *Strukturwandel der Frauenarbeit 1880–1980*, ed. Walter Müller, Angelika Willms, and Johann Handl (Frankfurt: Campus, 1983), 132, 135. The phrase, "stille Reserve," was often used in discussions of women's labor force participation in the 1950s. See, for example, Erna Hamann, "Die Frau auf dem Arbeitsmarkt," *Arbeitsblatt* (1949): 423.

51. On the totally inadequate nature of daycare provision by the early 1960s, see "Bericht der Bundesregierung über die Situation der Frauen in Beruf, Familie und Gesellschaft," prepared by Bundesminister für Arbeit und Sozialordnung, Deutscher Bundestag, *VdBT*, 5. Deutscher Bundestag, Drucksache V/909, 28–31, 337.

optimistic accounts of Schelsky and Oeter, not the neo-Marxist approach offered by the Frankfurt School.[52] As for other critical perspectives from the Left, when Engels's *Origins of the Family* was quoted in the discussion of family policy in the 1950s, it was by Wuermeling as a negative example, not by Social Democrats for whom it was an inheritance that they did not acknowledge.[53]

Potential criticism of the assumptions underlying the "normal family" was further diluted by the differences that continued to divide middle-class women's organizations, the heirs to the bourgeois feminist tradition, from women in the SPD and the trade union movement. The critique that emerged—and behind which bourgeois and socialist women could join forces—focused on the reform of marriage and family law and the achievement of wives' formal equality with husbands. It left untouched the concept of the "normal family" and its implications for specific measures like *Kindergeld*. In part, these priorities reflected the discussion of gender difference, which had taken place among German bourgeois feminists since the late nineteenth century. In the 1950s women activists of all political stripes reaffirmed their insistence that equality should not violate, but rather should reinforce and allow the emergence of, "natural" distinctions and they endorsed motherhood as the epitome of womanhood.[54]

In addition, although women in the SPD and the trade union movement placed greater emphasis on the economic needs motivating women to work outside the home, they would not be outdone in their assertion that "socially just wages" for men would insure that "no mother of preschool or school-aged children should be forced to work out of economic necessity."[55] Women in the SPD also subscribed completely to the belief in the essential bond between mother and child and prescribed the "Vitamin of Mother's Love" for the physical and psychological well-being of children.[56] This was a medication best administered in the home.

The split among women's organizations along confessional lines further complicated possibilities for any consistent or unified feminist critique. Catholic women's organizations, often directly tied to the church, were not willing to accept all clerical prescriptions for a scripturally based female

---

52. See Max Horkheimer, ed., *Studien über Autorität und Familie* (Paris: Librairie Félix Alcan, 1936); and Martin Jay, *The Dialectical Imagination: A History of the Frankfurt School and the Institute of Social Research 1923–1950* (Boston: Little, Brown & Co., 1973), 124–33.

53. Wuermeling, "Keine Bevölkerungspolitik, sondern Familienpolitik!" *Bulletin des Presse- und Informationsamtes der Bundesregierung*, no. 231 (1955): 1967–68.

54. For example, see Ann Taylor Allen, "Mothers of the New Generation: Adele Schreiber, Helene Stöcker, and the Evolution of a German Idea of Motherhood, 1900–1914," *Signs* 10 (Spring 1985): 418–38.

55. See, for example, "Zentrale Frauenkonferenz in Köln vom 29. bis 31. Mai 1953," *Gleichheit* 16, no. 7 (1953): 221. This demand was repeated by socialist women and women trade unionists throughout the 1950s.

56. A. Grossmann, "Vitamin Mutterliebe," *Gleichheit* 15, no. 11 (1952): 355–56.

subordination, but they were certainly far from questioning the sanctity of the family. The clear "gender gap" in favor of the CDU/CSU throughout the 1950s indicated, moreover, that women preferred political parties that could boast Christian, not Social or Free Democratic credentials.[57]

Finally, the emphasis on the "normal family" in social theory captured a central experience of Germans in the war's aftermath. In an insightful essay, Lutz Niethammer describes how the family promised protection, security, organized self-help, and survival in the face of the collapse of other sources of constituted authority. For women, in Niethammer's words, the family became "an obligation, a phantom, and a project." This vision of the family—what Niethammer rightly describes as the "product of fantasy" and a "concrete utopia"—was for Schelsky and others an unquestioned reality that justified making the family the foundation of a comprehensive social policy.[58] They advocated reinforcing that reality, not facilitating the formulation of other "concrete utopias." The absence of alternative conceptual frameworks greatly restricted the possibilities for women to imagine structuring their lives in other ways. Sociological studies of the career objectives of young women in the 1950s concluded that although they recognized the importance of occupational training, they ultimately sought work as wives and mothers. Studies of working mothers stressed that most women would prefer to leave wage work.[59] To describe women's lives in terms of choice and preference, however, was to posit options where few existed.

The categories that *did* emerge to describe gender relations and women's proper place indicate important characteristics of postwar West German society. Unlike the psychoanalytic terms that were so central to British postwar approaches to the problems of women and children, the German discussion was unselfconsciously sociological and economistic.[60] The language of social policy in the West German context was appropriate to a nation that found itself in the throes of economic reconstruction according to a capitalist blueprint and that was seeking to overcome its historical ambivalence toward capitalism. The division between production and reproduction was not always clear when families became agents of human capital accumulation. These categories emphasized the family's indispensability; they also did nothing to mystify its economic func-

---

57. In general, see Gabriele Bremme, *Die politische Rolle der Frau in Deutschland: Eine Untersuchung über den Einfluss der Frauen bei Wahlen und ihre Teilnahme in Partei und Parlament* (Göttingen: Vandenhoeck & Ruprecht, 1956).

58. Lutz Niethammer, "Privat-Wirtschaft: Erinnerungsfragmente einer anderen Umerziehung," in *"Hinterher merkt man,"* 48, 54.

59. See in particular, Elisabeth Pfeil, *Die Berufstätigkeit von Müttern* (Tübingen: J.C.B. Mohr [Paul Siebeck], 1961); and Edith Hinze (with the assistance of Elisabeth Knospe), *Lage und Leistung erwerbstätiger Mütter: Ergebnisse einer Untersuchung in Westberlin* (Cologne: Carl Heymanns Verlag, 1960).

60. On the English discussion, see Denise Riley, *War in the Nursery: Theories of the Child and Mother* (London: Virago, 1983).

tions or the work of women within it. Indeed, in terms reminiscent of the debate among feminists in the early 1970s over the value of women's unpaid labor in the home, sociologists and economists in the 1950s calculated women's non-wage contribution to economic development to the last pfennig. Of course, for them women's unpaid work was in the service of the "nation," the "family," and the *Volk*, not capitalism or patriarchy.[61]

At the same time that women's reproductive work was praised as essential to the smooth functioning of the "market economy," it was also women's responsibility to raise children to resist the consumer temptations offered by the "economic miracle" (*Wirtschaftswunder*) of postwar recovery. Inculcating children with the right values was clearly among a mother's tasks. The family, women's proper place, was in the market economy but not of it. Mothers preserved and transmitted to their children values that would abate the worst excesses of unbridled competition and would prevent West Germany from becoming a materialistic nation. Women also needed to police themselves. Those who worked outside the home constantly threatened to cross that boundary separating need from desire. Men *had* to go out to work; women *chose* to go out to work. For mothers, the choice meant turning their backs on their primary responsibilities; their motivations were under particular scrutiny.[62]

Family policy also became an important vehicle in the ideological move to a classless postwar society. This was most clearly expressed in Mackenroth's distinction between *"kinderarm"* and *"kinderreich,"* and in Schelsky's description of the "levelled-out petit bourgeois-*mittelständisch* society." It was apparent as well in analyses that acknowledged the value of women's unpaid domestic labor and concluded that all women worked, while triumphantly pronouncing that a working class no longer existed.

The reconstitution of a private family sphere was vital to reaching the "end to ideology" in the 1950s. It also embodied a critique of the ideological alternatives presented by Germany's recent past and by a communist East Germany in the present. In the confused categories of totalitarian theory, it was possible to reject both at the same time; the family could serve as a vehicle for anti-Nazi *and* anticommunist rhetoric. The emphasis on the family as an intimate, inviolable sphere reflected the widely held perception that National Socialists had attempted to subordinate the individual to the nation directly by weakening the link—the family—that should hold the two together while preserving the indi-

---

61. See, for example, Jessen, esp. 141–49. For the discussion among socialist feminists in the 1970s, see the summary in Michèle Barrett, *Women's Oppression Today: Problems in Marxist Feminist Analysis* (London: Verso, 1980), 172–86.

62. These priorities were underwritten by the marriage law as well. Even after its reform in 1957, the marriage law dictated that women's wage work outside the home must not impede fulfillment of "marital and family obligations." These provisions were not altered until 1977. See the summary in Harry G. Shaffner, *Women in the Two Germanies: A Comparative Study of a Socialist and a Non-Socialist Society* (New York: Pergamon Press, 1981), 28–29.

vidual's privacy. Particularly in the formulations of the ruling CDU/CSU coalition, it was communists who continued to attempt what National Socialists had not accomplished—to rob parents of authority over their children, to transform youth into charges of the state, and to reduce the family to the site "where children are brought into the world; but children, so says the state, belong to it."[63] Communists and Nazis alike sought to transform private spheres into public places.

In Wuermeling's words, both the "inhuman National Socialist rule of force" and the "Soviet terror that reduces the value of humanity to a soulless machine" attempted to transform individuals into "slaves of the collective." In the arena of family policy, Nazi and communist intentions became immediately apparent.[64] By undermining the family, both regimes most directly threatened the status of women. Although both acknowledged women's contributions to the social order, they sought to make women into servants of the state. In a democratic Germany, this equation would be reversed; the state would serve the needs of women and the family, securing women's status and supporting her vital domestic labors as wife and mother. Social policymakers in a new Germany sought to secure the family as society's most essential building block, safe from state intervention. Strengthening the family insured women the true equality that they could achieve only within the private sphere. In contrast, for both National Socialists and communists, women's "forced emancipation" brought them only the right to work alongside men in Nazi war industries or in East German uranium mines.[65]

West Germans also renounced a past in which the Nazis had sought political stability in *Lebensraum* (literally, "living space") in a conquered eastern Europe; they replaced it with a search for security in the *Lebensraum* of the family in which a "free" West Germany would grow and in which a new generation would be socialized.[66] The "communist-ruled peoples of the east"—a geographic designation that could be conveniently extended from the border

---

63. Hans Köhler, a professor at the Free University in Berlin, at *Dritter Parteitag der Christlich-Demokratischen Union, Berlin, 17.–19. Oktober 1952* (Cologne: Kölnische Verlagsdruckerei, n.d.), 52.

64. See Wuermeling's comments in Bundesgeschäftsstelle der Christlich-Demokratischen Union Deutschlands, ed., *Deutschland, sozialer Rechtsstaat im geeinten Europa (= 4. Bundesparteitag, 18.–22. April 1953, Hamburg)* (Hamburg: Sator Werbe Verlag, n.d.), 67–68.

65. See Wuermeling, *VdBT*, 2. Deutscher Bundestag, 15. Sitzung, 12 Feb. 1954, 493; and Ingrid Langer, "In letzter Konsequenz . . . Uranbergwerk! Die Gleichberechtigung in Grundgesetz und Bürgerlichem Gesetzbuch," in *Perlonzeit: Wie die Frauen ihr Wirtschaftswunder erlebten,* ed. Angela Delille and Andrea Grohn (Berlin: Elefanten Press, 1985), 72–81.

66. Wuermeling, "Ein machtvolles Bekenntnis zum katholischen Glauben," *Fränkische Nachrichten,* 21 June 1954 (copy in ACDP, I-221-005); and a speech delivered on 15 Sept. 1956, "Familie und Staat," in which he refers to "Freiheitsraum Familie" (typescript in ACDP, I-221-017). An SDP observer, Kurt Fiebig, although less virulent in his tone, reached the same conclusion. See his "Ostzonale Bevölkerungspolitik," *Gleichheit* 14, no. 10 (1951): 304–5. On the gender-specific understandings of *Lebensraum* under National Socialism, see Koonz, 13–14.

with East Germany to Shanghai—produced many more children than the West Germans who threatened to "die out." The "free civilization" of the west and the sanctity of the family's *Lebensraum* were challenged by the "natural dynamic of expansion" apparent in the east. The advocates of "money for children" in the Federal Republic argued that Nazis and communists alike pursued population policy, not policies to strengthen healthy families. Whether for women in the SPD or Wuermeling, the implication was the same: communism threatened the family, and an effective family policy was a bulwark against communism.[67]

The particular form of the "political reconstruction of the family" in post-1945 West Germany guaranteed that the *Wirtschaftswunder* would not be so miraculous for women. Biology had defined women's status under the Nazis; it remained women's destiny in a democratic republic. The "collapse" of 1945—that convenient description that made it unnecessary to go too far in ascribing agency and responsibility—did not leave Germans at the *Stunde Null* (zero hour).[68] The Federal Republic was neither Weimar nor the Third Reich, but it did embody certain elements that linked it to its own most recent history. In the language of pronatalism, motherhood, the sanctity of family relations, and in the state's attempts to shape these private relationships, there were striking continuities across the divide of 1945.[69] The new German constitution had guaranteed individuals the right to self-fulfillment, but the message of family policy in the 1950s was that for women, self-fulfillment was to be found in the home.

The debates around the protection of the family did identify genuine needs. As in almost all other societies, German women in the 1950s carried extraordinary burdens of biological motherhood and socially constructed burdens of housework and childcare. However, by locating women in "normal families" with male "providers," policy makers guaranteed that these needs would be addressed only in certain ways. In their categories, women's place was reasserted and reified, not redefined.

---

67. Wuermeling, transcript of speech in Nordwestdeutscher Rundfunk, 10 Nov. 1953, ACDP, I-221-017; "Für den Schutz der Familie," *Union in Deutschland*, no. 86, 4 Nov. 1953 (copy in ACDP, I-221-004). And, for similar sentiments from the SPD, see, e.g., Louise Schroeder, "Sozialpolitik in der Sowjetzone," *Gleichheit* 16, no. 7 (1953): 228–29.

68. See the reflections in Inge Stolten, *Das alltägliche Exil: Leben zwischen Hakenkreuz und Währungsreform* (Bonn: J.H.W. Dietz Nachf., 1982), 130. A comprehensive survey of women in the Weimar years and under the Nazi regime is provided in Renate Bridenthal, Atina Grossmann, and Marion Kaplan, eds., *When Biology Became Destiny: Women in Weimar and Nazi Germany* (New York: Monthly Review, 1984); and Koonz.

69. See the parallels in James M. Diehl, "Change and Continuity in the Treatment of German *Kriegsopfer*," *Central European History* 18 (June 1985): 170–87 (republished in this volume).

Public Service Personnel in West Germany in the 1950s: Controversial Policy Decisions and their Effects on Social Composition, Gender Structure, and the Role of Former Nazis

Curt Garner

Although a half century has elapsed since the end of World War II, comparatively little research has been done on German social history in the period after 1945. Instead, social historians have concentrated on examining events and processes in the nineteenth and the first half of the twentieth centuries. One major reason for the continuing focus on this era is the understandable desire to identify social factors which help to explain the failure of Weimar democracy, the rise of National Socialism, and its widespread acceptance in the German population. As a consequence of this emphasis, however, the period after 1945 has been neglected. The extensive research by contemporary historians on the postwar era has provided little corrective, since it deals predominantly with developments in the political sphere. More than a decade has gone by since the prominent contemporary historian Hans-Peter Schwarz criticized this bias and challenged his colleagues "to discover the society of the Federal Republic in its beginning phases as a field of historical research."[1] But only few heeded his call. The author of a recent survey observes that there is still a notable lack of consensus as to which concepts, key terms, types of explanations, and

---

1. Hans-Peter Schwarz, "Modernisierung oder Restauration? Einige Vorfragen zur künftigen Sozialgeschichtsforschung über die Ära Adenauer," in *Rheinland-Westfalen im Industriezeitalter,* vol. 3, ed. Kurt Düwell and Wolfgang Köllmann (Wuppertal, 1984), 278.

theoretical models might be most helpful in analyzing the phenomena at hand. Moreover, there is a need for empirical studies dealing with the specific social constellations and groups that played an influential role in postwar developments.[2]

Within this context, this chapter deals with the development of a particularly large and important social group during the 1950s. The focus on this decade might seem surprising, since the 1950s are commonly seen as a socially static, even boring, period during which most West Germans were preoccupied with economic reconstruction. Only in the 1960s, according to popular conception, did social stagnation give way to upheaval and rapid transformation. However, recent scholarship has revealed the complex character and historical significance of West German social evolution in the 1950s. Continuity was indeed the dominant feature of some areas of society, but other sectors were marked by momentous changes, some of which occurred quite rapidly. It is still too early for a definitive reassessment of the 1950s, for our knowledge of social developments in many areas remains fragmentary. Nevertheless, more and more historians now regard this decade as a key period, during which numerous processes of far-reaching importance set in and others, whose roots can be traced back to earlier decades, now prevailed. The dynamic thrust of these developments would lead to a metamorphosis of the social structure, way of life, and value systems in the Federal Republic within a relatively short period of time. As a result, West German society left behind the world of the 1920s and 1930s, which had been the explicit or implicit prototype for its reconstruction. What emerged was a "modern industrial society" with all its contradictions, social costs, ecological hazards, and problems of political governability.[3]

---

2. Paul Erker, "Zeitgeschichte als Sozialgeschichte. Forschungsstand und Forschungsdefizite," *Geschichte und Gesellschaft* 19 (1993). Four other theoretical articles written by contemporary historians also appeared in 1993; the publication of five such pieces within one year's time reflects recognition of the need for a fundamental change of perspective in German contemporary history. See Anselm Doering-Manteuffel, "Deutsche Zeitgeschichte nach 1945. Entwicklung und Problemlagen der historischen Forschung zur Nachkriegszeit," *Vierteljahrshefte für Zeitgeschichte* 41 (1993); Hans Günter Hockerts, "Zeitgeschichte in Deutschland. Begriff, Methoden, Themenfelder," *Historisches Jahrbuch* 113 (1993); Michael Prinz, "Demokratische Stabilisierung, Problemlagen von Modernisierung im Selbstbezug und historische Kontinuität—Leitbegriffe einer Zeitsozialgeschichte," *Westfälische Forschungen* 43 (1993); Axel Schildt, "Nachkriegszeit. Möglichkeiten und Probleme einer Periodisierung der westdeutschen Geschichte nach dem Zweiten Weltkrieg und ihrer Einordnung in die deutsche Geschichte des 20. Jahrhunderts," *Geschichte in Wissenschaft und Unterricht* 44 (1993).

3. For a particularly important contribution to the discussion about the reevaluation of the 1950s see Axel Schildt and Arnold Sywottek, eds., *Modernisierung im Wiederaufbau. Die westdeutsche Gesellschaft der 50er Jahre* (Bonn, 1993). The volume contains articles on aspects of the political system, the economy, society, and culture of the Federal Republic. It includes an earlier version of this article, which has been utilized with kind permission of the publisher, J. H. W. Dietz

Until now, research on the social history of the Federal Republic has virtually ignored those working in the public service.[4] This is surprising, given the size of this group and its traditional importance within German society, politics, and economics. Both a longstanding bureaucratic tradition and the increasingly active role of the state in economic and social policy had contributed to a massive expansion of the public service since the mid-nineteenth century. It eventually reached proportions unique on an international scale, as comparative figures for the first part of the twentieth century show. In 1925, and thus even after a sharp reduction in the number of those working in the German public service as a consequence of territorial losses in World War I and severe economic problems, there were still over 2.72 million public employees—more than in any other country in central or western Europe and nearly as many as in the United States, although the U.S. population was almost twice as large as Germany's.[5] The percentage of the German work force employed in the public service was also singularly high (8.50%).[6] Remarkably, the Federal Republic emerged with a public service that was no smaller when viewed in relative terms—despite the turbulence and the upheavals of the Nazi era and the occupation period. Indeed, its dimensions had increased even further. The 2.1 million people employed in the West German public service in 1950 constituted

---

Nachfolger. For publication in English, the study has been further developed at many points, and new primary sources have been consulted.

4. The term *modern industrial society,* now used by many historians to characterize the social formation which has evolved since the founding of the Federal Republic, doubtlessly contributes to the tendency to overlook the public employees. The term points specifically to the area of industrial production and distracts attention from the tertiary sector, although the growing significance of public and private services is said to be a prime characteristic of "modern" societies.

5. In the United States, 3.11 million persons worked for government units at all levels in 1929. The population of Germany numbered 62.4 million in 1925; in the same year, the figure for the United States was estimated to be 115.8 million. For these and the following statistics see Peter Flora et al., *State, Economy, and Society in Western Europe 1815–1975. A Data Handbook in two Volumes,* vol. 1 (Frankfurt a.M./London/Chicago, 1983), 193–243; *Historical Statistics of the United States. Colonial Times to 1970* (Washington, D.C., 1975), 8, 126–8, 1100–4 (all figures exclude military personnel). The number of public employees in Germany was actually even larger; Flora's statistics do not include personnel employed by the public utility companies, the social insurance agencies, the public utility companies, the social insurance agencies, the public utility companies, and state-run welfare institutions (such as public assistance agencies and homes for the elderly).

6. Not until after World War II did some other western European countries evidence similar percentages. In the following decades, though, many would overtake Germany permanently—as the result of a secular trend to accelerated growth in the public sector on an international scale. For a general discussion of the causes and varying pace of this development see Richard Rose et al., *Public Employment in Western Nations* (Cambridge, GB, et al., 1985). The statistics for the United States reflect a similar pattern of growth: whereas 6.48% of the work force were employed in the public service in 1929, the proportion had risen to 7.56% by 1940. It reached 8.96% in 1948 and then swelled to 15.28% by 1970 (computed on the basis of the figures in *Historical Statistics,* 126–7, 1102–4).

almost one-tenth of the entire work force and more than one-seventh of all wage earners actually employed at the time.[7]

These public employees performed a wide variety of tasks. Many worked in administration at the city, county, state, or federal levels, others worked for the police, for fire departments, hospitals and other health-care institutions, the public schools, or the (exclusively state-run) university system. Still others were employed in a multitude of public utilities and enterprises, such as gasworks and water companies, sewage treatment plants, most electric companies, and virtually all urban transport systems. In addition, more than a quarter of a million worked for the Federal Postal Service (*Bundespost*) in 1950. It was not only responsible for delivering letters and packages, but also ran the telephone and telegraph systems. Furthermore, all local post offices provided banking facilities as well as a savings and loan service, both of which were widely used. Last but not least, the public service included the Federal Railway (*Bundesbahn*), which employed more than half a million persons in 1950. The national railway system handled the bulk of the country's commercial shipping and was the most important means of passenger travel and commuter transportation. Thus the public employees were not only a social factor of considerable significance, they also played a central role in the country's economy.[8]

The public service differs from other sectors of the economy in that political decision makers can directly influence the social composition of the employees, their legal and economic status, and their working conditions. In Germany, government has traditionally determined the exact number and duties of those working in all areas of the public service, the prevailing recruitment policies, promotion rules, and basic salary regulations. Political decisions regarding such questions have had far-reaching consequences not only for the character of the public service, but for the structure of German society and the degree of social mobility in general. If, for example, recruitment policies allowed members of the middle and lower classes to enter the public service in increasing numbers, and if promotion regulations enabled them to work their way up from one level of administration to the next on the basis of merit, then they had better access to the higher levels of the public service—and upward social mobility increased overall. If, on the other hand, political decisions restricted access to the

---

7. In 1950, there were 2,104,103 full-time employees in the public service; the entire work force numbered 23,489,000 persons *(Erwerbspersonen),* and 14,163,100 wage earners were actually employed *(beschäftigte Arbeitnehmer).* See *Bevölkerung und Wirtschaft 1872–1972,* hg. vom Statistischen Bundesamt (Stuttgart/Cologne, 1972), 140, 236–7; *Statistisches Jahrbuch für die Bundesrepublik 1952,* 87.

8. In 1950, the Federal Statistical Office listed the number of those working for the Federal Postal Service as 279,508; they constituted 13.3% of all public service employees. The office reported that 525,429 persons worked for the Federal Railway; they represented 25.0% of all public service employees. See *Bevölkerung und Wirtschaft,* 236, 241.

public service or limited the chances for advancement on the basis of individual achievement, then this reinforced existing social hierarchies and reduced chances for social mobility. The history of the German public service in the nineteenth and early twentieth centuries offers numerous examples of such restrictions. There were formal barriers to social mobility such as the requirement that applicants for higher administrative positions must have a university degree in law (*Juristenmonopol,* "lawyers' monopoly"). At the same time, many positions in the lower levels of the civil service were traditionally reserved for those who had served as non-commissioned army officers for a certain number of years (*Militäranwärtersystem*). There were also informal barriers: discrimination against candidates on the basis of their political views, social origins, religion, and sex was widespread.[9]

This chapter deals with important aspects of this complex subject in the formative years of the Federal Republic. It examines four major decisions in personnel policy, each with far-reaching social consequences:

1. the decision on the part of the first Adenauer government and the first federal parliament, the Bundestag, to reject all proposals for a fundamental reform of the public service. Instead, the traditional personnel structure and the unique system of legal relationships on which it was founded were to be retained;

2. the decision taken by Dr. Konrad Adenauer and his political allies to avoid a decisive break with the past when recruiting personnel for the new federal ministries in Bonn. Priority was given to hiring former civil servants from the Prussian and Reich ministries in Berlin, even though it was well known that such persons had usually belonged to the Nazi Party and that some had been even more directly involved in the injustices and criminal acts perpetrated by the Nazi regime;

3. the decision of the first Bundestag to require all parts of the public administration and all public enterprises to recruit at least 20% of their personnel from among those who had lost their public service positions as a consequence of the war or in the process of denazification. This measure also mandated priority hiring of former professional soldiers and officers of the paramilitary Reich Labor Service. This controversial legislation was a major determinant of the recruitment policies of the

---

9. For a discussion in long-term perspective see Hartmut Kaelble, *Soziale Mobilität und Chancengleichheit im 19. und 20. Jahrhundert. Deutschland im internationalen Vergleich* (Göttingen, 1983), 73–102. In his discussion of social mobility in the public service after 1945, Kaelble had to confine himself mainly to formulating cautious hypotheses, because the empirical data available to him were of limited value. This detracts in no way from the theoretical importance of his pioneering work.

federal government, the states (*Länder*), and the municipalities in the 1950s and early 1960s;
4. the decision taken at several different levels to drastically reduce the proportion of female employees, whose number had increased considerably during the war years. Particular attention was devoted to forcing married women out of the public service. In doing so, administrators did not hesitate to continue to apply pertinent regulations decreed by the National Socialists.

1.

In 1952–53, after years of contention, all proposals for a fundamental reform of the public service were finally rejected. The traditional personnel structure and the peculiar system of legal relationships on which it was founded had been defended against all onslaught.

The issue had been an object of conflict since 1945. After the war, both the British and the American military governments had declared their determination to "democratize" the German public service.[10] First of all, a fundamental reform of the personnel structure was viewed as being essential. Traditionally, public employees were divided into a strict hierarchy of three groups with widely differing social and legal status: manual workers (*Arbeiter*), salaried employees (*Angestellte*), and civil servants (*Beamte*). The sharp distinction between the first two groups, blue-collar workers and white-collar salaried employees, was characteristic for German society on the whole. Legislative measures passed around the turn of the century had reinforced and strengthened the dividing line between them. Motivated by the desire to create a social bul-

---

10. The policies of the other two occupying powers had no direct consequences for developments in the Federal Republic. The Soviets favored sweeping reforms, and by 1949 the traditional German civil service system had actually been abolished in their zone. The French were the sole occupying power which considered only limited reform necessary. The measures enacted in their zone met nonetheless with stubborn German resistance and had no lasting effects. See Curt Garner, "Schlußfolgerungen aus der Vergangenheit? Die Auseinandersetzungen um die Zukunft des deutschen Berufsbeamtentums nach dem Ende des Zweiten Weltkrieges," in Hans-Erich Volkmann, ed., *Ende des Zweiten Weltkriegs, Ende des Dritten Reiches. Eine perspektivische Rückschau* (Munich/Zurich, 1995), 607–9, 615–6, 633–40, 652–62. For American policy see ibid., 612–5, 627–9; Hermann-Josef Rupieper, *Die Wurzeln der westdeutschen Nachkriegsdemokratie. Der amerikanische Beitrag 1945–1952* (Opladen, 1993), 173–83; Wolfgang Benz, "Versuche zur Reform des öffentlichen Dienstes in Deutschland 1945–1952," *Vierteljahrshefte für Zeitgeschichte* 29 (1981); for a detailed study of British policy see Ulrich Reusch, *Deutsches Berufsbeamtentum und britische Besatzung. Planung und Politik 1943–1947* (Stuttgart, 1985). Reusch's interpretation requires modification in fundamental points, however; see Curt Garner, "'Zerschlagung des Berufsbeamtentums'? Der deutsche Konflikt um die Neuordnung des öffentlichen Dienstes 1946–1948 am Beispiel Nordrhein-Westfalens," *Vierteljahrshefte für Zeitgeschichte* 39 (1991).

wark against the rise of the workers' movement, these laws had given salaried employees a privileged legal and economic status.[11]

Civil servants, in turn, enjoyed a special status that clearly distinguished them from the other two groups. The relationship between civil servant and employer was not founded by signing a mutually binding contract—that would have been considered tantamount to reducing civil servants to the status of salaried employees, who were alleged to be interested foremost in the pecuniary rewards of their work. Instead, the relationship between the civil servant and the state was supposed to be of a higher ethical quality. It also evidenced roots reaching back into the feudal past: the civil servant was appointed in an "act of state" (*Hoheitsakt*), received an official letter of commission and swore a formal oath of loyalty to the *Dienstherr* (literally: "master to whom service is owed"). The further conditions of service were regulated by a specific legal construct within the field of public law, the civil service status (*Beamtenverhältnis*). Central tenets of this status were the understanding that those involved would spend their entire working careers in the civil service (*Berufsbeamtentum*) and that they would in return receive lifelong tenure as well as emoluments, which were regarded not as earnings, but as a maintenance grant consistent with social status. The material provisions included not only a substantially higher salary than employees received, but also significantly better provisions for sick pay, a generous non-contributory pension, and, on death, dependents' allowances.[12]

The singular nature of the civil servants' status and their proximity to authority had traditionally encouraged their perception of belonging to a coherent

---

11. See Jürgen Kocka, "Class formation, interest articulation, and public policy: The origins of the German white-collar class in the late nineteenth and early twentieth centuries," in Suzanne Berger, ed., *Organizing interests in Western Europe. Pluralism, corporatism, and the transformation of politics* (Cambridge, GB, et al., 1981).

12. The historical origins and basic features of the *Berufsbeamtentum* are discussed in the introductory survey by Bernd Wunder, *Geschichte der Bürokratie in Deutschland* (Frankfurt a.M., 1986); it not only makes reference to the older literature, but also contains much new and important information. The general treatments available in English are less satisfying; see Fritz Morstein Marx, "Civil Service in Germany," in Leonard D. White et al., *Civil Service Abroad. Great Britain, Canada, France, Germany.* The Commission of Inquiry on Public Service Personnel, Monographs 2–5 (New York/London, 1935), 161–275; Erich Angermann, "Germany's 'Peculiar Institution': The *Beamtentum*," in Angermann and Marie-Luise Frings, eds., *Oceans Apart? Comparing Germany and the United States* (Stuttgart, 1981). The best English-language discussion by far has appeared in the context of research on the history of German professionalization in international perspective: Jane Caplan, "Profession as Vocation: The German Civil Service," in Geoffrey Cocks and Konrad H. Jarausch, eds., *German Professions, 1800–1950* (New York/Oxford, 1990). Two important monographs dealing with developments in the decades before 1945 have also appeared in English: Andreas Kunz, *Civil Servants and the Politics of Inflation in Germany, 1914–1924* (Berlin/New York, 1986); Jane Caplan, *Government Without Administration. State and Civil Service in Weimar and Nazi Germany* (Oxford, 1988).

and self-contained social estate or corporate group (*Standesbewußtsein*). This mentality was reinforced by the long-standing doctrine that service to the state was an especially valuable and morally superior way of life. Such notions had always been most pervasive in the higher ranks of bureaucracy, but they also played a considerable role in the lower levels of the civil service—in part as psychological compensation for the disquieting fact that, in reality, income levels in this part of the service were frequently lower than theory would have dictated. Lower-grade civil servants who earned less than highly qualified manual workers could still experience a feeling of moral superiority, because only they had the privilege of serving the state and, indeed, of being regarded as a veritable "incarnation of the idea of the state."[13]

Representatives of the American and British military governments criticized the hierarchical personnel structure in the public service as undemocratic. For one thing, manual workers and salaried employees had virtually no chance of working their way up to a higher level on a merit basis. Moreover, the special status and traditional mentality of the civil servants were considered highly problematic. This "privileged official class" with its distinctive "caste consciousness" and disdain for elected representatives was deemed a major obstacle to Allied efforts to create a democratic state in Germany. Military government officials were especially critical of the higher ranks of the civil service, which were perceived as being full of persons with an upper-class background and a fundamentally militaristic or authoritarian cast of mind. Virtually all were regarded as politically compromised, not only due to their obvious involvement in the National Socialist regime, but also because it was well known that many higher civil servants had retained their preference for a monarchical system after 1918 and regarded the Weimar Republic with scorn.

In order to effect a fundamental change in the political and social composition of the public service, both military governments sought to restructure its legal underpinnings. They tried to convince the German state governments that Anglo-American notions of reform were in fact superior to the status quo and that it would thus be a good idea to draft new state civil service laws based on these concepts. On the whole, German representatives showed little interest. The American military government eventually abandoned its efforts to achieve

---

13. *Verkörperung der Staatsidee*. The relevant body of academic teachings, *Staatsrecht*, dealt with the nature and authority of the (German) state. By no means did these doctrines and their proponents disappear along with the German state itself in 1945. After the first shock of defeat had worn off, well-known representatives of this field (who were themselves civil servants) moved quickly to reassert the continued validity of their earlier teachings; see, for example, the influential work by Carl Heyland, *Das Berufsbeamtentum im neuen demokratischen Staat. Eine staatsrechtliche Studie (Nach dem Stande vom 1. Oktober 1948)* (Berlin, 1949). Heyland was professor at the University of Gießen, where he had been teaching without interruption since 1923.

reform through democratic persuasion and put the governments of the three states in its zone under pressure. As a result, they promulgated new civil service laws in October/November 1946. But even then, none of these laws was fully consistent with American policy goals.[14] British representatives proved unable to persuade even one state government in their zone to introduce a law corresponding to the reform model they had drawn up in 1945–46.[15] After the two zones were merged and the Economic Council, a type of legislature for the Anglo-American Bizone, was created in June 1947, British and American representatives also tried to convince its members to pass a reform law for the jurisdiction of the bizonal administration. These efforts proved similarly unsuccessful.[16]

Finally, in early 1949, the military government authorities for the Bizone lost their patience and dictated a reform law. Such a step was unusual at this late date and sparked a heated public debate. "Military Law No. 15" officially pertained only to those employees working in the bizonal administration, but its authors intended to use it as an instrument to predetermine the future situation in the Federal Republic as a whole. Five aspects of the military law are of particular significance in our context:

1. Several provisions were designed to broaden the social base of the civil service. The decisive role which formal education had previously played in hiring practices was modified, and members of the middle

---

14. These state laws were published in *Bayerisches Gesetz- und Verordnungsblatt* 1946, 349–68; *Regierungsblatt für die Regierung Württemberg-Baden* 1946, 249–62; *Gesetz- und Verordnungsblatt für Groß-Hessen* 1946, 205–15. For an evaluation written by an avid proponent of the traditional civil service system see Heyland, 140–56.

15. Bark and Gress, the authors of the largest and most recent English-language history of West Germany, have—for reasons known only to them—come to a diametrically opposite view of these developments, for example: "In 1946 the Allied military governments . . . introduced laws . . . [which] abolished the bureaucracy's historical status as a special group under public law and transformed the Beamter's relationship with his employing institution into a simple contract like that between any employee and his employer." This stunning misjudgment could have been avoided, had the authors more carefully read the German work which they cite. See Dennis L. Bark and David R. Gress, *A History of West Germany*, vol. 1: *From Shadow to Substance, 1945–1963,* 2nd. ed. (Oxford, GB/ Cambridge, MA, 1993), 81–5 (the quotation is on p. 83). In addition to studies in German, there are also a number of helpful contemporary accounts available in English, written by scholars who had worked for the military government, among them: Harold Zink, *The United States in Germany 1944–1955* (Princeton, NJ, et al., 1957) 332–4; Arnold Brecht, "Personnel Management," in Edward H. Litchfield and Associates, *Governing Postwar Germany* (Ithaca, NY, 1953); J.F.J. Gillen, *State and Local Government in West Germany, 1945–1953, With Special Reference to the U.S. Zone and Bremen,* Historical Division, Office of the U.S. High Commissioner for Germany (1953), 69–91.

16. The author is presently engaged in a detailed investigation of the reasons why the American and British military governments did not find ways to implement their reform objectives in the critical first years of occupation. For first results of this project see Garner, "Schlußfolgerungen."

and lower classes were given greater opportunities to work their way up into the higher ranks on the basis of merit. Traditionally, advancement from one level or career track (*Laufbahn*) to the next was an anomaly. It was virtually impossible within the administrative service and more common only in the lower reaches of the railway and postal service. Military Law No. 15 widened the existing avenues and opened up new ones. In addition, many positions at higher levels were no longer to be restricted to those with legal degrees; college graduates in other relevant fields were to have equal access. The law also guaranteed equal treatment regardless of gender, thus prohibiting the further application of a number of regulations explicitly discriminating against women.

2. "Outsiders" were to receive greater opportunities to enter the civil service. This disparaging but time-hallowed term referred to those who had not become career civil servants after completing their formal education, but taken jobs in other fields. Military Law No. 15 allowed such persons to take an examination which would verify whether they were qualified to be admitted to the civil service. On the whole, experience in other fields of work was no longer to be regarded as objectionable, but as a potential enrichment.

3. The category of salaried employees was to be eliminated completely, and those holding this status were to be promoted to "civil servants subject to notice" (*Beamte auf Kündigung*). By reducing the rigid distinction between salaried employees and civil servants, this provision would help do away with the "caste system" which Allied officials considered so undemocratic. Other measures were aimed at improving the job security and economic situation of the salaried employees, since they could be dismissed easily and their earnings were comparatively low.

4. A civil servant could be dismissed if the employing agency was able to convince an impartial board that the individual lacked the necessary ability or motivation. This provision was condemned by advocates of the traditional system as contradicting the basic principle of lifelong tenure for career civil servants.

5. The law required the creation of an independent civil service commission to coordinate and monitor the processing of personnel matters throughout the entire administration. This measure was intended to ensure impartial recruitment and promotion decisions based on merit. The commission would be responsible for publicly advertising all available positions and conducting written examinations to determine the most qualified applicants. The civil service commission was also

charged with protecting employees from arbitrary actions by administrators and government officials.[17]

In September 1949, parallel to the formation of the Federal Republic, the military governors of the three Western zones were formally relieved from duty and superseded by the Allied High Commission, which was based in Bonn. As one of its first measures, the Allied High Commission announced that Military Law No. 15 would also pertain to the employees of the new federal agencies and would remain in force until the Germans had worked out a civil service law of their own. This step was intended as a diplomatically indirect way of assuring that the Allied reform measures would be applied during the crucial formative phase of the Federal Republic. All experts agreed that drafting a comprehensive new civil service law would take many months, and that the subsequent deliberations in the cabinet and the Bundestag would take even longer. Yet the Adenauer government countered with an unexpected move: within a matter of weeks, the cabinet approved the bill for a brief preliminary measure, a Federal Personnel Law which essentially mandated the application of a "denazified" version of the German Civil Service Law of 1937. While this legislation was pending, federal agencies did not implement Military Government Law No. 15. The Bundestag worked quickly, approving the Federal Personnel Law in a final vote on March 2, 1950. But the Allied High Commission refused to sanction the measure. Chancellor Adenauer, a staunch advocate of the traditional German civil service system,[18] negotiated intensively with Allied representatives to achieve approval. He argued that the Federal Personnel Law was intended only as a short-term measure, necessary to provide an adequate basis in German law for hiring the civil servants so urgently needed to staff the federal ministries. Adenauer assured the commissioners that a more comprehensive permanent law would soon be drafted, taking the main points of the Allied reform program into account. After the cabinet consented to minor modifications, the Allied High Commissioners permitted the Federal Personnel Law to be promulgated in June 1950. Parallel to this, they suspended Military Law No. 15, but only until December 31.

---

17. For the text of Military Government Law No. 15 see *Gesetzblatt der Verwaltung des Vereinigten Wirtschaftsgebietes,* 1949, Beilage 2. On this and the following see Udo Wengst, *Beamtentum zwischen Reform und Tradition. Beamtengesetzgebung in der Gründungsphase der Bundesrepublik Deutschland 1948–1953* (Düsseldorf, 1988), 32ff., 108ff.; Garner, "Schlußfolgerungen," 640–51; Rupieper, 183–99; Benz, 239–45.

18. Adenauer's commitment was not only motivated by political considerations, but also influenced by biographical factors. The chancellor could well identify with the interests of the higher civil servants, since he himself had once studied law and then set off on a career in the higher administrative service. Only later did he enter into politics. Adenauer's father had also been a civil servant.

In the period following, the Allied High Commission repeatedly reminded the chancellor of the assurances he had made and pressed for speedy passage of a law conforming to its reform objectives. In order to win greater support for this goal among Germans, the commission even dropped some particularly controversial aspects of the original conception.[19] Nonetheless, the opponents of reform in the Adenauer government and in the conservative majority parties—the Christian Democratic Union (CDU), the Christian Social Union (CSU), the Free Democratic Party (FDP), and the German Party (DP)—postponed final legislation as long as possible. The longer the tug-of-war lasted, the less leeway Allied reform advocates had: with the intensification of the Cold War, issues of foreign and security policy were given higher priority. The governments of the Western powers asked the Federal Republic to make a substantial financial contribution to Western defense efforts, for example, and the Allied High Commission had to negotiate with Chancellor Adenauer over a treaty determining the amount his country would pay. Under such circumstances it must have appeared unwise to upset Adenauer and his cabinet by insisting on a program for civil service reform which they so adamantly opposed.[20] Finally, in early 1952, the Allied High Commission announced that it was giving the Germans full freedom to decide the issue for themselves. Military Law No. 15, which had repeatedly been suspended but had continued to hang over the heads of Adenauer and his ministers like a Damoclean sword, was officially annulled on March 27, 1952.

Nine months previously, in July 1951, the federal cabinet had approved the bill for a comprehensive Civil Service Law which took several of the Allied reform wishes into account. Most of these concessions were now deleted during the deliberations in the Bundestag, and the ones that remained were mainly cosmetic in nature. The Federal Civil Service Law, passed on July 14, 1953, has thus rightly been characterized as a measure which preserved the traditional civil service system while "warding off Allied reform efforts."[21]

This decision also spelled the end of all plans to open the civil service to a broad range of candidates from different social backgrounds. Conservative

---

19. Above all, the plan to abolish salaried employees was abandoned. This proposal had been criticized even by those Germans in favor of reform.

20. The course of the negotiations between Chancellor Adenauer and the Allied High Commission on December 14, 1951, illustrates the dilemma resulting from this conflict of interest on the Allied side. The German record is published in: Hans-Peter Schwarz in connection with Reiner Pommerin, ed., *Adenauer und die Hohen Kommissare 1949–1951* (Munich, 1989), 428ff. For a good introduction to the main foreign policy issues of the period see Thomas Alan Schwartz, *America's Germany. John J. McCloy and the Federal Republic of Germany* (Cambridge, MA/London, 1991).

21. Wengst, *Beamtentum*, 108, 253. For details of the changes effected by the law and an evaluation of their actual significance see Reusch, 20–1. The contrasting interpretation provided by Bark and Gress (p. 296) is completely and utterly wrong; they also predate the passage of the Federal Civil Service Law by two years (p. 84).

politicians, who had condemned proposals to promote upward social mobility as "an effort to reduce the educated to the same level as the uneducated,"[22] had successfully fended off what they perceived as an attack on traditional values. In broader terms, the legislative affirmation of the old hierarchy of career tracks also helped shore up the system of social stratification which had been destabilized by the twin shocks of total war and total defeat.

The degree of formal education which individuals acquired *before* entering the public service was now once again the main determinant of their later career chances. Only university graduates were admitted to the highest of the four levels of administrative service, the higher service (*höherer Dienst*). Graduates of the most demanding type of secondary school, the *Gymnasium,* were considered only for positions in the second highest level, the superior service (*gehobener Dienst*). Those with a diploma from another type of high school were limited to jobs in the third level, the intermediate service (*mittlerer Dienst*), and all others were accepted only for positions in the lowest level, the elementary service (*einfacher Dienst*). Exceptions were rare, and advancement from one level to the next was highly unusual, if indeed possible at all. The traditional prescript that those entering the higher administrative service should have a legal degree, a rule which had been relaxed during the Nazi period and the immediate postwar years, now came to be more strictly enforced.[23] The admission of "outsiders" was also restricted.

The successful defense of the traditional system had fundamental consequences not only for the social structure of the civil service, but for civil servants' mentality and self-perception as well. During the Nazi era and the occupation period, the public image of this group had suffered seriously. As a result, the foundations of their proverbial corporatist mentality and the sense of moral superiority which often accompanied it had been severely shaken.[24] Now, however, federal legislation had acknowledged and confirmed their traditional legal and social standing. Civil servants were once again something special, on a different level than the rest of the work force. This affirmation of traditional positions encouraged the revival of a specific group mentality based

---

22. Thus Hans Schuberth (CSU), who castigated the "angestrebte Nivellierung der Gebildeten schlechthin" during a conference of leading representatives of the CDU and the CSU on January 8–9, 1949. Schuberth, born in 1897, was a university graduate and director of the Postal Service for the Bizone since 1947; in the autumn of 1949 he became the first postal minister of the Federal Republic. For the record of the conference see *Die Unionsparteien 1946–1950. Protokolle der Arbeitsgemeinschaft der CDU/CSU Deutschlands und der Konferenzen der Landesvorsitzenden* (Düsseldorf, 1991), 252ff. (the quotation is on p. 333).

23. See Rudolf Morsey, ed., *Verwaltungsgeschichte. Aufgaben, Zielsetzungen, Beispiele* (Berlin, 1977), 241–2. The remarks there relate to the situation in the federal administration; a similar development occurred in most state administrations. The central role of the *Juristenmonopol* in administrative practice in the 1950s is also stressed by Reusch, 21.

24. See Garner, "Zerschlagung," 63ff., 91ff.

on elements of the old corporatist outlook. Even the undemocratic concept of the civil servant as the incarnation of the "idea of the state," transcending party politics and the constitution, regained some of its former influence. This group mentality fostered persistent efforts to emphasize and bolster the financial and social line dividing civil servants from "ordinary" employees.[25]

2.

When setting up the new federal ministries, Konrad Adenauer and his political allies gave priority to hiring former civil servants from the higher levels of the Prussian and Reich ministries. This decision was prompted in part by the desire to take advantage of the years of experience which such persons had acquired in ministerial work, so that a well-functioning administration could be established as quickly as possible. But party-related motives and power politics also played an obvious role.

A closer look at Konrad Adenauer's methods of operation shows that these often conflicting goals were in practice pursued simultaneously. He repeatedly emphasized his determination to restore order in the public administration by rebuilding a career civil service comprised of well-trained experts who were politically neutral. Such assertions were often accompanied by the accusation that his political opponents—and most particularly the Social Democratic Party (SPD)—were not advocating more flexible personnel guidelines because they were truly interested in democratization, but because they were eager to hoist their own supporters into administrative positions, regardless of qualification. Sources that have become available in the last few years reveal, however, that Adenauer often failed to heed the principles he espoused in public. In the years between 1946 and 1949, for example, when he was head of the CDU in the Rhineland, he consistently endeavored to have CDU members appointed to key posts in public administration. In such matters, Adenauer was much more purposeful than many of his political opponents, because he had a clear sense of the political significance of personnel decisions: he was convinced that bringing one's influence to bear early on, during the initial process of selecting administrative *personnel*, was the best way to affect the outcome of subsequent administrative *decisions*.[26]

Adenauer and his political allies showed similar resolve when setting up the federal administration. They rejected the widespread view that it would be most sensible to build on the bizonal administration already at work in Frank-

---

25. Inversely, substantial portions of the population harbored considerable animosity toward the civil servants. See, for example, the results of the polls conducted by the Institut für Demoskopie in Allensbach: *Jahrbuch der öffentlichen Meinung 1947–1955* (Allensbach, 1956), 211–2; *Jahrbuch der öffentlichen Meinung 1958–1964* (Allensbach/Bonn, 1965), 348.

26. For some important examples see Garner, "Zerschlagung," 68–9, 98–9.

furt, arguing that much of the civil service personnel employed there had no previous ministerial experience. This situation was, however, to a considerable extent the result of Allied denazification regulations designed to prevent the hiring of politically compromised civil servants. Another factor contributed to the skepticism and animosity with which Adenauer and other conservative leaders viewed the agencies in Frankfurt: they suspected that there were quite a few SPD supporters among the bizonal employees. An alternative presented itself in late 1948: a group of former high-level civil servants from the Reich Ministry of the Interior approached Adenauer and offered him their services. He encouraged them to contact as many former colleagues from the Berlin ministries as possible, and they began to compile personnel lists which could be used to fill future positions. These lists contained information on the age and the religious affiliation of those concerned, the positions they had held until 1945, and the classification they had received during denazification. Adenauer and his aides must have known that the systematic recruitment of such individuals would be controversial. To avoid a possible misunderstanding, a spokesman of the group of Reich civil servants had explicitly pointed out that those involved were "essentially" persons "who had at least had formal connections to the NSDAP [Nazi Party]," and he emphasized that some of them had held "prominent positions" in the Reich administration until 1945.[27]

The preparations made by these former Reich civil servants influenced personnel policy in Bonn all the more directly, once leading members of the group assumed important positions in the new federal administration. One of them was Hans Ritter von Lex, the first state secretary in the Federal Ministry of the Interior.[28] Another was Dr. Hans Globke, who soon became Adenauer's "most important aide," acting as "virtual head" of the Federal Chancellery from 1949 on. Globke had a voice in all important personnel decisions in the federal ministries and has therefore been characterized as the "key person in setting up the apparatus of state in Bonn."[29]

This was one reason why many regarded Globke as the very personification of Adenauer's personnel policies. The other was that Globke's own career

27. Keßler to Blankenhorn, 25 Jan. 1949: Bundesarchiv Koblenz (hereafter: BAK), B 106/45737. Blankenhorn was Adenauer's personal secretary *(persönlicher Referent)*. See Rudolf Morsey, "Personal- und Beamtenpolitik im Übergang von der Bizonen- zur Bundesverwaltung (1947–1950). Kontinuität oder Neubeginn?," in Morsey, ed., *Verwaltungsgeschichte;* Udo Wengst, *Staatsaufbau und Regierungspraxis 1948–1953. Zur Geschichte der Verfassungsorgane der Bundesrepublik Deutschland* (Düsseldorf, 1984), 89 ff., 135 ff.

28. The state secretary was the highest-ranking civil servant in a ministry and its administrative head. He was also the official representative of the minister.

29. Wengst, *Staatsaufbau*, 143; Klaus Gotto, "Hans Globke (1898–1973)," in Kurt G.A. Jeserich and Helmut Neuhaus, eds., *Persönlichkeiten der Verwaltung. Biographien zur deutschen Verwaltungsgeschichte 1648–1945* (Stuttgart et al., 1991), 467; Hans-Peter Schwarz, *Die Ära Adenauer. Gründerjahre der Republik, 1949–1957* (Stuttgart/Wiesbaden, 1981), 38. See also Arnulf

provided a controversial example of how representatives of the old administrative elite managed to retain their social position in spite of the twofold change in political regimes in 1933 and 1945. Globke had entered the Prussian civil service in 1921, after earning a doctorate in law, and had been transferred to the Prussian Ministry of the Interior in Berlin in 1929. Such an assignment was considered a distinction, indicating good career chances in state administration. When the Prussian and Reich Ministries of the Interior were merged in 1934, Globke was taken into the Reich civil service and put in charge of the section of the ministry handling matters of personal and family legal status (*Personenstandssachen*). One year later he was given the responsibility of co-authoring all papers dealing with the "racial questions" involved in marital law—i.e., questions involving the segregation of those with "Jewish blood" from the "Aryan" majority. From 1936 to 1939 Globke also co-authored all papers on "general racial issues." In collaboration with Dr. Wilhelm Stuckart, state secretary in the interior ministry and an ardent Nazi, he wrote a semi-official commentary on the notorious "Nuremburg Laws." These measures, adopted in the fall of 1935, prescribed the systematic discrimination of the Jewish population in order to "protect German blood" and "German honor." (The very notion of their being "endangered" was grotesque; the Jews comprised less than 1% of the country's inhabitants.) The commentary told the authorities and the courts how this "German racial legislation" was to be applied.[30] Thus Globke was actively involved in organizing the implementation of Nazi racial policy—and the persecution of the Jews which it entailed.

Most accounts of Globke's conduct during the Third Reich fail to mention that, unlike most civil servants, he had not acted under economic pressure. He would not have lost all means of support had he refused to cooperate and possibly risked dismissal. On the contrary, he had good connections to private business circles and married the daughter of an industrialist in 1934.[31] Nonetheless, Globke chose to remain in the service of the Reich Interior Ministry. After the beginning of the Second World War, he applied his

Baring, *Im Anfang war Adenauer. Die Entstehung der Kanzlerdemokratie,* 2nd ed. (Munich, 1982), 15ff. For the following see: Gotto.

30. Stuckart-Globke, *Kommentare zur deutschen Rassengesetzgebung, Bd. I: Reichsbürgergergesetz vom 15. September 1935. Gesetz zum Schutze des deutschen Blutes und der deutschen Ehre vom 15. September 1935. Gesetz zum Schutze der Erbgesundheit des deutschen Volkes (Erbgesundheitsgesetz) vom 18. Oktober 1935. Nebst allen Ausführungsvorschriften und den einschlägigen Gesetzen und Verordnungen erläutert von Dr. Wilhelm Stuckart, Staatssekretär, und Dr. Hans Globke, Oberregierungsrat, beide im Reichs- und Preußischen Ministerium des Innern* (Munich/Berlin, 1936).

31. Although Ulrich von Hehl pointed this out in 1979, this important fact has gone unmentioned in later accounts. See Ulrich von Hehl, "Hans Globke (1898–1973)," in *Zeitgeschichte in Lebensbildern. Aus dem deutschen Katholizismus des 19. und 20. Jahrhunderts,* vol. 3, eds. Jürgen Aretz, Rudolf Morsey, Anton Rauscher (Mainz, 1979), 251. Von Hehl does not, however, specify the year of marriage; it can be found in *Wer ist wer?,* vol. I (Berlin, 1962), 431.

legal talents to solving problems in new areas: he assumed responsibility for the issues involved in organizing the administration of the annexed and occupied territories.[32]

Although Globke's controversial past was public knowledge in 1949, Konrad Adenauer had "no reservations whatsoever" about making him "his closest aide and adviser." In the years to follow, the chancellor continued to defend him "against every attack."[33] There seem to be three main reasons for this. First, the two men shared a common background and outlook inasmuch as both had been shaped by the Catholic environment of the Rhineland. Second, Globke undoubtedly had a remarkable talent for organization. He showed considerable proficiency in managing the establishment of the federal ministries and in coordinating the operations of the new administration—quietly, effectively, and according to Adenauer's wishes. Third, Globke was not only capable and diligent, he was absolutely dedicated to serving the chancellor. Indeed, Globke's controversial past left him virtually no leeway for independent political action or disloyalty. He "was only tenable" in his prominent position "as long as Adenauer acted to shield him."[34]

---

32. Globke's defenders argue that the preface of the commentary, which contains a blatant celebration of Nazi race ideology, was penned solely by State Secretary Stuckart; that Globke never belonged to the Nazi Party (he had, however, tried to join in 1940, with Stuckart's support, but his membership application was rejected by Martin Bormann); that Globke later declared that he had only agreed to co-author the commentary because he wanted to use the chance to prevent a more stringent interpretation of the Race Laws by anti-Semitic ideologues; and that he maintained regular contact with the Catholic bishop of Berlin, providing him with confidential political information from within the Reich administration. These arguments are advanced in particularly detailed fashion in Klaus Gotto, ed., *Der Staatssekretär Adenauers. Persönlichkeit und politisches Wirken Hans Globkes* (Stuttgart, 1980). Bark and Gress also devote considerable attention to these aspects of the case (pp. 85, 247–8); their assertion that Globke worked in the Reich Ministry of Justice is erroneous.

33. Hans-Peter Schwarz, *Die Ära Adenauer. Epochenwechsel, 1957–1963* (Stuttgart/ Wiesbaden, 1983), 214. See also Henning Köhler, *Adenauer. Eine politische Biographie* (Berlin/ Frankfurt a.M., 1994), 725–31 (this recent work represents an important addition to the historical literature on Adenauer's policies in general, offering many new insights and a stimulating critical discussion of judgments in earlier works.) In 1953, Globke was officially named state secretary of the Federal Chancellery (it is notable that this decision was not announced until after the parliamentary elections held that year). He retained this position until Adenauer resigned in October 1963.

34. Wengst, *Staatsaufbau,* 143. In the last several years, the conflict that once raged over the problem of an adequate historical evaluation of Globke's activities during the Third Reich gradually subsided, and it seemed as though elements of a general consensus were emerging. However, the most recent account to be published should provoke further debate. Manfred Kittel tries to put Globke's commentary on the German Race Laws of 1935 in a more favorable light by calling the work "a scholary commentary" ("einen wissenschaftlichen Kommentar")—as though it were somehow possible to reconcile the concept of scholarship with the authoring of a manual on the practical application of Nazi race ideology. In addition, Kittel does not mention that Globke

In addition to Globke and Ritter von Lex, numerous other former civil servants from the Prussian and Reich ministries had been hired by the federal administration since 1949. Many initially worked at subordinate posts, yet growing numbers were employed in the politically influential position of ministerial department head (*Abteilungsleiter*). As early as August 1950, 47.2% of all department heads were former Reich civil servants; an additional 22.9% had been civil servants in ministries at the state level or in other areas of administration prior to 1945. After 1950, the percentage of department heads who had once worked in Reich ministries rose even further. One factor contributing to this increase was the hiring of "a considerable number of civil servants who had held high-level positions at the end of the Third Reich."[35]

Administrative experience and professional qualifications were by no means the only criteria used in selecting ministerial personnel. Party politics also played an obvious role. Rudolf Morsey points out that the "flood of applicants for the federal service" offered "optimal recruitment possibilities."[36] But figures on the political affiliation of the department heads in the federal ministries reveal that supporters of the government parties predominated overwhelmingly. As of February 1953, 74% of the department heads can be identified as members or supporters of a particular political party. Of this group, less than 5% were affiliated with the SPD. Almost two-thirds are known to have been members or supporters of one of the governing parties: approximately 53% CDU/CSU, 6.5% FDP, and 4% DP. Only the remaining 32% were regarded as neutral.[37]

Particular controversy was sparked by the manner in which the Adenauer government dealt with the political problems inherent in appointing former Nazi Party members as civil servants in the ministries. Everyone knew that only a portion of them had joined the NSDAP out of conviction; many had become members for opportunistic reasons or because they were pressured to do so. Therefore most experts considered it justifiable—and sensible—to rehire qualified civil servants who had only been nominal party members to fill less profiled

---

wrote and published the commentary in collaboration with a prominent National Socialist. Other aspects of Kittel's monograph have already sparked considerable controversy, in particular his thesis that West German society did a much more adequate job of coming to terms with the Nazi legacy during the Adenauer years than previously believed. See Manfred Kittel, *Die Legende von der "Zweiten Schuld." Vergangenheitsbewältigung in der Ära Adenauer* (Berlin/Frankfurt a.M., 1993), 80–6 (the quotation is on p. 80).

35. Wengst, *Staatsaufbau*, 177–8; see Gerold Ambrosius, "Funktionswandel und Strukturveränderung der Bürokratie 1945–1949: Das Beispiel der Wirtschaftsverwaltung," in Heinrich August Winkler, ed., *Politische Weichenstellungen im Nachkriegsdeutschland 1945–1953* (Göttingen, 1979), 193.

36. Morsey, "Personal- und Beamtenpolitik," 224.

37. See Wengst, *Staatsaufbau*, 175–6. Unfortunately, he does not state the absolute numbers involved.

positions (such as *Referent*).[38] In 1950, a speaker of the SPD opposition in the Bundestag stressed that his party explicitly supported such a policy.[39] It was commonly assumed, however, that particularly stringent standards would have to be applied when filling the higher positions in the ministries.

The Adenauer government showed little sensitivity in this respect. If it seemed obvious that a former party member would not be considered for a post as state secretary, more generosity was displayed when filling positions on the level immediately below. As early as August 1950, more than a quarter of all department heads in the federal ministries were former NSDAP members; in addition, three officials in personnel departments had also belonged to the Nazi Party.[40] The federal minister of the interior, Gustav Heinemann (CDU), tried to halt this development but failed due to resistance from his fellow cabinet members. They were unwilling to agree to a clearly worded policy resolution which Heinemann had drafted, siding instead with the chancellor, who preferred to decide "from case to case."[41] Under these circumstances, the number of former party members in politically influential positions increased steadily. "No less than 60%" of all department heads appointed between August 1950 and February 1953 had belonged to the NSDAP. In 1951, an ex-party member was appointed state secretary; a second such appointment occurred in 1952.[42]

Adolf Arndt, a well-informed representative of the SPD, had already taken issue with the government's recruitment policies in July 1950. Speaking to the Bundestag, he criticized what he perceived to be an esprit de corps among the former ministerial civil servants from Berlin. It was all too often strengthened and reinforced by a feeling of solidarity among the politically compromised, he observed. In some areas, including the Foreign Service, Arndt saw a "tacit alliance of former members of the NSDAP." These employees did their best to hold open positions for former colleagues and to turn away other applicants. Furthermore, Arndt charged, "some key positions" in federal ministries were held by men "who were filled with resentment against those who were politically uncompromised or who had been persecuted" and who were therefore

---

38. A *Referent* was a subject-matter specialist employed in one of the sections of a ministry *(Referate)* and subordinate to the section head *(Referatsleiter)*. Several sections constituted a branch *(Unterabteilung)*, and the branches were in turn grouped into departments *(Abteilungen)*.

39. See *Verhandlungen des Deutschen Bundestages, Stenographische Berichte* (hereafter cited as: *DBT, StBer*), 12 July 1950, 2631. The SPD representative went on to declare that if this stance should lead to "attacks" on the party from forces domestic or foreign, he and his colleagues were prepared to "take this in their stride."

40. See Wengst, *Staatsaufbau*, 179.

41. *Die Kabinettsprotokolle der Bundesregierung,* vol.2, 1950 (Boppard am Rhein, 1984), 667–8.

42. Wengst, *Staatsaufbau*, 179–80.

doing their best to thwart efforts to hire such persons now working in administrations at the state level.[43]

Arndt's criticism did not appear to make much of an impression on the government, but a series of articles in the *Frankfurter Rundschau* in 1951 finally triggered hectic activity. The newspaper examined the recruitment policy of the Foreign Office and made a number of disturbing accusations. The Bundestag appointed an investigating committee to look into the matter. The committee's report, which was adopted unanimously, declared that some of the information in the newspaper articles was exaggerated or false.[44] Beyond that, however, the report noted that there definitely were problems which would have to be addressed. First, the head of the personnel department of the Foreign Office was not only a former NSDAP member, but had also worked "in the personnel department of the Foreign Office under Ribbentrop." The committee considered this "highly questionable." Second, the committee was convinced that "a group of former National Socialists has been at work" trying "to reactivate" persons for the Foreign Service "who had by no means displayed irreproachable behavior during the National Socialist regime." "The immediate superiors" of this group knew about and tolerated its actions. Third, the Foreign Service had already hired some former career diplomats who had definitely been more than nominal members of the NSDAP. They had once worked with obvious dedication to further Nazi foreign policy goals. One, for example, had served in the Political Department of the "Ribbentrop Ministry" and participated in the conception of Nazi foreign propaganda; another had not only helped formulate the country's "European policy" during the National Socialist era, but had even been involved in the organization of Jewish deportations abroad. Fourth, applicants not belonging to the in-group of former career diplomats had been turned down summarily. The investigating committee had received "a large number of complaints" in this regard.

Since Konrad Adenauer was in charge of foreign policy, he bore the political responsibility for this situation. In 1949, he had directed that the Foreign Service be set up as a department within the Federal Chancellery; after an independent ministry of foreign affairs had been established in 1951, Adenauer had assumed the office of foreign minister while continuing to serve as chancellor.[45] When responding to the report of the investigating committee, Adenauer obviously felt that a good offense was the best defense. Thus the chancellor claimed in his speech to the Bundestag on October 22, 1952, that the reputation

---

43. *DBT, StBer,* 12 July 1950, 2631–2.

44. The report was dated June 18, 1952, and published as *DBT, Drucksache (Ds.) 3465.* The following quotations are on pp. 9, 12, 36, 40.

45. One of Adenauer's closest aides, Herbert Blankenhorn, had been a career diplomat from 1929 to 1945. From 1949 on he played an important role in determining who was hired for the new Foreign Service. See Wengst, *Staatsaufbau,* 184–9; Baring, 34ff.

of the Federal Republic had not been damaged by the personnel policy of the Foreign Office, but rather by "the excessive attacks by the press." He further maintained that these "attacks" had served to disrupt the previously "gratifying development" of the office and had "repeatedly . . . hampered the effectiveness of this instrument of German foreign policy." Adenauer declared that if this were to occur again in the future, he would take legal action to have offenders prosecuted for "libel of the Foreign Service." Public "attacks on members of the civil service" would not be tolerated.[46]

Adenauer justified the policy of rehiring civil servants from the Ribbentrop Ministry, contending that it would have been impossible to proceed any other way. "One can not set up a Foreign Office without filling at least the leading positions with people who understand something about how things used to be done in the past." During the parliamentary debate, however, a well-informed FDP representative pointed out that the issue at hand was by no means a matter of a few individuals in leading positions: of the 82 section heads in the new Foreign Ministry, he declared, 64 had belonged to the Foreign Service prior to 1945 (78%). After repeated queries from the opposition, Adenauer finally revealed the percentage of former NSDAP members among the civil servants in the Foreign Office: "from the specialists in the sections (*Referenten*) on up, . . . approximately 66% had formerly belonged to the Nazi Party." The proportion was thus even higher than during the Third Reich, since recent research has shown that 59% of such civil servants were NSDAP members as of 1940 (71 of 120).[47] Adenauer showed little interest in further debate on such questions. Instead, he demanded a stop to the practice of "sniffing around for Nazis."

It is still too early for a definitive statement about the extent and significance of the controversial lines of personnel continuity extending across the political rift of 1945. Our picture of the situation is incomplete, for many important aspects have yet to be investigated. We know little, for example, about personnel movements in the federal ministries after 1952–53—and even less about the social and political backgrounds of the civil servants in positions below the level of department head. A broader focus seems all the more important, as

---

46. *DBT, StBer,* 22 Oct. 1952, 10724–5. For the following, including the Adenauer quotes, see pp. 10735–6, 10742.

47. See Hans-Adolf Jacobsen, "Zur Rolle der Diplomatie im 3. Reich," in Klaus Schwabe, ed., *Das Diplomatische Korps 1871–1945* (Boppard am Rhein, 1985), 187. See now also the recent English-language treatment by Gordon A. Craig, "Konrad Adenauer and His Diplomats," in Craig and Francis L. Loewenheim, eds., *The Diplomats, 1939–1979* (Princeton, 1994). That account makes no mention of the developments discussed here, however, and in fact comes to the opposite conclusion that, during the first formative years, "former diplomats . . . were exceptions to the general rule" (p. 205).

some individuals who were clearly compromised were deliberately assigned to relatively low-ranking positions at first in order to avoid public censure. They were later promoted to higher and more influential positions. One case in point is former Major General Werner Kreipe, one-time air force chief of staff and recipient of the "Blood Medal," which Hitler commissioned to honor those early Nazi supporters who took part in his attempted Putsch in Munich in 1923. Kreipe was hired by the Federal Ministry of Transportation in 1951 and first given a position as a salaried employee. After the political controversy sparked by his appointment died down, he moved further and further up the career ladder. Finally, in 1961, he was named head of the ministry's department for air transportation affairs and assistant chairman of the board of directors of the government-owned Lufthansa Airlines.[48]

The investigation of such phenomena should not, however, distract attention from an equally significant form of social continuity—namely the line that bridged not only the political rift of 1945, but the cleft of 1933 as well. Militant National Socialists who first received positions in the Reich administration after January 30, 1933, or who were promoted to leading posts soon afterward on the strength of their political convictions played no significant role in the Bonn ministries. Instead, the former NSDAP members in the federal agencies were to a considerable extent members of an older administrative elite which had evolved prior to 1933—and which, on the whole, continued to serve under the National Socialists. Most members of that older elite adapted quickly to the new political circumstances in 1933, whether out of nationalist conviction, opportunism, or fear. After 1945, they once again adjusted their behavior to suit the change in the political environment.[49]

Bonn's personnel policy was oriented to the past, in that priority was given to reinstating members of the old administrative elite. Yet it was very "modern" in one crucial point: the influence of the political parties, already reflected in the affiliations of higher-ranking civil servants in the early 1950s, was to increase perceptibly during the course of the decade. It gradually extended into the middle and lower levels of the ministerial bureaucracy as well. Although those involved took pains to transact such matters behind the scenes,

---

48. See the file in the "Sammlung Personalia" of the Archiv der sozialen Demokratie, Bonn (hereafter: AsD); *Die Kabinettsprotokolle der Bundesregierung,* vol. 4, 1951 (Boppard am Rhein, 1988), 259.

49. Further research on these topics should also include comparisons with developments in state and local administration, about which we know very little as yet. One important study now underway investigates the social composition of portions of the administrative elite in the states of Baden and Württemberg from 1930 to 1952. For first results see Michael Ruck, "Administrative Eliten in Demokratie und Diktatur. Beamtenkarrieren in Baden und Württemberg von den zwanziger Jahren bis in die Nachkriegszeit," in Cornelia Rauh-Kühne and Michael Ruck, eds., *Regionale Eliten zwischen Diktatur und Demokratie. Baden und Württemberg 1930–1952* (Munich, 1993).

considerations of party loyalty played such an obvious role in many hiring and promotion decisions that the issue had become a subject of public debate by the end of the 1950s.[50] The mounting criticism had little practical effect, however: in the years to follow, the party organizations would lose their remaining inhibitions and intervene actively in personnel decisions at all levels of the ministerial bureaucracy.[51]

Viewed from this perspective, the 1950s were a decade with a dual character. On the one hand, representatives of the old administrative elite gathered once again in Bonn and re-formed their ranks. On the other hand, the recruitment criteria which came to prevail gradually led to the formation of a new administrative elite subject to growing party domination and thus far less autonomous than the old civil service elite had once been.

3.

"The crassest error in a democratic sense was Article 131 of the Basic Law, along with the laws and ordinances regulating its implementation. The Federal Republic has been suffering under the consequences since its founding and will long continue to do so."[52] This pointed judgment by Karl-Hermann Flach, an influential journalist and politician on the left wing of the FDP, conveys an impression of the intensity with which contemporaries disputed the issue during and well beyond the 1950s. Even today the discussion of this topic is far from dispassionate, in part due to misconceptions and false information. For example, a well-respected and widely read introduction to postwar German history characterizes the legislation based on Article 131 as having applied to "members of the public service who had lost their positions due to denazification"; the provisions are said to have resulted in these persons regaining "their pension entitlements and the opportunity to work for the state." This account touches on an unquestionably important aspect of the topic, but mentions only

---

50. See, for example, the influential critique of party patronage practices since 1949 written by Theodor Eschenburg, *Ämterpatronage* (Stuttgart, 1961).

51. For the extent and consequences of such practices in the 1960s and 1970s see Kenneth H.F. Dyson, *Party, State, and Bureaucracy in Western Germany* (Beverly Hills/London, 1977); Dyson, "Die westdeutsche 'Parteibuch'-Verwaltung. Eine Auswertung," *Die Verwaltung* 12 (1979); Klaus Seemann, "Die Politisierung der Ministerialbürokratie in der Parteiendemokratie als Problem der Regierbarkeit," *Die Verwaltung* 13 (1980); Renate Mayntz and Hans-Ulrich Derlien, "Party Patronage and Politicization of the West German Administrative Elite 1970–1987: Towards Hybridization?" *Governance* 2 (1989).

52. Karl-Hermann Flach, *Erhards schwerer Weg* (Stuttgart, 1963), 23. The Basic Law was the provisional constitutional document worked out in 1948–49 by the Parliamentary Council, which was made up of 65 representatives of the states in the three Western zones. Leading West German politicians had decided to reserve the term *constitution* for a later document which would apply to Germany as a whole.

one feature of a series of measures with several goals and complex social ramifications.[53]

What was really at issue? When the Parliamentary Council drew up the Basic Law, it stipulated in Article 131 that the Bundestag had to pass legislation regulating the legal status of those persons "who on May 8, 1945, were employed in the public service . . . and who till now have not been employed or are not employed in a position corresponding to their former position." This provision affected a variety of groups: former employees of the Reich and of the state of Prussia whose employing agency no longer existed; former professional soldiers as well as civilians who had worked in the Wehrmacht administration; expellees and refugees (i.e., those who had been expelled from the former Eastern provinces and the Sudetenland or had fled from the Soviet zone) who had previously worked in the public service; and, finally, public employees who had once worked in the area now constituting the Western zones but lost their positions in the course of denazification.[54] In addition, Article 131 stipulated that federal lawmakers had to pass legislation regulating the legal status of those persons "who on May 8, 1945, were entitled to a pension or other assistance and who no longer receive any assistance or adequate assistance." This referred mainly to pensioners and surviving dependents who no longer received the customary support payments because the appropriate regional authorities had ceased to exist or, as was the case in the Soviet zone, because they now refused to honor such claims. This second part of Article 131 also pertained to a wide variety of groups with very different social and political backgrounds—all the way from widows of prominent Nazis to, say, the impoverished dependents of a mail carrier from East Prussia killed in wartime fighting.[55] In view of the complex nature of the subject and its political explosiveness, the Parliamentary Council deliberately refrained from making any decision as to how these various groups were to be treated. Instead, it left the matter entirely up to the future Bundestag.

---

53. Christoph Kleßmann, *Die doppelte Staatsgründung. Deutsche Geschichte 1945–1955.* 5th, revised and expanded ed. (Göttingen, 1991), 254. So far there has been no detailed research on the social consequences of this legislation. For a first brief discussion see Wunder, 164–7. Unfortunately, Wunder's account is of limited usefulness, because important details—including statistics—are presented without any reference to the sources from which they have been drawn. The English-language literature contains at most very short accounts of this legislation, which is probably why its significance for West German politics and society tends to be overlooked. The most reliable and detailed presentation is still the summary published in 1953 by Brecht, "Personnel Management," 269–71.

54. See *Parlamentarischer Rat. Verhandlungen des Hauptausschusses* (Bonn, 1948/49), 493ff. For more on the genesis of Article 131 see *Jahrbuch des öffentlichen Rechts,* N.F 1 (1951), 858ff.; Werner Sörgel, *Konsensus und Interessen. Eine Studie zur Entstehung des Grundgesetzes für die Bundesrepublik Deutschland* (Opladen, 1985), 120ff.; Wengst, *Beamtentum,* 60ff.

55. Although the legislative treatment of this delicate subject is not without interest, the following remarks will concentrate on those measures designed to reintegrate former employees into the public service.

At the time, no one knew how many people were affected by Article 131, and there was no reliable information on the social and political structure of the group. In order to obtain dependable data, the federal government commissioned the Statistical Office of the Combined Economic Area (i.e., the three Western zones) to take a detailed survey of those involved. The final results were presented in a report dated June 10, 1950. It circulated in only a limited number of copies and, until now, has never been analyzed by historians.[56] The report stated, first of all, that 430,306 persons were affected by Article 131 as of February 1, 1950. These "131ers," as they soon came to be called, were divided into two groups: 344,927 former employees and 85,379 entitled to pensions or other forms of assistance (including surviving dependents). The Statistical Office emphasized, though, that the number of persons involved was actually even greater. Despite extensive efforts, it had "by no means" been possible to find and register all those affected; the figures in some categories were regarded as "much too low." Moreover, these statistics did not include the large number of former employees and pensioners who had once worked for the Reich Railway and the Reich Postal Service. These individuals had been registered separately by the federal railway and postal administrations, which had reported directly to the Federal Ministry of the Interior.[57] In addition, the Statistical Office had primarily confined its efforts to registering those who had belonged to the public service for ten years or more.

As shown in table 1, the official statistics divided the former public employees into two groups: "former professional soldiers" and "displaced civil servants" (*verdrängte Beamte*). Both terms were diffuse and misleading, as the further breakdown of these categories reveals. Particularly questionable was the decision to subsume those dismissed during denazification in the Western zones—the so-called "denazified 131ers"—under the category of "displaced civil servants." The latter expression was commonly understood as referring to civil servants from the Soviet zone and the former Eastern territories; thus the unusual manner in which the statisticians defined these terms served to remove the "denazified 131ers" from the public eye. There is reason to believe that this did not happen inadvertently. A similar predilection for misleading terminology can be observed in another presentation which the Statistical Office published

---

56. See *Verdrängte Beamte und ehemalige Wehrmachtsangehörige. Statistische Erhebung über den unter Artikel 131 des Grundgesetzes fallenden Personenkreis. Endgültige Gesamtergebnisse für das Bundesgebiet.* Herausgeber: Statistisches Amt des Vereinigten Wirschaftsgebietes, mit der Führung der Statistik für Bundeszwecke beauftragt, June 10, 1950 (Statistische Berichte. VII/7/2), in: Archives of the Federal Statistical Office, Wiesbaden (hereafter cited as: *Verdrängte Beamte*).

57. Ibid., 4. The railway and postal services registered approximately 81,000 persons: circa 12,800 had been dismissed during denazification; 9,000 were being paid a monthly allowance and were to be given a new position as soon as one became available *(Wartegeldempfänger)*; and 60,000 were retired employees, widows, or orphans. See "Bundesfinanzminister an Kabinettsmitglieder, 19 May 1950, Anlage": BAK, B 136/507.

TABLE 1. Number and Structure of Those Falling under Article 131 of the Basic Law, as of February 1, 1950. Final Results for the Area of the Federal Republic

Total Number		**430,306**
comprised of:		
—Former employees		344,927
—Recipients of pensions and other forms of assistance		
(including surviving dependents)		85,379
Structure of the former employees:		
1. "Former professional soldiers"		
—Professional commissioned officers	33,535	
—Professional non-commissioned officers	70,932	
—Professional officers of special armed units	9,835	
—Male and female officers of the Reich Labor Service	14,808	
—Civil servants who had worked in the administration		
of the Wehrmacht or the Reich Labor Service	18,485	
Total "former professional soldiers"	147,595	(42.8%)

2. "Displaced civil servants" (in reality: former employees of public enterprises and administrative units)

—Manual workers and salaried employees		33,397	
—"Displaced civil servants"		163,935	
comprised of:			
—Expellees	76,389 (46.6%)		
—"Other immigrant civil servants"	25,208 (15.4%)		
(esp. refugees from East Berlin and Soviet Zone/GDR)			
—Civil servants whose former employing agency no longer exists	6,970 (4.3%)		
—Civil servants dismissed in the course of denazification	55,368 (33.8%)		
Total "displaced civil servants"		197,332	(57.2%)
Former employees, total		344,927	(100.0%)

Sources: Verdrängte Beamte und ehemalige Wehrmachtsangehörige. Statistische Erhebung über den unter Artikel 131 des Grundgesetzes fallenden Personenkreis. Endgültige Gesamtergebnisse für das Bundesgebiet. Herausgeber: Statistisches Amt des Vereinigten Wirtschaftsgebietes, mit der Führung der Statistik für Bundeszwecke beauftragt, 10 June 1950 (Statistische Berichte. VII/7/2), pp. 3, 5–6, in: Archives of the Federal Statistical Office, Wiesbaden; calculations based on these data.

in early 1950. In an article on the preliminary results of the survey, the percentage of "denazified" civil servants had been computed in a way that made it seem considerably smaller than it actually was.[58]

Table 1 contains newly calculated figures on the relative size of this group, showing it to be larger than historians have previously assumed. But even these statistics offer only a partial answer to the controversial question as to the degree to which the 131ers were politically compromised. Further significant information can be found in the appendix to the report compiled by the Statistical Office: it contains detailed figures revealing how those registered had been classified during denazification.[59] Since 1946, denazification involved the investigation of an individual's past by a special prosecutor's office and, in many cases, a subsequent hearing before a tribunal or panel of jurors. This process resulted in classification based on a system of five categories: I. major offenders (war criminals); II. offenders (activists, militarists, and profiteers—i.e., active participants or supporters of National Socialism, or recipients of excessive or unjust profits); III. lesser offenders (a probationary group, mainly for activists who could be expected to fulfill their duties as citizens of a peaceful democratic state after proving themselves in a period of probation); IV. followers (those who had belonged to the NSDAP or had been official candidates for party membership but were never more than nominal Nazis); V. exonerated persons (those who, in spite of formal membership or candidacy, had been involved in active resistance against the National Socialist regime and therefore suffered disadvantages). Finally, persons whose answers to the obligatory written questionnaire provided no grounds for suspecting any National Socialist activity were normally subject to no further examination and referred to as "not affected" (by denazification legislation).[60]

An evaluation of these statistics reveals a complex mixture of politically compromised and uncompromised persons in *all subgroups* of the 131ers. First, even among the "denazified civil servants"—those 55,368 persons who had been dismissed in the course of denazification in the Western zones because they were considered serious political offenders—only 83.3% had been

---

58. See *Wirtschaft und Statistik,* N.F. 2 (1950):10. The percentage had been calculated after augmenting the total number of "displaced civil servants" by including groups which most would not have considered to belong to this category. The members of some of these groups were not even civil servants (for example: "salaried employees and manual workers," "relatives of deceased or missing civil servants," or "recipients of pensions or dependents' allowances"). As a result, the percentage of "denazified civil servants" was stated to be 23.1%. It increases to 32.6% if these additional groups are subtracted. The lower, "official" figure has been accepted at face value in the historical literature so far; see, for example, Wunder, 166–7.

59. See *Verdrängte Beamte,* Tables 1c, 11c, and 21c. The following statistics have been computed on the basis of the data in these tables.

60. For a good introductory survey of the course of denazification see Clemens Vollnhals, ed., *Entnazifizierung. Politische Säuberung und Rehabilitierung in den vier Besatzungszonen 1945–1949* (Munich, 1991), 7–64. The work includes a detailed bibliography.

formally classified as politically compromised in subsequent investigations by denazification panels (46,135 in categories I–IV). An additional 10.7% were now viewed as "exonerated" (5,930 persons in category V), and 6.0% had even been declared "not affected" (3,303 former civil servants). Second, the remaining 108,567 "displaced civil servants" (expellees from the Eastern territories, refugees, and civil servants whose employing agency no longer existed) were by no means all uncompromised. Only 54.3% of these individuals were classified as "not affected" or "exonerated," while 33.8% were considered politically compromised (36,654 in categories I–IV). This figure included several war criminals. The percentage of those who were politically compromised was probably even higher, since 254 civil servants submitted no information on the results of their denazification, and another 12,738 (11.7%) were listed as "not classified."

Among the "former professional soldiers," the proportion classified as compromised was distinctly lower. In evaluating these figures, however, two factors must be taken into consideration. First, professional soldiers had traditionally been urged to abstain from party politics, and this notion of propriety continued to influence the behavior of many officers after 1933. Thus many refrained from joining the NSDAP, even though they agreed with its goals and supported its policies in practice. This restraint worked to their advantage after 1945, since party membership was one of the main criteria used to determine political culpability in the denazification process.[61] Second, many denazification panels had no way of verifying the information which officers submitted about their activities during the war. Nevertheless, there was still sufficient evidence to classify 16,172 of the 147,595 professional soldiers and Wehrmacht civil servants as politically compromised (11.0%). That figure included several war criminals. Moreover, the number registered as "not classified" was quite high: 32,428 (22.0%). This means that even at this late date, over one-fifth of the "former professional soldiers" had not yet taken part in the denazification procedure. Thus no definite statement on the degree of their political incrimination can be made.

Two further considerations give reason to view all official figures on the proportion of politically compromised 131ers as minimum values. First, these statistics were compiled on the basis of questionnaires filled out by those falling under Article 131 and gathered with the assistance of their interest groups.[62] Second, research on the history of denazification has shown that the classification standards were relaxed considerably after a short opening phase

---

61. The comparative advantage enjoyed by former professional soldiers in this respect generated strong resentment among other Germans. See Lutz Niethammer, *Entnazifizierung in Bayern. Säuberung und Rehabilitierung unter amerikanischer Besatzung* (Frankfurt a.M., 1972), 387, note 192. (This seminal work was reissued in 1982 as: *Die Mitläuferfabrik. Die Entnazifizierung am Beispiel Bayerns.*)

62. See *Verdrängte Beamte*, 2–3.

in 1946.[63] For example, many denazification panels hesitated to assign civil servants to categories I or II, since these classifications automatically entailed the prohibition of any further employment in the public service. It was often decided to put compromised civil servants in category III, the "probationary group," so as not to deprive them of their previous means of livelihood.

One example may serve to demonstrate how imperfectly such categorizations reflected the complex political realities of the Nazi period. Dr. Werner von Bargen, born in 1898, belonged to the group of career diplomats scrutinized by the investigating committee of the Bundestag in 1951–52. He had entered the Foreign Service in 1925 and joined the Nazi Party as of May 1, 1933. While serving as representative of the Foreign Office in occupied Belgium, von Bargen was involved in the organization of Jewish deportations. In 1943 he advanced to head of the Section for Western Europe in the Political Department of the Foreign Office. Later, however, von Bargen could show that he had been in contact with nationally minded officers connected with the plot to kill Hitler in 1944 (they had hoped to overthrow the Nazis, restore German honor, and—last but not least—salvage their country's standing as a major European power). As a result, the main denazification panel in von Bargen's home town of Stade decided in 1947 to classify him as category V ("exonerated"). Thus he was able to apply for a position in the Foreign Service of the Federal Republic and was reinstated in 1951. The investigating committee of the Bundestag took a sharply different view of his past, however: it considered him "unsuitable for further employment in the Foreign Service . . . in any form." This decision was prompted by several factors, among them: "Only after being confronted with the documents did Dr. von Bargen cease asserting that he could not remember, etc., and give an approximately truthful statement about the role he played in the Belgian Jewish deportations. Even then, his testimony was characterized by many reservations."[64]

In summary, a critical appraisal of the denazification statistics shows that the number of politically compromised 131ers was considerably larger than is suggested by the official percentage figures. Persons with doubtful records were to be found not only among the "denazified civil servants," but in all other subgroups as well. Nevertheless, it is important to keep in mind that many 131ers were not compromised. Thousands had been summarily dismissed from the public service in the Soviet zone, others had been forced to flee from the former

---

63. The most detailed account of this development is still the one provided by Niethammer, 335ff.

64. *DBT, Ds. 3465,* 18 June 1952, 6. In spite of this vote, von Bargen was not dismissed. His career in the Foreign Service ended with a tour of duty as ambassador to Iraq 1960–63. For more on the controversial role which German diplomats played in the organization of the murder of the European Jews see Hans-Jürgen Döscher, *Das Auswärtige Amt im Dritten Reich. Diplomatie im Schatten der "Endlösung"* (Berlin, 1987); Christopher R. Browning, *The Final Solution and the German Foreign Office. A Study of Referat D III of Abteilung Deutschland 1940–43* (New York/London, 1978).

Eastern provinces and were unable to find employment in the Federal Republic. These individuals and their families posed a social problem and, since they soon flocked to the banner of interest groups clamoring for financial compensation, a political one as well.

How did federal legislators deal with this complicated and potentially explosive issue? The "Law Regulating the Legal Status of those Persons Falling under Article 131 of the Basic Law" was promulgated on May 11, 1951. It prescribed far-reaching measures to compel reintegration of the 131ers into the public service. In principle, every person with at least ten years of service was to receive a position "equivalent" to the one held until 1945. To this end, the law mandated that all government units and public enterprises had a "placement obligation" (*Unterbringungspflicht*—literally: "duty to provide accomodation or shelter"). At least 20% of all regular positions had to be reserved for the "participants in the placement program" (*Unterbringungsteilnehmer*); in addition, every unit of the public service was obliged to disburse at least 20% of its total pay expenditures for the salaries of such employees. Any government agency or enterprise failing to fulfill this twofold requirement had to pay a commensurate "compensation fee" to the federal government. Moreover, such units were penalized by the loss of their discretionary powers in personnel matters: until the 20% quotas had been reached, they were obligated to hire "placement program participants" for all positions that became vacant or were newly created. Those 131ers still waiting for placement were to receive a monthly "transitional payment" from the federal government. Finally, the law also provided for pensioners and surviving dependents who were not covered up to that time: if no other government unit in Western Germany was responsible for meeting their claims, the federal government accepted the financial liability.[65]

The law included special regulations addressing the delicate problems posed by the politically compromised 131ers. Closer examination reveals, however, that these provisions were inconsistent and dubious:[66]

---

65. For a useful introduction to this complex piece of legislation see the semi-official commentary: *Gesetz zur Regelung der Rechtsverhältnisse der unter Artikel 131 des Grundgesetzes fallenden Personen. Für den praktischen Gebrauch erläutert von Dr. Georg Anders, Ministerialdirigent im Bundesministerium des Innern,* 2nd ed. (Stuttgart/Cologne, 1952) (hereafter cited as: Commentary Anders). See also the commentaries written by Ambrosius and by von Werder/Ortmann/Otto. For a detailed account of the drafting of the bill and the protracted deliberations in the cabinet and in parliament see Wengst, *Beamtentum,* 152ff. For new insights into the previously neglected but important role of veterans' lobbyists, among them several former generals and admirals, see the perceptive study by James M. Diehl, *The Thanks of the Fatherland: German Veterans after the Second World War* (Chapel Hill/London, 1993), 141ff.

66. The following in contrast to the assessment by Hans-Peter Schwarz, *Epochenwechsel,* 214. He argues that large numbers of politically compromised civil servants were able to gain reinstatement in the 1950s due to the questionable manner in which the courts interpreted the law.

1. The law declared that punishments imposed in the course of denazification were "unaffected" and thus remained in force (sec. 8). But since most of these penalties consisted of temporary demotions or salary cuts for a five-year period, they ran out in 1951–52 anyway. As a result, this section of the law applied essentially to the limited number of individuals who had been permanently dismissed from the public service. An examination of the figures compiled by the Statistical Office shows that this group comprised a mere 0.4% of all cases registered in 1950 (1,227 of the 344,927 former public employees).[67] Dr. Georg Anders, an official in the Federal Ministry of the Interior who wrote an influential commentary on the law, emphasized that hope existed even for these persons. Because the occupying powers had transferred the responsibility for the conclusion of denazification to the state governments, it was now possible for earlier classification decisions to be revised "in accordance with the stipulations of state law." Proceedings completed before 1949 could be reopened, or a pardon could be granted. Anders also pointed out that state legislatures were free to pass new regulations on denazification if they so wished.[68]

At the time Anders wrote his commentary, it was in fact obvious that denazification proceedings conducted under state law had in some cases already resulted in a perversion of the standards which had earlier applied. In 1950, for example, the denazification panel in Hanover had classified Dr. Wilhelm Stuckart, the former State Secretary in the Reich Interior Ministry, as category IV—thus deeming him a mere "follower" with only nominal membership in the Nazi Party. Yet the facts testifying to the contrary were clear. Stuckart had been an ardent Nazi before 1933 and had subsequently taken part in translating his party's racial theories into practical policy. His role in the drafting of the Nuremburg Laws was well known, for example, and his participation in the Wannsee Conference on the "final solution" of the "Jewish question" was documented. Due to the denazification panel's mild ruling in 1950, Stuckart was able to apply for reinstatement in the civil service according to the provisions of the law implementing Article 131. He could not, however, lay claim to the salary of a state secretary, since the panel had "punished" him by demoting

---

We will show, however, that the law itself contained provisions enabling the readmittance of many such individuals from the very start. Nevertheless, the fact remains that many courts did their best to facilitate the return of even more.

67. See *Verdrängte Beamte,* Tables 1c, 11c, 21c.

68. Commentary Anders, 44. Anders, who devoted detailed attention to this question, was himself a 131er. He had joined the NSDAP as of May 1, 1933, and worked as *Ministerialrat* in the Reich Ministry of Justice until 1945; after the end of the war, he was without work for some years. In 1949 he was hired by the Federal Ministry of the Interior and served as *Referent* in the Department for Civil Service Law; during this period he played a major role in drafting the law implementing Article 131. Anders was subsequently promoted to head of this department and, in 1957, appointed state secretary in the interior ministry.

him to the next lower rank, that of *Ministerialdirektor*—still one of the highest positions in German administration.[69]

2. The approximately 55,000 former public employees who had lost their positions during denazification in the Western zones were expressly excluded from participation in the placement program (sec. 63). This did not mean that such individuals could not be rehired, if public employers so desired; but there was no particular advantage to it, insofar as government units were not allowed to take these persons into account when computing the quota of 131ers among their employees. Furthermore, this group received no assistance from the Federal Compensation Agency (*Bundesausgleichsstelle*), which had been set up to aid 131ers who had not yet found an adequate position. In the light of such provisions, the "denazified 131ers" seemed to be at a significant disadvantage. This appearance was deceiving. Another clause of the same section 63 granted them the same claim to monthly transitional payments as the other 131ers. The responsibility for these payments did not, however, lie with the federal government, as in all other cases, but had to be assumed by the former employing agency. As a result, many state and municipal administrations decided to save money by filling as many empty positions as possible with such individuals. This consequence of section 63 was not accidental, nor did it come as a surprise to experts. The sources show that this roundabout solution to the problem of the "denazified civil servants" was in fact discussed and agreed upon behind the scenes during parliamentary deliberations. It was even referred to explicitly on the floor of the Bundestag—though only once, by a representative who apparently violated a tacit agreement that this aspect of the law was not to be debated in public.[70]

3. The law prohibited former members of the Gestapo and the Waffen-SS from participating in the placement measures (sec. 3 subs. 4, sec. 56 subs. 6). However, a provision in a later section of the law determined that this stipulation did not apply to persons who had been transferred to the Gestapo or the Waffen-SS "for official reasons" (*von Amts wegen*) during the Nazi era (sec. 67). This pertained, for example, to a substantial number of the more experienced Gestapo members, since they had worked for the Political Police until 1933 and then been integrated into the newly created Gestapo. In his commentary, Anders stressed that members of the Criminal Police, which had worked closely with the Gestapo, were not affected by any of these provisions. The

---

69. Due to an unexpected twist of fate, the case ended on a different note: before Stuckart's claim could be decided, he died as the result of a traffic accident. Contemporary newspapers contain numerous reports on his controversial denazification proceedings. For assistance in confirming details of the case as well as for additional information I would like to thank Dr. S. Brüdermann of the Hauptstaatsarchiv Hannover, Dr. S.-H. Schmidt of the Landesarchiv Berlin, and Dr. A. Castrup-Steidle of the Archiv der sozialen Demokratie, Bonn.

70. Dr. Miessner (FDP) criticized section 63 because—in his opinion—it did not do enough to rehabilitate the "denazified 131ers." See *DBT, StBer,* 6 Apr. 1951, 5036.

same was true, he stated, for members of the "Reich Security Service" (*Reichs-sicherheitsdienst*). This term was not commonly employed prior to 1945; Anders used it to allude to a particularly sensitive subject which he treated ex-plicitly only in a footnote: the wording of section 67 even opened the door for the reinstatement of former staff members of the *Reichssicherheitshauptamt*, the headquarters of the Nazi "security" apparatus led by Heinrich Himmler.[71]

The law implementing Article 131 sparked heated public debate even before it was promulgated. The problematic way it dealt with politically com-promised employees was only one aspect of the controversy, however. Even more criticism focused on the federal lawmakers' financial generosity. When Interior Minister Heinemann introduced the bill in the Bundestag in 1950, he reminded the representatives that, in addition to the 131ers, "many other groups" were also awaiting federal assistance. He pointed to "the disabled war veterans and victims of bombing, those who lost the savings they held prior to 1945, the victims of Nazi persecution, the persons who were abducted by foreign troops during the war, victims of Allied dismantling of factories, bond creditors, suppliers of the Reich, and, finally, the large number of expellees from the former Eastern territories."[72] But none of the parties in the Bundestag agreed with the moderate financial settlement for the 131ers which the bill con-tained, even though the finance minister spoke strongly in its favor. Instead, they competed with each other to advance proposals for increased benefits. This was true not only of the conservative parties, but of the SPD as well: well-known Social Democrats did their best to distinguish themselves as advocates for the cause of the expellees and professional non-commissioned officers suf-fering under social degradation. Even the Communist Party (KPD), whose speakers had ritually castigated the civil service as a "haven for reactionaries," now demanded more money for the 131ers. The cost of the initial proposal, which the finance minister had endorsed, was to have been 350 million marks a year. After the Bundestag had completed its voting on proposals for increased benefits, the annual cost was projected to be 750 million marks.[73]

When the bill came up for the final vote in the Bundestag on April 10, 1951, the speaker for the SPD, Fritz Erler, voiced his disapproval of the em-bittered public criticism. He granted that "a rather generous settlement" had indeed been reached, and accepted that "some who are themselves in dire straits may be filled with envy when looking at those favored by this law." But envy, asserted Erler, is "always an evil emotion." In the future, priority would have to be given to bringing the other "victims . . . up to the same level that we have

---

71. See Commentary Anders, 33. On the notable degree of personnel continuity between the Political Police and the Gestapo, as well as on the close working relationship between the Gestapo and the ostensibly "unpolitical" Criminal Police, see Robert Gellately, *The Gestapo and German Society. Enforcing Racial Policy 1933–1945* (Oxford, 1990), 50ff., 69ff.

72. *DBT, StBer,* 10 Apr. 1950, 3143.

73. Ibid., 3144; *DBT, StBer,* 6 Apr. 1951, 5026.

granted this particular group."[74] This statement and the results of the following vote belie the common assumption that the 131er legislation was a "reactionary" measure put through by a rightist coalition. On the contrary, the bill received virtually unanimous approval. Not one member of the Bundestag voted against it, and only two abstained.

What was the rationale behind the stance of the SPD and the KPD? After all, both parties had always had a strained relationship to the conservative civil service apparatus, and the active role which state authorities played in the persecution of the Left between 1933 and 1945 had created even further animosity. A closer look at the policy of the SPD, the major opposition party, shows that it appears to have been prompted by several motives, some of which were extremely pragmatic:[75]

— The sheer size of the electoral constituency which the law affected must have been a major consideration. The 131ers and their families numbered well over a million persons, and most were of voting age. Clearly, SPD leadership could not want the conservative coalition to be seen as the sole force endowing this group with long-term financial benefits.

— Influential Social Democrats were concerned that the party would acquire a negative image if it opposed virtually everything the government proposed. Kurt Schumacher, the SPD's forceful and headstrong leader, took every opportunity to emphasize that he disagreed with Konrad Adenauer on nearly all key foreign policy issues. As a counterbalance, SPD representatives in the Bundestag strove to play a constructive role in the resolution of major domestic problems. From the very beginning, Social Democratic leaders left no doubt that they were willing to cooperate with the government on legislation to implement Article 131. During the committee deliberations on the government's draft law, SPD representatives worked resolutely (if often unsuccessfully) to amend it and change its focus.

---

74. *DBT, StBer,* 10 Apr. 1951, 5091. For the following see ibid., 5110.

75. There is no previous scholarly analysis of the motives of the SPD and the KPD. Most authors even fail to mention that the Left supported the 131er legislation. Remarkably, this is true even of the major work on the SPD in this period: Kurt Klotzbach, *Der Weg zur Staatspartei. Programmatik, praktische Politik und Organisation der deutschen Sozialdemokratie 1945 bis 1965* (Berlin/Bonn, 1982). See for the following the—unfortunately brief—records of the SPD executive committee's meetings on 21–22 Jan., 12 March, and 17 Nov. 1949; 24 June and 16 Sep. 1950; and 20–21 Jan., 10 March, and 25 May 1951: AsD, Parteivorstandsprotokolle; the very informative "Rede Dr. Schumacher vor Parteivorstand und Parteiausschuß auf der Tagung vom 14.3.1950 in Bonn": AsD, PV, Schumacher, Q 11; *Die SPD-Fraktion im Deutschen Bundestag. Sitzungsprotokolle 1949–1957,* 1. Halbband, bearbeitet von Petra Weber (Düsseldorf, 1993), pp. LXXXVI, 43–4, 166–7, 179, 208–11, 218, 220, 224–5, 255, 259–60; *DBT, StBer,* 13 Sep. 1950, 3142–61; 14 Dec. 1950, 3988–4000; 5 Apr. 1951, 4984–5017; 6 Apr. 1951, 5020–47; 10 Apr. 1951, 5099–110; *Protokoll der Verhandlungen des Parteitages der Sozialdemokratischen Partei Deutschlands vom 20. bis 24. Juli 1954 in Berlin* (Bonn, [1954]), 306–8.

—Concern over growing support for groups on the radical Right was another important factor. The success of the neo-Nazi Socialist Reich Party was particularly alarming. Although it had just been founded in October 1949, its members soon included two Bundestag representatives and several state legislators.[76] Lobbyists for the 131ers tried to capitalize on nationalist sentiment in a manner quite similar to the radical Right, attacking the new republic for ignoring the plight of those former civil servants and professional soldiers who had served the Reich so faithfully.[77] Viewed against this backdrop, a generous settlement of the 131ers' claims appeared to be an expedient way of thinning the ranks of the economically discontent, thus reducing the number of potential protest voters. Rapid social integration of this large and articulate group would bolster the political stability of the Bonn Republic and help preclude a backslide into the unsettled conditions of the Weimar era. Nevertheless, even if such action seemed prudent, it was still distasteful to many SPD activists. Some leading Social Democrats looked at the situation from a positive angle, however, perceiving it as an opportunity to sow the seeds for future electoral victories. Kurt Schumacher argued that it would be irresponsible to shun the millions who had once belonged to the Hitler Youth, the Nazi Party, and the Wehrmacht officers' corps as though they were all equally guilty. That would drive them into the arms of radical groups on the right and the left, sounding the death knell for democracy in Germany. In his effort to expedite the political integration of these uprooted elements—and broaden the electoral base of the SPD—Schumacher interspersed his socialist rhetoric with recurrent appeals to nationalist sentiment. He condemned the Communists as agents of a foreign power and castigated Konrad Adenauer for allegedly being too cooperative toward the Western powers, even calling him "Chancellor of the Allies" and insinuating that Adenauer had betrayed German interests.[78] SPD leadership complemented this strategy by establishing behind-the-scenes contacts to groups lobbying for the 131ers. Talks with representatives of the

---

76. They had been elected on other tickets and subsequently joined the Socialist Reich Party. In May 1951, the party received 11% of the vote in state elections in Lower Saxony. After lengthy hearings, the Federal Constitutional Court declared the party unconstitutional on October 23, 1952, and decreed its immediate dissolution. See Horst W. Schmollinger, "Die Sozialistische Reichspartei," in Richard W. Stöss, ed., *Parteien-Handbuch. Die Parteien der Bundesrepublik Deutschland 1945–1980,* vol. 2 (Opladen, 1984), 2274–336.

77. For several examples see Wengst, *Beamtentum,* chapter 4.

78. See Klotzbach, 188–236; Schwartz, 55–6, 78–83, 145–6; Dietrich Orlow, "Delayed Reaction: Democracy, Nationalism, and the SPD, 1945–1966," *German Studies Review* 16 (1993): 84–7; Willy Albrecht, ed., *Kurt Schumacher. Reden—Schriften—Korrespondenzen 1945–1952* (Berlin/Bonn, 1985), 153–80, 714–894, 994–8 (for the quotation see p. 732).

nascent confederation of former professional soldiers began as early as 1949 and intensified during parliamentary deliberation on the bill. Subsequently, Schumacher even met secretly with members of the controversial Mutual Aid Society, the veterans' organization of the Waffen-SS.[79]

— The debate over German rearmament, fanned by the outbreak of the Korean War in June 1950 and the resultant heightening of East-West tensions, led Social Democratic leaders to recognize that armed forces would soon be a factor in domestic and foreign policy once again. Although many in the party's socialist rank and file were solidly pacifist, Schumacher and other top SPD officials met secretly with former Wehrmacht generals to discuss the conditions under which both sides could work together to establish a new, democratic army. One major obstacle was obvious: prominent military figures had repeatedly declared that they and their former colleagues deeply resented the way they had been "defamed" and "discriminated against" since 1945. They vehemently rejected the notion that Wehrmacht officers shared a "collective guilt" for German war crimes. Numerous former officers refused to entertain any thought of participating in future defense efforts until the Bundestag settled their claims under Article 131. They asserted that such action was needed to restore their "dignity" and the "equal rights" of which they had been deprived.[80]

— Even among the large majority of civil servants not affected by Article 131, there was a widespread feeling that the issue was of great symbolic importance. Official recognition that former civil servants were still entitled to privileges guaranteed to them by the Reich was deemed necessary to reestablish the "honor" of the professional civil service. Even if they did not share this view, Social Democrats serving in elected office on the local and state levels were dependent on a good working relationship with the bureaucracy. In addition, party representatives in Bonn profited from informal links to civil servants in some of the federal ministries, repeatedly surprising political adversaries with con-

---

79. The press eventually gained knowledge of some of these activities. The ensuing reports led to considerable unrest within the SPD. See Georg Meyer, "Zur Situation der deutschen militärischen Führungsschicht im Vorfeld des westdeutschen Verteidigungsbeitrages 1945–1950/51," in *Anfänge westdeutscher Sicherheitspolitik 1945–1956,* ed. Militärgeschichtliches Forschungsamt, vol. 1, *Von der Kapitulation bis zum Pleven-Plan* (Munich/Vienna, 1982), 639–46; Diehl, 154–6; Albrecht, 178–9, 895–8; David Clay Large, "Reckoning without the Past: The HIAG of the Waffen-SS and the Politics of Rehabilitation in the Bonn Republic, 1950–1961," *Journal of Modern History* 59 (1987): 97–102.

80. See *DBT, StBer,* 13 Sep. 1950, 3142, 3145–6, 3149; 5 Apr. 1951, 4983–4; Hartmut Soell, *Fritz Erler—Eine politische Biographie,* vol. 1 (Berlin/Bonn-Bad Godesberg, 1976), 143–7, 570–1; Albrecht, 171, 177–8, 899–901; Diehl, 143–54; Klotzbach, 210–9; Meyer, 652–4, 692–707.

fidential information during parliamentary deliberations. Had the SPD opposed legislation to implement Article 131, the pragmatic efforts to establish a cooperative relationship with the higher ranks of bureaucracy could well have suffered a considerable setback. Members of the party leadership must have perceived this as a serious risk to take. Representatives of the rank and file took a different view, however, censuring what they perceived as privileged treatment of civil servants—who had been restored to their old positions as if they were the only group "who did not lose the war, whereas the other groups have to shoulder the entire burden alone."[81]

— More than a few SPD representatives in the Bundestag felt that it was now time to return to "normality" and, after two decades of political turbulence, let bygones be bygones. This tendency was a response to a widespread mood in West German society. Efforts to come to terms with the past were increasingly unpopular; most wanted to look to the future and forget National Socialism—and denazification as well.[82]

Finally, the law implementing Article 131 was rendered more palatable to many on the Left by coupling it with a restitution act for all former public employees who had been victims of Nazi persecution. Many of the beneficiaries had belonged to the SPD or KPD, or were of Jewish ancestry. The Bundestag approved the restitution act on April 5, 1951, five days before the legislation on Article 131, and the two laws were promulgated simultaneously. When subsequently attacked by representatives of the rank and file for approving the 131er law, SPD leaders defended their position by pointing to the restitution act. The Bundestag would never have passed it, they asserted, had the Social Democrats refused to vote for the 131er bill.[83]

This claim may well have been a conscious misrepresentation of the facts in order to mollify party critics. Recent scholarship has shown that the

---

81. This remark was part of a severely critical speech by a delegate at the SPD national convention in 1954 (it was the first national convention after passage of the 131er legislation). Fellow delegates responded enthusiastically, the speaker was interrupted several times by "strong applause" and "lively calls of approval," as the official record notes. He demanded that the SPD members of the Bundestag cease cooperating with the government in efforts to increase benefits for 131ers even further, closing with the impassioned assertion that this legislation was nothing of which German democracy could be proud. The other delegates demonstrated their concurrence by applauding "for minutes." See *Protokoll der Verhandlungen*, 302–3.

82. This is one important topic addressed by Dr. Norbert Frei (Institut für Zeitgeschichte, Munich) in a major study, [published after completion of this chapter as *Vergangenheitspolitik: Die Anfänge der Bundesrepublik und die NS-Vergangenheit* (Munich, 1996), —Ed.] on the way West German politics dealt with the legacy of the Nazi past in the 1950s. Frei examines a series of legislative, administrative, and judicial decisions, as well as the public debate which they sparked.

83. Thus Walter Menzel, speaking for the SPD leadership at the party's national convention

conservative coalition did not have to be coerced by the Left at all. Indeed, the government began preparing the restitution act back in 1949, parallel to the 131er bill, and conservative leaders were equally interested in passing both measures simultaneously—because, as one historian concludes, the restitution act was "basically an alibi for the settlement of the 131ers' claims, which . . . actually had priority." The government fully realized that, without the accompanying restitution act, its proposals for the 131ers would have met with moral and political censure at home and abroad, since they would have awarded this group more generous compensation than public employees persecuted by the Nazis. Since a general restitution law for all Nazi victims was not on the immediate agenda—for financial reasons, it was said—the government drew up this special measure applying solely to former public employees. It awarded them a considerably higher rate of compensation than that planned for the remaining victims who would be dealt with later—because without such privileged treatment, the beneficiaries of the restitution act of 1951 would still have received less than their former colleagues, the 131ers.[84] Even so, the results of the two laws were not really comparable: the restitution act applied to fewer than one thousand persons, whereas the number of 131ers was more than four hundred times as large.

What precisely were the effects of the 131er legislation on the social structure of the public service in the 1950s? This important question has never previously been investigated by historians. The following remarks cannot provide an exhaustive answer, but highlight key aspects of the complex process which ensued.

Let us begin by examining the situation in two particularly large and important government enterprises, the federal railway and the postal service. A closer look reveals that the number of 131ers was comparatively high even before the law was passed. This was the result of management efforts to accommodate former employees from the Eastern provinces and the Soviet zone as well as the colleagues who had once worked in the corresponding Reich ministries. In addition, both enterprises had already reinstated tens of thousands who had been dismissed during denazification.[85] These policies were motivated

---

in 1954. See *Protokoll der Verhandlungen,* 307.

84. See Constantin Goschler, *Wiedergutmachung. Westdeutschland und die Verfolgten des Nationalsozialismus (1945–1954)* (Munich, 1992), 234–41 (the quotation is on p. 238); Wengst, *Beamtentum,* 222–35.

85. See, also for the following, Kurt Wiesemeyer, "Die wichtigsten Aufgaben im Personalwesen der Post seit 1945," *Jahrbuch des Postwesens* 6 (1955/56); Kurt Wiesemeyer, "Die Personalverhältnisse der Deutschen Bundespost," *Jahrbuch des Postwesens* 10 (1960); "Unterbringungsverfahren der Deutschen Bundesbahn," *Hinweisblatt der Bundesausgleichsstelle* (hereafter cited as: *Hinweisblatt*) 1 (No. 9, 5 Dec. 1952): 1; Josef Fries, "Wiederaufbauprobleme im Personalwesen und ihre Lösung," in *Zehn Jahre Wiederaufbau bei der Deutschen Bundesbahn, 1945–1955* (Darmstadt, 1955); Theodor Mölter, "Personalfragen des höheren Dienstes seit 1945,"

by several factors. Social concern played a role, as did conservative group mentality. Economic considerations were an additional component: such one-time employees were already familiar with technical procedures and did not require extensive training. As a result, the railway and the postal service had already rehired most of their "own" 131ers before the law even went into effect.

Nevertheless, the relatively high number of 131ers in these enterprises was by no means sufficient to fulfill the 20% quotas. At the end of 1951, only 14.2% of all regular positions in the postal service were held by 131ers. At the railway, the percentage was even lower and did not reach a similar level until nine months later (14.1% as of September 30, 1952). By this point in time, the federal railway had reinstated approximately 60,000 former civil servants from the ranks of the 131ers "in regular positions at the level to which they were entitled (or higher)," as the personnel department emphasized.[86]

Such figures already reflected the first results of the law based on Article 131. Starting in 1951, the railway and the postal service had to pay substantial compensation fees and were obligated to fill empty positions with additional 131ers. Most of the persons now hired had no previous work experience in these enterprises; the majority were former non-commissioned officers and Reich Labor Service officers. Other candidates were older, for example those who had once worked in the Wehrmacht administration, and could only be put to use in a narrow range of jobs, for which they had to be specially trained. This hiring policy was not only costly, but left little leeway for recruiting younger employees. Thus the age structure of the staff grew even more unbalanced than it already had been as a result of the war. At the beginning of 1955, only 20.6% of all railway civil servants were under 40 years of age; the proportion of those between 50 and 65 was twice as high (40.6%).[87] The prominent role which 131ers played in parts of the higher service can be illustrated with data from the federal railway in 1955: 85% of all civil servants employed in that career track were 131ers (1,785 of approximately 2,100); 975 of them were "civil servants who had been relieved from their positions due to the denazification laws," the other 810 were "expellees or displaced civil servants."[88]

Information about the implementation of the law in the other parts of the public service is provided by statistics compiled by the Federal Compensation Agency. At the time the law took effect, only the federal administration was in a favorable position with regard to the 20% quotas. Indeed, as of July 1, 1951, the proportion of 131ers in regular civil service positions was already 23.7% (excluding the railway, the postal service, and the Federal Social Insurance Agency

---

in ibid.

86. "Unterbringungsverfahren"; see Wiesemeyer, "Aufgaben," 97; *Hinweisblatt* 2 (1953): 98, 105.

87. Computed on the basis of the data in Fries, 156.

88. Mölter, 162–3. These categories illustrate how self-evidently the personnel department of the postal service distinguished between "denazified 131ers" and "displaced civil servants"—in

for Salaried Employees). In state government, where a considerably larger number of civil servants was employed, the figure comprised only 13.6%, and at the local level a mere 8.3%.[89] The changes which the law brought about in less than four years can be seen by comparing the data for March 31, 1955: at the state and local levels, the quotas had now leaped to 19.0% and 15.1%, respectively, and even at the federal level the percentage had risen further, to 24.3%. The particularly large increase in local administration, where the proportion of 131ers had almost doubled, came as a direct result of the pressure exerted by high compensation fees. Municipalities that refused to hire politically compromised civil servants could literally not afford to maintain such a policy for very long. Initially, five major cities had to pay over one million marks per year; in one case, the annual sum amounted to 2.7 million marks. In the period up until March 31, 1955, state and local units had incurred a total of 190 million marks in compensation fees. City and county governments bore approximately 70% of this burden.[90]

The pressure on the public service subsided only gradually in the later 1950s. The reestablishment of armed forces in 1955 eased the situation considerably, since it provided new jobs for former professional soldiers. But many disabled veterans in this group were no longer suited for active military service and continued to crowd into other branches of the public service.[91] In addition, the federal government amended the 131er law and the regulations on its implementation several times in order to increase the number of those entitled to benefits. Moreover, refugees and displaced persons continued to stream in from East Berlin, East Germany, and the former Eastern provinces, putting in claims for positions in the public service.[92] Finally, on August 21, 1961, the placement obligation which had weighed on government units for more than a decade was lifted. This step was taken in the context of the third supplement to the law, which included generous provisions designed to facilitate the settlement of all cases still open.[93]

Both the increase in the number of persons eligible to make claims and

---

clear contrast to the misleading terminology of the Federal Statistical Office discussed above.

89. The situation varied considerably from region to region. The proportion of 131ers in state government units in Lower Saxony was 27.2%, for example, but only 6.7% in Hamburg and 5.8% in Rhineland-Palatinate. See *Hinweisblatt* 2 (1953): 105–6.

90. Calculated on the basis of the data in *Hinweisblatt* 4 (1955): 86, 149. All further figures have been taken from these sources.

91. For example, 26% of the former professional soldiers and Reich Labor Service officers registered in 1950 were partially disabled veterans. The same is true for 19% of the former civil servants of the Wehrmacht administration. Computed on the basis of the data in *Verdrängte Beamte,* Tables 11c, 21c.

92. See, for example, the yearly accounts written by the personnel department of the postal service: *Deutsche Bundespost, Geschäftsbericht,* 1955: 74; 1956: 85; 1957: 77; 1958: 75.

93. See *Hinweisblatt* 10 (1961): 70–1.

the repeated extension of the range of benefits were results of the political parties' continuing competition for the votes of the 131ers and their families—and of civil servants in general. Each of the supplements to the law was passed immediately prior to a Bundestag election: in July 1953, September 1957, August 1961, and, for the fourth and last time, in July 1965. Each led to a substantial rise in costs. On July 1, 1965, just before the Bundestag cast its final vote on the fourth supplement, a speaker for the CDU/CSU proudly quoted statistics on the financial consequences of the 131er legislation: expenditures up to the end of 1964 had amounted to approximately 19.5 billion marks—not including the substantial expenses incurred by the federal railway and the postal service. Following the approval of the fourth supplement to the law, he stated, the annual costs would "exceed 3 billion marks by far."[94] Two decades later, there were still more than 200,000 persons receiving monthly benefits. The cost to the public was approximately 4 billion marks a year.[95]

4.

After the end of the Second World War, administrators at all levels of government strove to reduce the number of female employees drastically. These efforts continued into the 1950s and were a major determinant of personnel policy. Nonetheless, the literature on the history of the public service in Germany usually fails to make any mention of this essential aspect of postwar development. Nowhere has this important topic been investigated systematically.[96]

In part, the widespread dismissal of female employees was a reaction to

---

94. *DBT, StBer,* 1 July 1965, 9938. The second figure included the expenditures expected to be incurred by the railway and the postal service.

95. See Werner Breidenstein, "Versorgungsempfänger des öffentlichen Dienstes am 1. February 1983," *Wirtschaft und Statistik,* N.F. 35 (1983).

96. The recently published, voluminous manual on administrative history since 1945 is a typical result of the traditional tendency to ignore this dimension of public service development: *Deutsche Verwaltungsgeschichte, Bd. 5: Die Bundesrepublik Deutschland* (Stuttgart, 1987). Some aspects of the topic are referred to in: Wunder, 163; Jutta Beyer and Everhard Holtmann, "'Auch die Frau soll politisch denken'—oder: 'Die Bildung des Herzens'. Frauen und Frauenbild in der Kommunalpolitik der frühen Nachkriegszeit 1945–1950," *Archiv für Sozialgeschichte* 25 (1985): 414–8; Doris Schubert, *Frauen in der deutschen Nachkriegszeit, Bd. 1: Frauenarbeit 1945–1949, Quellen und Materialien* (Düsseldorf, 1984), 101–3, 325–31; Maria Höhn, "Frau im Haus und Girl im Spiegel: Discourse on Women in the Interregnum Period of 1945–1949 and the Question of German Identity," *Central European History* 26 (1993): 65–6; Klaus-Jörg Ruhl, *Verordnete Unterordnung. Berufstätige Frauen zwischen Wirtschaftswachstum und konservativer Ideologie in der Nachkriegszeit (1945–1963)* (Munich, 1994), 117–21. Ruhl's book is one of two recent monographs offering a wealth of information on women's history of the period in general. The second is the impressive study by Robert G. Moeller, *Protecting Motherhood. Women and the Family in the Politics of Postwar West Germany* (Berkeley et al., 1993). See also the useful document collection assembled by Klaus-Jörg Ruhl, ed., *Frauen in der Nachkriegszeit 1945–1963* (Munich, 1988), here: 72ff.

developments during the war. Since 1939, many government agencies had hired women as "temporary helpers" (*Aushilfskräfte*) to replace male employees who had volunteered or been inducted for military service. Often such women did not have the formal education normally required for the position. Thus once the war was over, employers not only discharged women whose male predecessors actually returned, but also tried to find better qualified replacements for many others as well. Frequently social considerations also played a role: most public administrations and enterprises tried to give less qualified and less demanding positions to disabled veterans and crippled fathers, because such individuals had little chance of finding a job in private industry.

In many cases, however, administrators simply wanted to return to "normal" conditions as far as gender was concerned. Women working in "men's positions" (*Männerarbeitsplätze*) were to be "exchanged" for members of the opposite sex (*austauschen*). City councils, district administrations, state employment offices, and regional authorities reviewed the lists of public service positions in their jurisdictions, deciding which were "typically male" and therefore to be officially designated as "exchange positions" (*Austauschplätze*) if women were holding them at the time.[97] The standards applied were based on the personnel structure of the prewar period, in which women had played only a subordinate role: traditionally, the percentage of female employees in the German public service had been low; women rarely attained higher-level positions and were predominantly hired for a limited range of "typically female" jobs, above all in nursing and health care, in secretarial and switchboard services, and in elementary schools. The administrative efforts to enforce a large-scale gender rollback after 1945 were viewed by many as a matter of course. Indeed, there was a historical precedent which many still remembered well: after the First World War, employers had dismissed hundreds of thousands of women who had been newly hired between 1914 and 1918 to work in the public service and in private industry.[98]

Well into the 1950s, officials in many government agencies were particularly determined to force married women out of the service. This policy was often justified by pointing to another historical precedent, the Reich Law on the Legal Status of Female Civil Servants of May 30, 1932. It permitted the dismissal of married female civil servants working in the Reich administration,

---

97. For examples of such policies in the cities of Kamen and Unna see Beyer and Holtmann, 414–7; for Duisburg: Schubert, 102, 330; for Wuppertal: *DBT, StBer,* 2 Mar. 1950, 1490. A more detailed study of such activities based on a wider selection of sources would be a valuable contribution to further research.

98. See especially Susanne Rouette, *Sozialpolitik als Geschlechterpolitik. Die Regulierung der Frauenarbeit nach dem Ersten Weltkrieg* (Frankfurt a.M./New York, 1993). Further details, embedded in a broader panorama of German social history in the postwar years, can be found in: Richard Bessel, *Germany after the First World War* (Oxford, 1993).

even though they had previously been awarded lifelong tenure. Only two conditions had to be met: the agency for which the woman worked had to file a formal request for her discharge, and an examination of her family's total income had to show that her "economic maintenance . . . seems to be permanently ensured." This measure clearly violated the Weimar constitution, which not only stipulated that men and women were basically equal before the law (Article 109), but also expressly prohibited discriminatory measures against female civil servants (Article 128). The 1932 law could only take effect because the Reichstag approved it with the two-thirds majority necessary to pass measures contravening the constitution.[99]

One factor prompting this legislation was obviously the unprecedented economic crisis of the early 1930s. Public criticism of working wives mounted, and they were castigated as "double earners" (*Doppelverdiener*) because their jobs enabled their families to enjoy a double income, whereas millions had none at all. Nevertheless, mass unemployment was by no means the only reason why the Reich law of 1932 came to be passed. It must also be viewed in the context of a long tradition of discriminatory measures against married women in the German public service. In fact, the law was a somewhat milder version of regulations which had been adopted in 1923 and abolished only in 1929. Another important factor was growing pressure exerted by religious forces. The Pope had condemned the increasing number of working mothers in his encyclical *Casti Connubii* on December 30, 1930. He maintained that the chief purpose of marriage was to bring forth children, who were to be raised as good Catholics, so that their number "may daily increase." The concept of women's economic and social emancipation was "a crime," propagated by "false teachers who . . . do not scruple to do away with the honorable and trusting obedience which the woman owes to the man." The married woman should not "be able to follow her

---

99. The law was published in *Reichsgesetzblatt* I, 1932, 245–6. In the past two decades, it has been examined by a number of historians under differing perspectives. See, also for the following, Helen Boak, "The State as an Employer of Women in the Weimar Republic," in W. R. Lee and Eve Rosenhaft, eds., *The State and Social Change in Germany, 1880–1980* (New York et al., 1990); Karen Hagemann, *Frauenalltag und Männerpolitik. Alltagsleben und gesellschaftliches Handeln von Arbeiterfrauen in der Weimarer Republik* (Bonn, 1990), 458–64; Ursula Nienhaus, "'Unter dem Reichsadler'. Postbeamtinnen und ihre Organisation 1908–1933," *1999. Zeitschrift für Sozialgeschichte des 20. und 21. Jahrhunderts* 5 (1990): 72–6; Caplan, *Government*, 97–100; Barbara Greven-Aschoff, *Die bürgerliche Frauenbewegung in Deutschland 1894–1933* (Göttingen, 1981), 172–9; Claudia Hahn, "Der öffentliche Dienst und die Frauen. Beamtinnen in der Weimarer Republik," in *Mutterkreuz und Arbeitsbuch. Zur Geschichte der Frauen in der Weimarer Republik und im Nationalsozialismus* (Frankfurt a.M., 1981), 71–6; Stefan Bajohr, *Die Hälfte der Fabrik. Geschichte der Frauenarbeit in Deutschland 1914 bis 1945* (Marburg, 1979), 180–8; Jill Stephenson, *Women in Nazi Society* (London, 1975), 81–9, 147–58. See also the semi-official yet very helpful survey of the history of women's employment in the German postal service by Josephine Doerner, "Neun Jahrzehnte Frauenbeschäftigung bei der Postverwaltung," *Jahrbuch des Postwesens* 7 (1956/57).

own bent and devote herself to business and even public affairs," but give her full attention to "children, husband, and family." This was "the essential order of the domestic society"; it corresponded with "the natural disposition and temperament of the female sex" and was founded "on the authority and wisdom of God, and so not changeable by public laws or at the pleasure of private individuals."[100] In the months following this papal pronouncement, the influential Catholic Center Party drafted a law permitting the dismissal of married female civil servants and brought it into the Reichstag. Catholic politicians also played a key role in ensuring passage of the bill, negotiating persistently with representatives of other parties until the broad coalition necessary to assure approval with a two-thirds majority had been forged.

Although the provisions of 1932 were cited again and again after 1945 as a historical precedent, they were not actually followed to the letter in the postwar period. Instead, a more drastic version decreed during the Nazi era was applied. As of June 30, 1933, the new Hitler government had prescribed important changes in the wording of the 1932 law: the regulations no longer applied solely to the Reich administration, but to married female civil servants at all levels. Furthermore, government agencies lost their discretionary right to retain female civil servants considered difficult to replace: dismissal upon marriage was now mandatory.[101] These revisions were not only aimed at battling mass unemployment, they were also part of an ideologically motivated effort to reinforce traditional gender roles by compelling married women to leave the work force. Thus it was only consistent that this measure was later incorporated into the German Civil Service Law of 1937 (*Deutsches Beamtengesetz,* DBG), as section 63. Similarly, the wage regulations decreed in 1938 for salaried employees in the public service also mandated that women who married were to be dismissed automatically.[102] During the war, these rules were relaxed or suspended as part of emergency provisions decreed by the Nazi authorities. But after the occupying powers annulled all such emergency provisions in 1945, the regulations dating from 1937–38 came back into force.

Efforts to alter this situation were made only in some states. In the American zone, the impetus came from the military government. When it demanded

---

100. For a reprint of the original translation published by the Catholic church see Claudia Carlen, ed., *The Papal Encyclicals 1903–1939* (Raleigh, NC, 1981), 391–413 (the quotations on pp. 393, 402–3). The Pope re-emphasized this position six months later in the encyclical *Quadragesimo Anno,* see pp. 415–444.

101. See *Reichsgesetzblatt* I, 1933, 433ff.; here: sec. 7.

102. The wage regulations decreed at the same time for manual workers in the public service contained no comparable stipulation—presumably because the prescribed term for giving notice was already so short that a special provision seemed unnecessary. See "Tarifordnung B für Gefolgschaftsmitglieder im öffentlichen Dienst," *Reichsarbeitsblatt* 1938: VI 489 ff.; for salaried employees: "Tarifordnung A," ibid.: VI 475 ff., here: sec. 17 ("Departure from the Service Due to Marriage"). For the German Civil Service Law see *Reichsgesetzblatt* I, 1937, 39 ff.

that the state governments of Hesse, Bavaria, and Württemberg-Baden prepare new civil service laws in 1946, there were explicit instructions to include a clause prohibiting discrimination of employees on the basis of sex. These state laws went into effect in October/November 1946, as shown in part 1 of this chapter. However, they did not apply for the many employees of the railway and the postal service in these states. These two enterprises continued to operate on the basis of Reich civil service law, and they made further use of the corresponding option to dismiss married female civil servants.[103]

In the British zone, the military government did not play such an active role. In August 1946 it issued a contradictory declaration stating that men and women should be treated equally, but at the same time permitting government units to decide for themselves whether to continue to dismiss married women. The British statement was all the more confusing, in that it also referred to a section of the military government's plan for reforming German civil service law with an even more restrictive slant: "Generally speaking, provision should be made for women to resign from the Public Service on marriage. . . ."[104] This perplexing amalgam of conflicting positions reflected basic differences of opinion in Britain itself, where married women were traditionally barred from public service. That rule had only been relaxed due to the exigencies of the world war, and there were strong forces in favor of restoring it after the conflict was over. It was only in September 1946 that the cabinet agreed to abolish the marriage bar in Britain once and for all—and not because there was an overwhelming desire to provide equal opportunity for married women, but mainly due to the critical manpower shortage in the immediate postwar years.[105]

Eventually, German politicians in the British zone took the initiative on their own. In North Rhine-Westphalia, the zone's largest and most important state by far, Interior Minister Walter Menzel (SPD) persuaded his colleagues to pass a cabinet resolution on February 9, 1948, declaring that the relevant

---

103. For the continued application of sec. 63 DBG by the railway in the Western zones see "Rundschreiben," 13 June 1949, *Die Reichsbahn* 23 (1949): 299.

104. Military Government Directive on Administration, Local and Regional Government and Public Services, Part II [June 1946], Appendix E, para. 11: Public Record Office, Great Britain, FO 371/55617. For the British declaration of August 1946 see *Grundsätze. Bestimmungen für die Bearbeitung der Beamten- und Personalangelegenheiten. Landesregierung Nordrhein-Westfalen, Innenministerium, Abt. II,* 3rd ed. (Düsseldorf, 1948), 56.

105. See Harold L. Smith, "The Womanpower Problem in Britain during the Second World War," *The Historical Journal* 27 (1984): 941–4. The marriage bar remained in effect for members of the British foreign service even after 1946; see Penny Summerfield, "Women, War and Social Change: Women in Britain in World War II," in Arthur Marwick, ed., *Total War and Social Change* (Houndsmills/London, 1988), 113. In her pioneering work *Women in Nazi Society,* Jill Stephenson warned against historians' implicit tendency to assume that policies in other countries were necessarily more enlightened than those in Germany in the 1930s. Explicit international comparisons, for which she then called, are still sadly lacking.

part of the German Civil Service Law was "no longer to be applied." In an announcement issued on February 26, Menzel explained that section 63 was incompatible "with the legal principles now in effect and the basic ideas of a modern democracy." In addition, he declared, it "indisputably" represented a "pure manifestation of National Socialist thought."[106] This policy was often ignored by local government units, however, and even agencies directly subordinate to the state government proved reluctant to implement it. Finally, on November 18, 1949, the state administrative court refused to acknowledge the cabinet resolution as legally binding. As a result, government units in North Rhine-Westphalia were free to continue dismissing married women.[107] Such formal difficulties did not arise in Lower Saxony, the second largest state in the British zone. There the state legislature passed a special law suspending section 63 DBG. But those responsible had waited long before taking action: the new law was dated June 17, 1949.

As a consequence of these developments on the state level, the regulations decreed by the Nazi regime retained their validity in important areas of the public service in the Western zones. These provisions continued to apply after the founding of the Federal Republic as well.[108]

But why did the Basic Law have no influence on this situation when it went into effect in 1949? After all, Article 3 contained a clear guarantee in paragraph 2: "Men and women have equal rights." This so-called "equality principle" *(Gleichheitsgrundsatz)* was even more explicitly restated in paragraph 3: "No one may be prejudiced or privileged because of sex. . . ." When the Parliamentary Council voted to incorporate these passages into the Basic Law, there were

---

106. The cabinet had approved a proposal first put forward by the Interior Minister on January 15, 1948; it was published in *Grundsätze*, 56–8, and has been reprinted in Ruhl, *Frauen,* 74–7. In this document, Menzel openly criticized the equivocal policy of the British military government. For the announcement of February 26, see *Ministerialblatt für das Land Nordrhein–Westfalen* 1 (1948): 78. In May 1949, Menzel issued a similar notice pertaining to female salaried employees, see ibid. 2 (1949): 649–50.

107. A married woman teacher dismissed by a regional government unit had sued for reinstatement, citing the text of the cabinet resolution and Menzel's public announcement. In its decision, the court declared that the minister's characterization of sec. 63 DBG as a "pure manifestation of National Socialist thought" seemed "incomprehensible"—since the provision differed little from the regulations passed by democratically elected governments in 1923 and 1932. For the text of the court's decision see Hauptstaatsarchiv Düsseldorf, NW 110–849, Bl. 93–103 (the quotation is from p. 8). This document has been published in abridged form in Ruhl, *Frauen,* 89–92; that version omits the passage cited here. For an evaluation of these developments from a different viewpoint see Ruhl, *Verordnete Unterordnung,* 118–20.

108. For a useful survey of the legal situation in the various states see Ernst Wichert, *Deutsches Beamtengesetz mit Ergänzungsgesetzen, Durchführungsvorschriften und Ausführungsbestimmungen. Allgemeine Fassung mit den Abweichungen im Bund und in den Ländern Bremen, Hamburg, Niedersachsen, Nordrhein-Westfalen, Schleswig-Holstein und Baden und den Vorschriften des Beamtengesetzes des Landes Rheinland-Pfalz* (Bonn, 1952), 201ff.

many older legal provisions contravening them, for example in the areas of family law, marriage law, property law—and civil service law. In order to give federal legislators time to revise these regulations to comply with the new constitutional norm, the Basic Law provided for a transitional period: all necessary changes had to be made by March 31, 1953, at the latest (Art. 117, par. 1). Thus section 63 DBG remained in force even after the Basic Law was promulgated. The same was true for the corresponding section of the 1938 wage regulations for salaried employees in the public service.

It quickly became apparent that the Adenauer government saw no need to set an example by complying with the constitutional principle of equality before it became compulsory. On the contrary, the bill for the provisional Federal Personnel Law which the cabinet passed on to the Bundestag on November 11, 1949, specifically retained the exact wording of the old section 63 DBG. However, the members of the appropriate committee of the Bundestag refused to go along: they voted to change the provision so that dismissals would no longer be possible.[109] Now Federal Postal Minister Hans Schuberth entered the fray, demanding that the original wording be retained. He cited economic arguments to support his case. For decades, the postal service had employed a substantial number of women; at that particular point in time the figure was approximately 70,000. If they married, they were usually dismissed forthwith. This policy had always been justified by claims that married women were not physically capable of shouldering the double burden of family and career. Schuberth cited statistics alleging that married women who had been permitted to remain in the postal service evidenced a considerably higher number of sick days and therefore a lower level of productivity than unmarried employees. He warned that any change in the present regulations would inevitably lead to an uncontrollable rise in the number of married female civil servants. The results of this development would make it impossible to run operations efficiently and economically, he maintained, and could very well lead to complete disruption of mail and telephone service. The conservative majority in the Bundestag soon agreed to a proposal more to Schuberth's liking. It was somewhat weaker than the 1937 statute, but still gave government units the opportunity to dismiss women upon marriage.[110]

---

109. The committee's spokesman, a member of the CDU, declared that he and his colleagues had taken this decision in view of "the importance of enforcing the equality principle": *DBT, StBer,* 15 Feb. 1950, 1269. For the wording approved by the committee see *DBT, Ds. 497,* p. 10.

110. Schuberth identified all the more strongly with the traditional personnel policies of the postal service, inasmuch as he had worked there for decades in high-ranking positions. After World War II he headed the Oberpostdirektion in Munich; in 1947 he was named director of the newly established postal service for the Bizone (see note 22). For a particularly detailed presentation of Schuberth's arguments see "Bundespostminister to Bundesinnenminister, 18 July 1951": BAK, B 136/492. The parallels between the situation in 1949–50 and the constellation in the years before

The Postal Minister's campaign to defend the status quo was all the more successful due to a supporting consideration: continued discrimination of married women guaranteed additional jobs for the 131ers. The interconnection of these two questions has never before been noted in the historical literature, perhaps because those in power at the time did their best to distract public attention from the issue. This linkage was, however, explicitly stressed by the state secretary of the interior ministry, Ritter von Lex, as he negotiated with representatives of the Allied High Commission to gain approval of the Federal Personnel Law in 1950. They criticized the measure because it violated the Allied requirement that men and women be treated equally. Ritter von Lex responded by pointing out that hundreds of thousands of former civil servants were looking for new positions in the public service. In view of this "very difficult situation" he saw no possibility of retaining any married woman whose husband's income afforded adequate support. Any other policy would cause "great embitterment" among the 131ers.[111] It went without saying that the dismissal of married women in order to accommodate more 131ers would lead to a shift in the gender structure of the public service. Everyone involved knew that the vast majority of the 131ers were men. According to the final results of the official survey presented seven weeks later, the exact figure was 96.4%.[112]

The representatives of the Allied High Commission proved reluctant to accept this part of the law. In order to allay their reservations, the emissaries of the federal government asserted that the provision was actually only intended as a "very temporary measure." In fact, they stated, it was the section of the law which was "the most provisional in nature," quite "definitely a transitional regulation."[113] But such assurances did not mean that the federal authorities would refrain from dismissing married women once the law received Allied approval. The postal service alone discharged several hundred female civil servants and salaried employees in 1951 and 1952.[114]

Furthermore, it soon became evident that many CDU/CSU representatives in the Bundestag were definitely not of the opinion that the regulation should be

---

1933 are striking. The Reich Postal Ministry had advocated a virtually identical policy, and it had played an important role in the efforts to put through the legislation required. Furthermore, in both instances Catholic politicians were instrumental in persuading their fellow lawmakers to approve measures restraining married women from working. For a general account of the parliamentary deliberations leading to the Federal Personnel Law of 1950 see Wengst, *Beamtentum,* 117ff.

111. "Niederschrift über die Besprechung auf dem Petersberg am 18. April 1950 betr. das vorläufige Personalgesetz," 15: BAK, B 136/489.

112. There were 332,351 men and 12,576 women among the 344,927 former employees (computed on the basis of the data in: *Verdrängte Beamte,* Tables 1b, 11b, 21b). The preliminary results of the survey, available since February 1950, must have offered the authorities similar information; see *Wirtschaft und Statistik,* N.F. 2 (1950): 10.

113. "Niederschrift . . . 18 Apr. 1950," 14–15.

114. See *DBT, Ds. 4086,* 13 Feb. 1953.

temporary. The deliberations on the bill for a permanent Federal Civil Service Law, which lasted from 1951 to mid-1953, were marked by persistent attempts to insert a section providing for the dismissal of married women. Surprisingly enough, a closer look at the forces behind these efforts reveals that Catholic women's organizations played a key role. These groups—among them professional societies for female public service employees such as the Association of Catholic German Women Teachers and the Professional Association of Catholic Women Social Workers—maintained that male and female civil servants should receive equal treatment in general, but women should still be dismissed in case of marriage. In a joint statement, these organizations declared that their demand was motivated by "impassioned concern for the *child,* which is endangered by the mother's employment, and by concern for the *family* in general, whose protection is viewed by the state as a particularly urgent task." Proposals to leave it up to the woman herself to decide whether to remain in the public service after marriage were specifically rejected: the issue raised questions "that deeply affect the basic character of our people" and had to be regulated by the state. Moreover, these Catholic women's associations argued that the state was obligated to protect its legitimate interests as an employer and thus had to dismiss married women because they were less productive and took more sick leave than unmarried women. It was also contended that this policy would be in the best interest of the population as a whole, since civil servants' salaries were paid for with taxpayers' money, which had to be spent responsibly and economically.[115]

Leading representatives of Catholic women's organizations continued to press for such measures even after a growing number of male CDU/CSU politicians had begun to waver. Many of the latter argued that the traditional dismissal practice was indeed desirable from a Christian point of view, but they had growing doubts about whether it would be sanctioned by the newly established Federal Constitutional Court. Article 3 of the Basic Law was so clearly worded that it seemed to leave little room for interpretation. Helene Weber, an outspoken CDU representative in the Bundestag, showed little sympathy for such vacillators and demanded a firm stand. Weber was the speaker of the women's committees of the CDU/CSU and a prominent Catholic women's leader (president of the Professional Association of Catholic Women Social Workers and vice president of the Catholic German Women's Federation). She had also worked for decades as a civil servant—which was only possible because she had adhered to the traditional ideal of chaste service for the common

---

115. "Zur Gleichberechtigung der Beamtin. Stellungnahme des Vereins katholischer deutscher Lehrerinnen, des Berufsverbandes katholischer Fürsorgerinnen, des Katholischen Deutschen Frauenverbandes und des Katholischen Fürsorgevereins für Mädchen, Frauen und Kinder," undated: Institut für Zeitgeschichte, Archive, Munich (IfZ), Helene Weber Papers, vol. 37. For the quotations see pp. 11–12.

good and remained unmarried. During the deliberations of the appropriate CDU committee in May 1952, Weber insisted that the party must ensure that the new civil service law included a section allowing for the dismissal of married women. The equality principle in the Basic Law should not be given a "stiff legalistic literal interpretation;" that would have "devastating consequences." Indeed, she pointed out, the Weimar constitution had also contained a similar provision—but that had never proved to be an insurmountable barrier. Weber's position was supported by the other woman on this committee, Josephine Doerner, who had been a civil servant in the postal service for decades and was thus also unmarried. Doerner now headed the newly created department for women's affairs in the postal ministry.[116]

Weber finally seized the initiative herself and introduced a proposal in the Bundestag which would allow continued dismissal of female civil servants at marriage. On May 13, 1953, she took to the floor to urge her fellow representatives to vote for the measure. She asserted that only unmarried women were able to fulfill the demands posed by a position in the civil service. It was unrealistic to expect that married women could meet the challenge of holding two occupations simultaneously, that of public servant and that of housewife and mother. They should therefore remain at home and devote "their entire energy" to building healthy families. Weber declared that this task was the key to repairing Germany's torn social fabric and thus a matter of national importance anyway. She concluded with the contention that employing married women in the civil service would also be unjust toward younger unmarried women, because they would then have no hope of finding jobs as "social workers, teachers, or postal employees."[117]

Clearly, the efforts to discriminate against married female civil servants were not only the product of conservative male politics, but also the result of a determined initiative on the part of influential unmarried professional women. Once this constellation is recognized, the historical precedent cited again and

---

116. See "Niederschrift über die Sitzung des Bundesausschusses [der CDU] für 'öffentliche Dienste', 19.–20.5.1952," 7–9: IfZ, H. Weber Papers, vol. 32. In 1957, Doerner still asserted that the postal service's traditional dismissal policy had not contradicted the Basic Law, obviously regretting that it had not been maintained. See Doerner, 378, 399. For biographical data on Weber see *Die Volksvertretung. Handbuch des Deutschen Bundestages* (Stuttgart, 1949), 254; Rudolf Morsey, "Helene Weber (1881–1962)," in *Zeitgeschichte in Lebensbildern.*

117. *DBT, StBer,* 13 May 1953, 13051; see "Änderungsantrag der Abgeordneten Frau Dr. Weber (Essen) und Genossen, Umdruck Nr. 914," 12 May 1953: Parlamentsarchiv of the Deutscher Bundestag, Bonn. An analysis of the broader public discussion of this issue would exceed the scope of this chapter but remains an important topic for further research. The aforementioned works by Moeller and Ruhl offer an excellent overview of the larger context—the general debate on the status of women in West German society. For details of Helene Weber's role in other controversies over government policy toward women and the family in the 1950s see Moeller, 63ff., 84–5, 89–90, 94, 198–9, 218, 221; Ruhl, *Verordnete Unterordnung,* 256, 269.

again in the early 1950s, the Reich law of 1932, also appears in a new light. A re-examination of the sources reveals that the cleavage between single and married women was an important factor leading to the very inception of that measure—an aspect which has gone unnoticed in previous scholarly accounts. Indeed, it was Helene Weber who played a key role then, too, as the records of the Center Party show. At that time she was a senior civil servant in the Prussian Ministry of Welfare, she chaired the Center Party's national women's committee (*Reichsfrauenbeirat*), belonged to the Reichstag, and was also a member of the steering committee of her party's parliamentary group. During a meeting of this committee on February 3, 1931, Weber broached the subject, "demand[ing] a draft law which would require married women to quit the civil service." On October 15, 1931, Weber presented the bill to the other members of the Center Party's parliamentary group, urging them to vote to submit it to the Reichstag. When the bill came out of the budget committee of the Reichstag on December 9, 1931, it was Weber who reported on it to the full house. Finally, on May 12, 1932, she took the floor to press for passage—in order to give "married women . . . back to their families." Weber's one regret, she stated, was that the final committee version of the bill restricted its application to the Reich administration and thus no longer pertained to women working at the state and local levels.[118] This concession, exacted by the SPD in exchange for its approval, meant that the controversial measure did not affect the great majority of married female civil servants.[119]

Two decades later, the parliamentary debate took an altogether different turn. Helene Weber introduced her proposal with the support of 25 other representatives of the CDU, among them three women. But in the heated exchange following her speech on May 13, 1953, another female representative of the CDU—a married woman—took to the floor and argued for rejection. Dr. Else Brökelschen was a professional teacher and mother. After marriage, she declared, she had voluntarily tendered her resignation, because she had felt "unequal to the double burden" of "a double occupation as housewife and teacher." But her school superintendent and the regional school authority had urged her to stay on, she asserted, because they believed a married female

---

118. *Die Protokolle der Reichstagsfraktion und des Fraktionsvorstands der Deutschen Zentrumspartei 1926–1933*, compiled by Rudolf Morsey (Mainz, 1969), 508; see ibid., 514, 518, 550–1; *Verhandlungen des Reichstags, Ds.* 1207, 15 Oct. 1931; *Ds.* 1269, 9 Dec. 1931; *Verhandlungen des Reichstags, Stenographische Berichte,* 12 May 1932, 2677–85 (the quotation is on p. 2684).

119. It was left to the Nazis to extend the coverage of the Reich law to state and local government—one year later, as seen above. The strong element of continuity in that step, often overlooked, is persuasive evidence in support of Jill Stephenson's argument that the truly unique features of Nazi policy toward women can only be discerned if viewed within the broader context of the policies pursued in the decades after the turn of the century. See Jill Stephenson, "Women and the Professions in Germany, 1900–1945," in *German Professions,* 277, 283–5.

teacher "would have to have a completely different view on social questions than an unmarried woman." After this jibe at Weber and other women's leaders who were single, Brökelschen demanded proof for the recurrent contention that the families of professional women were "not in good order," whereas the families of women who remained at home were. She had to admit that she spoke for no more than "a small number" of CDU representatives. Nevertheless, they were determined to vote against the proposal.[120]

Even a relatively small number of dissenting votes was enough to dash the hopes of those supporting the proposal, because the conservative coalition had a majority of only seven seats in the Bundestag. Yet Weber's motion was defeated by a much larger margin. Many conservative politicians were now convinced that the Federal Constitutional Court would eventually declare the measure null and void, so that voting for it would be an exercise in futility, serving only to expose its supporters to public ridicule. A second factor probably also played a considerable role: the next Bundestag elections were only a few months away. Since the SPD demanded a roll call vote, anyone casting a ballot in favor of the proposal risked criticism during the election campaign. The possible consequences were difficult to assess, but everyone knew that, as a consequence of the Second World War, women constituted a clear majority of the voters.[121] This might well be the reason why an exceptionally large number of CDU/CSU representatives refrained from committing themselves publicly. More than 40% abstained or did not participate in the vote at all.[122]

Only after this vote on May 13, 1953, was it finally clear that the new Federal Civil Service Law would not include a section permitting the dismissal of married women.

In view of the attitudes and policies prevailing at the federal level, many state and local administrators also made no effort to conform to the constitutional principle of equality before it became mandatory. They continued to apply the old regulations after 1949 as if nothing had changed, and indeed sought to cut back on female personnel even further. Conditions were particularly favorable, inasmuch as the currency reform of June 1948 had led to a sharp rise in the unemployment rate. As a result, even those branches of the public service which had complained about an insufficient number of male job appli-

---

120. *DBT, StBer,* 13 May 1953, 13055.

121. According to the official census returns for the resident population in 1950, women constituted 17.8 million of the 32.3 million persons aged 21 years and older (55.1%). Only 14.5 million were male (44.9%). Computed on the basis of the figures in: *Die Bevölkerung der Bundesrepublik Deutschland nach der Zählung vom 13.9.1950,* Statistik der Bundesrepublik Deutschland, vol. 35 (Stuttgart/Cologne, 1952), 8–11.

122. This was true of 59 of the 146 CDU/CSU representatives (among them Konrad Adenauer). Of those who did vote, 63 supported the proposal and 24 were opposed. For the official record of how the individual representatives voted see: *DBT, StBer,* 13 May 1953, 13106–9.

cants in the immediate postwar years now had better chances of realizing their goals of "personnel exchange." In the public transportation sector, for example, the female streetcar conductors who had been sustaining operations in most cities since 1939–40 became the targets of such programs. Until the war, this occupation had been a male domain. Klaus-Jörg Ruhl has shown that the systematic efforts to replace female conductors with men were challenged by the influential Union of Public Service and Transport Employees. In the important Rhine-Ruhr area, the union managed to reach an agreement with public transport authorities guaranteeing further employment of women in this occupation. But even this apparent victory proved hollow; it was practically impossible to stem the tide of gender rollback.[123] A closer look at these developments reveals that the situation was more complex, however; union initiatives in support of female conductors not only met with resistance from public employers, but were also undermined by opposition from within the union ranks. Influential men in the local union councils showed little sympathy for the leadership's efforts to guarantee women the right to work at "men's jobs." The union's secretary for women's affairs at the federal level made no effort to conceal her indignation over this development. In a public statement, she termed it "extremely bitter."[124]

The steps taken against women regarded as "double earners" were particularly rigorous. Government authorities investigated the financial circumstances and family status of their female employees to determine whether dismissal could be justified. If such evaluations did not produce the desired results, they could be repeated periodically. Some administrators interpreted the term "double earner" so broadly that it even applied to young unmarried women living in a common household with their parents. If the father's income seemed adequate, the working daughter could be dismissed.[125]

But even under the particularly favorable conditions prevailing in the early 1950s, it was not always possible to replace women with men to the extent desired. The new demographic constellation sometimes prevented full implementation of such policies. In retrospect, it seems obvious that the war-related drop in the relative size of the male population necessarily entailed a lasting shift in the gender structure of the work force. But in the postwar era, many Germans only gradually came to comprehend the full implications of the new situation. The economy was in a state of transition, unemployment remained high, and refugees continued pouring in from the East.

---

123. See Ruhl, *Verordnete Unterordnung,* 121; Ruhl, *Frauen,* 72–3, 100–101.

124. Gewerkschaft Öffentliche Dienste, Transport und Verkehr (ÖTV), *Geschäftsbericht 1949–1951* (Stuttgart, [1952]), Part I, 173. See Gewerkschaft ÖTV, *Geschäftsbericht 1952–1954* (Stuttgart, [1955]), 323; *Gleichheit* 14 (1951): 59.

125. For the case of a female employee in Bremen who went to court to fight her dismissal on these grounds and lost, see *Gleichheit* 14 (1951): 171.

TABLE 2. The Female Employees in the Public Service in 1952: Number, Structure, and Percentage of Total Personnel

	Absolute number of female employees	Distribution according to status (%)	Total public service personnel	Women as a percentage of total personnel
Entire public service				
Civil servants	93,566	24.0	890,971	10.5
Salaried employees	198,251	51.0	490,254	40.4
Manual workers	97,239	25.0	764,892	12.7
Total	389,056	100.0	2,146,117	18.1
Federal government				
Civil servants	181	1.1	50,748	0.4
Salaried employees	12,228	77.5	32,539	37.6
Manual workers	3,379	21.4	21,751	15.6
Total	15,788	100.0	105,038	15.0
State government				
Civil servants	48,776	39.6	332,211	14.7
Salaried employees	51,064	41.4	136,506	37.4
Manual workers	23,487	19.0	96,730	24.3
Total	123,327	100.0	565,447	21.8
Local government				
Civil servants	11,879	9.1	112,479	10.6
Salaried employees	76,194	58.3	210,079	36.3
Manual workers	42,649	32.6	224,279	19.0
Total	1,300,722	100.0	546,837	23.9
Total federal, state, and local government				
Civil servants	65,216	22.2	525,245	12.4
Salaried employees	154,248	52.6	413,752	37.3
Manual workers	73,946	25.2	361,248	20.5
Total	293,410	100.0	1,300,245	22.6
Federal Postal Service				
Civil servants	26,672	39.5	152,724	17.5
Salaried employees	33,331	49.4	42,185	79.0
Manual workers	7,519	11.1	91,636	8.2
Total	67,522	100.0	286,545	23.6
Federal Railway				
Civil servants	1,591	9.3	210,584	0.8
Salaried employees	215	1.3	2,451	8.8
Manual workers	15,330	89.5	309,934	4.9
Total	17,136	100.0	522,969	3.3
Public law institutions				
Civil servants	87	0.8	2,418	3.6
Salaried employees	10,457	95.2	31,866	32.8
Manual workers	444	4.0	2,074	21.4
Total	10,988	100.0	36,358	30.2

Sources: Personal der öffentlichen Verwaltung am 2.10.1952. Statistik der Bundesrepublik Deutschland, vol. 84 (Stuttgart/Cologne 1954), 7, 23, 30, 33; calculations based on these data. (Figures exclude municipalities with less than 1,000 inhabitants; they include the personnel of the municipal savings and loan institutions; the figures for state governments do not include the *Hansestädte* Hamburg and Bremen.)

Thus many hopes of rehiring men to fill positions which they had "normally" occupied before the war still seemed realistic. It was only later, as a result of the first powerful economic upswing, that the consequences of demographic constraints for hiring policies would become fully evident. This process set in somewhat earlier in the public sector, however, because salaries there were distinctly lower than in most areas of private industry. Thus many men considered a job in the public service less desirable, and they transferred to the private sector as the opportunity arose. Those willing to take their places were frequently women. As a result, many public employers proved unable to reduce the number of female employees as far as they would have liked.

What, then, was the net effect of these conflicting forces on the gender structure of the public service? The earliest detailed statistics available are from the year 1952. According to these data published by the Federal Statistical Office, 22.6% of the employees at the federal, state, and local levels were women (293,410 of 1,300,245). This official figure suggests an overly favorable picture of the situation, however, since it does not include the 845,872 persons working for the postal service, the railway, and the public law institutions. The percentage drops to 18.1% if they are taken into account.[126]

Table 2 presents detailed information on the female employees according to employment status and sector. The breakdown according to employment status (columns one and two) reveals that most women held positions as salaried employees. Of the rest, the majority were manual workers. Less than one-quarter of all women in the public service enjoyed civil service status and thus life tenure—as long as they refrained from marrying. The percentage of male employees with civil service status was almost twice as high (45.4%). Conversely, the percentage of men working as salaried employees was only 16.6%—less than one-third of the corresponding figure for women (51.0%).

The view from another angle is even more revealing. The data on female employees as a percentage of total public service personnel (column four) show that 40.4% of all salaried employees, but only 10.5% of all civil servants, were female. This difference was even more significant when one considers that the number of civil servants was almost twice as large as the number of salaried employees. The figures indicating a somewhat higher percentage of female civil servants at the state and local levels should not be misinterpreted as proof of

126. See *Personal der öffentlichen Verwaltung am 2.10.1952,* Statistik der Bundesrepublik Deutschland, vol. 84 (Stuttgart/Cologne, 1954), 7, 14, 23, 30, 33. A comparison with the situation in preceding decades is difficult, since most earlier surveys contain no data on gender structure. It is, however, possible to find some partial figures which illustrate the magnitude of the decrease after the war in certain areas: in 1945, 35.8% of all local government employees in Bavaria were women; by 1949 the figure had dropped to 30.1%, by 1952 to 23.3%. During these seven years, the absolute number of local government employees had risen from 82,793 to 102,401, but the number

more liberal recruitment policies in the administrative units there. They chiefly reflect the large number of female teachers working in the public schools. Most schoolteachers in West Germany were employees of state governments; a smaller number worked for municipalities. Women comprised 38% of all teaching staff at these levels.[127] As the statistics show, the highest proportion of female civil servants was to be found in the postal service. This was the result of a unique personnel policy with a long historical tradition. Since the latter part of the nineteenth century, the postal service had employed a considerably larger number of women than other parts of the public service; most worked as telephone operators, as sorters and bookkeepers in the financial divisions, or in counter and secretarial services. Because personnel fluctuation posed a problem, efforts had been made to increase the incentive for long-term service: female salaried employees who had worked for the postal service for a number of years received the opportunity to take an examination enabling them to enter the civil service at the intermediate level. The traditional prerequisite for receiving such a civil service position was, however, the understanding that the woman would have to abstain from marriage ("celibacy clause").[128]

Finally, most women with positions as civil servants or salaried employees worked in subordinate positions. The degree to which they were concentrated in the lowest levels of service can be seen in table 3. First of all, it contains statistics on gender structure in the non-technical areas of the public service in 1950 (excluding the railway and the postal service).[129] The percentage of male employees in the two lowest levels was conspicuously smaller. Conversely, the proportion of men working in the two highest levels was almost three times as large as that of women. The gender gap was even greater in the postal service, as can be seen from the figures for 1952. There were almost no female employees in the highest level of service, and very few in the second highest. Indeed, women were to be found almost exclusively in the two lowest levels: 97.9% of all female civil servants and 99.8% of all female salaried employees held positions in the intermediate or elementary service.[130]

---

of women decreased from 29,640 to 23,865. In the Reich Postal Service, women constituted 50.1% of the three main personnel groups (full-time civil servants, salaried employees, skilled workers) as of September 30, 1944. On March 30, 1949, the corresponding figure for the Western zones was 28.3% This was still clearly higher than the percentage of women working for the Federal Postal Service in 1952 (23.6%). The author is preparing a study on the social history of the German public service 1945–1949, in which these and other developments in the turbulent postwar years will be analyzed.

127. See ibid., 14.

128. Statistics from the year 1950 show that the postal service had been largely successful in maintaining this policy in spite of the extraordinary conditions prevailing during and after the war: approximately 19,000 of 21,000 female civil servants were unmarried (90.5%). See "Bundespostminister to Bundesinnenminister," 18 Jan. 1951, p. 1: BAK, B 136/492. For more information on specific policy developments see Doerner, 385ff., 394–5.

129. In official statistics, public employees were traditionally divided into two categories:

TABLE 3.   The Distribution of Female and Male Employees According to Service Level, 1950–1952

| | | Percentage in the | | | |
	Absolute number	higher service	superior service	intermediate service	elementary service
Non-technical areas of the public service, all levels, 1950:					
Female salaried employees	136,320	0.8	10.4	65.0	23.8
Male salaried employees	257,729	7.1	24.1	46.3	22.5
Female civil servants	10,609	6.4	17.3	64.7	11.6
Male civil servants	444,484	13.3	49.6	32.3	4.9
Federal Postal Service, 1952:					
Female salaried employees	33,331	0.009	0.2	88.8	11.0
Male salaried employees	42,185	2.5	32.2	61.4	4.0
Female civil servants	26,672	0.007	2.1	97.9	—
Male civil servants	152,724	0.8	13.1	24.7	61.4

Sources: Personal der öffentlichen Verwaltung am 2.9.1950. Statistik der Bundesrepublik Deutschland, vol. 55 (Stuttgart/Cologne 1952), 20, 27 (excluding teachers); *Personal der öffentlichen Verwaltung am 2.10.1952,* Statistik der Bundesrepublik Deutschland, vol. 84 (Stuttgart/Cologne 1954), 8, 33; calculations based on these data.

5.

The consequences of the controversial policy decisions discussed in this chapter were far-reaching:

— The successful defense of traditional civil service law reaffirmed the old hierarchy of career tracks based on formal education, reduced opportunities for upward mobility, and helped shore up the system of social stratification which had been destabilized by the twin shocks of total war and total defeat. The confirmation of civil servants' privileged legal status also encouraged the revival of a specific group mentality characterized by a sense of moral and social superiority.

— In Bonn, priority hiring of former civil servants from the Prussian and

---

(a) personnel in the non-technical areas of the public service *(Hoheits- und Kämmereiverwaltungen)* and (b) personnel in economic enterprises (gas, water, and electrical companies; local public transportation; agriculture and forestry enterprises). In 1950, 15.6% of all federal, state, and local government employees worked in economic enterprises (199,837 of 1,282,530). A breakdown of this group into the four service levels is not available. Had the official statistics taken them into account, the results would have shown female employees to be at even more of a disadvantage.

130.   The postal administration did not allow women to take on jobs in the elementary level of the civil service. It was primarily reserved for mail carriers, who were hired after leaving school at age 14 to 15; officials feared "that the working conditions and demands . . . could be dangerous for girls in their developing years . . . and detrimental for their future duties in marriage and motherhood" (Doerner, 394).

Reich ministries reestablished clear lines of continuity with the period before 1945. Many members of the old administrative elite now served in the upper echelons of the new federal ministries. Among them were numerous civil servants who were compromised by the role they had played during the Third Reich. The repercussions of these developments were by no means confined to the capital city. They had a manifest influence on the political climate in the country as a whole.

— Similarly, the legislation implementing Article 131 of the Basic Law also had a broader, symbolic significance. These measures did not merely address the social problems of many uprooted public employees, but compelled government units to rehire large numbers of them, thus intensifying personnel continuity with regard to the period before 1945. Moreover, this legislation provided the basis on which almost all of the civil servants discharged during denazification could be reinstated. At the same time, the 131er legislation left little opportunity for the recruitment and training of younger employees in many parts of the public service. The skewed age structure of the staff gave rise to long-term personnel problems—and thus to further costs not included in the official statistics on the billions awarded to the 131ers and their families.

— A gender rollback was the result of persistent efforts to discharge women holding "men's jobs," all married women, and as many other female "double earners" as possible. Women were once again relegated to the position which traditional role concepts accorded them: to sectors outside of the core areas of the civil service, to subordinate posts with little employment security, to jobs for which men could not be found—or, as far as married women were concerned, to home, hearth, and family.

Nevertheless, an interpretation of the social history of the public service from this perspective alone would be incomplete. A closer look at developments in the latter part of the 1950s shows that this was also a decade in which signs of long-term social change became increasingly apparent in this sector as well. Some processes took place against the will of many administrators and government officials, or as a result of decisions which proved to have unintended consequences. Above all, important elements of social change can be discerned in two areas:

1. The overall percentage of women in the public service began to increase once again—slowly, but perceptibly. The driving force behind this development was the "economic miracle" *(Wirtschaftswunder)*, the unprecedented economic upsurge characterized by years of rapid and continuous growth lasting well into the 1960s. The situation on the labor market changed drastically, eventually

forcing modification of traditional policies toward women in the public service. The boom led to a dramatic drop in the unemployment rate: it fell from 11.0% in 1950 to 5.6% in 1955, finally shrinking to only 1.3% in 1960.[131] As a consequence, government authorities had an increasingly difficult time finding men who were willing to accept positions in the lower echelons of the public service. Administrators admitted openly that they had no other alternative but to hire more women once again.[132] The total percentage of female employees in the public service increased, from 18.1% in 1952 to 22.8% in 1960. The proportion of women working in administrative units at the federal, state, and local levels rose even higher, climbing from 22.6% in 1952 to 28.1% in 1960.[133] Some officials hoped that this development was only temporary and that it could later be reversed under more favorable conditions. In reality, it marked the beginning of a long-term shift in the gender structure of the public service. This trend, alternatively sustained by economic factors and political forces, has continued up to the present day.

2. The 1950s witnessed the emergence of a personnel structure clearly different from that prevailing in the Weimar Republic. By the end of the decade, the proportion of civil servants had dropped to a level previously unknown. Conversely, the percentage of salaried employees and manual workers rose substantially. A significant, though apparently unintentional, consequence of this process was a gradual broadening of the social base of the public service.

This momentous shift was not the result of central directives, but of a multitude of individual decisions at various levels. One obviously important factor contributing to the destabilization of traditional personnel structures was the war: the percentage of civil servants dropped dramatically due to military inductions and casualties. Yet even after the war was over, the proportion of civil servants remained unusually low.[134] To some extent, this was a consequence of denazification. The percentage of NSDAP members among civil

131. See *Bevölkerung und Wirtschaft,* 148. For background information see the useful survey by Alan Kramer, *The West German Economy, 1945–1955* (New York/Oxford, 1991), 177–221.

132. So, for example, Kurt Wiesemeyer, a senior official in the federal postal administration. In an article on the personnel situation in the latter part of the 1950s, he noted that the postal service had experienced growing difficulties in its search for "suitable personnel"; thus it proved necessary "to resort to accepting a greater number of female employees"—"even for positions normally reserved for men." See Wiesemeyer, "Personalverhältnisse," 78–9.

133. Computed on the basis of: *Personal von Bund, Ländern und Gemeinden, 2. Oktober 1960,* Finanzen und Steuern, Reihe 4 (Stuttgart/Mainz, 1961), 4, 43.

134. Here is just one example: among local government employees in Bavaria, the proportion of civil servants sank from 53.2% in 1933 to 29.5% in 1945; it finally reached 19.3% in 1949. This and other developments referred to in the following will be discussed in the author's above-mentioned study on the social history of the public service 1945–1949.

servants had been considerably higher than among salaried employees or manual workers. Thus a particularly large number of civil servants lost their jobs after 1945. A second factor was the cautious hiring policy of many authorities due to the uncertain prospects of political and economic development. Since the future financial situation and personnel needs could not be clearly assessed, employers often refrained from making long-term commitments. Administrators now often hired salaried employees or manual workers for jobs previously performed by civil servants. Persons without civil service status were less expensive and could later be dismissed if so desired.

As conditions stabilized in the 1950s, the percentage of civil servants gradually settled at a level higher than during the turbulent war years and the occupation period, but conspicuously lower than the level considered "normal" during the Weimar Republic. For example, the proportion of civil servants in local government was 18.1% in 1960, as compared to 59.5% in 1927. During the same period, the percentage of civil servants in state government dropped from 83.5% to 60.4%. The corresponding figure for the federal government was 30.5% in 1960, as compared to 56.9% for the Reich government in 1927.[135]

Within each of these government levels, however, the situation differed greatly from sector to sector. There had been little change within the ministries and other traditional core areas of the public service such as police, justice, finance, and defense (the so-called *Hoheitsverwaltung*). In these sectors, most employees continued to enjoy civil service status. But the situation was quite different in the more newly established service administration (*Leistungsverwaltung*), for example in health care and public welfare, in the compensation agencies, in public construction and housing authorities, and in the social insurance agencies. Here the percentage of civil servants was markedly lower than it had been previously. Moreover, political decisions led to a considerable expansion of the service administrations in the 1950s. This shift in the character of the public service contributed to an even faster decrease in the overall proportion of civil servants.[136]

---

135. A similar shift occurred in the postal service: in 1927, 74.2% of the employees were civil servants, but only 61.2% in 1960. All percentages have been computed on the basis of the data in: *Bevölkerung und Wirtschaft,* 236–7.

136. The periodic reports on the number of public service employees published by the Federal Statistical Office also contain important information on sectoral differences in development in the 1950s. For detailed statistical material with comparative figures for 1930 and 1966 see Jörg Jung, *Die Zweispurigkeit des öffentlichen Dienstes. Eine Untersuchung über die Veränderungen der Personalstruktur im öffentlichen Dienst und die Verankerung des Berufsbeamtentums im Grundgesetz* (Berlin, 1971).

Thus the 1950s were a period in which lawmakers unmistakably confirmed the special legal and social status of career civil servants, but at the same time the point at which this group lost its dominant position in the public service, at least in numerical terms, once and for all. Only the traditional core areas remained largely untouched by change. There, civil servants—and often the old conservative esprit de corps—still dominated. But these areas were increasingly surrounded by others in which civil servants constituted just a small portion of total personnel, occupying only the highest positions. The great majority of the staff consisted of salaried employees and manual workers. Their understanding of their role as public employees differed radically from the old corporate mentality once common among civil servants, and they often came from other social backgrounds.

The question of the extent to which contemporaries perceived this momentous structural shift and, if so, how they interpreted it, is a subject for future research. At present, most evidence suggests that popular conceptions of the public service were predominantly influenced by traditional images and ideologies. This perception was encouraged by the policy of the Adenauer governments and the conservative parties, which deliberately propagated the old ideals and values. This policy proved to be so effective that many who criticized the Adenauer era as a period of veritable "restoration" cited the public service as a prime example—though some important developments in this sector might better be viewed as an example of how futile political intentions can be in the face of long-term social change. Even in the 1970s and 1980s, well-known historians and political scientists continued to depict the development of the public service during the Adenauer era solely in terms of "restoration." Thus the significance of the controversial political decisions of the early 1950s lies not only in the fact that they represented a major contribution to the social consolidation of the public service under conservative auspices. In addition, these measures apparently had such a strong influence on people's perception of the public service that signs of long-term social change were either overlooked or underestimated by many for years to come.

Part 3.
Coming to Terms with the Past

The Historic Triangle:
Occupiers, Germans and Jews
in Postwar Germany

Frank Stern

In April 1945, American troops liberated some 700 survivors of the concentration and work-camp Dora-Nordhausen. 2,000 citizens of Nordhausen were ordered to help with the burial of the dead. A Jewish intelligence officer found 120 Jews. "They had boarded the evacuation train like the rest," he noted, "but were quickly thrown off by antisemitic fellow prisoners." Later, while taking a tour of the camp conducted by one of the Jewish prisoners, he stood in "dazed silence before the crematorium. All the sudden his guide climbed up and stood upon a pile of white ashes near by. 'You know what I'm standing on?' he asked him matter-of-factly, and began to answer, 'I'm standing on the bodies of . . .' 'I screamed at him to get off,'" the officer remembered, "'and he looked at me very puzzled, like what kind of morality is that? I realized I didn't understand him, and he didn't understand me, and there was a great barrier between us.'"[1]

In Nuremberg, a young woman had survived racist persecution. She recalled the following about her liberation on April 20th, 1945: "How happy we were! Twenty years young. We'd survived! How beautiful the world was! The brownshirts were gone and done with! Hitler was finished! Hard to describe the mood. The population of Nuremberg, afflicted by anxiety and sadness, slinked with lowered eyes through the streets . . . The only ones who were really overjoyed were the people who'd been liberated from the various concentration camps, camps for foreigners, and those who'd been living in hiding."[2]

This chapter was translated from German into English by Bill Templer. [Citation form conforms with the German style of the *Tel Aviver Jahrbuch für deutsche Geschichte,* the original place of publication, —Ed.].

1. Robert H. Abzug, Inside the Vicious Heart. Americans and the Liberation of Nazi Concentration Camps, New York, Oxford 1985, 41f.; see also Margaret Bourke-White, "Dear Fatherland Rest Quietly." A Report on the Collapse of Hitler's "Thousand Years," New York 1946, 74.

2. Inge Protzner-Kaufmann, Nicht mehr "Mischling 1. Grades" in: Peter Altmann (ed.), Hauptsache Frieden, Kriegsende, Befreiung, Neubeginn 1945–1949. Vom antifaschistischen Kon-

On April 15, after American tanks had rumbled on through his town Ernst Jünger noted down in his journal: "There is still a sense of unreality. It is the astonishment of people who remain standing after a heavy wheel has passed over and through them."[3] And on May 6: "In the morning, six Jews who had been liberated from Belsen came into the courtyard. The youngest was eleven. He was looking at picture books with the voracity of a child who'd never seen such a thing before in all his life. Our cat was also made the object of his great surprise and wonder—as though a gigantic dream image were now moving toward him."[4]

These three modes of perception contain certain key contradictory elements of the immediate German postwar reality. They point to the manifold tensions and complex relations between Allied soldiers, defeated Germans and liberated Jews. The Allied occupation policies in Germany were intended to realize certain objectives which had been agreed upon in the European Advisory Commission in London and at Yalta. German expectations and fears aside, these goals defined the very beginning of Allied-German conflicts and tensions for the period to come. At the same time, this was also a period of confrontation of surviving Jews with their liberators and with the Germans. Hence, attitudes of Germans toward Jews, and toward matters in any way connected with Jews, were unavoidably marked by these relations, at whose base lay an extremely antagonistic experience.

This pattern entailed different recollections and reflections of a social, political and psychological situation which had not been determined solely and exclusively by the confrontation of Germans with the occupying forces. However, that confrontation is usually what most historical writing deals with in terms of occupation policies, scrutinizing the legacy of the Nazi past or elaborating on a democratic future. The different spheres of German society after 1945 have been the subject of painstakingly detailed historical research in a growing number of studies.[5] With very few exceptions, however, the Jewish chapter of this period, as an integral part of postwar German history, has been left out.[6] On the other hand, there is a body of research on the Jewish remnant,

---

sens zum Grundgesetz, Frankfurt/M. 1985, 34f.

3. Ernst Jünger, Jahre der Okkupation. April 1945–Dezember 1948, Stuttgart 1958, 20.

4. Ibid.

5. See Wolfgang Benz, Deutsche Geschichte nach dem Zweiten Weltkrieg. Probleme und Tendenzen zeitgeschichtlicher Forschung in der Bundesrepublik, in : *Tel Aviver Jahrbuch für deutsche Geschichte*, vol. XVI, 1987, 398ff.

6. See Ursula Büttner (ed.), Das Unrechtsregime. Internationale Forschungen über den Nationalsozialismus, 2 vols., Hamburg 1986, with an article by U. Büttner on German Jews in the

She'erith Hapletah, but principally only on the Jewish displaced persons from Eastern Europe; frequently, there is only very minor reference to the German social and political scene to which the survivors had to adapt.[7] Both ways of dealing with the German postwar period must be questioned, keeping additionally in mind that Jewish topics have been treated mainly by Jewish scholars.

Though such shortcomings are a significant and traditional peculiarity of German-Jewish historiography, it is not enough to make critical reference to their existence or refer only to their ideological implications. It will be argued here that the Jewish aspects of the postwar period ought to be an integral part of the analysis of German postwar history. Since the 9th of November 1989, at least, we are now compelled to reconsider the "Jewish question" within the "German question."[8] And because there is much writing and discussion about historical continuity, one ought to regard the peculiar Jewish continuum—at least in order to understand some of the discontinuities of German and Jewish history. In the following, I will sketch the three focal points of this triangle and their relationship in the context of the emerging West German state down to the beginning of the 1950s:

The political and social framework.
The state bureaucracy and the survivors.
The Jews as a touchstone of democracy.

The Political and Social Framework: "Maybe it would be better if not too many came back"

Julius Posner, a Jewish officer in the British army, reported this statement by a young German woman in this analysis of the changes in the attitudes of Germans towards Jews during the course of 1945–1946.[9] A survey analysis of the Office of Military Government, U.S. in Germany (OMGUS) in November 1945 focused on "the current thought and conditions in a new Germany—a Germany that had been given a breathing period in which to recover somewhat from the numbness caused by losing the war." If one sums up the statements on Jews, Jewish persecution and its consequences described and quoted in this report, the

British Zone of Occupation, and Martin Broszat/Klaus-Dieter Henke/Hans Woller (eds.), Von Stalingrad zur Währungsreform. Zur Sozialgeschichte des Umbruchs in Deutschland, Munich 1988, with an article by Juliane Wetzel on Jewish survivors in Bavaria. An exceptionally positive example is (since 1985) the *Dachauer Hefte* series, with an English edition since 1988, and many local studies on the history of Jews.

7. See Wolfgang Jacobmeyer, Jüdische Überlebende als "Displaced Persons," in: *Geschichte und Gesellschaft* 3, vol. 9 (1983), 421f.

8. See Anson Rabinbach, The Jewish Question in the German Question, in: *New German Critique* 44 (1988), 159f.

9. Julius Posner, In Deutschland 1945–1946, Jerusalem 1947, 112.

following picture emerges: "Few people defend the way in which the Jews were treated, but most feel it was good to break their power." People claimed they knew nothing about the mass murders and believed the American reports were exaggerated. In addition, it was felt that Jews were "economically too influential." People argued that as a result of the Allied air-raids and the losses suffered by the German civilian population, a balance had been created: a scale in which there were victims set off against victims. The slave laborers, it was contended, had been well treated, and the suffering that had been inflicted on them had been in retaliation for plundering and violent acts on their part after the German defeat. Likewise, the practice of appointing returning emigrés to official posts was criticized "because these emigrés have lost the contact with the people; they have not endured the hardships of war and of anti-Nazi fighting, but have lived comfortably and safely in neutral or allied countries. They are estranged from their people and have lost their confidence."[10]

After a few months under occupation, the results of the first steps in re-education turned out to be more of a readjustment to the everyday situation, including the readoption of anti-Jewish biases. Times had changed. "In the summer of 1945," Posner noted down, "it was considered the proper tone *(der gute Ton)* to think that something had to be done for the Jews."[11] But by that autumn, German popular sentiment had begun to show its darker and more traditional colors.

Wherever Germans had encountered Jews in the spring and summer of 1945, they had not been less astonished than the victorious soldiers that some Jews were indeed still alive. About 15,000 German Jews had survived inside the Third Reich. Approximately 50,000 Jews from numerous countries had been liberated in slave labor camps or on death marches between March and May 1945. Some had been in hiding, some had lived on borrowed time with false papers, some had had a privileged status or were alive thanks to contradictions in the Nazi hierarchy, and some had succeeded in buying their share of "love thy neighbor," whatever the material or moral price might have been.

Already before liberation, all this had involved individual and collective encounters between Germans and Jews. Now, in May/June of 1945, Jews were trying to adjust to the hardship of the postwar crisis in about 500 German towns as well as a number of camps for displaced persons (DPs). By far the largest number of Jewish survivors were situated in the American Zone, and this number was constantly on the increase, due to the steady influx from Eastern Europe. These developments, totally unforeseen by the Allied postwar planners, created a highly problematic challenge for the occupation powers, for the

10. OMGUS, Report USFET, The German View (19. 11. 1945), National Archives (NA). Rg. 260.

11. Posner (fn. 9), 109.

emerging German administrations and particularly for the Jewish survivors. It took some time, but gradually a framework for interaction developed between the occupation powers, the Germans and the Jews.

On a political, institutional, social, cultural and psychological level, one can attribute to this framework the structural qualities which justify the term *triangle*. This triangle existed for a few short years. It was a tension-ridden part of a more comprehensive triangle that included the United States with its American Jewish community, Germany with the Jewish remnant, and the Jewish settlement in Palestine as the precursor of the State of Israel.[12]

Let us briefly consider the Jews in Germany as one component of this triadic relationship. Shortly after liberation, survivors came together in several cities and re-established the Jewish Communities *(Religionsgemeinden)*. A few days after the occupation of Cologne on March 6, 1945, for example, the American Education and Religion Officer granted Jewish survivors permission to hold religious services. The Community, numbering approximately 80 members, was refounded on April 28. In Munich, a Jewish lawyer who had survived by working in a munitions factory in the city made formal application for re-establishing a Jewish community there.[13] It should be stressed here that the *readmission* of Jewish communities into German society was brought about at local Jewish request through the occupation authorities.

Such reestablished communities structured along decentralized lines meant the creation of a collective social and religious bond among survivors as a group vis-à-vis the bureaucracy of the occupying powers and the local municipalities.[14] Within the DP camps, the Jewish inmates also began with self-organization, usually assisted by Jewish officers or army chaplains. But as a whole, they too had to rely on themselves for a number of early and crucial weeks.

Most Jewish DPs as well as the overwhelming majority of surviving younger German Jews and children were often waiting for the chance to emigrate to Palestine or the United States. It was more than doubtful at that time whether there were—or would in future be—any long-term prospects for some sort of Jewish life in Germany. This perception frequently not just shaped the

---

12. This context will be dealt with in an introduction to documents on German-Israeli relations, edited by Yeshayahu Jelinek (forthcoming 1997).

13. See Juliane Wetzel, Jüdisches Leben in München 1945–1951. Durchgangsstadium oder Wiederaufbau, Munich 1987.

14. See Monika Richarz, Jews in Today's Germanies, in: *Year Book Leo Baeck Institute* 30 (1985), 265f.; Michael Y. Bodemann, Staat und Ethnizität: Der Aufbau der jüdischen Gemeinden im Kalten Krieg, in: Michael Brumlik, Doron Kiesel, Cilly Kugelmann, Julius H. Schoeps (eds.), Jüdisches Leben in Deutschland seit 1945, Frankfurt/M 1986, 49ff.; Juliane Wetzel, op. cit. (fn. 13); Abraham J. Peck, Zero Hour and the Development of Jewish Life in Germany after 1945, in: A Pariah People? Jewish Life in Germany after 1945. A Symposium held on November 18, 1988 at KK Bene Israel, Cincinnati, Ohio 1988, 3f.

sense of identity among Jews, but also molded their attitude toward the Germans and their reliance on American help—not to mention their opposition to the British and their highly reluctant handling of the Palestine question.

It is still difficult to assess the cost—in psychological terms and in resulting social difficulties—of the adjustment efforts to the German postwar situation.[15] It was a time of crisis for the whole of German society; millions of Germans and millions of displaced persons were on the move attempting to return "home," to places where they had once belonged or thought they would now be welcomed. Jewish survivors from the concentration camps who returned to their hometowns often had a frightening experience: "One left the German Jews to their fate after liberation. The Allies considered it to be their natural duty to take their own nationals as quickly as possible from the camps and return them home. The German Jews had to find their way home alone. The only helping hand they were offered was by those Jews who had lived in hiding during the final years of the Nazi regime."[16] The most pressing problems involved clothing, food, housing and—right from the beginning in this connection—the return of Jewish property and the question of restitution.

In contrast with the majority of German *Heimkehrer,* the Jews no longer had any families or friends, no homes, no clothes or personal possessions. Their former homes, businesses, offices and workplaces were now occupied by others. The end of Nazi terror did not imply that every anti-Jewish measure had been revoked and eradicated. When anti-Jewish acts were formally in accordance with law—as was the case with the so-called Aryanisation of Jewish property—then Jewish survivors could only peek through their former windows from the outside.

In June, an active member of the Cologne community mentioned in a letter what the state of the so-called *guter Ton* was at that juncture: "We have been living in freedom since March of this year, but have yet to receive any assistance from anyone. We are without any means whatsoever."[17] In the autumn, before the formation (January 1946) of the Landesverband jüdischer Gemeinden in Nord-Rhein-Westfalen (State Association of Jewish Communities), Posner visited returnees in Solingen, Wuppertal and Remscheid. "They felt abandoned by God and the world. And especially by the Jews. 'You're the first

---

15. See Harry Maòr, Über den Wiederaufbau der Jüdischen Gemeinden in Deutschland seit 1945, Mainz 1961; Ralph Giordano (ed.), Narben, Spuren, Zeugen, 15 Jahre Allgemeine Wochenzeitung der Juden in Deutschland, Düsseldorf 1961; Juliane Wetzel (fn. 13); Cilly Kugelmann, "Tell Them in America We're still Alive!": The Jewish Community in the Federal Republic, in: *New German Critique* 46 (Winter 1989), 129f.

16. Quoted in Giordano (fn. 15), 15.

17. See Günther Bernd Ginzel, Phasen der Etablierung einer Jüdischen Gemeinde in der Kölner Trümmerlandschaft 1945–1949, in: J. Bohnke-Kollwitz, W. P. Eckert a.o. (eds.), Köln und das rheinische Judentum. Festschrift Germania Judaica, Cologne 1984, 451.

visit we've had . . . We hadn't counted on any help when we were in the East. But we thought then that once we were in the Rhineland, we would be swamped with Anglo-American shlichim [representatives] . . ."[18] (Neither, by the way, were they swamped by shlichim from the Yishuv, the Jewish settlement in Palestine.)

During this initial period, the regulations and instructions of the Supreme Headquarters of the Allied Expeditionary Forces in Europe (SHAEF) were still enforced: "Military Government action should stress treatment of Jews equal to that of other citizens of the Reich. As a general rule, Military Government should avoid creating the impression that the Jews are to be singled out for special treatment, as such action will tend to perpetuate the distinction of Nazi racial theory."[19] Emendations in these guidelines were generally not heeded by the responsible officers. "This meant that German-Jewish concentration camp inmates did not receive the same consideration as others persecuted by the Nazis but were, in fact, treated by Allied soldiers as Germans and thus former enemies."[20] According to reports of Jewish-American soldiers and official statements by investigative committees, that situation did not change until the summer.

Following the issuance of a directive by General Eisenhower, attributable in part to Jewish pressure in Washington, German Jews and Jewish DPs received preferential treatment. Jewish DP camps were set up. The State Department insisted on changes in occupied Germany which would be to the favor of the Jewish survivors. The Third Army under the command of General Patton had some quite notorious problems dealing with their own homemade anti-Jewish and pro-German attitudes until Patton's replacement. He was replaced for two reasons: his failure to implement denazification and his obvious shortcomings and reluctance in responding to the needs of the Jewish displaced persons.

Much of Jewish life developed in small and medium-sized towns which, after having been declared *judenfrei* only a short time before, were now faced with Jews demanding their rights at municipal offices. The names of these localities generally reappear in reports on antisemitic incidents. This point should be underlined, since in order to draw a complete picture of developments in the early months and years of the postwar period in Germany, it is essential to take a closer look at such smaller towns, and not just the Jewish centers in the larger metropolitan areas.

It is astonishing to note that recent publications on the social history of

---

18. See Posner, op cit. (fn. 9), 115f.

19. See Leonard Dinnerstein, America and the Survivors of the Holocaust, New York 1982, 13.

20. See Ursula Büttner, Not nach der Befreiung. Die Situation der deutschen Juden in der britischen Besatzungszone 1945–1948, in: Büttner, op. cit. (fn. 6), 388.

such towns after 1945 neglect anti-Jewish activities and the fate of Jewish survivors. Many publications on the somehow fading mythical "zero hour" show this lack of sensitivity when it comes to Jewish issues or anti-Jewish phenomena.[21]

The most typical and outstanding publication which is characterized by this historiographical omission is *From Stalingrad to the Currency Reform*. It includes an excellent article dealing with Jewish DPs and, less extensively, with surviving German Jews. Except for this article included in the book's section on "perpetrators and victims," nothing else is elaborated upon in an extensive manner when it comes to Jews or antisemitism. The chapters on the churches and the Wehrmacht fail to discuss this subject at any length. The underlying approach is sketched in the introduction to the book. Here the *dauerhafte Überwindung des Antisemitismus* (permanent overcoming of antisemitism) is mentioned as one of the central objectives of the occupation policy. That is followed by the remark: "The complex chapter of restitution (*Wiedergutmachung*) was not included in the present volume," since this topic was to be dealt with in a separate publication.[22] It seems to me a rather questionable thesis which would contend that the social history and the relationship of German and Jews in the period from "Stalingrad to the currency reform" can be reduced basically to the problem of *Wiedergutmachung*. The preface mentions antisemitic phenomena after 1945 and "gestures of reconciliation" by German politicians. But this, then, is another stereotype of avoidance: namely the attempt to sidestep any analysis of German-Jewish contemporary history within the context of social life, political reconstruction, or in relation to the churches, and especially to the former Wehrmacht soldiers.

Whenever relations to Jews in the German postwar were discussed, the term *reconciliation* became almost a cultural code-word. Its content avoided a genuine confrontation with the crimes and their consequences; its medium was philosemitism and its goal was not so much a new attitude in German-Jewish relations, but a normalizing reconciliation of West Germany with its own past. Historical writing which focuses predominantly on the Jewish DPs, *Wiedergutmachung* or "reconciliation" is a highly inadequate contribution to the analysis of the Jewish postwar experience in Germany. To keep antisemitism and the Jewish experience partially outside the writing of German history contradicts

---

21. On this lack of sensitivity or even use of antisemitic clichés, see Monika Richarz, Jewish History and Local Politics. Contemporary German Historiography on Jewish Communities. Paper given at the International Conference "How Can Jews live in Germany Today?" in Toronto, November 1989.

22. See Broszat et al., op. cit. (fn. 6), XXXVI; Ludolf Herbst/Constantin Goschler (eds.), Wiedergutmachung in der Bundesrepublik Deutschland, Munich 1989. See also the review of "Von Stalingrad . . ." by Jürgen Kocka in: *Der Spiegel*, Nr. 36 (5. 9. 1988), 45ff.

the key impact this topic had and has on German society. This, of course, poses certain questions as to continuities in German historiography.[23]

Against the background of international reports about German anti-semitism in 1945–1946,[24] for example, it becomes understandable that numerous Jewish personalities abroad reacted negatively to a reconstruction of Jewish institutions in Germany: some found it incomprehensible, others expressed their criticism or even pointed rejection. Posner noted: "Our national institutions have written off these shattered remnants of peoples right from the start." He spoke with Jewish personalities abroad. "Let them stay where they are." Adler-Rudel told Posner in London, when he called his attention to the distressful state of the German Jews. "May they wait in their beloved fatherland until their throats are slit too."[25]

The Jewish communities quite naturally gave this dilemma some serious thought. Their own self-identity oscillated between being a "community in transit," a "community in the process of liquidation" and a "Jewish new beginning." For this reason, cooperation with the Military Government and with the German authorities in the phase of renewed early activity of the Jewish communities was necessarily fraught with difficulties. The individual and institutional contacts between Germans and Jews evolving in many places in Germany at the time, naturally more intensive in the proximity of DP camps, were ridden with various contradictions.

There were a number of elements which all served as sufficient cause for Germans to link long-standing prejudicial attitudes against Jews with newfound bias. Most prominent among these were the actual (or imagined) material assistance which Jews received from the occupying powers, the struggle for return of property and belongings, along with resentment over the ongoing process of denazification. To this can be added the confiscation of apartments of former

---

23. See Otto Dov Kulka, Die deutsche Geschichtsschreibung über den Nationalsozialismus und die "Endlösung." Tendenzen und Entwicklungsphasen 1924–1984, in: *Historische Zeitschrift* 3/240 (1985), 599ff.; Konrad Kwiet/Helmut Eschwege, Selbstbehauptung und Widerstand. Deutsche Juden im Kampf um Existenz und Menschenwürde 1933–1945, Hamburg 1984, 11ff.

24. The first surveys on antisemitism by OMGUS indicated: "Results of an October 1945 survey made in the American Zone showed that a fifth of the people went along with Hitler on his treatment of the Jews. They were presented with three alternative statements for agreement or disagreement: 1) Hitler was right in his treatment of the Jews; 2) he went too far in his treatment of the Jews, but 'something had to be done to keep them within bounds'; and 3) the actions against the Jews were in no way justified. A majority agreed with the third statement. However, 19% chose the second alternative and thus ranged themselves on the side of anti-semitism." (OMGUS, Opinion Survey Section, Report No. 5, 1. 4. 1946, NA. Rg. 260).

25. Posner, op. cit. (fn. 9), 115.

Nazis for Jewish DPs. In Munich, for example, Jewish children living in these apartments had recurrent fist-fights with their "reeducated" schoolmates, who repeated in the streets what they had heard at home about the new Jewish neighbors. Later legal disputes regarding title to property, return of property and restitution were more or less "programmed" during these first months and years. As a result, Jews developed a fundamental and justifiable mistrust; and many Germans continued to have a prejudiced bureaucratic, authoritarian attitude vis-à-vis surviving victims.

Viewed against this general background, Posner's assessment of the changes taking place down to the autumn of 1945 becomes understandable: the *guter Ton* toward Jews had, after a short period, lost its topical public interest. Indeed, interest in returning Jews flagged fairly rapidly among the general populace. Posner describes this change of public opinion in sarcastic terms: "They were around again, and that was a good thing. And because they were Jews, they'd probably have a good life. (Jews know how to make a nice life for themselves.) So while the great flood of words on the injustice done to Jews continued to gush and foam, and while the individual German did not tire to assert how he felt about these matters, he was always embarrassed by the question as to what he and his friends, what his city had in fact done to make pleasant the lot of those few who were once again back among them."[26]

The journalist and writer Ralph Giordano characterized the period from the spring to autumn of 1945 in much more critical terms as far as relationships with Jews were concerned. He referred to the fear of retaliation and vengeance in certain sections of the population and emphasized that up until September 1945, no antisemite had dared to admit so publicly. "However, then the masses closely allied with National Socialism, who had an enormous fear of retaliation, had discovered that their anxieties about vengeance existed mainly in their own imagination."[27]

In early November 1945, an editorial in the Berlin *Tagesspiegel* addressed itself, under the title "Politische Gefahren" (Political dangers), to widespread German attitudes: "There has been an unmistakable change in the type of letters sent to us in the last few weeks. It is too soon to speak about a shift. But the stagnation appears to be over, people are now daring to come out in the open. A number of letters are quite baffling. They start out by condemning National Socialism and end with accusations against those who have accepted responsibility for its legacy. It is difficult to cast off the feeling of suspicion that the matter-of-factness with which all are in agreement in their judgment of Mr. Hitler is only a kind of international alibi."[28] At the same time, one should

---

26. Ibid., 111.
27. Ralph Giordano, Die Zweite Schuld oder Von der Last Deutscher zu sein, Hamburg 1987.
28. *Der Tagesspiegel* (6. 11. 1945).

ask: how did the newspaper *Tagesspiegel* in fact fulfill its responsibilities when it came to the Jewish topic? In reading through issues of the paper published between September and December 1945, one is struck by the following characteristics: beginning with the very first number, almost everything centers around the "lost war." In a bid to gain solidarity and identification among its readership, there are reports about the "emaciated," "pale," "rag-torn and tattered" soldiers returning home from the front.[29] A regular column entitled "Our Prisoners of War" is given considerable space. The paper contains a feature, "Greetings from Berliners in English Camps." For the readers of the *Tagesspiegel, camp* was not associated primarily with concentration or extermination camps, but rather with POW camps in England, France, the Soviet Union and the United States. This contextual aspect illustrates the ongoing antagonistic perception of a contemporary past. Those who had suffered were Germans: German men, German sons—there was little room for the suffering of others, for the hardships endured by "foreigners." This emotionalizing aspect is especially evident if one compares the articles dealing with Jews and Jewish topics.

In an article entitled "Jews in Germany: Emigration or Assimilation," the paper presented its Berlin readers with a piece dealing with the murder of the Jews of Berlin and the situation of those Jews who had survived: "One might ask whether, given this situation, the Jewish problem for Germany and the world deserves the attention being given it by leading statesmen in America and England. Nothing would be more dangerous to believe—for the Jews themselves as well as for the European peoples—than the notion that with the disappearance of the 'Third Reich,' the Jewish problem also suddenly vanished . . . Nothing would be more wrong today than to reverse cause and effect, like after 1918, and then make these homeless Jews—who even today, eight months after their liberation, still for the most part find it necessary to live in camps—responsible for the aggravation of the Jewish problem . . . One can only hope that the millions of victims were not in vain, but that it will now prove possible, after hundreds of years of effort, to solve the Jewish problem in its entirety. This can be accomplished by the emigration of homeless Jews, on the one hand, and by the complete assimilation of Jews who wish to remain in Europe . . . The German people are called upon to make an important contribution toward this end."[30]

Initially, what is surprising about this article is the sheer naiveté with which the German people are once again given the task of "solving the Jewish problem." Now as before, it is a problem of the Jews—i.e., the point of departure is not the problem of the non-Jewish majority, antisemitism, racism and

---

29. Ibid., 27. 9. 1945.
30. Ibid., 5. 12. 1945.

persecution of the Jews; rather, the author deals with a "Jewish problem" which extends beyond the compass of the Third Reich. Though he is aware of the causes for the existence of Jewish displaced persons, he suggests that such DPs have been made responsible in the eyes of the populace for the "aggravation of the Jewish problem." In addition, the millions of Jewish victims are given a special "significance," one which should make it possible now to "solve the Jewish problem in its entirety": namely, emigration for the homeless DPs and "complete assimilation" for those who have returned home. These, however, were prescriptions that had been advanced back in the Weimar Republic and which, after 1945, were hardly imbued with any consciousness of German responsibility.

State Bureaucracy and the Survivors: "As far as the town official is concerned, they can sleep on the floors"

Support for Jewish concerns coming from individual personalities and politicians was very often counteracted by the behavior of the German administration. Available archival materials from Cologne substantiate "thousands of cases of bureaucratic muddle and arbitrariness"[31] toward Jews during this period. At the same time, the Jewish community took an active role in the search for Nazi mass murderers and in providing housing and assistance for Jewish DPs. Naturally, this resulted in constant contacts with public offices, landlords, etc., and such contacts often entailed a certain amount of friction.

An extreme, though not uncommon, example is reported for May 1945. In the town of Celle, following instructions by British authorities, officials had distributed ration cards to German Jews who had been freed from the Belsen camp. At the same time, and in keeping with good Nazi practice, they stamped the cards with the word *Jew*.[32] In the French Zone, the Military Government had forgotten to instruct the police and registry offices that official documents, e.g., the marriage registry or new identity cards for survivors should not include the first name Israel or Sara. And since there had not been any *Behördenvorgang* (administrative order) until January 1946, the old instructions were dutifully obeyed by the state employees—to the horror of elderly Jews returning from France. But there seemed to have been some leniency in the reversal of the former official state antisemitism. The administration was instructed again in July 1946 to permanently eliminate the special additional first names enforced by the Nazis, not to note in copies of the marriage registry that the names had changed and to correct the addresses for the "Adrema" addressing machines. To

---

31. Ginzel, op. cit. (fn. 17), 456f.

32. See Wolfgang Jacobmeyer, Vom Zwangsarbeiter zum heimatlosen Ausländer. Die Displaced Persons in Westdeutschland 1945–1951, Göttingen 1985, 44.

underscore the instituted changes, these had to be published in the *Amtsblatt der Landesverwaltung Baden.*[33] In the American Zone, state officials were legally prosecuted in 1946 for issuing documents with these prenames and the word *Jude* as indication of the applicant's nationality instead of German. Judah Nadich, advisor for Jewish affairs to General Eisenhower, came across the presence of some 60 Jews in September 1945 in Bad Nauheim, located in the American Zone. They were housed in a number of inferior, unheated rooms and apartments in the town. Former Jewish homes were still in German possession. Buildings previously owned by the Jewish *Gemeinde* were being used by U.S. troops, though they were still officially the possession of the municipality, since the latter had confiscated and seized all institutionalized Jewish property during the Third Reich. Return of such property had not yet been regulated during the first several months of the occupation by the Allied authorities. Thus, the municipality of Bad Nauheim was not paying the rent to the Jewish community for the buildings being used by the occupation troops, but rather to the municipal administration, i.e., to itself—in bureaucratic overzealous fulfillment of the orders of Military Government. The representatives of the Jewish survivors protested, but in vain. Nadich went together with these representatives to the town mayor, "a pompous, autocratic and sly individual, determined to cooperate as little as possible with the Americans and, certainly not at all with the Jews, yet without getting himself into difficulties with the occupational authorities."[34] The mayor, when asked about the food situation, referred to the State Council and the State Office of Nutrition and to their regulations regarding ration cards for Jewish citizens, stating that he was unable to do anything without first consulting the State Council. In respect to the question of housing, he stated that he would have to consult the Housing Office first and that he envisaged many bureaucratic difficulties standing in the way of an exchange of living quarters between Germans and Jews.[35]

The complaints voiced by the 600 Jews in Bamberg, whom Nadich visited in October 1945, were even more serious: "When they had brought their requests for additional housing to the German official in charge of the municipal housing bureau, he told them that he did not 'give a damn where Jews lived—as far as he is concerned they can sleep on the floors.'"[36] Such experiences are mentioned by various staff members of the American and French military administration, Jewish representatives from abroad and journalists. Changes had to be brought about by intervention of the occupation authorities, thus making it

33. Commissariat pour le Land Bade. Délégation Provinciale Pour le Bade-Sud, 2–636. Affaires Politiques. Section politique—Culte Israelite, Archives de l'Occupation Française en Allemagne et en Autriche, Colmar.

34. Judah Nadich, Eisenhower and the Jews, New York 1953, 145f.

35. Ibid., 147.

36. Ibid., 204.

clear to the German administration where Jewish survivors could enforce their rights.

The critical situation in respect to the material well-being, social relations and health of the previously persecuted and disenfranchised Jewish minority made German administrative bureaus and offices, alongside those of the Military Government, into the central point of reference for the reestablishment of a "normal" Jewish postwar existence based on the exercise of full civil rights. At the same time, the German administrations began to react to the genesis of an institutionalized Jewish life. In mid-May 1946, one year after liberation, the Representative Body of Jewish Communities and Religious Associations appealed to the state governments in Germany, noting that the returnees from the concentration camps "had still not obtained the property stolen from them when deported, or their movable possessions."

Immediately after this open letter, the *Jüdisches Gemeindeblatt* published two reports. One stated that in the budget of the province of Westfalia, one million Reichsmark had been set aside for the surviving relatives of the SS. Another article described the visit by an official from the Municipal Tax Office of Düsseldorf to the Gemeinde. This official had come armed with a distraint order for 3,348.46 Reichsmark claimed in back property taxes from 1938 to 1945 levied on the land on which the synagogue was located. The synagogue had been set on fire and burned down by the Nazis in November 1938. The head of the Association of Jewish Communities (*Länderverband der jüdischen Gemeinden*) reacted angrily in a letter in which he pointed out that until 1945 "the tax offices participated as first-rate hangman's assistants in the exploitation of the Jews."[37] The reply from the tax office was a brief, strictly formal note of apology.

The examples mentioned here, culled from the everyday work routine of the German official offices, based on indifference, impudence and obtuse bureaucratic behavior, illustrate the political and social dimension associated with individual Jews and Jewish institutions. They are manifestations of the social and institutional aspect of surviving antisemitic relicts. Furthermore, one comes to realize that the re-emancipation of the Jews was in no way brought about as a result of Allied order; rather, it was a complicated process the Jews had to struggle for with the support of the occupation authorities.

This also provides an insight into the existing continuity of various phenomena in an administrative apparatus that had remained basically unchanged and connected with the legacy of preceding decades: "A social-conservative ethos and style penetrated from here into the politics, society and culture of the young republic; pre-democratic patterns of authority and non-liberal traditions

---

37. *Jüdisches Gemeindeblatt für die Nord-Rheinprovinz und Westfalen* (7. 6. 1946).

were passed on down in this manner, accompanied, to be sure, by administrative competence and efficiency."[38]

This competence and efficiency was also accorded a certain degree of importance in the eyes of the American occupation forces in view of the massively chaotic conditions they were faced with. It gave the German corps of government officials a form of self-confidence which the Jewish victims of previous German "thoroughness" must have perceived as exceptionally unpleasant, even hostile. The fact that antisemitism was no longer official state ideology and that German officialdom thus was no longer supposed—by dint of professional ethos and bureaucratic loyalty—to implement antisemitic policies, was a result of the abolition of antisemitic Nazi legislation by decrees of the Allied Control Council. Yet it proved to be rather difficult to switch to non-antisemitic efficiency, since it was not only a question of a change in socially binding norms, but of deeply rooted anti-Jewish bias. Thus, one has to be careful not to reduce German postwar antisemitism to racist traditions leading to genocide. When the Allied authorities initiated denazification, there was a wave of dismissals, arrests, internments and trials which culminated in the proceedings at Nuremberg. Yet it should be borne in mind that the judgments against state officials were comparatively lenient and that in the judgments rendered against the principal defendants, only in a small number of cases did crimes against Jews play a role as a clear factor in the decision.

OMGUS reports point out that pressure had to be exerted by the occupying powers and their appointed state commissioners in the German bureaucracy to deal with the problems and needs of the persecuted and the victims of the Nazi regime. This had led once again to the creation and intensification, though under changed conditions, of an immediate link between German officialdom, the emerging new German *Länder* and the "Jewish problem." The evolving postwar relationship of Germans to Jews and Jewish topics had thus been extended very quickly from the realm of opinions, views and public exposure of the crimes to the institutional sphere. It can be ranked among the structural aspects inseparably connected with the path leading to the formation of a new German state.

The early contacts between public administration, official politics and the Jews in Germany shaped the attitude of both Germans and Jews to each other. This involved a structural element of that evolving relationship, an institutional intermediation, which served to confirm and actualize existing attitudes among all concerned, or even create new views and attitudes. The racial antisemitism leading to extermination had indeed been overcome, but only to be replaced by

---

38. Jürgen Kocka, 1945: Neubeginn oder Restauration? in: Carola Stern/Heinrich August Winkler (eds.), Wendepunkte deutscher Geschichte 1848–1945, Frankfurt/M. 1979, 154ff.

traditional and redefined anti-Jewish stereotypes repeatedly in evidence throughout the 40-year history of the Federal Republic. However, one is struck by the lack of any treatment of this dimension in the majority of publications dealing with the genesis and the historical development of the Federal Republic.

The antisemitic conceptual clichés adapted themselves to the new reality, with more than 230,000 Jewish DPs living temporarily in occupied Germany. In November 1946, the Bavarian State Commissioner for the Victims of Fascism, Philipp Auerbach, who had himself spent several years in German concentration camps, found it pertinent to address the Bavarian public about the attitudes of the bureaucracy and the anti-Jewish reactions among the populace: "That antisemitic mood is now once again on the rise, a mood we thought we had overcome. People operate with the same method, in that they wish to construe differences between the small number of surviving German Jews and foreign Jews."[39] Hence it was the Jews from Eastern Europe who had become the main focus for early postwar German antisemitism.

Jews as the Touchstone for Democracy: "Don't underestimate Jewish power"

"In the occupation zone, thousands of young Americans come into contact with Jewish DPs whose nerves have been rubbed sore by abnormal living conditions and by the constant Jew-baiting of German officialdom and private individuals. The deteriorating economic position of the DP's, their mounting political disillusionment and moral despair, the social tensions throughout Germany, due in large part to the breakdown of economic life . . . —all these factors make for friction between the occupation forces and the DP's."[40] Such was the summary of Samuel Gringauz, a German Jew who had survived the concentration camps, was then among the first to organize the Jewish DPs and chaired the Central Committee of the Liberated Jews of Bavaria until he emigrated to the United States.[41]

The Central Committee was fundamentally opposed to a Jewish renewal in Germany and built its activities solely on international assistance. It considered itself as speaking for all Jews in Germany, propagated emigration and was

---

39. The biography of Philipp Auerbach has not yet been written, as is the case with most other leading Jewish personalities in the German postwar period. See the excellent chapter on Auerbach in Christian Pross, Wiedergutmachung. Der Kleinkrieg gegen die Opfer, Frankfurt/M, 1988, 73ff.; see also Constantin Goschler, Der Fall Philipp Auerbach. Wiedergutmachung in der Bundesrepublik Deutschland, Munich 1989, 77ff.

40. Samuel Gringauz, Our New German Policy and the DP's, in: *Commentary*, June 1948, 509.

41. See Wetzel, op. cit. (fn. 13), 54.

soon in conflict with the reestablished Jewish communities. For some years, a Jewish double structure existed; that came to an end in the early 1950s when the DPs had largely left Germany, aside from some 20,000 still remaining.

But until that time, the Jews constituted one of the main concerns of American Military Government—and after 1949 of the U.S. High Commission for Germany, not to mention the different American and international Jewish organizations and the representatives of the State of Israel.[42]

Let us take a closer look at the American side. As already indicated, it can be easily seen from numerous OMGUS reports since 1945 that the behavior of many of the military who had the task of dealing with DP affairs was riddled with contradictions. Orders were not always clear, nor was the average American GI as a rule in a position to successfully handle the psychologically highly complex situation of the Jewish survivors—or even deal with his own prejudices and biases. Symptomatic of this is one of the most important documents on the situation of the Jews in 1945, the Harrison Report.

In July 1945, Earl G. Harrison was commissioned by President Harry S. Truman—who had been informed about the desolate situation of the DPs by American representatives of Jewish organizations and by Henry Morgenthau, Secretary of the Treasury, among others[43]—to report on Jewish camps in Germany and Austria. The report contains a detailed description of the situation. First, the Harrison Report emphasized the need to recognize the true status of the Jewish DPs—i.e., their status as Jews, and not simply as nationals from their respective countries of origin, as wanted by the British. Second, it stressed the decisive importance of helping to facilitate the emigration of all who wished to do so. He regarded Palestine as the main solution, a position which influenced the reaction of the British government to the report as a whole.

"Up to this point," Harrison wrote, "they have been 'liberated' more in a military sense than actually. . . . they feel that they, who were in so many ways the first and worst victims of Nazism, are being neglected by their liberators. . . . it is difficult to understand why so many displaced persons, particularly those who have so long been persecuted and whose repatriation or resettlement is likely to be delayed, should be compelled to live in crude, overcrowded camps while the German people, in rural areas, continue undisturbed in their homes . . ." There are "very few places where fearless and uncompromising military officers have either requisitioned an entire village for the benefit of displaced persons, compelling the German population to find housing where they can, or have required the local population to billet a reasonable number of

---

42. See Yehuda Bauer, Out of the Ashes. The Impact of American Jews on Post-Holocaust European Jewry, Oxford, New York 1989; Yeshayahu Jelinek, Like an Oasis in the Desert: The Israeli Consulate in Munich, 1948–1953, in: *Studies in Zionism* IX (1988), 81ff.

43. See Dinnerstein, op. cit. (fn. 19), 9ff.; Bauer, op. cit. (fn. 42), 46ff.

them . . . At many places, however, the military government officers manifest the utmost reluctance or indisposition, if not timidity, about inconveniencing the German population. They even say that their job is to get communities working properly and soundly again, that they must 'live with the Germans while the DP's are a more temporary problem.' . . . Actually, there have been situations where displaced persons, especially Jews, have found it difficult to obtain audiences with military government authorities because ironically they have been obliged to go through German employees who have not facilitated matters."[44]

This report kept the War Department and the State Department in Washington busy since, quite suddenly and only a few weeks after V-Day, a civilian had (at least temporarily) rearranged the moral priorities of military occupation—and thus the tension-ridden triangle. Truman ordered changes, and Eisenhower reacted immediately. The British found Harrison's demand for the admission of 100,000 Jews to Palestine rather inconvenient.

Eisenhower issued a directive which stated, among other things: "Persons discharged from concentration camps, if their loyalty to the Allied cause has been determined, will receive all of the benefits granted United Nations displaced persons even if they were originally of enemy origin, such as German and Hungarian Jews, labor leaders or others put into concentration camps because of political activities or racial or religious persecution . . . These persons are accorded priority of treatment over the German population."[45] On the level of policy-making, the uncertainties of the first weeks were over, although this did not imply the immediate implementation of such directives. The orders and directives pertaining to Jews constituted only a small fraction of the myriad tasks which the Military Government had to grapple with, quite aside from the fact that such directives were not received with the requisite positive attitude by certain military organs lower down. A report by the United Nations Relief and Rehabilitation Administration (UNRRA) issued in the spring of 1946 stated: "The directives of General Eisenhower have not been and are not being properly implemented in the field. The majority of officials are woefully ignorant of the problem and the few officers remaining who have knowledge of, and sympathy for it, are unable to make their influence felt at the troop level."[46]

This was also reflected in the fact that a substantial number of Germans felt that their antisemitic "pre-education" had been confirmed in spite of the beginning reeducation. How insensitive the reactions even of influential American military leaders were was demonstrated likewise by Lucius D. Clay:

---

44. Earl G. Harrison, The Plight of the Displaced Jews in Europe. Report to President Truman, Washington D.C. 1945.
45. See Nadich, op. cit. (fn. 32), 43f.
46. See Dinnerstein, op. cit. (fn. 19), 49.

in October 1945, he stated that the German police should be given weapons and be deployed in the DP camps.[47] The cooperation with German police authorities strengthened the impression that Germans and Americans should together ensure that law and order prevailed—even enacting this by force against DPs. As a consequence, several Jewish DPs were shot by German police officers. In Stuttgart in March 1946, 200 armed German police, accompanied by shepherd dogs, raided an assembly center, killing a concentration camp survivor. Three others were wounded. Protest meetings in several DP camps and press reports led to an order barring German police in future from entering the DP camps and temporarily removed DPs from German legal jurisdiction.

The irritation among many Germans was also spurred by the fact that a large number of American GIs chose to prefer the company of well-bred, modest, neat and tidy Germans to the company of what appeared to them as impoverished, filthy and depressing DPs. In a letter an American GI expressed this attitude quite typically: ". . . the average soldier of our Army . . . cannot understand that the nice and clean-looking people with their well-kept homes and their sense of law and order could be dangerous or guilty of any crime. As for the adults, they strike most Americans in Germany as decent, pleasant, rather kindly people, who respect their parents, love children, and lavish affection on pets; they are admirably clean and orderly, and have all the solid qualities favored by Ben Franklin."[48]

German realities, especially in rural areas, looked a bit different from what had been suggested by many a propaganda film from Hollywood. The impracticable prohibition on fraternization was unable to do much to prevent these American-German encounters. Judah Nadich reported from Bavaria that it was lower military ranks in particular which had been influenced by contact with the Germans: "The German secretaries and clerks who worked in American military offices, the Germans whose homes were visited socially by American officers, the German frauleins whom American officers escorted— all accused the Jewish displaced persons of all the crimes committed in Germany."[49]

This was not primarily an instance of a traditional antisemitic attitude looking for a scapegoat, but involved a multi-layered complex of attitudes, suspicions, conjectures and a new developing sense of self-esteem. In encounters with the victors, many Germans were in search of a common bond that was directed toward and rooted in the present, after the Third Reich had seemingly become past history. Now, it was only "natural"—for one's own sense of

---

47. Ibid.

48. See Leonard Dinnerstein, German Attitudes towards the Jewish Displaced Persons, 1945–1950, in: Hans L. Trefousse (ed.), Germany and America. Essays on Problems of International Relations and Immigration, New York 1980, 243.

49. Nadich, op. cit. (fn. 32), 70.

self-esteem—to try to integrate any inkling of philo-Germanism, proclivities toward a bourgeois-Philistine "orderly" world and antisemitic hints into one's own post-defeat world-view.

Truman had every reason to send Eisenhower a long letter in which he stressed: " . . . we have a particular responsibility toward these victims of persecution and tyranny who are in our zone. We must make clear to the German people that we thoroughly abhor the Nazi policies of hatred and persecution. We have no better opportunity to demonstrate this than by the manner in which we ourselves actually treat the survivors remaining in Germany."[50] Eisenhower, in turn, answered with a long letter referring to several of the key longer-term problems: "With respect to the Jews, I found that most want to go to Palestine . . . However, the matter draws practical importance for us out of the possibility that caring for displaced persons may be a long-time job. Since I assume that most countries would be unwilling to absorb masses of these people as citizens in their respective countries, the only alternative is that of hoping they will gradually voluntarily disperse in the areas of Western Europe and try to establish them in a self-sustaining life. To this end we encourage everybody to go out and get a job if he possibly can, and have been trying to explore the possibilities of agriculture and small business in the hopes of establishing small colonies of these people near their present locations. One great difficulty is that they do not desire to look upon their present locations as any form of permanent home. They prefer to sit and wait rather than to attempt, as they say, 'forcing themselves into a population where they would never be welcome.'"[51]

Throughout these years, OMGUS staff studies repeatedly analyzed the contradictions of camps and resettlement, of emigration and integration of antisemitism and democracy. It was usually pointed out that the possibilities of the U.S. Government were limited and that there was no certainty that all Jews—or even the major part of the Jewish population then living in Germany—could be transported to Palestine, the United States, or other areas of the globe for resettlement. In addition, compared with the British Zone, there was the development of an awareness and recognition of Jewish victims as a special group.

In contrast, British occupational policy made a clear distinction between German Jews and Jewish DPs or emigrants. German Jews were treated as Germans, not as DPs: this led to disastrous human and social consequences. An English rabbi's entry visa to Hanover in the British Zone was canceled "because British citizens were not permitted to engage in temporary assistance work under Germans," under enemies who, in this case, were a group of

---

50. See ibid., 114.

51. The Papers of Dwight D. Eisenhower, Occupation 1945: VI (Editors: Alfred D. Chandler/Louis Galambos), Baltimore, London 1978, 358.

Jewish survivors. British officers were warned not to give Jews preferential treatment. Delays in granting permits to Jews to return were connected with the fact that the Military Government planned to settle the survivors in very small groups in Germany, "so that prejudice would not be able to fix on a visible object."[52] It is worth noting here that the British policy of attempting to prevent a massive emigration to Palestine confronted the U.S. authorities with the task of suggesting activities to the DPs which would ultimately amount to economic and social integration for some of them within the German environment.

It is therefore not accurate to link the matter of whether Jewish DPs remained or emigrated solely to the question of Palestine. To put it briefly, Zionism was not the only answer of Americans, Germans or surviving Jews to the moral, political and social challenges confronting Jews in the immediate postwar period. Although this is a highly emotionalized chapter of Jewish history, one ought to rely on the facts, and not ideology.

A confidential report on the situation of the Jewish DPs indicates what nonsensical proportions the uncertainty about their future could take on as a result of rumors. This report observed that in DP camps there was "a firm belief that if Palestine is inaccessible to them, a Jewish state will be set up in Bavaria."[53]

The postwar crisis in Germany and the contradictory experiences with the occupation policies led to attitudes in the populace which were not confined only to nonsensical rumors about the Soviets erecting their border along the Rhine, but also to openly voiced anti-Jewish opinions and hostile reactions to Jewish activities. The almost shock-like, antisemitic "speechlessness" which had emerged after the military defeat and initial anti-Nazi measures by the Allies began to evaporate under the impact of changing political priorities. As a result, it became obvious, at least to the American observers and Jewish personalities, that there was a vital connection between antisemitism and the weak, formal character of the "new" emerging political culture. Antisemitism, it was feared, would develop in an inverse proportion to the evolution of German democracy.[54]

The reaction of the new political parties and their leadership seemed to be totally insufficient. Investigations and interviews show that most party leaders refrained from dealing with Jewish topics or fighting antisemitism openly, being afraid to lose support of potential voters. Jewish topics were simply not a popular issue. It was no longer a matter of shock and guilt, bad conscience and adapting to the regime of occupation—but rather, an adaptation to the

---

52. See Büttner, op. cit. (fn. 6), 383.

53. OMGUS, Office of the Political Advisor, Munich, Confidential Report, 2.2. 1946, NA. Rg. 84.

54. OMGUS, Weekly Report, 2. 11.–9. 11. 1946, NA. Rg. 260.

given nationalistic potential. The usually praised capacity of the postwar parties to integrate the postwar Germans into the new Germany contradicted—at least in terms of the OMGUS orientations—the necessary new stance in German-Jewish relations. Relations toward Jews became more a matter of expediency and less a matter of morality.

The Office of Military Government for Bavaria made reference in 1946 to the political opposition to antisemitism of a large group of Bavarians "for opportunistic reasons" and elaborated upon this "new style 'philosemitism,'" citing as an example the following event.[55] The chairman of the CSU(Christian Social Union) tells an inner-circle discussion group of the CSU in August 1946: "Unfortunately I have to leave now, since I've got an important meeting with the rabbi of Munich . . . We have agreed that there is just as much place in our party for a decent and upstanding Jew as for a Catholic or Protestant. You can well imagine that this will have a very positive effect for the party in a certain direction."[56]

On March 4, 1947, the Bavarian Minister of Agriculture Baumgartner spoke in that same circle about the problems of the food crisis after the difficult winter 1946–47 and the problems for provisions to the population resulting from the merger of the zones.[57] He mourned the loss of the eastern territories, criticized the SPD, polemicized against the KPD and the overly "soft" policy of the Western powers toward the Soviet Union. In regard to the American occupational authorities, he noted: "Yet almost the biggest difficulty is the fact that—and I hope we're among ourselves here—that today almost all you find is Americans of third and fourth level ability here in Germany. Very often, they don't have a clue when it comes to objective knowledge." A lively discussion developed among those present. Baumgartner was asked whether the American intention was not simply to let the Germans die. Not satisfied with Baumgartner's reply, the man continued to press his question: "But you can see everywhere that the overwhelming majority of Americans with power and authority here are freemasons and Jews! And their attitude toward us, and most especially toward the church, is in line with this." Dr. Baumgartner responded: "My dear friend, you shouldn't be unjust when it comes to this matter, and you should be especially careful to avoid being imprudent! We will never be able to get along without the Jews—and especially the Jewish merchants in the US and elsewhere in the world: We need them in order to reestablish our old trade relations! Though as far as all the Jews from Eastern Europe here in Bavaria are

---

55. OMGUS, Trend. A Weekly Report of Political Affairs and Public Opinion, No. 23, 11. 11. 1946, NA. Rg. 260.

56. See Klaus-Dietmar Henke, Hans Woller (eds.), Lehrjahre der CSU. Eine Nachkriegspartei im Spiegel vertraulicher Berichte an die amerikanische Militärregierung, Stuttgart 1984, 92.

57. The following quotations, ibid., 122f.

concerned, I have a different view. Gentlemen, unfortunately I was forced to take part in the convention held by Jews in Reichenhall. The only positive and encouraging thing for me at that convention was the final unanimous resolution: 'Get Out of Germany!' (laughter)." The discussion turned again to the food situation and the party profile of the CSU as compared with the SPD. After this, Baumgartner made a final comment which sheds light on the evaluation of the much-needed Jewish merchants and the large numbers of superfluous Jews from Eastern Europe: "He especially emphasized the necessity for taking action against the thesis of the collective guilt of the German people. That thesis had guided the entire previous occupation policy of the Four Powers and perhaps would stamp that of the Moscow Conference as well. It was important now, he argued, before the Moscow Conference, publicly—in the press, on the radio, in speeches—to take a stand against collective guilt. It would be best if all four parties could do this jointly, or at least reach an agreement on their position. Actually it was quite ridiculous: for years, we had been listening illegally to broadcasts with those Anglo-Saxon slogans that this war was being fought against the Nazis and militarists, and that a new future would be opened up for the rest of the population. Instead of this, he said, we were now all being treated like scum and all regulations were based on the thesis of the guilt of the entire German people." The economic scarcities, forced democratization by the Military Government, the ideological pressure of the thesis of collective guilt— these form central social filters which helped shape the relationship with Jews. Even in this internal, semi-public circle, specific statements and unstated allusions blend one into the other: the speaker can be assured of the assenting positive associations of his audience. And this in both directions: the development of prudent economic relations with Jews around the world, and, simultaneously, the emotionally charged rejection of the presence of Jewish DPs in Germany, and of the demands of German Jews for restitution. All this illustrates that the gulf between the hopes of the Jews at the time of liberation or return and the political realities of the German postwar was rapidly widening.

To the extent that the hold of the occupation authorities became weaker, traditional and stereotypical biased attitudes toward Jews surfaced again. In the discussions of the *Länderrat* and other German institutions preparing the genesis of a new German state, one seeks in vain for a public and self-critical declaration addressed to the remnants of German and European Jewry. Reeducation for humanism and against antisemitism soon shifted to reeducation for integration into the West and anticommunism. The intended elimination of the antidemocratic complex of Jewish-Bolshevist stereotypes was easily reversed by simple truncation of the tabooed Jewish part of this social-psychological and political pattern. The intermingling of antisemitism and anticommunism in the German antidemocratic tradition was simply disregarded. The contradiction between a new value orientation and morality on the one hand, and incomplete structural changes, along with new political and international priorities implying a partial return to the old conservative and anticommunist values on the other, is one of the most frightening experiences of the Jewish survivor; and not only of those who were unable to get an entry visa to the United States because of their antifascist or socialist past—a problem many East European collaborators with the Nazis did not have.

As a result, those Jews within the American administration and in the media who had leftist leanings or adhered to the original intentions of democratic reeducation found themselves in 1947/48 at the margins of a political culture that was more restored than renewed. Many departed, mostly to the United States, some to East Germany. The dream of cultural change, of a reformed mentality, was shattered with the advance of the politics of containment. Major Gehlen, the reliable spy-master, was more useful for the reconstruction of West Germany than Franz Neumann, Stefan Heym or even Hans Habe.

The disturbing news about the worsening of German reactions and attitudes toward Jews, newspaper articles published in the United States and the unbroken activities of some OMGUS branches, for instance the Religious Affairs Branch.[58] led to decisions and plans to combat antisemitism. It was obvious now that basic democratic elements had to be introduced into the political culture on an institutional level. OMGUS insisted on immediate action: "Community organizations should be set up and strengthened which devote themselves to the promotion of democratic ideas . . . Civil liberty leagues, associations for human rights etc. based on membership drawn from all important groups and strata of leadership would serve as a useful purpose. These groups could exert pressure on the state agencies to grant effective protection to all citizens . . . Forms of community cooperation on problems of joint interest and benefit should be developed in which all elements (including the Jews) take part. (Religious cooperation, cultural and recreational activities, better government associations, etc.)"[59]

The dilemma of these recommendations is evident from the year they were issued—1947. Quite apart from what might have been possible to realize or what was still realizable in pragmatic terms at the time, the report came two years too late. Within the overall policy toward Germany, geared toward its integration into the West, reeducation for democracy did not necessarily have to entail a total break with all antidemocratic traditions, in addition to which it seemed quite impossible to solve the knotty problem of reeducating the educa-

---

58. See Frank Stern, The Whitewashing of the Yellow Badge. Antisemitism and Philosemitism in Postwar Germany 1945–1952, Oxford 1992; and idem, Deutsch-Jüdisches Neubeginnen nach 1945? Ein Rückblick auf die Gründungen der Gesellschaften für Christlich-jüdische Zusammenarbeit, in: *Journal Geschichte* 6, 1989.

59. OMGUS, Information Control Division, Report on Survival of Anti-Semitism, 24. 7. 1947, NA. Rg. 260.

tors. Regardless of special conditions—an extended period of time is required for economic, political, and cultural changes to have an impact on the history of mentality. *La longue durée* is usually on the side of the historian, but it almost never sides with political decision-makers.

The same holds true for the fate of denazification. John H. Herz, then working for the U.S. government, referred already in 1948 to denazification as a fiasco: ". . . denazification, which began with a bang, has since died with a whimper, . . . it opened the way toward renewed control of German public, social, economic and cultural life by forces which only partially and temporarily had been deprived of the influence they had exerted under the Nazi régime. . . . Nothing could be more revealing than the strange modification of meaning that the term 'denazification' itself has undergone. While at first signifying the elimination of Nazis from public life, it has now in everyday German language come to mean the removal of the nazi stigma from the individual concerned, that is, the procedure by which he gets rid of certain inhibitions and restrictions ('Mr. X was denazified yesterday'—he can now take up his former profession again)."[60] The "factory for fellow-travelers," as Lutz Niethammer termed it, proved to have an enormous output.[61]

To understand this development, it is instructive to examine discussions of administrative and political bodies of the German *Länder* dealing with social and economical problems. The economic recovery made demands for restitution of Jewish property more pressing. The Council of States in the U.S. Zone deliberated in March 1947 on a draft of the Law of Restitution, intended to deal with the restitution of still determinable objects of property. Preliminary work in which OMGUS was involved had been available since the summer of 1946. Representatives of Jews in Germany had been demanding the immediate return of their property since liberation, international Jewish organizations had been active for a long time, and various draft plans had been the object of debate in Washington.

Starting in the late 1930s, there had been claims for restitution raised by various Jewish organizations—first, among others, by Adler-Rudel and in a memorandum by Siegfried Moses, later to become the first state comptroller of the State of Israel.[62] The verbal agreement to reparations by the various new German institutions had, as rule, been followed by a "vehement rejection"[63]

60. John H. Herz, The Fiasco of Denazification in Germany, in: *Political Science Quarterly* 63 (1948), 569f.

61. See Lutz Niethammer, Die Mitläuferfabrik, Berlin, Bonn 1982².

62. See Rolf Vogel (ed.), Der deutsch-israelische Dialog, Teil I: Politik, vol. 1, Munich, New York a.o., 1987; Yeshayahu Jelinek, Israel und die Anfänge der Shilumim, in: Herbst, op. cit. (fn. 21), 119ff.

63. Bundesarchiv, Institut für Zeitgeschichte (eds.), Akten zur Vorgeschichte der Bundesrepublik Deutschland 1945–1949, vol. 2, Munich, Wien 1977, 270.

when it came to implementation. Thus, the discussants in the *Länderrat* rejected the draft of the law though they were "quite aware that this could not be clearly articulated, due to political reasons and out of consideration for the military government."[64] It was feared that antisemitism would increase once the law was made public. Hence, the recommendation was made only to consider those Jews "who had sold their property under compulsion, but not those who emigrated 'in the early period.'"[65] A further official statement by the heads of the state governments also expressed their "misgivings," after fundamentally affirming the notion: "This concerns the long deadline given for registration of claims until December 31, 1948, as well as the very extensive rights of appeal of the claimant, which will lead to hardships for credulous and decent assignees."[66] One should note that the end of 1948 appeared then to be too distant a deadline for claims whose formal registration alone was to take many years. The representatives of the highest German political body anticipated "hardships" only for the "credulous and decent assignees." Decency, as a matter of fact, was the code-word, when nothing else could be said about one's individual behavior during those years before May 1945. Afterwards, the political mechanism was worked out perfectly by Konrad Adenauer: since the German population was antisemitic, it seemed to be better not to touch Jewish topics. If this was unavoidable, then Allied deliberations, certain American circles with particular interests, or at least, the German suffering as a result of Allied bombing had to be mentioned. The discussion of the *Länderrat* in 1947 can be understood as some sort of prologue to the negotiations of 1951–52, although not yet cloaked in the language of diplomacy.

In the Jewish media in Germany, on the other hand, a broad discussion was underway: how to alleviate the distressful social situation of Jewish survivors, how to arrive at the necessary social rehabilitation, how to contribute to the struggle for establishing a Jewish state in Palestine. But the most burning question was: Can Jews remain in Germany or return here, since, as was remarked in a letter to the editor of the *Jüdisches Gemeindeblatt*, "no life can flower, no human beings can live in a cemetery."[67] A sense of disappointment and frustration among German Jews, especially younger survivors, was noted by OMGUS: "The fact that the German people feel no compulsion to make amends for the crimes of Nazism is the most important reason why a substantial part of the few surviving German Jews have decided to emigrate."[68]

Starting in May 1947, there were finally also certain noteworthy counter-responses from the German side, carried out in part jointly together with

---

64. Ibid.
65. Ibid.
66. Ibid., 271.
67. *Jüdisches Gemeindeblatt für die Nord-Rheinprovinz und Westfalen*, 19. 3. 1947.
68. Moses Moskowitz, The Germans and the Jews: Postwar Report, in: *Commentary* 1/1

representatives of Jewish organizations. A protest meeting was organized in the center of Bremen after a ridiculously lenient sentence had been handed down in the case of a Nazi found guilty of having murdered a Jew in 1938. Similar rallies took place in other cities.

In the summer of 1947, representatives of Jewish communities and Jewish DPs organized separate meetings where the development of official German politics was criticized. The Central Committee of Liberated Jews passed on a memorandum to General Clay, in which it recommended legislative measures against antisemitism and submitted a draft proposal for a "Bill to Combat Incitement Against Jews." Its first article reads as follows: "Whoever makes utterances verbally or in writing or acts to impair the esteem or offends the honour of the Jewish people, or one or more of its members, will, unless heavier punishment is provided for under existing other laws, receive prison terms, and if the offense is committed publicly, a prison sentence of not less than 6 months."[69] General Clay, in his response two months later, deplored antisemitism, but refrained from supporting this draft legislation, since "such legislation, in seeking to suppress oral and written statements, would undoubtedly be considered unconstitutional in the United States; and it is wholly at variance with the American belief that the public good is best advanced in the long run by the free expression of ideas, however misguided or odious the particular opinions may be . . ."[70]

Reference to the United States was a common practice, but like in so many matters when it came to the policy of occupation, the mere formal transference of basic elements from American political culture into the emergent political culture of West Germany did not correspond with German traditions and the social realities two short years after the downfall of the Nazi regime. A liberal-democratic public sphere was indeed targeted as a future goal, yet in 1947 it was not present as a relevant social-political factor. Precisely the fact that half-measures were generally the rule when it came to pursuing antisemitic activities led to a strengthening of such phenomena and to a growing gulf between surviving Jews and the "new Germany."

The successor of Lucius D. Clay as head of the American administration in Germany, John McCloy, could not refrain from repeating on several occasions the necessity for change in German-Jewish relations, necessary in terms of the new German state. In the summer of 1949, he addressed representatives of the Jewish communities and said that the behavior of Germans toward the few Jews in their midst will "be one of the real touchstones and the test of Germany's progress."[71] A few days later, a demonstration of approximately 1,000 Jews took

---

(1946), 13.

69. OMGUS, Letter to General Clay, 12. 8. 1947, NA. Rg. 260.

70. OMGUS, Letter to the Central Committee of Liberated Jews, 6. 10. 1947, NA. Rg. 260.

71. John McCloy, Remarks at the Heidelberg Conference, 1949, Truman Library, Papers of

place in Munich, against the publication of an antisemitic letter in the *Süddeutsche Zeitung,* which responded to McCloy's speech. The demonstration led to a violent clash between German police and demonstrators. The American authorities were rather reluctant to react. Overzealousness in political interference in public did not appear to be particularly opportune at the time. Combating antisemitism was left to the Germans—who were on their way to becoming a Republic. When it came to Germany there were more important problems. A few days later the elections to the first Bundestag took place.

When Adenauer issued the declaration of the new government in September 1949, it hardly touched at all on the topic of the relationship toward Jews and their persecution. The historical responsibility for the crimes committed against the Jews was given no consideration. Adenauer's commitment reads as follows: "Let me comment in this connection on antisemitic phenomena that have apparently surfaced here and there. We unequivocally condemn these efforts. We consider it disgraceful and in itself uncredible that after all that occurred in the Nazi period, there could still be individuals in Germany who persecute or hate Jews because they are Jews. Ladies and Gentlemen!" his speech went on, "I come now to an especially serious and important chapter. Through its new political organization, Germany is now in a position to deal more energetically and forcefully than before with the problem of German prisoners of war and deportees."[72]

This seemed somewhat inadequate in the light of McCloy's speech and in the light of experiences and fears among Jews in Germany. It appeared to be a veritable reversal of the touchstone of democracy. And such it remained—in spite of later publications addressed to Jews or the beginning negotiations on restitution and reparation following Adenauer's statement in this context in September 1951. Different interpretations of these negotiations do not basically change the fact that the depicted triangle was fading away as West Germany "paid off" its Jewish problem. Neither do different interpretations of Adenauer's intentions or the hunt for the last hidden briefings by the chancellor alter a clear fact: the metaphor of Jews as a touchstone of democracy had turned out in reality to be a touchstone of foreign policy, integration into the West and economic reconstruction.

In 1966, Konrad Adenauer gave an interview in which he said: "We had done the Jews . . . so much injustice, we had committed so many crimes against them, that somehow these had to be expiated, there had to be recompense if we

H. N. Rosenfield, Box 16. I would like to thank Y. Jelinek, Beer Sheva for making the original text of this speech available to me. See also *Die Neue Zeitung* (1. 8. 1949); *Allgemeine Wochenzeitung der Juden in Deutschland* (5. 8. 1949).

72. Peter Pulte (ed.), Regierungserklärungen 1949–1973, Berlin, New York 1973, 21f.

wished once more to gain respect and standing among the world's nations. Moreover, the power held by the Jews, even today, especially in America, should not be underestimated."[73]

Summary: The Waning Coherence of the Triangle

By the mid-1950s, the small Jewish remnant of German and East European origin that had survived in the *Altreich* or migrated into the western zones of occupation and did not emigrate further had become a part of the new German present. They too became integrated to a certain extent into the German postwar society. They also belonged to the "success story" of German society which "emerged more homogeneous and therefore more politically representable than ever before."[74]

But insofar as those survivors decided to remain in Germany, they had—for the most part—to deal with also an insurmountable and lasting alienation. They were alienated from their German *Mitbürger,* their fellow-citizens. They were alienated from the Jewish past in Germany through the heavy and ineradicable burden of the dead. They now lived, as Hans Mayer termed it, "in einer deutschen Fremde," in a Germany that was foreign.

This was aggravated by an additional fact; there was obviously no need in the young republic to officially and openly ask the survivors of German Jewry, now scattered all over the world, to come back. The impact of power politics between East and West, coupled with the successful reconstruction of a West German society—and the equally successful establishment of a conservative political culture—left no place for a Jewish re-definition of German-Jewish relations. Neither did it appear necessary for the German side to restore a "symbiosis" that had only existed as a wishful illusion.

The political process of integration into the West, in the specific way it was carried out, put an end to the moral, humanist and historic quality of the depicted triangle. By 1952, the incomplete democratic and humanist reconstruction of West Germany resulted in a fast-growing gap between the incomplete rehabilitation and formal re-emancipation of the Jews in Germany. Some OMGUS branches had questioned this development at the very outset of the Federal Republic. In August 1949, Jack Hain, a visiting expert, assumed that "the revival of a healthy Jewish community in Germany will, in a real sense, be a barometer of German's rehabilitation as a democratic force." He emphasized the necessary efforts by the Military Government in the field of education which "must be redoubled, and be equal to our efforts in the economic reconstruction

---

73. *Deutschland Berichte* 1/2 (January 1966).

74. Peter Baldwin, Postwar Germany in the Longue Durée, in: *German Politics and Society* 16 (1989), 6.

of Germany." But the period of Military Government came to an end in 1949, and the High Commission was not particularly interested in renewed reeducation.

The visiting expert gave a rather resigned recommendation concerning the Jews in Germany: "Those who are here must attempt to forget what has gone by, and make an effort to identify themselves with the general German community. The losses of the Jews have been incalculable and their reluctance in establishing a rapport with their German neighbors who, in the main, were at least silent accomplices to the wrongs to which the Jews were subjected, is understandable. Yet, this rapport will have to be established if the Jews are to expect the Germans to accept them on a parity with themselves."[75]

The pledge for a new mental, moral and cultural attitude toward Jews based on the values of emancipation and equality was paid off, finally, with the Luxemburg Agreement on restitution and reparations. The moral call for the total change in German-Jewish relations within Germany could now be substituted by foreign policy, as Eleonore Sterling pointed out already in 1965. This strengthened the German-American side of the triangle and significantly weakened the Jewish-German side.

The rehabilitation of the Jews embracing all spheres of society was never completed. That side of the triangle which linked the interests of the Jews in Germany and those of the occupiers, at least certain segments of the U.S. authorities, vanished into oblivion. The German-Jewish side of the triangle became a matter of pragmatism. Jews either had to adapt to the realities of Germany's relations with its allies or to leave. Their usual response was to keep busy economically along with the rest of the Germans, retire into intellectual life in one of the two Germanys or have their trunks ready and close at hand. For almost two decades, the very content of German-Jewish relations was largely reduced to the German context of *Wiedergutmachung*.

The war against the Jews thus had a strange aftermath in Germany when compared with the horrendous historic rupture the politics of antisemitism had brought upon German Jewry. The Jews living in West Germany had become the moral hostages of Germany's integration into the West. The problem is that they usually did not even realize how and why they again had become instrumental for purposes outside their concern.

Yet in the ensuing years, even the most private encounters between Germans and Jews contained a political and psychological dimension when projected against the historical background. The triangle was no longer of any importance, except for a certain impact in religious and academic life and in the media. However, the enormity and uniqueness of the mass extermination,

---

75. OMGUS, Status of Jewish Workers and Employers in Post-War Germany by Jack Hain, Visiting Expert Series No. 10 (August 1949).

of the Shoah, left its imprint on German society. It continues as a lasting component of the contemporary identity of Germans and Jews in Germany, and this quite apart from any subjective understanding of contemporary history. When looking today at the triangle sketched here and at postwar history in Germany as a whole, it becomes quite obvious that the politics of antisemitism in Nazi Europe were not only the end-point in a long chain of developments, but also the point of historical departure for the German postwar era. To put it quite bluntly: In the beginning there was Auschwitz—not Adenauer, and most certainly not the division of Germany.

The Attitude towards Jews in
Bavaria after the Second World War

Constantin Goschler

In May 1947, two years after the end of Nazi rule in Germany, Rabbi Philip S. Bernstein, the Jewish Adviser to the American Military Governor, made a speech to the UN Commission for Palestine in the Bavarian capital of Munich. The scenario he depicted was bleak:[1] "Gentlemen, if the United States Army were to withdraw tomorrow, there would be pogroms on the following day." This comment throws a harsh light on the problem of German attitudes towards the Jews after the collapse of Hitler's rule. Was Bernstein dramatising the situation in an attempt to impress his audience, or were his fears justified by actual developments? Did conditions in Bavaria on this issue differ from those in other regions of Germany? The following chapter will investigate the course of events, paying particular attention to the vital and turbulent years between the end of the war and the beginning of the 1950s.

The first answers to these questions can be obtained by assessing a number of surveys of public opinion. On the basis of interviews with approximately 3,400 people in its occupation zone and in West Berlin during 1946, the American Military Government for Germany produced a report on antisemitism in the U.S. Zone on 3rd March 1947. The survey distinguished five groups: "those with little bias (20%), nationalists (19%), racists (22%), antisemites (21%), and intense antisemites (18%)."[2] The Military Government came to the alarming conclusion that antisemitism had actually increased in recent months.[3] If the

---

1. Thomas P. Liebschütz, *Rabbi Philip S. Bernstein and the Jewish Displaced Persons,* Diss., Cincinnati 1965, p. 105, quoted in Juliane Wetzel, *Jüdiches Leben in München 1945–1951, Durchgangsstation oder Wiederaufbau?*, Munich 1987, pp. 356–357.

2. Report No. 49 (3rd March 1947): 'Antisemitism in the American Zone', in Anna J. Merritt and Richard L. Merritt (eds.), *Public Opinion in Occupied Germany. The OMGUS Surveys, 1945–1949*, London 1970, p. 146.

3. *Neue Zeitung*, 5th May 1947, 'Steigender Antisemitismus. Die Ergebnisse einer Umfrage der Nachrichtenkontrolle', p. 2.

categories of racists, antisemites and intense antisemites are amalgamated, then 59% of interviewees in Bavaria fell into that group. In the *Länder* (states) of Hesse (63%) and Württemberg-Baden (65%), which were also part of the American Zone, the proportion was even higher, while in West Berlin it was comparatively low at 45%.

Dislike of the Jews was not equally distributed among all social groups. Communists showed least antipathy towards them; dislike increased as the educational level declined; Protestants were to be found among the antisemites more frequently than Catholics, although in both denominations it was the regular churchgoers who showed greater hostility; the agricultural population was more hostile than the urban population, but Munich provided a much greater percentage of antisemites than other cities; women were more prejudiced than men, a factor which was probably connected to their lower level of education.[4]

A full year later the investigation in the U.S. Zone was repeated in order to detect how attitudes had developed in the interim. The overall share of the prejudiced groups—intense antisemites, antisemites and racists—remained virtually the same in April 1948. The first two of these categories had actually declined somewhat, but that of the racists had increased.[5]

Any attempt to follow the course of developments over time is hampered by problems with the available data, since both the regions covered and the questions asked were different in later polls. In these circumstances no direct comparison is possible. However, it is clear from investigations conducted in the territory of the U.S. Zone under the auspices of the American High Commissioner, and from data gathered by a German opinion research institute and covering the whole of the Federal Republic, that negative attitudes towards the Jews remained widespread even after the beginning of the 1950s. In December 1946, 48% of those questioned in the American Zone took the view "that some human races are more fit to rule than others"; by October 1949, after some swings above and below, the figure was still 44%.[6] A study covering the entire Federal Republic even detected a clear increase in negative attitudes towards the Jews between 1949 and 1952.[7] In the following decades the extent of

---

4. See 'Antisemitism in the American Zone', loc. cit.

5. See Report No. 122 (22nd May 1948): 'Prejudice and Antisemitism', in Merritt and Merritt (eds.), *Public Opinion in Occupied Germany*, op cit., pp. 239–240.

6. See Report No. 1 (30th December 1949): 'The State of German Nationalism following the Founding of the West German Republic', in Anna J. Merritt and Richard L. Merritt (eds.), *Public Opinion in Semisovereign Germany. The HICOG Surveys, 1949–1955*, Urbana–Chicago–London 1980, pp. 53–54.

7. To the question "What is your attitude toward Jews?", in August 1949 15% of those sampled in West Germany gave ambivalent answers and 23% of answers were clearly antisemitic. In December 1952 these responses were 18% and 34% respectively. See Elisabeth Noelle and Erich Peter Neumann (eds.), *Jahrbuch der öffentlichen Meinung, 1947–1955*, Allensbach 1956, p. 128.

antisemitic views declined strongly, though without ever disappearing completely.[8]

What these figures show is that antisemitism—or at least negative attitudes towards Jews—affected a considerable proportion of the German population in the first decade after the Second World War. This is certainly shocking but, in view of recent history, not altogether surprising. What do the figures mean when applied to Bavaria, our own area of inquiry? Insofar as the figures allow distinctions or comparisons to be made with other German regions, they reveal a gradual though not a fundamental difference in the prevalence of such attitudes. However, the potential peculiarities of the Bavarian example are not apparent if the investigation is confined to opinion research data. It is, therefore, necessary to analyse specific problem areas which will enable us to clarify details of developments in Bavaria.

First and foremost, it is essential to recall the situation and composition of the Jewish community in Bavaria after the end of the Nazi persecutions. There are two crucial factors to be taken into account. Firstly, between 1945 and 1950 more Jews were living in Bavaria than in the whole of the rest of Germany. Secondly—and closely connected with the first point—there was hardly any continuity of Bavarian Jewish life before the destruction of the Jewish communities in Hitler's Germany and after the end of Nazi rule.

After the war, there were two very different spheres of Jewish life in Bavaria. One of them, the remnant of the Bavarian Jewish communities, began to reorganise in many localities. The example of Munich is typical. In 1933 the Munich Jewish community had numbered approximately 9,000 people. By the end of June 1945 there were 430 Jews there, forming the core of a new Jewish community. Of these 84 were so-called "full Jews" who had managed to go into hiding in the Nazi years; over 300 were baptised Jews or those living in "privileged mixed marriages," who had been protected from deportation; and there were a number of survivors returning home from Theresienstadt and other camps. By spring 1946 the Jewish remnant in Munich had grown to around 700 people, including a number of re-emigrants from abroad.[9]

---

8. The proportion of people believing that no Jews should live in Germany declined from 37% in December 1952 to 19% in March 1965. See Elisabeth Noelle and Erich Peter Neumann (eds.), *Jahrbuch der öffentlichen Meinung 1965–1967*, Allensbach–Bonn 1967, p. 96. In October 1981 14% were against working with Jewish colleagues or living together in the same house. The responses for black people were 23% for both. See Elisabeth Noelle-Neumann and E. Piel (eds.), *Allensbacher Jahrbuch der Demoskopie 1978–1983*, Munich–New York–London–Paris 1983, p. 79.

9. See Juliane Wetzel, '"Mir szeinen doh". München und Umgebung als Zuflucht von Überlebenden des Holocaust 1945–1948', in Martin Broszat, Klaus-Dietmar Henke and Hans Woller (eds.), *Von Stalingrad zur Währungsreform. Zur Sozialgeschichte des Umbruchs in Deutschland*, Munich 1988, pp. 334, 340.

Alongside the small number of surviving German Jews in Bavaria, however, there was a significant concentration of Jewish people from a different background. In numerical terms this group was far more important. These were the Jewish Displaced Persons (DPs). According to Allied definition the DPs were "civilians outside the national boundaries of their countries by reason of the war," who needed assistance to return or to resettle.[10] They included Jews who had been liberated from Nazi concentration camps and forced labour camps, as well as people who had poured into the Western occupation zones, particularly the American Zone, only after the end of the war. In 1946 alone, when the influx reached its high point, more than 100,000, mainly Polish Jews, crossed into the American Zone—mostly into Bavaria—where they were given DP status.[11] One reason for this influx of East European Jews lay in post-war Polish antisemitism; another was the attempt of Jewish organisations to create a mass problem in the American Zone in order to intensify the pressure for the opening of Palestine to Jewish immigrants.[12] As far as Bavaria was concerned, the result was that the number of Jewish DPs increased from approximately 25,000 in spring 1946 to around 80,000 by the end of the year.[13] Due to the subsequent emigration of Jewish DPs, the total then declined rapidly until the beginning of the 1950s.

The vast majority of these DPs lived in camps. These were administered by the American Military Government for a transitional period, before coming under the control of the United Nations Relief and Rehabilitation Administration (UNRRA) and later the International Refugee Organisation (IRO). Most Jewish DPs in the camps were waiting for the chance to emigrate, usually to Palestine/Israel or the USA. In their own view, they were completely outside German society. For a short period Jewish life blossomed in the camps, though this came to an end as most of the Jewish DPs left the country.[14] By the beginning of the 1950s the majority of camps were closed, and the remain-

10. See Supreme Headquarters, Allied Expeditionary Force (SHAEF), Administrative Memorandum No. 39 (revised—16th April 1945), subparagraph 5b, Archiv des Instituts für Zeitgeschichte, München (IfZ-Archiv), Fi 01.06.

11. See Wolfgang Jacobmeyer, 'Die Lager der jüdischen Displaced Persons in den deutschen Westzonen 1946/47 als Ort jüdischer Selbstvergewisserung', in Micha Brumlik et al. (eds.), *Jüdisches Leben in Deutschland seit 1945*, Frankfurt a. Main 1986, p. 37.

12. See Wolfgang Jacobmeyer, 'Jüdische Überlebende als "Displaced Persons". Untersuchungen zur Besatzungspolitik in den deutschen Westzonen und zur Zuwanderung osteuropäischer Juden 1945–1947', in *Geschichte und Gesellschaft*, 9 (1983), pp. 434–435.

13. IfZ-Archiv, Fi. 01.30–01.34, ITS-Arolsen; see also Wetzel, 'München und Umgebung als Zuflucht', loc. cit., p. 349.

14. See Abraham J. Peck, 'Jüdisches Leben in Bayern nach 1945. Die Stimme von She'erit Hapletah', in Manfred Treml and Josef Kirmeier (eds.), *Geschichte und Kultur der Juden in Bayern. Aufsätze*, Munich–New York–London–Paris 1988, pp. 505–516; Wetzel, 'München und Umbegung als Zuflucht', loc. cit., pp. 352–354.

ing few thousand Jewish DPs were transferred to German responsibility in mid-1951.

However, a smaller proportion of Jewish DPs settled outside the camps and integrated into German society and the economy. There they became members of the newly established Jewish religious communities, the structure of which was thereby changed in a fundamental way. After a short time the old-established German Jews were frequently in the minority in these communities, a fact which inevitably led to cultural, political and religious tensions. In part this was the result of the contrast between the *Ostjuden* (eastern European Jews)—much more traditional in religious matters—and the old-established German Jews. The tendency was intensified by the fact that, as a consequence of the Nazi persecutions, it was the Jewish partners in mixed marriages who had been much more likely to survive—the very people who were already on the periphery of, or even outside, the Jewish faith.

The composition of the Jewish religious community in Bavaria at the end of the 1950s can be described with some accuracy. In Munich there were 1,800 former DPs and approximately 400 German Jews, while the proportion of DPs to German Jews was generally similar among the 850 Jews who were scattered among seven other Bavarian Jewish religious communities.[15] While the gathering of tens of thousands of DPs in UN-administered camps had been a passing—though highly significant—phenomenon of the early post-war years, the fundamental restructuring of the Jewish communities was a factor of lasting importance. Nowhere was the change so radical as in Bavaria.

The "DP question" was also a factor in shaping Bavarian attitudes towards the Jews in the early post-war period, even though the DPs included other groups. In this respect the attitude of the American Military Government, which had custody of the camps during this period, is also significant. At first no distinction was made between Jewish and non-Jewish DPs. This could lead to situations in which the Jews were accommodated alongside their former persecutors, since the DPs clearly included people who had collaborated with the Germans or who had actually taken an active part in the persecutions.[16]

In these circumstances the conduct of the first American Military Governor for Bavaria, General George S. Patton, was notorious. It was Patton who ensured that the DP camps were surrounded with barbed wire and watch

---

15. Nuremberg (43 former DPs, 164 German Jews), Regensburg (84 former DPs, 88 German Jews), Augsburg (85 former DPs, 64 German Jews), Würzburg (25 former DPs, 80 German Jews), Straubing (79 former DPs, 9 German Jews), Bamberg (65 former DPs, 10 German Jews), Amberg (60 former DPs, 9 German Jews). See Harry Maòr, *Über den Wiederaufbau der jüdischen Gemeinden in Deutschland seit 1945*, Mainz 1961, pp. 29–30.

16. Leonard Dinnerstein, *America and the Survivors of the Holocaust*, New York 1982, pp. 17–24.

towers and were generally ill-equipped to give their inhabitants any sense of liberation. The Jewish DPs were often physically and spiritually shattered by their experiences, which inevitably had a damaging effect on social standards in many cases; consequently, they made a much less favourable impression on Patton and some other Americans than the physically clean, well-turned out Germans.[17]

Measures were taken to remedy the situation in August 1945, after the Americans were appalled by the results of a commission of investigation under Earl G. Harrison, the former American Immigration Commissioner. In his report Harrison had concluded:[18]

> As the matter now stands, we appear to be treating the Jews as the Nazis treated them except that we do not exterminate them. They are in concentration camps in large numbers under our military guard instead of S.S. troops. One is led to wonder whether the German people, seeing this, are not supposing that we are following or at least condoning Nazi policy.

Patton regarded these reproaches as the result of a Jewish conspiracy in Washington. He wrote in his diary: "Harrison and his ilk believe that the Displaced Person is a human being, which he is not, and this applies particularly to the Jews who are lower than animals."[19]

Eisenhower acted to remove Patton, as well as the barbed wire. Moreover, the Jewish DPs were now accommodated in separate camps. From then on, the American occupying power adopted a positive attitude towards the Jewish DPs in Bavaria as elsewhere. To this end the post of Adviser on Jewish Affairs to the Military Governor was created and appointments made on the suggestion of the big American Jewish organisations. One such Jewish Adviser was Rabbi Bernstein, whose remarks opened this chapter.

The Military Government also adopted a positive approach to the German Jews living outside the camps. At the same time, the Americans took care that antisemitic tendencies did not emerge in Bavarian politics, and it was a major contribution of the American Military Government that antisemitism ceased to be socially acceptable in any form. In October 1945 the American Military Government also instructed the Bavarian government to give preferential treatment to the Jews.[20] Subsequently the Bavarian government established a

---

17. See *The Patton Papers: 1940–1945*, ed. by Martin Blumenson, Boston 1974, pp. 750–755.

18. See Earl G. Harrison Report to President Truman on 'The Plight of the Displaced Jews in Europe', August 1945, p. 12, reprinted in Dinnerstein, op. cit., Appendix B.

19. *The Patton Papers*, op. cit., p. 751.

20. See Bayerischer Ministerrat, 24th October 1945, IfZ-Archiv, S1 Hoegner, ED 120, folder 354.

Staatskommissariat zur Betreuung der Juden (state commission for the care of the Jews). At first this was headed by Hermann Aumer, an *Achteljude* ("one eighth Jew") according to the definition of the Nuremberg Laws. His task was "to take all necessary measures in order to give all necessary assistance to the Jewish population of Bavaria [which had been] persecuted on racial grounds." At the same time he was also to ensure "that the Jewish part of the population of *Land* Bavaria again becomes a healthy factor in the Bavarian economy."[21]

After the dismissal of Aumer for corruption, a *Staatskommissariat für rassisch, religiös und politisch Verfolgte* (state commission for the victims of racial, religious and political persecution) was created by amalgamating Aumer's organisation with the *Staatskommissariat für die politisch Verfolgten*, which had been created in the interim. At its head was appointed Philipp Auerbach, a member of an old-established Hamburg Jewish family. He had spent four and a half years in German prisons and concentration camps and, after liberation, had initially worked for the government of North Rhine Province in the care of victims of persecution and refugees. After the British Military Government had dismissed him over political differences, Auerbach had worked as Chairman of the zonal office of the Jewish communities in the British Zone and as Vice President of the *Zentralkomitee für die befreiten Juden* (Central committee for liberated Jews) in the British Zone.[22]

Before Auerbach took office in Bavaria, the main principles of his work were outlined by his future boss, the Social Democratic Minister of the Interior, Josef Seifried. Firstly, good will must be demonstrated to the Americans; "but at the same time we have to help the DPs to move on, because more refugees are already pressing behind them."[23] This was a reference to the German expellees from the East whose presence, indeed, was creating a source of intense social rivalry.

In June 1947 the Bavarian *Ministerrat* (council of ministers) discussed the mass influx of Jews from the East into Bavaria. *Ministerpräsident* Hans Ehard of the *Christlich-Soziale Union* (Christian-Social Union, CSU) predicted that it could lead to the rise of antisemitism in a previously unknown form. State Secretary Gentner poured oil onto the flames by declaring that of the 600 Polish Jews in his *Landkreis*, only two were willing to work while all the others were involved in the black market. "The consequence was a hatred of Jews which

---

21. Bestallungsurkunde für Hermann Aumer, 26th October 1946, signed Wilhelm Hoegner, Bayerisches Hauptstaatsarchiv, München (BayHStA), MA 114 262.

22. See Constantin Goschler, 'Der Fall Philipp Auerbach. Wiedergutmachung in Bayern', in Ludolf Herbst and Constantin Goschler (eds.), *Wiedergutmachung in der Bundesrepublik Deutschland*, Munich 1989, pp. 78–79.

23. See testimony of Josef Seifried, 31st August 1951, Archiv des Bayerischen Landtags, München (Archiv-BayLT), Protokoll der 6. Sitzung des Untersuchungsausschusses zur Untersuchung der Vorgänge im Landesentschädigungsamt, p. 106.

was previously completely unknown."[24] The fact that the German police had no right to enter the DP camps was a particular source of irritation.

While the German Jews in Bavaria came under the control of the Bavarian authorities, these had no rights where the DP camps were concerned. Persistent friction was the result. Because of their experience, the Jewish DPs in the camps were overwhelmingly hostile towards the Germans and regarded their stay as no more than a temporary stop.[25] Naturally enough there was some law-breaking amongst the Jewish DPs and, as a result of the persecution they had suffered, scarcely any feeling that injustice was being done to the German population. Yet the criminal element among the DPs was very small.[26] Nevertheless, Jewish participation in the black market and other crimes specific to the post-war situation was often highlighted. Stories on the subject were eagerly circulated among the Bavarian population and became part of the inventory of a new generation of prejudices. Symbol of the trend was Munich's *Möhlstraße*, which until 1949 was a well-known centre both of Jewish life and also of the black market.[27] Another fertile breeding ground for antipathy was the fact that Bavaria had to pay considerable sums to finance the DPs, over and above the occupation costs.[28] One particular stumbling block was created when German homes had to be evacuated to accommodate DPs, a process which inevitably caused hardship.[29] Furthermore, the German side felt scarcely any responsibility or obligation regarding the Jews from Eastern Europe, who had come into the area only after the end of the war.

In attitudes towards the Jews in Bavaria as a whole, however, some distinctions were made. Typical of this is a comment made at the beginning of 1947 by Josef Baumgartner, the Bavarian *Landwirtschaftsminister* (minister of agriculture) and later chairman of the *Bayernpartei*. In a closed political discussion of the CSU he remarked:[30]

---

24. See Bayerischer Ministerrat, 20th June 1947, IfZ-Archiv, N1 Hoegner, ED 120, folder 364.

25. See Peck, loc. cit., p. 505.

26. See Jacobmeyer, 'Jüdische Überlebende als "Displaced Persons"', loc. cit., pp. 439–441.

27. See Wetzel, 'München und Umgebung als Zuflucht', loc. cit., pp. 354–355.

28. See Institut für Besatzungsfragen, *Das DP-Problem. Eine Studie über die ausländischen Flüchtlinge in Deutschland*, Tübingen 1950, pp. 87–91.

29. See 'Mündlicher Bericht des Ausschusses für Sozialpolitik zu den Anträgen des Abgeordneten Stock und Genossen betreffend Freigabe der von der UNRRA beschlagnahmten Arbeitersiedlung "Kaltherberge" in München', *Verhandlungen des Bayerischen Landtags*, Steno-graphische Berichte, 45th meeting on 16th January 1948, pp. 576–581.

30. Josef Baumgartner on 4th March 1947 at the "Dienstag-Club", in Klaus-Dietmar Henke and Hans Woller (eds.), *Lehrjahre der CSU. Eine Nachkriegspartei im Spiegel vertraulicher Berichte an die amerikanische Militärregierung*, Stuttgart 1984, p. 122. Baumgartner is referring to the second congress of liberated Jews at Bad Reichenhall in 1947.

Without the Jews and particularly the Jewish businessmen in the USA and the rest of the world we will never manage: We need them for the resumption of our old trade relations! As regards the many *Ostjuden* here in Bavaria I am of a different opinion: Gentlemen! I was unfortunately compelled to take part in the Jewish congress in Reichenhall: The one pleasing thing at the meeting for me was the resolution which was unanimously adopted: "Out of Germany"! (Laughter).

In an attitude with echoes dating from the 1920s—for example the expulsion of *Ostjuden* from Bavaria ordered by *Generalstaatskommisar* von Kahr in 1923[31]—the Jews from the East were regarded as more or less undesirable elements. By contrast, the German Jews tended to be seen as important helpers in the re-establishment of international trade relations.

This contrast between the German Jews and the *Ostjuden* also coincided with tensions within the Jewish community itself. From the point of view of foreign Jewish organisations, the Jewish communities in Germany were acting as virtual collaborators for a time, in so far as they did not follow the goal of their own disbandment. In 1948 the World Jewish Congress in Montreux had decided that there should be no new Jewish society on the "blood-soaked soil" of Germany. This attitude was changed only gradually.[32] On the other side, the German Jews continued to harbour traditional resentments against their co-religionists from the East.[33]

The post-war Jewish communities in Bavaria were thus in a quandary. On the one hand—at least until the beginning of the 1950s—they were looked at askance by the vast majority of foreign Jewish organisations and the Jewish DP organisations. On the other, they lived in an environment which was bound to seem highly insecure. When post-war antisemitism flared up again from 1947 it appeared even more threatening now that it was no longer encouraged and exacerbated from above as in the Nazi years, but bore the character of an "indigenous" antisemitism with its roots in popular sentiment.

Alongside the difficulties arising from the DP problem, this antisemitism was associated mainly with the fact that most of the Jews were now completely without means and in need of support. Though the privileges granted to them were really very modest, they aroused envy amongst the Bavarian population.

---

31. See Reiner Pommerin, 'Die Ausweisung von "Ostjuden" aus Bayern 1923. Ein Beitrag zum Krisenjahr der Weimarer Republik', in *Vierteljahrshefte für Zeitgeschichte*, 34 (1986), pp. 311–340.

32. See Hendrik George van Dam, 'Die Juden in Deutschland nach 1945', in Franz Böhm und Walter Dirks (eds.), *Judentum. Schicksal, Wesen und Gegenwart*, vol. II, Wiesbaden 1965, p. 896.

33. See Maòr, op. cit., pp. 25ff.

Other needy groups, such as the victims of political persecution and the German refugees and expellees, also felt the force of this resentment. However, the last of these had one major socio-psychological advantage; since the Germans were not directly to blame for the injustices they suffered, this group could ultimately count on greater sympathy.

A dangerous brew had been created by the mixing of traditional prejudices against the Jews with resentment at privileged treatment as compensation for their sufferings under Nazism and their supposed massive participation in the black market. At the beginning of 1948 the CSU deputy Georg Stang told the Bavarian *Landtag* (parliament) that he detected a "spontaneously increasing wave of antisemitism." He continued:[34]

> I am sorry for the decent Jews who must now suffer in the judgement of the people for the bad performance of many of those of their race . . . I think that there is no need to stir up antisemitism, which we all rigorously reject, artificially; the flame [will] rise up on its own if things go on as before with many members of the Jewish race.

In view of such tensions, *Staatskommissar* Auerbach had already published an appeal to the Jewish communities in Bavaria in March 1947. Here he had called on them not to behave in a provocative manner in public. In particular, Auerbach urged the Jews not to make unjustified attacks on people as "German pigs" or as Nazis on public transport or in the street; nor should they provoke people by a "public display, on trains and in trams, of foodstuffs and luxuries which are not accessible to the general population." Incidents of this kind, he thought, had contributed to the spread of an antisemitism previously unknown in Bavaria.[35] This appeal brought Auerbach sharp criticism in the New York journal *Aufbau*.[36]

However, when Auerbach let it be known through the press and radio that the Jews in Bavaria were to be granted more favourable rates of exchange in the currency reform of June 1948, the result was the spread of numerous rumours about the preferential treatment of the Jews, in which the antisemitic undertones were unmistakable. There were other more aggressive reactions. The American Military Government reported "attempted student demonstrations before American Joint Distribution Committee Agencies and rumors of a

---

34. See *Verhandlungen des Bayerischen Landtags*, Stenographische Berichte, 52nd meeting on 6th February 1948, p. 834.

35. See Philipp Auerbach, 'An alle Jüdischen Gemeinden', 7th March 1947, IfZ-Archiv, Nl Hoegner, ED 120, folder 138.

36. See *Verhandlungen des Bayerischen Landtags*, Stenographische Berichte, 45th meeting on 16th January 1948, p. 578.

march of Bavarians upon the home of Dr. Auerbach."[37] Eventually the Americans debated whether Auerbach's tactically unwise public statements had been responsible for stirring up antisemitism, and whether he should consequently be dismissed. However, they came to the following conclusion regarding Auerbach's comments: "If they have roused anti-semitism that is evidence of a hangover of Nazism in the Bavarian mind, rather than the fault of Dr. Auerbach."[38]

One of the most striking symptoms of increasing post-war antisemitism was an extensive series of desecrations of Jewish cemeteries. From the beginning of 1948 there were fresh reports of such attacks each week in the newspaper, especially in Franconia. The incidents developed into a wave, which lasted for months before ebbing once again. But it was not limited to Bavaria; similar incidents occurred in other German *Länder*. Though deliberate antisemitic conduct did not lie behind every single attack, the incidents were nevertheless only the tip of the iceberg. Beneath them lay a wide range of attitudes towards the Jews and their places of worship, ranging from indifference to outright hostility.

After protests from Auerbach and others, the Bavarian *Ministerrat* debated whether an appeal to the population—of the kind issued by the governments of Hesse and North Rhine-Westphalia—was a suitable method of stopping the incidents. But *Ministerpräsident* Ehard and his ministers believed that such a step would only attract unwanted attention. Their main fear was that Bavaria would be depicted in foreign press headlines as the stronghold of antisemitism. The *Ministerrat* eventually agreed "that these destructions of cemeteries were not a sign of antisemitism, but provocative acts by terrorist circles."[39]

In reality, the problem could not be overcome by adopting an ostrich-like policy of this kind. Complaints about the ineffectiveness of the Bavarian police grew more frequent. With the argument that "this news and the commentaries associated with it [are] . . . liable to do considerable damage to the reputation of Bavaria abroad,"[40] a question was asked in the Bavarian *Landtag* in July 1948 regarding the desecration of Jewish cemeteries. *Innenminister* (minister of the interior) Willi Ankermüller defended the *Landpolizei* under his control against

---

37. OMGB, Monthly Report for Period Ending 30 June 1948. Education and Cultural Relations Division. Religious Affairs Branch, IfZ-Archiv, MF 260, OMGUS-By, 10/51–3/3.

38. Louis G. Kelly, Chief/OMGUS-Displaced Persons Branch, 28th July 1948, IfZ-Archiv, MF 260, OMGUS-CAD, 3/173–1/19.

39. See minutes of the meeting of the Bayerischer Ministerrat, 16th April 1948, Bayerische Staatskanzlei, München.

40. See Interpellation der Abgeordneten Dr. von Prittwitz und Gaffron und Hausleiter und Genossen betreffend Schändung israelitischer Friedhöfe (Beilage 1615), *Verhandlungen des Bayerischen Landtags*, Stenographische Berichte, 79th meeting on 22nd July 1948, p. 1650.

the charge that it had not intervened sufficiently or been successful in hunting for the perpetrators. He indicated that of 21 desecrations which had been notified, 15 cases had been cleared up. Of these, seven were attributed to "natural processes of decay" and in six more the perpetrators had been "children and youths playing." In only two cases had criminal offences been attributable to adults, and in one of these the perpetrator had been trying to demonstrate the need for a permanent watch on the cemetery. (In fact, mounting a guard was not an entirely effective method: in Regensburg shortly before, an auxiliary policeman given the job of protecting the Jewish cemetery had himself been responsible for desecrating it.[41]) Referring to the fact that numerous Christian cemeteries had also been desecrated during the same period, Ankermüller rejected the view "that the damage done to the Jewish cemeteries had been the affair of a Nazi underground movement. All these occurrences must be seen much more as symptom of a general brutalisation caused by the Nazi dictatorship and the war."[42]

In the background to this debate was an attack in the press by *Regierungsrat* Bachmann of the *Innenministerium* against the President of the Bavarian *Landpolizei, Freiherr* von Godin. Bachmann was himself a Jew who had survived the Nazi period by spending a number of years underground. He had reacted with bitter sarcasm to the publication of the *Landpolizei* findings that the destruction in Jewish cemeteries could be attributed to the weather and to children at play, and to the refusal to perceive any signs of antisemitism in these developments. His letter to the Franconian *Main-Post* contained the following remarks:[43]

It is thus clearly established who is guilty of these scandalous incidents, and that is none other than the American government. It appears that German children have eaten their fill of school meals to such an extent that they are now capable of overturning hundreds of heavy gravestones.

In the Bavarian *Landtag*, Bachmann's comments provoked a storm of indignation which had much wider implications than its original cause, namely the desecration of Jewish cemeteries. The CSU deputy Hans Hagn argued furiously:[44]

---

41. See *Süddeutsche Zeitung*, 6th July 1948, 'Neue Schändungen jüdischer Friedhöfe'; *Verhandlungen des Bayerischen Landtags*, Stenographische Berichte, 81st meeting on 28th July 1948, p. 1756.

42. See *Verhandlungen des Bayerischen Landtags*, Stenographische Berichte, 79th meeting on 22nd July 1948, pp. 1748–1749.

43. See *Verhandlungen des Bayerischen Landtags*, Stenographische Berichte, 81st meeting on 28th July 1948, p. 1752. Bachmann was alluding to the U.S.-financed "Hoover Program", which provided extra food rations for German schoolchildren.

44. Ibid.

No person in this house approves when memorials to the dead are damaged in any way. But we must not go so far as artificially to create an atmosphere in which our efforts to achieve a good understanding with previous victims of racial persecution are seriously impaired simply because of the effects of the climate or the stupidity of little children.

Bachmann was marked out as a "calumniator," his comments as a tasteless gaffe which damaged Bavaria's reputation in the world. The Bavarian *Landtag* was unanimous in its judgment (even *Staatskommissar* Auerbach agreed); amid applause, *Innenminister* Ankermüller announced the "disciplinary assessment" of the *Regierungsrat*, who was now regarded as a man who had fouled his own nest.[45]

In many ways this episode is symptomatic of Bavarian relations with Jews and antisemitism after the war. Of course none of the deputies approved of the desecration of Jewish cemeteries—this was sheer common sense. But at the same time, hardly anyone was ready to come to grips with the potential antisemitism which these acts expressed. The existence of such sentiments was freely admitted in other circumstances, and could even be used as a political argument. For example, during efforts to block unwanted measures concerning the DPs there were constant references to the danger of encouraging the growth of antisemitism.[46] It is thus more than an unfortunate coincidence that the Bavarian *Landtag* showed its greatest resolution in reprimanding Bachmann for breaking the silence about the deeper causes behind the desecration of Jewish cemeteries.

Neither the harsh Bavarian climate nor the games of Bavarian children, however, could be used as an excuse in August 1949, when the liberal *Süddeutsche Zeitung* published a reader's letter signed "Adolf Bleibtreu." The letter included the following remarks:[47] "I am employed by the Amis and many of them have already said that they forgive us everything except for one thing, and that is that we did not gas them all, for now America is blessed with them." The letter had been chosen from many with a similar content and published without comment.

Next day, following a protest meeting, some 600 Jewish demonstrators gathered with banners expressing their anger and tried to make their way to the *Süddeutsche Zeitung*. Their route was barred by the German police. The attempt to disperse this unauthorised demonstration led to bitter street fighting in which demonstrators hurled paving stones in response to the use of police

---

45. Ibid., p. 1757.

46. See *Verhandlungen des Bayerischen Landtags*, Stenographische Berichte, 45th meeting on 16th January 1948, p. 577.

47. *Süddeutsche Zeitung*, 9th August 1949, 'Leserbriefe'.

truncheons. One policeman—in self-defence, according to the commission of enquiry—fired his gun and severely wounded two demonstrators. Order was finally restored only with the help of the American military police.[48]

The publication of this letter and the subsequent conduct of the German police were both bitterly criticised, particularly by the Jewish press abroad. Nevertheless, the Munich Jewish religious community made a full apology to the German guardians of order.[49] The American High Commissioner, John J. McCloy, who had to consider possible proceedings against the *Süddeutsche Zeitung,* decided to accept its editor's excuse that the matter had been a regrettable oversight:[50]

> It appears to me to be far better to allow the free democratic forces in Germany and the reaction of a vigorous public conscience to rebuff and combat Nazi and antisemitic sentiments wherever they appear, than to intervene with arbitrary Military Government action in every instance of this sort and thereby discourage the initiative and sense of responsibility of the German public.

The publication of the "Bleibtreu letter" had drawn clear attention to the existence of antisemitic attitudes in the Bavarian and German population. However, it was highly significant that its publication had met with the unanimous condemnation of the German media. The American High Commissioner, who regarded the resolution of problems between Jews and Germans as the litmus test of German democracy, placed his hopes for the future on the process of change which this development reflected, proceeding more or less from the top down.[51]

At the beginning of the 1950s, however, Bavaria was still making the headlines. A series of events there culminated in a sensational trial which many Jews regarded as an attempt to make new antisemitic propaganda. On 10th March 1951, the President of the Bavarian *Landesentschädigungsamt* (compensation office) was arrested in Munich. The man was Philipp Auerbach, who was also a board member of the *Zentralrat der Juden in Deutschland* (Central Council for Jews in Germany) founded in 1950.[52] He was accused of a whole series of of-

---

48. See Murray D. van Wagoner to C. Montieth Cilpin, 26th August 1949, IfZ-Archiv, MF 260, OMGUS-By 13/144–2/7; *Neue Zeitung,* 11th August 1949, 'Schwere Tumulte in München. Antisemitischer Leserbrief verursacht Straßenschlacht'.

49. See van Wagoner to Cilpin (as note 48).

50. John J. McCloy to Murray D. van Wagoner, 3rd September 1949, IfZ-Archiv, MF 260, OMGUS-By 13/134–3/11.

51. See Kurt Grossmann, *Germany's Moral Debt. The German-Israel Agreement,* Washington D.C. 1954, p. 14.

52. See Goschler, loc. cit., pp. 77–98.

fences committed while in office, some of which were ill-founded, but the fundamental argument was that Auerbach and others had enriched themselves from the reparations for the victims of Nazi persecution. Accused along with Auerbach was the Bavarian *Landesrabbiner* Aaron Ohrenstein, who had compared his position with that of a bishop. In consequence, the two most prominent representatives of post-war Bavarian Jewry were taken before a Bavarian court.

Before Auerbach's arrest the police had occupied the Bavarian *Landesentschädigungsamt*, which was responsible for organising reparations in Bavaria, in January 1951. This action was described by a furious Auerbach as a "frontal attack on reparation and Jewry."[53] The trial, in 1952, was seen by foreign observers in particular as a test case for German attitudes towards the Jews. Seven years after the end of Nazi rule, was a German court now to pass judgement on two Jews, when three of its five judges had been associated with the Nazi Party in some way?

The Bavarian *Justizministerium* (ministry of justice) showed a lack of sensitivity in dealing with questions of this kind. Its response to reproaches was as follows:[54] "I fully concur with you when you reject all collective discrimination, e.g. of racial or religious kind. But I must dismiss equally resolutely the attempts to discriminate against a judge because he was once a member of the Nazi Party, for this too is a matter of a collective prejudice." The presiding judge, *Landgerichtsdirektor* Mulzer, contributed a large number of maladroit observations during the trial. When Auerbach's defence counsel, Klibansky, asked for the postponement of the trial because it coincided with a Jewish festival, Mulzer interrupted him to say that he could not be expected to listen to endless details of Jewish rites. Klibansky replied that his client had spent five years in a concentration camp waiting for the chance to state his views, to which Mulzer responded by referring to his own "period of waiting" as a prisoner-of-war of the Russians.[55] While there is no need to read overt antisemitism into these exchanges, at the very least they reveal a profound lack of sympathy for the Jewish situation. However, there was another major indication that this was no normal or unpolitical trial, and that was the active propaganda made against Auerbach by *Justizminister* Müller during the entire investigation.

When judgement was finally given on 14th August 1952, the main elements of the original accusation had collapsed. Nevertheless, the court

---

53. See *Süddeutsche Zeitung*, 29th January 1951, 'Entschädigungsamt unter Polizeibewachung'.

54. Dr. Koch (Under Secretary at the Bayerisches Staatministerium der Justiz) to Bruno Weil, 22nd September 1952, Archives of the Leo Baeck Institute, N.Y. (LBIA), Axis Victims League Inc. (Siegfried Moses)—box 1 (47/3).

55. See Committee on Fair Play for Auerbach, April 1952, LBIA, Axis Victims League Inc. (Siegfried Moses), box 1 (47/3), *Neue Zeitung*, 27th April 1952, 'Gefahrvolle Entwicklungen', by Eberhard Körting.

sentenced Auerbach to $2^1/_2$ years' imprisonment and a fine of DM 2,700 for using the title "Dr." when he was not entitled to do so (which Auerbach admitted), and for a number of other offences which he continued to deny.[56] Auerbach talked of a "terror sentence" and protested that a second Dreyfus case had been created.[57] But the appeal he had lodged never took place: three days after sentence was passed, Auerbach committed suicide.

Had a Jew been driven to his death by an antisemitic judiciary, as many observers suspected?[58] To provide at least some answers to this question, it is necessary to look into the background of the trial. Through his work for Jewish and other victims of Nazi persecution, Auerbach had acquired an extremely influential position in Bavaria. In the process he had also acquired enemies. His main opponent was the Bavarian *Justizminister* and deputy *Ministerpräsident* Josef Müller, known as *"Ochsen-Sepp."* Müller told the press that Auerbach was behaving like a *Gauleiter*;[59] about Hendrik George van Dam, later Secretary General of the *Zentralrat der Juden in Deutschland*, he said that Bavaria had no desire to be ruled by a Jewish "king."[60] Various earlier attempts by Müller to destroy Auerbach had failed because Auerbach initially had considerable support, not only from the victims of racial and political persecution but also from the Bavarian government itself. The latter was particularly pleased that Auerbach had managed to accelerate the emigration of the Jewish DPs to a considerable degree. By linking the payment of reparations to DPs with emigration, he was said to have persuaded 80,000 Jewish DPs to leave Bavaria. Not all the measures he adopted were irreproachable from a bureaucratic point of view, but the authorities had been more than willing to tolerate them; for the Bavarian government, the main thing was that the DPs left Bavaria.[61]

Auerbach's balancing act between the interests of the Jewish and other victims of persecution on the one hand, and the Bavarian state on the other, became increasingly difficult to maintain. After he had broken away from the increasingly Communist-dominated *Vereinigung der Verfolgten des Naziregimes* (Union of those persecuted by the Nazi regime, or VVN), many victims

---

56. See Urteil in der Strafsache gegen Auerbach und drei Andere, ausgefertigt am 5.12.1952, Akten der Staatsanwaltschaft München I, Az. 2 KLs 1/52.

57. See *Neue Zeitung*, 16th August 1952, 'Gericht begründet das Urteil gegen Auerbach und Ohrenstein'.

58. See for example Rabbi D. Wilhelm Weinberg, 'Randbemerkungen zum Freitode Auerbachs', (1952), LBIA, Kurt Grossmann Collection.

59. See *Neue Zeitung*, 14th October 1948, 'Auerbach heftig angegriffen'.

60. See minutes of a meeting of *Landgerichtsrat* Aman and van Dam, 27th July 1951, Staatsanwaltschaft München I, Akten des Prozesses gegen Auerbach und drei Andere, Az. 2 KLs 1/52.

61. See testimony of von Gumppenberg, 1st February 1952, Archiv-BayLT, Protokoll der 18. Sitzung des Untersuchungsausschusses zur Untersuchung der Vorgänge im Landesentschädigungsamt, p. 18.

of political persecution began to oppose him. To the German Jews his behaviour was often "too ostentatiously Jewish," too little *deutsch korrekt* (properly German). By contrast, the Jewish DPs were frequently disturbed by his closeness to the German state.[62] Among his bitterest opponents was the Jewish Restitution Successor Organisation (IRSO) because Auerbach, in the struggle between the post-war German-Jewish communities and the IRSO for the inheritance of the destroyed Jewish communities, had energetically espoused the cause of the German Jews. In this conflict the IRSO gained a valuable ally in Benjamin Buttenwieser, the Deputy American High Commissioner, a Wall Street man and himself a Jew. Only when the Jewish organisations had signalled to Auerbach's arch rival Müller that they were no longer ready to protect him, and indeed would even be interested in an action against him, could Müller inaugurate a political action which led to the accusation against Auerbach.[63]

In fact, from a purely judicial point of view Auerbach was not an entirely innocent victim. Once action was taken, the judiciary had no alternative but to investigate the matter and to pass judgement accordingly. A search through the extensive documentation of the trial reveals no indications that the investigating authorities and the judges were motivated by hostility to Jews in the course of their work. On the contrary, Auerbach's co-defendent (and rival) Ohrenstein was actually able to make tactical use of his status as a Jewish rabbi during the trial.[64]

The real problem lies in the decision to take action at all. It was an open secret that Auerbach's work was not all done "by the book." But under the special circumstances of the post-war years such idiosyncrasies were quietly tolerated. Otherwise it would have been impossible for him to achieve the truly extraordinary results that he did, to the benefit of the persecuted and the Bavarian state alike. One commission of enquiry established by the Bavarian *Landtag* declared:[65] "Such tasks were not to be solved by normal means nor by individuals who were used to working faithfully to the letter of the law but would have been somewhat helpless in face of the extraordinary situation confronting them." These arguments receded into the background only after the

---

62. See report of Paul W. Freedman (American Jewish Committee), 'The Philipp Auerbach Tragedy', 17th September 1952, p. 31, Archives of the YIVO, New York, N.Y., RG 347, AJC, records, GEN–10, box 36.

63. See report of Paul W. Freedman, 'Auerbach Jailed', 20th March 1951, pp. 18ff., YIVO, RG 347, AJC records, GEN–10, box 36.

64. See Staatsanwaltschaft München I, Akten des Prozesses gegen Auerbach und drei Andere, Az. 2 KLs 1/52.

65. Schlußbericht des Untersuchungsausschusses zur Prüfung der Vorgänge im Landesentschädigungsamt (LEA) vom 10.12.1953, *Verhandlungen des Bayerischen Landtags*, 1953/54, Beilage 5128, p. 15.

creation of the disparate coalition of interests described above. The Stuttgart lawyer Benno Ostertag, himself a Jew, put the matter well:[66] "Auerbach was the broom of his government who could be stuck in the corner whenever it suited his government and used again whenever they wanted it."

What significance did the trial have for attitudes towards the Jews? Undoubtedly the effect was negative, partly because the *Justizminister*'s public campaign created the impression that something was seriously amiss in the question of reparations and the Jews. Such opinions only confirmed and strengthened prevailing prejudices. For this reason the *Zentralrat der Juden in Deutschland* became anxious to distance itself from Auerbach and to treat the issue as an ordinary criminal trial.[67] It must be said, however, that the trial was not the anti-Jewish tribunal that Auerbach and his defenders liked to claim.

Nevertheless, the issue involved a number of circumstances which make talk of a political trial appear justified. These include matters relating to attitudes towards the Jews in Bavaria. In this affair, Jews were to be found on both sides—that of the victim and that of the wire-pullers—though the dominating image is the tragic fate of Auerbach himself. For our purposes, the vital point is that his entire conduct cannot be understood without taking into account attitudes towards the Jews in Bavaria, including the problem of a powerful post-war antisemitism. To this Auerbach reacted with aggressive counter-measures on one hand, but with efforts to reduce the conflict—particularly by encouraging the emigration of Jewish DPs—on the other. Auerbach tried to combine resolute advocacy of the rights of Jews in post-war German society with strong loyalty towards the Bavarian state. The complexities of his conduct demonstrate the exceptionally complicated situation facing the German Jews after the end of Nazi rule.

In 1965, Hendrik George van Dam claimed that the continued existence of potential antisemitism in the German people was "basically an antisemitism without Jews."[68] As we have seen, at least in the first years after the war, conditions in Bavaria were different: here there was an antisemitism *with* Jews. The exceptional concentration of Jewish people in Bavaria in the early years after Nazi rule was not repeated to the same extent anywhere else in Germany. In Bavaria there were conditions which, together with the profound legacy of anti-Jewish prejudices from the Nazi era, created the foundations for a distinct post-war antisemitism. This was notably *volkstümlich*, while at the level of official policy—partly due to the influence of the American Military Govern-

---

66. Benno Ostertag, 'Auerbach und die bayerische Regierung', in *Allgemeine Wochenzeitung der Juden in Deutschland*, 22nd February 1952.

67. See report of Paul W. Freedman, 20th March 1951, pp. 18–20 (as note 63).

68. See van Dam, loc. cit., p. 912.

ment—it was no longer acceptable.

Decisive for the post-war development of attitudes towards the Jews was the disappearance of the political conditions in which undoubted latent anti-Jewish or antisemitic sentiments could have made a breakthrough. Equally, in politically responsible circles in Bavaria after the war there is evidence of attitudes which, though not overtly antisemitic, nevertheless reflected group dislikes and prejudices and frequently resulted in unsympathetic or narrow-minded modes of conduct and speech. Later, particularly from the 1960s, this gave way to a somewhat awkward rapprochement.[69]

Antisemitic attitudes in the population declined slowly, in a process which will not be investigated further here. There were setbacks throughout, and these attitudes have not entirely disappeared even today. This can clearly be seen in the development of the internationally famous Oberammergau Passion Play, which despite several revisions of the text, still contains anti-Jewish passages, and which, therefore, regularly comes under attack from Jewish critics.[70] Criticism of this kind was also made on the occasion of the most recent performance in 1990.[71] Such local incidents aside, Bavaria—once the exceptional situation of the post-war years had ceased to exist—was no longer different from other German regions as regards attitudes towards the Jews.[72]

---

69. See ibid., p. 913.

70. See Hans Lamm, 'Und wieder: Traditionsreiches Oberammergau . . . Neuer Bürgermeister und neuer Geist?', in *Münchener Jüdische Gemeindezeitung*, No. 28 (1984), pp. 13–14.

71. See *Abendzeitung* (Munich), 15th June 1990, 'Neue Kritik an Oberammergaus frommen Spielen: Judenfeindlicher Ballast'.

72. With reference to the general developments in both the *Bundesrepublik* and the former *Deutsche Demokratische Republik*, see a.o., Monika Richarz, 'Jews in Today's Germanies', in *LBI Year Book XXX* (1985), pp. 265–274.

The Homosexual Man Is a "Man," the Homosexual Woman Is a "Woman": Sex, Society, and the Law in Postwar West Germany

Robert G. Moeller

Are there essential differences in the drives of men and women that also have an effect on same-sex activity?

In what way does male homosexuality, on the one hand, and lesbian love, on the other, represent a social danger? In the family and in society, are their effects and outward manifestations different? . . .

Is there a difference in the activity and lack of inhibition in same-sex relations between men on the one hand and women on the other, so that associated with them there is a difference in the degree of propagation of such relations and the danger of seduction, especially of youth? Does male homosexuality appear in the public sphere more frequently than lesbian love? Is there prostitution among male homosexuals and lesbians?[1]

My thanks to Jane Caplan, John Fout, and Lynn Mally, whose comments on earlier drafts of this chapter helped me focus my argument. I also benefited from a discussion of the chapter by members of the Gender, Politics, and Society Study Group of Harvard University's Center for European Studies. Work on this project was completed with support from the European Society and Culture Research Group of the Center for German and European Studies at the University of California, Berkeley, and the Organized Research Initiative, "Woman and the Image," of the University of California, Irvine. All translations from German in this chapter are my own.

1. *Entscheidungen des Bundesverfassungsgerichts*, vol. 6 (Tübingen, 1957), pp. 398–99 (hereafter cited as *EdB*). The published proceedings amount to over fifty pages of text. All quotations from the German are my own. The case is widely cited in the German-language literature as an important moment in the history of homosexuality in the postwar period. For a useful summary see Hans-Georg Stümke and Rudi Finkler, *Rosa Winkel, Rosa Listen: Homosexuelle und "Gesundes Volksempfinden" von Auschwitz bis heute* (Reinbek, 1981), pp. 356–65; also Hans-Georg Stümke, *Homosexuelle in Deutschland: Eine politische Geschichte* (Munich, 1989), p. 134; Claudia Schoppmann, *Nationalsozialistische Sexualpolitik und weibliche Homosexualität* (Pfaffen-

These questions were posed in 1957 not by Alfred Kinsey, the American sex researcher, nor by the Wolfenden Committee, the parliamentary task force charged with reporting on "Homosexual Offences and Prostitution" in postwar Britain, but by the West German Federal Constitutional Court (Bundesverfassungsgericht) in its response to the appeals case of Günter R., a cook, and Oskar K., a merchant, both of whom had been sentenced in the early 1950s to jail terms for numerous violations of the Criminal Code's Paragraph 175, the statute prohibiting homosexual relations between men.[2]

Günter R. and Oskar K. charged that they had been convicted under a National Socialist law. Paragraph 175 had been revised by the Nazis in 1935, and they claimed that this revision embodied principles of "National Socialist racial teaching" (*Rassenlehre*); it represented a "striking violation of democratic principles."[3] In addition, prohibition of same-sex sexual relations among men was at odds with the promise of the Basic Law (Grundgesetz)—the postwar West German constitution adopted in 1949—that every individual had a right to develop her or his personality freely. Sexual relations between consenting adults fell solidly within the inviolable private realm where the state had no business. Finally, the appellants claimed that Paragraph 175 represented an unconstitutional form of discrimination against male homosexuals, because lesbians were exempt from prosecution. The Basic Law guaranteed the equality of women and men; thus, Paragraph 175 embodied a sexual double standard that violated the rights of male homosexuals.

---

weiler, 1991), p. 255; Peter Kröger, "Entwicklungsstadien der Bestrafung der widernatürlichen Unzucht und kritische Studie zur Berechtigung der §§ 175, 175a, 175b StGB de lege ferenda" (Doctor of Law diss., Free University, Berlin, 1957), p. 100; and Ralf Dose, "Der § 175 in der Bundesrepublik Deutschland (1949 bis heute)," in *Die Geschichte des § 175: Strafrecht gegen Homosexuelle*, ed. Freunde eines Schwulen Museums in Berlin e.V. in Zusammenarbeit mit Emanzipation e.V. Frankfurt am Main (Berlin, 1990), pp. 125–33. Stümke and Finkler also provide an extended excerpt from the case, *Homosexuelle und "Gesundes Volksempfinden,"* pp. 460–77.

2. See Alfred Kinsey, Wardell B. Pomeroy, and Clyde E. Martin, *Sexual Behavior in the Human Male* (Philadelphia, 1948); Alfred Kinsey et al., *Sexual Behavior in the Human Female* (Philadelphia, 1953); and the useful introduction to the significance of these reports in Paul Robinson, *The Modernization of Sex: Havelock Ellis, Alfred Kinsey, William Masters and Virginia Johnson* (New York, 1976), pp. 42–119; and John D'Emilio and Estelle B. Freedman, *Intimate Matters: A History of Sexuality in America* (New York, 1988), pp. 285–95. On the report of the Wolfenden Committee, see *The Wolfenden Report: Report of the Committee on Homosexual Offenses and Prostitution,* with an introduction by Karl Menninger (New York, 1963); Jeffrey Weeks, *Sex, Politics, and Society: The Regulation of Sexuality since 1800,* 2d ed. (London, 1989), pp. 239–44, and idem, *Coming Out: Homosexual Politics in Britain, from the Nineteenth Century to the Present* (London, 1977), pp. 164–67; Stephen Jeffrey-Poulter, *Peers, Queers, and Commons: The Struggle for Gay Law Reform from 1950 to the Present* (London, 1991), pp. 28–46; and the contemporary commentary of Charles Berg, *Fear, Punishment, Anxiety and the Wolfenden Report* (London, 1959), pp. 11–50.

3. *EdB,* 6:413.

From the published account of the appeals case, it is impossible to learn much about the two men who challenged the constitutionality of the criminal code and called on the court to define Nazi "racial teaching." All personal details about Günter R. and Oskar K. are carefully purged in the court's official record. Like other legal proceedings, this case thus provides a source, at once tantalizing and frustrating, for the historian for whom the outcome of a trial is potentially no more interesting than the personalities involved in the proceedings and the circumstances that lead individuals to challenge the authority of the courts and the constitutionality of the law. The published transcript offers no hints of what motivated the appellants to initiate and pursue an appeals process that lasted for more than six years. We are told only that Oskar K. died a little over a year before the court reached its decision, allowing the court flatly to conclude that his case had thus been "settled."[4]

However, what the case does provide is a framework for understanding postwar West German conceptions of sexuality and homosexuality, the differences between lesbianism and male homosexuality, and the boundaries between sexual equality and sexual difference. This chapter uses the case as a means to illuminate these issues. It attempts to identify a set of questions, not to exhaust all possible means for finding answers; it is an invitation to future research, a single contribution to a much larger project of writing the history of sexuality in the postwar period.[5]

In addition, as historians of sexuality repeatedly have emphasized, at least since the nineteenth century, discussions of sexuality are always more than that; they are discussions of social relations, the "surrogate medium through

---

4. *EdB*, 6:442–43.

5. The history of homosexuality in modern Germany is still very much in the making. However, at least for the Kaiserreich, Weimar, and the years of the Thousand Year Reich, important works have helped outline the terrain. For a sampling of key contributions to the English-language literature, see, for example, John C. Fout, "Sexual Politics in Wilhelmine Germany: The Male Gender Crisis, Moral Purity, and Homophobia," *Journal of the History of Sexuality* 2 (1992): 388–421; George L. Mosse, "Nationalism and Respectability: Normal and Abnormal Sexuality in the Nineteenth Century," *Journal of Contemporary History* 17 (1982): 221–46; Isabel V. Hull, "The Bourgeoisie and its Discontents: Reflections on 'Nationalism and Respectability,'" *Journal of Contemporary History* 17 (1982): 247–68; James D. Steakley, "Iconography of a Scandal: Political Cartoons and the Eulenburg Affair in Wilhelmine Germany," in *Hidden From History: Reclaiming the Gay and Lesbian Past,* ed. Martin Bauml Duberman, Martha Vicinus, and George Chauncey, Jr. (New York, 1989), pp. 233–57, and idem, *The Homosexual Emancipation Movement in Germany* (Salem, N.H., 1982); and Harry Oosterhuis, "Homosexual Emancipation in Germany Before 1933: Two Traditions," *Journal of Homosexuality* 22 (1991): 1–27. In addition to the overview of Stümke and Finkler, particularly important German-language works include Burkhard Jellonnek, *Homosexuelle unter dem Hakenkreuz: Die Verfolgung von Homosexuellen im Dritten Reich* (Paderborn, 1990); and Schoppmann, *Nationalsozialistische Sexualpolitik.* For the 1950s, the scholar confronts a historiographic landscape that looks far more barren.

which other intractable battles could be fought."[6] From this perspective, the chapter also explores what insights the case can offer into the anxieties and discontents of West Germans as they sought to come to terms with their own most recent history, to specify what constituted the legacy of National Socialism, to identify who was to qualify as a victim of the Nazi regime, and to move from the Third Reich to a postwar democratic order.

When the Federal Republic was founded in 1949, it maintained the criminal penalties against male homosexuality put in place by the Nazis fourteen years earlier. Since the establishment of a unified criminal code for Bismarck's unified Reich in 1871, sexual relations between men were grouped with bestiality, and both activities were deemed criminal offenses. However, before 1935, legal action depended on evidence of violence, seduction of a minor, or "intercourse-like behavior." At least for consenting adult men, prosecution virtually required being caught in flagrante delicto or being subject to third-party denunciation.[7]

From the late 1890s on, this formulation of Paragraph 175 had been the target of a repeal campaign that was headed by sex reformers and advocates of homosexual rights, who maintained that homosexuality was wrongly labeled as deviance and who drew additional strength from some liberal and Social Democratic critics of any restrictions on the sexual activity of consenting adults. Headed by Magnus Hirschfeld, the *Wissenschaftlich-huminitäres Komitee* (Scientific humanitarian committee) repeatedly introduced petitions to the Reichstag demanding the abolition of Paragraph 175. Hirschfeld, a noted sexologist who had a profound influence on turn-of-the-century European theories of homosexuality, was also among the most vocal advocates of the theory of the "third sex," according to which homosexuality should be understood not as a deviation from a male or female norm, but as another sexual variant. Hirschfeld maintained that homosexuality was an innate condition; homosexuals were born, not made. Indeed, the "ineradicability of homosexuality" (*Unausrottbarkeit der Homosexuali-tät*) made it senseless to hope that criminal prosecution or other forms of discrimination and persecution could serve as deterrents. Hirschfeld did not ask that the homosexual be pitied because of his or her immutable state; rather, homosexuality should be recognized as normal and legitimate, a form of love "different only in

---

6. Jeffrey Weeks, *Sexuality and its Discontents: Meanings, Myths, and Modern Sexualities* (London, 1985), p. 74.

7. There is a useful summary of the law's history in Kröger, "Entwicklungsstadien und Studie." See also Jürgen Baumann, *Paragraph 175: Über die Möglichkeit einfache, die nichtjugendgefährdende und nicht öffentliche Homosexualität unter Erwachsenen straffrei zu lassen* (Berlin, 1968), pp. 40–46.

direction, rather than in kind."[8]

Amplified by an increasingly visible gay male and lesbian subculture, particularly in large urban areas such as Berlin, voices calling for the repeal of Paragraph 175 grew louder in the Weimar Republic. Still, even supported in parliament by Communists, Social Democrats, and the liberal German Democratic party, reform advocates were unable to achieve their objective in the 1920s. Although de facto the police largely reduced their prosecution of male homosexuality to investigations of third-party complaints, de jure Paragraph 175 remained unchanged.[9]

The Nazi takeover in January 1933 completely silenced the wide-ranging discussion of sexuality and sexual reform that had flourished in the Weimar

8. Magnus Hirschfeld, *Was muss das Volk vom dritten Geschlecht wissen!*, cited in Fout, "Sexual Politics," p. 398; and for a survey of legal reform attempts before 1914, see Baumann, *Paragraph 175*, pp. 123–28. Fout does a very effective job of analyzing the significance of Hirschfeld's theory in the context of late-nineteenth-century moral purity movements and the crisis of gender relations in the imperial period. See also the useful discussions of Hirschfeld in Hull, "Bourgeoisie and Discontent," pp. 262–65; Gunter Schmidt, "Allies and Persecutors: Science and Medicine in the Homosexuality Issue," *Journal of Homosexuality* 10 (1984): 127–40; James W. Jones, *"We of the Third Sex": Literary Representations of Homosexuality in Wilhelmine Germany* (New York, 1990), pp. 43–113; Stümke and Finkler, *Homosexuelle und "Gesundes Volksempfinden,"* pp. 48–66; Günter Dworek, "'Für Freiheit und Recht': Justiz, Sexualwissenschaft und schwule Emanzipation 1871–1896," in *Die Geschichte des § 175*, pp. 42–61; Jörg Hutter, "§ 175 RStGB im Zweiten Deutschen Reich von 1890–1919," in *Die Geschichte des § 175*, pp. 62–80; and the general contexualization of Hirschfeld's theory in David F. Greenberg, *The Construction of Homosexuality* (Chicago, 1988), pp. 404–18. Hirschfeld's best-known work is his massive study, *Die Homosexualität des Mannes und des Weibes,* 2d ed. (Berlin, 1920) (originally published in 1914); for another useful set of representative writings by Hirschfeld, see *Documents of the Homosexual Rights Movement in Germany, 1836–1927* (New York, 1975); and on Hirschfeld's life, the highly sympathetic, uncritical treatment of Charlotte Wolff, *Magnus Hirschfeld: A Portrait of a Pioneer in Sexology* (London, 1986). Wolff, a medical doctor, was also active in the Weimar sex reform movement. For other contemporary commentaries, see the documents in Ilse Kokula, ed., *Weibliche Homosexualität um 1900 in zeitgenössichen Dokumenten* (Munich, 1981).

9. Jellonnek, *Homosexuelle unter dem Hakenkreuz,* pp. 39–50; on legal pressures for reform, Baumann, *Paragraph 175*, pp. 96–116, 129–40; Manfred Baumgardt, "Das Institut für Sexualwissenschaft und die Homosexuellen-Bewegung in der Weimarer Republik," in *Eldorado: Homosexuelle Frauen und Männer in Berlin 1850–1950: Geschichte, Alltag und Kultur,* ed. Berlin Museum (Berlin, 1984), pp. 31–41; Ilse Kokula, "Lesbish leben von Weimar bis zur Nachkriegszeit," in *Eldorado,* pp. 149–58; Katharina Vogel, "Zum Selbstverständnis lesbischer Frauen in der Weimarer Republik: Eine Analyse der Zeitschrift 'Die Freundin' 1924–1933," in *Eldorado,* pp. 162–68; Bodo Mende, "Die antihomosexuelle Gesetzgebung in der Weimarer Republik," in *Die Geschichte des § 175,* pp. 82–104; Manfred Baumgardt, "Geschichte der Schwulenbewegung in Berlin 1850–1933," in *Dokumentation der Vortragsreihe "Homosexualität und Wissenschaft",* ed. Schwulenreferat im Allgemeinen Studentenausschuss der Freien Universität Berlin (Berlin, 1985), pp. 171–76; Ilse Kokula, "Freundinnen: Lesbische Frauen in der Weimarer Republik," in *Neue Frauen: Die zwanziger Jahre,* ed. Kristine von Soden and Maruta Schmidt (Berlin, 1988), pp. 160–66; Stümke and Finkler, *Homosexuelle und "Gesundes Volksempfinden,"* pp. 19–48; on cultural representations, Richard Dyer, "Less and More than Women and Men:

era. Hirschfeld escaped persecution only because he was outside Germany. In early May, the Nazis unleashed the SA (*Sturmabteilung,* or Stormtroops), their paramilitary wing, on Hirschfeld's Institute of Sexual Science, one of the most visible symbols of the Weimar sex reform movement and according to the Nazis, "an unparalleled breeding ground of dirt and filth."[10] However, in the first instance the Nazis did not identify gay men among the most visible targets of the discriminatory policies of the Third Reich. This distinction was reserved for the political left, particularly communists, and Jews. In the easily decoded categories of Nazi ideology, it was possible to associate pressures for homosexual rights in Weimar with Jews and communists, and Nazi rhetoric emphasized the "indissoluble joining of Marxism, pederasty, and systematic Jewish contamination."[11] By explicitly mentioning any part of this mixture, Nazi true believers could implicitly invoke the others. Still, Nazi priorities of anti-Bolshevism and anti-Semitism meant that "Magnus Hirschfeld and his racial comrades"[12] were demonized as much for their religion and leftist political beliefs as for their sexuality.

National Socialist policy remained trapped between homophobic theory and pragmatic considerations in part because the homosexuality of key Nazi leaders was an open secret. At the level of official rhetoric, gay men were excoriated not simply as "deviants"; in the context of the profoundly racialist Nazi worldview, they also represented a threat to the biological integrity of the nation. They were agents of the "death of the *Volk*" because they refused to participate in ensuring the future of the "Aryan race." However, particularly within the SA, homosexuality not only was tolerated; in the case of Ernst Röhm, the organization's leader and a longtime confederate of Hitler, it was loudly celebrated as part of a full-scale rejection of bourgeois society. For

Lesbian and Gay Cinema in Weimar Germany," *New German Critique* 51 (1990): 5–60; and Claudia Schoppmann, *"Der Skorpion": Frauenliebe in der Weimarer Republik* (Hamburg, 1985); on the Left's response to homosexuality, W. U. Eissler, *Arbeiterparteien und Homosexuellenfrage: Zur Sexualpolitik von SPD und KPD in der Weimarer Republik* (Berlin, 1980); and for a contemporary perspective, Magnus Hirschfeld, "Die Homosexualität," in *Sittengeschichte des Lasters,* ed. Schidrowitz (Vienna, 1927), pp. 303–18, reprinted in *Documents of the Homosexual Rights Movement in Germany, 1836–1927.*

    10. Erwin J. Haeberle, "Swastika, Pink Triangle, and Yellow Star: The Destruction of Sexology and the Persecution of Homosexuals in Nazi Germany," in *Hidden from History,* ed. Duberman, Vicinus, and Chauncey, pp. 368–69; Steakley, *Homosexual Emancipation Movement,* pp. 104–105; and in general, Atina Grossmann, *Reforming Sex: The German Movement for Birth Control and Abortion Rights, 1920 to 1950* (New York, 1995).

    11. *Völkischer Beobachter,* October 31, 1928, quoted in Jellonnek, *Homosexuelle unter dem Hakenkreuz,* p. 55.

    12. Wilhelm Frick, *Verhandlungen des Reichstags,* 3. Wahlperiode 1924/28, Stenographische Berichte, vol. 393 (Berlin, 1927), p. 10993, quoted in Jellonnek, *Homosexuelle unter dem Hakenkreuz,* p. 53.

Röhm, the anticipated "second revolution," the true Nazi revolution that would mark a dramatic rupture with Germany's past, would tremendously enhance the status and power of the SA and would also include a sexual revolution, an all-out war on the "narrow-minded (*Spiesser*), hypocrites (*Muckern*), and apostles of morality."[13]

Before 1933, it was precisely Röhm's hardly closeted homosexuality that had opened him to attack, not from Nazi leaders, but from the Social Democratic party (SPD), which offset its support for the repeal of Paragraph 175 with sensationalist press reports about Röhm, strongly suggesting that inclinations toward National Socialism and perverse sexual practices went hand in hand.[14] Still, while the SPD sought to claim that its revelations about Röhm reflected not Social Democratic hypocrisy but rather the hypocrisy of the National Socialists, Röhm kept his leadership position in the Nazi party, and SPD charges prompted no response from Hitler. Thus, even after the Nazis came to power, when the regime moved quickly and forcefully to establish itself as a guardian of morality, destroying the bars and clubs of male homosexuals, outlawing all forms of "smut and pornography," and prohibiting nude bathing—that well-known practice of "marxists, Communists, and psychopaths"[15]—it took no action against homosexuals within its own ranks.

On June 30, 1934, the tide turned decisively, and the Gestapo silenced Röhm permanently. To be sure, the "night of long knives," the assassination of Röhm and purge of the SA leadership, was prompted less by Röhm's vision of a sexually liberated *Lebensraum* than by the threat to the Reichswehr explicit in his aspirations to expand dramatically the military responsibilities of his organization. However, the need to rid the SA of homosexuals quickly emerged as the ostensible reason for the murder of Röhm and many of his followers, and there is much evidence to suggest that the revelation of Röhm's sexual proclivities was crucial to Hitler's ability to win broad popular support for his move against the SA. Apparently, most Germans preferred an enforced sexual orthodoxy to Röhm's alternative. June 1934 thus marked a dramatic reduction in the power of the SA, the solidification of Hitler's authority, and the ascendance of the SS (*Schutzstaffeln*); it also ended any benign neglect of male homosexuality in the Thousand Year Reich.[16]

13. Jellonnek, *Homosexuelle unter dem Hakenkreuz*, p. 83.

14. Stümke and Finkler, *Homosexuelle und "Gesundes Volksempfinden*," pp. 119–43; Jellonnek, *Homosexuelle unter dem Hakenkreuz*, pp. 62–72; Eissler, *Arbeiterpartein und Homosexuellenfrage*, pp. 106–112; and Friedrich Koch, *Sexuelle Denunziation: Die Sexualität in der politischen Auseinandersetzung* (Frankfurt, 1986), pp. 23–30.

15. Jellonnek, *Homosexuelle unter dem Hakenkreuz*, p. 81.

16. Robert Gellateley, *The Gestapo and German Society: Enforcing Racial Policy, 1933–1945* (Oxford, 1990), pp. 201–203; Koch, *Sexuelle Denunziation*, pp. 15–21; Ian Kershaw,

Key to the intensified persecution of homosexual men after June 1934 was the reform of Paragraph 175, according to which prosecution was no longer restricted to incidents of "intercourse-like behavior" but was justified by "any form of same-sex immorality." This elastic definition did not even require physical contact and might involve only walking arm-in-arm or "gazing with lustful intention." Determining what constituted lust and intent was left to the police and the courts. In theory, even certain dreams were now illegal.[17]

To be sure, the Nazi solution to the problem of male homosexuality was not of necessity final; unlike Jews or Sinti and Roma ("gypsies"), who could not alter the blood that flowed through their veins and defined their difference in the categories of scientific racism, gay men could be "reeducated" and "healed." Heinrich Himmler of the SS, who claimed to be one of the leading National Socialist experts on homosexuality, judged homosexuality to be a pathology but not an immutable biological trait. At least in theory, gay men could escape criminal prosecution if they agreed to abandon specific types of sexual activity, and within the SS, the branch of the Nazi state largely responsible for implementing racial policy, there was a willingness to distinguish between "seducer"

The "Hitler Myth": Image and Reality in the Third Reich (New York, 1987), pp. 92–93; and Jellonnek, *Homosexuelle unter dem Hakenkreuz,* pp. 95–96.

17. In general, on the persecution of male homosexuals under the Nazis, in addition to Jellonnek, *Homosexuelle unter dem Hakenkreuz,* see also Propser Schücking and Martin Sölle, "§ 175 StGB—Strafrechtliche Verfolgung homosexueller Männer in Köln," *Verführte Männer: Das Leben der Kölner Homosexuellen im Dritten Reich,* ed. Cornelia Limpricht, Jürgen Müller, and Nina Oxenius (Cologne, 1991), pp. 104–119; Rüdiger Lautmann, "Hauptdevise: bloss nicht anecken': Das Leben homosexueller Männer unter dem Nationalsozialismus," in *Terror und Hoffnung in Deutschland 1933–1945,* ed. Johannes Beck et al. (Reinbek, 1980), pp. 366–90, idem, "Categorization in Concentration Camps as a Collective Fate: A Comparison of Homosexuals, Jehovah's Witnesses and Political Prisoners," *Journal of Homosexuality* 19 (1990): 67–88, idem, "The Pink Triangle: The Persecution of Homosexual Males in Concentration Camps in Nazi Germany," *Journal of Homosexuality* 6 (1980–81): 141–60, and idem, *Der Zwang zur Tugend: Die gesellschaftliche Kontrolle der Sexualitäten* (Frankfurt am Main, 1984), pp. 156–80; Harry Oosterhuis, "Male Bonding and Homosexuality in German Nationalism," *Journal of Homosexuality* 22 (1991): 247–52; Haeberle, "Swastika, Pink Triangle, and Yellow Star," pp. 365–79; Harry Wilde, *Das Schicksal der Verfemten: Die Verfolgung der Homosexuellen im "Dritten Reich" und ihre Stellung in der heutigen Gesellschaft* (Tübingen, 1969), pp. 16–38; Stümke, *Homosexuelle in Deutschland,* pp. 132–35; Stümke and Finkler, *Homosexuelle und "Gesundes Volksempfinden,"* pp. 212–301, 356–67; Michael Burleigh and Wolfgang Wippermann, *The Racial State: Germany, 1933–1945* (Cambridge, 1991), pp. 182–97; Erhard Vismar, "Perversion und Verfolgung unter dem deutschen Faschismus," in *Seminar: Gesellschaft und Homosexualität,* ed. Rüdiger Lautmann (Frankfurt, 1977), pp. 309–24; Rüdiger Lautmann, Winfried Grikschat, Egbert Schmidt, "Der rosa Winkel in den nationalsozialistischen Konzentrationslagern," in *Seminar,* ed. Lautmann, pp. 325–65; Heinz-Dieter Schilling, ed., *Schwule und Faschismus* (Berlin, 1983); Günter Grau, "Verfolgung und Vernichtung 1933–1945: Der § 175 als Instrument faschistischer Bevölkerungspolitik," in *Die Geschichte des § 175,* pp. 105–17; and Günter Grau, ed., *Homosexualität in der NS-Zeit: Dokumente einer Diskriminierung und Verfolgung* (Frankfurt am Main, 1993).

and "seduced" and to differentiate between those with "strong" and "weak" homosexual tendencies.[18] However, these distinctions in no way inhibited the significantly intensified persecution of male homosexuals after 1935 and the dramatic expansion in the number of those charged and convicted on the basis of Paragraph 175. Of 41,116 Germans convicted for violating morals laws from 1931 to 1933, 2,319 were prosecuted under Paragraph 175. From 1937 to 1939, the total number of those found guilty of morals offenses increased by a third to 65,155, but the number charged with violating Paragraph 175 had increased more than tenfold to 24,447.[19]

The Nazi legal experts who drafted the new version of Paragraph 175 also discussed the advisability of extending its scope to include lesbianism, because lesbians might seduce heterosexual women, removing them from the potential pool of "mothers of the *Volk*." Ultimately, however, they concluded that lesbians could remain exempt, because lesbianism presented less serious a threat to population growth than male homosexuality. Justifying this position, the Nazi Ministry of Justice temporized that "in the case of [homosexual] men, procreative power is wasted, they are for the most part excluded from reproduction; in the case of women this is not the case or at least not in the same measure." As another jurist put it, the "woman inclined toward lesbianism" would "nevertheless [remain] capable of reproducing." Female homosexuality did not jeopardize Germany's future because women were reproductive Boy Scouts, "always sexually prepared," while homosexual men were far more likely to become "psychologically impotent."[20] Linking in one office the administrative agency charged with prosecuting violations of antiabortion laws with that responsible for controlling male homosexuality was by no means arbitrary; for the Nazis, both homosexuality and abortion threatened the future of

18. Jellonnek, *Homosexuelle unter dem Hakenkreuz,* pp. 122–75; and for a useful review of theories of homosexuality under the Nazis, see Schoppmann, *Nationalsozialistische Sexualpolitik,* pp. 126–62. On the prosecution of homosexuals in the army, SS, and Hitler Youth during the war, see Franz Seidler, *Prostitution, Homosexualität, Selbstverstümmelung: Probleme der deutschen Sanitätsführung 1939–1945* (Neckargemünd, 1977), pp. 193–232; and documents in Grau, ed., *Homosexualität in der NS-Zeit,* pp. 209–51.

19. According to Baumann's figures, 1,801 men were sentenced on the basis of Paragraph 175 in the first two years of Nazi rule. The figure climbed to 2,106 in 1935 and 5,320 in 1936. With the start of the war and the SS's increasing preoccupation with solving the "Jewish Question," the numbers of those sentenced declined to 3,773 in 1940; 3,739 in 1941; 2,678 in 1942; and 2,218 in 1943. See Baumann, *Paragraph 175,* p. 61; Rudolf Klimmer, *Die Homosexualität als biologisch-soziologische Zeitfrage,* 3d ed. (Hamburg, 1965), p. 277, a work originally published in 1958; and Grau, ed., *Homosexualität in der NS-Zeit,* p. 197.

20. Quoted in Schoppmann, *Nationalsozialistische Sexualpolitik,* pp. 22–23; see also Klimmer, *Homosexualität als Zeitfrage,* p. 191; documents in Grau, ed., *Homosexualität in der NS-Zeit,* pp. 101–15; and Claudia Schoppmann, "Zur Situation lesbischer Frauen in der NS-Zeit," in Grau, ed., *Homosexualität in der NS-Zeit,* pp. 35–42.

the "master race."[21] But Nazi constraints on female sexuality did not extend to the criminal prohibition of lesbianism, and lesbians were not subject to the same aggressive persecution accorded by the Nazis to gay men.

In its 1957 decision, the Federal Constitutional Court did not provide anything approaching a full account of the revision of Paragraph 175 under the Nazis. This reflected no lack of interest in the history of criminal penalties against male homosexuality, and the court carefully traced the origins of the laws punishing sodomy back to the Old Testament and outlined the implementation of specific measures from the early sixteenth century up to the present. The message communicated by this lengthy litany was unambiguous: precedent was on the side of those favoring the legal prohibition of male homosexuality. However, while acknowledging the link between the assassination of Röhm and the intensified persecution of homosexuals and comparing the terms of the criminal statutes before and after the Nazi reform of 1935, the court's account of the law's history in the Thousand Year Reich was highly selective. The justices eschewed all mention of the connection between Paragraph 175 and racialist population policies and based their rejection of the appellants' claim on the example of the Allied forces of occupation and the West German parliament, neither of which had shown any inclination to revise Paragraph 175 or to suspend the expanded provisions introduced by the Nazis.[22] This silence on the part of the Allies and the Federal Republic's founding fathers, reasoned the justices, was evidence that they need have no fears that Paragraph 175 was anything but legitimate and necessary. Not every law introduced in the Thousand Year Reich was indelibly tainted by the "National Socialist body of thought" (Gedankengut), and the justices were confident that by 1957 there had been ample opportunity for the legislature to suspend any law that was compromised on this basis.[23] Indeed, when it came to learning how most effectively to criminalize certain forms of sexual activity, it seemed that there was much to learn from the Nazis.

---

21. Kröger, "Entwicklungsstadien und Studie," p. 57; Stümke, Homosexuelle in Deutschland pp. 111, 113; Nina Oxenius, "Zucht und Unzucht: Homosexuelle und die NS-Bevölkerungsideologie," in Verführte Männer, ed. Limpricht, Müller, and Oxenius, pp. 48–55.

22. EdB, 6:390–95, 413–19. The Federal High Court (Bundesgerichtshof) had taken the same position in a judgment of March 13, 1951, Entscheidungen des Bundesgerichtshofs in Strafsachen (Detmold, 1951), 1:81; see also the commentary in Juristenzeitung 6 (1951): 561–64. For other examples of cases upholding the expanded interpretation of "same-sex offense" (gleichgeschlechtliche Unzucht) and "stimulating immorality" (Unzuchttreiben), see the decisions of the Federal High Court, September 22, 1953, Entscheidungen des Bundesgerichtshofs in Strafsachen (Detmold, 1954), 4:323–25; and November 13, 1955, Entscheidungen des Bundesgerichtshofs in Strafsachen (Detmold, 1954), 5:88–90. In general, on legal and judicial reform in the early postwar period, see Hans Wrobel, Verurteilt zur Demokratie: Justiz und Justizpolitik in Deutschland, 1945–1949 (Heidelberg, 1989), pp. 101–5.

23. EdB, 6:414–19.

The court's terse rejection of the appellants' charge that Paragraph 175 embodied Nazi "racial teaching" contrasted sharply with its lengthy response to
the question of what differentiated male homosexuality from lesbianism. A
satisfactory answer was essential, because the appellants maintained that the
criminalization of male homosexuality violated the Basic Law's promise of
equal rights for women and men; either gay men and lesbians should have equal
rights to end up behind bars or equal rights to exercise their sexual preferences
freely.

Determining the constitutionality of laws was the chief business of the
Federal Constitutional Court. The postwar creation of an agent of judicial
review marked a break with Germany's codified law tradition, according to
which the executive and the legislature, not the judiciary, bore responsibility for
defining the law to the fullest extent possible. Two-thirds of the court's justices
were chosen by the major political groupings, the Social Democratic party
(SPD) and the conservative Christian Democratic–Christian Social Union
(CDU-CSU) coalition. Another third were ostensibly nonpartisan, although in
practice those chosen were closely affiliated with one of the major political parties. Common to all justices was that their pasts were carefully scrutinized for
any history of loyalty to the Nazi regime; the highest priority was placed on
finding "clean" candidates. None had held a major position under the Nazis,
several had either survived the Third Reich in exile or had otherwise experienced direct forms of discrimination or persecution under the regime, and most
had earned their positions because of the leading roles they had played in restoring political order in the immediate postwar years. The court was divided into
two chambers. Cases dealing with fundamental constitutional rights—including
Articles 2 and 3 of the Basic Law—were directed to the first Senat, where the
SPD held a slight margin among the twelve justices, earning it the label of the
"Red" Senat and often setting it at odds with Konrad Adenauer's conservative
government. This chamber passed judgment in the appeals case of Günter R.
and Oskar K.[24]

The court's particular concern with the constitutional guarantee of the
equal rights of women and men had intensified significantly after April 1953.
By this date, according to the Basic Law, it was the task of the West German
parliament to revise any existing laws that contravened the constitutional prescription of the equality of the sexes. The Bundestag had failed to meet the
1953 deadline, bogged down by its inability to reformulate key parts of the explicitly patriarchal 1900 family law in order to bring it into accord with the
1949 constitution. While there was general agreement that provisions restricting married women's right to enter into contracts or to own property violated

---

24. Donald P. Kommers, *Judicial Politics in West Germany: A Study of the Federal Constitutional Court* (Beverly Hills, 1976), pp. 100, 120–32.

any notion of equality, consensus collapsed over the question of who should have the last word in instances of irreconcilable differences between wife and husband. With the backing of Chancellor Konrad Adenauer and the highest ranks of the Catholic clergy, the overwhelming majority of the ruling conservative CDU-CSU coalition maintained that husbands and wives must subordinate individual interests for the good of the relationship formed out of their union. This in turn required establishing a court of last resort in cases of serious disagreement; for the CDU-CSU, it was self-evident that the husband should be judge and jury. When conflicts over children's welfare were at stake, then parental authority should become paternal. In Adenauer's words, "Just as the mother fundamentally has to subordinate herself to the father, so should the wife also be expected to do the same in relation to the husband."[25] To violate the principle of patriarchal authority, Adenauer argued, was to threaten the stability of the family.

Because by April 1953 Adenauer's government could find no clear majority for its position in the Bundestag, parliamentary debates over the meaning of equality and family law reform continued after this date, but determining precisely what equality meant also became a preoccupation of the courts. The Basic Law had specified that should the Bundestag fail to complete reform of the family law by the 1953 deadline, it would become the responsibility of the courts to fill the void, determining the constitutionality of specific laws on a case-by-case basis while waiting for more precise instruction from the government and the legislature. Overriding the objections of some judges and legal experts that the courts had no authority to act in the absence of legislative guidelines, the Federal Constitutional Court had ruled in late 1953 that it was not only the right but the responsibility of jurists to fill the void left by parliamentarians. Its decision affirmed that equality did not mean "comparable worth" or senseless "leveling" (*Gleichmacherei*); rather, the justices reasoned that equality had meaning only if coupled with a recognition of difference, affirming the position unanimously accepted by the drafters of the Basic Law. In the context of family law, this recognition meant that "objective biological or functional" differences that defined a "division of labor" (*Arbeitsteilung*) between the sexes necessitated "particular legal regulation," such as "measures for the protection of the woman as mother, [and] differentiation of the types of work [of wives and husbands] for the community of the family."[26]

It was thus the Bundestag's inability to reach agreement on how best to regulate legally sanctioned heterosexual relationships that structured the arena

---

25. Adenauer to Bundesminister and Chef des Bundespräsidialamtes, September 2, 1952, B106/3432, Bundesarchiv (Koblenz); and in general, Robert G. Moeller, *Protecting Motherhood: Women and the Family in the Politics of Postwar West Germany* (Berkeley, 1993), pp. 76–108.

26. Decision of December 18, 1953, *EdB*, 3:232, 239–42; see also Moeller, *Protecting Motherhood*, pp. 181–84.

in which the Federal Constitutional Court found itself discussing illegal sexual relationships between adult men and venturing well beyond the provisions of the family law that were the focus of the legislature's work. What tied Günter R. and Oskar K.'s case to other legal controversies over the meaning of the Basic Law's guarantee of women's and men's equal rights was the court's attempt to determine what constituted those "biological or functional difference[s]" that justified exceptions to the principle of equal treatment under the law. For the most part, the court addressed these issues in cases involving conflicts over the sexual division of labor within marriage and the rights of husbands over wives and fathers over mothers;[27] in this case, however, it was asked to determine not whether sexual difference justified male privilege but rather whether it justified women's exemption from criminal sanctions exclusively applicable to men.

Although there were some legal precedents from the early 1950s that upheld the exemption of lesbianism from criminal prosecution, these cases had stopped far short of any detailed discussion of the differences between male and female homosexuality. They affirmed that only truly similar circumstances were ensured the same legal treatment and invoked the "naturally given differences between the sexes" to justify maintaining Paragraph 175, but no case had specified precisely what those "naturally given differences" were.[28] The Federal Constitutional Court justices clearly believed that the time for a definitive answer had come, and they took the extraordinary step of calling in reinforcements to assist in illuminating the mysteries of human sexuality. While the court solicited no outside assistance in determining the character of Nazi racism, it marshalled a broad range of experts to aid in determining what distinguished women from men and male homosexuality from "lesbian love" (*lesbische Liebe*). In addition to the questions with which this chapter began, it also asked for testimony on the potential correlation between the "surplus of women" (*Frauenüberschuss*) created by the high incidence of adult male death in World War II and an increase in "communal housekeeping arrangements between two or more women," a context in which social relationships might become sexual. The opinions solicited by the court came from a panel of "expert witnesses," including a psychologist, two neurologists, a specialist in forensic medicine, a sociologist, a criminologist, a criminal investigator, and the director of a state youth welfare agency.

Particularly prominent on this panel was Helmut Schelsky, a leading proponent of an empirical sociological method that claimed to be more concerned

---

27. Moeller, *Protecting Motherhood*, pp. 187–90.

28. Decision of Federal High Court, June 22, 1951, *Neue juristische Wochenschrift* 4 (1951): 810; and decision of State High Court (Oberlandesgericht), Braunschweig, October 2, 1953, *Neue juristische Wochenschrift* 6 (1953): 1929–30.

with problem solving than with grandiose theories. He had greatly advanced his reputation with a major study of expellees who fled to West Germany in front of the Red Army as it moved westward at the end of the war. Schelsky argued forcefully that the family's stability in the face of a general societal collapse justified making it the central focus for social policy in the postwar era, and his authority on the subject won him a place on a blue-ribbon advisory board that counseled the Ministry of Family Affairs in Adenauer's administration.[29]

Outspoken in his criticism of women's emancipation, Schelsky maintained that the "emancipation out of necessity" of the war and postwar years was a dubious gain. Misguided bourgeois feminists who championed equality for women on the same terms as men represented the interests of only a few upper-middle-class women. Their lives were reduced to the duties of representation and giving orders, and their lack of accomplishment and sense of dissatisfaction, argued Schelsky, led them to seek other experiences outside the home. In their private lives, they tended to place "inordinate emphasis and extraordinary demands on personal relations, in particular romantic relations between the sexes, in short, a heightening of the erotic."[30] According to Schelsky, the highest priority of most women was not liberation to go out to work but an emancipation to labor at only one job—for their husbands and children.

Although these concerns about professional women and the sanctity of private families resounded in Schelsky's testimony before the Federal Constitutional Court, what doubtless justified his inclusion among the "expert witnesses" was his book, *Soziologie der Sexualität: Über die Beziehungen zwischen Geschlecht, Moral und Gesellschaft* (Sociology of sexuality: On the relationships among sex, morals, and society) which had gone through seven reprintings and 100,000 copies by 1957 as part of an inexpensive "pocketbook encyclopedia" series.[31] According to Schelsky, sexuality was no timeless essence, but rather a phenomenon structured by culture and society. The forms of sexual relations in any society were thus determined by the "condition and development of religious beliefs, technology and art, social and political relations among social strata, and so forth."[32] The only constant seemed to be that

---

29. Helmut Schelsky, *Wandlungen der deutschen Familie in der Gegenwart: Darstellung und Deutung einer empirisch-soziologischen Tatbestandsaufnahme,* 4th ed. (Stuttgart, 1960); and Hans Braun, "Helmut Schelsky's Konzept der 'nivellierten Mittelstandsgesellschaft' und die Bundesrepublik der 50er Jahre," *Archiv für Sozialgeschichte* 29 (1985): 199–223.

30. Helmut Schelsky, "Die Gleichberechtigung der Frau und die Gesellschaftsordnung," *Sozialer Fortschritt* 1 (1952): 130–31; and Moeller, *Protecting Motherhood*, pp. 117–20.

31. Helmut Schelsky, *Soziologie der Sexualität: Über die Beziehungen zwischen Geschlecht, Moral und Gesellschaft* (Hamburg, 1955).

32. Helmut Schelsky, "Die sozialen Formen der sexuellen Beziehungen," in *Die Sexualität des Menschen: Handbuch der medizinischen Forschung* (Stuttgart, 1955), p. 251.

virtually all societies were constituted around the "sexually polarized" extremes of male and female, however much the contents shoved into these categories might differ from one society or historical period to another.[33] Schelsky was well aware that his insistence on the "'cultural' relativity" of sexual relations challenged any notion of an absolute sexual morality, whether based on religion or metaphysics or grounded in biology and conceptions of what was natural. Explicitly critical of the "veneration of 'nature'" and the "dogmatic biologism of our age," Schelsky argued that nature was no more than "what the individual makes of it or is forced to make of it."[34]

Biology could provide no adequate explanation of homosexual tendencies, but Schelsky was far from ready to see homosexuality as one form of socially constructed sexual variation among others. Rather, it was a symbol of a society in disequilibrium, a phenomenon particularly characteristic of periods of social chaos and instability. Not only political disruption and profound changes in social structure, but also economic collapse, inflation, and crises of provisioning brought in their wake a "flood of sexual perversions," and homosexuality was among them. The aftermath of two world wars in the twentieth century offered ample evidence, Schelsky argued. The "revolutionary removal of inhibition" leading to an increase in homosexuality was greater after World War I than after World War II, but there could still be little doubt that a "proliferation of sexual uncertainty and the increased incidence of sexual abnormality were the consequences of the massive social uprootedness, inflicted on German society by the war and the events of the postwar period," topics Schelsky had discussed at length in his study of the postwar German family.[35]

In his *Soziologie der Sexualität*, Schelsky offered no insights into lesbianism, but on the subject of male homosexuality he had much to say. In general, social situations that promoted intensive contact among men were hotbeds of potential homosexuality. Young men sent off to all-male schools and adult men sent off to war were denied "female contact," a prerequisite for "sexual development conforming to norms." In addition, the "flight from masculinity," a characteristic of all advanced industrial societies, led away from heterosexuality, not into women's arms, and in the postwar period there were many pressures driving men toward other men. The harsh competition characteristic of a "western economic order," depressions, unemployment, wars, and fear of renewed

---

33. Ibid., pp. 245, 251, 254–55.
34. Ibid., pp. 254–55.
35. Schelsky, *Soziologie der Sexualität*, p. 82. See also Ludwig von Friedeburg, *Die Umfrage in der Intimsphäre* (Stuttgart, 1953). Many of the same concerns emerged in studies of returning prisoners of war. See, for example, *Die Sexualität des Heimkehrers: Vorträge gehalten auf dem 4. Kongress der Deutschen Gesellschaft für Sexualforschung in Erlangen 1956* (Stuttgart, 1957); and Albrecht Lehmann, *Gefangenschaft und Heimkehr: Deutsche Kriegsgefangene in der Sowjetunion* (Munich, 1986), pp. 89–90, 146–53.

global conflict all combined to make it increasingly difficult for men to be men, and there was never any question that proper men were heterosexual. Rather than providing beleaguered men with comfort and support, women seemed only to make matters worse. They confronted men as competitors in professional life even as they placed ever greater demands on male breadwinners in their role as "rulers of consumer desires."[36] The pressure for female emancipation also leveled the differences between the sexes, leaving men more uncertain of their identity and stripped of the social significance that once shaped their subjective experience. Echoing a central theme of his study of the postwar German family, Schelsky also argued that equilibrium within families had been disrupted during the war and the postwar years because mothers' responsibilities had expanded dramatically. The consequent decline in fathers' authority represented an additional impediment to the establishment of stable heterosexual relationships and accelerated the "flight from masculinity."

It was possible to hear many of these themes in Schelsky's testimony before the Federal Constitutional Court. Schelsky also directly addressed the court's request for information about the differences between male and female homosexuality in postwar West Germany. He asserted that the growing public and professional status of women made lesbianism no less dangerous than male homosexuality. Once lesbians were supervisors, they would be just as likely as men to exploit their positions "to seduce their subordinates for lesbian friendly relationships." However, mitigating circumstances included the fact that "for a large portion of women, there would be a stronger family connection and a greater need for privacy, so that, on balance, their lesbian activity should not be subject to the same criminal penalties as those [that applied] to male homosexuals"; it represented "a less serious social danger." Lesbians were also more likely to keep their relationships private, "entering less frequently into public," and they would be less inclined to "build cliques or to tend to other asocial forms and to prostitution."[37]

Figuring even more prominently than Schelsky's sociological analysis in the court's final decision were the opinions of those witnesses who emphasized that male and female sexuality differed fundamentally because of physiological differences and the destinies linked inextricably to biology. This position, articulated most fully by Hans Giese, the director of the Institute for Sexual Research in Frankfurt, described in detail the "biological or functional" differences that could justify differential legal treatment of women and men. In contrast to Schelsky, Giese was less interested in the pressures of modern society and the particular characteristics of postwar West Germany than in the egg and the sperm.

---

36. Schelsky, *Soziologie der Sexualität*, pp. 83–84.
37. *EdB*, 6:408–409.

Giese wrote prolifically on human sexuality in the 1950s and early 1960s, illuminating his subject with the bright light of psychological method and theory. He modestly offered his *Psychopathologie der Sexualität* (Psychopathology of sexuality), a collection published in 1962, as no less than a sequel, equal in quality and representativeness, to Richard von Krafft-Ebing's pathbreaking *Psychopathia Sexualis,* which had defined the state of research into sexuality in the late nineteenth century.[38] An advocate of reforming Paragraph 175 in the early 1950s, Giese acknowledged that he and the Frankfurt institute were seen as "pioneers" by supporters of homosexual rights. In his testimony to the court, he made clear his conviction that when it involved only consenting adults and remained "in the realm of monogamous relations or long-term relations with the same partner behind one's own door," homosexual "deviance" presented no social danger.[39] However, Giese did not use his testimony to try to convince the court that Paragraph 175 should be abolished or even significantly reformed. Rather, he placed greatest emphasis on the biological differences between women and men that translated into profoundly different sexual tendencies, making it far more likely that male homosexuals would engage in practices that were a threat to society because they ran a greater risk of crossing the line that separated innocuous "deviance" from potentially dangerous "perversion."

In language that the court borrowed explicitly in its final decision, Giese distinguished between the two fundamental aspects of human sexuality: "on the one hand, a procreative-instinctual (*generativ-vegegativer*) one, that is, an aspect of unconscious bodily function in relationship to sexuality, and on the other hand, a social aspect." Elaborating on the attributes of normal heterosexual sexuality, he maintained that women's sexuality was much more profoundly influenced by the "procreative-instinctual" aspect, men's sexuality by the social. Fatherhood was not a creation of "insemination (*Zeugungsvorgang*) . . . a short-term act," but of society, whereas for a woman, motherhood was reached along a "procreative-instinctual" path that began with conception.

In his testimony, Giese emphasized that these differences in women's and men's respective "contributions" to procreation translated into fundamental differences in male and female sexuality. Male sexuality, "'freed' from the procreative-instinctual aspect," was endangered by an "excess of drives" that resulted in greater promiscuity, more sexual activity, and a greater emphasis on

---

38. Hans Giese and Victor E. von Gebsattel, eds., *Psychopathologie der Sexualität* (Stuttgart, 1962); and Hans Giese, ed., *Mensch, Geschlecht, Gesellschaft: Das Geschlechtsleben unserer Zeit gemeinverständlich dargestellt,* 2d ed. (Baden-Baden, 1961).

39. Hans Giese, *Der homosexuelle Mann in der Welt,* 2d ed. (Stuttgart, 1964), p. 7. This study, based on the case histories of 131 homosexual men, was completed in the winter of 1957–58. See also Dose, "§ 175," pp. 124–25. For Giese's testimony, *EdB,* 6:404.

"mere sexual pleasure." Men's excessive drives were evident in their ability to be aroused more rapidly, and, relative to women, more often, and in sexual behavior that was "aggressive [and] demanding." This in turn led to the "characteristic experience of pleasure of male sexuality," greater tendencies toward promiscuity, limited abilities to form lasting relationships, and the danger of pursuing sex merely for "lustful gain." Women, no matter what the object of their lust, apparently used different balance sheets. They were more inclined toward abstinence, less interested in sex, and less promiscuous.

This lengthy discussion of the relationship between reproduction and sexuality was an essential prologue to Giese's analysis of what distinguished male homosexuality from lesbianism; understanding "insemination" and "conception" was the key to any understanding of the "natural dissimilarity of the sexes," no less for lesbians and male homosexuals than for heterosexual women and men. Lesbians, spared from the "excess of drives" that plagued men, were better able to endure sexual abstinence, far more likely to form lasting stable relationships with other women, and far less likely to be unattached than homosexual men. Because their sexuality was rooted in the "procreative-instinctual" aspect, "their organism, which is meant for motherhood, shows them how to compensate by acting like a mother, when they are not biologically mothers."[40]

Of particular concern to Giese was the potential seduction of minors by homosexuals. Girls and boys were equally subject to "undesirable maturation crises" if they were the victims of homosexual adults, but there was also no doubt that the structure of male sexuality with its greater sex drives, its voracious appetite, and its tendency toward "excessively heightened activity" meant that male homosexuals were more likely than their female counterparts to prey on youth. Men "more easily land on the track toward perversion" which could lead toward pederasty, and Giese saw no "tendency analogous to pederasty among homosexual women."[41]

The themes outlined by Giese were repeated with variations in the testimony of many other witnesses.[42] The seduction of youth was a central concern,

---

40. *EdB*, 6:403.

41. *EdB*, 6:405.

42. In *Psychopathologie der Sexualität*, Giese continued to maintain that "homosexuality as such was not yet perverse." Rather, it was the "abnormal form of sexual activity" that "expressed an 'inability,' 'to find the (natural) way to the other sex.'" He emphasized the "sterility" of homosexual sexual activity as defining its abnormality and described fatherhood and motherhood as the likely means to diminish or totally obliterate "homosexual desire." Completely rejecting the "theory of the 'third sex,'" he asserted that "the homosexual man is in fact a 'man,' the homosexual woman, a 'woman,'" the same position he took in his testimony to the court. In *Psychopathologie der Sexualität*, Giese also noted the parallels between the persecution by the Nazis of Jews and homosexuals, both attacked as threats to the "continuance of the species," although for Giese, only anti-Semitism qualified as a form of racism. This line of argument was absent from his testimony before the court. See Giese and Gebsattel, eds., *Psychopathologie der Sexualität,* pp. 403–8, 416–20; also, Hans

and this emphasis echoed a much larger debate over the future of the generation that had come of age after the war. In particular, sociologists and social psychologists worried that young people would find few adequate role models. The older generation was discredited by its association with National Socialism and could not win the confidence or admiration of the "skeptical generation."[43] In their testimony before the court, experts emphasized that puberty was a phase of particularly great uncertainty, because young people were still not sure where their sexual drives might propel them. This made them particularly susceptible to sexual abuse, and the seduction of youth by homosexuals could have permanent consequences. However, there was a general consensus that homosexual seduction presented different potential dangers for young women and men. Ellen Scheuner, head of the state youth and welfare education office in Westphalia and Lippe and the only woman among the witnesses, testified that young women's "natural sense of the sexual order . . . and also . . . their heterosexual involvement at an earlier age with older partners" tended to protect them from seduction by lesbians and made them less susceptible to the advances of older women.[44] Apparently the normative social path to fatherhood that contained men's "excess of drives" also included the responsibility for the heterosexual initiation of younger women. The court accepted the considered opinion of the director of the criminal investigation division of the Cologne police, Chief Superintendent O. Wenzky, that "youthful lesbians do not exist."[45] Young men were unsure of themselves around the opposite sex, although also inherently more active. Girls, by contrast, were "far more . . . protected by a natural sense for the sexual order, in part, because girls settle on heterosexual relations at a much earlier age relative to boys." Unlike the adult male homosexual who preferred young men, moreover, the "desire of active lesbians" aimed not at young women, but at "sexually experienced women."[46]

Many witnesses also underscored their belief that men's "aggressive and demanding" sexual "function" contrasted sharply with women's, which was "more accepting and ready for submission."[47] Men were "basically always prepared for sexual activity," while women, according to the testimony of Roland

---

Giese, "Gesellschaftsunterschiede im homosexuellen Verhalten," in *Mensch, Geschlechte, Gesellschaft*, ed. Giese, p. 873.

43. Helmut Schelsky was a major contributor to the discussion of the problems of youth as well. See *Die skeptische Generation: Eine Soziologie der deutschen Jugend* (1957; reprint, Frankfurt, 1984); also Curt Bondy et al., *Jugendliche stören die Ordnung: Bericht und Stellungnahme zu den Halbstarkenkrawallen* (Munich, 1957); and Günther Kaiser, *Randalierende Jugend: Eine soziologische und kriminologische Studie über die sogenannten "Halbstarken"* (Heidelberg, 1959).

44. *EdB*, 6:427.

45. *EdB*, 6:409.

46. *EdB*, 6:427.

47. *EdB*, 6:411, testimony of Kroh of the Psychological Institute of the Free University of Berlin.

Grassberger, head of the Institute for Criminology of the University of Vienna, were not only more passive but "because of menstruation, are impeded one fourth of the time."[48] For Wenzky, these differences translated into the far greater public presence of male homosexuals, perpetually in search of venues for "making friendly connections" and ubiquitous in "train stations with their waiting rooms, the squares in front of train stations, restrooms, pubs with a clearly homosexual milieu, [and] homosexual dance groups."[49] Citing Grassberger's data from Austria, where lesbianism was subject to the same criminal penalties as male homosexuality, the court concluded that twenty-five times more men than women were sentenced for "same-sex immorality."[50] This difference in quantity was one more indication of a difference in quality. Male prostitution was another obvious consequence of the differences between male and female sexuality. If not, like the youthful lesbian, an impossibility, the lesbian prostitute was a rarity, restricted to a "few, discrete cases."[51] Where there was little demand, there would be little supply.

The justices also heard much testimony confirming Giese's observation that the difference between lesbians and male homosexuals was fundamentally determined by the fact that lesbians remained potential mothers. Grassberger, the professor of criminology, declared that women, whether homosexual or heterosexual, "are reminded again and again that their sexual lives are associated with burdens."[52] The court agreed, acknowledging the broad consensus among the witnesses that for women, whomever they slept with, sexuality was always associated with reproduction, and reproduction, in turn, with maternal duties. The linkage woman-mother thus defined the sexuality of even those women whose sexual activity could not lead to conception. Indeed, because for lesbians, "feminine, motherly feelings predominate," policing female homosexuality was extremely difficult; it was "not possible to define the boundary between a lesbian relationship and a tender friendship between women."[53]

Ernst Kretschmer, a psychiatrist and the director of a neurological clinic in Tübingen, acknowledged that there were differences between male and female homosexuality, but, departing from his medical brethren, he argued that

---

48. *EdB*, 6:406. Grassberger was the author of *Psychologie des Strafverfahrens*, 2d ed. (Vienna, 1968), first published in 1950. He continued to lobby against suspension of Paragraph 175 into the 1960s. See Baumann, *Paragraph 175*, p. 158.

49. *EdB*, 6:410.

50. *EdB*, 6:425.

51. *EdB*, 6:410, testimony of Wenzky.

52. *EdB*, 6:406, testimony of Grassberger.

53. *EdB*, 6:407, testimony of Wiethold, whose professional affiliation is not provided. He was among those recruited to provide an "expert" opinion on the nature of homosexuality for the parliamentary commission charged with a reform of the criminal code in 1958. In this context, he reaffirmed his rejection of any conception of innate homosexuality and argued for maintaining all provisions of Paragraph 175. See Baumann, *Paragraph 175*, p. 148.

these differences were "more of a quantitative than a qualitative nature," and he explicitly "dispute[d] genuine psychological differences between the sexes of the type that would justify differing legal treatment."[54] Kretschmer contended that it was precisely the criminalization of male homosexuals that resulted in their apparently greater presence in public life; the law, not natural sexual differences, made male homosexuals far more visible than lesbians.

The author of a *Textbook of Medical Psychology* that had already gone through ten editions by 1950, Kretschmer had established his credentials in the 1920s as a principal advocate of a psychiatric theory that linked body type, physical appearance, psychological makeup, character traits, and heredity. Although variations on this theme were developed to a fine point by Nazi doctors, Kretschmer had lost influence after 1933 because he refused to renounce his respect for Freud, to endorse the concept of an "ideal race," and to abandon his belief that racial mixture did not hinder, but rather benefited, cultural development. Never a member of the Nazi party, he had returned to prominence in the medical community after the war and had headed the Tübingen clinic since 1946.[55]

While acknowledging that in many cases, homosexuality was "inborn," exhibiting "definite anomalies of a dysglandular nature or abnormal functioning of the diencephalic sex-centres," in his writings on the subject Kretschmer maintained that in other instances, it depended "on constitutional factors or brain-injury" or was "predominantly psychogenic" and "determined by environmental factors." As he concluded in his testimony, "it is senseless to argue about whether homosexuality is innate or acquired. There is a reciprocal relation between biological disposition and external influences." Whether caused by nature, culture, or some combination of the two, homosexuality should be

---

54. *EdB*, 6:401.

55. Ernst Kretschmer, *Medizinische Psychologie*, 10th ed. (Stuttgart, 1950), published in English as *A Text-Book of Medical Psychology*, trans. E. B. Strauss (London, 1952). Kretschmer's other major work, *Körperbau und Charakter: Untersuchungen zum Konstitutionsproblem und zur Lehre von den Temperamenten,* 21st ed. (Berlin, 1955), was first published in 1922 and was reissued in 1936; it also appeared in an English translation, *Physique and Character: An Investigation of the Nature of Constitution and of the Theory of Temperament,* trans. W. J. H. Sprott (London, 1925). See also Ernst Kretschmer, *Gestalten und Gedanken* (Stuttgart, 1963), pp. 155–58, and idem, "Das Ende des Rassenwahns (1945)," in *Psychiatrische Schriften 1914–1962,* ed. Wolfgang Kretschmer (Berlin, 1974), pp. 179–81; Wolfgang Kretschmer, "Ernst Kretschmer: Das Ringen um die medizinische Psychologie," *Deutsche medizinische Wochenschrift* 114 (1989): 922–26; Geoffrey Cocks, *Psychotherapy in the Third Reich: The Göring Institute* (New York, 1985), pp. 18, 109–110, 237–38; Annemarie Tröger, "The Creation of a Female Assembly-Line Proletariat," in *When Biology Became Destiny: Women in Weimar and Nazi Germany,* ed. Renate Bridenthal, Atina Grossmann, and Marion Kaplan (New York, 1984), p. 252; and Ulfried Geuter, *The Professionalization of Psychology in Nazi Germany,* trans. Richard J. Holmes (Cambridge, 1992), pp. 121, 123.

classified as the "most important perversion,"[56] and Kretschmer emphasized the potential dangers, particularly to youth, of homosexual seduction. However, in this regard, lesbians presented no less a danger than male homosexuals and should be subject to no different criminal penalties; in the case of consenting adults, he "could only recognize a public interest in prosecution [of homosexual activity] if public scandal were provoked."[57]

The expert testimony "completely convinced" the court that criminalizing only male homosexual activity was not a violation of the Basic Law's guarantee of equal rights. What the justices needed was proof of fundamental "biological or functional" differences that distinguished women from men, thus justifying an exception to the constitutional guarantee that "men and women have the same rights." Science obliged, and the court reasoned that even in his dissent over the appropriateness of criminal penalties, Kretschmer never questioned the fundamental sexual differences between women and men. Summing up the testimony presented to them, the Federal Constitutional Court justices concluded that

> as different sexual beings, man and woman are also able to practice same-sex immoral activity (*gleichgeschlectliche Unzucht*) only in the form that their sex makes possible. The particular sexual character of homosexual immorality is apparent both in different methods of bodily acts as well as in different psychological attitudes during these acts.[58]

Acts and attitudes were determined in turn by those "biological differences" that distinguished women from men. Equal treatment was justified only in cases where women and men were subject to the same circumstances, not where "the peculiarity of woman as sexual being and the peculiarity of man as sexual being so fundamentally and decisively determine the facts that the comparable element, the abnormal turn of desire to one's own sex, retreats from view, and lesbian love and male homosexuality appear as non-comparable in a legal sense."[59]

The court also justified its decision by comparing the differential treatment of male and female homosexuality to other instances where sexual difference took precedence over gender equality. In citing precedents that had established the limits of "biological or functional" difference, the court pointed out that neither the woman worker, whose hours of work were restricted, nor the "woman, who becomes a mother" had any "legal advantages or disad-

---

56. E. Kretschmer, *Text-Book,* pp. 175–76, and *Körperbau und Charakter,* p. 132. For his testimony, *EdB,* 6: 401–2.

57. *EdB,* 6:400–402.

58. *EdB,* 6:424.

59. *EdB,* 6:431–32.

vantages" because of state-mandated measures to which men were not entitled.[60]

In affirming that special treatment in no way violated the principle of equality, the justices clearly echoed the sentiments of those Social Democratic drafters of the Basic Law, who had insisted that the fundamental guarantee of the equal rights of women and men be enshrined in the constitution. The SPD's Elisabeth Selbert, who led the fight for the equal rights clause, had addressed head-on the potential tension between demands for equality and demands for special treatment in the deliberations over the Basic Law in 1949. According to her, a conception of equality that "acknowledge[d] difference" incorporated a recognition of the particular demands of motherhood. CDU critics of Selbert's equal rights language in the debates over the Basic Law charged that unequivocal guarantees of equality would threaten the "protection of mothers" at the workplace. Complete equal rights would mean "protecting 'male motherhood'"; because this was nonsensical, placing women on completely equal footing with men would mean eliminating their claims to special treatment. If men could not be mothers, and women and men were equal in all respects, then mothers could claim no special treatment. However, Selbert countered that the protection of motherhood in no way privileged women; rather, it represented only "compensation for the burdens . . . that arise because of a woman's natural obligations as mother."[61]

Selbert's position, shared by advocates of women's rights from across the political spectrum in the 1950s, had been repeatedly affirmed by the courts and was implicitly invoked in the justices' response to Günter R. and Oskar K.'s appeal. In its judgment the court emphasized that protective legislation for women workers and paid maternity leaves for wage-earning women did not discriminate against men; rather, they took "into account the need for protection of the biological peculiarity of the woman in the context of her working conditions."[62] Similarly, by upholding the differential treatment of male and female homosexuals, the court did not violate the principle of the equal rights of men and women; rather, it affirmed the existence of those "biological or functional" differences that defined men, justified criminalizing their homosexual activity, and made it necessary to protect society from dangers that lesbianism simply could not present.

---

60. *EdB,* 6:422–23.

61. Parlamentarischer Rat, Hauptausschuss, Bonn 1948/49, 42. Sitzung, January 18, 1949, p. 539 (a copy of this published protocol is available in Parlamentsarchiv des deutschen Bundestages); and Moeller, *Protecting Motherhood,* p. 159.

62. *EdB,* 6:422. On protective legislation, particularly the maternity law of 1952 (*Mutterschutzgesetz*), see Robert G. Moeller, "Protecting Mother's Work: From Production to Reproduction in Postwar West Germany," *Journal of Social History* 22 (1989): 413–37, and idem, *Protecting Motherhood,* pp. 142–79.

In Germany the brand of Anglo-American feminism that advocated that sexual differences were of no social or political consequence and that equality should be based on the common humanity of women and men had never found a substantial audience.[63] The court stressed that German supporters of women's rights had also never championed the equal status of male and female homosexuals. Rather, "in the battle for equal rights of the sexes there was never any mention of the equal treatment of male and female homosexuality."[64] Here the court oversimplified the intense debates within the bourgeois women's movement in 1910–11, when at least some women's rights advocates had proposed that extending Paragraph 175 to cover lesbianism would represent a welcome acknowledgment of women's equality with men.[65] However, on balance there was no question that the rights and status of lesbians and homosexual men had never been high on the agenda of any part of the German women's movement, nor did these issues concern politically active women in the 1950s.[66]

Expert testimony and legal opinion confirmed that homosexuality violated the laws of nature. The court left no doubt that it also violated the laws of morality, and it was on this basis that the justices rejected the appellants' claim that criminalizing male homosexuality unconstitutionally restricted the "lives of individuals who have homosexual feelings—in most cases, an innate characteristic—because they are not given the possibility to translate their feelings into practice."[67] The court upheld the principle that there was an "inviolable arena of human freedom, . . . exempt from being influenced by any form of

---

63. See in particular Barbara Greven-Aschoff, *Die bürgerliche Frauenbewegung in Deutschland, 1894–1933* (Göttingen, 1981); Ann Taylor Allen, *Feminism and Motherhood in Germany, 1800–1914* (New Brunswick, N.J., 1991); and Irene Stoehr, "Housework and Motherhood: Debates and Politics in the Women's Movement in Imperial Germany and the Weimar Republic," in *Maternity and Gender Policies: Women and the Rise of the European Welfare States, 1880s–1950s,* ed. Gisela Bock and Pat Thane (London, 1991), pp. 213–32. By the 1920s, the SPD was also closer to this position as it moved farther away from any variant of the Marxist prescription that women's true equality would be reached via her entry into "productive" labor. See Karen Hagemann, *Frauenalltag und Männerpolitik: Alltagsleben und gesellschaftliches Handeln von Arbeiterfrauen in der Weimarer Republik* (Bonn, 1990). On the continuity in these views in the 1950s, see Moeller, *Protecting Motherhood,* pp. 57–61.

64. *EdB,* 6:431.

65. Mecki Pieper, "Die Frauenbewegung und ihre Bedeutung für lesbische Frauen (1850–1920)," in *Eldorado,* pp. 116–24. A number of contributions to the debate are republished in Kokula, *Weibliche Homosexualität;* see also Anna Rüling, "Welches Interesse hat die Frauenbewegung an der Lösung des homosexuellen Problems?" *Jahrbuch für sexuelle Zwischenstufen* 7 (1905): 131–51, printed in *Lesbianism and Feminism in Germany, 1895–1910* (New York, 1975).

66. Among the Federal Constitutional Court justices was at least one who could speak with some authority on this subject. Erna Scheffler, the only female justice, was an outspoken advocate of women's rights in the 1950s, and her selection for the court was in part an acknowledgment of her reputation as a steadfast campaigner against the patriarchal vestiges of the family law. See Moeller, *Protecting Motherhood,* pp. 185–86.

67. *EdB,* 6:422.

public authority." Such sentiments took on particular significance in the aftermath of Nazi attempts to transform private spheres into public places and to subordinate individual freedoms to the collective good of the *Volk*.[68] However, the court emphasized that there were other spaces that were on the "border between private and social spheres." The bedrooms of male homosexuals apparently were among them, places where the state was free to tread. Quite simply, "homosexual activity unequivocally violates the moral law"; moral law could establish a *"legal* boundary to the right to the free development of personality"; it legitimated "an intervention by the lawgiver into the individual's freedom"; and it was binding on the community.[69]

Science alone did not define the moral law or the danger male homosexuality presented to society. In establishing that Paragraph 175 did not violate the rights of individuals to develop their personalities freely, the court also invoked the opinion of the church to bolster its position, accepting the claims of organized religion to a privileged position in the political legislation of morality in postwar West Germany. In the late 1940s and 1950s, both Protestant and Catholic churches quickly emerged as representatives of the "other Germany," the Germany that had not completely succumbed to National Socialism, and the court stressed that "in particular both large Christian confessions . . . provide[d] much of the population with the standard of measurement for their moral behavior."[70] That standard was undeniably heterosexual. No less than the doctors of the mind and body did the doctors of the soul condemn "same-sex offences." In addition to religious authority, the court also cited legal precedents that invoked the "healthy sensibility of the people" (*gesunde[s] Empfinden des Volkes*)[71] to confirm that "homosexual activity unequivocally violates the moral law," never pausing to comment on how this same "healthy sensibility" (*gesundes Volksempfinden*) had been used to justify the systematic persecu-tion of "community aliens"—among them, homosexual men—in the Third Reich.[72]

According to Günter R. and Oskar K., West Germany's refusal to de-

---

68. These concerns were central to debates over family policy and family law reform in the 1950s. See Moeller, *Protecting Motherhood*, pp. 38–141.

69. *EdB*, 6:432–34.

70. *EdB*, 6:435. There is an immense literature on religion, particularly Catholicism, and the CDU in the early postwar period. For an introduction, see, for example, Rudolf Uertz, *Christentum und Sozialismus in der frühen CDU: Grundlagen und Wirkungen der christlich-sozialen Ideen in der Union 1945–1949* (Stuttgart, 1981); Hans Maier,"Der politische Weg der deutschen Katholiken nach 1945," in *Deutscher Katholizismus nach 1945: Kirche, Gesellschaft, Geschichte,* ed. Hans Maier (Munich, 1964), 190–99; and Albrecht Langer, ed., *Katholizismus im politischen System der Bundesrepublik* (Paderborn, 1978).

71. *EdB*, 6:436.

72. In general, see Burleigh and Wippermann, *Racial State;* and Detlev J. K. Peukert, *Inside Nazi Germany: Conformity, Opposition, and Racism in Everyday Life,* trans. Richard Deveson (New Haven, 1987).

criminalize homosexual activity was at odds with the norms of the "occidental cultural world" (*dem abendländischen Kulturkreis*) and contradicted the Federal Republic's professed commitment to uphold the 1950 European Convention on Human Rights, the postwar agreement among western European nations that included guarantees of fundamental rights to freedom and privacy. By the late 1950s, the list of countries without criminal penalties against homosexual relations between consenting adults included France, Italy, Denmark, Sweden, Switzerland, and the Netherlands.[73] By calling for West Germany to subscribe to trends in the "occidental world," Günter R. and Oskar K. invoked the authority of a Cold War ideology that bisected the universe along lines of latitude, separating a communist East from the "free world." There could be no question that under Adenauer's leadership, West Germany had marched resolutely into a military and political alliance with the West. The appellants called for it to declare itself part of an enlightened Western cultural order as well.[74]

The court conceded that "new research data might lead to understanding homosexuality as an unavoidable bodily-spiritual deviation from the norm," which in turn would make it meaningless to prosecute it criminally, and it also granted that other European states diverged from German practice by placing no restrictions on the sexual activity of adult male homosexuals.[75] However, it completely rejected the appellants' charge that by maintaining Paragraph 175, the Federal Republic abandoned claims to belong to the "occidental cultural world." In addition, a commitment to human rights need not preclude laws "for the protection of health and morality or [laws] necessary for the protection of the rights and freedoms of others," an umbrella that the justices easily extended to cover Paragraph 175.[76] What seemed to be a liberalization of laws prohibiting homosexuality elsewhere might reflect nothing more than the admission that it was difficult to prosecute violators. In any event, actions by other states need in no way influence Germans to accept that "homosexuality is no longer morally condemned."[77]

---

73. Klimmer, *Homosexualität als Zeitfrage*, pp. 329–33, 397–404; Kröger, *"Entwicklungsstadien und Studie,"* pp. 20–26; Baumann, *Paragraph 175*, pp. 67–73; and Armand Mergen, "Einspruch gegen die generelle Kriminalisierung der Homosexualität," in *Plädoyer für die Abschaffung des § 175*, ed. Tobias Brocher et al. (Frankfurt am Main, 1966), p. 55.

74. The significance of identification with the *Abendland* for the formulation of social policies affecting women and the family in the 1950s is discussed at length in Moeller, *Protecting Motherhood*; see also Jost Hermand, *Kultur im Wiederaufbau: Die Bundesrepublik Deutschland 1945–1965* (Munich, 1986), pp. 44–47, 84.

75. *EdB*, 6:436.

76. *EdB*, 6:441. Also see Arthur H. Robertson, and John G. Merrills, *Human Rights in Europe: A Study of the European Convention on Human Rights*, 3d ed. (Manchester, England, 1993), pp. 1–14, 129.

77. *EdB*, 6:437.

Rejecting all parts of Günter R. and Oskar K.'s appeal, the Federal Constitutional Court unambiguously expressed its view that the criminalization of male homosexual activity violated no part of the Basic Law nor did it undermine the foundations of a "free democracy." Pressures to reform or completely suspend Paragraph 175 were not completely absent in the Adenauer era, and proposals by sex reformers and liberal jurists to eliminate criminal penalties resumed the Weimar agenda.[78] However, the court's unwillingness to revoke the Nazis' expanded version of Paragraph 175 reinforced a similar unwillingness on the part of the West German Ministry of Justice to consider reform appeals. Indeed, Hans-Georg Stümke, a leading German historian of homosexuality, characterizes government discussions of the criminal law reform in the late 1950s and early 1960s as offering little more than an "encyclopedic collection of anti-enlightenment buzzwords about the criminalization of homosexuality" when they came to Paragraph 175.[79] The review of reform proposals led to the conclusion that any lessening of criminal penalties against male homosexuality would open the floodgates to the public organization of homosexuals as pressure groups and the entry of homosexuals into same-sex institutions such as the police and the military, directly endangering the larger society. In debates over proposals to reform the criminal law, opponents of liberalizing or abolishing Paragraph 175 explicitly cited the 1957 judgment of the Federal Constitutional Court and its unequivocal dismissal of the contention that Paragraph 175 violated the Basic Law's promise of equal rights for women and men. The 1957

78. See, for example, Heinrich Ackermann, "Zur Frage der Strafwürdigkeit des homosexuellen Verhaltens des Mannes," in *Sexualität und Verbrechen: Beiträge zur Strafrechtsreform*, ed. Fritz Bauer et al. (Frankfurt, 1963), pp. 153–54; Theodor Adorno, "Sexualtabus und Recht heute," in *Sexualität und Verbrechen*, ed. Bauer et al., pp. 307–8; and Stümke and Finkler, *Homosexuelle und "Gesundes Volksempfinden,"* pp. 340–48. The most comprehensive review of contemporary arguments for reform is provided by Klimmer, *Homosexualität als Zeitfrage.* Rudolf Klimmer, himself a homosexual, had been a member of the Communist Party of Germany (KPD) and was active in the sex reform movement in Weimar. His major work, a comprehensive refutation of the contemporary arguments in favor of criminalizing homosexuality, was denied publication in the German Democratic Republic (GDR), where Klimmer lived and worked after the war. It was ultimately published in Hamburg in 1958. On Klimmer and in general on the discussion of homosexuality in the GDR in the 1950s, see Gudrun von Kowalksi, *Homosexualität in der DDR: Ein historischer Abriss* (Marburg, 1987), pp. 16–25; and on the application of Paragraph 175, Baumann, *Paragraph 175*, p. 52. In the GDR, the expanded penalties instituted by the Nazis were no longer applied after 1950, but the prohibition of "intercourse-like" relations—the provision of the 1871 Criminal Code—was not suspended until 1968. See the decision of the State High Court, Halle, September 20, 1948, *Neue Justiz* 3 (1949): 143–47. Also see Bert Thinius, "Verwandlung und Fall des Paragraphen 175 in der Deutschen Demokratischen Republik," in *Die Geschichte des 175*, pp. 145–62.

79. Stümke, *Homosexuelle in Deutschland*, p. 136; see also Klimmer, *Homosexualität als Zeitfrage*, pp. 409–13; and in general, Siegfried Seelbach, *Gleichgeschlechtliches Verhalten als Straftatbestand: Die Beratungen der grossen Strafrechtskommission* (Stuttgart, 1966).

decision left no doubt that such charges against Paragraph 175 were "without any significance whatsoever" for lawmakers.[80]

The complete rejection of proposals to reform or eliminate Paragraph 175 provides one indication that in the restorative climate of the post–World War II period, there was even less room for a discussion of progressive sexual reform than there had been in the Weimar era.[81] The extensive gay and lesbian subculture that emerged in many urban centers in the 1920s, the public debates over sexuality among policymakers, legal experts, medical practitioners, psychologists, and academic sex researchers, and the pressure from politicians and a well-organized homosexual rights movement for the suspension of Paragraph 175 were all forces that found no counterparts in the early history of the Bonn Republic.

Behind the court's condemnation of homosexual deviance was an idealized vision of heterosexual normalcy that implicitly tied the discussion of homosexuality to a powerfully resurgent postwar pronatalism. West Germany's need for an expanding birthrate and the priority of women's work as mothers were central themes in all discussions of social policies affecting women and the family in the 1950s. Although the immigration of expellees (*Vertriebene*) and others fleeing before the Red Army at the end of the war and the steady stream of migration from East to West Germany before the closing of the border in 1961 registered as net gains in the population of West Germany in the 1950s, the Federal Republic remained obsessed with fears that Germany was "dying out" and that high rates of war deaths combined with long-term trends toward family size limitation would present insurmountable obstacles to sustained economic growth. West Germans were constantly reminded of their responsibility to produce more West Germans.[82] Seen against this background, the court's focus on the tie between fatherhood and normative sexual development for men took on an added layer of meaning; fatherhood not only served to

---

80. Excerpts from the summary of the parliamentary discussion are republished in Brocher et al., *Plädoyer für Abschaffung*, pp. 144, 146; and in addition to Seelbach, an informative review of debates is found in Baumann, *Paragraph 175*, pp. 147–99. The potential seduction of youth by male homosexuals continued to be a major argument in favor of maintaining Paragraph 175. See, for example, Walter Becker, *Homosexualität und Jugendschutz* (Hamm/Westphalia, 1961).

81. Joachim S. Hohmann, ed., *Keine Zeit für gute Freunde: Homosexuelle in Deutschland 1933–1969* (Berlin, 1982), pp. 17–29. The absence of initiatives to eliminate Paragraph 218, the criminal prohibition of abortion, is another example of the Federal Republic's retreat from the Weimar agenda. A highly significant political issue in Weimar, abortion virtually vanished from the public debates of the organized women's movement or any political party in the 1950s and early 1960s. On the Weimar discussion, see Atina Grossmann, "Abortion and Economic Crisis: The 1931 Campaign Against Paragraph 218," in *When Biology Became Destiny*, ed. Bridenthal, Grossmann, and Kaplan, pp. 66–86, and idem, *Reforming Sex*; Cornelie Usbourne, *The Politics of the Body in Weimar Germany: Women's Reproductive Rights and Duties* (Ann Arbor, Mich, 1992), pp. 156–201; and Hagemann, *Frauenalltag und Männerpolitik*, pp. 276–305.

82. Moeller, *Protecting Motherhood*, p. 137.

contain excessive male sexual drives, but it also ensured the growing population essential to postwar reconstruction.

No expert witness responded directly to the constitutional court's request for reflections on the potential correlation between the postwar "surplus of women" and an increase in lesbianism, but the implicit consensus seemed to be that such a correlation did not exist. In addition, Grassberger, the criminologist, maintained that lesbians might well "continue to have intercourse in a normal fashion" and thus would have "substantially greater" fertility than their male counterparts, for whom there was "often a lasting inability to engage in heterosexual acts," a commentary that startlingly echoed arguments of Nazi opponents of the criminalization of lesbian relations in the 1930s.[83]

However, for those fixated on the declining birthrate in postwar West Germany, the "surplus of women" created even graver problems; there were many adult women who were relegated to "half-families" or "incomplete families"—families with no adult males—or, worse yet, were left "standing alone" (*alleinstehend*) by the "scarcity of men" (*Männermangel*), thus excluded from contributing to the birthrate. This only intensified the ideological pressure to be fruitful and multiply on those women fortunate enough to "get a man." The politics of pronatalism reduced sexuality to reproductive heterosexuality and placed yet another barrier in the path of anyone seeking to return to the expanded sexual agenda of the Weimar period. Postwar reconstruction was grounded in conceptions of a productive order of private ownership, capitalism, and the "social market economy" (*soziale Marktwirtschaft*); it was also grounded in a reproductive order that equated sexuality with heterosexuality and heterosexuality with women's "natural obligation" to be wives and mothers. In May 1957, only a week before the Federal Constitutional Court's announced its judgment in the case of Günter R. and Oskar K., the parliament finally completed the work of revising the family law to bring it into accord with the constitutional prescription of the equal rights of women and men. With support from all political parties, the Bundestag legislated provisions specifying that a wife's right to work outside the home was limited by the fulfillment of her "obligations to marriage and family," and no one questioned that those obligations included bearing and raising children.[84]

Family and motherhood took on added significance as institutions that had survived Nazi intervention and bomb attacks and the privation of the chaotic years immediately following the war, sources of uniquely German

---

83. *EdB*, 6:407; also Schoppmann, *Nationalsozialistische Sexualpolitik*, p. 255.

84. See Ingrid Laurien, "'Wie kriege ich einen Mann'? Zum weiblichen Leitbild und zur Rolle der Frau in den Fünfziger Jahren," *Sozialwissenschaftliche Informationen* 15 (1986): 32–44; Moeller, *Protecting Motherhood*, p. 201; Stümke, *Homosexuelle in Deutschland*, pp. 141, 146; and Dietrich Haensch, *Repressive Familienpolitik: Sexualunterdrückung als Mittel der Politik* (Reinbek, 1969).

values that could provide a solid basis for reconstructing postwar West Germany and defining clearly the border with the Communist East. In the context of the Cold War, any challenges to this "natural" heterosexual order could be viewed as subversive; threats to the family were threats to society's fundamental building block, essential for the preservation of "occidental" values and the first line of defense in the struggle against communism.[85]

The reconstruction of postwar West Germany included the reconstruction of gender relations, and the Federal Constitutional Court's assessment of the constitutionality of Paragraph 175 underscored that those relations should only be heterosexual. Even in its analysis of homosexuality, the court ultimately relied most heavily on normative conceptions of what separated heterosexual men and women in its attempts to define what distinguished male homosexuality from "lesbian love." When the court uncritically recorded Hans Giese's testimony that "the homosexual man is a 'man,' the homosexual woman is a 'woman,'"[86] sexuality and heterosexuality became indistinguishable.

Nowhere in the case did Hirschfeld's "third sex" reappear, nor was there any mention of the late-nineteenth-century stereotype of the "sexual invert" or the "mannish" lesbian. As John Fout convincingly demonstrates, by adopting an "essentialist position," Hirschfeld was "arguing that homosexuality was deeply rooted in a biological imperative" and "challeng[ing] all those who argued that individuals could 'become' homosexual." Fout and others have rightly emphasized that the optimistic belief among late-nineteenth- and early-twentieth-century sexologists that science would establish legitimacy for homosexuals and create a society of justice and tolerance was unfounded; science was as likely to limit, restrict, label, and confine as to liberate.[87] However, at least for Hirschfeld, biology left room for homosexual desire. In the testi-

---

85. For the much more fully documented record of the United States, see John D'Emilio, "The Homosexual Menace: The Politics of Sexuality in Cold War America," in *Passion and Power: Sexuality in History,* ed. Kathy Peiss and Christina Simmons with Robert A. Padgug (Philadelphia, 1989), pp. 226–40, and *Sexual Politics, Sexual Communities: The Making of a Homosexual Minority in the United States, 1940–1970* (Chicago, 1983), pp. 40–53; Allan Bérubé, *Coming Out Under Fire: The History of Gay Men and Women in World War Two* (New York, 1990), pp. 258–60, 265–70; and Elaine Tyler May, *Homeward Bound: American Families in the Cold War Era* (New York, 1988).

86. *EdB,* 6:405.

87. Fout, "Sexual Politics," pp. 398, 400; Hull, "Bourgeoisie and Discontents," pp. 263–64; Schoppmann, *Nationalsozialistische Sexualpolitik,* pp. 121–22; and Schmidt, "Allies and Persecutors," p. 128. On the theory of "sexual inversion," see George Chauncey, Jr., "From Sexual Inversion to Homosexuality: The Changing Medical Conceptualization of Female 'Deviance,'" in *Passion and Power,* ed. Peiss and Simmons, pp. 87–117; Carroll Smith-Rosenberg, "Discourses of Sexuality and Subjectivity: The New Woman, 1870–1936," in *Hidden from History,* ed. Duberman, Vicinus, and Chauncey, pp. 267–71; Esther Newton, "The Mythic Mannish Lesbian: Radclyffe Hall and the New Woman," in *Hidden from History,* ed. Duberman, Vicinus, and Chauncey, pp. 287–89; Martha Vicinus, "'They Wonder to Which Sex I Belong': The Historical Roots of Modern

mony to the Federal Constitutional Court, science still reigned supreme, but it allowed no independent existence to homosexuality; homosexuals were not only limited, but virtually erased, understandable only as deviant or perverse incarnations of normal heterosexuals.

In the court's judgment, homosexuals were not born, but made when heterosexuality ran amok, and the court accepted that the possibility of "innate homosexuality" was "so rare that for practical purposes it can be disregarded."[88] The appellants' claim that to have "homosexual feelings" was "in most cases, an innate characteristic" received no further commentary. The difference between male and female homosexuality was reduced to the difference between the relationship of "insemination" to fatherhood and "conception" to motherhood. All men were manly, and they shared an "excess of sexual drives"; no more than mannish lesbians did effeminate male homosexuals emerge in the testimony to the court. All women were motherly and united by bodies that tied sexuality to weighty responsibilities, "reduc[ing] the joy of sexual experience." Properly domesticated by a social institution, fatherhood, the potentially perverse qualities of male sexuality could be channeled. However, the naturally "stronger sexual need of men," when not adequately tempered by society, might lead to "sexual deviance." For women, the dangers were far less great, because even for lesbians, "feminine, motherly feelings predominate." As the court concluded, summarizing the testimony that it had heard:

> Differences in sex life are possibly even more significantly expressed in homosexual than in heterosexual relations, because women's organism, destined for motherhood, involuntarily points toward how to function in a womanly-motherly fashion in a social sense, even if she is not biologically a mother, while there is no corresponding compensation for men.[89]

Lesbian Identity," *Feminist Studies* 18 (1992): 484–86; and for turn-of-the-century examples, Arduin, "Die Frauenfrage und die sexuellen Zwischenstufen," *Jahrbuch für sexuelle Zwischenstufen* 2 (1900): 211–23, republished in *Lesbianism and Feminism in Germany*; and Anne v. den Eken, *Mannweiber-Weibmänner und der § 175: Eine Schrift für denkende Frauen* (Leipzig, 1906), reprinted in *Lesbianism and Feminism in Germany*. For examples of the continuing influence of this psychopathological model in the United States, see Jennifer Terry, "Lesbians Under the Medical Gaze: Scientists Search for Remarkable Differences," *Journal of Sex Research* 27 (1990): 317–39; Henry L. Minton, "Femininity in Men and Masculinity in Women: American Psychiatry and Psychology Portray Homosexuality in the 1930s," *Journal of Homosexuality* 13 (1986): 1–21; Elisabeth Lapovsky Kennedy and Madeleine Davis, "The Reproduction of Butch-Fem Roles: A Social Constructionist Approach," in *Passion and Power,* ed. Peiss and Simmons, pp. 241–42; and Donna Penn, "The Meanings of Lesbianism in Post-War America," *Gender & History* 3 (1991): 190–203.

88. *EdB,* 6:407, testimony of Wiethold.

89. *EdB,* 6:426.

Collapsed into the categories of normative heterosexuality, homosexuality all but vanished in the court's analysis of the differences between women and men. Homosexuality differed in quantity, not quality. Gay men and lesbians marched to the same drummer, they simply were unable to keep the beat.

The Bonn Republic was neither Weimar nor the Third Reich. In many respects, 1949 and the founding of the Federal Republic marked a turning point in modern German history. By the late 1950s, most West Germans could feel a sense of satisfaction at their postwar accomplishments. They had broken with the National Socialist past, and they had established a democratic political order on foundations much firmer than those of the Weimar Republic. Only slightly more than a decade after defeat in war and the destruction of the Nazi regime, West Germans measured the success of their second experiment with democracy on their broad acceptance of parliamentary politics, their establishment of a tremendously expanded welfare state, and their complete integration into a Western political and military alliance. The "economic miracle" (*Wirtschaftswunder*), the postwar boom of unprecedented, sustained growth and prosperity, provided the solid basis for these achievements and eliminated the economic volatility that had caused the chronic instability of Weimar, paving the way for National Socialism.

However, the Federal Constitutional Court's 1957 judgment in the appeals case of Günter R. and Oskar K. indicated clearly that in other respects, the Federal Republic's break with the past was anything but clean. Between 1953 and 1965, the police reported 98,700 violators of Paragraph 175; nearly 38,000 of these were found guilty and sentenced. This figure exceeded the number of those prosecuted in the twelve years of the Thousand Year Reich.[90] Only in 1969 did the Bundestag lift criminal sanctions against sexual activity between men over the age of twenty-one, and this move entailed no ex-post acknowledgment of the victimization of many gay men by the National Socialist regime. A decade later, the West German government explicitly limited restitution for losses caused by the crimes of the Third Reich to those who were persecuted because of their "race, belief, or world-view" while excluding from any special consideration those "who were carried off to concentration camps because of [their] homosexuality." There was still no willingness to entertain the issue raised in the 1957 case that Paragraph 175 embodied Nazi "racial teaching."[91] In 1986, the West German parliament reaffirmed the Federal Con-

---

90. Baumann, *Paragraph 175*, pp. 63–66; and Jellonnek, *Homosexuelle unter dem Hakenkreuz*, p. 11. See also Wilfried Rasch, "Die Frage nach der strafrechtlichen Verantwortlichkeit," in *Psychopathologie der Sexualität*, ed. Giese and Gebsattel, p. 606.

91. Stümke and Finkler, *Homosexuelle und "Gesundes Volksempfinden,"* pp. 353–55, 418. For assessments of the continued discrimination against homosexuals after the reform of Paragraph 175, see Rüdiger Lautmann, "Wie man Aussenseiter draussen hält: Zur Kriminal- und Ordnungspolitik gegenüber homosexuellen Männern und Frauen," *Kritische Justiz* 12 (1979): 1–21;

stitutional Court's view that prosecution for violations of Paragraph 175 by the Nazis did not constitute a case of "National Socialist injustice." Not until the end of the decade did the political pressure of the West German gay liberation movement and the Green party achieve the inclusion of homosexuals among the "forgotten victims" of the National Socialist regime, and even then, material compensation was limited to those who could verify incarceration in a concentration camp, a 50 percent disability caused by their imprisonment, and particular need. By 1989, only nine homosexual men had made application for such compensation, and only one application had been approved.[92]

To be sure, postwar West Germany was characterized neither by the political turmoil of Weimar nor the repressive qualities of the Nazi state, but in its denial of fundamental civil rights to gay men, the Federal Republic revealed its narrow conception of what was to be included among the crimes of the Thousand Year Reich and set limits to what it was willing to learn from its most recent history.[93] The Federal Constitutional Court did not view the expansive discriminatory laws against male homosexuals, introduced by the Nazis in 1935, to embody the abhorrent characteristics of National Socialism. Rather, a new West Germany explicitly endorsed this Nazi legacy as completely consistent with a "democratic political order."

Writing a decade after the Federal Constitution Court had explicitly upheld the Nazis' version of Paragraph 175, the psychologists Alexander and Margarete Mitscherlich analyzed West Germans' "inability to mourn," the apparent lack of interest in directly assessing the meanings of National Socialism. In the postwar era Germans had avoided the past, argued the Mitscherlichs, by throwing themselves into the future. By placing an emphasis on "entrepreneurial spirit" and "restoring what was destroyed," West Germans cleared a path to selective memory, circumventing key aspects of the Thousand Year Reich.[94]

---

and Hanns Wienold and Rüdiger Lautmann, "Antihomosexualität und demokratische Kultur in der BRD," in *Seminar,* ed. Lautmann, pp. 383–416.

92. Schoppmann, *Nationalsozialistische Sexualpolitik*, pp. 257–58.

93. Male homosexuals were not the only "forgotten victims" in the 1950s; the list also includes those subject to involuntary sterilization, other "asocials," Sinti and Roma, and members of the Communist party who opposed the "free democratic" order of the Federal Republic. For an excellent overview, see Burleigh and Wippermann, *Racial State*; also Heinz Düx, "Wiedergutmachung gegenüber den Opfern von NS-Verbrechen," in *Recht, Justiz und Faschismus: Nach 1933 und heute*, ed. Helmut D. Fangmann and Norman Paech (Cologne, 1984), pp. 108–9; and Klaus Scherer, *"Asozial" im Dritten Reich: Die vergessenen Verfolgten* (Münster, 1990). In general, on the complex politics of restitution to victims of National Socialism, see Ludolf Herbst and Constantin Goschler, eds., *Wiedergutmachung in der Bundesrepublik Deutschland* (Munich, 1989); and Constantin Goschler, *Wiedergutmachung: Westdeutschland und die Verfolgten des Nationalsozialismus (1945–1954)* (Munich, 1992).

94. Alexander Mitscherlich and Margarete Mitscherlich, *Die Unfähigkeit zu trauern: Grundlagen kollektiven Verhaltens* (Munich, 1967), p. 19.

In responding to the appeals case of Günter R. and Oskar K., the Federal Constitutional Court showed not an inability, but rather an unwillingness, to mourn. It could not avoid the Nazi legacy; the case unambiguously posed the questions of what constituted "Nazi racial teaching" and what qualified as "National Socialist ideas." Rather, the court explicitly accepted the Nazis' dramatic expansion of the bases for the persecution of gay men as part of a past that required neither rationalization nor rejection, a past that should be accepted and endorsed, not overcome.

When contemporaries prided themselves that Bonn was not Weimar, they contrasted the political and economic instability of the 1920s with the stability of the 1950s.[95] The court's decision also underscored the desire of West Germans to distance themselves from the *sexual* instability of Weimar, the Nazi vision of a revolutionized family subordinated to the state in the 1930s, and the "ruins of families" (*Familientrümmer*) left by Allied bombs and war deaths in the 1940s; it was part of a postwar effort to restore an imagined past where society made men into fathers, biology made women into mothers, and nature made everyone heterosexual. The judgment against Günter R. and Oskar K. suggests how postwar reconstruction included setting clear limits to what constituted the Nazi past and specifying the links between the social and the sexual contract in a democratic Federal Republic.

---

95. See, for example, Fritz René Allemann, *Bonn ist nicht Weimar* (Cologne, 1956).

Part 4.
Ideology and Political Identities in the "Economic Miracle"

The Organic Society and the 'Massenmenschen': Integrating Young Labour in the Ruhr Mines, 1945–58[1]

Mark Roseman

Introduction

In the immediate post-war period, the key to German and indeed Western European economic recovery lay in increasing coal production in the Ruhr. This, in turn, depended on finding new labour for the colliery workforces which, after the liberation of the wartime conscripts in April 1945, were almost 50 percent under strength. The shortfall was so large not only because of the very considerable number of German miners who had died at the front but also because of a failure to take on youngsters in the pre-war era. Moreover, many of those miners still in the pits in 1945 were over-aged or under-strength. Such deficiencies could not be made good overnight and even after the currency reform Germany's economic development was to remain in no small part dependent on the degree to which the mining industry was able to regenerate its workforce. For more than a decade after the capitulation, therefore, rebuilding the colliery workforces was to be a task of eminent economic importance.[2]

---

1. I would like to thank the German Academic Exchange Service, the Leverhulme Trust, and the German Historical Institute for funding the research work on which this piece is based. For full references and a more detailed account, see Mark Roseman, 'New Miners in the Ruhr. Rebuilding the workforce in the Ruhr mines, 1945–1958' (Ph.D thesis, Warwick University, 1987), later published under the title *Recasting the Ruhr, Manpower, economic recovery and labour relations 1945–1958* (Oxford, 1992).

2. For more detail on the economic issues, see Mark Roseman, 'The uncontrolled economy: Ruhr coal production 1945–1948', in Ian Turner (ed.), *Reconstruction in post-war Germany: British Occupation policy and the Western Zones 1945–1955* (Oxford, 1989), 93–123.

Yet the historian who happens upon the reports, letters, and journal articles which remain as testimony to this huge enterprise is apt to be struck as much by ideology as by economics. Beyond prosaic questions of productive integration, an astonishing amount of ink was devoted to the task of shaping the newcomers' mentality. In industrial journals normally more concerned with the merits of the latest coal-plough, the reader prepared to plough through the coal will find grand proposals for reshaping the workforce. Romantic notions—of revitalizing the lost spirit of the pre-industrial miner, of rooting the newcomers in local soil—abound. From the pens of regional labour administration officials flow poetic broadsides about creating a new juvenile élite among the miners. There is a hidden battle, almost a *Kulturkampf,* between churches (and behind them, the employers) and unions over control of and access to young miners' hostels. And alongside the hopes for the future are continual references to the dangers of the present, to the threats of collectivism, nihilism, and radicalization which only the right sort of integration can keep at bay.

Much of this rhetoric and ideology was directed at the mines' juvenile intake, in particular at the apprentices, rather than at the industry's adult recruits. The apprenticeship, with its formal status and lengthy training, was new to mining[3] and many both inside and outside the industry hoped that its implementation might lead to the formation of a new élite within the workforce. In addition to the hopes attached specifically to the apprenticeship, there was the fact that many of the youngsters entering the industry were refugees, coming from outside the Ruhr and from quite different social backgrounds. Not only colliery managers but also social services departments, clergymen, and others saw in this situation an important opportunity for post-war social engineering. The aim of the present chapter is to look in detail at the aspirations, motives, and fears that lay behind the policies adopted towards the youngsters and to draw some conclusions about the ideology and outlook of Germany's bourgeoisie in the post-war period.

The Apprenticeship Strategy before 1945

To do that, we must first cast a brief glance backward into the 1920s and 1930s. It was shortly after the founding of the Deutsches Institut für technische Arbeitsschulung (DINTA; German Institute for Technical Work Training) in 1925 that mines began to seek ways of systematically shaping the workforce's outlook and behaviour. New training programmes were adopted, involving strong elements of character training. Works newspapers started appearing around this time, with their aim of enhancing company loyalty. Traditional elements of

---

3. It had been formally established in 1941.

company welfare policy, the provision of housing, kindergarten, holiday homes, and so on were also extended.[4]

During the 1930s many mines realized that they faced a fundamental problem on the labour market. At the prices they were allowed to charge, they could not afford to pay the wages necessary to win adequate new labour and create a stable workforce. One reason for this was that mining was seen in the Ruhr as a low-status occupation. To be seen as a miner was to be seen to have failed. Engineering, on the other hand, benefited from that fascination with technology that characterized young Germans in the 1930s. As a Wirtschaftsgruppe Bergbau (Mining Association) study noted in 1942, every 6-year-old knew the exact technical details of every plane, car, and radio produced in Germany, but the difference between hard coal and lignite was a closed book even to most 60-year-olds.[5]

To compensate for these factors, mining's wages had to be well ahead of its competitors. Yet this was impossible; apart from anything else, the coal price was pegged at the low level of 1932, thus limiting the size of the collieries' wage bill. So mining employers began to give thought to ways in which they might improve the situation without requiring major injections of resources. The main strategy adopted was to build on the training initiatives of the 1920s and create for the first time a formal, officially recognized apprenticeship, a goal finally realized in 1941. To a certain extent this proposal was advisable on purely technical grounds, but the real hope behind it was that it would restore mining's status, increase recruitment, and create a new core of loyal, stable, and highly qualified young workers. The more the industry faced recruitment and wastage problems in the 1930s, the more this goal of workforce stability became the employers' dominant consideration.

The idea was that apprenticeships would have a twofold effect. On the one hand, they would convince parents and youngsters "that in the field of mining the training that is offered will be qualitatively just as valuable as in other industries."[6] On the other hand, they would enable the employers to bring to bear "educational influences . . . that aim to create a workforce that is aware of its responsibilities."[7] Ultimately, the influx of high-quality and closely supervised new recruits would transform what the employers regarded as the

---

4. See Michael Zimmermann, *Schachtanlage und Zechenkolonie, Leben, Arbeit und Politik in einer Arbeitersiedlung 1880–1980* (Essen, 1987), 146ff.

5. Cited in Hanns W. Brose, 'Eine Gemeinschaftswerbung zur Gewinnung von Nachwuchs für den Bergbau', *Sonderdruck* of the journal *Die Werbung,* July 1950.

6. Archive of the Landesoberbergamt, Dortmund (OBADA) 16300, GMSO, Circular No. 138, Nov. 1945, annex 2.

7. Rudolf Schwenger, *Die betriebliche Sozialpolitik im Ruhrkohlenbergbau,* Munich 1932, cited ibid.

unstable and unreliable workforce of the 1920s into a permanent, responsible, and co-operative one.[8]

To supplement and accelerate the apprenticeship's impact, mines began to use modern advertising methods to alter the way the miner was perceived both inside and outside the industry. The mines hoped to win apprentices from groups previously unwilling to send their offspring to the mines and set about constructing special apprentice hostels to accommodate outsiders to the Ruhr. However, the needs of total war forced a halt to the construction programme, and a number of the hostels were given over to housing forced labour.[9]

New Labour Policy 1945–48

In the immediate post-war period there was little room for anything more than the most short-term policies, aiming directly to increase production immediately. For one thing there was the sheer scale of the mines' labour shortages, for another the dependence of West German and Western European recovery, indeed survival, on sizeable and immediate injections of Ruhr coal. Labour had to be had at any price and, under British Military Government direction, policy consisted in little more than recruiting almost any available able-bodied man, providing very basic accommodation and the most rudimentary training programme, and thrusting him before the coal face. Between 1945 and 1948 over 200,000 adults, the vast majority coming from quite different working backgrounds, entered the mines under these conditions.

This situation did not prevent the employers from giving thought to the industry's longer-term needs. Proposals, ranging from formal documents on how to recognize the industry down to mutterings in the *Kasino* (dining room) about those terrible British, were in the air almost from the start of the occupation. Just a few weeks after its creation in autumn 1945, the German Mines Supplies Organization—a skeleton employers' association revived by the British to help run the industry—sent the collieries a circular reminding them of mining's long-standing efforts to upgrade training within the industry and expressing the hope that the training programme would enhance the industry's status and the size and quality of its young intake. The circular was accompanied by a directive from the also revived Oberbergamt Dortmund—the state mining inspectorate for the region—which laid down detailed guidelines for apprentice

8. See ibid. and H. Büttchereit, 'Probleme des bergmännischen Bildungswesens', *Mitteilungen der WBK*, 5 (1957), 5–10.

9. Brose, 'Eine Gemeinschaftswerbung', passim; Michael Zimmermann, 'Ausbruchshoffnungen. Junge Bergleute in den dreißiger Jahren', in Lutz Niethammer (ed.), *"Die Jahre weiß man nicht, wo man die heute hinsetzen soll". Faschismuserfahrungen im Ruhrgebiet* (Berlin/Bonn 1983), 97–132, here p. 114; Hans-Georg Erzmoneit, 'Was tut der Ruhrbergbau für seinen Nachwuchs?', *Bergbau*, 7 (1956), 168–75, here p. 172.

training. Even before the currency reform considerable numbers of youngsters were recruited.[10] By 1948, therefore, the strategy of promoting apprentice recruitment enjoyed almost universal endorsement in the Ruhr.

It was in that year that the industry gained more freedom to shape its own labour policy. Military Government had begun to relax its controls and in November 1947 had created a German body, the Deutsche Kohlenbergbauleitung (DKBL; Director of the German Coal Mining Industry), to run the industry. Over the following twelve months the urgency of European coal demand abated (though it by no means disappeared), thus lifting some of the pressure from the Ruhr administrators' shoulders. Management was at last able to begin implementing its broader and longer-term goals.

Before looking at the collieries' actions, however, it is worth saying a word or two about the distribution of power within the industry in 1948. Certainly the establishment of the DKBL meant the return to power of the *Bergassessoren* (mining engineers). Yet management's control was far from absolute. At the highest levels, the Allies continued for several years to exercise influence on the industry's policy. American plans for deconcentration rendered the future of many mining companies uncertain, and senior industrialists remained embroiled in discussions with the Allies about reorganizing the industry until as late as 1952–3.

Considerable leverage in the industry was enjoyed also by the German state, above all because it held the purse strings. Despite Erhard's liberalization of the economy, the coal price remained fixed and the mines found themselves heavily dependent on state help to provide vital investment in plant and miners' housing. The quid pro quo was a state say in industrial policy making.

Labour too was not without influence. True, as managers gained more confidence, they were keen to roll back labour's power. Yet the state, in the form of the labour administration and the North Rhine Westphalian regional ministries, proved to be very concerned to win the support of organized labour and was often able to force the industry to involve labour representatives. In addition, the importance of maintaining a closed front vis-à-vis the Allies meant that the DKBL could not afford to drive the miners' union, the Industriegewerkschaft Bergbau (IGB; Industrial Union of the Mining Industry), into open opposition. Indeed, to prevent the more radical American plans for deconcentration from being realized, the DKBL allowed the IGB to become closely involved in the formulation of alternative German proposals.

---

10. Paul Breder, *Geschichten vor Ort. Erinnerungen eines Bergmannes* (Essen, 1979). See especially the chapter on new miners; OBADA I6300/1080/45, Oberbergamt Dortmund (OBAD) to all Bergämter (BÄ), 17 Nov. 1945; I6300, GMSO, Circular No. 138, Nov. 1945; I6301/1339/45, Präsident of Landesarbeitsamt (LAA) Westfalen-Lippe) to Arbeitsämter (AÄ), 28 Oct. 1945; Public Records Office (PRO) FO942, 509, North German Coal Control (NGCC), 'Steinkohle production in the British occupied Zone of Germany. Review of production', May 1946.

Apprenticeship, Status, and Recruitment

With regard to young labour, the most important initiative in 1948 was the drive to expand apprentice recruitment. Over the following years, extensive and carefully structured recruitment campaigns and propitious labour-market conditions secured the mines a stream of apprentices which continued to grow after adult recruitment ran into difficulties. By 1954 there were some 35,000 apprentices in the Ruhr mines, a healthy figure by any standards. Considerable resources were committed to the construction of apprentice hostels. By 1954 there were no less than 118 mine-apprentice hostels in the region and a further 24 youth villages.[11]

But what was the appeal of the apprentice scheme? Young labour was cheap, of course, but the financial argument should not be given too much weight. It was cheaper to take on youngsters as juvenile trainees (*Bergjungleute*), with their lower wage and more rudimentary training. The fact that *apprentice* recruitment was given priority proved that wage costs were not the main argument in their favour. Moreover, apprentices in mining were extremely well paid in comparison with their counterparts in other industries, receiving two-and-a-half times as much as the average. If the financial argument is far from compelling, the mines' clear need to rejuvenate the workforce is equally inadequate as an explanation. After all, rejuvenation would have proceeded far faster if juvenile trainees or young adults, with their shorter induction period, had been preferred to the apprentices.

There is, moreover, little evidence to suggest that the apprentices' lengthy training made them more productive members of the workforce. They were less susceptible to accidents, certainly, and perhaps more flexible and useful at times of crisis, but it was noteworthy that neither the mines nor the DKBL produced any statistics comparing the efficiency of former apprentices and adult recruits. And, when one looks closely at training practice within the mines, it is clear that the employers were often hard put to it to find things for the apprentices to do; in productive or technical terms, the apprenticeship was undoubtedly far too long.[12] This was certainly the view of an NCB party which visited the Ruhr in the mid-1950s. For the British managers, the most striking thing they encountered during their stay was the elaborate apprentice training which had no parallel in British practice. They acknowledged the ideological benefits ("it seemed clear that the apprenticeship produced a good type of miner and citizen"), but could see no concrete evidence to suggest that it produced any better results than other types of training. In particular, the marked difference in treat-

---

11. Roseman, 'New Miners', 280–1.

12. Hans Dieter Baroth, *Aber es waren schöne Zeiten* (Cologne, 1978), 132–8; OBADA I6303/1004/46, BA Werden to OBAD, 10 June 1946.

ment accorded the apprentice, on the one hand, and the juvenile trainee, on the other, seemed to have no justification at all in terms of production.[13]

And yet, as they correctly observed, that difference could be enormous. In the pre-currency reform period, for example, when conditions in the adult camps were frequently appalling, the apprentice hostels were generally in good order. This was not simply a mark of the employers' humanity towards the young. There was an almost total lack of provision for those non-local youngsters who were not on the apprenticeship scheme. The point was that the employers did not want to dilute the special atmosphere of the apprentice hostel or undermine the attempts to create a new élite by allowing in other types of young labour.[14]

In short, the apprenticeship's real virtues must be sought elsewhere. They lay, first of all, in what one might call its "public relations" aspect and secondly, in the potential for transforming the workforce's character.

As before the war, the employers argued that the apprenticeship would persuade potential recruits (and their parents) of mining's status and worth and thus avoid future recruitment problems. After all, mining's ability to increase its wages remained fairly limited. Controlled prices did not give the industry much room for manoeuvre and, in any case, its low productivity would prevent it from keeping up with the wage competition from iron and steel. And so the strategy of increasing the *immaterial* gratification, above all the status, associated with mining work, was as attractive as ever. Discussions about the apprenticeship were often dominated by the public relations aspect; considerations of status, not productivity, prevailed.[15]

The possibility of tapping new reserves of high-quality youngsters seemed particularly good in 1947/8 because in the next few years there would be a very large number of school-leavers for whom training opportunities would be limited. Refugee parents, in particular, might be persuaded of the worth of mining training and wish to avail their children of the undoubtedly good earnings and possibilities for upward mobility which the apprenticeship

---

13. National Coal Board (NCB), *Training and education in the Ruhr coalmining industry* (printed NCB paper 1955), 39–41.

14. Hauptstaatsarchiv, Düsseldorf (HStaD) NW41, 746, Social Ministry NRW IIIB/6 to colliery directors, 17 June 1947; Archive of the Industrie-Gewerkschaft Bergbau und Energie (IGBEA) BR7, Außenstelle Bergbau (ABB) to Industrieverband Bergbau (IVB), 28 Apr. 1947; HStaD NW41, 761, Social Ministry IIIB/6, Memo, 7 Aug 1948; OBADA I6303/2672/47, minutes of meeting on 5 Sept. 1947.

15. See 'Zur Pflege bergmännischer berufsethischer Gesinnung', *Arbeitsblatt für die britische Zone,* 1 (1947), 259–62; 'Das Nachwuchsproblem im Bergbau', *Bundesarbeitsblatt,* 9 (1950) 331–3, here p. 332f.; 'Männer von Morgen', *Junior Magazin,* 12 (1952), 474–6; OBADA I6301/1339/45, LAA Westfalen-Lippe, circular to labour exchanges No. I65/45. 28 Oct. 1945; I6301/1004/46, BA Werden to OBAD, 10 July 1946; I6303/85/48, OBAD to AA Gelsenkirchen, 21 Jan. 1948.

represented. Thus the post-war situation presented the mines with a perhaps unique opportunity to achieve a large influx of new blood.[16]

An additional, though related, virtue of the apprenticeship was that state officials found it morally reassuring and politically important to be able to offer young refugees an officially recognized training programme and a proper qualification, rather than just shoving them down the mines. Particularly outside mining areas, many labour-exchange officials were reluctant to send youngsters to the pits. On the other hand, they were well aware of mining's importance and aware too that other training opportunities were limited. The promise of a formal and supervised apprenticeship made it palatable to propose mining as a career. Similarly, it made it politically and psychologically easier for Federal Ministries, particularly the Refugee Ministry, to provide funds for the mines. Well before the currency reform, there was a recognition in Ruhr circles that state and industry's interests might run in parallel here, and the DKBL was at pains to draw attention to the economic, social, and pedagogical virtues of mining apprenticeships and the comparatively good opportunities for youngsters from poor families to rise up within the industry. Indeed, for some colliery managements not quite convinced of the need for apprenticeships, it may well have been the promise of state support for hostel-building programmes that galvanized them to prefer apprentices to other types of young labour. Certainly they found themselves under strong pressure from labour administration officials to increase their training provision.[17]

At a fairly early stage, the idea of using the apprenticeship to tap new sources of recruitment gained added impetus from the view that the outsiders, or at least a proportion of them, were of a particularly high quality. Whereas within the Ruhr region school-leavers with good results tended to avoid the mines and go into more desirable trades, outside the Ruhr the mines faced little competition on the juvenile labour market. So it was not surprising that the collieries soon found they were able to obtain youngsters with very good school results. Moreover, the attraction of the outsiders went further. As a local union official angrily noted, many employers were arguing that it was better to recruit

16. OBADA I6301/927/46, LAA Westfalen-Lippe, circular, signed Dr. Herwegen, 25 Apr. 1946; I6301/969/47, ABB, circular to colliery managements and labour exchanges, 17 Mar. 1947; HStaD NW45, 210, *Informations-Rundbrief zur sozialen Lage der Jugend,* 4/12 (1952), 12.

17. OBADA I6301/969/47, ABB, circular to colliery managements and labour exchanges, 17 Mar. 1947; I6301/2448/49, Deutsche Kohlenbergbauleitung (DKBL) (ed.), *Die Berglehrlignsheime des Steinkohlenbergbaus der Nordzone . . . im Dienste der Bekämpfung von Berufsnot und Arbeitslosigkeit unter den Jungendlichen* (Hamborn, 29 Oct. 1949); I6303/273/48, OBAD to AA Gelsenkirchen, 31 Jan. 1948; HStaD NW73, 458, Arbeitsminister NRW, Hauptabt. LAA, Memo, 8 Feb. 1949; NW45, 210, 'Objektive und subjektive Berufsnot der Jugend', and 'Maßnahmen zur Behebung der Not der berufslosen und heimatlosen Jugend in NRW', both in *Informations-Rundbrief zur sozialen Lage der Jugend,* 4/4 (1952) 1ff.; NW41, 769, report on an interministerial meeting at the Federal Economics Ministry (BWiM), 6 June 1950.

youngsters "who come from the countryside [i.e., from outside the Ruhr], because in general they are substantially above average, they have a different upbringing, and in addition they are educationally at a higher level; thus, it is possible to do much more with them."[18] Often from non-working-class or small-town backgrounds, the outsiders were sometimes seen by the employers as bringing desirable values and attitudes to the mines. Above all, they would remove the low behaviour and negative attitudes which the culturally and racially inferior Poles had brought in at the end of the nineteenth century. Dr. Herwegen, from the Mining Section (Außenstelle Bergbau, or ABB) of the NRW Regional Labour Office (LAA) observed that "the hiring of people from outside, who for the most part were on a lower cultural level, has led to a mode of behaviour in the world of the miners, which seems intolerable to many who are willing to work." "Intellectually suitable" outsiders could play a key role in introducing new standards of behaviour. There would thus be a virtuous circle whereby the status of a proper qualification would attract outsiders and the outsiders' standards and behaviour would, in turn, enhance mining's standing in the community.[19]

Creating a Stable and Contented Workforce

These last remarks indicate that the apprenticeship's raison d'être was not solely to make mining more attractive to potential recruits. The further goal of altering the workforce's behaviour and changing its attitude to the mining profession remained just as attractive to the employers as before the war. Perhaps even more attractive, because management's feeling that the workforce needed to be licked into shape had been considerably strengthened by long years of dealing with unskilled newcomers, first in the shape of Soviet prisoners of war and secondly in the new miners of the post-war years, many of whom were unproductive and left the mines after the first few shifts.

The miner who had gone through the apprenticeship, so it was argued, would have a new self-esteem, be unlikely to leave the mine, and also be better disposed to company and employers. When, at a major conference of colliery

18. Archive of the Deutscher Gewerkschaftsbund (DGBA) Protokoll-Sammlung. 'Protokoll des 1. Verbandsjugendtags der IGB' (Bochum, 1950). See also Manfred Daberkow, 'Die Seßhaftmachung der vom westdeutschen Steinkohlenbergbau aus bergfremden Gebieten angeworbenen Berglehrlinge' (*Examensarbeit, Sozialschule* Gelsenkirchen, 1955), 15; OBADA I6301/2448/49, DKBL to OBAD, 5 Nov. 1949, annex: 'Stellungnahme zu dem von der Verwaltung für Wirtschaft erbetenen Bericht . . . '.

19. HStaD NW41, 746, minutes of a meeting of the 'Ausschuß zur Ausarbeitung eines Lehrganges für Heimleiter' on 16 Dec. 1948, 27 Dec. 1948. See also HStaD NW41, 768, Sozialwissenschaftliche Arbeitsgemeinschaft zur Erforschung von Jugendproblemen (ed.), 'Maßnahmen zur Behebung der Not der berufslosen und heimatlosen Jugend in NRW' (unpublished MS, no date (1951)); Daberkow, 'Seßhaftmachung', 50ff.

training directors in 1953, DKBL General Director Heinrich Kost[20] listed what he saw as the most important virtues of the traineeship, he put in first place not its contribution to productivity but its potential for creating a stable workforce.[21]

These aspirations were frequently linked to a myth of the miner as he had once been. Indeed, they are explicable only once the power of that myth has been understood. In a 1948 article for the mining industry's journal, *Glückauf*, Karl Bax evoked this image when he wrote:

> For the occupations in primary production it is not sufficient just to have knowledge and skills. Farmer, fisherman, and miner . . . need a special attitude towards life: A worldview that is determined by corporate occupational identification. All primary production struggles with nature. It discovers nature's secrets, and dares to do battle with its powers.[22]

The miner of yore was thus bound to his profession by deep inner ties to the earth and an almost mystical desire to unlock its secrets and bring its treasures to the surface. A perceptive correspondent from the *Neue Zeitung* noted in 1951 that both union and employers were trying to create out of the young miners members of

> a class of miners with a strong corporate consciousness (*Standesbewußtsein*), invoking the vision of the almost legendary old miner, who considered his work in the pit not only as a means to earn money, but also as the chance and adventure of constantly wrestling with the primal power of the mountain.[23]

The key word here was *Standesbewußtsein*. The miner of yore was seen as being secure in his social position. At peace with the world, he was characterized by self-esteem, loyalty, and respect for his employers. By contrast, the high wastage rates and recruitment problems of more recent times and the militancy of the mining community seemed to the employers to denote a loss of self-respect and security. The works newspaper of the Gelsenkirchener Bergwerks A.G.'s Hamborn Group, for instance, bemoaned the passing of workers of past generations who were "whole, harmonious, and fulfilled by their profession."[24]

---

20. Kost was also one of the individuals most closely associated with promoting apprenticeships since the early 1940s.

21. HStaD NW41, 761, Senft, report on the conference of training directors at the DKV Haus Essen, 15 Jan. 1953.

22. Karl Bax, 'Die Nachwuchssorgen des Steinkohlenbergbaus. Gründe des nachwuchsmangels und Versuche zu ihrer Behebung', *Glückauf*, 85, 27/28 (1949), 477–85, here p. 478.

23. 'Der "Lager Mensch"—Symptom einer Entwicklung'. *Neue Zeitung*, 7 Aug. 1951.

24. *Der Förderturm*, June 1948, 1–2; 'Zur Berufsethik des Bergmanns', *Arbeitsblatt für die britische Zone*, 1 (1947), 170–2, here p. 171.

Linked to the image of the miner of the past was the view that a general social process of modernization was at work in removing the miner's sense of self-worth and the worth of his profession. Job changing was seen as a sign of a lack of social roots and the consequent loss of a rounded personality. In his guidelines for constructing and running hostels for apprentices, Klaus von Bismarck attributed wastage primarily not to material causes but to "loss of home and property, dissolution of societal order and obligations, the floundering of corporate groups, the general lack of security and sense of belonging in a world that has become materialistic and impersonal."[25] In a speech to mining employers, the influential Pastor Dannenmann argued that high levels of wastage in mining were ultimately a spiritual problem: "It is, in the end, the quest for the meaning of life."[26] The hope, therefore, was that the apprenticeship flanked by additional measures in the field of education and housing, could provide a stable social framework in which the young miner could find pride and contentment.

Clearly, this type of thinking fitted rather well to a situation where mining was condemned by limited resources to tackle its wastage problem with immaterial means. But it was not simply a reflex of mining engineers to their industry's own peculiar problems. It was part of a more general tendency on the part of the post-war bourgeoisie to see the dangers threatening German society and the problems of the past as being the result of materialism and the mass age. The fact that the two men quoted above were no industrialists but rather churchmen involved in social work with the miners tends to confirm this point.

The Apprenticeship's Political and Moral Function

Particularly in the post-war period, the proper integration of young miners came to be seen not just as a means to achieve workforce stability, but also as a sort of political and spiritual immunization against the dangers of the modern age. Very often, when they wished to convey this idea, contemporaries juxtaposed two concepts, namely *Persönlichkeit* and *Vermassung*. Indeed, this antithesis, *Persönlichkeit* (individual personality) or *echte Persönlichkeit* (genuine individuality)[27] or *Personalkern des Individuums* (core of the individual),[28] on the one hand, and *Vermassung* (creation of a mass)[29] or *Kollektivierung*

---

25. HStaD NW41, 747, *Sozialamt der evangelischen Kirche,* 'Vorschläge zum Bau und zur Führung von Knappenheimen', 15 Oct. 1951.

26. Archive of the Sozialforschungsstelle, Dortmund (SoFoStA), file 'Dr. Jantke Sozialausschüsse der ev. Kirche, 4.11.1951. 12', Pastor P. Arnold Dannenmann, *Das Jugendproblem heute,* reprint of lecture given on 22 Jan. 1952 in Essen, no date [1952].

27. 'Statt Kasernengeist die echte Persönlichkeit', *Rheinischer Merkur,* Koblenz, 5 Feb. 1949.

28. HStaD NW17, 141, lecture from Sieburg, 'Ziele staatsbürgerlicher Willensbildung in der kulturellen Bergmannsbetreuung', in report on the RAG conference at Kronenburg, 21–26 Sept. 1953.

29. Dannenmann, *Das Jugendproblem heute.*

(collectivization),[30] on the other hand, was so widespread that it became a sort of shorthand, which could be communicated and understood without the need for thought or explanation. Here, for example, is Jürgen Heuer, writing about the work in apprentice villages:

> It is not only because of the necessity to curtail the sense of collectivism, already during adolescence, that the factor of developing individuality is most important; in addition, it is also essential to inculcate in the future miner from the very beginning a solid sense of occupation in accord with the tradition of the mines.[31]

On the one hand, Heuer is talking about recreating a mining tradition and establishing a strong commitment to mining. On the other, there is the more fundamental danger of collectivism. The notion of *Persönlichkeitsbildung* (development of individuality) meant trying to prevent the individual personality from being swallowed up by mass society. For, whereas in an organic society the individual has firm roots, a clear social picture, and strong values, in mass society these are lost and the individual is open to the dangers of extremism and radicalization. That was why policy makers took as their goal "to cut the people of today free from mass society and to make possible the transition to organic forms of matrimony, the family, and settlement on their own property."[32]

In part, this simply revived a long-standing conservative criticism of mass society, mass politics, and democracy. Here is Adolf Hitler, for example:

> I am no friend of mass society. I juxtapose individuality to mass society. Only men, not the masses, make history. The masses need to be led . . . The *Volk* has to be integrated into an authoritarian order.[33]

The difference was that, for the post-war bourgeoisie, Nazism was seen as the *product* of mass man. It is clear, though it was seldom said at the time, that the explanatory and emotional power of the juxtaposition between mass and personality derived in part from the way many middle-class Germans were at-

---

30. Report on speech from Heinrich Kost, in HStaD NW41, 761, Senft, Tagungsbericht von der Ausbildungstagung im DKV-Haus, Essen, 15 Jan. 1953.

31. Jürgen Heuer, 'Pestalozzidorf—Sozialleistung des Bergbaus, Aufbau und Probleme', in H. J. Seraphim (ed.), *Siedlungen und Wohnungen von heute* (Münster, 1952), 54–72, here p. 62.

32. HStaD NW41, 747, *Sozialamt der evangelischen Kirche*, 'Vorschläge zum Bau und zur Führung von Knappenheimen', 15 Oct. 1951.

33. See E. Calic, *Ohne Maske, Hitler-Breitling Geheimgespräche 1931* (Frankfurt, 1968), 47–8, cited in Reinhard Kühnl, *Faschismustheorien. Texte zur Faschismusdiskussion* 2 (Rheinbek bei Hamburg, 1979), 67.

tempting to deal with the experience of fascism and war. It is evident that their attitude towards the fascist era was to reject its "excesses," which they interpreted as the excesses of a "mass age" in which conventional values had disappeared. No doubt there was something to this, but it also sanitized National Socialism and allowed its crimes to be referred to almost anonymously under the heading of "problems of the modern age."

It was in keeping with this approach that the Nazi era was generally referred to only under the euphemism *jüngste Vergangenheit* (most recent past). Wartime destruction and the expulsions *were* referred to by name but they too were placed in this broader context of modern age and mass society. Many bourgeois commentators saw the disruption caused by war and its aftermath as quintessentially modern experiences, intensifying the more general negative effects of the modern age, above all eroding roots and creating mass man.

For example, in Klaus von Bismarck's comments about "creation of the mass" and the origins of labour wastage, noted above, the writer moves effortlessly from specific features of the war and post-war period ("loss of home and property") to the more general lack of security and protection in the modern world ("general absence of security in a world that has become impersonal and materialistic").[34] Many other contemporaries employed *Vermassung* in this way, and part of the term's appeal seems to have been precisely its ability to subsume Germany's recent experience under broader categories of modern social change.

Concealed behind this type of analysis was clearly a great deal of anxiety about the political dangers of the present and an ambivalent attitude towards democracy and the mass politics it represented. This found expression in a concern about the ostensible propensity to extremism on the part of the younger generation—the generation which had been most strongly exposed to National Socialist ideas and had missed out on proper education in wartime and the immediate post-war years. In a draft paper for a conference of hostel wardens, a Dr. Herwegen jotted down as key words on the situation of youngsters in post-war society "neglect, impoverishment, endangerment, demoralization, criminality."[35] Refugees and other groups who had been swept away from their homeland or their former life by war and the consequences of war were also believed to be vulnerable to the call of the mass. One of the field workers involved in cultural welfare policy observed that the refugees had a high educational level but had lost a sense for genuine morality and ethics as a result of brutal wartime and post-war experiences.[36]

---

34. Ibid.

35. HStaD NW41, 746, Dr Herwegen, 'Entwurf für die Tagesordnung einer Heimleiter-Tagung', no date [1948/9].

36. Bergbau-Archiv, Bochum (BBA) 8, 191, copy of report from Fischer, 'Alkohol in Bergarbeiterwohnheimen', 27 Apr. 1950.

There was felt to be a danger that radical organizations would exploit and intensify the negative consequences of this *Vermassung*. The "personalities" of the youngsters needed rescuing not just from their past experiences but from the machinations of extremist organizations, above all from the KPD and the influences emanating from the GDR. In 1951, the socialist Curt Bondy presented his thoughts on welfare policy after visiting miners' hostels and, in a section of the paper underlined by Bondy, warned of the danger that the youngsters could become the followers of extreme left- or right-wing parties if not handled in the right way.[37]

The solution, so it was hoped, lay in *Verwurzelung* (rootedness) through the apprenticeship. The apprenticeship would not only provide the means to create a better workforce but also offer rootless and endangered youngsters a firm place in society. When Heinrich Kost, for instance, emphasized the importance of the apprenticeship for creating a stable workforce, he went on to say that it had the important additional function of protecting youngsters from the dangers of political extremism.[38]

At an even deeper level, the notion that the young and the dispossessed needed guidance to return to the values and behaviour of an ordered society was a way of suppressing the anxiety that it was precisely the older generation and the established classes who had been compromised by fascism, whose values had been called into question, and who could no longer provide convincing leadership for the young. An inner uncertainty was being turned outwards into a mission to rescue the "uprooted" and transmit firm values. The employers, the churchmen, and others were struggling to make something *within themselves* strong. As the Bochum director of apprentice education, Dr. Herwick, said in a talk about the moral and educational goals beyond the schools' narrower technical curriculum:

Stein's word served as our guidepost: "What we have lost in external glory, we have to win back through our inner values." Our faith is sustained by the eternal values of the German soul which may have been covered by the rubble, but, as Goethe knew, are of such abundance that all the lands and oceans are not large enough to contain them.[39]

---

37. HStaD NW41, 747, Curt Bondy, 'Gedanken zur außerbetrieblichen Beeinflussung von Bergbaulehrlingen, Knappen und jungen Neubergleuten', Hamburg, No. 1951; BBA 32, 267, Höcker to Premer, 3 June 1950.

38. HStaD NW41, 761, Senft, report on the conference of training directors at the DKV Haus Essen, 15 Jan. 1953: NW41, 746, Dr Herwegen, 'Entwurf für die Tagesordnung einer Heimleiter-Tagung', no date [1948/9].

39. Archive of the Westfälische Berggewerkschaftskasse (WBKA), photocopied extract from *Mitteilungen der WBK1950*, Nr 3, Vortrag des Bezirksschuldirektors Herwick, 'Unsere Bergberufsschule als Erziehungsschule'.

One piece of evidence that tends to confirm the view that the bourgeoisie was talking as much about its own certainty as about any real threat is that the extent of radicalism within the camps and hostels was continually exaggerated, particularly in the early years. Churchmen, for instance, were continually warning about the Marxist spirit pervading the camps. Yet in reality, left-wing radicalism had at no point been a danger in the hostels, and from the very beginning the communists found it hard to mobilize a following amongst the newcomers.[40]

The significance attached in the mines' rhetoric and policy to these broader political, cultural, and psychological issues undoubtedly owed a lot to the influence of the state. It was vocational training officers in the labour administration, officials in the refugee ministries, and parliamentarians who most frequently and forcefully expressed the deeper spiritual and political concerns of Germany's post-war bourgeoisie. Churchmen, often brought in by the state to help supervise voluntary-aided institutions and projects, also played a major role in getting the mines to take such questions more seriously.[41] Since the mines could not do without state funding or administrative support, they made a point of stressing that they were not just trying to get workers for a job but were embarked on a high moral mission. That sort of thing went down well with the responsible officials. After a visit to the Ruhr in October 1952 by a parliamentary committee for youth welfare, the chairman reported to the chancellor that they were very impressed by what they saw and, above all, "the unequivocal acknowledgment of Director General Kost that when the mining companies took on the obligation of occupational training they were not willing to renounce the educational and ethical values of Christianity."[42] Apparently the chancellor himself was very pleased and promised to praise Kost at the appropriate opportunity.[43] Of more significance than such praise, however, was that the mines were frequently reminded that funding was conditional on the right pedagogical measures being adopted.

Apprentice Hostels

More than any other group, youngsters who came from outside the Ruhr and were separated from their parents presented the employers with new responsibilities and new opportunities. Many of them refugees, they were a manifestation of one of the most pervasive and revolutionary features of the

---

40. Roseman, 'New Miners', 447.

41. HStaD NW45, 210, 'Objektive und subjektive Berufsnot der Jugend', and 'Maßnahmen zur Behebung der Not der berufslosen und heimatlosen Jugend in NRW', both in *Informations-Rundbrief zur sozialen Lage der Jugend,* 4/4 (1952), 1 ff.; NW41, 769, report on an interministerial meeting at the BWiM, 6 June 1950.

42. Bundesarchiv, Koblenz (BAK) B102, 3306, Hensel to Ullrich, 23 Oct. 1952.

43. Ibid.

post-war experience: the massive population upheaval which had for a brief period seen almost 40 percent of the German population on the move. As youngsters under the age of consent, they brought with them certain legal obligations of guardianship and protection for the employees. In addition to such statutory matters, a number of different state administrations let it be known that they expected the employers to look after their charges.

Because they lived in a mass and because most of them were young, unattached former refugees, many having lost their parents as well as their homeland, the hostel occupants were seen as being particularly endangered by *Vermassung* and susceptible to radicalism. In some guidelines produced by the Catholic church, seminary students were advised to spend several months working and living in the hostels, "to get to know the modern mass man."[44] At the same time, the apprentices—and to a certain extent their young adult counterparts—represented an impressionable and captive audience who could be reached and fashioned not only at the workplace and within the formal confines of the training programme but in their leisure hours as well.

It was therefore not surprising that the employers took considerable care over designing the apprentice hostels. In the pre-currency reform period, when conditions in the adult camps were frequently appalling and colliery managers were doing little more than passively and resignedly watching the great mass of often unwilling labour flow through the mines, the apprentice hostels were generally in good order. After the currency reform, the standard of amenities and facilities improved rapidly. In many there were no more than three beds to a room and the hostels were equipped with table-tennis rooms, small gymnasia, dark rooms, their own libraries, and so on. Given the high standard of the hostels and the fact that apprentices earned less than their adult colleagues, it is not surprising to find that they were heavily subsidized, even more than their increasingly subsidized adult counterparts.[45]

As well as making the hostels attractive places to live, employers also tried to design an environment which would reinforce the goals of the apprentice programme. Here they ran into a dilemma which throughout the 1950s was to bedevil attempts to integrate the apprentices. On the one hand, the employers wanted the newcomers to strike roots in the Ruhr and become permanent members of the workforce. On the other hand, they did not want them to assume the worst habits of the existing workforce. In addition, the controlled environment in the hostels represented a marvelous opportunity to transmit the

---

44. 'Vorschläge zum Bau und zur Führung von Berglehrlings- und Knappenheimen', *Mitteilungen der Kommission für soziale Aufgaben (KFSA)*, 1/2 (1952), 3; Bistumsarchiv, Münster (BM) A201, 47, *Merkblatt für Theologen im Bergbau*, no date.

45. 'Männer von Morgen', *Junior Magazin*, 12 (1952), 474–7; Hibernia Konzern (ed.), *Sozialbericht 1956*, 15 and 20.

"right" values to a captive and impressionable "audience." The dilemma, therefore, was: integrate or segregate?[46]

On the whole, segregation seems to have been emphasized at the expense of integration. This was in part because both state and church reinforced the mines' wishes with their own fears and ambitions. There was widespread anxiety about the negative impact of proximity to the adult community. Drunken new miners and promiscuous miners' daughters seem to have been among the dangers facing apprentices. Thus most hostels were built a good distance away from the mining estates, and at least one reason for the comprehensive provision of facilities in the hostels was the desire to keep the apprentices out of the wrong company.[47]

Perhaps the most innovative experiment, and a sign of just how far the employers were prepared to go to create their new workforce, was the establishment of special youth villages to house the apprentices. In 1948 the Pestalozzi Association—an organization dedicated to disseminating the educational ideas of the eighteenth-century Swiss educational theorist Pestalozzi—persuaded the Vereinigte Stahlwerke's (United Steelworkers') housing associations to try an experiment with two Pestalozzi villages, one in Lohberg, the site of a mine belonging to the GBAG's Hamborn group, and the other in Bochum. The idea then caught on elsewhere and by 1956 there were thirty-three villages with, in all, 5,500 places, equivalent to almost a third of all the accommodation provided for apprentices and *Knappen* (young miners).[48] Generally, the villages consisted of a series of large houses with big gardens in the manner of the *Kleinsiedlung* (small settlement), each house occupied by a "parent" family and six youngsters. Each village had its own leader and, with time, its own community centre. The village parents obtained their accommodation free plus a monthly payment from which to feed the

---

46. HStaD NW41, 747, 'Zusammenstellungen des Sozialamtes der evangelischen Kirche in Westfalen über die in einigen Berglehrlingsheimen angefallenen Erfahrungen', no date [1951].

47. For a powerful example of this fear of predatory women leading the innocents astray, see Erwin Jochum, 'Das sexuelle Problem unserer heutigen Jugend und der Beitrag der Bergberufsschule zu seiner Lösung', *Mitteilungen für die Bergberufsschulen*, 6 (1954) esp. p. 10; the KfSA's guidelines conceded it might be possible to build a hostel near 'einer modernen Bergmannssiedlung'. Presumably what they had in mind was a new estate of owner-occupied properties where they felt that the behaviour of the residents might be expected not to set a bad example. *Mitteilungen der KfSA*, 1/2 (1952), 5.

48. HStaD NW41, 764, Forstmann, 'Ausführung in der Aufsichtsratssitzung vom 21.11.1949': Arbeitsgemeinschaft Heimstatthilfe im Lande NRW (ed.), *Verzeichnis der Jugendheimstätten in NRW* (NRW, 1956); private papers from the Jugendheimstättenwerk Pestalozzi-Vereinigung e.V. in possession of Herr Klinkert, Gelsenkirchen (Klinkert Papers), file 'Sammlung Vorstandssitzungen', minutes of executive meeting of Jugendheimstättenwerk e.V. Pestalozzidorf Vereinigung (JHStW PV), 17 Oct. 1956.

youngsters. The village leader supervised the parents and watched over the youngsters.[49]

The attractions of the village concept were manifold. Although the cost factor was probably not decisive, it was certainly significant that the villages cost the employers less than conventional hostels.[50] In addition, the houses could in the future be used as normal housing. Yet the real logic to the village concept was that it was seen as a way of overcoming the conflict between integration and segregation. The idea was to introduce the youngsters to the best of the mining community in a controlled and monitored environment. The parents would be carefully chosen so as to avoid contaminating the youngsters with the *Untugenden* (bad habits) of the mining community and to transmit the appropriate values and outlook. The villages themselves were carefully situated well away from the miners' estates, "a little jewel-case in the midst of a green landscape," as Walter Forstmann put it. Thus the dangers of the wrong sort of company would be avoided, but at the same time so would the risks associated with communal living in a large hostel.[51]

The resonance which the idea of the miners' village enjoyed and the way in which it was implemented reveal many of the myths about the integration process which abounded in the mining industry. The houses were built on the *Kleinsiedler* (small holder) pattern, in part so that the youngsters could be rooted by means of garden work. Here the notion of deep roots in local soil emerged very strongly:

We want the young miners to become familiar right away with the work in the sty and the garden, and in particular we want to awaken their inclination and love for small animal husbandry and gardening, so that they will one day become rooted close to the mines as smallholders or as tenants [of a farmer]."[52]

---

49. Otto-Wilhelm Roelen, 'Die Bedeutung der Pestalozzidörfer für die Gewinnung eines bergbaulichen Nachwuchses' (Diss., Cologne University, 1956), passim.

50. A point stressed by the Gruppe Hamborn's training director when asked for his view on the Pestalozzi villages. See Klinkert Papers, minutes of the first meeting on the JSHtW PV, 31 July 1948; HStaD NW41, 764, minutes of meeting on 21 Nov. 1950 in Essen with DKBL, 23 Nov. 1950; Roelen, 'Die Bedeutung der Pestalozzidörfer', 163–4, which shows the enormous difference between the repayments burden on a typical apprentice hostel and that in the case of the Pestalozzi village—the former being almost four times as high per occupant.

51. Walter Forstmann, 'Die Erziehung zum Eigentumsgedanken', *Die Volksheimstätte, Monatszeitschrift des Deutschen Volksheimstättenwerks*, 7/5 (1955), 1–5; JHStW PV (ed.), *Pestalozzieltern im Pestalozzidorf* (Essen. 1952), cited in Roelen, 'Die Bedeutung der Pestalozzidörfer', 25ff.; see also Roelen, op. cit., 72.

52. HStaD NW41, 764, Forstmann, 'Ausführung in der Aufsichtsratsitzung vom 24.11.1949'; see also 'Die Pestalozzidörfer des Bergbaus', *Bergfreiheit*, 8 (1951), 17–19.

At work here was that romantic image of the authentic miner which we have already encountered in discussions about the apprenticeship. Garden work was seen as confirming and sustaining the close relationship to nature and the earth which was the mark of the true miner. The idea that there was a link between farmer and miner, a symmetry between two different types of battle with nature, continually resurfaced. To this, the Pestalozzi villages had added a related "romantic" vision, namely that of the newcomer "growing roots" through work in the garden. The semi-rural atmosphere and large garden were seen as vital ingredients in settling the newcomers and tying them to mining and the Ruhr. This image, too, frequently surfaced over the following years. A paper on how to treat the youngsters in (conventional) hostels argued that "We should never lose sight of the goal of educating young men to become self-sufficient miners, able to found a family, and to establish a life with a garden and a sense of rootedness in their surroundings."[53]

Though there was talk of *Ausgleich*, of pleasant compensation for the work underground, it was evident that the garden work in the Pestalozzi estates was far more than that because it was actually a duty for the youngsters. When at a meeting of the village leaders it was suggested that the youngsters were not necessarily all that interested in gardening, the chairman of the Pestalozzi Association came down very strongly on the issue, reminding all present that the villages had been created specifically "to bring the youth close to land and the soil."[54] The designation *Dorfälteste* (village elder) rather than *Dorfleiter* (village leader) for the village leaders indicated the desire to resurrect the notion of an intact, quasi-rural community. Another virtue of the housing design in the eyes of the village founders was that the apprentices would feel encouraged to become owner-occupiers. "The goal is finally achieved," wrote Walter Forstmann, "when we have paved the [miner's] way to the establishment of a home of his own."[55]

Ultimately, of course, the Pestalozzi villages were another attempt to undo *Vermassung* and strengthen *Persönlichkeit*. Jürgen Heuer's words, quoted above, were written in the context of a study on the Pestalozzi villages. Above all, argued Heuer, it was

necessary . . . to awaken a feeling for the mentality of the miner. Conveying a genuine sense of tradition that is related to well-founded professional

---

53. *Mitteilungen der KfSA*, 1/2 (1952), 3. See also Roseman, 'New Miners', 356ff., and Walter Forstmann's comments in 1949 about the function of the Pestalozzi villages. HStaD NW41, 764, Forstmann, 'Ausführungen in der Aufsichtsratssitzung am 21.11.1949 über den Zweck und den Bau der Pestalozzisiedlungen in Dinslaken-Lohberg', 21 Nov. 1949.

54. Klinkert Papers, file 'Niederschriften der Arbeitstagungen und Vortragsveranstaltungen', minutes of meeting of village leaders, 10 Dec. 1958.

55. Walter Forstmann, 'Die Erziehung zum Eigentumsgedanken', 5.

pride and a corporate consciousness that keeps the miner in high standing is one of the most important tasks that is primarily the duty of the foster parents of the Pestalozzi village.[56]

Supervision and Control in the Hostels

A natural consequence of the anxieties and hopes aroused by the young hostel occupants was that the employers were at pains to keep works councillors and unions well away from them. Here, however, the employers found themselves from the start in a difficult situation. Under Control Council legislation, there was no doubt that works councillors had a right to co-determine social and cultural policy. Particularly during the immediate post-war years, employers did not feel strong enough to prevent works councillors from nominating hostel wardens. In addition, the DKBL was unwilling to antagonize the unions openly on social questions. Indeed in 1948, under British pressure, it formed the Kommission für soziale Aufgaben (Commission for Social Duties), an organization jointly run with the miners' union to provide better services for the newcomers.[57]

However, the churches stepped forward to offer a solution. Ever since 1947 or so, they had seen in the apprentice hostels a chance to influence the future character of the mining community. As the Caritas organization argued in a pamphlet devoted to its new apprentice hostel in Bottrop, "if we point the apprentice of today in a Christian direction, we will also have a Christian workforce tomorrow." In 1950 the Arbeitsgemeinschaft katholische Heimstattbewegung für heimatlose Jugend im Lande NRW (Task Force of the Catholic Movement for Settling Homeless Youths in North Rhine Westphalia) was formed to co-ordinate these initiatives for the Catholic side. Similar initiatives emanated from the Christlicher Verein Junger Männer (Young Men's Christian Association) and the Innere Mission (Inner Mission) on the Protestant side.[58]

Initially the employers themselves were very cautious in their response to the church's initiative. Nevertheless, it did not take them long to see that handing hostels over to the churches was the best way to keep union and works

---

56. Heuer, 'Pestalozzidorf', 62.

57. Control Council Law No. 22, Works Council Law, reprinted in *Military Government Gazette for the British Zone*, 9 (1946), 197–9, esp. Article V (f): BM A101, 251, DKBL, to Bischöfl. Gen. vikariat, 29.4. 1948 Westfälisches Wirtschaftsarchiv, Dortmund (WWA) S22 (OMGUS) BICO BISEC 11/104-2/2, UK/US CCG, report to BICO for Dec. 1948.

58. *BM* A101, 251, T. Fennemann, Director St. Johannesstift der Salesianer to Kardinal Frings et al., 12 July 1947; BM A101, 253, 'Caritas Berglehrlingsheim Bottrop. Ein Beitrag zum christlichen Nachwuchs des Bergmanns' [1949/1950]; BM A101, 253, paper, 'Die religiöse Situation und die seelsorgliche Betreuung in den Wohnheimen und Lagern des Industriegebiets', no date.

council at bay. From 1950 onwards, the DKBL felt confident enough actively to promote the establishment of church-run hostels. "I do not need to over-emphasize," wrote the DKBL's Lorenz Höcker to the director of the mine Emscher-Lippe, "that in our opinion the spirit of Christianity must shine forth everywhere, particularly in the hostels. After all, this spirit is the only force that can oppose the spectre that rules in the East and elsewhere."[59] It is worth noting that the churches also saved the employers money, in some cases because they were able to tap external sources of funding but more generally because church hostels were not covered by the agreement and their employees cost considerably less.[60]

These moves were, understandably, a source of considerable unease to the miners' union which felt the question of hostel regime to be one of fundamental importance. A quiet war developed, with church representatives wooing the employers and union representatives trying to prevent the mines from putting their hostels in the churches' hands. The union, however, suffered a decisive disadvantage in that the state gave the churches a great deal of covert support. An official in the LAA (Landesarbeitsamt, or State Labor Office) Mining Office informed the diocese of Münster that funds could be diverted to enable Catholic hostels to be built; another official in the same administration offered to segregate incoming apprentices on confessional lines to facilitate the founding of Catholic hostels. In October 1951, Hensel, one of the mining specialists in the Economics Ministry, sent a letter to the NRW Social Ministry's youth officer Willi Weber. In response to an IGB circular condemning Christian initiatives, Hensel asked Weber if he could not get the religious organizations to show the absurdity of the union' accusations. In the same breath, however, he continued: "The Christian element in mining must not be smothered on any account, least of all among the mining youth. This would remove the last brake on the radicalization, which is already far too advanced."[61]

In view of the support for the churches, it is not surprising to discover that they made rapid headway. By the end of 1952, according to IGB calculations, some 108 apprentice and *Knappen* hostels had been completed. Of these, thirty-three, or just under a third, had been removed from colliery control.

59. BBA 35, 267, Höcker to Premer, 3 June 1950.

60. BM A101, 251, DKBL to Bischöfl. Gen. vikariat, 29 Apr. 1948; HStaD NW41, 747, Soz. Min. NRW IIIB/6, memo, 25 Jul. 1948; BM A101, 251, Julius Angerhauen to Bischof Michael Keller, 9 Apr. 1948.

61. IGBEA File 'Jugend', August Enderle to August Schmidt, 12 May 1949; IGB Abteilung Schulung u. Bildung to Enderle, 1 June 1948; IGB Hauptverwaltung, circular Nr. 88/51 to works councils and social representatives, 23 July 1951; IGBEA V3, IGB, two internal memos from Abteilung VII to Geschäftsführenden Vorstand, both dated 17 June 1952; IGBEA V6, IGB, memo, 10 May 1954; BM A101, 252, B. v. Heyden to Bischof Keller, 15 Mar. 1951; B. v. Heyden to Gen. vikar, 3 Aug. 1951; Winkelheide to Gen. vikar, 27 Nov. 1951; BAK B102, 33189, Hensel to Weber, 13 Oct. 1951.

Thirteen were in the hands of Caritas, fifteen run by the Innere Mission, and five by other church organizations. Of the thirty hostels then under construction virtually half were church controlled, so that by 1954 the church would be in charge of between one-third and two-fifths of young miners' hostels.[62]

However, the Co-determination Law began to affect the situation, as the labour directors were appointed and extended their influence. Because of the lower costs, the labour directors were very often well disposed to the church hostels, but they were able to insist on agreements that ensured union and works council free access. It was in recognition of this situation that the IGB abandoned its hard line against the church hostels. Thus although, in hostels covered by existing agreements, the union sometimes continued to have problems of access, new agreements with the church caused less concern. From the employers' viewpoint, they therefore offered less protection from the union than before and were probably inspired more by the desire to save money than by anything else.[63]

Apart from the church, the state also exerted a considerable amount of influence. Ever since 1947, the regional social ministry had been one of the prime movers in calls for more supervision, education, and entertainment for the hostel occupants. The employers' lack of cash and the DKBL's desire in the early years to find a neutral solution to the question of who should actually lecture and entertain the miners resulted in the state actually getting involved in providing the entertainment. In 1949, negotiations between the DKBL and the Ministry for Education and Culture led to the creation of a Fachstelle für Bergarbeiterbetreuung (Office of Miners' Welfare), run by the regional association for adult education (Landesverband der Volkshochschulen). The Fachstelle was wound up in 1949 and replaced by the Revierarbeitsgemeinschaft für die kulturelle Bergarbeiterbetreuung (RAG, or Association for the Cultural Care of Miners in the Mining District) an organization that persists to this day. Five field workers were appointed to stimulate and co-ordinate cultural activities in the miners' hostels. The sums invested were not large, but the RAG, in conjunction with local wardens and *Volkshochschulen* [public schools that were designed largely for adult education], did organize a considerable number of events.[64]

---

62. Calculated from figures in DGBA Protokoll-Sammlung, IGB, Hauptverwaltung, Abteilung Jugend (ed.), *Geschäftsbericht 1950–1952* (Bochum, 1953), 87; and figures in IGBEA V6, IGB, memo concerning transfer of hostel to outside organizations (*Trägerverbände*), 10 Mar. 1954.

63. IGBEA Handakten Rudi Quast, file 'Arbeitskreis-Arbeitsdirektoren 1952–1956', meeting of Arbeitskreis der Arbeitsdirektoren, Bezirk Recklinghausen, 30 Sept. 1953; IGBEA V6, IGB, memo concerning transfer of hostels to outside organizations (*Trägerverbände*), 10 May 1954; IGB Bezirksleitung Essen (ed.), *Geschäftsbericht 1954/1955*, 117; IGB (ed.), *Jahrbuch 1956*, 252.

64. WWA S22 (OMGUS) CO HIST BR 3/404-1/7, minutes of 18th meeting of UK/USCCG, 6 Aug. 1948; HStaD NW17, 136, Landesverband der Volkshochschulen NRW, circular to members of the Landesverband, 10 Jan. 1950.

Supervision and Propaganda in the Hostels

Turning to the actual propaganda and rhetoric directed towards young labour by employers, church, and state, we find many of the themes and aspirations noted above. Understandably, a lot of energy was expended trying to increase the youngsters' pride and interest in mining. A theatrical attempt to emphasize continuity with the past and to celebrate the steadfastness of the miner was a ceremony at the Diergardt-Mevissen mine. The 250,000th newcomer to be found a job in the Ruhr was symbolically presented with the miners' tools by the oldest miner in the pit. The celebration was attended by the 50,000th newcomer, the 100,000th, and so on, as well as a mining family of grandfather, father, son, and son-in-law, all of whom worked at the Hugo mine. Of course, not all the attempts to encourage integration were in this romantic-historical mould. A glance through the standard lecture topics offered to the miners in 1953 shows a large number of more straightforward subjects, though the programme was not without lectures on the history of mining and the mentality of the miner.[65]

Both state and employers shared a burning desire to communicate to the young. Over the following years, virtually no entertainment or service was offered the miners without in some way carrying a moral or political message. Even when in reality all that was being provided was a little entertainment, the employers and other German groups involved were simply unable to concede that that was all they were doing. There was a compulsion to find a higher purpose, a deeper mission to everything that was done.

This was one of the most striking differences between the British and American attempts to help in the new miner programme and the Germans' approach. If there was any "higher" aim in British suggestions than providing entertainment, it was to give the youngsters a taste of democracy by letting them organize their own clubs.[66] The German proposals at the time have a completely different tone. They are full of anxieties and hopes, of the dangers of doing nothing, and of the high moral ideals towards which the youngsters must be led by wise elders. When, for instance, the KfSA suggested that films might be provided at some of the hostels because the inhabitants had no going-out

---

65. HStaD NW41, 746, copy, Caritasverband Bottrop, Berglehrlingsheim Erziehungsgrundsätze, Bottrop, 21 Oct. 1948; Curt Bondy, 'Gedanken zur außerbetrieblichen Beeinflussung'; 'Sechs Jahre Außenstelle Bergbau', 79; *Der Förderturm*, June, July, Aug., and Oct. 1948 and Oct. 1949; Archive of the Gesamtverband des deutschen Steinkohlenbergbaus, Essen (Ges. Verb.), file 'Unternehmensverband 662–668', *Tätigkeitsbericht der Revierarbeitsgemeinschaft für die kulturelle Bergmannsbetreuung* (RAG) (1953).

66. OBADA 16303/1757/47, copy, Elphick, 'Die Bedingungen junger Arbeiter in den Zechen. 2RCD u. 3RCD Bereich', 15 Jan. 1947; Public Opinion Research Organisation, Political Division (PORO) (ed.), *A social survey. The mining trainee 1947* (Bielefeld,1948), 30.

clothes or lacked local cinemas, it was immediately proposed that only culturally valuable films should be shown so as to raise the intellectual and spiritual
level of the miners. And a further justification for showing the films was
found—it would help keep the newcomers away from *abwegigen Vergnü-
gungsrummeln* ("misguided pleasure-sprees") in the local towns.[67] This compulsion to have a mission, and to guide rather than to let speak, seems to have
been a fundamental characteristic of bourgeois culture in post-war Germany. It
reveals very clearly the way the bourgeoisie's suppressed uncertainty was psychologically transmuted into a mission to "rescue" the young.

There was a general consensus that the new miners should be educated to
be good democrats.[68] State representatives, like the employers, stressed the
duties and responsibilities of the citizen, rather than his freedom or participation. As Herwick, the director of apprentice education, declared: "We hope . . .
to shape people who later will be ashamed to utter in the streetcars things like
'Democratic freedom means that everyone can do what they want.'"[69] The
older generation's anxiety, natural authoritarianism, and burning sense of mission all tended to preclude much practical democracy. Again this was a striking
contrast between the British initiatives and those of their German counterparts.
Consider the closing words of the British survey of trainees in 1947:

> Finally, there is presented here a golden opportunity to introduce demo-
> cratic practices. The trainees should not be nursed and cosseted but
> induced to do things for themselves. It might be recommended to the
> trainees in each camp that they set up a social committee. A house commit-
> tee is also indicated, to decide upon those day to day matters and questions
> of conduct and discipline which fall outside the general supervisory func-
> tions of the pit management or camp leader. Such a committee could also
> act as the representative voice of the trainees in dealing with the manage-
> ment of the pit or with outside bodies. A seat on the Works' Council should
> be reserved for a representative elected by this committee.[70]

In German hands, by contrast, instruction and moral education were often realized in a very authoritarian manner, particularly in relation to the young
apprentices. There was a general feeling that the uprooted young needed to be
brought up within a firm and a religious environment. They had been deprived
too long of the "firm guiding hand of the father."[71] The hostel rules produced by
the Caritas in Bottrop reveal this particularly clearly. Beginning with the men-

---

67. Ges. Verb. File 'I.II', Section 024.3, minutes of 2nd meeting of Arbeitskreis II, 24 Aug.
1948.
68. Sieburg, 'Staatsbürgerliche Willensbildung in der Bergmannsbetreuung'.
69. Herwick, 'Unsere Bergberufsschule'.
70. PORO (ed.), *The mining trainee 1947*, 30.
71. Jochum, 'Das sexuelle Problem', 8.

acing greeting, "Our hostel should be your 'home.' We want you to feel comfortable here," it goes on to tell the youngster when to get up, how to wash, and in what state the room must be left. No matter what the weather, the windows must be opened on awakening—"We are all friends of the fresh morning air." Only on two weekdays and Sundays did the youngsters have free use of their leisure time. (Needless to say, church-going was compulsory.) They were trained to sing grace in canon at mealtimes. But outside the hostels, even local-born youngsters experienced a new religious-authoritarian spirit in their schools. Indeed, it pervaded the way mining employees brought up their own children, as the memoirs of mining engineer Rudolf Wawersik make clear.[72]

Free discussions were difficult and often unrewarding because so many areas were taboo. This applied particularly to the state-sponsored activities because of the state's strong desire to appear politically and religiously neutral. Both *Volkschochschulen* and NRW ministries felt their work could not be effective if their neutrality was placed in jeopardy. If this neutrality were not seen to be preserved, the speakers would lose credibility and there was a danger of losing the youngsters or driving them to extremes. Thus lectures tended to concentrate on formal issues. As a speaker at a conference for hostel wardens said, a good topic was not "socialism or capitalism" but "the refugee and equal rights," "I read a constitution," and "what is politics and is it necessary." Religious questions too were evidently seen as dangerous if they dragged the lecturers into any area that could be considered denominational. At a conference on cultural policy in 1953, the question was raised whether religious issues should be discussed. Yes, was the answer, and the field-workers must be in a position "to answer the frequently potentially explosive questions." Again, there was a strong sense of danger here, of balancing on the slippery tightrope of "neutrality."[73]

Finally, of course, there were inner uncertainties that made any discussion dangerous. "How many of the German people have really spiritually dealt with the events of the last twenty years?" asked Oberkirchenrat Kloppenburg, in a lecture to mining educationalists whose refreshing openness contrasted strongly with so much that was said after the war.[74] The speaker continued,

---

72. HStaD NW41, 746, Caritasverband Bottrop, Berglehrlingsheim *Hausordnung*, 21 Oct. 1948; Bondy, 'Gedanken zur außerbetrieblichen Beeinflussung'; 'Statt Kasernengeist die echte Persönlichkeit', *Rheinischer Merkur*, 5 Feb. 1949; Hans Diether Baroth, '*Aber es waren schöne Zeiten*' (Munich, 1982), 58; Rudolf Wawersik, *Ausbeute eines Bergmannslebens. Erinnerungen an den oberschlesischen, saarländischen und westfälischen Bergbau* (Essen, 1981), esp. p. 131.

73. HStaD NW17, 136, Kultusministerium NRW IIE5, internal memo to Minister Teusch, 8 Nov. 1950; NW42, 912, Simons, report on a course for wardens of hostels for apprentices and young miners, 6–10 Oct. 1947, 18 Jan. 1948; NW17, 141, RAG, report on the conference in Kronenburg 21–26 Sept. 1953, Oct. 1953.

74. Kloppenburg, 'Jugend in Beruf und Freizeit', *Mitteilungen für die Bergberufsschulen der WBK*, 15 (1957).

"How should we expect youth to respond in a healthy fashion when we have become hysterical in discussions of these things?"

If the Nazi era was mentioned at all, it was rushed through discussion under the euphemism of "most recent past." This same inner uncertainty made discussion of many contemporary issues also very rigid. In a revealing phrase in his dissertation about the Pestalozzi villages, Roelen observed that religious groups had been set up in a number of villages where the youngsters could discuss religious issues and "eliminate religious doubts."[75] There was no room for doubt. This fear of admitting uncertainty or embarking on contentious issues gave a lot of the political and religious messages a rather sterile quality.

Because of the danger of embarking on the central issues, a lot of the thrust of the educational programmes went into the secondary virtues, into restoring proper behaviour and a respect for authority. No programme for cultural welfare was complete without a reference to reviving an "active Christian attitude,"[76] to the "educational and ethical values of Christianity,"[77] or the values of "occidental culture that rests on a Christian foundation."[78] Exactly what was meant by Christian values was never specified, but the value on which greatest emphasis was placed was undoubtedly respect for authority. "I use every opportunity, every utterance, to fight against immodesty, lack of respect, and the rejection of all authority," reported one of the field-workers in cultural welfare.[79]

Controlling sexual behaviour was another priority, and many hostels instituted dancing classes as a way of regulating how young men and women came together. There was a discussion in 1953 about whether youngsters should be allowed to take their girlfriends on trips. Yes, was the answer, because the young miner then has

a healthy ambition to prevail against the others with that girl. He will choose his companion and will behave accordingly. These are things that are on the agenda of the cultural care and control of the miners.[80]

---

75. Roelen, 'Die Bedeutung der Pestalozzidörfer', 77.

76. Klinkert Papers, file 'Niederschriften der Arbeitstagungen und Vortragsveranstaltungen'. Vormbrock, 'Überblick über die bisherige Arbeit des Jugendheimstättenwerks und den Entwicklungsstand der Pestalozzidörfer', 7 Oct. 1953.

77. *BAK* B102, Hensel to Ullrich, 23 Oct. 1952.

78. Pestalozzidörfer des Bergbaus', 17; Roelen, 'Die Bedeutung der Pestalozzidörfer', 26.

79. HStaD NW17, 10, Erich Burrisch to *Kultusministerium*, 2 Dec. 1949, annex; see also the list of requirements of village parents in JHStW PV (ed.), *Pestalozzieltern im Pestalozzidorf*, cited in Roelen, 'Die Bedeutung der Pestalozzidörfer', 27ff.

80. HStaD NW17, 141, lecture from Fischer in report on the RAG conference at Kronenburg, 21–26 Sept. 1953; see also Roelen, 'Die Bedeutung der Pestalozzidörfer', 84; BBA 32, 1186, 'Shamrock Berglehrlinge widmen sich begeistert dem Tango nach der Schicht', clipping from *Westfälische Rundschau*.

Suitable lectures were also offered to influence the youngsters' choice of partner, on "healthy and unhealthy female beauty," for example, which presumably warned the young miners against flashy girls wearing too much make-up. The hostel wardens were instructed how to help prevent premature sex and masturbation. General social behaviour too, needed improving, and fitting lectures with titles such as "We behave ourselves again" were given to meet this need.[81]

These "secondary virtues" became the symbols of the struggle to preserve or revive a past moral order. Two examples will suffice to show the strength of the anxieties that were aroused here. In a lecture given in 1954, Erwin Jochum talked about the way in which the apprentice schools could help to shape apprentices' sexual behaviour. He described some of the shocking cases that had come to his attention, the worst being that of two miners who, invited to spend the night at the house of a widow, slept with her two daughters after drawing straws to see who slept with whom. Leaving aside the fact that the story, in the form in which it is presented, seems rather apocryphal, it is noteworthy that Jochum went on to say: "The abyss that opens there must fill us with disgust and dread. But this is how things are these days . . . this is the sinister smoldering fire under the surface, which can break out into a ravaging blaze."[82]

Less apocalyptic, but no less striking, was a paper delivered in the previous year at a conference for field-workers and other interested participants in cultural welfare policy. Without embarrassment, but with an emotion that comes through clearly in the text, Dozent Fischer had this to say about the cultural value of organized outings with young miners:

> It is said so often that the young people no longer have any feeling for ethical values. But this is not entirely true. It is always quite an experience to see how these people become still and silent in the cathedral and even put their hands together in prayer. This alone could justify the work to take care (of the young miners).[83]

There is a sort of shuddery feeling of pleasure here at that little physical gesture of bourgeois propriety. The decently held hands, though in reality indicating nothing more than that their owners were intimidated by the atmosphere of a large cathedral and uncertain as to how to behave, symbolize for the speaker an acceptance of proper values. The values themselves remain undefined. Such

---

81. HStaD NW42, 912, Simons, Bericht über den Lehrgang für Heimleiter von Berglehrlingen- und Ledigenheimen vom 6.10.1947, 18 Jan. 1948; NW17, 10, Report on cultural events in the hostels of mine Lohberg during January 1950; lecture from Fischer in HStaD NW17, 141, RAG, report on the conference in Kronenburg, 21–26 Sept. 1953, October 1953.

82. Jochum, 'Das sexuelle Problem', 10.

83. HStaD NW17, 141, lecture from Fischer in report on the RAG conference at Kronenburg, 21–26 Sept. 1953.

gestures—decent behaviour, respectful demeanour, and so on—become the focal point of cultural policy, because of the difficulty in actually specifying what the deeper values might be.

As well as integrating the newcomers into the moral order, the cultural policy makers also felt the need to communicate a genuine aesthetic. Lecture topics and works newspaper articles such as "beautiful world," "healthy and unhealthy female beauty," "German music or jazz," and so on were meant to lead the youngsters to an appreciation of true culture. There was a sense of returning—or attempting to return—to a valid, German aesthetic. In a 1950 article on cultural activities in the hostels and mining community, *Der Förderturm* praised a recent concert of much-loved tunes: "Heart and soul rejoice in those happy memories of childhood and home, memories that the turmoil of the war and post-war years, but not least of all also the jazz and Negro rhythms of the present, threatened to suffocate completely."[84]

Some hoped that not only the newcomers but also the established miners could be drawn into the wider community through appreciation of the classics of national culture. An experiment in exposing the whole workforce to improving cultural events had in fact been underway at the GHH mines since 1949. This was also the goal of another organization, the Association of Friends of Art and Culture in Mining. One of its members wrote of the need to assist the miners in aesthetic judgments about furnishing their houses. His article is worth quoting at length because of the way many of the motifs and anxieties we have observed elsewhere are brought together here. After stressing the need for caution and subtlety in approaching what was after all part of the miners' private family lives, Winkelmann outlined what was wrong with the miners' choice of furniture:

> The huge, bulging kitchen buffets which convey restlessness, the heavy ostentatious beds and vanities—in short, all that we call "Gelsenkirchen Baroque" these days—is in reality foreign to the simple inner values of the miner . . . Precisely because these issues of housing penetrate the most intimate sphere of our miners, their family life and their inner life, they constitute a task of fundamental significance for us. The education of a sensitivity for form, a sense of harmony between space and furniture, the step toward true form and color are preconditions for the development of

---

84. 'Gesang und Instrumentalmusik im Rahmen der kulturellen Bergmannsbetreuung', *Der Förderturm* (Mar. 1950); see also HStaD NW17, 10, Städtische VHS Bochum, Dozent für kulturelle Bergmannsbetreuung, Berich, 1 May 1950; 'Rückschau auf die Kulturveranstaltungen die in den Heimen der Zeche Lohberg im Januar 1950 durchgeführt wurden', *Mitteilungen der KfSA*, 4 (1949), 4.

a new design for living (*Wohnkultur*) that corresponds to our inner being, our present situation, and our quest for authenticity.[85]

Winkelmann expresses perfectly the Ruhr bourgeoisie's ambiguous approach to the miners. On the one hand, the image of the true and simple miner is very strong here. Like so many of his contemporaries, Winkelmann aspired to revive the spirit of the miner of yore, a man characterized by both *Standesbewußtsein* (a sense of occupational status) and modesty, who knew his place and had been uncorrupted by the *Vermassung* of modern times. On the other, there was the goal of creating a new *Wohnkultur* (style of living), of educating the miner to find balance and harmony in the post-war social order. Both goals were conservative in intent, but embodied different types of conservatism and different images of social integration. Whereas some employers and officials were clearly still immersed in the patriarchal relations of years gone by, indeed hoped to recreate the labour relations of the pre–First World War period, others sought to find a new type of integration, creating out of the miner a deproletarianized citizen. Often, as in this case, the two vocabularies co-existed unresolved, indicating a fair degree of uncertainty as to what the ideal post-war society should look like. Moreover, Winkelmann's statement contains not just uncertainty, but also a clear anxiety about the kind of statement that the "Gelsenkirchen Baroque" style was making. The robust, pompous showiness that characterized a lot of miners' furniture at that time was anathema to a nervous bourgeoisie anxious to restore restraint, modesty, and propriety.

Conclusions

To note the rhetoric and ideology associated with the apprenticeship and the integration of the mines' young recruits, to take it seriously and to analyse it, is not to make the mistake of assuming that the hard-headed *Bergassessoren* (mining engineers) were in the first instance ideologues or combatants in the class war and only secondarily businessmen in pursuit of financial rewards. The bottom line for the employers was hard coal and hard currency, and no little part of the speechifying and the cultural policy was just a smoke-screen, designed to conceal the quiet dictatorship of the balance-sheet or to impart a moral tone to the fact that thousands of young refugees were being sent down the mines because there was no other employment for them.

---

85. Heinrich Winkelmann, 'Heim und Herd und Sport und Spiel des Bergmanns', *West-deutsche Wirtschafts-Monographie*, Pt. 1, 'Steinkohle Ausgabe', Apr. 1953; see also HStaD NW41, 747, Dr. Hoernecke, Wiesbaden, Gedanken zur kulturellen Bergmannsbetreuung im Steinkohlenbergbau, 15 May 1952; Ges. Verb. Fiel '"K" vol. 2', minutes of the 7th meeting of KfSA, 11 Nov. 1948; File 'III.IV', meeting of Arbeitskreis III, 24 Sept. 1952.

Yet at the same time it is clear that wider social and ideological influences did play (and indeed always will play) a key role in influencing the industrialists' behaviour. Ruhr mining managers pursued policies quite different from those envisaged by the British mining engineers initially involved in the Ruhr. The way the Ruhr employers defined their ideal labour force, the wider ideological and political goals they allowed to trickle into that definition, and the strategies they developed to achieve their ends all reveal underlying social perceptions, myths, and hopes as much as they did any objective economic interests.

Above all, the Ruhr employers' traditionalism comes shining through, both in that they behaved and thought much as they had done fifty years earlier and in that they consciously aspired to recreate a type of workforce and community that lay in the past. The language and aspirations of the colliery managers were redolent of the patriarchal labour relations of the nineteenth century. The apprenticeship programme aspired to fashion the workforce in a nineteenth-century image, to forge a, one is tempted to say, "bucolic" figure— modest, rooted to locality and profession, and fulfilled by his work and social position. The employers believed, or chose to believe, that the job changing of the present was a sign of incomplete personality and tried to foster the steadfastness which they believed the miners of the past had exhibited. The employers' approach to labour relations was very far from the pragmatism and co-operativeness which are conventionally seen as the hallmarks of the 1950s German manager. Instead, as their alliance with the churches showed, they tried to weaken the power of the union and keep it at arm's length from the apprentices.

The point is not simply that there are different ways of getting a productive workforce and that the particular *strategy* adopted in the Ruhr after the war was influenced by wider social and ideological currents. It is also that noneconomic *goals*—moral and political—played a key role in shaping labour policy. This had a lot to do with the state's involvement.

For the state, the economic importance of Ruhr coal was but one of many reasons prompting its intervention or assistance. The openly moral and political goal of offering young refugees suitable employment was at least as significant. True, many officials felt unhappy about sending young refugees down the mines, but that only intensified their desire to give recruitment and training programme a moral aspect. And there were other ambitions, too, many of them deriving from the state's sense of responsibility for the youngsters in the mines. Behind these ambitions, the state articulated fears about the threat posed by refugees and the young to the established order. It is not too far-fetched to say that in its treatment of displaced and dispossessed youth, in its approach to providing workers' housing and in other matters, the state was trying not just to solve an economic problem but at the same time to provide the foundations for a healthy, stable society.

This forced the employers to take issues seriously which they might otherwise have ignored. Not a few of the employers' statements of high moral purpose were stimulated more by the desire for state funding than by any personally held conviction. Many of the welfare measures adopted, Pestalozzi villages and so on, owed their rapid introduction to state financial help. By setting priorities and offering financial inducements, the state, if you like, made it financially and economically rational for employers to espouse moral and political aims.

Yet one should not see the employers simply as responding to state pressure. They shared with their colleagues in the civil service and the clergy a strong sense of mission, an urgent need to influence and "improve" the young miners. The mining engineers, civil servants, and bishops had in common deep anxieties about the nature of post-war Germany's younger generation and a suppressed unease about their role in the Nazi era. Here, too, there were strong similarities with Ruhr society before 1914.[86] Thus, at a time when the British bourgeoisie, for instance, was increasingly reticent about casting society in its own image—as the approach of British officers in the Ruhr showed—their German counterparts retained much more of the evangelism of earlier times.

What exactly the goal of that evangelism was, what the young miners should be turned into, was unclear. This was partly because two contradictory images existed alongside each other, unresolved. On the one hand, there was, as already noted, the notion of returning to the organic society and simple worker of the past, of shoring up the simple working man against the anomie of modern times. On the other, there was the goal of creating the democratic citizen, of educating the worker in bourgeois values. It is worth noting that the coexistence of these two goals applied not only to apprentice policy but to other aspects of the mines' social policy as well. In housing design, for instance, a romantic, agrarian conservatism sometimes complemented, sometimes contradicted the desire to modernize the taste and living style of the miner.[87]

There was, in fact, a fundamental uncertainty about what the ideal future society should be, a conflict between the "organic" and the democratic. Indeed, uncertainty and anxiety generally debilitated attempts to produce a coherent moral and political message. The state's nervous desire to be seen as neutral and hypersensitivity to questions about the Nazi era often forced the speech makers and social workers to concentrate on secondary virtues and reduced

---

86. See Franz Brüggemeier, *Leben vor Ort. Ruhrbergleute und Ruhrbergbau 1889–1919* (Munich, 1983), 142ff.

87. Roseman, 'New Miners', 356ff.

them to stiff and sterile authoritarian figures, with little chance of really reaching their young audience.

The other factor which vitiated the employers' attempts to reshape the workforce was the influence of the labour movement. It was not that the unions were particularly powerful in their own right. But many state institutions felt that the legitimacy and stability of the new post-war order depended on state neutrality and union participation. The state made its funding conditional on the union's having a say in the committees. Gradually, state pressure saw to it that IGB was represented on every cultural and housing committee. The co-determination law put labour directors in charge of colliery social policy. And even if the DKBL had felt inclined to resist this pressure, the need to present a united front to the Allies ensured that it would not. Thus all the moves against the union in cultural policy had to be engaged in quietly and surreptitiously and were ultimately largely abandoned.

What then did the employers and their helpers achieve? The mines never really succeeded in establishing mining as a desirable profession and the number of apprentice recruits fell rapidly from 1954 onwards. Secondly, they failed to create a *Stammbelgeschaft* (loyal crew of workers). In 1953, wastage was such that 60,000 hirings were necessary to achieve a 3,000 increase in workforce size! Even more disappointing for the employers was the fact that neither the former apprentices in general, nor those outsiders who had been subject to the intensive nurturing in the youth villages and hostels, showed any greater propensity to stay than miners who had not gone through these training programmes.[88]

To a certain extent these results were inevitable whatever the employers did. Mining work was unattractive. The physical conditions were unpleasant and taxing, the dangers associated with the work considerable, and the prospect of almost certain ill-health in old age most uninviting. Not surprisingly, most other European countries were experiencing similar difficulties.

Yet the weaknesses of the apprentice strategy were not simply the result of mining's inherent unattractiveness. In the first place, it was readily apparent to recruits that the apprenticeship was an ideological artefact of no real substance. A lot of the training period was spent rather aimlessly or without supervision because there simply were not enough things to learn. Because of high wastage rates, the industry continued to hire 50–60,000 adult recruits a year and these men did exactly the same jobs and earned exactly the same wage after their few weeks' training as the apprentices earned at the end of three years. So there could be no genuine élite consciousness. Secondly, the employers had fundamentally misunderstood their wastage problem. It was often not the rootless personalities but precisely the well integrated, confident, and easily adaptable

---

88. Ibid. 281ff., 292, 328.

workers who were most inclined to leave their jobs and seek something more convivial. A lot of the employers' effort was therefore misplaced. Finally, as far as outsiders were concerned, what the policymakers were doing was contradictory. On the one hand they wanted the youngsters to settle, but on the other they actually kept them at arm's length from the existing mining community. Small wonder that a great many of the apprentices left the industry as soon as they had obtained their qualification.

It was symptomatic of management's conservatism that it did not do the one thing which, if the evidence of a great many contemporary observers is to be believed, could have made a significant impact on the industry's retention rates. It did not modernize management styles within the collieries. Again and again surveys showed that, next to mining's inherent unattractiveness, the main problem of working life was the character of management and human relations. Though some figures in the industry were willing to recognize this, the majority view remained that wastage was the result of inadequacy, rootlessness, and lack of steadfastness on the part of the recruits. Instead of looking to the United States or to other industries for different styles of management, the *Bergassessoren* kept their sights firmly fixed on their idealized miner of days gone by.[89]

What about the wider moral, political, and cultural goals of employers, state, and church? Of course, this is a particularly difficult area to assess, yet, even here, the sources are so rich that we can venture a number of conclusions. The employers failed to drive a wedge between the apprentices and the labour movement. Unionization amongst apprentices was almost 100 percent and it was noteworthy that in what was virtually the only mining strike since the currency reform, the "Reusch strike" of 1955, considerable numbers of apprentices took part. Yet this did not mean that the employers' worst nightmares were confirmed. On the contrary, much of the employers' ideological work was simply unnecessary, in that it was impelled by fears that were understandable but inappropriate. The union soon proved to be dominated by moderates and conservatives and, as we have seen, the Communists had never had much of a following in the hostels.

The bourgeoisie's rigidity, nervousness in relation to contentious issues, and lack of a clear core message all limited the possibility of any real communication. If they managed to communicate anything, it was that a large range of issues were better left undiscussed. In most cases, the hostel occupants seem to have "subverted" what was on offer for their own purposes, attending courses and events according to their entertainment value and ignoring those that seemed out merely to improve.[90]

---

89. Ibid. 309, 339–47, 460ff.
90. Ibid. 445ff.

By the mid-1950s, the employers were sadder and wiser but also more re-laxed and secure. By then the apprentice drive and the cultural welfare policy were running out of steam. Such activities as did continue were handed over to the labour directors and ceased to have any great ideological content. The churches lost both their sense of mission and their anxiety and gradually wound down their activities in the mines. A number of institutions continued to tick over, indeed some still exist, but more from institutional inertia than from any other reason. By 1960 or so the stream of apprentices from outside the Ruhr had virtually dried up. The great experiment was over.

The Fight for the "Christian West": German Film Control, the Churches, and the Reconstruction of Civil Society in the Early Bonn Republic

Heide Fehrenbach

By 1949, the postwar political organization of West Germany had been settled, but the task of reconstructing German civil society and achieving social consensus remained largely incomplete and contested. The normalization of German public life was marked in part by negotiation and cooperation, but also provoked impassioned rhetoric, public resistance, and heated debates over the limits, as well as social and moral implications, of the new democratic order. Catholic and Protestant church leaders, in an attempt to reclaim social and cultural power denied them under Hitler, quickly entered—and in large measure shaped the nature of—these debates, particularly in the area of film policy and culture.[1]

I would like to thank Victoria de Grazia, Miriam Hansen, Harold Poor, and John Gillis for their comments and criticisms on earlier drafts of this chapter as well as Eric Rentschler for sharing his invaluable insights and film collection. Special thanks to Bob Mensel for his generous contributions to this project as critic, editor, and friend. Earlier versions of this chapter were presented at the 1989 German Studies Association Meeting in Milwaukee and at the Center for the Critical Analysis of Contemporary Culture at Rutgers University in April 1989. The Deutscher Akademischer Austauschdienst provided crucial financial support for the research upon which this chapter is based.

1. The churches actively engaged in expanding their influence in the other media during the postwar period as well. Film, however, received an inordinate amount of attention because of its unprecedented popularity after the war and because of contemporaries' post-Hitler perception that its control was crucial to the rehabilitation of the German nation. Theater and literature were the

Cinema policy became a battlefield almost immediately after the occupation of the country. The defeat of National Socialism and the Allied occupation forced government officials, representatives of religious communities, and educators to confront the task of reeducating the population to "democratic" ideals. In this drive for democratization, Allied leaders, and later their German counterparts, were especially concerned to regulate and control the mass media.

Apart from its popularity as entertainment, film in Germany was historically an important product for export as well as international prestige. During the 1920s, the German film industry had the distinction of being Hollywood's only serious challenger on the world market. After 1945, the large American film companies fought fiercely to retain their commercial advantage internationally by attempting, through their trade association, to convince American Information Control officers in the military government that a rapid resurgence of the German film industry would threaten the democratization process initiated by the Western Allies. However, this strategy had only limited success in winning the support of American Information Control officials and was not sufficient in itself to insure the international demise of the German film industry. The fate of the postwar German film industry cannot be told as a simple story of a powerful Hollywood muscling its German competitor out of the international market.

The inability of the (West) German film industry to recapture a measure of prestige and commercial success on the international market was also the result of church intervention in the area of film control and censorship. These initiatives, in conjunction with the American principles for industry reorganization, prodded the German film industry into provinciality and commercial failure by directly affecting the aesthetic, moral, and narrative qualities of German films.

Catholic and Protestant churchmen and lay leaders were responding to what they perceived as threats to their cultural authority on the domestic level. With the demise of Nazi control over cultural production, the specter of a reemergent German film industry, regulated solely by market imperatives and operating according to American principles, began to haunt German social conservatives. Vehemently rejecting the Soviet model of political, social, and

targets of less vehemence because they were not, and were not understood to be, "mass" entertainments. Furthermore, religious and state elites identified unregulated film as potentially more dangerous than radio or the press to German reconstruction precisely because of its visual immediacy and potent appeal to certain "vulnerable" sectors of the population. Film occupied an exceptional place in the imaginations and rhetoric of West German churchmen and conservative state officials. For a discussion of postwar ecclesiastical involvement in radio, television, and the press, as well as film, see Karl-Werner Bühler, *Die Kirchen und die Massenmedien. Intentionen und Institutionen konfessioneller Kulturpolitik in Rundfunk, Fernsehen, Film und Presse nach 1945* (Hamburg: Furche Verlag, 1968).

cultural organization offered for the reconstruction of German society, West German social conservatives also harbored serious reservations about the American vision. In response to the cultural challenges from East and West, some local religious and government leaders advocated a third alternative based upon aspects of the Weimar experience. While shunning the artistic experimentation and leftist social criticism characteristic of that period, these individuals sought to salvage earlier native forms of cultural management and censorship. In their "Fight for the Christian West," German social conservatives resisted what they considered to be threats to their renascent national community and cultural traditions, both from communism and from American consumer culture. Religious leaders resolved to resume their pre-Nazi roles as cultural arbiters, and attempted to resist, or at least control, the forces of secularization and commercialization.

In challenging commercial film products released in West Germany, church leaders typically employed the old argument that films which threatened a "religious or morally-endangering influence upon the viewer"[2] should be banned. This idea of *Filmwirkung*, or psychological susceptibility to the film medium, was important in the development of film censorship in twentieth-century Germany and served as a justification for the expurgation of various films throughout the Adenauer period. An examination of the tactics and rhetoric used in the public fights against one particular German film, director Willi Forst's *Die Sünderin* (The Sinner), exposes the assumptions upon which public leaders based the refashioning of German society in the West. It also offers a closer view of church-state relations, and of the reactions of social conservatives to the threat posed by the internationalization of consumer culture.

Film politics, in the early years of the Bonn republic, were characterized by skirmishes between economics and ideology. And astonishingly, ideology won. Why couldn't the capitalist industry better defend itself from ideological attacks? Was the industry complicit in its own demise? And finally, what social and cultural implications did this triumph of ideology have for German reconstruction in the West?

The Renewal of Confessional Film Work After Hitler: A New Course

Beginning with the Occupation period, church leaders actively engaged themselves in the pressing issues of reconstruction. As leaders of the only German institutions to emerge from the war intact, Catholic and Protestant bishops

---

2. Bayerisches Hauptstaatsarchiv (hereafter BayHStA), MK 51750. Press Release of Kirchliche Hauptstelle für Bild und Filmarbeit, 27 November 1948.

immediately assumed the role of German ambassadors to the occupying powers, dispensing often unwelcome advice and criticism and intervening in political affairs over which they had no jurisdiction. Perhaps because of their unwillingness to remain publicly passive during the Occupation, even in the face of Allied opposition and irritation, church leaders generally enjoyed a great deal of prestige in the eyes of the local population.[3]

Consequently, church leaders possessed a large degree of de facto public authority immediately following the capitulation of Germany.[4] Catholic bishops, in particular, worked to strengthen and institutionalize their informal public authority during the Occupation and the first years of the Adenauer era.[5] The result of these efforts was a network of alliances involving coreligionists, Protestant counterparts, and, increasingly, sympathetic state officials.

Toward the end of the Occupation period, the Catholic Church very consciously began to build a network of offices and publications to advise their congregations on film matters. By 1951, the Church was able to launch a large-scale mobilization of believers against the film *Die Sünderin*. This mobilization provided the Catholic Church with the leverage to wage a successful attack against the prevailing values of commercial culture, and in the process bolster its own authority. For although church leaders cast their rhetoric in religious terms, they were actually participating in a serious political debate over the nature of postwar German social and cultural reorganization.

The Catholic leadership considered the struggle to control the potential effect of film viewing a matter of crucial social importance. Postwar Catholic film activity distinguished itself from earlier Catholic initiatives by its broad scope, passionate lobbying, and occasionally flamboyant tactics. Prior to 1933, Catholic film groups had sought to reshape the market, and produced Catholic films intended to compete with the commercial industry. However, by 1934 even the largest Catholic film companies had collapsed due to financial difficulties related to Hitler's rise to power.[6] What little confessional film activity

---

3. Martin Greschat, "Kirche und Öffentlichkeit in der deutschen Nachkriegszeit (1945–1949)," in A. Boyens, M. Greschat, et al., *Kirchen in der Nachkriegszeit* (Göttingen: Vandenhoeck & Ruprecht, 1979), 115–16.

4. See Armin Boyens, "Die Kirchenpolitik der amerikanischen Besatzungsmacht in Deutschland von 1944 bis 1946," *Kirchen in der Nachkriegszeit,* 7–57; Greschat, 107. See also Frederic Spotts, *The Churches and Politics in Germany* (Middletown, Conn.: Wesleyan University Press, 1973), 55, who mentions that the "churches were tacitly recognized as the sole institutions above direct military control, as national bodies not generally subject to varying zonal regulations and exempt from 'reorientation' into directions determined in Washington, London, or Paris."

5. See Spotts, 149–58, on the importance the German Catholic episcopate placed on founding and organizing lay movements, professional associations, a Catholic press, radio station, trade union, and university.

6. These included the impressive Leo-Film Gesellschaft with branches in Switzerland, Spain, and Austria.

remained was sharply regulated, and by 1943 all such activity had ceased.[7] After the war, Catholics recognized that the prewar strategy was no longer viable. In the light of the overwhelming popularity of commercial films, Catholic film commissioner Anton Kochs devoted his energies to reforming the commercial product.[8]

Protestant film work was historically rather less organized. Prior to World War II, the Protestant clergy tended to view film as antithetical to the mission of the church. Film work was confined to the efforts of lay organizations, which produced and distributed films chronicling the accomplishments of missionaries or church social workers. After the devastation wrought by the war, however, Protestant leaders increasingly recognized the need to educate "the homeless, uprooted and neglected" German youth.[9] Thereafter, Protestant leaders, like their Catholic counterparts, shifted their attention to altering the nature of the products released by the domestic film industry.

Sharing a common goal and philosophy for the social role of film in postwar Germany, these confessional groups modeled new strategies for influencing commercial film production and policy. Early in the postwar period, both Catholic and Protestant churches created organizations to deal with film questions. In 1946, Catholic bishops founded the *Kirchliche Hauptstelle für Bild und Filmarbeit in den deutschen Diözesen*, a central office for film matters. By the following year, two publications, *Filmdienst der Jugend* and *Filmüberschau*, appeared which advised Catholics on the moral quality of films released in the Western zones.

The Protestant churches took somewhat longer to organize and were never as cohesive a force. They did not issue a film journal until late in 1948, when *Evangelischer Film-Beobachter* appeared in Munich. In the spring of 1949, the Evangelical Church appointed Pastor Werner Hess as special commissioner for film matters.[10]

7. Heiner Schmitt, *Kirche und Film. Kirchliche Filmarbeit in Deutschland von ihren Anfängen bis 1945* (Schriften des Bundesarchivs, no. 26) (Boppard am Rhein: Harald Boldt Verlag, 1979), 64–87, 151–89, 205–30, 244–54; Charles Ford, *Der Film und der Glaube*, trans. Pierre Pascal (Nürnberg: Glock und Lutz, 1955), 200–203; and Stefan Bamberger, *Christentum und Film* (Aschaffenburg: Paul Pattloch Verlag, 1968), 7–24, for discussions of early film activity by German ecclesiastics.

8. Anton Kochs, "Wunsch an den deutschen Film," supplement to *Film Korrespondenz*, no. 7 (1 August 1950). Also Anton Kochs, "Kirche und Film in Westdeutschland," *International Film Revue* 1 no. 4 (1951–52). Kochs's discussion closely follows Werner Hess's argument in his talk entitled "Gibt es den religiösen Film?" which appeared in published form in *Film und Kirche. Die wichtigsten Referate der Schwalbacher Tagung, 21.–25. Juni 1950* (Munich: Verlag des Evangelischen Presseverbandes für Bayern in München, 1950), 18–38.

9. Werner Hess, "Die Filmarbeit der Evangelischen Kirchen in Deutschland," *Internationale Film Revue* 2 no. 6 (1954–55): 42; and Schmitt, 105–39.

10. Hess later argued that 1949 represented a turning point in the EKD's understanding of its responsibility for film content and control.

Recognizing this convergence of purpose with respect to the film industry, church representatives initiated an informal policy of interconfessional cooperation in film affairs. This move grew out of the domestic political atmosphere and paralleled the tone of confessional conciliation and cooperation best symbolized by the creation of the Christian Democratic and the Bavarian Christian Social Unions.

Initially, both the Protestant and Catholic film commissioners attacked the indiscriminate use of religious motifs, settings, and ceremony in feature films, a practice they charged was becoming particularly widespread in the early years of renewed German film production.[11] According to Pastor Hess, there was "hardly a comedy, a criminal thriller," or any other type of film in which

> a church scene wasn't inserted, [or] somewhere a pastor or monk cropped up. . . . [T]his type of employment of religious motifs . . . is . . . distressing, because one notices they are not affirmations of Christ but of mammon.[12]

Catholic film commissioner Anton Kochs seconded Hess's objections to religious kitsch, complaining that "[c]louds of incense smoke and burning candles, friendly monks and almond-eyed acolytes" did not ensure that a film was religious.[13] Hess and Kochs clearly objected to the commercial exploitation and cooptation of religiosity by the film industry. Yet their statements can also be read as metaphors for their opposition to the trivialization of religion in a period marked by the abrupt release of culture from Nazi state control and the influx of American cultural forms. Struck by the rapid secularization and renewed commercialization of German society, churchmen feared the loss of their traditional social and cultural authority. They needed to strike back.

For a New, Moral Film Control

The most obvious place to start in this campaign was with a modification of the postwar film censorship apparatus, the *Freiwillige Selbstkontrolle der Filmwirtschaft* (FSK), which churchmen generally viewed as a foreign imposition and the outgrowth of an Allied policy unresponsive to their cultural and social concerns. In 1949, the American occupiers had replaced state censorship of film, practiced under the Nazi regime, with self-censorship by the film industry, a principle based on the experience of the Hays Commission in the

---

11. The accuracy of these allegations cannot, of course, be established without a thorough analysis of pre- and postwar film content.

12. Werner Hess, "Der Wille der Kirche zur filmischen Gestaltung," *Kirche und Film* no. 20 (14 October 1949): 2.

13. Anton Kochs, "Kirche und Film in Westdeutschland." Also Kochs, "Wunsch an den deutschen Film."

United States. The censorship standards to be applied were never an issue of contention. But the Americans were pressured by local state officials to modify the U.S. model to include the "public voice." This was a contest for cultural influence, and the agreement could be reached only after elaborate negotiations and concessions.[14]

Thus the new postwar film censorship settlement actually represented a blending of old and new principles. The American model of exclusive censorship by film producers was merged with the principle of representation by social welfare and religious groups, which had its roots in the Weimar film control legislation (*Reichslichtspielgesetz*) of 1920. However, it was clear from the beginning that church and state representatives considered this new arrangement a temporary expedient. These groups had been compelled by occupation officials to accept, albeit with modification, the American principle of industry self-censorship, yet they refused to consider the situation permanent. Shortly after the FSK began operation, Dr. Walter Keim, ministerial counselor in the Bavarian Cultural Ministry and a staunch Catholic, emphasized that the current arrangement would go forth on a "trial basis."[15]

Despite church representation on the censorship board, it quickly became, in the words of Werner Hess, the "target of passionate ecclesiastical criticism." Church leaders expressed grave misgivings about the "laxity" of the film review process. The cause of this "laxity" was, according to the churchmen, the voting strength of the secular, commercial interests in that body and the corresponding weakness of the churches.

Apparently anticipating such circumstances in the months before the FSK began operation, the Catholic Church consolidated its film activity, founding a Catholic Film Commission for the purpose of reviewing and rating all films— domestic and imported—shown in Germany, and awarding prizes for the "year's best" films. Shortly thereafter the Catholic Film Commission united *Filmdienst der Jugend* and *Filmüberschau* to create a single, official organ,

---

14. Debate centered on the makeup of the film review board and, in particular, the proportion of representation allotted to the commercial film industry, state bodies, churches, and the confessionally linked youth offices. The final agreement permitted minority representation by the State Ministries of Culture, the churches, and youth offices. However, the film industry retained an absolute majority of votes: four seats out of six on the Working Committee, which reviewed films for permission for release in West Germany, and eight out of fifteen on the Main Committee, which ruled on contested decisions. See Johanne Noltenius, *Die Freiwillige Selbstkontrolle der Filmwirtschaft und das Zensurverbot des Grundgesetzes* (Göttingen: Verlag Otto Schwartz & Co., 1958). For a discussion of Bavarian officials' efforts to counter the American plans for purely industry-controlled film censorship, see chapter two of Heide Fehrenbach, *Cinema in Democratizing Germany: Reconstructing National Identity after Hitler* (Chapel Hill: University of North Carolina Press, 1995).

15. Walter Keim, "Die Freiwillige Selbstkontrolle der deutschen Filmwirtschaft," *Kulturarbeit* no. 9 (1949).

Filmdienst, which printed the commission's opinions on all films shown in western Germany. The judgments of the Film Commission were posted "on almost all church doors and in many public showcases."[16] Such activity obviously paralleled in part the functions of the FSK, and it is unclear why industry and American officials did not object immediately to this organization. Presumably the Americans considered it an internal church affair instituted to "advise" congregations on the moral content of films, and not a body which sought to usurp or subvert the work of the censorship board. Members of the German commercial film industry learned by bitter experience that the work of these organizations would have broader repercussions.[17]

Writing for an international Catholic journal, Catholic film commissioner Anton Kochs summarized the issues and attempted to cast the debate in terms congenial to the Catholic position by asking a series of questions which, for him, must have been rhetorical, but which were indicative of the demands to be made on the industry. The responses were only to be worked out over the course of the Adenauer era:

> Does film . . . assist in the reconstruction of the Christian West? Does it counter the destructive powers of the present with something positive? Does it provide something that actually helps people? or does it undermine and corrupt that which responsible people wish to construct, since the destruction of the war, in the home, in public and in the church?[18]

The Case of "Die Sünderin"

In early 1951, members of both the Catholic and Protestant churches took up arms to protect Christian morality, and with it, the "Christian West." This first battle for the "Christian West" took the form of a fight against director Willi Forst's film *Die Sünderin.* Initiated in the chambers of the FSK, the debate about the film quickly transcended narrow bureaucratic confines and exploded into the public arena, resulting in a mobilization of civil society. The film became a cause célèbre, around which debates concerning the reorganization of

---

16. Bamberger, 26–27, and Ford, 204–6.

17. In fact, shortly after the creation of the Catholic Film Commission, Rolf Meyer, a film producer from the Jungen Film Union, lodged a legal complaint charging that the negative rating of one of his films by the Catholic Film Commission in their publication *Filmdienst* violated the constitutional guarantee of freedom of opinion and resulted in reduced business for the film. See the response to this complaint by Walter Keim in "Geniessen wir Katholiken verfassungsmässige Meinungsfreiheit auf dem Gebiet des Films?" originally published in *Münchner Katholische Kirchenzeitung* (5 and 12 March 1950), reprinted in *Film-Korrespondenz* 1/1950 (1 May 1950): 3–4.

18. Kochs, "Kirche und Film in Westdeutschland," 289.

social roles and relationships, as well as issues of cultural authority, were played out.

Die Sünderin, a melodrama told in flashbacks and voiceovers, portrays the life and death of a woman named Marina.[19] It shows her descent into prostitution as a result of the disintegration of her bourgeois family during the war; her redemption through her love for Alexander, a reformed alcoholic artist; and their deaths at Marina's hands. Marina performs the mercy killing at Alexander's request because he is suffering from a debilitating brain tumor. Her suicide, of which he is unaware, takes place in the dying man's arms and unites the pair in death.

Willi Forst very self-consciously heralded his film as an innovation, both in terms of his own, personal style of filmmaking as well as within the tradition of German cinema. Best known as a director of musicals during the Nazi period, Forst claimed to have reconsidered his career and decided to forsake the "dream factory" school of filmmaking in favor of a German realism based on postwar experience: films "the public could identify with."[20] Implicit in his campaign was a rejection of the hegemony of the "UFA" style of escapist filmmaking that flourished in the 1930s and 1940s.[21]

The film was criticized during an evaluative screening before the censorship board, on which Protestant film commissioner Werner Hess and an unidentified Bavarian Catholic representative sat.[22] Although no firm decision was made about the advisability of the film's release, the committee agreed that it contained objectionable scenes, including Marina's resort to prostitution to

---

19. For a discussion of melodrama as a genre, see *Home is Where the Heart Is. Studies in Melodrama and the Woman's Film*, ed. Christine Gledhill (London: British Film Institute, 1987); esp. Christine Gledhill, "The Melodramatic Field: An Investigation," 5–42; and Lea Jacobs, "Censorship and the Fallen Woman Cycle," 100–112.

20. Forst called *Die Sünderin* a "Reportage des wirklichen Lebens"—a chronicle of real life—yet emphasized that it was mild compared to some Italian, French, and American films. He had not, after all, depicted the "sin itself . . . that he would never do!" See Julieanne Eisenführ, *Die Sünderin. Geschichte und Analyse eines Kinoskandals* (Magisterarbeit, Universität Osnabrück, 1982), 228 and 256.

Aside from the inclusion of social problems such as prostitution, incest, adultery, and alcoholism, the film has no thematic or stylistic similarities to Italian Neo-Realism. Filmed in the studio, *Die Sünderin* is characterized by sanitized sets as well as sanitized treatments of social problems.

21. See Eric Rentschler, "Germany: The Past that Would Not Go Away," *World Cinema Since 1945*, ed. William Luhr (New York: Ungar Publishing Co., 1987), 208–51. Named for the largest film monopoly (*Universum Film A.G.*) in interwar and Nazi Germany, "UFA" was used as shorthand to describe "escapist . . . extravaganzas, . . . the well-crafted, technically solid films with attractive casts, lavish sets, and—for all of their ideological insidiousness—no apparent relationship to the real world."

22. The following description of events surrounding the *Sünderin* affair is based heavily on Julieanne Eisenführ's unpublished thesis.

help her financially pressed and ailing lover, as well as the portrayal of mercy killing and suicide. There were indications that if appropriate editorial cuts were made, the committee would license its release.

Forst adamantly refused, however, to make cuts, calling a summons to appear before the censorship board "a personal insult." And although the board's main committee ultimately authorized the film's release,[23] it warned that *Die Sünderin* pressed "hard on the limits of the permissible."[24] The following day, Pastor Werner Hess resigned his position as the FSK representative of the Evangelical Church. Anton Kochs resigned shortly thereafter.[25]

Over the next few months it was precisely the question of who would wield cultural authority in the new Germany that was debated and to some extent resolved. And because *Die Sünderin* was one of the first postwar German films to benefit from the newly created state and federal film credit programs, the controversy would facilitate the reentry of state involvement in cultural production and regulation, a situation the Americans had been determined to block.

The Mobilization of Pressure Groups and Public Protest

The Catholic Church quickly moved to the forefront of the organized fight against the film on the local level. It became a subject of church sermons and protest activity, often by "believers" who had not viewed the film but relied on the reports of their local priest or film journal to supply details.[26]

---

23. Eisenführ, 234. The committee was composed of four representatives named by the film industry, three named by the public institutions (one representative each from the Catholic church, the Protestant church, and a confessional youth group), and three representatives of the state governments. The release of *Die Sünderin* was approved by a vote of nine to four for audiences "over the age of 16 years but not for screenings on religious holidays."

24. This decision coincided exactly with the premiere of the film at the Turmpalast in Frankfurt. The film's producer, distributor, and exhibitor decided to screen the film even without the board's approval, an action that further eroded the trust of church representatives in the authority of the institution as well as its effectiveness in curbing renegade behavior by industry members. Questions concerning the effectiveness of the FSK had been raised in the Catholic press during the previous year. See "Die Tätigkeit der Selbstkontrolle," *Filmkorrespondenz* no. 3 (1 June 1950); "Die befehdete Selbstkontrolle," *Filmkorrespondenz* no. 4 (15 June 1950); "Nachrichten aus der Filmwirtschaft," *Filmkorrespondenz* no. 5 (1 July 1950); as well as correspondence in the BayHStA MK 51750.

25. "Zum Fall Sünderin," *Kirche und Film* no. 3 (1 February 1951). Both resignations occurred at the request of the respective bishops in charge of film affairs, Protestant Bishop Lilje and Catholic Archbishop Berning. Also "Die Sünderin—Fall der Selbstkontrolle" in *Filmblätter* no. 4 (26 January 1951): 77; and "Filmkontrolle ohne Evangelische Kirche?" *Evangelische Film-beobachter* 3 no. 3 (1 February 1951): 17–18. Also Eisenführ, 246.

26. Eisenführ, 249–50.

Protests began in central and northern Germany, following the trail of the film's release.[27] Within a month, disturbances had broken out all over West Germany.[28] The film was banned in dozens of small- and medium-sized towns. Screenings were interrupted by tear gas in Frankfurt and Mannheim and by the release of white mice in Duisburg. Anti-*Sünderin* protests occurred after promptings by local clergy in Koblenz and Bielefeld, as well as in Düsseldorf and Regensburg, where street scuffles broke out and stink bombs were thrown into theaters.

Clergymen led schoolboys in street marches in Lüneberg, Munich, Regensburg, Ulm, and elsewhere. In Aschaffenberg, some 150 Catholic youths blocked access to the theater, banged on the exit doors, and stinkbombed the building. In Karlsruhe, 200 Catholic students staged a silent protest march. In Lüneberg, Catholic minors sent a letter of protest to the theater owner stressing the spiritual crisis of postwar youth. And in Erlangen, confessional students demanded local film censorship and disseminated leaflets protesting the film's "glorification of the new heathendom."

It is unclear exactly how local priests and religious teachers throughout the country decided to take to the streets using such similar tactics,[29] and whether this action was encouraged or even orchestrated by the Catholic hierarchy. It is clear, however, that the calls of Catholic bishops for the defense of "Christian humanity" were considered justification for their actions. Furthermore, neither Catholic leaders nor the religious press ever publicly criticized anti-*Sünderin* protests, even when they resulted in violence, and in one case, in the sensational trial of a Catholic priest.[30] Instead, they stuck with the strategy

---

27. Following the Frankfurt premiere, the film opened in "Hamburg, Düsseldorf and Essen, etc." *Filmblätter* no. 4 (26 January 1951): 78.

28. Eisenführ has separate, dated entries for every disturbance for which she had been able to find press reports. Among the towns she lists are: Oberhausen, Bonn, Koblenz, Münster, Nordhorn, Papenburg, Meppen, Lingen, Herne, Beilngries, Opladen, as well as those mentioned in the body of the text. Eisenführ, 251–95.

While it is not possible to get an accurate count of the number of people involved in street demonstrations nationwide, press reports seem to confirm that local action typically involved anywhere from several dozen to several hundred protestors. To a certain extent, the actual numbers do not matter. What was more important was that local and state government officials and the conservative and confessional press perceived and characterized the scattered demonstrations as widespread civil unrest.

29. There was, nonetheless, a historical precedent for the lobbing of stinkbombs and release of mice in German movie theaters: precisely the same tactics were employed by the Nazi SA against the American film *All Quiet on the Western Front* upon its release in Berlin in late 1930. See Modris Eksteins, "War, Memory, and Politics: The Fate of the Film *All Quiet on the Western Front*," *Central European History* 13 no. 1 (1980): 60–82.

30. "Klinkhammer-Prozeß in Düsseldorf," *Kölnische Rundschau* (16 October 1952). Father Klinkhammer was arrested and accused of disturbing the public peace, disseminating stinkbombs, and impeding police activity. Klinkhammer countered that the police physically and verbally

of blaming the film itself for domestic unrest, charging that it, not the protestors, posed a "threat to democracy" and the German nation.

The rallying point for this campaign was "Christian morality," and generalized rhetoric centered on the "good," "true humanity," and "honor," all values with unimpeachable appeal. Yet in the heat of the Cold War, concepts like "Christian morality" and the "Christian West" had more than an ethical appeal: they had a political thrust. Indeed, a church message in Osnabrück entitled "exemplary Soviet Union" praised that nation's lack of erotic decadence in the press, commenting pointedly that one shouldn't be surprised if those "unbroken youths someday become masters of the lustful boys" in the West.[31] Such pronouncements played upon the anticommunist sentiments prevalent among Catholics, to create an atmosphere of moral and political crisis. And the source of that crisis was identified with the burgeoning commercial culture which accompanied the democratization of West Germany, and with the avid consumption of the messages and values implicit in that culture.

Filmwirkung and Social Conservatism

"Cr[ying] out from a plagued heart" shortly after he resigned his seat on the censorship board, Hess inquired "who will help hinder such spiritual murder of our young people and women, tested by suffering, and our broken-bodied men?"[32] The question was rhetorical: it was clear from its source which institutions would claim the leadership of such a campaign. But the peculiarity of the images conjured in his question, of violence and ruin, of gender and generation, bears further scrutiny.

Hess explained that his resignation was a necessary response because the film "called into question the last vital forces of morality during a time of distress for our *Volk*."[33] The assumption was that the film itself was to blame; that it, by working directly on the mind of the viewer, could influence individual desire and social behavior, thus corrupting the "spiritual" health of the fatigued and susceptible national community and shredding the weak moral fibers which held it together.

The rhetoric of conservative cultural critics reveals that they considered women and youth to be most susceptible to the attractions and "insidious" influences of film and commercial culture. This appears in such images as "the

---

abused him due to their antireligious bias. He explained that he was stimulated to act against the film after he had heard the cardinal of Cologne's pastoral letter and sermon calling for the defense of the Church. The article noted that the cardinal had not objected to Klinkhammer's behavior in this instance.

31. Quoted in Eisenführ, 281.

32. From a film review by Anton Kochs in the *Evangelischer Filmbeobachter* no. 3 (February 1, 1951) as quoted in Eisenführ, 247.

33. Quoted in Eisenführ, 243.

lustful boys in the West" falling prey to the "unbroken boys in the East" and in the widely held opinion that mothers could not be trusted with the regulation of their own children's film attendance. This state of affairs was used as justification for moral intervention by an outside authority, be it church or state. A letter from the Office of the President of Upper Bavaria to the Bavarian Ministry of Education and Culture maintained, that

> [a]s much as one, at this time, may greatly dread . . . that which smacks of censorship, a means and a way must be found to redress this deplorable state of affairs, which exposes the already greatly endangered youth to further dangers. This is not served by appealing to the reason of parents . . . [b]ecause experience shows that parents oftentimes lack the necessary understanding. . . . Otherwise it would not happen that mothers appear at film screenings with small children in their arms.[34]

How could one expect "parents," more specifically, mothers, to be responsible for the moral development of their charges, when the mothers themselves were seduced by the very source of the corruption?

What emerges from such rhetoric is the fear that postwar German women were at least in part unable to fulfill their social and moral mission as mothers. One consequence of this was the curious spectacle, in February 1951, of activist (male) priests recruiting armies of schoolboys and leading them onto the streets across West Germany, demanding a new public morality and the "protection of our women's honor."[35] Their espousal of the concept of *Filmwirkung*,[36] with its corollary notion of the film itself as agent, allowed church leaders to characterize their mobilization as defensive. In the words of Cardinal Frings, which rang from the pulpit on Palm Sunday, 1951: "If nothing else works, we will embrace self-defense!"[37]

The rhetoric of "defense" remained, for the most part, overtly apolitical, lodged in the preservation of traditional values of home, family, and "woman's honor." Yet after 1945, this line was highly political and framed the debates over the reconstruction of gender relations and the position of women in the new democracy, as well as in the home.[38] Church and state leaders energetically assumed the task of reconstructing stable social relations after the disruption

---

34. BayHStA MK 51766, letter from Regierungspräsident, Oberbayern, to Bayerisches Staatsministerium für Unterricht und Kultus, 4 March 1947.

35. Eisenführ, 264.

36. Noltenius, 85. The ideal of *Filmwirkung* was not new to this postwar period, nor peculiar to the churches. Film censorship, since the *Reichslichtspielgesetz* of 1920, was justified on the basis of potential moral degradation of the viewer as well as "later, potentially illegal or otherwise disapproved of actions of the viewer under the influence of film."

37. Eisenführ, 299.

38. See Robert Moeller, "Reconstructing the Family in Reconstruction Germany: Women and Social Policy in the Federal Republic, 1949–1955," *Feminist Studies* 15 no. 1 (Spring 1989):

caused by the war, and a prime concern was the redomestication of women, as well as the reestablishment of the normative family and the ideology of motherhood.[39]

These priorities were considered particularly pressing well into the 1950s. In the beginning of the decade, just over half of all West Germans lived in "intact families"[40]; the divorce rate was high and would continue to rise for several more years. Furthermore, in 1950, even "after most prisoners-of-war had returned, nearly one-third of the slightly more than fifteen million German households were headed by divorced women or widows." In those cases in which a man was present in the household, he was "often physically or psychologically scarred, unwilling or unable to work, or disqualified from some jobs because of [his] National Socialist loyalties."[41] He could not, therefore, easily resume his traditionally defined social role as husband or father. The familiar social order was threatened.

Die Sünderin exemplified that threat by depicting a woman, outside of the traditional family arrangement, who could boast a measure of economic independence, who exhibited a materialist streak in her clothing and furnishings, and who controlled, and at times marketed, her sexuality. Here was a woman who literally abandoned the family for the marketplace and the culture of consumption.

In the film, prostitution brings no decline in economic status for Marina. In fact, it initially intensifies desire and provides access to clothing and jewelry previously possessed only in a limited amount by her mother. Furthermore it bestows knowledge, satisfies her sexual curiosity, and teaches her, from her first sexual encounter, that "she could gain power over men."

Marina gains economic independence, indeed wealth, by playing on the desires of military officers (Nazi and American) and society men. The film presents a secularized vision of the world: Marina moves from one urban setting to another (Hamburg, Munich, Vienna), acquiring material finery. The film

---

137–69. While I find his argument convincing that German sociology and family policy was predicated on the assumptions that women's proper place was in the home, not out in the labor force, that "it was . . . women's responsibility to raise children to resist the consumer temptations that the economic miracle offered . . . [and] inculcat[e] children with the right values," I would argue that there were lingering misgivings and feelings of ambivalence among traditional (male) political and religious leaders regarding the ability of women to suppress their own desires and fascination with consumer society in order to fulfill their moral and social mission. For further discussion of this point, see Fehrenbach, *Cinema in Democratizing Germany*.

39. Angela Vogel, "Familie," *Die Bundesrepublik Deutschland. Band 2: Gesellschaft*, ed. Wolfgang Benz (Frankfurt a.M.: Fischer Taschenbuch Verlag, 1985), 98–126; and Moeller, "Reconstructing the Family," 137–69.

40. Vogel, 99.

41. Moeller, 140. Also Sibylle Meyer and Eva Schulze, *Von Liebe sprach damals keiner. Familienalltag in der Nachkriegszeit* (Munich: C.H. Beck Verlag, 1985).

could be interpreted as creating the desire for consumer goods and a cosmopolitan life-style at a time when the bishop of Würzburg was demanding that legal means be adopted to ban films "meant to enervate the body of the *Volk* and, particularly in the villages, to encourage flight from the land."[42]

Conservative critics also objected to Marina's high degree of sexual independence. Her extramarital relations included, shockingly, sexual relations with her stepbrother and a long-term adulterous relationship with Alexander, who, while separated, was still married to another woman. The free use by an independent woman of her own sexuality was a theme that caused deep disturbance among conservative political and religious leaders, and one which was not peculiar to *Die Sünderin*. Officials at the Bavarian State Youth Office were outraged by a report they received from the *Regierungspräsident* of Upper Bavaria, which quoted an advertisement that had been making the rounds in local newspapers, for the Italian film *Bitter Rice:*

> . . . 17 year old Silvano Mangano [*sic*], discovered for this film, the overnight sensation, the nubile Roman girl! A young woman, without inhibitions, totally natural, without shame! Silvano Mangano [*sic*], the erotic super-atomic bomb—in a stormy, passionate, tumultuous film. Everybody wants to see her—Silvano Mangano [*sic*]![43]

The author of the report questioned how their social programs could successfully "place a 17-year-old girl in a home or under protective supervision for moral degeneracy, while 'girls without inhibitions and . . . shame' are at the same time being publicly prized." The problem that faced the churches was how to make mothers and daughters once again out of war-shattered women, how to corral German women back into the newly reconstructed home. Films, like *Bitter Rice* and *Die Sünderin*, which openly celebrated sexuality, were perceived as grave dangers to this effort.

Germans flocked to the cinema to watch *Die Sünderin*, despite, or perhaps because of, widespread clerical campaigning against the film and the difficulty of viewing it in many localities. Enough people ignored the churches' proscription to make it the most popular German film in the Federal Republic in 1951.[44] Simple curiosity spurred by church sermons and reports in the press may account for its overwhelming popularity, yet film viewing as a method of

42. BayHStA MK 51766. Copy of letter from Bischöfliches Ordinariat Würzburg to Dr. Hans Ehard, Bayerischer Ministerpräsident, 6 March 1951.

43. BayHStA MK 51766. Copy of Letter from Dr. Kneuer, Regierungspräsident Oberbayern to the Bayerische Landesjugendamt, 24 April 1951. Kneuer likely had no first-hand knowledge of the film, *Bitter Rice*, nor its notorious star, Silvana Mangano, to judge from the consistency with which her name was misspelled throughout the letter.

44. *Filmblätter* no. 4 (26 January 1951): 78.

resistance to the circumscription of civil liberties surfaced in various locations. Perhaps the most dramatic show of disapproval occurred in the Bavarian city of Regensburg, where thousands of citizens gathered in front of the town hall for two consecutive evenings to protest the actions of local priests against *Die Sünderin* and the mayor's decision to ban the film. The pro-film demonstrators milled around peacefully until the police, who were equipped with steel helmets and rifles, began pushing into the crowd with their nightsticks. Radicalized by the violence, the indignant citizens cried out, "What about democracy?" and "Down with the Black dictatorship!" and marched to the film theater to protest the prohibition of the film. On the way through town, demonstrators broke the windows of a clergyman's house.[45] The strength of the new democracy was being tested, and in this case it was found to be sadly lacking.

Certainly these actions demonstrate that the churches' power was by no means consolidated and unquestioned, even in Bavarian towns known for their robust Catholicism.[46] The position and role of the churches in the new democracy remained an object of intense debate. Certain sectors of the German public rejected the churches as cultural arbiters and refused to obey restrictions on leisure activity and cultural consumption imposed by local religious and governmental authorities. And while the level of political organization remained neophyte, one can assume, on the basis of the Regensburg example, that the churches did not serve as the unequivocal voice of the masses. In fact, the strong voice of the informal, socially conservative church-state coalition in cultural matters was challenged, in this case, as an infringement on the population's new constitutional rights.

The dramatic tactics of the confessional campaign against the film were also criticized as undemocratic in the more liberal press as well as in film trade papers. Perhaps one can suspect the impartiality of the trade paper for German cinema owners which condemned the "mob-like practices" of Catholic groups by charging that their efforts "[t]o disrupt the guarantees of constitutional law is a crime against the *Volk* and against our young democratic state."[47] But criticisms of Hess's and Kochs's walkout from the FSK by nontrade papers called into question the political loyalties of church leaders and their vision of where they fit in the new democracy:

---

45. Eisenführ, 263–80.

46. Counterprotests surfaced in other Bavarian towns as well. In Weissenburg, disgruntled viewers forced the theater owner to show *Die Sünderin* against his will; and in Freising, where the film was banned, a group of people took a bus to Munich to see it. Told there that admission tickets had been sold out, they continued on to Garmisch-Partenkirchen, where they fulfilled their mission, and where, by the way, half of the population had seen the film. These incidents were harvested from local newspaper accounts by Eisenführ, 283–84.

47. "Schutz zugelassener Filmvorführungen," *Film-Echo* 5, Sonderausgabe (30 January 1951): 97.

[The FSK] . . . is supposed to be a democratic forum, a true parliament; but today who sits in a democratic parliament if he believes he has to resign his seat as soon as his view has not prevailed?[48]

The implication was that the churches had to adjust to the democratic system, to the condition of being just one interest group among many.

The Protestant response to this type of criticism was not to deny the charges but to subvert them. Agreeing that the FSK was a democratic institution, a Protestant commentator and pastor then questioned whether it was proper that the Christian churches possessed only one vote out of fifteen (on the Main Committee), given the fact that the body dealt with issues crucial to "the foundation of Christian belief." He went further, suggesting that the matter went beyond democratic politics:

This does not concern an attempt of the church to secure power, but rather the understanding that the Ten Commandments, which the Church must preach, can never be subjugated to a democratic vote.[49]

Industry Reaction and the Threat of Cultural Provincialism

Ecclesiastical attacks on the film's content, based on the concept of *Wirkung*, were interpreted by members of the film industry as threatening to the very existence of a national cinema. From the beginning of the controversy, Willi Forst defined the issue for German filmmakers when he asked: "Will there ever again be a German film?" The economic strength of the German film industry had been severely weakened by the war and Allied regulation. Studio space had been "lost" to the Russians or destroyed, film raw stock was difficult to secure, and Allied licensing of new production had been slow and stringent. Even when these political and material hindrances were alleviated, German film companies continued to have great difficulty securing funding for production.

The situation was even bleaker with regard to the international marketing of German films. The export of German films outside of Central Europe declined drastically during the 1930s. Economic autarky and ideological considerations under Hitler dictated that foreign productions be excluded from the German market. Affected countries responded in kind, closing their markets to German films. The industry suffered a further blow in the aftermath of the war when American officials insisted on the breakup of the powerful UFA

---

48. Quoted from *Münchner Merkur* in "Presse-Echo zur . . ." *Film-Echo* 5, Sonderausgabe (30 January 1951): 98.

49. Pfarrer Robert Geisendörfer, "Filmselbstkontrolle ohne Evangelische Kirche?" *Evangelischer Film-Beobachter* 2 no. 3 (1 February 1951): 18.

film concern, which resulted in the proliferation of small, and often economically unviable, production companies. Postwar German film companies engaged in a life and death struggle to win back a portion of the international market. And in order to accomplish this goal, they needed a stronger economic base as well as a cosmopolitan look. The issue here was not merely the intellectual and moral content of future German film production, but industry survival and international competitiveness as well.[50]

Industry representatives correctly expected that the churches' fight for a narrowly defined Christian culture, with its limitations on film content and form, would produce "provincial" pictures which would be difficult to peddle on anything other than the domestic market. Industry spokesmen attacked church initiatives as interventionist and unconstitutional, charging that they infringed upon freedom of opinion, the press, and artistic expression. The industry had much to lose if the vision of a church-mediated culture triumphed.

After the premier of his film in Frankfurt, Forst asked the press not to create more chaos by opposing the release of his film, for fear that the future would then beget only the "Third Black Forest Girl from the right," a new hybrid combining the worst of the old UFA film genres.[51] Comparing his film to those on the international market, and to Italian, French, and American films released in West Germany, Forst maintained that his film was "suitable for showing at a children's matinee."[52] This bit of hyperbole conveyed the perception of filmmakers that moral censorship by the churches in West Germany was excessive and potentially fatal to the reestablishment of an internationally competitive industry.

---

50. For discussions of the postwar reconstruction of the German film industry, see: Peter Pleyer, *Deutscher Nachkriegsfilm 1946–1948* (Münster: Verlag C.J. Fahle, 1965); Klaus Kreimeier, *Kino and Filmindustrie in der BRD. Ideologieproduktion und Klassenwirklichkeit nach 1945* (Kronberg: Scriptor Verlag, 1973); Wilfried von Bredow and Rolf Zurek, eds., *Film und Gesellschaft in Deutschland. Dokumente und Materialien* (Hamburg: Hoffmann und Campe Verlag, 1975), 237–371; Wilhelm Heerman, *Die Entwicklung der deutschen Filmwirtschaft von 1945 bis 1955* (Universität Osnabrück, Fachbereich 7: Kommunikation/Ästhetik, 1983 unveröffentlicht); Thomas Guback, *The International Film Industry: Western Europe and America Since 1945* (Bloomington: Indiana University Press, 1969); and Rentschler, "Germany: The Past That Would Not Go Away."

51. Forst's pejorative comment was a play on words which merged the titles of two popular, current German films: *Black Forest Girl (Schwarzwaldmädel)*, a sentimental *Heimatfilm* of the previous year, which celebrated the unspoiled beauty of the Black Forest, local traditions, and the rural life, with *Third from the Right (Dritte von Rechts)*, which was part detective film, part musical revue. See "Der Strudel," *Filmblätter* no. 4 (26 January 1951): 79 and "Lassen Sie mich nicht in Stich," *Film-Echo* 5 no. 4 (27 January 1951): 74. Also Richard C. Helt and Marie E. Helt, *West German Cinema since 1945: A Reference Handbook.* (Metuchen, N.J.: Scarecrow Press, 1987), 111.

52. Quoted in *Film Echo* 5 no. 4 (27 January 1951): 74.

Curiously, filmmakers and industry officials never launched a major effort to refute the theory of *Filmwirkung*, but typically sought to establish the reasons a particular film could not be considered dangerous to an average viewer. They did, however, question the motives and mentalities of moral critics. In a handwritten note in the confidential files of the FSK, industry representative Fritz Podehl rhetorically asked:

> How tainted must those be, who assume that the viewers of such a film, also the younger ones among them, could be induced either to become a prostitute, or kill a suffering relative, or to commit suicide. The morally healthy could not possibly react with the wish to imitate.[53]

But the churches did not need to address the issue of film's effect on a society that was healthy, morally or otherwise. In a postwar Germany inhabited by victims of material want, physical weakness, psychical despondency, and moral decay, the vulnerability of the population was assumed. By stressing these exceptional social and moral conditions in West Germany, they sought to create in the public a sense that the social order was so precarious and tenuous that even a single film could jeopardize its existence.

The "Sünderin" Aftermath: Industry Capitulation and the Triumph of the Christian (Democratic) West

Although the content and artistic value of *Die Sünderin* continued to be criticized in the press and in angry letters to state ministries, public debates rapidly transcended the disputed film and focused on the validity of the current form of film censorship and subsidization.[54] At stake was the issue of who should control and regulate the resurgent national culture and the principles upon which such control should be based.

The most obvious target for reform was the censorship body in which the conflict began. Hess's resignation from the board was a sign of his strong dissatisfaction with its methods of operation and the tendency of licensing decisions to favor the position of the film industry. He complained that the "public voice" in the decision-making process was disproportionately small, and that church participation on the board was being exploited by the industry to serve "propagandistic purposes".

When joined by Kochs, Hess's action challenged the board's claim that its censorship activity was an outgrowth of public consensus. This situation was

---

53. Notes on *"Die Sünderin"* from confidential papers of the FSK, quoted in Eisenführ, 240.

54. Eisenführ, 247–49.

further exacerbated when at least one state representative withdrew from the FSK in a show of solidarity with the clerics.[55] Several days later Protestant and Catholic representatives met with industry representatives to affirm their willingness to work with the censorship board, provided certain reforms were made.

This gesture of reconciliation caused industry representatives to declare that there would be "no *Kulturkampf* . . . neither now nor later." Film trade papers pointedly reminded readers that the resignation of church representatives had not disrupted the operation of the censorship board; film screenings and evaluations continued.[56] This fact may have led to the clerics' sudden moderation. In any event, the churches had apparently reached the limits of their subversion of the FSK.

Despite the triumphant tone of the film trade press, the industry was ultimately forced to capitulate to demands for a stronger "public voice" in the censorship body, due to pressure applied by the State Ministries of Culture.[57] Although the demands of the churches were not met in toto, the final settlement established a parity between industry and public representatives on the Working Committee, which evaluated films for release.[58] Indeed, due to the modifications in the censorship board, the "public voice" was essentially represented by only one party: the Christian Democrats.[59]

The *Sünderin* controversy also set off a wave of demands on the federal government by local and state officials to tighten up the criteria for the public credit (*Bürgschaften*) for film projects. The day after Werner Hess resigned from the FSK, journalists and parliamentary representatives walked out of a special screening of the film in Bonn to protest the use of public funds for its production.[60] The press quickly took up this line of argument and demanded that stricter moral criteria be instituted for films receiving public funds.

In 1950, government officials had finally addressed the industry's financial problems by creating a system of state (and later federal) support designed to bolster the production of German films that could compete on the international market. This was largely intended as a method to increase export revenues. In the first year, 1950–51, 75 percent of all German feature films

---

55. Eisenführ, 253–54. This individual was Professor Walter Hagemann, CDU founder, noted film sociologist at the University of Münster, director of the Institut für Publizistik, and representative for the state of North Rhine Westphalia.

56. See *Film-Echo* 5, Sonderausgabe (30 January 1951): 97.

57. Eisenführ, 313–21.

58. The number of members on the Working Committee was increased to eight, four of whom now came from the "public sector." These four seats were distributed to the Catholic and Evangelical churches and the Jewish religious community (in alternation); State Ministries of Culture; the federal youth office; and for the first time, the federal government.

59. Eisenführ, 313–20. See also *Film-Echo* 5, Sonderausgabe (30 January 1951): 97–99.

60. Eisenführ, 251.

were supported by state or federal funds;[61] Willi Forst's film *Die Sünderin* was one of them.[62]

These credit programs gave state and federal governments a strong voice in film production. This voice was not, however, one of moral authority. The regulation of film credit fell to the state and federal Ministries of Economics, a situation which lead to interministry squabbling. In Bavaria, for example, Cultural Ministry officials fought for inclusion in the decision-making process, but were rebuffed by Economics Ministry officials, who indicated that credit decisions would be based strictly on financial and profit considerations. Issues of moral content would not be entertained.[63]

Interestingly, it is probable that this position led to the funding of *Die Sünderin*. Willi Forst was a well-known filmmaker from the Nazi period, and the credit commissions screened for both professional experience and the likelihood of a film's commercial success. This method of assessment led to financial support for "sure bets" like Forst, a situation which reinforced the continuation of the same worn-out genres and technically polished, but artistically disappointing, films which were produced by UFA.[64]

Consequently, financial credit was not extended to innovative or experimental films, but to the comfortably familiar. Chairman Rudolf Vogel of the Parliamentary Committee for Press, Radio and Film in Bonn insisted that:

> The German film, as in earlier times . . . possesses a great possibility for the future if it once again returns to . . . musicals, landscape films, and *Kulturfilme* and thereby achieves that which is rightfully expected of it by foreigners based on its earlier tradition.[65]

Government representatives never believed in a *Stunde Null* in terms of film style and genre, but assumed that the industry should resume production based upon the historical "specialization" of the German film industry in the world

---

61. Willi Höfig, *Der Deutsche Heimatfilm 1947–1960* (Stuttgart: Ferdinand Enke Verlag, 1973), 88–90. Also Wilfred von Bredow and Rolf Zurek, eds., "Neuanfang und Kontinuität nach 1945," *Film und Gesellschaft in Deutschland*, 239–47.

62. Ironically, the public funds in this case had been well invested, and the government did not lose a groschen. The film was an immense success, seen by an estimated 6.5 million Germans. See Claudius Seidl, *Der deutsche Film der fünfziger Jahre* (Munich: Wilhelm Heyne Verlag, 1987), 180, and Eisenführ, 301.

63. "Gemeinwohl geht vor Individualismus" in the Presse Archiv Sammlung der Bayerischen Staatsregierung no. 17, 1950; and BayHStA MK 51766.

64. Eisenführ pointed with irony to the possibility that Willi Forst's reputation for making musicals during the Third Reich may have contributed to the decision to subsidize his film. Eisenführ, 8.

65. Quoted in Eisenführ, 7.

market and in line with "the old UFA tradition," a strategy which would fail them this time around.[66]

Stymied by the application of purely economic criteria to credit decisions made by the Economics Ministry, the Cultural Ministries created their own economic incentive but dispensed it according to ideological criteria. In 1951, the German *Länder* created a Film Rating Board of the German States (*Filmbewertungsstelle der Länder*, later *Filmbewertungstelle Wiesbaden*).[67] This body had no mandatory authority over film content but was authorized to grant significant tax breaks to the producers of approved films.[68] In practice, it supplemented the censorship functions of the FSK by encouraging the production of old-style, seemingly apolitical feature films. This shaped an "acceptable" if provincial style of filmmaking, which might have satisfied some political and social conservatives but reinforced the scorn of serious film critics and the indifference—indeed, disinterest—of international distributors and audiences.

The final stroke was administered later that year when Catholic bishops called for the creation of *Filmliga*, or film leagues, in every diocese throughout the country. Membership in the *Filmliga* was voluntary but required one to take an oath not to attend films which were rejected by the Catholic Film Commission and to support those they endorsed.[69]

---

66. A decade later, in 1962, the "angry young men" at Oberhausen were reacting against the formal, ideological, and economic constraints of the reconstructed domestic film industry when they issued their Manifesto. For a discussion of the rebirth of film culture after National Socialism, the "Oberhauseners'" evaluation of the cinematic status quo, and of the importance of their experiences in the German film club movement and film festivals for the formulation of their critical stances vis-à-vis postwar cultural politics, see, for example, Anne Paech, "Schule der Zuschauer. Zur Geschichte der deutschen Film Club-Bewegung," *Zwischen Gestern und Morgen. Westdeutscher Nachkriegsfilm 1946–1962* (Frankfurt: Deutsches Filmmuseum, 1989); Fernand Jung, "Das Kino der frühen Jahre. Herbert Vesely und die Filmavantgarde der Bundesrepublik," *Zwischen Gestern und Morgen*; and chapters four and five of Fehrenbach, *Cinema in Democratizing Germany*.

67. The FBW began operation on 20 August 1951, but had been under discussion by the German states since 1950. The actual proposal for a state-sponsored film rating board with national jurisdiction occurred only in April 1951, no doubt spurred by the *Sünderin* affair. George Roeber and G. Jacoby, *Handbuch der filmwirtschaftlichen Medienbereiche. Die wirtschaftlichen Erscheinungsformen des Films auf den Gebieten der Unterhaltung, der Werbung, der Bildung und des Fernsehens* (Pullach, 1973), 483–87.

68. Hermann Krings, *Was heißt wertvoll. Über Grundlagen und Maßstab der Filmbewertung*, 2. Auflage. (Wiesbaden-Biebrich: Der Filmbewertungsstelle Wiesbaden, 1961), 14–17; H.G. Pflaum and H.H. Prinzler, *Film in der Bundesrepublik Deutschland* (Munich: Carl Hanser Verlag, 1979), 105–6; Roeber, 483–87; and Anton Kochs, "Kirche und Film in Westdeutschland," *International Film Revue* 1 (1951–52): 289. The evaluation board of the FBW was comprised of government officials (40 percent), professionals (*freie Berufe*) (30 percent), film journalists (19 percent), and representatives of the film industry (11 percent). The churches were also represented in the body in an advisory capacity.

69. Quoted in Bühler, 42.

Characterized as a *"Volks* movement," the leagues were intended to counter "the highly organized film industry with a correspondingly highly organized consumer group."[70] And although the trade association for the film industry strenuously protested the creation of the *Filmliga*, the campaign apparently worked. Membership in the *Filmliga* rose from one million in 1951 to three million the following year.[71] Furthermore, the strength of this "consumer group" pressured the German film industry to produce films which were morally and socially unobjectionable to the Catholic Film Office throughout the 1950s.

Transgressions proved costly. A negative rating in the Catholic film journal *Filmdienst* typically resulted in public rejection of the film outside of the major German cities.[72] In smaller towns and rural villages, attendance at a film rejected by the Catholic film press could lead to public censure and suspicion of one's moral character. The clergy in the small Catholic towns of Alt- and Neuötting in Bavaria, for example, attempted to coerce public behavior during the *Sünderin* campaign by insisting that those "who attended a film which glorified prostitutes, betrayed a prostitute's spirit."[73] Film attendance was perceived as implied support for the values and messages the film allegedly conveyed. In this schema, consumption revealed character.[74]

Did the church leadership fear that consumption would replace contrition, religious or otherwise? Certainly they were reacting to both consumer culture and the political novelty of democracy. Their goal was somehow to stabilize their position and survive the onslaught of both. They did so by mediating between the media and the public. Public debates, pronouncements, and lobbying all served to determine the types of films screened in cinemas and to color the way German audiences interpreted what they saw, and indeed the ways they decided what to see.

---

70. P. Max Gritschneder S.J., "Bilanz der katholischen Filmarbeit," *Petrusblatt* (15 July 1952).

71. These figures are quoted in Bühler, 42. See also "Die Ziele der Katholischen Filmliga," *Nürnberger Nachrichten* (4 July 1951); P. Max Gritschneder, S.J., "Bilanz der katholischen Filmarbeit," *Petrusblatt* (15 July 1952); "Wo liegen die Grenzen?," *Filmwoche* (10 May 1952); "Hirtenwort der deutschen Bischöfe zur Filmfrage," BayHStA MK 51763; and Eisenführ, 303–4. The Evangelical Church also founded a similar organization, the *Filmgilde*, with less public fanfare and fewer members. For an explanation of the organization and activities of the *Filmgilde*, see Werner Hess, "Evangelische Filmgilde," *Kirche und Film* 21 (1 November 1951): 4.

72. An article in *Kirche und Film* in 1954 noted that "between 30 to 35 percent of all theater owners could no longer decide to screen films which have been rejected by one of the two churches [Catholic or Evangelical]; in small cities and rural areas this percentage has already reached 45 percent." Furthermore, distributors estimated that films rejected by the churches showed profits of up to a third less than what otherwise would have been expected. See "Kirchliche 'Streitmacht für den guten Film'" in *Kirche und Film* 4 (April 1954): 7.

73. Quoted in Eisenführ, 294.

74. For a discussion of film viewing as consumption, see Jeanne Allen, "The Film Viewer as Consumer," *Quarterly Review of Film Studies* 5 no. 4 (Fall 1980): 481–500.

Church influence in film affairs was much greater after 1945 than it had been at any time previously. The churches adroitly capitalized on the circumstances of the early postwar period, bolstering their initially strong position as the sole remaining institutions in defeated Germany, forging close ties with the reigning Christian Democratic Party, encouraging lay involvement in party politics, and crafting their rhetoric to underscore the need to protect the national community during a time of exceptional material and moral crisis. Through these means, the churches claimed a prominent role in German cultural reconstruction. In effect, religious leaders were able to achieve after 1945 what they had been striving for with little success since the early 1920s: sustained influence over the types of films produced and marketed in West Germany. By 1951, the structure for church influence was in place, and throughout the Adenauer era there was no need to launch a campaign similar in scale or passion to that launched against *Die Sünderin*.

Yet industry charges that the churches alone were to blame for German cultural provincialism remain problematic. The industry exhibited little tendency to produce socially or formally innovative work prior to 1951 and rarely attempted to confront political and social issues outside of the melodramatic form. Willi Forst, in spite of his call for a new type of German film, never delivered on his word, and shortly afterward resorted to making his own *Heimatfilm*, which was released the year after *Die Sünderin*.[75]

The peculiarly German genre of the *Heimatfilm*, the picture "postcard panorama" set in the rural hills of the Black Forest or the heathered fields of the *Lüneberger Heide*, featuring close-knit communities and townsfolk in traditional dress, became the staple fare of West German cinema during the 1950s. Fully one fifth of all German film production was devoted to this genre.[76]

Heimatfilme were popular entertainment as well and provided postwar Germans with "a strikingly authentic reverse image of the period":

Untouched nature replaces ruined cities, church bells resound instead of ubiquitous jackhammers, quaint panel houses offer a hominess the city's ugly and quickly erected concrete edifices could not.[77]

Yet perhaps more importantly, these films provided Germans the opportunity to participate, for a couple of hours, in a never-never land of lost German tradition. *Heimatfilme* always contained the requisite village festival or dance celebrating

---

75. The film, *Im Weißen Rößl*, filmed at Wolfgangsee in the Austrian Salzkammergut, was released in 1952.

76. Rentschler, 215. Also see Seidl, 52–102; Gerhard Bliersbach, *So Grün war die Heide* (Weinheim: Beltz Verlag, 1985); and Höfig, *Der Deutsche Heimatfilm 1947–1960*.

77. Rentschler, 215.

local traditions and community ties, inviting the audience to visually participate in the ritual. In large measure, the *Heimatfilm* itself "reinvented" a reassuring, though not necessarily "authentic," German tradition for consumption by the postwar German viewer.[78]

Heimatfilme presented a conservative and sometimes reactionary agenda for social, and particularly gender, relations. Metaphorically speaking, they portray the social and spiritual redemption of Marina, the heroine of *Die Sünderin*. In a typical *Heimatfilm*, a female city dweller makes a foray into the countryside to visit an elderly relative. There she experiences a conversion of sorts and becomes initiated into the ways of the local community, falling in love with some strapping, nature-loving woodsman or country squire. He stands in sharp contrast to her effete, urban boyfriend, who disturbs the peace of the countryside and village life with the intrusive noise of his sportscar and his disrespectful ways. Often she must return to the city to fully recognize that she belongs with the morally solid countryfolk, insulated from technological and social change by their strong notions of moral and social order. Ultimately, she forsakes the city, with its jazz music and mass culture, and returns to the slow pace of the closed community. She abandons the marketplace for the home, affirming tradition over innovation, religion over secularization, and community over autonomy.

Heimatfilm, the reigning film genre of the 1950s, reinforced the conservative agenda for the social reconstruction of postwar Germany. Indeed, there would be no more *Sünderins* in store for German audiences in the 1950s; rather, the traditional escapist and "politically-insidious" *Heimatfilm*, first popularized under the Nazis, would become the national product of Bonn.

---

78. See Eric Hobsbawm, "Introduction: Inventing Traditions," *The Invention of Tradition*, eds. E. Hobsbawm and T. Ranger (New York: Cambridge University Press, 1988), 1–14. Also David Thelen, "Memory and American History," in *The Journal of American History* 75 no. 4 (March 1989): 1117–29.

Alice in the Consumer Wonderland: West German Case Studies in Gender and Consumer Culture

Erica Carter

Changing Gear: A Reappraisal of the Politics of Style

People say . . . well, what don't they say about teenagers?! They start with the accusation that we have no manners or sense of good behaviour, and that we're hopelessly lacking in all religious belief. Then we are told off, either for dressing too sloppily, or looking too old for our age . . . 'Either', we are told, 'you run around like tramps in floppy jackets buttoned up at the back and drainpipe trousers which are far too tight—or else you slavishly follow the latest fashion trends'.

We would like for once to give our point of view . . . We teenagers have our own style. And that's what makes many people see red. (Advertisement for 'Triumph' underwear, *Bravo* magazine, no. 42, 1958)

Since the beginning of the 1970s, theorists of youth subcultures in Britain have appropriated the notion of 'style' from marketers of teenage fashion commodities, and mobilised it for their studies of oppositional subcultures in the postwar period. Recalling a tradition of cultural studies which reaches back to Richard Hoggart's *Uses of Literacy* (Hoggart 1958), early analysts of subcultural deviance and opposition[1] seem implicitly to share his distaste for the

My thanks are due to Brigit Cramon-Daiber, Ryszard Gagola, Angela McRobbie, and Maureen McNeil, whose critical comments and eminently helpful suggestions have been incorporated at various stages in the writing of this article.

1. The seminal work in this field was Phil Cohen's 1972 study of "Subcultural Conflict and Working-class Community" (Cohen 1972). Other works to which both explicit and implicit reference will be made in the following pages include Hall and Jefferson 1976, Hebdige 1979 and Willis 1977.

plastic glamour of commercialised youth culture; their gaze falls rather on visible subversions of dominant forms. The discordant notes sounded by Teds, rockers, mods, rastas or punks are seen to be pitched against the harmony of mass consumer culture; appropriating commodities from fashion, music and media industries, subcultural youths reassemble them into symbolic systems of their own which, if only at the moment of their birth, strike chords of disenchantment, rebellion and resistance. Like the phenomena which they examine, the analyses themselves are founded on a number of unspoken oppositions: conformity and resistance, harmony and rupture, passivity and activity, consumption and appropriation, femininity and masculinity.

In a discussion of sexism amongst the working-class lads of his 'Hammertown' study, Paul Willis finds himself slipping with ease into the discourse of consumerism.

> The male counter-school culture promotes its own sexism—even celebrates it as part of its overall confidence. Girls are pursued, sometimes roughly, for their sexual favours, often dropped and labeled 'loose' when they are given. Girls are asked to be sexy and inviting as well as pure and monogamous; to be consumed and not be consumed. (Willis 1977, 146)

In a study from which girls are largely absent, the moment of their appearance is profoundly significant. Girls, it seems, are written into youth cultural theory in the language of consumption; initially—though not, as we shall see, of necessity—as objects for consumption by men. Under the regime of Althusserian structuralism in British cultural theory, this led to the perception of girls at best as an absence, a silence, a lack which could perhaps only be filled in some separate world of autonomous female culture. Ideology was an 'instance', consumption a 'sphere', severed from its tangled roots in the social institutions with which structuralism was primarily concerned—the family, ideology and the repressive State. Feminist researchers then turned towards the family as the pivotal point around which the existence of teenage girls revolved.

> If women are marginal to the male cultures of work (middle and working class) it is because they are central and pivotal to a subordinate area, which mirrors, but in a complementary and subordinate way, the 'dominant' masculine arenas. They are 'marginal' to work because they are central to the subordinate, complementary sphere of the family. (McRobbie and Garber 1976, 211)

Following working-class girls into the closed arena of the family allowed the researchers of female culture privileged insights into the possibilities of specifically female cultural forms. So-called 'bedroom culture' was analagous to

male subcultures, in that here too dominant signs and symbols were appropriated, reassembled and reproduced in homology[2] with an already existing set of
social relations. In male youth subcultures, these homologies existed between
the lived culture of a subordinate *class* and the symbolic systems through
which its members made that culture 'mean'. In bedroom culture, gender relations overlaid, overlapped and took precedence over relations of race and class.

Yet the search for autonomous female cultural forms in the bedroom hide-
aways of teenage girls has been consistently dogged by nagging doubts as to
the creative, productive and potentially subversive power of this mode of femininity. The study of 'teeny bopper culture', for example, was recognised as a
key which might unlock the potentialities of specifically female forms; on the
other hand, teenage adulation of male pop idols remained a symbol of the
'future general subordination' of adolescent girls (McRobbie and Garber 1976,
219). One problem with taking subculture theory as a starting point for studies
of female culture was that the homologies which 'profane culture' moulded
and shaped for itself were always performed—and more readily reformed at
the slightest hint of female autonomy—by an ever-watchful capitalist market.

The spectacle of working-class subcultures erupted into a yawning gap
between class relations as they are lived by working-class youth and the classless categories according to which capitalist markets are structured. Ever
since Warner's classic study of social class in America (Warner 1960) the marketing establishment has measured consumers against typological grids on
which 'class' appears primarily as an attribute of personal status and income;
working-class subcultures are, in part, a raucous rejection of a consumer culture which has continually repressed the seamier side of class subordination
from view. Gender, on the other hand, operates as a dominant variable for the
structuring of consumer groups. Thus not only have market researchers developed a vast apparatus of consumer surveillance which ensures the immediate
recuperation and reassimilation of new—or hitherto unheeded—facets of femininity; the 'image industries' (fashion, cosmetics, the female mass media)
have also consistently drawn on these marketing data to produce symbolic representations which fit skintight to female experiences. Hence the difference in
mood, tone and resonance of masculine and feminine revolts into style. Male
'semiological guerrillas' plunder the symbolic treasure chests of consumer culture, recreating their booty as signifiers of resistance whose signifier—the

---

2. The term *homology* is used in subcultural theory to describe the "degree of fit" between
the structure of group experience and the cultural forms through which that experience is expressed. Thus, for example, in Paul Willis's studies of hippy and bike-boy culture, the music of
each group was seen to exist in a relationship of homology with its lifestyle and values. "The preferred music must have the potential, at least in its formal structure, to express meanings which
resonate with other aspects of group life" (Willis, "The Cultural Meaning of Drug Use" in Hall and
Jefferson 1976, 106).

disaffection of subordinate class fractions—was until recently banished from the symbolic landscape of the teenage mass market. Conversely, even the un-pleasures of femininity find continual, if oblique, reflection in commodities on the female market, from perfect cures for the imperfections of the female body (slimming pills, aerobic outfits, beauty aids), to more expensive and corre-spondingly drastic remedies for the psychic ailments of the female condition—from nerve-tonics to psychoanalysis, with Babycham to add a touch of sparkle.

Deviance, resistance, autonomy, revolt: in the sociological tradition of the academic Left, these are located beyond the hostile walls of an impassive monolith—the Market. Analyses of subcultural style represented an attempt to freeze commodities-as-signifiers into fixed relations of subversive opposition; the (re)marketing of punk safety-pins and crazy-colour hairstyles was dubbed a 'recuperation'—silencing, defeat. The first punk safety-pin to spill off the end of the mass production line did indeed dislodge punk from its anchorage in the adolescent culture of the urban working classes; yet at the same time, it carried the meanings and values of punk into a wider field of teenage mass culture, where its progress has yet to be properly charted.

If subculture theory has traditionally remained standing somewhat suspi-ciously on the sidelines of commercial youth culture, the same has not always been true of research into girls' culture. Women researchers have had to plunge, head-on at times, into the seething morass of capital flows, emerging with a proliferation of critiques of the commodities which pattern the fabric of girls' lives: advertising images, fashionable clothes, mass magazines, popular fiction. In feminist theory too, the theoretical terrain for a re-engagement with market mechanisms has been prepared since the beginning of the break with Althusser and structuralism. The market is not an institution with rigidly de-fined (if consistently subverted) hierarchies, structures, orders and conventions; neither is it a tightly-knit subculture whose practices and rituals can be traced onto frozen 'maps of meaning'. It is instead a vast machine for the regulation of interconnecting circulatory flows: the flow of capital and labour through the production process, the flows of money, commodities, visual and textual signi-fiers through the circuits of consumption unlocked by capital.

Recognising market practices as constant and unbroken flows demands a similarly supple set of categories for their analysis; the homologies and oppo-sitions of structuralist symbolic deconstructions offer only one of many routes into the fragmented and splintered realities of female consumption. Shifting onto more fluid epistemological ground will not entail a feminist farewell to subcultures: charting the labyrinth of female market practices, we will be led to girls and women within *and* outside subcultures, all of whom participate in the regulation and organisation of market processes. The machine itself, if vast and apparently all-embracing, is never intrinsically monstrous; it is both manipulative and manipulated, controlled and controlling. Girls and women surface on a multitude of levels as both objects and agents of market processes; so, for example, the eighties boom in the second-hand rag trade owes its greatest debt to the 'nouvelle entrepreneuse' of New Wave subculture (and signals, incidentally, a successful attempt to divert fashion's commodity flows from their source in monopoly capitalist production).

An 'Archaeology' of Female Consumption

Across the landscape of post-war mass markets, female consumers, too, emerge both as 'objects' (of market research, advertising campaigns, sexual consumption by men) and as active agents in consumption processes. The work presented in the following pages—studies of specific instances of female 'consumer culture' in post-war West Germany—represents a first step towards a latter-day 'archaeology' of female consumption; an attempt to grasp and represent aspects of female consumerism in all their myriad complexities; and an appeal for the postponement of premature outrage at the 'co-option', 'recuperation', 'objectification' of women and girls in post-war consumer culture.

The nascent Federal Republic of Germany may seem an unlikely point of departure. Yet the very distance between areas of study (in this case, both geographical and conceptual in nature) forces the disruption of established modes of understanding, pointing the way towards potentially more fertile theoretical terrain. In the first instance, looking at German attempts to build a new democracy out of the shattered ruins of Germany's Nazi past can shed light on processes which, in Britain, took on less visible forms. Germany in 1945 lacked the cozy security of the cultural institutions in which British democratic values were founded—from fair play in English cricket to resonances of Empire in the British cup of tea. Analogous cultural forms and practices in post-war Germany resounded still with echoes of Nazism; meanwhile, the allied Western powers demanded tangible evidence of a decisive break with the totalitarian past. The West German constitution of 1949, then, was offered as an anchorage point for the fragile floating remnants of Weimar democracy; it contained, importantly, explicit guarantees of the equality of women and men before the law. The first section of the following study traces some of the processes whereby these constitutional promises came to be realised in the course of the 1950s. In practice, the explicit inscription of women as equal subjects in legal discourse as negotiated through their installation as consumers in a 'social market economy'; citizenship for women thus came to be defined through consumption on a capitalist mass market.

This, then, is a study of the ways in which the post-war market colonised and rooted itself in political discourses and institutions. The caesura of 1945 in Germany; attempts to suffocate a Nazi past under the cushion of consumer democracy; these may throw into sharper relief analogous developments in the consumerism of post-war Britain. Here as in Germany the middle-class house-wife enacted her political enfranchisement through the exercise of economic rationality: choosing to buy or not to buy, to spend or to save, to covet or to shun.

Certainly in 1950s West Germany, this was part of the 'political' future to which teenage girls were widely urged to aspire; at the same time, the expand-ing market in teenage leisure commodities transported adolescent consumption into a separate dimension of 'symbolic' and 'hedonistic' pleasures (Woods 1960). In the second section, then, I look at some aspects of fifties' leisure con-sumption for girls; at the symbolic systems of teenage lifestyles; and at one specific instance of female mass consumption: artificial 'silk' stockings for teenage girls. Heavily laden though nylons may be with predetermined 'sexist' meanings, a cool appraisal of the actual mode of their consumption reveals teenage girls engaged in the production of meanings and values more appropri-ate to their own needs. Nylon stockings, imported en masse from the USA, may appear simply as one of the more visible manifestations of American cultural hegemony. Yet a closer look at this one element in an emergent, and largely im-ported, teenage culture of consumption, points towards different questions to be asked of the process of consumption itself. Passive manipulation or active ap-propriation, escapist delusion or Utopian fantasy, consumerism can be all or none of these. The first step in its analysis is *rapprochement*, the dismantling of fronts in the youth cultural struggle, a recognition and reformulation of de-mands (our own included) for the pleasures which consumerism offers. 'Saying yes to the modern world is much more controversial and more provocative than saying no' (Freiwillige Selbstkontrolle, on West German rock).

Women and Girls in the Consumer Public

The history of the public sphere in Germany has been documented in detail by Habermas in his *Structural Change in the Public Sphere*, first published in Ger-many in 1962. In it he traces the history of the transition in Germany from the 'representative public' of feudal times, marked, not by the later strict division between public and private spheres, but by the investment of public status in particular representative figures—the aristocracy, representatives of the Church and of the Crown. In the transition to bourgeois society, 'public' and 'private' came to be understood as distinct and separate spheres, the family and the workplace being primary sites of 'private' activity, against which the notion of a public sphere was defined. *Öffentlichkeit* (the public sphere) becomes the field of public discourse within institutions which understand themselves as bearers of a 'public opinion', a dominant consensus to which members of soci-ety purportedly subscribe.

From the eighteenth century onwards, the preferred institution of the bourgeois public, within which the interests of collectivities of individuals could find objective representation, was the press; and it is with the transformation of that institution through economic and technical innovation (primarily, through the increasing concentration of the press in late capitalism and the development of the electronic media) that a transformation of the bourgeois public also takes place. According to the liberal model of a free press, the medium retained its objective and unbiased character through its ownership by private individuals, who were by definition free from the partiality of State institutions. In the twentieth century, however, the increasing commercialisation of the press through its ever greater dependence on advertising revenue, as well as processes of economic and technological concentration, have called into question this equation of free speech with private ownership. Indeed, the legitimation crisis in the twentieth-century press is symptomatic of fundamental dislocations in the traditional bourgeois public. In an economic system founded on giant national and multinational corporations, economic power coalesces in ever larger blocks, opaque to the 'average' individual and clearly no longer always representative of her or his interests. Definitions of equality as equality in private ownership must, then, give way to new terms which reinvest power in the hands of the individual. In West Germany in the fifties precisely this shift took place, with the development of so-called 'consumer democracy'.

Ludwig Erhard, Minister for Economic Affairs under Adenauer, is remembered primarily as the prophet and founder of West Germany's social market economy. He defines the basic economic freedoms of the post-war German state in the following terms:

> by this is meant first and foremost the freedom of all citizens to shape their lives in a form adequate to the personal wishes and conceptions of the individual, within the framework of the financial means at their disposal. This *basic democratic right of consumer freedom* must find its logical counterpart in the freedom of the entrepreneur to produce or distribute whatever he thinks necessary and potentially successful in a given market context . . . Every citizen must be conscious of consumer freedom and the freedom of economic enterprise as basic and inalienable rights, whose violation should be punished as an assault on our social order. Democracy and a free economy belong as logically together as do dictatorship and a State economy. (Erhard 1960, 14; author's emphasis)

Democracy realised, then, in the equality of producers and consumers as social partners towards a common goal: *Wohlstand für alle* (Prosperity for all). The rhetoric of consumer democracy borrows connotations of 'freedom,'

'equality' and 'democratic rights' from classic notions of a critical and rea-
soning public, grafting these on to the concept of a mutual dependency
between two equal partners, producer and consumer. The consumer public ex-
ercises its critical faculties in the 'rational' choice of those commodities which
best correspond to its needs; power is invested in the hands of consumers, insofar as they may refuse products which fail to meet those needs.

If, in the fifties, consumer democracy became a byword of parliamentary
rhetoric, then this was not simply the result of a single shift between two separate spheres, public and private. The 'public' is never unitary, always fragmentary; there is no unified public sphere, but instead an 'accumulation of
public forms' (Bommes and Wright 1982, 260)—television, the press, the educational apparatus, political parties, the army, church and legal establishment.
Relations between public institutions and the organs of a monopoly capitalist
economy are diverse; the managing director of a multinational company may
be nominated for the post of government minister;[3] the same multinational may
finance sports meetings or other cultural events; its sales director may frequent
the same night club as well-known media magnates. Or those relations may be
more ephemeral, locatable on the level of representation: the recurrence of
single signifiers (freedom, humanity, femininity) across a range of discourses
and the associative chains thereby forged. Or again they may be rooted in
interconnecting networks of finance; thus, for example, German marketing experts in the late 1950s advocated state financing of commercial market
research, to be carried out by state educational institutions, universities and
other research bodies, and used by commodity producers for forward planning.
To study transformations in the public sphere is, then, both to examine specific
sites on which a 'public' is constructed and, at the same time, to trace the wider
network of relations through which these disparate elements are assembled into
an ideological unity, the 'public sphere' at large. The notion of the 'rational
consumer' slots in neatly here, as a link forged on a multiplicity of sites between the post-war state and an expanding capitalist economy. Capital was
hungry for new markets, the German nation for democracy. Conflating concepts of freedom and democracy with images of a critical consumer was an
indispensable mechanism in the organisation of public consensus in the emergent social market economy. Thus Erhard, in a section of his book *Prosperity
for All* entitled 'The Will to Consume', makes consumption the very foundation of liberation and human dignity.

---

3. A recent case in point was the so-called Schwarz-Schilling affair in West Germany in the
winter of 1982–83. Christian Schwarz-Schilling, the new telecommunications minister in the Kohl
cabinet, came under attack for his plans to inject at least DM1 billion of state money into cable TV
projects, after it had become known that he himself had private interests in the cable industry.

Only if the economy is subject to continuous pressure from the consumption sphere will the production sphere retain the strength and fluidity to accommodate increased demand and free the population from material deprivation and difficulty . . . Increased wealth . . . is the necessary basis for the liberation of human beings from primitive and purely materialist modes of thought. (Erhard 1960, 234)

Women and Citizenship

Within eighteenth- and nineteenth-century political discourse, 'citizenship', though never marked as such, was in fact a masculine category; in state institutions which claimed to represent the interests of the collectivity at large, women's economic and political freedoms were severely curtailed, if not in some areas non-existent. Within 1950s definitions of the citizen-as-consumer, the position was reversed. The 'consumer', too, was a non-gendered category. Yet in relation to family consumption, it was women—specifically housewives—to whom it was applied. By the end of the fifties, the voices of official political and social scientific orthodoxy in West Germany were proclaiming that patriarchy was dead. Anchored in Article III of the constitution, women's formal equality was seen to have been realised in the gradual restructuring of gender relations at work and in the home, according to an overriding principle of 'equality in difference'. Equal rights legislation passed in 1957 outlined the practical effects of Article III ('Men and Women are equal') for the private lives of married couples. Wife and husband were to be mutually responsible for all decisions relating to their life together; the one significant exception to this rule was Paragraph 1356, which began: 'The wife carries sole responsibility for the running of the household'. Domestic labour remained in law the exclusive province of the married women; legally, the assumption of this housewifely role was defined at one and the same time as a woman's right and as her duty, both to her husband and to the community at large.

In this sense, women could be seen to be fulfilling a public role in performing the daily tasks of domestic labour. Yet it was not enough for women to continue practising traditional forms of childcare, cookery, shopping and cleaning; as Erhard had emphasised, true integration into the democratic public demanded more sophisticated modes of consumption, which alone could fuel the economy on which democracy depended. More importantly, equating the rights of citizenship with women's right to consume allowed a neat integration of women's demands for equality into a consumer-oriented economy. Thus it was as consumers that women were called upon by public institutions to work for the good of the community at large. Housewives' organisations were regularly called in by government bodies for advice and information on consumer affairs. In 1956, the Adenauer government passed a bill revising and expanding Federal regulations on food standards and labelling. Not only had the bill been drafted almost exclusively by fifty-two female members of the Bundestag; the campaign for the revision of existing regulations had also been carried by women's organisations, who had worked together with nutritional scientists and consumer pressure groups.

The 7 percent of the female population organised in housewives' associations constituted a powerful pressure group in itself; at the same time, the non-organised housewife was commonly depicted as having similar power to influence state legislation and market trends. One such grandiose claim was made by consumer expert Ingrid Landgrebe-Wolff on behalf of the American housewife, whom she saw in 1957 as actively participating in the development of world food markets, in ways as yet unfamiliar to German women. She cites as a classic example the coffee market of the mid-1950s, when demand fell rapidly as a result of rising prices. Even for a beverage so central to the diet of the average American, housewives were unwilling to pay the exorbitant prices demanded. They turned instead to tea, milk or malt drinks, leaving coffee companies in despair over mounting stockpiles. The housewife demanded cheaper coffee, and in the end not only packaging companies, but also growers of coffee for the international market, were forced to comply. World prices sank, breathing new life into the American home market. 'Thus', concludes Landgrebe-Wolff, 'the American housewife finally had her way' (Landgrebe-Wolff 1957, 56).

Teenage Girls in the Consumer Public

There are no simple connections to be made between women's position within relations of consumption for the fifties family and the situation of adolescent girls as consumers on a mass teenage market. On the one hand, it was clearly the case that women taking up their new position of equality were seen to be lacking in the qualities necessary for democratic citizenship. Since women's assumed tendency to be over-emotional was said to hamper them in the exercise of rational consumer choice, it became the task of both state and private institutions (centrally, of course, the advertising establishment) to educate women into the required patterns of consumption.

There is, then, indeed a sense in which drives towards the end of the decade to initiate girls into new modes of consumption were simply preparing them for their entry into an adult female world. On the other hand, teenage consumption, revolving as it did around leisure commodities, was clearly distinct from that practised by housewives. Why, after all, should girls with a well-trained eye for fashionable colour combinations—the right shade of lipstick to set off matching gloves and shoes—necessarily be similarly adept at differentiating between an increasingly confusing variety of washing-powder brands?

Yet via the notion of the 'public', there are crucial links to be made. For the fifties housewives, one component of domestic labour—shopping—was lifted out of the enclaves of home and the local street, and transferred to the 'public' terrain of the supermarket and the neighbourhood or regional shopping centre. Abstract promises of a public identity for women as consumers took concrete form in the reorganisation of public space around centralised loci of commodity exchange. Shops and stores gradually abandoned earlier styles of personal service, in favour of more up-to-date self-service methods. A number of stores introduced the so-called 'Kiebitz' system, displaying placards or badges which invited the customer to 'come in and look around', with no obligation to buy. Shop displays were reordered accordingly, with an emphasis on the commodity as image and spectacle; at the same time, posters and labels on or near individual articles drew the customers' attention to their particular advantages. Firms originally specialising in mail-order delivery expanded their department store chains; in urban centres in particular, specialist shops began to lose customers to larger department stores and supermarkets.

Developments in town planning further accelerated the centralisation of the consumption process. West Berlin was particularly interesting in this respect; having sustained heavy bombing in the Second World War, the city centre was a blank page across which architects and town planners would write the forms of their social Utopias. In 1946, a town planning collective under the directorship of Hans Scharoun opened debates on the future of the city with an exhibition, 'Berlin plant' (Berlin plans). They proposed using the wide-open spaces left by bomb damage to break with previous traditions of high-density housing and closed communities in which living, sometimes also working-space had been integrated with leisure facilities—the obligatory *Eckkneipe* (local bar)—and other points of commodity exchange: the equally indispensable *Tante-Emma-Laden* ('Aunt Emma's corner shop'). The post-war Berlin of Scharoun was to draw sharp boundaries between these diverse spheres of city life; strips of parkland and fast, wide roads were to divide off residential areas from commercial quarters, and from sites of work and leisure—including centralised shopping areas.

Through their integration into an expanding teenage market, adolescent girls were drawn in increasing numbers into this new public space. The new generation of young consumers were particularly attracted to self-service and department stores, where they were free to look, compare and admire at their leisure, with no immediate compulsion to buy. A 1957 Intermarket survey of West German consumer habits records the preference of teenagers for these more impersonal stores, as well as their predilection for the 'Americanised' off-the-peg fashions still regarded with suspicion by their older compatriots.

If girls are absent from subcultures, then, they become visible at the point of consumption. Working-class girls in particular have never been entirely absent from the street, the cinema or the dancehall; they have not lived a life of seclusion away from the eyes of predatory men. A favourite occupation of young female factory workers in 1950s West Germany was an evening stroll along main streets, in search of excitement and the company of contemporaries. Again, it was shopping which drew them onto the street and into public life. In a series of sociological monographs published in 1958 (Wurzbacher and Jaide 1958, 169–70), Bärbel—fifteen years old at the time of the study and employed since leaving school in a knitwear factory—relates how she is sent out every evening to fetch milk for the family (a duty she is only too happy to perform, since the dairy is a favourite meeting place for a large proportion of the local village youth).

> Here new films and the latest fashions are discussed. The boys at first set themselves a little apart, in order to be able to pass comment on the girls; later they make attempts to pick them up. This is a place for young people to talk together; this is the place where dates are made. There is always something going on at the dairy.

If the market offers itself to women and girls as a stage for the production of themselves as public beings, then it does so on particularly unfavourable terms. Bärbel's dairy was a meeting place for separate groups of boys and girls: the girls, whatever their own motives for assembling there, found themselves on display to boys angling for a date—or something more. It is this overwhelming power of men to position women as sexual prey that has made the feminist search for autonomous female subcultures so consistently difficult. Doubtless, though, the difficulty resides equally in the subculturalists' choice of object, cultural resistance being located chiefly in formal innovations by an adolescent avant-garde. If anything is to be learned about the lived realities of consumption, then we must shift the terms of the youth culture debate, looking first at the dominant forms of a supposedly conformist culture of consumerism (as well as its everyday subversions). One route into this project is the examination of teenage lifestyles: of their assemblage on the production line of commodities for the teenage market, and their deconstruction, appropriation, subversion and reassemblage by teenage girls themselves.

Girls in West Germany and the Teenage Dream

The word *teenager* first entered the German language in the 1950s, imported like chewing gum and Coca-Cola from the USA and vibrant with connotations of crazy styles, zany humour, rock'n'roll parties, Elvis, James Dean, loud music and soft park-bench romance. Its partner, the *Twen*, arrived around the same time and is of somewhat more dubious origin. Signifying 'young people in their twenties', it relied on associations of Americanness ('false' ones, inso-far as the *Twen* does not exist outside Germany) to construct an image of the older, more responsible, but nonetheless fun-loving party-going free-spending twenty-year-old. The average marital age in late 1950s Germany was twenty-six, and the relatively high disposable income of unmarried *Twens* made them particularly attractive to producers of consumer goods in the upper price range of the leisure market. A survey carried out by the DIVO Market Research Institute in 1961 estimated the disposable income of twenty-one to twenty-four-year-olds by 1960 at DM192 per month for men (compared with DM91 for seventeen- to twenty-year-olds), and DM180 per month for women (com-pared with DM100 for their seventeen- to twenty-year-old counterparts).

It was on the teenage market, then, that girls represented a particularly at-tractive target group for the leisure industries. During their late teens (from the age of fifteen onwards) girls in general drew a higher income than boys, but dropped back below their male contemporaries on reaching the age of twenty. In part, this resulted from their greater store of 'cultural capital' (Bourdieu 1967); girls leaving school in their mid-teens were likely to be initially better qualified for jobs requiring school certificates (*Volksschulabschlüsse*), while boys tended to make up for their lack of academic qualifications by entering an initially lower-paid apprenticeship or trainee post. The most lucrative section of the female market, then, was the group of *Angestellte* (clerical and secretar-ial workers); their disposable income amounted to three or four times that of their grammar school and college counterparts, or of working-class girls in un-skilled factory work. Girls on the margins of the middle income bracket were, in a sense, the deviants of marketing discourse, and *Angestellte* the norm against which teenage market potential was measured.

To the marketing establishment, it was clear that the golden egg of the female market had to be cracked with care. The male leisure market offered no adequate model for marketing to girls for whom leisure and pleasure were elas-tic and unstable terms. Female consumption constantly slipped between the grey world of work on the one hand and, on the other, the glittering but (above all sexually) dangerous domain of unbounded hedonism. The leisure com-modities favoured by boys offered pathways to present and immediate pleasures; for girls, on the other hand, so-called 'leisure' commodities embod-ied their more sober demands for future security in a precarious world. Girls in the middle to higher income brackets spent a significant portion of their income as unmarried females on collecting objects for their bottom drawer. This tradi-tional feminine institution, having gone into decline in the austerity years of the forties and early fifties, celebrated its comeback towards the end of the decade, when girls began once again to collect bedclothes, table linen, crock-ery, cutlery, glasswear—the accoutrements of the bourgeois domestic idyll. Teenage boys and young men, meanwhile, were busily buying motor-bikes,

cars, cameras, sports equipment and other consumer durables: the only piece
of technical equipment more highly favoured by female consumers was the
typewriter (Scharmann 1965, 33–8). Like the bottom drawer (which raised
women's value on the marriage market), the typewriter represented an investment in a comfortable future, girls' production of themselves as desirable
commodities on a competitive job market, and a key to the door of future financial security.

Private Faces in Public Places

As girls and women entered the post-war market place, whole new areas of
their lives began to become the 'public' property of marketing institutions.
Modern surveillance systems were installed in shops and supermarkets for the
observation and control of consumer behaviour: consumer panels were constituted as a source of information on attitudes to specific commodities and
brands: 'in-depth' psychological testing came into vogue with the rise of motivation research. Investigations into consumer behaviour required a massive
apparatus for the gathering and processing of data on consumer habits, preference, tastes and whims; hence the post-war boom in market research, when the
five major West German institutes (DIVO, EMNID, GfM, IFT, INFRATEST)
were founded in the space of as many years, between 1945 and 1950. The unifying principle of diverse market research techniques was the regulation of
information flows, which were to proceed in one direction only: from the consumer upwards to the institutions of the image production industries. Here,
data on consumers would be 'reprocessed', before being returned to them in
the shape of commodity representations: product design, packaging, advertising, public relations. Until reaching the stage of its reproduction in these more
palatable forms, knowledge of the consumer was channeled through scientific
discourses within which she was placed only as object, never as subject of the
consumption process. In commodity representations the situation was reversed.
The same knowledge was used by the image industries to construct image
commodities-as-symbols, from advertising images to fashionable clothes for a
teenage mass market. First, however, it had to be 'translated' from the terms of
social science into those of what may be called the 'commodity aesthetic'
within which, importantly, consumers were replaced as subjects of consumption practices.

Since the second half of the nineteenth century, the proliferation and increasing differentiation of public images of and for women has been intimately
bound up with their role as consumers. The effects of market research have
been visible for almost a century in the newspaper industry; as early as the
1890s in America, newspapers began to extend society news and entertainment sections, after they discovered that women—the audience at whom these

features were primarily aimed—carried the greatest potential as a future consumer market (Noelle 1940, 92). Yet it was not until well into the 1950s that market research in Germany first turned its attention to the younger generation of female consumers. In 1959, the Gesellschaft für Marktforschung carried out a survey of 1,500 male and female teenagers between the ages of fourteen and nineteen. The study was supplemented by further investigations in 1960, which aimed both 'to re-examine certain findings of the previous year' and 'to gain further basic insights into this important consumer group' (Scharmann 1965, 17). While sociological and media research carried out earlier in the decade had confined itself to quantitative studies of adolescent leisure pursuits, the GfM study was the first to focus specifically on the teenager as consumer and to attempt a broad sociometric analysis of teenage habits, preference and tastes.

In 1961, DIVO followed the GfM lead with a report commissioned by the advertising editors of *Bravo* magazine, a music, film, television, fashion and fiction teenage weekly which had been launched five years previously in 1956. By the early sixties, *Bravo* had already established itself as a leading light on the developing market for magazines aimed at a specifically teenage (male and female) readership. The 1961 survey aimed to spotlight the potential of the teenage market for the advertisers on whose revenue the magazine increasingly depended. *Bravo*, they argued, could operate as a bridge to span the gap between commodity producers, advertisers and consumers; its potential for success lay in its proven ability to capture and sustain a loyal readership amongst young people between the ages of twelve and twenty-four. In offering advertising space to the producers of commodities for a teenage market, it could ensure the dissemination of commodity representations amongst a teenage public constituted as such primarily through their role as consumers. *Bravo* readers, the publishers claim, are to be 'taken seriously' as consumers; for it is as such, they say, that teenagers primarily understand themselves.

> Confronted daily with literally hundreds of magazines and newspapers, young people may, it is true, pick up any one of them at any given time. Yet the only medium which will truly appeal to them is one which they feel is meant for and aimed only at them. They want, rightly, to be taken seriously enough for efforts to be made directly on their behalf. This is why *Bravo* has to be the way it is. (DIVO 1961)

In the face of moral outrage on the part of teachers, parents, academics and other guardians of Culture, Decency and Good Taste, *Bravo* was out to legitimise its own innovations in the field of popular taste. If teenagers were to assert themselves in a hostile world, they needed, it was argued, a mouthpiece through which their grievances could be aired, and it was in this capacity that

Bravo offered its services, claiming itself to be the only forum in which teenage protest could—and should—find expression. The mode of teenage rebellion was to be, not 'political', but aesthetic: 'We teenagers have our own style. And that's just what makes so many people see red' ('Triumph' advertisement, 1958). In the opening pages of the DIVO survey, *Bravo* then offered its services as an open site on which new teenage forms could be built and subsequently assembled into smoothly polished consumer lifestyles.

Girls in Teenage Lifestyle

The discourse of marketing defines lifestyles in terms of the specific configurations of commodity ownership which characterise particular consumer groups. In Germany, the Nürnberg Gesellschaft für Marktforschung (Society for Market Research) was the first marketing institution to develop its own theory of lifestyle; it was not until the mid-fifties that other market research establishments began to look in earnest to sources outside classical economics for more finely differentiated analyses of potential target groups. Taking up the work of Thorstein Veblen, Margaret Mead, Freud, Jung and others, consumption theorists now set about recuperating information gathered in the academic disciplines of cultural anthropology, sociology and psychology to feed the data banks of the capitalist market. Classical political economy had tended to neglect the consumer, or to consider consumption only in relation to the economics of commodity production and distribution. In opposition to this, the new wave of consumption theorists, with Bengler and Vershofen in Nürnberg as their avant-garde, argued consistently for a more sophisticated awareness of the social and aesthetic dimensions of commodity use. Wilhelm Vershofen proposed that the concept of commodity use value should be broken down into three analytical components: basic, or original use value; and social use value, measured against variables such as social prestige; and aesthetic use value, measured against given standards of social taste (Vershofen 1954, 12). Members of the artistic and literary establishment were taken to task for their confinement of Culture to a discrete and autonomous sphere, floating freely above the colourless wasteland of everyday life. The mutual dependence of economy and culture was seen by Vershofen to take active form in the daily exercise of consumer choice, determined as much by aesthetic as by economic or socio-psychological considerations.

The aesthetic principle regulating consumer lifestyles was a unity of form which bound the separate elements through which they were constructed. Part of the function of teenage commodities was to provide aesthetic forms for a cultural 'space' (adolescent leisure culture) which was differently inhabited by female and male consumers. For middle-class and working-class girls, home, the workplace and the street, where they shopped in the daytime and strolled by night, were always simultaneously sites of labour and of leisure. For the female consumer, the focal point of leisure, pleasure and personal freedom is not traditionally any fixed geographical location, but the female body itself. It was therefore the 'image industries'—the female mass media, and fashion and cosmetics industries—which constituted the largest sector of the post-war market in leisure commodities for girls.

The unity of post-war consumer lifestyles demanded new forms, too, for the feminine woman, produced in part on the production lines of the fashion, cosmetics and beauty-care industries. A glance at 1950s fashion images shows designers engaged in the business of sculpting, shaping and moulding ever more imaginative feminine forms: in 1954, the H-line, in spring 1955, the A-line, Dior's 'sack' in 1957, the trapeze line in spring 1958, into 1959 with the Empire line. At the same time, rigorous beauty-care regimes ensured that female bodies slipped smoothly into these new forms. Young girls turning for advice to *Bravo*'s beauty-care columnist were taught techniques of body culture and maintenance whereby each part of the body could be separately shaped and trained. When skirt hems rose to just above the knee, attention was focused on the female leg:

> From Paris comes the news that skirts are getting shorter—and short skirts show more leg! Are your legs in a fit state for public display? Nylon stockings show up every little blemish: do your stockings highlight the soft sheen of your well-cared-for skin . . . or is it the hard rough patches on thighs and knees which show up most? If it is, then something must be done at all costs! (*Bravo*, no. 10, 1958)

Tips on leg maintenance in *Bravo* between 1957 and 1959 included regular gymnastics, massage with 'slimming cream' (*sic*), visits to the chiropodist for sufferers from flat feet, lukewarm saltwater compresses for fat thighs, cycling for thin legs, trips to the doctor for red and inflamed skin. In conjunction with the beauty column, representations of women in the popular cultural discourses which traversed the pages of *Bravo* (film, television, fashion, rock and pop music and so on) reproduced certain common conventions of pose, gesture and body shape. For the perfect female leg, the general emphasis was on long, sweeping lines, further accentuated by high-heeled shoes tapering down to a pointed toe. Perfection was seen as embodied in particular representative female figures; Marlene Dietrich's legs, like Sophia Loren's hips and Brigitte Bardot's curves, were the talk of fifties beauty columns. Yet *Bravo* did not offer film star pin-ups as models of an ideal to which teenage girls should necessarily aspire; the ideal was displaced from visual representations and located instead in the masculine gaze. 'Fashion has made skirts shorter', said the *Bravo* beauty tip in March 1958, 'More than ever, eyes are drawn to your legs'. That these were the eyes of men had been made clear in the same column in an earlier edition of the magazine, which sounded the following note of comfort for girls whose legs, despite hours of tortured beauty treatment, remained stubbornly inelegant.

> A lot of men—for whose sake, after all, we go to all this trouble—don't have anything against legs that are a little stocky. A true man doesn't fall in love with external appearances. And if he does, he's the wrong one for you! (*Bravo*, no. 44, 1957)

On the one hand, girls were exhorted to invest time and energy into the labour of body maintenance, grooming and careful dressing; on the other, the desired product of their labours remained persistently out of reach. The 'perfect female self' to which girls were urged to aspire was mirrored in the gaze of the men and boys with whom they shared their everyday lives; thus it remained unknowable, not signified in visual or textual representations, but in the ambiguous amorous attentions of men.

'Bravo girls' were offered one route out of this predicament; it led, not directly towards, but around and between the images of women which peopled the pages of the magazine. Mass media icons (film stars, fashion models, pop idols) were mediated to female readers by authoritative experts on fashion and beauty care—'Ilse' in 'Triumph' underwear advertisements, or 'Trixi' in *Bravo*'s own fashion column. The information they filtered down to the female reader concerned, not *what* she should look like, but instructions on *how* to make the best of her own resources. They celebrated, not any single image of femininity, but a set of aesthetic principles as possible instruments for the construction of a more beautiful self. Tailored to the modest resources of the *Angestellte* who were *Bravo*'s most lucrative market, the mode of aesthetic production propagated here was rule by principles of sobriety, discretion, restraint, moderation and self-control.

> Our 'style' may perhaps tend at times to copy adult fashions. But in general it is still *more restrained, less changeable and less expensive* . . . Slaves to fashion? We're convinced . . . and we hope you are too—that that's the last thing we want to be ('Triumph' advertisement, *Bravo*, no. 42, 1958; author's emphasis)

'Consumption' as Cultural Practice

In the preceding sections of this survey of fifties consumer culture, I have outlined some of the ways in which capital organised commodity markets to expand the boundaries of female consumption. From this analysis of dominant forms, perspectives for future work on gender and consumption now begin to emerge. In the first instance, it is capital which dictates the forms which commodity consumption takes; yet the market remains dependent on the development by the female consumer of specific sets of social competences and skills: from the rational decision-making of the thrifty housewife to teenage girls' production of themselves as aesthetic objects in the symbolic configurations of teenage lifestyles. The category of 'consumption' covers a multitude of sins: symbolic readings of commodity representations, processes of sensual gratification, practices of economic and cultural exchange. The so-called 'sphere' of consumption can thus be dismantled into a multiplicity of complex forms, relations and practices, which operate on diverse and discrete market sites. On each of these 'levels' of consumption, female consumers engage differently with the market machine, activating multiple sets of functions, meanings and values in the commodities they consume. Rules and conventions governing these consumer practices are laid down in consumer law, advice and information; thus we have seen *Bravo*'s fashion advisors setting out implicit and explicit rules for the production of teenage style through the consumption of fashion commodities.

Analyses of these rules and conventions are indispensable to, yet at the same time inadequate for feminist research into female practices of consumption. Highlighting the mechanisms of control which capital deploys, they fail to grasp the experiential quality of consumer culture for women and girls. Biographical narratives offer one way of bridging this gap, by tracing the paths whereby social subjects negotiate dominant forms; thus I have chosen to end this series of case studies in gender and consumer culture with two short narratives: a fictional filmic narrative and a biography taken from an account of ethnographic field-work in the fifties. Positioned within radically different contexts, their common feature is the central significance accorded to one commodity: stockings. By 1961, nylons had swamped the young female market in West Germany; *Bravo*'s DIVO survey shows 85 percent of 'Bravo girls' between the ages of twelve and twenty-four (compared with 80 percent of non-readers in the same age group) to be wearing seamless stockings; the percentage of female *Bravo* readers who did not possess either Perlon or nylon stockings was nil (DIVO 1961, 137). These figures can neither be read as indicators of girls' blind submission to the dictates of the market, nor do they signify female capitulation to fetishistic 'male' fantasy. The all-pervasiveness of synthetic silk stockings begs different questions: what were the sources of their popularity, and how were they actually 'consumed'?

Ninotchka

In the late fifties, *Bravo* ran a series of half-page advertisements for 'Opal' seamless stockings, depicting crossed female legs, long and sophisticated, emerging from the folds of an elegant black dress. Parallel to the 'Opal' campaign, the magazine carried reports on *Silk Stockings*, Cole Porter's musical remake of Ernst Lubitsch's *Ninotchka* (1939). In the fifties' musical, Wim Sonneveld plays a Russian people's representative in Paris, whose loyalty to the Party is beginning to fade. Three Soviet commissars are ordered from Moscow to Paris: their mission—to rescue their colleague from the clutches of that decadent capital. When they in turn disappear, super-activist Ninotchka (Cyd Charisse) is sent on their trail. She soon recognises the American, Edwin Canfield (Fred Astaire), as her main adversary; he meanwhile, is amused, fascinated, but never convinced, by her fervent defence of socialism and the Soviet way of life. He guides her instead down the boulevards of Paris, knowing that no woman—'above all no woman with the charms of Ninotchka'—can withstand the 'democratic temptations' of their dazzling window displays. The 'fortress Ninotchka' finally falls; she succumbs to the charms of Edwin, and of the Western world he represents.

> Moscow—and politics—have lost Ninotschka for ever. Silk stockings may be thin, but in the end and above all, they are more attractive than the best of political convictions. (*Bravo*, no. 4, 1958)

Consumers of 'symbolic commodities' have preferred textual sources from which they draw the meanings with which those commodities are invested. *Bravo* is one such source for teenage consumers, and in 1958 it offered its readers a range of texts ('Opal' advertisements, fashion and beauty tips, reviews of *Silk Stockings*) in which synthetic silk (nylon or Perlon) stockings were encoded into new configurations of meaning. In part, these were drawn from the symbolic field of meanings around genuine silk, with its traditional associations of exoticism, sensuality, luxury and mystery: the legend of the Chinese princess said to have discovered the secret of the silkworm more than five thousand years ago or the two sixth-century monks reputed to have smuggled the eggs of the silkworm out of China to the court of the Byzantine Emperor Justinian. But the additional glamour of the American nylon has specific origins elsewhere. On post-1945 black markets, American soldiers were well known as the main purveyors of nylon stockings; by the 1950s, poster graphics were using images of stockinged female legs for comparative representations of rising productivity rates in European countries. In popular representations of the Cold War period, the stocking became a dominant signifier of freedom, democracy and the American way of life; the musical *Silk Stockings* was Hollywood's contribution to this modern myth. In the *Silk Stockings* narrative, real anxieties over a simmering East-West conflict are played out in fantastic form across the female body. Ninotchka first becomes a 'true' woman through romantic association with a Western man—and through her consumption of fashion commodities for the feminine woman. In *Bravo*'s review, the resolution of the romantic narrative is couched in terms of military defeat ('the fortress Ninotchka . . . falls'); in the person of Edwin Canfield, America emerges victorious, not only over Ninotchka herself, but over the red threat she represents.

Reconstructing the *Silk Stockings* narrative, *Bravo*'s review becomes instrumental in the production of a store of meanings around synthetic silk hose, from which teenage consumers might potentially have drawn. Those meanings cannot, however, simply be read off the *Bravo* text. Post-structuralist studies of narrative as complexly codified systems of representations have shown meaning to be the product of relationships between reader and text, and thus not an intrinsic characteristic of the narrative itself. In order to make sense of any given narrative, the reader engages differently with each of its multiple 'codes', reproducing in her/his signifying practices the relations of tension and contradiction which exist between those codes. In *Bravo's Silk Stockings* review, the so-called 'hermeneutic' and 'cultural' codes may be seen to produce just such contradictory meanings and values. The 'hermeneutic code' is the one which poses the central questions of the narrative, delaying the answers until the final moment of narrative resolution. The enigma of Ninotchka's narrative is the question of her possible transformation into a 'true' woman—a question answered at the end of the narrative in the language of female submission. Ninotchka capitulates to imperialist drives to colonise enemy continents, drives which are encapsulated here in the sexual passion of Edwin Canfield.

According to Barthes' definition in *S/Z*, the 'cultural code' of narrative refers the reader to meanings and values in the social world beyond the text (Barthes 1970). The social meaning of synthetic silk stockings is not exhausted in the *Bravo* narrative alone; indeed, connotations from other sources may badly disfigure the patterns of meaning constructed by 'internal' narrative codes (which are, in Barthesian terms, the hermeneutic and the semic codes). The following example of a second 1950s 'stocking narrative' shows one of the forms which these potentially oppositional meanings might take.

Annette

Between 1955 and 1957, a West German social worker, Renate Wald, put together a collection of biographical monographs of working-class factory girls, which were later published in Wurzbacher's *Die junge Arbeiterin* (1958). She drew on a pool of ethnographic research conducted by a team of participant observers, all of whom had lived and worked as factory employees for a number of months or years.

One of the girls, Annette, works with her mother in a textile factory;

an only child, she spends much of her 'leisure time' at home with the family, helping her mother around the house, or enjoying precious moments of lazy conversation when the chores are finally done. Annette's mother, wary of the dangers of possible sexual adventures, is unwilling to allow her to develop close friendships with young people of either sex; even female friendships, she fears, would ultimately lead to perilous encounters with the opposite sex. At the age of fifteen, Annette still amicably complies with her mother's wishes, remaining a model daughter in almost all respects. Even her taste in clothes is dictated by her mother's preferences for careful but unobtrusive dressing:

> She wears plain . . . dark clothes; although she uses powder and lipstick, she does so with care and in moderation; her hair is well-groomed and simply styled. She has an air, not so much of homeliness, as of exceptional respectability. (Wald, in Wurzbacher 1958, 161)

Although mother and daughter rarely clash, there is one niggling point of conflict. The Perlon stockings which Annette wears to work every day cannot stand the rigours of shopfloor labour; inevitably, she wears out two or three pairs a week. Since Annette spends her weekly pocket money on biscuits and sweets, her mother has constantly to replenish her stock of nylons out of the housekeeping money. Her acid comment on her daughter's prodigality: 'She oughtn't to spend so much on tidbits to eat. There's plenty of fruit and sweets to be had at home' (Wald, in Wurzbacher 1958, 150). A striking characteristic of Annette's biography is the dreary regularity of her everyday life. Up at six in the morning to snatch a quick breakfast, stack the washing up, air the bedrooms and make the beds before setting out for work: nine hours at the production line: arriving back home at six-thirty in the evening to dust the rooms and clean the stairs before sitting down to eat with the family: retiring to bed by ten o'clock at the latest to recoup energy for the day ahead. Both at home and at the workplace, time, space, experience and action are regulated for Annette by institutions and agents of social control—the family and parents, the factory, overseers and management. In this context, Annette's conflict with her mother over stockings becomes more than a whimsical and inconsequential detail. A moment of disorder and disruption, it marks the displacement of potentially more grandiose demands for self-determination onto the only site where they may realistically be met. Annette is financially and emotionally dependent on the security of family life; she cannot allow herself prolonged struggles over points of generational difference. Repressed from the placid routine of everyday family life, these (inevitable) differences find expression in tangential conflicts and struggles.

It has been suggested that similar processes of displacement were in play in the formation of post-war youth subcultures (Cohen 1972, 26). Yet subcultural resistance was no solution for Annette; isolated as she was from her contemporaries, her struggles necessarily took more minutely personal forms. Her conflicts with her mother centered on practices of day-to-day consumption—the money she wasted on frivolous treats and her (mis)use of Perlon stockings. Perlon is made to be used and thrown away; mending stocking ladders is difficult and diminishes aesthetic appeal. The 'built-in obsolescence' of Perlon stockings allowed Annette to use them to express an aberrant disregard for her mother's principle of moderation in all things, a principle to which she otherwise strictly adhered. Mass commodities demand to be consumed to excess: Annette, unconsciously perhaps, took them at their word.

Conclusion

As work on male youth subcultures has traced the 'hidden contradictions' which they 'magically resolve' (Hebdige 1979, 18), so Annette's biography can shed light on some of the ways in which girls may live out the contradictions of their lives through an everyday culture of consumption. Her individual reformulation of the logic of built-in obsolescence took place *within* a teenage consumer culture; for her, hedonic consumption itself became a practice of refusal vis-à-vis dominant codes of social taste.

Feminists have commonly represented the 1950s as an age of repressive quiescence, in which women's disaffection with their feminine lot was successfully obscured and silenced. Since Betty Friedan's *Feminine Mystique* (1963), the blame for a widespread fifties' female malaise has been laid predominantly at the door of capitalist marketeers, to whom is ascribed the ability to dupe and seduce women into slavish submission to the authority of the market. But was 'consumerism' an adequate name for the problems of the female condition? Is there a hidden history of authentic female experience to be unearthed from beneath the glossy façade of fifties' femininity? Or could it not equally be the case that the façade itself 'speaks' the problems (and the delights) of the female condition? Consumerism not only offers, but also continually fulfills its promise of everyday solutions—albeit limited and partial ones—to problems whose origins may lie elsewhere. In post-war West Germany, women were constrained to search beyond national boundaries for female cultural forms untainted by aftertastes of Nazism. To don the accoutrements of an American female ideal—nylon stockings, scarlet lipstick, narrow skirts and high-heeled shoes—was in part to register a public disavowal of fascist images of femininity: scrubbed faces shining with health, sturdy child-bearing hips sporting seamed stockings and sensible shoes. Fifties consumerism, while it held many traps for women, nonetheless offered ways and means of negotiating a cultural history of militaristic discipline and rigorous control. Female 'resistance' of the period was perhaps not so much silenced, as pitched at a different level from earlier campaigns for women's equality (which in the fifties was proclaimed to have been achieved) or later feminist struggles against women's commoditisation and objectification on a capitalist market. At specific moments in post-war history, the market has become a target for the rhetoric of a necessary and well-founded feminist opposition; yet in relation to the fifties—and possibly in the eighties too—there was, and is, little to be gained from 'oppositional' postures of aloof distaste.

> For me, the eighties are more than this: love the things that bring you down. I can't change things, I can't think plastic out of my world, so I try to turn the tables on it and see what's actually good about it. Do you see . . . I can drape myself with as much silk and linen as I want, and the plastic still won't go away. So I try to look at it differently. Love the things that bring you down. (Annette Humpe, Ideal)

Sources Cited

Barthes, Roland. 1970. *S/Z.* London: Jonathan Cape.

Bommes, M., and P. Wright. 1982. Charms of residence: The public and the past. In *Making histories: Studies in history-writing and politics,* edited by R. Johnson, G. McLennan, B. Schwartz, and D. Sutton. London: Hutchinson.

Bourdieu, P. 1967. Systems of education and systems of thought. *International Social Science Journal* 19, no. 3.

Cohen, P. 1972. Subcultural conflict and working-class community. *Working Papers in Cultural Studies,* no. 2 (spring).

DIVO/Kindler und Schiermeyer Verlag AG, eds. 1961. *Bravo-Leser stellen sich vor.* Munich: Kindler und Schiermeyer.

Erhard, L. 1960. *Wohlstand für alle.* Düsseldorf: Econ-Verlag.

Habermas, J. 1962. *Strukturwandel der Öffentlichkeit.* Darmstadt und Neuwied: Luchterhand.

Hall, S., and T. Jefferson, eds. 1976. *Resistance through rituals: Youth subcultures in post-war Britain.* London: Hutchinson.

Hebdige, D. 1979. Hiding in the light. *Ten* 8, no. 9.

Hoggart, R. 1958. *The uses of literacy.* Harmondsworth: Penguin.

Landgrebe-Wolff, I., and AID (Land- und hauswirtschaftlicher Auswertungs- und Informationsdienst e.V.), eds. 1957. *Mehr Käuferbewusstsein! Verbrauchererziehung und Ernährungsberatung in den USA, mit Anregegung für Deutschland.* Frankfurt am Main: Kommentator.

McRobbie, A., and J. Garber. 1976. Girls and subcultures. In *Resistance through rituals: Youth subcultures in post-war Britain,* edited by S. Hall and T. Jefferson. London: Hutchinson.

Noelle, E. 1940. *Massenbefragungen über Politik und Presse in USA.* Frankfurt am Main: Diesterweg.

Scharmann, D-L. 1965. *Das Konsumverhalten von Jugendlichen.* Munich: Juventa.

Vershofen, W. 1954. Rationalisierung vom Verbraucher her. *Deutshe Wirtschaft im Querschnitt* (Beilage zu *Der Volkswirt*), no. 28.

Warner, W. L. 1960. *Social class in America.* Evanston, Ill.: Harper and Row.

Willis, P. 1977. *Learning to labour: How working class kids get working class jobs.* London: Saxon House.

Willis, P. 1976. "The cultural meaning of drug use. In *Resistance through rituals: Youth subcultures in post-war Britain,* edited by S. Hall and T. Jefferson. London: Hutchinson.

Woods, W. 1960. Psychological dimensions of consumer decision. *Journal of Marketing* 24, no. 3.

Wurzbacher, G., and W. Jaide, eds. 1958. *Die junge Arbeiterin: Beiträge zur Sozialkunde und Jugendarbeit.* Munich: Juventa.

Rock 'n' Roll, Female Sexuality, and the Cold War Battle over German Identities

Uta G. Poiger

When rock 'n' roll crossed the Atlantic to Germany in the second half of the 1950s, it dramatically—and relatively suddenly—brought young women into the public eye as consumers and sexual beings. In 1956, a cartoon in the East Berlin daily *Berliner Zeitung* showed a small, emaciated Elvis Presley performing under larger-than-life female legs in front of a crowd of girls much bigger than he was. They were throwing off garter belts and bras and licking their thick lips in obvious sexual excitement. The accompanying article identified girls as the main consumers of American "nonculture" and commented that rock 'n' roll appealed to primitive humans.[1] West Germans had similar worries: According to one commentator, the behavior of female rock 'n' roll fans illustrated the dangerous "sexualization of the 15-year-olds."[2] Another West German saw rock 'n' roll dancers as "wild barbarians in ecstasy."[3]

An earlier version of this article was presented at the Ninth Berkshire Conference on the History of Women, "Transformations: Women, Gender, Power," Vassar College, June 1993. For helpful comments and criticisms on earlier drafts, I would like to thank Lucy Barber, Volker Berghahn, Mari Jo Buhle, Carolyn Dean, Jane Gerhard, Mary Gluck, Edward Gray, Elaine Tyler May, Donna Penn, Jessica Shubow, the two anonymous reviewers for the *Journal of Modern History,* and especially Ruth Feldstein and Melani McAlister.

1. "Appell an den Urmenschen," *Berliner Zeitung* (December 13, 1956). Throughout this article, I use the terms "girls" and "boys" to refer to American and German rock 'n' roll fans. The German sources from the 1950s on rock 'n' roll and on adolescent behavior employed *Mädchen* ("girls") and *Jungen* ("boys") to denote the relatively young ages of their subjects. While it is difficult to ascertain the exact ages of rock 'n' roll fans, many of them were sixteen or younger.

2. H. Heigert, "Ein neuer Typ wird produziert: Der Teenager," in *Deutsche Jugend,* no. 3 (1959), pp. 117–21, quoted in Christine Bertram and Heinz-Hermann Krüger, "Vom Backfisch zum Teenager—Mädchensozialisation in den 50er Jahren," in *"Die Elvistolle, die hatte ich mir unauffällig wachsen lassen": Lebensgeschichte und jugendliche Alltagskultur in den fünfziger Jahren,* ed. Heinz-Hermann Krüger (Opladen, 1985), pp. 84–101, quote on p. 94.

3. "Außer Rand und Band," *Beratungsdienst Jugend und Film* 1 (November 1956): BVII.

In this article I will locate the rebellious actions of female rock 'n' roll fans in the context of cold war struggles over East and West German national identities and explore how their public behavior at dances, at concerts, and in the streets challenged the traditional norms of female respectability that authorities in East and West Germany had made central to their respective reconstruction efforts.[4] Both East and West German authorities, albeit in increasingly different ways, politicized the actions of female rock 'n' roll fans.[5]

Two interrelated concerns shaped East and West German reactions to rock 'n' roll: worries about uncontrolled female sexuality on the one hand and about alleged racial differences on the other.[6] Commentators linked consumption, sexuality, and femininity. While these links had characterized discourses on consumer culture since the nineteenth century, alleged connections among the consumption of mass culture, the oversexualization of women, and the fem-

---

4. For the purposes of this article, I focus on how young women entered the public sphere through their consumption of rock 'n' roll. For the United States this has been suggested by Alice Echols, "'We Gotta Get Out of This Place': Notes toward Remapping the Sixties," *Socialist Review* 22 (April 1992): 9–33, esp. 28. On the attraction of rock 'n' roll for teenage girls in the United States and Britain, see also Wini Breines, *Young, White and Miserable: Growing up Female in the Fifties* (Boston, 1992), pp. 151–66; Barbara Ehrenreich, Elizabeth Hess, and Gloria Jacobs, *Re-making Love: The Feminization of Sex* (New York, 1986). Angela McRobbie, most recently in *Feminism and Youth Culture: From Jackie to Just Seventeen* (Boston, 1991), has pointed to the importance that popular culture consumption has had for girls as a way to enter the public sphere. On women and the consumption of American popular culture, see also Susan J. Douglas, *Where the Girls Are: Growing up Female with the Mass Media* (New York, 1994); Jackie Stacey, *Star Gazing: Hollywood Cinema and Female Spectatorship* (New York, 1994). Scholars of West German youth cultures have mostly failed to see any political implications of female rock 'n' roll consumption. See the otherwise excellent study by Kaspar Maase, *Bravo Amerika: Erkundigungen zur Jugendkultur der Bundesrepublik in den fünfziger Jahren* (Hamburg, 1992), p. 131; Peter Kuhnert and Ute Ackermann, "Jenseits von Lust und Liebe? Jugendsexualität in den 50er Jahren," in Krüger, ed., pp. 43–83; Bertram and Krüger, p. 99. However, there are some important exceptions: Erica Carter, "Alice in the Consumer Wonderland: West German Case studies in Gender and Consumer Culture," in *Gender and Generation*, ed. Angela McRobbie and Mica Nava (London, 1984), pp. 185–214 [republished in this volume], has warned against quick judgements about girls as "objectified" in postwar consumer culture. See also Angela Delille and Andrea Grohn, eds., *Perlonzeit: Wie die Frauen ihr Wirtschaftswunder erlebten* (Berlin, 1985).

5. My focus thus is not on how girls themselves experienced rock 'n' roll. Nevertheless, I suggest what frameworks were available to them for understanding their actions and, later, for constructing their histories. For connections between cold war political rhetoric and gender norms brought forward in popular culture in the United States, see Elaine Tyler May, *Homeward Bound: American Families in the Cold War* (New York, 1988). The most comprehensive treatment for Germany is Robert G. Moeller, *Protecting Motherhood: Women and the Family in the Politics of Postwar West Germany* (Berkeley and Los Angeles, 1993).

6. For developing these ideas, I am indebted to long discussions with Ruth S. Feldstein. See also her "'I Wanted the Whole World to See': Race, Gender and Constructions of Motherhood in the Death of Emmett Till," in *Not June Cleaver: Women and Gender in Postwar America, 1945–1960*, ed. Joanne Meyerowitz (Philadelphia, 1994), pp. 263–303.

inization of men were particularly worrisome to East and West Germans in the 1950s. After the defeat of National Socialism and in the face of the cold war, authorities in both states saw the success of reconstruction as dependent on reconfiguring and revalidating Germanness; defining normative gender roles was important to these reconstruction projects.[7] Although East and West German officials differed greatly, for example, in their approval of female employment, both sides relied on the image of the asexual female caretaker and the controlling and controlled male protector in their construction of ideal gender roles.[8] In the mid-1950s, young male and female rebels with a penchant for American music and fashions challenged these norms and exacerbated East and West German concerns about the consumption of American popular culture. Indeed, worries about the actions of female rock 'n' roll fans were intimately linked to concerns about male rebelliousness. Authorities in East and West Germany invoked American and German women as instigators of, victims of, and solutions to the problems they associated with consumer culture.[9]

The need to affirm racial differences between Germans and African-Americans also emerged in East and West German discourses on rock 'n' roll. Although many attacks against musicians and fans employed racial slurs and stereotypes, race has hardly been used as a category of analysis in histories of the German post-Nazi period.[10] Debates about rock 'n' roll reveal that after

---

7. Reconstruction has been used mostly to describe West Germany after 1945, but it is a useful concept for both Germanies. James Sheehan, "National History and National Identity in the New Germany," *German Studies Review* 15 (Winter 1992): 162–74, has warned against treating the two Germanies as if they had two separate histories, "joined only at their beginning and their end" (p. 170). My thanks to Mary Gluck for urging me to think carefully through the changing relationship of culture and politics.

8. For West Germany, see Moeller; Heide Fehrenbach, *Cinema in Democratizing Germany: Reconstructing National Identity after Hitler* (Chapel Hill, N.C., 1995); Maria Höhn, "Frau im Haus und Girl im *Spiegel*: Discourse on Women in the Interregnum Period of 1945–1949 and the Question of German Identity," *Central European History* 26 (1993): 57–90. For East Germany, Ina Merkel, . . .*Und Du, Frau an der Werkbank: Die DDR in den 50er Jahren* (Berlin, 1990), has pointed to the reproduction of a gender division of labor in spite of socialist claims for women's equality. See also Barbara Einhorn, *Cinderella Goes to Market: Citizenship, Gender, and Women's Movements in East Central Europe* (New York, 1993); Atina Grossmann, *Reforming Sex: The German Movement for Birth Control and Abortion Reform, 1920–1950* (New York, 1995).

9. Popular culture and especially such commercialized products as rock 'n' roll have been investigated in the framework of cultural studies, most notably in scholarship that grew out of the Centre for Contemporary Cultural Studies at Birmingham. Anna Szemere, "Bandits, Heroes, the Honest and the Misled: Exploring the Politics of Representation in the Hungarian Uprising of 1956," in *Cultural Studies*, ed. Lawrence Grossberg, Cary Nelson, and Paula Treichler (New York, 1992), pp. 623–39, has pointed out that, while this work has enabled a critique of liberal capitalism, very few scholars have yet tried to apply the frameworks developed in this scholarship to the study of the countries that used to be east of the iron curtain.

10. George L. Mosse, *Toward the Final Solution: A History of European Racism* (New York, 1978), p. xi, e.g., conceives of the Holocaust as the culmination and endpoint of European

World War II Germans continued to define Germanness in racial terms. Since the nineteenth century, race had clearly been central to German identities. German conceptions of racial hierarchies had manifested themselves most forcefully in anti-Semitism, but many Germans also saw blacks, along with other groups like Sinti and Roma ("Gypsies"), as racially inferior.[11] For example, hostilities toward blacks were pronounced in the 1920s when the French occupation army in the Rhineland included many Senegalese. The Nazis forced the children that German women had by these soldiers to undergo compulsory sterilization.[12] Anxieties surfaced again when black soldiers came to Germany as part of the American occupying forces after World War II. Yet Germans have not needed black people within their own country in order to make blackness a quality against which to define their Germanness.[13] Rock 'n' roll in 1950s West Germany was radical precisely because of its associations with blackness; unlike many Americans, Germans did not perceive it as "whitened" music.[14]

In the German debates on rock 'n' roll, hostilities toward black culture combined with fears of the destruction of gender mores: East and West German authorities rejected rock 'n' roll fans and stars as transgressors of both racial and gender boundaries. Asserting traditional gender norms allowed authorities on both sides of the iron curtain to distinguish civilized Germanness from the alleged threats of African-American culture.

---

racism. For a recent exploration of postwar German attitudes toward Jews, see Frank Stern, *The Whitewashing of the Yellow Badge: Antisemitism and Philosemitism in Postwar Germany* (New York, 1992); for East Germany, see Jeffrey Herf, "German Communism, the Discourse of 'Antifascist Resistance,' and the Jewish Catastrophe," in *Resistance against the Third Reich, 1933–1990*, ed. Michael Geyer and John W. Boyer (Chicago, 1994), pp. 257–94.

11. For overviews on German racism, see Michael Burleigh and Wolfgang Wippermann, *The Racial State: Germany, 1933–1945* (New York, 1991); Mosse; Detlev J. K. Peukert, *Inside Nazi Germany: Conformity, Opposition, and Racism in Everday Life,* trans. Richard Deveson (New Haven, Conn., 1987); Paul Weindling, *Health, Race, and German Politics between National Unification and Nazism, 1870–1945* (New York, 1989).

12. See Peukert, *Inside Nazi Germany,* p. 217; Reiner Pommerin, *Sterilisierung der Rheinlandbastarde: Das Schicksal einer farbigen deutschen Minderheit, 1918–1937* (Düsseldorf, 1979).

13. See Katherine Pence, "The 'Fräuleins' meet the 'Amis': Americanization of German Women in the Reconstruction of the West German State," *Michigan Feminist Studies* 7 (1992–93): 83–108, esp. 87–89; Sander L. Gilman, *On Blackness without Blacks: Essays on the Image of the Black in Germany* (Boston, 1982).

14. Rainer Erd, "Musikalische Praxis und sozialer Protest: Überlegungen zur Funktion von Rock and Roll, Jazz und Oper," *German Politics and Society,* no. 18 (Fall 1989): 18–35. For the transgressions of racial boundaries in rock 'n' roll in the United States and Britain, see Greil Marcus, *Mystery Train: Images of America in Rock 'n' Roll Music* (New York, 1982); George Lipsitz, *Time Passages: Collective Memory and American Popular Culture* (Minneapolis, 1990). For the importance of race in attacks on rock 'n' roll, see Linda Martin and Kerry Segrave, *Anti-Rock: The Opposition to Rock 'n' Roll* (Hamden, Conn., 1988).

The 1950s were hardly the first time that American popular culture seemed subversive to Germans. Since the 1920s many Germans had equated America with modernity—an association that raised both hopes and fears. During the Weimar Republic, for example, Germans were not just fascinated with American management and production methods; in big cities like Berlin, American popular culture, especially music and movies, also made a splash.[15] With the arrival of American jazz in the early 1920s, Germans had to come to terms with a music that they saw as black and that came to define one aspect of modernity. As many young people embraced jazz and the musicians who brought it to Germany, conservatives and fascists leveled antiblack and anti-Semitic attacks: jazz was a music created by "niggers," linked to "primitive sexuality," and marketed by Jews. Together with lascivious women, jazz allegedly endangered Germany's young men.[16]

During the Third Reich, the National Socialists sought to root out all cultural products perceived as non-Aryan, and jazz was one of their prime targets. In the 1940s the Nazis viciously prosecuted "swing youths," groups of young women and men who listened to jazz together and wore distinctive clothes. Yet even the National Socialists, caught between their racial utopia and the need to accommodate a population under the conditions of war, never banned jazz completely from the air waves.[17]

After 1945, with the Allied occupation and the opening of its market, West Germany experienced an unprecedented influx of American products, from nylon stockings to popular music. The impact of these imports was by no means restricted to West Germany; especially via Berlin it reached well beyond the iron curtain. Until the construction of the wall in August 1961, a constant stream of people flowed back and forth between East and West Berlin. Large numbers of East Berliners and East Germans came to shop and to enjoy

15. For Germans' fascination with America, see John Willet, *The New Sobriety: Art and Politics in the Weimar Period* (New York, 1978); Mary Nolan, *Visions of Modernity: American Business and the Modernization of Germany* (New York, 1994); Frank Costigliola, *Awkward Dominion: American Political, Economic, and Cultural Relations with Europe, 1919–1933* (Ithaca, N.Y., 1984). For American movies, see Victoria DeGrazia, "Mass Culture and Sovereignty: The American Challenge to European Cinemas, 1920–1960," *Journal of Modern History* 61 (1989): 53–87; Thomas J. Saunders, *Hollywood in Berlin: American Cinema and Weimar Germany* (Berkeley and Los Angeles, 1994).

16. Quotes from Michael H. Kater, "The Jazz Experience in Weimar Germany," *German History* 6, no. 2 (1988): 145–58, 154.

17. On swing youths, see Michael Kater, *Different Drummers: Jazz in the Culture of Nazi Germany* (New York, 1992). Studies of American popular culture in the Third Reich have pointed to its function as a source of resistance as well as of Nazi manipulation. See Kater, *Different Drummers;* Peukert, *Inside Nazi Germany*; Hans Dieter Schäfer, "Amerikanismus im Dritten Reich," in *Nationalsozialismus und Modernisierung,* ed. Michael Prinz and Rainer Zitelmann (Darmstadt, 1991), pp. 199–215.

themselves in West Berlin. Sometimes whole East Berlin school classes would cross into the Western sectors to watch movies. Many East Berlin boys and girls frequented West Berlin music halls, and young people from all over the German Democratic Republic (GDR) would go to West Berlin to buy jeans, leather jackets, or records, in spite of prohibitive exchange rates. At home some of them would tune into Western radio stations, including the American Forces Network (AFN) and Radio Luxembourg, to listen to the latest American hits. Thus, when rock 'n' roll hit West Berlin in 1956, its impact was felt in both Germanies.

Because of associations with blackness and unbridled sexuality, rock 'n' roll, like its predecessor jazz, represented a threat in postwar East and West Germany; neither East nor West German officials considered the activities of rock 'n' roll fans harmless. Further, while the two German sides of the cold war developed their political and cultural visions in constant reference to each other, both German states also had a common point of reference in America. Given this day-to-day exposure to American influences, it is hardly astonishing that American popular culture received special attention in East and West German attempts to regulate cultural consumption by their citizens. Both Germanies were facing the difficult task of constructing German national identities out of the rubble left by National Socialism, World War II, and the tensions of the cold war, and it was frequently in relation to the United States—long recognized as the most developed consumer culture—that each state laid claim to a German heritage and tried to define what being a German meant. Youth cultures—and the youthful taste for the latest U.S. imports—thus became one battleground for struggles over German identities.

Rock 'n' roll challenged East and West German constructions of national identity precisely because Germans saw it as a black or black-influenced music that undermined gender norms. Critiques of rock 'n' roll fans and stars drew heavily on intersecting racial and gender stereotypes; authorities on both sides treated uncontrolled female sexuality as un-German and marked it as unacceptable by associating it with blackness.[18] This investigation will help us understand how political reconstruction on both sides of the iron curtain shaped and was shaped by normative ideas of German culture. In the context of the continuing politicization of culture in the postwar period and of the renewed fears concerning consumer culture in the 1950s, many commentators in East and West Germany perceived the behavior of rock 'n' roll fans as an outright youth rebellion. They saw the involvement of young women in rock 'n'

---

18. For the complicated relationship between race and gender under National Socialism, see e.g., Gisela Bock, "Equality and Difference in National Socialist Racism," in *Beyond Difference and Equality: Citizenship, Feminist Politics and Female Subjectivity,* ed. Gisela Bock and Susan James (New York, 1992), pp. 89–109; Marion Kaplan, "Jewish Women in Nazi Germany: Daily Life, Daily Struggles, 1933–1939," *Feminist Studies* 16 (1990): 579–606.

roll culture and the connections of rock 'n' roll to black American culture as threats with political implications worthy of the attention of politicians and requiring the creation of youth policies.

Making gender a central category of analysis, exploring intersections of gender with race, and inserting young women into the story of rock 'n' roll challenges the frameworks that scholars have thus far established to interpret 1950s youth cultures (when they have not completely ignored them). Jost Hermand, for example, has claimed that West German adolescents from the lower class perceived rock 'n' roll as rebellious for a while; but, in accordance with the Marxist idea of negative co-optation, he has concluded that the culture industry channeled the potential dissatisfaction of the lower classes, and their potential political resistance, into the arena of compensatory entertainment.[19] For East Germany, Timothy Ryback has rejected the notion that rock 'n' roll could assume any political significance other than highlighting the repressive stance of East Bloc authorities.[20] His interpretation echoes liberal assessments that have evaluated 1950s West German youth cultures as apolitical from the outset.[21] Like most scholars of 1950s youth, these authors have focused almost exclusively on male rebels. Even Kaspar Maase, who has recently reasserted the significance of West German youth cultures in the 1950s, has downplayed

---

19. Jost Hermand, *Kultur im Wiederaufbau: Die Bundesrepublik Deutschland, 1945–1965* (Munich, 1986), pp. 294–95, 357–63. Joachim Kaiser, "Phasenverschiebungen und Einschnitte in der kulturellen Entwicklung," in *Zäsuren nach 1945: Essays zur Periodisierung der deutschen Nachkriegsgeschichte*, ed. Martin Broszat (Munich, 1990), pp. 58–74, in his overview of West German culture ignores the youth rebellion altogether: he describes the years 1956–67 as "the real 1950s," a period of economic security and "babbittry," which only intellectuals like Günter Grass or Peter Weiss resisted. For the United States, George Lipsitz, *Class and Culture in Cold War America: A Rainbow at Midnight* (South Hadley, Mass., 1982), p. 218, has argued that, if one defines politics as the social struggle for a good life, rock 'n' roll songs "represented politics of the highest order." Yet Lipsitz, too, has ignored the female component of this rebellion in his validation of rock 'n' roll.

20. Timothy Ryback, *Rock around the Bloc: A History of Rock Music in Eastern Europe and the Soviet Union* (New York, 1990), p. 34. This is in marked contrast to Ryback's interpretation of the 1960s and recent assertions that rock music was improtant in the political transformations that led to the demise of socialism in 1989. See Sabrina P. Ramet, *Social Currents in Eastern Europe: The Sources and Meaning of the Great Transformation* (Durham, N.C., 1991); Peter Wicke, "The Times They Are A-Changin': Rock Music and Political Change in East Germany," in *Rockin' the Boat: Mass Music and Mass Movements*, ed. Reebee Garofalo (Boston, 1992), pp. 81–92. For rock music fans in the GDR in the 1950s and 1960s, see also Michael Rauhut, *Beat in der Grauzone: DDR-Rock, 1964–1972—Politik und Alltag* (Berlin, 1993); Dorothee Wierling, "Jugend als innerer Feind: Konflikte in der Erziehungsdiktatur der sechziger Jahre," in *Sozialgeschichte der DDR*, ed. Hartmut Kaelble, Jürgen Kocka, and Hartmut Zwahr (Stuttgart, 1994), pp. 404–25.

21. These interpretations follow Helmut Schelsky, *Die skeptische Generation: Eine Soziologie der deutschen Jugend* (Düsseldorf, 1957). See, e.g., Viggo Graf Blücher, *Die Generation der Unbefangenen: Zur Soziologie der jungen Menschen heute* (Düsseldorf, 1966).

the importance of female rebels and has explicitly located the actions of male adolescents in the "semiotic wars of everyday life" and "not on the political stage."[22] Western Marxists and liberals alike have seen 1950s youth cultures as consistently nonpolitical and have relegated young women to their sidelines.

Yet, as I have pointed out, a close examination of the public debates over youth cultures in the 1950s shows that authorities in East and West Germany did define Germanness in terms of both race and stereotyped gender roles and that they also politicized rock 'n' roll. In this article I hope to explain the disjunction between the reactions of both East and West German authorities to youth cultures in the 1950s, on the one hand, and the treatment of these cultures in subsequent scholarship, on the other. My questions are thus both historical and historiographical: How were gender and race obliterated from accounts of the 1950s youth rebellion? How did this youth rebellion come to be represented as a nonpolitical stance in both East and West Germany—and internationally—despite the political attention it received at the time? What are the implications of these representations for a history of young women in the 1950s?

As I will suggest, present assessments of the 1950s rebellion as nonpolitical are the result of what I call a cold war liberal understanding of culture in West Germany.[23] In the late 1950s, many West Germans ceased to see rock 'n'

---

22. Maase (n. 4 above), pp. 12–13. In the course of his study, Maase mentions West German girls and racism but does not make race a central category of analysis. See also Rainer Dorner, "Halbstark," pp. 233–43, and Andi Brauer, "Schaukeln und Wälzen," pp. 245–57, both in *Bikini: Die Fünfziger Jahre: Kalter Krieg und Capri-Sonne* (1981; reprint, Reinbek, 1983). Hermann Glaser, *Die Kulturgeschichte der Bundesrepublik Deutschland,* vol. 2, *Zwischen Grundgesetz und Großer Koalition, 1949–1967* (Frankfurt am Main, 1990), pp. 239–40, devotes two pages in his cultural history of the Federal Republic to Americanized youth cultures and identifies challenges to established gender norms associated with rock 'n' roll without putting them into a larger framework.

23. A consensus is emerging among scholars of West Germany that the years after 1956 saw important social and political transformations. See Anselm Doering-Manteuffel, "Deutsche Zeitgeschichte nach 1945: Entwicklung und Problemlagen der historischen Forschung zur Nachkriegszeit," *Vierteljahrshefte für Zeitgeschichte* 41 (January 1993): 1–29; Paul Erker, "Zeitgeschichte als Sozialgeschichte," *Geschichte und Gesellschaft* 19 (1993): 202–38. The question whether West Germany indeed developed into a liberal system has been the subject of much concern. See Ralf Dahrendorf, *Society and Democracy in Germany* (Garden City, N.Y., 1967); David P. Conradt, "From Output Orientation to Regime Support: Changing German Political Culture," in *Social and Political Structures in West Germany: From Authoritarianism to Postindustrial Democracy,* ed. Ursula Hoffmann-Lange (Boulder, Colo., 1991), pp. 127–42. Konrad H. Jarausch and Larry Eugene Jones, "German Liberalism Reconsidered," in *In Search of a Liberal Germany: Studies in the History of German Liberalism from 1789 to the Present,* ed. Konrad H. Jarausch and Larry Eugene Jones (New York, 1990), pp. 1–23, have asserted that liberalism has shaped West Germany's political landscape (p. 20). On cold war liberalism in the United States, see Robert J. Corber, *In the Name of National Security: Hitchcock, Homophobia, and the Political Construction of Gender in Postwar America* (Durham, N.C., 1993).

roll as a danger, while East German authorities continued to fight it. The West German view that culture was not a central site of political struggle emerged in the years after 1957 when scholars and politicians like Helmut Schelsky and Ludwig Erhard employed psychological theories to explain rebellious adolescent behavior and to define it as nonpolitical. While I see the existence of a cultural realm completely divorced from politics as conceptually impossible, I do want to consider the historical and political significance of these efforts to define culture as nonpolitical and thereby to affirm a division between culture and politics that liberalism assumes. I interpret the move on the part of West German cold war liberals to define culture as nonpolitical not as a "depoliticization" but, rather, as a renewed politicization of culture on different terrain. I will also investigate how the reframing of rock 'n' roll consumption as a nonpolitical activity was related to efforts to accommodate and alter adolescent behavior. And finally, I will examine the significance of this shift for a history of young German women in the context of the cold war of the 1950s.

Thus I will argue that the consumption of American popular culture and German reactions to it were important forces in changing sexual norms in the two Germanies as well as in transforming the overall German cold war battle. In recent years Americanization has become a contested framework for the study of West European—and specifically West German—postwar history. In some treatments, successful Americanization in Europe has been equated with the successful installation of liberal states and market economies.[24] However, other treatments of postwar West European culture have often been critical of American influences, as signified by the term "Coca-Colonization" used by historians of West Germany and Austria.[25] My focus on Americanized youth cultures in both East and West Germany moves beyond the tropes of liberation, negative co-optation, and fascistization that have characterized many debates among cultural critics, social theorists, and politicians in the past and that many

---

24. For a treatment celebrating the stablizing American impact (stable families, revived democracies, improved national sentiments) in postwar Europe, see Peter Duignan and L. H. Gann, *The Rebirth of the West: The Americanization of the Democratic World, 1945–1958* (Cambridge, 1992). For a much more nuanced study that focuses on American economic hegemony, see Volker R. Berghahn, *The Americanization of West German Industry, 1945–1973* (New York, 1986).

25. Ralph Willet, *The Americanization of Germany, 1945–1949* (New York, 1989), p. ix; Reinhold Wagnleitner, *Coca-Colonization and Cold War: The Cultural Mission of the United States in Austria after the Second World War,* trans. Diana M. Wolf (Chapel Hill, N.C., 1994). For useful critiques of the concept Americanization in the West German context, see Maase, pp. 21–40; and Arnold Sywottek, "The Americanization of Everyday Life? Early Trends in Consumer and Leisure-Time Behavior," in *America and the Shaping of German Society, 1945–1955,* ed. Michael Ermath (Providence, R.I., 1993), pp. 132–52. Recently scholars are paying more attention to the prejudices Europeans have brought to their encounters with the United States. See Dan Diner, *Verkehrte Welten: Antiamerikanismus in Deutschland* (Frankfurt am Main, 1993); Richard Kuisel, *Seducing the French: The Dilemma of Americanization* (Berkeley and Los Angeles, 1993).

scholars have reaffirmed since. In this way I will explore how the politicization of culture in both states was interlinked with the reconstitution of gender and racial norms that were central to (re)constructions of Germanness on either side of the iron curtain. Battles over the meaning of American popular culture in the 1950s were sites for reconfiguring culture and politics in both Germanies, even though the two states conceived of the relationship between culture and politics very differently.

German Reactions to Elvis Presley and His Female American Fans

When the West German weekly *Der Spiegel* ran a cover story on Elvis Presley in December 1956, it described his American fans as girls steeped in "orgiastic hysteria." According to *Der Spiegel,* the American music industry had pushed Presley after "the first symptoms of collective erotic eruptions" appeared.[26] In late 1956 and in 1957, many more West German newspapers reported extensively on female American teenagers who were said to swarm around Presley wherever he showed up and who would even go so far as to tear his clothes off in ecstasy. The West German press thus made a clear connection between rock 'n' roll and white American female sexual aggressiveness.[27]

Just two months earlier, West German papers had evaluated rock quite differently—namely, as instigating male rebellion. In September 1956, *Der Spiegel* reported in an article on Presley's success that riots had occurred at American rock 'n' roll concerts; here *Der Spiegel* treated Presley's fans as male delinquents. This resonated in both Germanies. Since 1955, youth riots with mostly male participants had also shaken many West German and some East German cities. In the West commentators worried about a rebellion of the *Halbstarke*—literally, the "semi-strong," a term that connoted working-class male delinquents. East Germans preferred the English word "rowdies" to describe young males who, like their counterparts in the West, roamed the streets attacking policemen and destroying public property. When the American movie *Blackboard Jungle* brought Bill Haley's song "Rock around the Clock"

---

26. "Elvis, the Pelvis," *Der Spiegel* (December 12, 1956).

27. For treatments of American girls tearing Presley's clothes off or girls fainting in hysteria, see Manfred George, "Liebesbriefe an einen Toten," *Tagesspiegel* (September 15, 1956); "Das Phänomen Elvis Presley," *Telegraf* (October 11, 1956); "Der Gorilla mit der Gitarre," *Depesche* (January 11, 1957); "Idol der Mädchen," *Telegraf* (February 9, 1957); "Über Geschmack läßt sich streiten," *Spandauer Volksblatt* (March 22, 1957); "New York empfindet anders als Berlin," *Telegraf* (May 26, 1957); "Ein Gesicht in der Menge," *B.Z.* (October 31, 1957). The West German youth magazine *Bravo* also reported about Elvis's female American fans: "Schwarm von Millionen," *Bravo* (December 2, 1956); "Mädchen schreien für Elvis," *Bravo* (December 9, 1956). Hysteria has historically been described as a female disease. See Elaine Showalter, *The Female Malady: Women, Madness, and Culture in England, 1830–1980* (New York, 1986).

to Germany in December 1955 (and implied a connection between the song and the juvenile delinquency shown in the movie), some commentators in Germany began to make rock 'n' roll into the culprit that instigated male misbehavior. These fears were exacerbated by reports of riots after Presley concerts in the United States and violence after showings of the movie *Rock around the Clock* in London and Oslo in the summer of 1956.[28]

Commentators linked their worries about the excessive aggressiveness of male youths to fears of black cultural influences and worries about the effectiveness of state power. One West German scholar saw the behavior of the *Halbstarke* as a regression into a "wild state" of "de-civilization."[29] *Der Spiegel* warned that American youths at Presley concerts were dancing by themselves "like haunted medicine men of a jungle tribe governed only by music"—namely, by rock 'n' roll. The article added a jab at the American occupation in Germany when it asserted that American papers reported news from the "rock 'n' roll front" with the same steadiness that German papers "reported on violent acts committed by American soldiers in Germany." That same month, in September 1956, the newly founded West German youth magazine *Bravo*, a chief promoter of the new American-influenced commercialized youth culture, announced the arrival of the first rock 'n' roll movie to reach Germany, *Rock around the Clock. Bravo* explained that the "wild rhythm" of Bill Haley's music was rooted in the ritual music of "Africa's Negroes." Moreover, the magazine printed pictures of male English rock fans and reported that they had rioted after viewing the movie. Proclaiming that under the influence of rock 'n' roll "cool Englishmen" had turned into "white Negroes," *Bravo* labeled rioting as typically black behavior. In the same article, the magazine urged its German audience not to behave like the English. Even as the magazine ostensibly admired the wild, black-influenced rock 'n' roll music, *Bravo*, like *Der Spiegel*, warned against its effects in racist terms.[30]

28. "Der Über-Rhythmus," *Der Spiegel* (September 26, 1956). On riots, see "Die Königin greift ein," *Spandauer Volksblatt* (September 19, 1956); for a report about riots abroad, see *National-Zeitung* (September 28, 1956). For the origins of the term *Halbstarke* as a reference to male working-class youth during the Wilhelmine period, see Detlev J. K. Peukert, "Clemens Schultzens 'Naturgeschichte des Halbstarken,'" in *Schock und Schöpfung: Jugendästhetik im 20. Jahrhundert,* ed. Deutscher Werkbund and Württembergischer Kunstverein (Darmstadt, 1986), pp. 391–93.

29. Hans Muchow, "Zur Psychologie und Pädagogik der Halbstarken," *Unsere Jugend,* nos. 9–11 (1956), quoted in Curt Bondy et al., *Jugendliche stören die Ordnung: Bericht und Stellungnahme zu den Halbstarkenkrawallen* (Munich, 1957), pp. 82–84.

30. "Der Über-Rhythmus"; "Die ganze Welt rockt und rollt," *Bravo* (September 30, 1956). For an analysis of the racial meanings of aggression in postwar U.S. political writings, see Ruth Feldstein, "Making 'Moms' and 'Matriarchs': Dangerous Women, Race, and American Liberalism, 1930–1965" (Ph.D. diss., Brown University, 1996), chaps. 2 and 3. On U.S. cultural politics in the cold war, see Melani McAlister, "Staging the American Century: Race, Gender, and Nation in U.S. Representations of the Middle East, 1945–1992," (Ph.D. diss., Brown University, 1996).

After December 1956, the attention German papers gave to Presley's American female fans transformed the discourse on rock 'n' roll: now it was not merely about male aggressiveness but also about feminized men and overly aggressive women. Once German commentators recognized that young women were Presley's most active fans, they began to describe the threat of rock 'n' roll in openly sexual terms. This shift went hand in hand with an effort to question Presley's masculinity.

As in the United States, gender ambiguity was one of Presley's outstanding characteristics for German promoters as well as opponents.[31] The music industry and press commentary worked together to feminize him. In 1956, RCA decided to market Presley in Germany with the slogan "He sings like Marilyn Monroe walks." Both West and East German papers picked up on the press releases from RCA, and sometimes they played with the slogan to underline Presley's gender ambiguity. An article in an East Berlin paper, for example, announced that Presley was trying to compensate for his bad voice by "wildly swinging his hips like Marilyn Monroe."[32] The close association with Monroe, who like the French actresses Marina Vlady and Brigitte Bardot had become a symbol of female sensuality in Germany, in fact made Presley into a rebel quite different from such predecessors as Marlon Brando. When describing Presley's concert performances, *Der Spiegel* doubted that Presley's moving hips were an allusion to male sexual behavior and instead described his gestures as those of a "talented female striptease dancer."[33] That description had also been used by American papers, and along with the American expression "Elvis, the Pelvis" it was taken up by many Germans.[34]

West German commentators again harnessed alleged racial characteristics to criticize Presley and his fans, but this time they used them to support the notion of *female* aggression and male weakness. Some West German reports on Presley drew a clear connection between his gender and racial ambiguities:

---

31. We may think of Elvis as hypermasculine, but in the 1950s German depictions of him were more complicated. On Elvis's challenge to respectable manhood, see Steven Simels, *Gender Chameleons: Androgyny in Rock 'n' Roll* (New York, 1985), pp. 14–16. For a reading of Elvis as a female impersonator, see Marjorie Garber, *Vested Interests: Cross-Dressing and Cultural Anxiety* (New York, 1992), pp. 365–74. She asserts that Elvis's racial crossover was read as a "crossover move in gender terms: a move from hypermale to hyperfemale" (p. 367).

32. Werner Micke, "Philosophie des Stumpfsinns," *Junge Welt* (February 5, 1957), quoted in Rauhut (n. 20 above), p. 31; "Elvis, the Pelvis"; Ker Robertson, "Elvis Presley, Idol von Millionen von Backfischen und bestürzendes Symptom unserer Zeit," *Depesche* (January 18, 1957); "Gold aus heißer Kehle," *Beratungsdienst Jugend und Film*, vol. 3 (February 1958): BI–BII. My thanks to Mark Cooper for first pointing me to RCA's marketing strategy.

33. "Elvis, the Pelvis." This comparison was also made in the United States. For a quote from the *New York Daily Mirror,* see Simels, p. 16.

34. See, e.g., "Gold aus heißer Kehle," *Beratungsdienst Jugend und Film.*

Presley's way of moving put not just his male gender but also his racial origins in doubt. Newspapers in the West suspected that Presley must have black blood in his ancestry to be able to move and sing in this extraordinary fashion.[35] In another attack, one West German paper directly referred to Presley's thick lips as an attribute of the ideal man in the United States—a country described as run by women ("Frauenstaat Amerika").[36] Such statements used references to racial stereotypes, like thick lips, to underline the notion that in the United States gender norms were reversed. Gender and racial ambiguities on Presley's part elicited and required gender and racial transgressions on the part of his female fans. Unlike earlier writers who associated rock 'n' roll with male over-aggressiveness and blackness, commentators now turned against female aggressivity: they reported that in the United States Presley's female fans attacked policemen and exhibited active sexual desire toward this feminized man with what they described as stereotypically black features. West German commentators thus conflated male weakness with blackness and linked both to female desire. These associations of blackness with both male overaggression and male weakness reaffirmed Western stereotypes of black men.[37]

East German officials, too, associated the public behavior of young women as consumers of rock 'n' roll with primitiveness and, implicitly, with blackness. The 1956 cartoon in the *Berliner Zeitung* that showed a small, thin Presley in front of a crowd of big girls clearly implied that rock 'n' roll turned gender roles on their heads: American girls, who were throwing off their garterbelts, were sexual aggressors who emasculated men. Their hairstyles marked some of these young women as possibly black (short curly dark hair) and others as white (blonde ponytails), but in portraying all of them with stereotypical "negroid" features (wide noses, thick lips) the cartoon labeled their behavior as typically black. The accompanying article also put this reversal of gender roles into a racial context: it claimed that young women were the main consumers of rock 'n' roll (described as American nonculture) and asserted that rock 'n' roll appealed to primitive humans. Thus, in both East and West German critiques of rock 'n' roll, allusions to gender upheaval and alleged racial transgressions reinforced one another to portray rock as dangerous.[38]

---

35. To explain Elvis's musical style, Manfred George asserted that at some point in Elvis's ancestry black blood must have entered his family. He also mentioned that music of the African jungle had been brought over by slaves forced to leave their homes, who today counted "15 million citizens working for their full emancipation" (*Tagesspiegel* [February 7, 1957]).

36. "'Rock ans Roll': öffentliches Ärgernis," *Badische Neue Nachrichten* (August 22, 1956).

37. See "Elvis, the Pelvis" (n. 26 above).

38. "Appell an den Urmenschen" (n. 1 above) was a direct response to the title story "Elvis, the Pelvis" in *Der Spiegel* on December 12.

East and West German Concepts of Civilization

On both sides of the iron curtain, the strong reactions against Presley's openly sexual American female fans were rooted in shared gender and racial assumptions that underlay East and West German concepts of civilization. Since the end of World War II, both sides had often formulated their cultural visions by explicitly rejecting American popular culture. For example, in the early 1950s West German authorities had attacked American dances like boogie-woogie as part of their youth protection efforts. (Germans used the term "boogie" to refer to both the American dance music and the dances associated with it.) Boogie and other types of fast-paced dance music became associated with primitivism and stigmatized for the threat they posed to proper gender roles. In West German discussions of dancing, concerns about premarital sex, especially by women, intersected with misgivings about working-class culture and with a hostility toward black culture. One West German official described the new dances as "intoxicating" and therefore as especially dangerous for young women.[39] Contemporaries criticized girls in working-class neighborhoods who hung out on the streets and danced to boogie-woogie, suggesting that they were potential sexual delinquents. Related attacks pointed to the emasculating and feminizing effects that "sultry negro songs" had on young men: as education manuals warned, they too had to restrain themselves in order to reach full manhood.[40] Both charges—those against female sexual expressiveness as well as those against the feminization of men—were reminiscent of Nazi hostility toward jazz and swing specifically and of Nazi attacks on Jews, blacks, homosexuals, and Sinti and Roma more generally. Moreover, West Germans had made these attacks a crucial part of their larger political vision, which linked mass culture to a lack of male restraint and female respectability and to the threat of fascism; politicians voiced such attacks on mass culture not only in the context of youth protection but also, for example, in the 1955 and 1956 debates on rearmament.[41]

---

39. Hans Engelbach, "Entwurf eines Gesetzes zum Schutze der Jugend in der Öffentlichkeit," n.d. [1949], (LAB) Rep. 13, Acc. 1046, Nr. 18. See also, "K.o. durch Töne," *Berliner Montag* (October 31, 1949); "So jung und schon . . ." *Illus* (January 20, 1952); "Weil's so schön war," *Blickpunkt*, no. 14 (1953); Erna Maraun, "Schutzaufsichtshelfer diskutieren über 'Jugend und Tanz,'" *Der Rundbrief* 5 (March 1955): 23–24, LAB, Rep. 13, Acc. 1022, Nr. 6. One Berlin social worker stated with some satisfaction in 1954 that not all adolescents were interested in boogie-woogie or jitterbug. Compare Hans-Dieter Wehowski, "Nicht nur Jazzfreunde," *Der Rundbrief* 4 (February 1954): 25, LAB, Rep. 13, Acc. 1022, Nr. 6.

40. See A. Gügler, *Euer Sohn in der Entwicklungskrise* (Stuttgart, 1952), pp. 32–48, reprinted in Kuhnert and Ackermann (n. 4 above), p. 50.

41. For the meaning of jazz in the Third Reich, see Kater, *Different Drummers* (n. 17 above). For examples of sexual deviance as the signifier of racial inferiority (and vice versa), see Burleigh and Wippermann (n. 11 above). On the threats that (American) mass culture allegedly

Taken together, these voices shaped a West German discourse in which a rejection of (female) sexual expressiveness was linked to definitions of black culture and working-class culture as sexual and therefore unacceptable. Thus, in spite of their commitment to a Western military and political alliance, West German authorities in the first half of the 1950s were seeking a third, "German" way between what they saw as the threat of Bolshevism on the one hand and the self-destructive, sexualizing, and emasculating powers emanating from American-style consumer culture on the other. To this end conservatives from the governing Christian Democrats (CDU/CSU) promoted the notion of a "Christian Occident." While the opposition Social Democrats (SPD) did not agree with this particular terminology, they, too, supported the government's gender conservatism. Believing that the West German family had survived National Socialism unscathed, these mainstream parties agreed that families of male breadwinner/protectors and female homemakers were central to postwar West German stability and that such families distinguished West Germany from its cold war enemies to the East. Across party lines, officials promoted self-restraint in both sexual matters and consumption, especially for women, as crucial to the preservation of the West German family and thus to West German reconstruction. Dances like boogie or, later, rock 'n' roll proved incompatible with that vision, and state officials tried to ensure that West German adolescents learned properly bourgeois and white dances like the waltz.[42]

On the other side of the iron curtain, East German officials used the notion of decadence to oppose Western influences.[43] In the early 1950s, East Germans had described "decadent" imports like boogie-woogie, jazz, and samba as part of a more general "American cultural barbarism" which they saw at the root of American and West German imperialism.[44] Historically, decadence had

---

posed to the restrained, postfascist, masculine West German soldier, see Uta G. Poiger, "Rebels with a Cause? American Popular Culture, the 1956 Youth Riots, and New Conceptions of Masculinity in East and West Germany," in *The American Impact on Postwar Germany*, ed. Reiner Pommerin (Oxford, 1995), pp. 93–124.

42. For the gender norms crucial to the vision of a "Christian occident," see Fehrenbach, *Cinema in Democratizing Germany* (n. 8 above), Moeller (n. 5 above).

43. Accusations of decadence by socialists were directed against the primal, the irrational (and implicitly feminine) aspects of modern life that they saw manifested in bourgeois culture. For hostilities toward mass culture, see Andreas Huyssen, *After the Great Divide: Modernism, Mass Culture, Postmodernism* (Bloomington, Ind., 1986). For the years before the founding of the GDR, see David Pike, *The Politics of Culture in Soviet-Occupied Germany, 1945–49* (Stanford, Calif., 1992). For KPD attacks on decadence, see Patrice Petro, *Joyless Streets: Women and Melodramatic Representation in Weimar Germany* (Princeton, 1989).

44. See HA Jugendhilfe und Jugenderziehung, "Entwurf: Präambel 'Verordnung zum Schutze der Kinder und der Jugendlichen'," Berlin, February 18, 1952, Landesarchiv Berlin, Außenstelle Breite Straße (LAB [STA]), Rep. 120, Nr. 2614. East Berlin officials sought to take measures to fight the American driven *Entartung* (degeneration) of social dancing and even wanted to purge radio archives of Western "Hott-Musik." See "Genosse Roesky zur Kenntnisnahme,"

connoted deviations from respectable womanhood and manhood, and Europeans had often used the term also to criticize behavior they perceived as racial transgression. East German officials indicted jazz music, for example, as "decadent" and supported this rejection with references to jazz's allegedly sexualizing effects. One cultural official spoke of the marks that brothels had left on jazz, and another was worried about the "public display of sexual drives" among jazz fans who danced.[45] Since East German officials did not have to negotiate between westward political integration and their hostility toward consumer culture, they geared their youth protection efforts explicitly against the "American way of life" and American *Unkultur,* a German expression that altogether denied American imports the status of "culture."[46]

The fact that many of the products of American culture were rooted in the culture of African-Americans, whom communists recognized as an oppressed group, did not dissuade East German authorities from attacks on American music and dances and especially rock 'n' roll. Race played a complicated role in these attacks. It would seem that the racialism and racism apparent in East German charges of "decadence" and "primitivism" against American popular culture were clearly at odds with East Germany's public stance against racism in the United States. After all, East German papers in the mid-1950s reported extensively on efforts to integrate schools and public accommodations in the American South. However, East German visions of racial equality relied on ideals of male restraint and female respectability, including female sexual passivity, across races. This insistence on specific norms of male and female respectability found one of its most powerful articulations in official rejections of jazz as a music associated with gangsters and prostitutes. With such condemnations of jazz, which they saw as a black music, East German officials reasserted racial hierarchies in the realm of cul-

---

November 17, 1953, LAB (STA), Rep. 121, Nr. 162. Samba and other "degenerations" of dancing were described as American cultural barbarism in "Bericht über die Privattanzschulen," n.d. [ca. 1954], LAB (STA), Rep. 121, Nr. 162. American-style dances were just one focus of East German officials; in the first half of the 1950s they also very actively fought against Western dime novels and movies.

45. Georg Knepler, "Jazz und die Volksmusik," *Musik und Gesellschaft* 5 (June 1955): 181–83; Ludwig Richard Müller, "Dekadenz und lebensfroher Neubeginn," *Musik und Gesellschaft* 5 (April 1955): 114–17. For an example of the use of decadence in racial terms, see Kater, "The Jazz Experience in Weimar Germany" (n. 16 above), p. 153. See also Sandra Siegel, "Literature and Degeneration: The Representation of 'Decadence,'" in *Degeneration: The Dark Side of Progress,* ed. J. Edward Chamberlin and Sander L. Gilman (New York, 1985), pp. 199–219.

46. The preamble of the 1955 GDR youth protection law turned explicitly against the "American way of life," propagated in the "Adenauer-state" (i.e., West Germany) ("Verordnung des Ministerrats der DDR zum Schutze der Jugend," *Gesetzblatt der DDR,* pt. 1, no. 80 [September 29, 1955]).

ture. Even though highlighting American racism was one way to fight the cold war against the United States and West Germany, East German authorities could not relinquish their own association between female sexual passivity, "civilization," and "whiteness."[47]

West German rhetoric against American influences shared many similarities with official East German reactions. West German authorities and the West German press also opposed racial segregation in the United States, yet they, too, felt threatened by the music and dance styles that they identified as rooted in black culture. These similarities between East and West German assumptions about what a viable civilization was and what role it should play in the construction of East and West German identities, respectively, led to a curious constellation. Indeed, these similarities even threatened to undermine the West German strategy of describing East Germany as inferior because its officials forced women into the workforce and thus allegedly destroyed families. On several occasions, West German church authorities, especially Catholics, praised policies in the East where, they claimed, adolescents were better protected from the dangers of consumer culture and from American imports. Conservative West German politicians, in turn, echoed these charges to fight the supposedly damaging effects of consumer culture within West Germany. In the face of the onslaught of American-style consumer culture, it appeared in the mid-1950s that West German authorities felt even more vulnerable politically than their East German counterparts.[48]

East and West German Female Rock 'n' Roll "Hysterics"

Perhaps because of their specific fears, many West German commentators still hoped, in the spring of 1957, that the American "mass hysteria" around Elvis Presley would not take hold in Germany. In spite of evidence to the contrary, they contrasted the "hysterical" behavior of American teenagers with the "more rational" reactions of their German counterparts. Journalists thus praised German girls who, confronted with the movie *Love Me Tender,*

---

47. I use "racialism" here to refer to the fact that race was one structuring force in discourses on decadence and primitivism (which also had racist implications). For the limits of racial liberalism and its intersections with racialized gender norms in the 1950s United States, see Feldstein (n. 6 above).

48. For a 1951 Catholic message praising the lack of decadence in the Soviet Union, see Heide Fehrenbach, "The Fight for the 'Christian West': German Film Control, the Churches and the Reconstruction of Civil Society in the Early Bonn Republic," *German Studies Review* 14 (February 1991): 39–63, esp. 46 [republished in this volume]. In an October 1956 speech to the West German parliament, Minister of the Interior Schröder referred to Bishop Dibelius, who had praised the GDR authorities for controlling youth consumption of mass culture (see "Ein Studienbüro für Jugendfragen," *Stuttgarter Zeitung* [October 26, 1956]).

allegedly urged Presley to get rid of his make-up.[49] One West German paper expressed relief that German women, unlike their American contemporaries, would not "melt" when they saw Elvis's wide, soft—and, implicitly, unmanly—face.[50] Allegedly, German women were not swayed by Elvis's American brand of eroticism.[51]

However, as other reports indicate, East and West German girls did like rock 'n' roll. In October 1956, a local Berlin newspaper reported that "rock 'n' roll reigned in the Hot-House," a West Berlin club. According to the article, women were the more accomplished rock dancers and preferred to buy their cokes themselves rather than have some guy step on their fashionable shoes. They would even turn their backs on clumsy young men and grab their girl-friends to "rock" on the dance floor! Rock 'n' roll dancing provided a dramatic contrast to traditional dance styles in which the man led and the woman followed. Consequently, one West German commentary in 1956 described rock 'n' roll dancers as "wild barbarians in ecstasy" and worried that their dancing "degenerated" into "vulgar and erotically expressive movements."[52] Women and men threw each other through the air. Also, rock 'n' roll dancers often held each other just by the hand and thus were able to design their movements individually. This "open dancing" even made it possible for women to dance with each other in public. Thus the new dynamic dance style associated with rock 'n' roll changed gender codes dramatically, as women asserted their independence in ever greater numbers and rejected the male control that older dance styles so effectively symbolized.[53]

The West German youth magazine *Bravo* now showed less hostility toward the black origins of rock 'n' roll and even referred to these black origins to market the music. When advertising the first German rock 'n' roll dance championship, *Bravo* stressed that rock 'n' roll came into existence among "Negroes": "They played it hotter, more convincingly, and danced it better, more freely and more elegantly." Comparisons with "Negroes" certainly served to underline the outrageous character of the new musical style, yet

---

49. "Nun ja, man lacht," *B.Z.* (April 15, 1957). See also "Zwischenrufe: So ein Himbeer-bubi!" *Der Tag* (April 13, 1957); "Ade, Du Himbeerbubi," *Berliner Morgenpost* (April 13, 1957); "New York empfindet anders als Berlin," *Telegraf* (May 26, 1957).

50. "Pulverdampf und heiße Lieder," *Die Welt* (April 13, 1957).

51. Allegedly, German girls did not value the erotic effect of the dark lines under Presley's eyes ("Nun ja, man lacht").

52. "Außer Rand und Band" (n. 3 above), p. BVII.

53. See "Waden aus Gummi rollen im Hot-House," *Depesche* (October 23, 1956); "Bravo sucht den deutschen Meister im 'Rock and Roll'," *Bravo* (November 13, 1956); "Selbstmördern empfohlen," *Junge Welt* (June 1957). For an exploration of youth dancing as a space for female display/victimization as well as for female pleasure, see Simon Frith and Angela McRobbie, "Rock and Sexuality," in *On Record: Rock, Pop, and the Written Word,* ed. Simon Frith and Andrew Goodwin (New York, 1990), pp. 371–89.

Bravo valorized black styles exactly because they were outrageous. It now urged German teenagers to try for themselves the dance styles developed by African-Americans.[54]

The shocking fashions of female rock 'n' roll fans further exacerbated fears in both East and West Germany. For critical contemporaries, their looks signified a loss of femininity.[55] A West German critique of an outspoken female Presley fan imagined her this way in 1958: "half-long pants, funny jacket, sauerkraut figure like a toilet brush."[56] Others commented on the boyish looks of girls with ponytails.[57] In the East, too, young women sported jeans, tight pants, and short sweaters, and they emulated Western models. As one paper put it: "Female creatures of this kind distinguish themselves from the males only in their hair, which is eaten regularly by rats, so that one ultimately doesn't know where these rodents wreak more damage—in or on the heads."[58] In an East German youth magazine, a report on East German male delinquents featured girls with tight pants and short jackets prominently among the boys.[59] Wearing men's clothes in public had formerly been reserved for women in times of emergency, like the war and the immediate postwar period. With their new fashions, many East and West German girls now directly countered the images of female respectability available to them: the model of the "clean" German woman with no makeup and with her hair in a German bun that the Nazis had promoted so forcefully and that West German cultural conservatives still saw as an ideal, as well as the model of the asexual East German worker/mother.[60]

54. "Wer wird deutscher Meister im Rock 'n' Roll?" *Bravo* (December 9, 1956). Maase (n. 4 above) overvalorizes *Bravo*'s antiracist efforts.

55. See pictures of rock 'n' roll dancers in "Bravo sucht den deutschen Neuster in 'Rock and Roll!'" *Bravo* (November 13, 1956). See also the description of female Elvis fans in tight jeans ("engbehoste Verehrerinnen") in "Unsere Meinung," *Die Welt* (October 5, 1958). For an insightful treatment of fashion as part of a larger struggle for political and social power, see Mary Louise Roberts, "Samson and Delilah Revisited: The Politics of Women's Fashion in 1920s France," *American Historical Review* 98 (June 1993): 657–84.

56. Letters to the editor *Nürnberger Nachrichten* (February 7, 1958).

57. West German commentary quoted in Helmut Lamprecht, *Teenager und Manager* (1960; reprint, Munich, 1965), p. 14.

58. East German press quoted in "Alter Feind—neu entdeckt," *Kölnische Rundschau* (August 6, 1958). One official report complained that even when members of a state youth club put up a portrait of the Russian cosmonaut Gagarin they contrasted it with a picture of a "lightly clad" girl from a West German magazine (see "Einschätzung der Entwicklung der Jugendclubs," August 8, 1961, LAB (STA) [n. 44 above], Rep. 121, Nr. 62).

59. See "Jugend zwischen 18 und 22 Uhr," *Junge Generation* 12, no. 1 (1958): 17–22.

60. For a vehement attack on girls wearing pants and especially tight jeans as an expression of weakness and "un-girl like casual male behavior" ("unmädchenhafte Burschikosität"), see "Sollen Schulmädchen Hosen tragen?" *Spandauer Volksblatt* (November 6, 1957). In the article, the wearing of pants was deemed justified only during war. Dress codes were established at times in East and West Berlin. In the West, e.g., they required girls to wear skirts to school. See Carter

In East and West, rock 'n' roll fans, with their behavior and looks, made the consumption of rock 'n' roll into a decidedly public event and thus brought up bourgeois fears of male delinquency and female prostitution historically associated with the streets. That young women now did the same things as young men was particularly worrisome to East and West German officials. Teens of both sexes danced during movie showings in West German cities. They copied their moves from movies like *Rock around the Clock* and *Love Me Tender,* and in some instances, in both East and West, they danced after the movies in the streets. Much to the horror of their elders, they sometimes also rioted.[61] As a witness of one such scene in a Munich street explained, the girls, who were present in lower numbers, were nonetheless much more prominent in their extravagant dress and casual behavior.[62] In West Germany, the "wild dancing" to rock 'n' roll, like that to boogie-woogie before it, was coded as working-class behavior, and commentators stressed increasingly that "respectable" middle- and upper-class jazz fans rejected such "public displays."[63] In East Germany, some state-run clubs where adolescents listened to rock 'n' roll and danced apart gained a bad reputation among the population. In 1957 one Karl-Marx-Stadt club was referred to alternately as a "rock 'n' roll hall" or a "youth brothel." Some parents refused to allow their daughters to frequent these clubs, and state officials were greatly worried about the situation.[64]

(n. 4 above), p. 201. In the East, jeans, e.g., were prohibited (interview with Wolfgang Hille, January 22, 1993). (All interviews were conducted by me from January to July 1993; names have been changed; recordings and notes are in my possession.) For images of women under National Socialism, see Christine Wittrock, *Weiblichkeitsmythen: Das Frauenbild im Faschismus und seine Vorläufer in der Frauenbewegung der 20er Jahre* (Frankfurt am Main, 1983); Rita Thalmann, *Frauensein im Dritten Reich* (Munich, 1984); Renate Wiggershaus, *Frauen unterm Nationalsozialismus* (Wuppertal, 1984).

61. See the report on a Munich showing of *Love Me Tender* (*Beratungsdienst Jugend und Film* 2 [March 1957]: BVIII); also the report on a West Berlin showing of *Loving You* in "Gold aus heißer Kehle," *Beratungsdienst Jugend und Film* (n. 32 above), p. BII. For a description of riots in West Berlin and West Germany, see Bondy et al. (n. 29 above), pp. 37–46. For East Germany, see Hentschel, Abteilung Kultur, Rat der Stadt Halle to Folkmann, Referat Musik, Ministerium für Kultur, September 24, 1957, Bundesarchiv Abteilungen Potsdam (BArch P), DR1 Nr. 243; "Protokoll über einen Erfahrungsaustausch über die Arbeit der Jugendklubs in der DDR," 1960, Jugendarchiv beim Institut für zeitgeschichtliche Jugendforschung, Berlin (JA-IzJ), A6724 (cited hereafter as "Erfahrungsaustausch," 1960, JA-IzJ, A6724).

62. "Außer Rand und Band 2. Teil," *Beratungsdienst Jugend und Film,* vol. 2 (January 1957).

63. See "Kann der Jazz unserer Jugend schaden?" *Die Welt* (July 21, 1957). In 1956 and 1957 rock 'n' roll was often not clearly differentiated from boogie-woogie.

64. "Erfahrungsaustausch," 1960, JA-IzJ, A6724. Rolf Lindner, "Strasse—Strassenjunge—Strassenbande: Ein zivilisationstheoretischer Streifzug," *Zeitschrift für Volkskunde* 79 (1983): 192–208, has made clear that definitions of deviance have been gender-specific (p. 193). For the Weimar Republic, see Detlev J. K. Peukert, *Jugend zwischen Krieg und Krise: Lebenswelten von Arbeiterjungen in der Weimarer Republik* (Cologne, 1987).

With the advent of rock 'n' roll, female rebels attracted widespread attention as sexual beings. To be sure, some young women had been taking an active part in the *Halbstarken* subcultures that had formed in many working-class neighborhoods after 1954 and that had created so much anxiety among both East and West Germans. A few had joined street gangs in working-class neighborhoods. While women undoubtedly played subordinate roles in gangs and riots, they were watched with some admiration by many female contemporaries. The East and West German press, however, had mostly ignored them. Generally, female members of youth subcultures found it more difficult than their male counterparts to gain public acknowledgment for their actions.[65]

As more and more female rock 'n' roll fans clearly challenged the East and West German ideals of female (sexual) passivity after 1956, the East and West German press oscillated between ignoring them and raging against them. Thus East and West German papers did not report that there were female rioters at a Bill Haley concert in Berlin in 1958, although pictures in the press clearly showed both boys *and* girls throwing chairs. At the other extreme, one West German paper mobilized the image of the (usually male) delinquent *Halbstarke* against female rock 'n' roll fans, criticizing a young West German woman who had spoken out in Presley's defense as a "typical female *Halbstarke*" with "an open mane, a face full of pimples, a purple loud mouth, and black eyeliner."[66]

In their most publicized challenges to dominant gender norms, young women often made use of their status as potential girlfriends and wives. Publicly making Elvis Presley into a male ideal, women in East and West Germany redefined norms of both masculinity and femininity. A female fan wrote a letter to the editor of a West German newspaper concerning a negative review of a Presley movie in which she accused the reviewer of being "a fat, old, nasty dwarf, a jealous dog and an old sack."[67] Also in 1958, girls from a West Berlin fan club from the upper-class district of Wilmersdorf announced that Elvis had

---

65. "Der Sportpalast-ein Hexenkessel," *Spandauer Volksblatt* (October 28, 1958); "Tumulte im Sportpalast," *Telegraf* (October 28, 1958). See also pictures that show girls next to boys throwing chairs: "Wer hat schuld an Rock 'n' Roll-Krawallen?" *Die Welt* (November 8, 1958). In their 1957 study, Bondy et al., pp. 23–28, defined *Halbstarke* as male adolescents "who dress conspicuously and are interested in a loose, casual, and unproductive togetherness with companions of their age and sex" (p. 28). Similar definitions were used in East Germany (see "Erfahrungsaustausch," 1960, JA-IzJ, A6724). However, Bondy et al. estimated that 5–12 percent of the participants in riots after music shows or movies were girls, who arrived on the backseats of their boyfriends' motorbikes (p. 53). For oral histories about girls' participation in riots, see also Bertram and Krüger (n. 2 above).

66. Letters to the editor, *Nürnberger Nachrichten* (February 7, 1958). See also the description of a female "*halbstarker* Teenager" in blue jeans and sweater in "Mit Caterina Valente in die Scala," *Mannheimer Morgen* (January 18, 1957).

67. Letters to the editor, *Nürnberger Nachrichten* (February 7, 1958).

more success with women than his critics did.[68] East Berlin girls stated their support for Presley by wearing his name on the back of their jeans.[69] These young women went public with their (sexual) desire, asserted their right to choose their mates and, further, constructed Elvis into a "softer, [more] understanding man." Thus they opposed the male machismo prevalent in the *Halbstarken* subcultures and rejected the image of the self-restrained, controlling man that had been the accepted ideal in East and West Germany. Authorities in both German states were promoting such men as ideal citizens and soldiers in the mid-1950s, at the same time as they began rearming.[70] The spread of rebellious behavior from the working class to a wider circle of young women from middle- and upper-class neighborhoods certainly threatened ideologies that, in both Germanies, had sought to confine women's sexuality to the sphere of marriage and motherhood.

It was exactly this double resistance to bourgeois norms of both male and female respectability and the transgression of racial boundaries that made rock 'n' roll an attractive dance style and Elvis an important figure for East and West German girls. In spite of, or perhaps because of, the negative reporting about American and German female rock 'n' roll fans in the press, many German girls made it known publicly that they liked Elvis. In Germany as in the United States, Presley's female fans supported his challenge to respectable masculinity; at the same time, their association with blackness through Elvis and rock 'n' roll made their own challenges to norms of female respectability all the more radical. Adopting styles with connotations of blackness was a radical act for young women in the German context, where blacks (along with Jews, Sinti and Roma, and Asians) had been portrayed as sexual aggressors under National Socialism and into the postwar years.[71]

While it is difficult to determine exactly what young women in the 1950s thought about their actions, the effects of their behavior were certainly subver-

---

68. Letter to the editor by Elvis Presley Club, Berlin Wilmersdorf, *Tagesspiegel* (February 2, 1958). For German hysteria, see "Der einzig richtige Mann . . . ," *Westdeutsche Allgemeine* (January 25, 1958). The most glaring example of Elvis mania given there was that of an eighteen-year-old girl who had committed suicide for love of Elvis—"the only true man" in her eyes.

69. "Elvis Presley und die schauen Puppen," *Berliner Zeitung* (August 8, 1958).

70. For a similar analysis of the meaning of rock stars for girls, see Frith and McRobbie (n. 53 above). Maase (n. 4 above), pp. 132–35, has raised the possibility that girls' ideals may have contributed to the development of a masculinity that did not rely on the soldier ideal. However, his analysis that girls' admiration for Presley and other stars was an exercise in female slave behavior overestimates the degree to which these girls were relying on approval from men for their self-definition. For a more extended discussion of East and West German constructions of masculinity, see Poiger (n. 41 above).

71. See Burleigh and Wippermann (n. 11 above). In the postwar years, rapists among the occupation forces were frequently described as black Americans in the West and as Mongolians in the East.

sive, clearly undermining the gender norms and sexual mores propagated by parents and state officials. Female rock 'n' roll fans may not have thought of their actions as political, but if we define as political all actions designed to effect larger social changes, they were indeed political. Clearly their actions challenged certain state-supported norms and thus positioned them as "bad girls." These young women used that position in interesting ways: they asserted their youthful difference and attempted to recast the dominant notions of masculinity and femininity, which were, as we have seen, at the heart of reconstruction in both states. Recognizing that cultural consumption took place in and reshaped the public sphere will allow us to examine how (re)constructions of (private) identities affected state politics. Certainly the reactions of authorities in East and West Germany left little doubt that female rock 'n' roll fans posed a political threat to the established order.

West German Repression and East German Vacillations

Female sexual impropriety was a central signifier for the threats that rock 'n' roll posed in West Germany (and vice versa). One West German newspaper article actually saw German women's admiration for Presley at the root of male *Halbstarken* behavior. Commenting on tumultuous scenes in a Berlin movie theater after a showing of *Love Me Tender* in 1957, the reporter wondered whether *halbstarke* boys would behave differently if *halbschwache* (semi-weak) girls did not show such a preference for guys like Presley.[72] In January 1957 the West German movie rating board (consisting of church and state officials and representatives of the movie industry) mandated cuts from the rock 'n' roll movie *Don't Knock the Rock* before it permitted showings to adolescents under sixteen: two scenes that showed "the loose and aggressive flirting of girls" had to be eliminated because the "materialist understanding of life" rampant among adolescents would otherwise be fostered.[73]

Rock 'n' roll became a symbol for the reversal of gender roles at the very time that West Germans were discussing the social role of women in the context of a new family law. This law was to legislate spousal property rights and parental rights. In the discussions, all German parties affirmed the notion that the woman's place was in the home. A cartoon "How to dance rock 'n' roll?" in the West Berlin youth magazine *Blickpunkt* showed a boy and a girl dressed in

---

72. "Pulverdampf und heiße Lieder," *Kurier* (April 13, 1957). See also H. Heigert, "Ein neuer Typ wird produziert: Der Teenager," *Deutsche Jugend*, no. 3 (1959), pp. 117–21, quoted in Kuhnert and Ackermann (n. 4 above), p. 94.

73. Arbeitsausschuß der FSK, "Jugendprotokoll: Außer Rand und Band," II. Teil, February 1, 1957, Landesbildstelle Berlin, Pressearchiv. A minority on the board wanted to ban the movie altogether for youths under sixteen because it would foster "loose behavior and propensity for hysteric mass behavior."

identical t-shirts and tight long pants. The boy was jumping up and kicking the girl right in her stomach. The caption read: "The woman has equal rights, treat her accordingly." In openly misogynist terms this cartoon made the same arguments that the West German opponents of equal rights were making at just the same time. Equal rights for women, like the fashions and individually designed movements of rock 'n' roll dancers (which erased gender differences), would mean a loss of the male protection that was at the center of the reconstructed gender system in postwar West Germany. While such references to explicitly political debates became increasingly rare, traditional gender norms remained—relatively unchanged—at the center of mainstream West German reactions to rock 'n' roll.[74]

West Germans found themselves even more on the defensive when, in 1956 and 1957, some East German voices suggested that teenagers' adoption of American-influenced fashions and styles could be part of the resistance to capitalist regimes and particularly to West German military service. During the period of greater flexibility after the Twentieth Party Congress of the Soviet Communist Party, the Central Council of the state youth organization Free German Youth (FDJ), for example, declared that the appearance of young West German rebels—who drew heavily on American imports—signified that they preferred a life "of personal freedom" to conscription. The movie *Berlin Ecke Schönhauser* ("Berlin Corner Schönhauser"), produced by the East German state-owned movie company, suggested that listening to fast-paced American music and wearing jeans was in fact compatible with the formation of male and female socialist personalities. Such opinions were always hotly contested in East Germany, and as the East German party elite reasserted its authority these lenient attitudes were quickly replaced by the earlier stance that American popular culture posed a consistent threat to socialism. After a brief phase of relaxation, East German authorities reverted to the earlier notion that American commercial music was decadent; rock 'n' roll was a special object of their scorn.[75]

As East German officials attacked rock 'n' roll, they drew heavily on the notion of female sexual impropriety and linked it to male rebelliousness. Their rhetoric was explicitly politicized. An East German flyer about Western immorality featured a picture of the Boogie Club, a West Berlin dance hall. On both sides of the club entrance were large signs, each depicting a young woman in half-long pants and a tight t-shirt. East German officials portrayed

74. "Wie tanzt man Rock 'n' Roll," *Blickpunkt* (November 1956). For the debates erupting around the new family law, see Moeller (n. 5 above), chap. 6. Moeller points out that those championing equal rights in the 1950s never questioned women's primary roles as housewives and mothers.

75. See Sekretariat des Zentralrats der FDJ, "Stellungnahme," suppl. 1 to "Protokoll," September 19, 1956, JA-IzJ (n. 61 above), 2608; "Berlin Ecke Schönhauser," *Progress Film Pro-*

such clubs as hotbeds of conspiracies to organize provocations in the East. A 1957 East Berlin report on juvenile delinquency made the "rock 'n' roll atmosphere" imported from the United States responsible for rowdiness, the formation of cliques, rape, and "perverted behavior" in the East.[76]

On their own territory, East German officials adopted an array of measures to curtail the impact of Western influences, specifically including rock 'n' roll. East German officials tried to prohibit rock 'n' roll dancing. In 1957 one Ministry of Culture official gave explicit orders to prevent the spread of rock 'n' roll since the music and dancing represented the "degeneration" (*Abart*) inherent in the American way of life.[77] In early 1958 the East German Ministry of Culture ordered that only 40 percent of any music program could consist of imports from the West. Certification procedures for bands were to insure that they played proper music (preferably no American imports) in a proper fashion (without "hot" rhythms).[78] Nonetheless, some of the youth clubs run by the state youth organization continued to tap Western radio stations or used bands and tapes to play almost exclusively Western music. In many cases, in the fifteen minutes before closing, visitors were still able to put in a round of the "open dancing" that appeared to change gender roles so fundamentally.[79] From 1958 officials promoted their own fashion dance, the Lipsi,

gramm, no. 75 (1957), Landesbildstelle Berlin, Pressearchiv; Horst Knietzsch, "Wo wir nicht sind . . . ," *Neues Deutschland* (September 3, 1957). For attacks on the greater leniency, see Alfred Kurella, "Einflüsse der Dekadenz," excerpt of speech held in July 1957, published in *Sonntag* (July 4, 1957); Alexander Abusch's speech at the thirty-second plenum of the Central Committee of the Socialist Unity Party (SED) in July 1957, "Es gibt nur eine Kulturpolitik"—both reprinted in *Dokumente zur Kunst-, Literatur- und Kulturpolitik der SED,* ed. Elimar Schubbe (Stuttgart, 1972), pp. 469–72, 473–78, respectively. See also Poiger.

76. See material published by the Zentralrat der FDJ and distributed "to enlighten youths about hardship and demoralization in West Germany," 1958, LAB (STA) (n. 44 above), Rep. 121, Nr. 230; Ständige Kommission für Jugendfragen, Stadtverordnetenversammlung Gross-Berlin, "Bericht über die Jugendkriminalität," October 10, 1957, LAB (STA), Rep. 119, Nr. 22, pp. 7–8.

77. Dr. Uszkoreit to state concert agency (Deutsche Konzert- und Gastspieldirektion), August 21, 1957, BArch P (n. 61 above), DR1 Nr. 243.

78. "Anordnung über die Programmgestaltung bei Unterhaltungs- und Tanzmusik," January 2, 1958, reprinted in Schubbe, ed., p. 515. Economic considerations likewise played a role: East Germany was paying DM 2 million per year for the rights to perform Western music. At a meeting with state officials, however, band leaders made clear that it would be difficult to follow the order, since audiences demanded Western hits. See "Protokoll zur Aussprache mit den Institutionen und Kapellenleitern," March 11, 1958, p. 2, LAB (STA), Rep. 121, Nr. 230. On protests against certification, see "Erfahrungsaustausch," 1960, JA-IzJ (n. 61 above), A6724.

79. See "Einschätzung der Entwicklung der Jugendclubs," August 8, 1961, LAB (STA), Rep. 121, Nr. 62. Especially popular was Radio Luxembourg; see "Erfahrungsaustausch," 1960, JA-IzJ, A6724. On the local level, the FDJ indeed advertised its program as distinctly different from "Sunday schools and ballroom dancing." East Berliners experienced the FDJ dances as quite a contrast to the stiff atmosphere elsewhere, especially in church leisure time offerings (interviews with Hannelore Diehl, Sigrid Tönnies, Margret Hamm, and Günter Schmidt, my files).

in which couples danced to a faster rhythm, but without any of the dangerous "openness" of dancing apart.[80]

West German Liberal Containment

In the second half of the 1950s West German cold war liberals were replacing the religiously inspired conservatives of the first half of the decade in positions of power. The impact of liberalism in postwar Germany was by no means confined to the small Free Democratic Party; rather, in the late 1950s and early 1960s, the whole West German political system underwent an important shift. In spite of many differences, the governing CDU/CSU and the opposition SPD moved toward a cold war liberal consensus. The SPD abandoned Marxism for good; and even as the Christian Democrats won the 1957 election with the slogan "No experiments," liberals made their presence increasingly felt within that party. Struggles between CDU liberals, clustered around Ludwig Erhard, the champion of the "social market economy," and the conservatives, who rallied around chancellor Konrad Adenauer, increased over the following years. Consequently, extreme conservatives like the Minister of Family Affairs Josef Wuermeling lost some of their appeal. Wuermeling resigned in 1962 and Erhard replaced Adenauer as chancellor in 1963. In the late 1950s and 1960s, conservatives remained vocal in West Germany (and especially so in discussions about youth), but the power of their perspective was diminished by the ascendancy of liberal policies and liberal ideas on culture, society, and politics that were increasingly shared by officials from both the CDU/CSU and the SPD.[81]

Two of the most important theorists of the West German brand of liberalism were Erhard himself and the sociologist Helmut Schelsky. In 1957 both published books that became blueprints for changing society and politics in West Germany: Erhard's *Wohlstand für alle* ("Prosperity for all") and Schelsky's *Die skeptische Generation* ("The skeptical generation").[82]

---

80. In October 1957 the East German Ministry for Culture ordered dance instructors to prevent the spread of rock 'n' roll. Also in 1957 the East Berlin Haus der Volkskunst offered courses for delegates from all Berlin firms to learn how to distinguish between good and bad dancing and to sponsor dances successfully, so that they would not have to "blame the West Berlin *Halbstarken-Problem*" for their failures (letter from Berliner Haus der Volkskunst, October 1, 1957, LAB [STA], Rep. 121, Nr. 162). See also Ryback (n. 20 above).

81. Jarausch and Jones (n. 23 above) have argued that liberal concepts had an impact on Christian Democrats and Social Democrats after World War II. Hermand (n. 19 above), pp. 263–76, distinguishes between "conservatives" around Adenauer and "neo-liberals" around Erhard. On Erhard's views of U.S. capitalism, see Berghahn (n. 24 above), pp. 158–59.

82. Ludwig Erhard, *Wohlstand für alle* (Düsseldorf, 1957). Schelsky (n. 21 above), p. 5, claimed to analyze the West German adolescent from 1945 to 1955. He indeed drew occasionally on empirical research from this period, but in the context of this article his work is more interesting as a blueprint for West German society. Moeller (n. 5 above), p. 191, has correctly called

Both authors embraced the consumer society that had emerged in West Germany by the mid-1950s. Erhard stressed the positive effects of softening the West German class structure through consumer culture. In his widely read study, Schelsky, too, spoke positively of the disappearance of class differences in youth behavior. They identified two opponents: conservatives in the West and the threat of socialism in the East. Yet their rhetoric showed them to be much less on the defensive than West German conservatives.[83]

Their most powerful move was to postulate an end to ideologies. Thus Schelsky praised the "skepticism" of West German youth because they had moved beyond the world of ideologies. In 1960, Erhard too urged his fellow CDU members to pursue a social policy beyond any ideology. In the German context this had multiple meanings. First, it helped liberals place themselves in a position superior to both Communism and National Socialism. Second, the notion of a move beyond ideologies included a rejection of the political divisiveness and the youth cultures that many believed to have contributed to the demise of the Weimar Republic. Finally, it enabled West Germans to integrate themselves rhetorically into the alliance of Western societies and to bring themselves closer to the mainstream of Western thought: in these very same years, many intellectuals in the United States and Western Europe were also promoting the idea of an end of ideologies.[84] Schelsky's thinking in particular was influenced by the American social scientist David Riesman, who—even as he voiced some worries about conformity—argued for the basic stability of consumption-oriented societies.[85]

For Schelsky and other West German liberals a lot was at stake: they sought to disconnect themselves from Weimar and from Nazism by erasing

---

Schelsky "a sociologist for all seasons." Schelsky had assumed his first university position during the Third Reich. In the first half of the 1950s he made a name for himself with his sociology of the family, which promoted the role of a female homeworker and a male breadwinner, and with his treatise against Kinsey. Also he served on an advisory board to conservative Minister of Family Affairs Wuermeling.

83. See Schelsky, p. 391; Erhard, *Wohlstand für Alle*. Erhard, on the one hand, defended the democratizing effects of the consumer society vehemently against conservative critics in the West. On the other hand, he frequently contrasted this to the threat of collectivization in the East and, thus, retained the East as his reference point. See Erhard, "Soziale Marktwirtschaft und Materialismus," *Sonntagsblatt,* January 29, 1956, and "Der Arbeit einen Sinn geben," speech to the Seventh Convention of the CDU, Hamburg, May 14, 1957, both reprinted in *Ludwig Erhard: Gedanken aus fünf Jahrzehnten,* ed. Karl Hohmann (Düsseldorf, 1988), pp. 466–70 and 490–506, respectively. See also Carter (n. 4 above), p. 192; Hermand, pp. 263–76. For similar arguments in the United States, see May (n. 5 above).

84. Most famous are Raymond Aaron and Daniel Bell.

85. Schelsky, pp. 84–95; speech by Erhard at the April 1960 CDU convention, "Wirtschaftspolitik als Teil der Gesellschaftspolitik," reprinted in Hohmann, ed., pp. 607–23, esp. 614. Schelsky wrote the introduction to the German translation of Riesman's *The Lonely Crowd*. See David Riesman, *Die einsame Masse,* introduction by Helmut Schelsky (Darmstadt, 1956).

differences between West Germany and other Western societies and by fully integrating themselves into the fight against Communism.[86] It is quite telling that Schelsky contrasted the "skeptical," depoliticized youth of the 1950s with what he called the "political" youth of the period before 1945. By asserting that his own contemporaries—the parents of 1950s youth—had transformed themselves from a "political" into a skeptical generation as well, Schelsky also whitewashed his own generation's association with Nazism.[87] He now proclaimed 1950s German youth to be "nonpolitically democratic" and thus put them at the center of a liberal system. If anything was still German about this generation of youth, it was the fact that it was fulfilling its "fate" with special German thoroughness.[88] Thus Schelsky suggested that West Germans were indeed better liberals than West Europeans or Americans, and he abandoned the fight for a third, specifically West German way between consumerism in the West and socialism in the East.

Schelsky's assessments rested on his reevaluation of the German youth rebellion of the 1950s as a "private" matter, in which rebellious youth behavior became a mere nonpolitical expression of style. He described the postwar generation as one that was tolerant, sober, and successful, one that had fled from societal pressures into the private sphere.[89] At the same time, Schelsky's rhetoric effaced gender and race as central components of the youth rebellion. He gave three examples of unruly adolescent behavior in his conclusion, referring to the "ecstatic devotion to the lively music of jazz sessions," to certain "acrobatic dissolved" forms of dancing, and to the "individual rage" of *Halbstarke* rioters, and thus explicitly connecting rebellious behavior to American influences. Yet, unlike other commentators, Schelsky did not refer to the challenges these forms of behavior posed to traditional gender roles, and he explicitly turned against those who described this youth behavior as a mere turn to primitivism. The rhetoric of primitivism and gender upheaval was dominant in conservative East and West German reactions that identified rock 'n' roll as a political threat. In contrast, Schelsky argued that these forms of youth behavior had no significance beyond being expressions of vitality in an increasingly technical world. He stressed that these were neither political challenges nor precursors of political challenges to come.[90]

---

86. This concept of totalitarianism was a feature of German (and Western) postwar thought and politics. See Doering-Manteuffel (n. 23 above), p. 109.

87. Schelsky, pp. 66–84, 456. Reviewers reiterated the positive traits of German youth. See "Die junge Generation," *Wirtschaftzeitung* (December 7, 1957); Hans Kudszus, "Eine Generation wird besichtigt," *Tagesspiegel* (March 30, 1958).

88. Schelsky, p. 493; Kudszus.

89. Schelsky, p. 488. This summary was reiterated by Kudszus; and Friedrich Herzog, "Die skeptische Generation," *Der Tag* (February 7, 1958).

90. Schelsky, pp. 494–97.

Schelsky was hardly the only one to foster this development: the West German fashion industry and some cultural commentators likewise sought to divorce cultural expression from the political realm. Thus, in 1958 the West German youth magazine *Bravo* ran the following advertisement: "Moscow— and politics—have lost Ninotschka forever. Silk stockings may be thin, but in the end they are far more attractive than the best of political convictions."[91] This slogan put female stylishness at the heart of the "end of ideologies" and suggested that a country like West Germany, where silk stockings were easily available, had an edge in the cold war battle. Some West German liberal intellectuals and some parts of the fashion industry therefore "cooperated" in a curious way to claim style as an apolitical category. The explicit references to the Soviet Union, however, reveal this ostensible depoliticization as merely a new form of politicization that pitted West Germany's reconstruction as a liberal haven of consumption against the "politics" of consumer deprivation in the East.

Along similar lines, a 1958 commentary on Elvis Presley in a West German paper rejected the notion that his gender ambiguity had any political implications. It described him as a "rock 'n' roll idol" for some and as a "singing acrobat of undefined gender" for others. This commentary argued a point of view favored by both liberals and the West German entertainment industry: how one behaved toward Elvis remained "a private matter."[92]

The editors of *Bravo* combined advocacy of an end of ideology with a rejection of "race hatred." In 1959, for example, teenager-advice columnist Steffi rejected the time "of different colored shirts"—that is, of street fights between Communist and National Socialist youths in the Weimar Republic. Like many other articles in *Bravo* that reported on the commitment of black and white American stars to desegregation, she also turned against "race hatred." What was unusual about the Steffi column was that she salvaged explicit political meaning for the youth culture. She defined politics as speaking out about freedom and war and claimed that teenagers' "bluejeans" prevented them from engaging in violence against people with different political convictions. Not unlike Schelsky, she concluded that adolescents were in fact swayed less by intolerant ideologies than their predecessors had been.[93]

Considering the hype that the youth rebellion was receiving in West Germany during these very years, it is clear that Schelsky's interpretation and the stance of the entertainment industry continued to be contested. Both Erhard and Schelsky contended with critics of the consumer culture. Schelsky himself

---

91. *Bravo,* no. 4 (1958), quoted in Carter, p. 209. ("Ninotschka" is a generic Russian female name.)

92. "Gold aus heißer Kehle," *Kasseler Post* (May 21, 1958).

93. *Bravo,* no. 15 (1959), quoted in Maase (n. 4 above), p. 144. The author of these columns was a retired male teacher.

echoed some of the concerns of cultural conservatives, worrying that German adolescents could succumb to vulgar materialism with consumerism as their life goal, or, worse, turn into criminals. And in 1963, in his first speech as chancellor to the West German parliament, Erhard responded to critics who bemoaned West Germany's growing materialism by urging his fellow West Germans not to lose track of Christian values.[94]

West German cold war liberals like Schelsky and Erhard did retain a fair amount of hostility toward cultural styles associated with unrespectable lower-class behavior and specifically with American popular culture. Yet these hostilities were not incompatible with their efforts to render youth cultures nonpolitical and to celebrate a consumption-oriented West German society. Reinscribing gender difference was also central to such liberal efforts to resolve the apparent threats posed by youth cultures. While avoiding open prohibition, liberals continued to portray styles like rock 'n' roll negatively and actively promoted alternatives. In the second half of the 1950s, for example, the West Berlin SPD-run government promoted ballroom dancing, especially in working-class neighborhoods. Subsidized lessons included instruction about correct behavior toward the opposite sex.[95]

The implications of such cultural visions became clear in a 1958 state-funded film, "Why are they against us?," which addressed the problems of teenage alienation and was made specifically for schools and youth groups. The movie associated its promiscuous girl character (who wore risqué clothing with a low neckline) directly with rock 'n' roll. The working-class male hero rejected this "bad" girl, who danced to rock 'n' roll at the local soda fountain and who "came on" to boys, for a "good," restrained, middle-class girl who went to museums. Like Erhard in his many public statements, the movie was critical of the middle-class father's prejudices against the working-class boy, but as part of legitimizing this critique the movie makers portrayed "working-class" cultural practices, "public" women, and the consumption of popular culture in very negative terms. The working-class boy, the movie suggested, could raise his status by adopting a bourgeois style of cultural consumption. Thus, in this movie, liberalism with respect to class (promoted also by people like Schelsky and Erhard) rested explicitly on gender and cultural conservatism.[96]

Taming Rock 'n' Roll in West Germany

In spite or perhaps because of these efforts, rock 'n' roll spread in West Germany during these years from working-class adolescents to middle- and

---

94. See Schelsky (n. 21 above), pp. 88–90; Erhard, "Politik der Mitte und der Verständigung," speech to the West German Bundestag, October 18, 1963, reprinted in Hohmann, ed. (n. 83 above), pp. 814–46.

95. Interview with Susanne Quandt, who attended one of these courses in 1958 (my files).

96. Siegfried Mohrhof, *Warum sind sie gegen uns?* (Seebruck am Chiemsee, 1958).

upper-class youths.[97] The shift of the working-class styles associated with rock 'n' roll to the middle and upper classes included a transformation—and taming—of these styles. Concurrently, the rhetoric against rock 'n' roll in West Germany turned more mild. Given the authorities' preoccupation in East and West Germany with the gender and racial ambiguities imported with rock 'n' roll, the taming of the "threat" of rock 'n' roll in West Germany rested on undermining the racial and gender transgressions in youth styles. As a result, race was effaced from discussions of rock 'n' roll.

Liberal critiques of rock 'n' roll relied on psychological explanations to account for the attraction of rock across classes and saw the institution of proper gender roles as a solution to the youth rebellion. Psychologist Curt Bondy and his team, in a study of the *Halbstarkenproblem* funded by the West German Ministry of the Interior, rejected the notion that rock 'n' roll was responsible for the recent youth riots; rather, they suggested, the two forms of behavior fulfilled the same needs for psychological and physical release. At the same time, Bondy's analysis mostly ignored the female consumers of rock 'n' roll who were clearly present in his sources. Instead, women became the solution to the problem: the study concluded that most boys gave up rioting as soon as they had steady girlfriends. This assessment was echoed in the West German press. West German cold war liberals rarely reacted to challenges of gender norms with outright prohibitions of cultural products. Rather, they portrayed both riots and rock 'n' roll as mere cultural styles whose threats could be resolved "privately."[98] This reframing of the youth rebellion as nonpolitical was facilitated by efforts on the part of state officials, the press, and the entertainment industry to alter the practices adolescents engaged in.

As rock 'n' roll caught on, a new West German female emerged: the "teenager." In Germany this American term had first been used to describe American female Presley fans, but from 1957 onward "teenagers" increasingly became a label for young German women of all classes. For many of these young women, the term "teenager" carried a much more modern image of femininity, one that included greater openness in sexual matters. It also had implications for female adolescent consumption: the image of the teenager ran counter to the traditional ideal image of the woman who exerted self-restraint in matters of consumption and sexuality. Initially used as a criticism, but quickly turned into a marketing tool, "teenager" carried less rebellious connotations than the term *Halbstarke*.[99]

---

97. See Maase.

98. Bondy et al. (n. 29 above), pp. 71–72, 86–89, 92. Bondy and his team even rejected the notion that attacks on policemen could be politically motivated. See also Klaus Eyferth, "Es reicht nicht zu Revolutionen," *Die Welt* (November 8, 1958); "Totenkopf bürgerlich," *Revue,* no. 19 (1962).

99. In 1956 German papers were still educating the public that "teenager" meant *Backfisch.* See "Das Phänomen Elvis Presley," *Telegraf* (October 11, 1956); "Das Phänomen Elvis Presley,"

As rock 'n' roll spread, its black origins were increasingly effaced from discourses on German youth cultures. At the same time, the fashion industry and the magazine *Bravo* worked to transform the styles that had posed challenges to gender norms. Deracialization and a clear separation of gender roles went hand in hand. Elvis's induction into the army in 1958 resolved his gender ambiguity: *Bravo* celebrated his new respectable appearance with short hair and no sideburns, and other commentators soon referred to him as a "tame" (yet now properly masculine) member of the occupying forces in West Germany.[100] At the same time, reviews of *King Creole,* released in 1958 in Germany, never even mentioned that large parts of the movie were set in a black nightclub.[101] In West German renditions of Presley's success story, his rise from truck driver to millionaire took center stage, while references to the black origins of his music all but disappeared. Thus Presley was "whitened" and masculinized as his story became compatible with the West German "economic miracle mentality" (*Wirtschaftswundermentalität*). While eliminating race from such discussions signified the greater acceptability of rock 'n' roll, it also diminished the acceptance of black culture in West Germany.

An increasing focus on a heterosocial realm with clearly defined gender roles for adolescents appeared to be successful in taming the radicalism of the youth rebellion. The effects were contradictory. On the one hand, public visibility became an option for women of all classes. On the other, female behavior that had transgressed racial and gender lines was tamed: women were allowed to become visible primarily as potential girlfriends and wives of men. Conversely, women were seen as taming men: in press commentaries and psychological research reports, *Halbstarke* were portrayed as harmless once they had girlfriends. And in popular usage the term "teenager" under-

---

Spandauer Volksblatt (October 12, 1956); "Teenager," *Blickpunkt,* nos. 48/49 (1956), p. 21. *Der Spiegel,* in its December 1956 feature on Elvis, switched between *Backfisch* and "teenager." See "Elvis, the Pelvis" (n. 26 above). See also the West German dictionary *Der große Herder,* vol. 8, (1956), quoted in Maase, p. 162. By 1958 the term had become common currency in Germany. See the teenager books directed specifically at girls: Eric Godal, *Teenagers,* ed. Rolf Itaaliander (Hamburg, 1958); and G. Hilgendorf, *Das Teenagerbuch* (Munich, 1958)—both cited in Maase; "Woran starb der Backfisch?" *Quick* no. 15 (1959), reprinted in Delille and Grohn, eds. (n. 4 above), pp. 18–19; "Der (Teenager)-Spleen," *Blickpunkt* (February 1960), p. 17. See also Kuhnert and Ackermann (n. 4 above); Bertram and Krüger (n. 2 above); Doris Foitzik, ed., *Vom Trümmerkind zum Teenager: Kindheit und Jugend in der Nachkriegszeit* (Bremen, 1992); Rolf Lindner, "Teenager— ein amerikanischer Traum," in Deutscher Werkbund and Württembergischer Kunstverein, eds. (n. 28 above), pp. 278–83; Maase, pp. 161–75.

100. *Bravo,* no. 12 (1958), quoted in Maase, p. 168. "I Like Elvis," *Abend* (October 10, 1958), described Presley as a modest young man and urged parents not to worry if their daughters had his picture on their walls.

101. See, e.g., reviews of *King Creole* in *Telegraf, Kurier, Die Welt,* all November 1, 1958.

went a significant shift in meaning: by 1960 it could include both young men and young women, and it now connoted generational difference rather than conflict.[102] This signified a feminization and taming of the *Halbstarken* youth rebellion.

This shift was certainly fostered by the systematic marketing of Peter Kraus and Conny Froboess as ideal teenagers. Initially, Kraus was sold as the "German Elvis." Racial ambiguity was not part of his image, and nobody referred to his thick lips (which he did have). Although Kraus, too, encountered "hysterical teenagers," he was mostly portrayed as a nice German boy, much "more likable in voice and behavior" than the American original.[103] When he was joined by a female mate, "Conny," his domestication was almost complete. "Conny and Peter" made movies together and were celebrated as West German rock 'n' roll stars. The West German fashion industry used their popularity to market teenage fashions and claimed to direct the "not so complaisant" wishes of adolescents into "pleasant forms."[104] "Conny" sweaters for young women, as well as "Peter Kraus pulls" (vests) intended for young men, stressed different cuts for women and men and thus tried to reinstate a larger measure of gender difference.

In the promotion of Conny Froboess and Peter Kraus traditional gender roles were partially resurrected. Thus Froboess had to be protected from association with too much "sexiness." Froboess's manager/father invoked the differences between *Halbstarke* and teenagers and criticized Kraus when he allegedly turned too "sexy": "That is something for *Halbstarke* and not for teenagers. . . . If teenager music declines into sex, then [it will do so] without me."[105] On the one hand, the duo was part of a heterosocial teenage world where young men and women together challenged older standards of respectable dancing or clothing; but on the other hand, they tried to steer away from open challenges to sexual mores.

Newer styles of rock 'n' roll dancing also stressed gender differences, developing from a "wild" style, in which men *and* women threw their partners through the air, to a "tamed" version in which the male partner hardly moved at all. In 1960 *Bravo* published directions for dancing rock 'n' roll as part of a series on ballroom dancing. The man depicted in the photograph wore a dark suit and guided a young woman dressed in a petticoat skirt while apparently avoiding any excessive movements himself. This style of rock 'n' roll dancing could be safely adopted at the private house parties that became the fashion among middle-class youth. It effectively symbolized the ideal female teenager

102. See Lamprecht (n. 57 above), p. 33, who referred to teenagers of both sexes.
103. "Vom Spieltrieb besessen," *Telegraf* (July 11, 1957). Erd (n. 14 above) sees Kraus, in contrast to Presley, as whitened in the German context.
104. Interview with teenager fashion producer quoted in Lamprecht, p. 39.
105. Quoted in ibid., p. 107. See also Maase (n. 4 above), p. 169.

as the acolyte of the controlled and controlling man, avoided allusions to black culture, and made rock 'n' roll compatible with a bourgeois gender system.[106]

While the subversive gender, racial, and class implications of rock 'n' roll consumption lessened, the greater acceptance of rock 'n' roll and sexuality as modes of "private" expression constituted a widening of options for West German adolescents, especially young women. The West German attempts to tame rock 'n' roll had only limited success. Many young Germans perceived the German rock 'n' roll songs as weak imitations and preferred the American originals. And fashion makers were hardly able or even willing to prevent girls from wearing Peter Kraus pulls along with James Dean jackets. Moreover, even with their tamed German version of rock 'n' roll, Froboess and Kraus introduced American words like "baby," "sexy," and "love" into the German vocabulary.[107] And the practice of petting—sexual touching without actual intercourse— became more acceptable for young men and women, at least in West Germany. So closely was the connection made between sexual expressiveness and American imports that teenagers as well as commentators in both East and West Germany believed that not just the word "petting" but even the behavior itself had come from the United States.[108] Ironically, East German critics used the writings of West German conservatives to criticize sex outside of long-term monogamous relationships and specifically to condemn petting in East and West.[109] That West German women were not able to express their dissatisfaction with the mixed blessings of this "sexual revolution" in political terms until the late 1960s is evidence of the effectiveness of the West German redefinition of sexuality and the consumption of popular culture as nonpolitical.

Cold War Battles

East German officials appealed to what one might call a petit-bourgeois morality and used the cold war even more forcefully than their West German counterparts to contain images and behavior that were perceived as public dis-

---

106. See "Bravo sucht den deutschen Meister im 'Rock and Roll'" (n. 53 above); "Erlaubt ist, was gefällt," *Bravo*, no. 6 (1960); interview with Renate Ebert (my files).

107. Maase, p. 164. He has correctly warned against seeing the teenage culture as devoid of all challenges to dominant norms. See also oral history with Klaus Woldeck, quoted in Maase, p. 169; and interviews with Susanne Quandt and Dietmar Iser (my files).

108. See Winfried Sträter, "'Das konnte ein Erwachsener nicht mit ruhigen Augen beobachten': Die Halbstarken," in *Vom Lagerfeuer zur Musikbox: Jugendkulturen, 1900–1960*, ed. Berliner Geschichtswerkstatt e.V. (Berlin, 1985), pp. 137–70, 154. Hans Giese and Günter Schmidt, *Studentensexualität* (Reinbek, 1968), p. 85, revised Giese's own conviction that petting was primarily practiced in the United States. For petting as a significant form of sexual behavior among West German adolescents in the 1950s, see Kuhnert und Ackermann (no. 4 above).

109. See, e.g., Walter Friedrich and Adolf Kossakowski, *Zur Psychologie des Jugendalters* (Berlin, 1962), p. 171.

plays of female sexuality with dangerous effects on men. For example, in 1957 an official East German manual on how the East German soldier was to think and behave made it very clear that knowing how to dance properly and how to resist Western ideology was crucial. The author accused the West German government and industrialists, both of whom he labeled fascists, of using boogie-woogie, rock 'n' roll, pornography, and the breasts of female movie stars to seduce male West German adolescents into the army and into aggression against East Germany and its allies. This statement reiterated the theme so important to both West and East German attacks on American popular culture: that the consumption of American popular culture was connected to female sexual expressiveness, male hyperaggression, and fascist behavior and was therefore incompatible with respectable German femininity and masculinity.[110]

To East German officials, rock 'n' roll seemed so threatening that in 1958 the East German Party leader Walter Ulbricht publicly indicted "its noise" as an "expression of impetuosity" reflecting the "anarchism of capitalist society." East German defense minister Willi Stoph supplemented this diatribe with warnings echoed in many papers that "rock 'n' roll was a means of seduction to make the youth ripe for atomic war." After riots broke out at a West Berlin Bill Haley concert, the official FDJ newspaper announced that West German defense minister Franz-Josef Strauß himself had ordered rock 'n' roll concerts to prepare adolescents for conscription.[111] In contrast, East German youth officials reported time and again about East German male youths for whom shedding bluejeans and learning to dance properly was the key to their conversion to the socialist cause.[112] Even as East Germany itself was rearming, East German authorities linked anti-Americanism and antimilitarism to attack their West German enemies and to repress Americanized youth cultures within their own borders.

After a brief hiatus in 1956 and 1957, East German authorities made drawing young people away from Western influences integral to the consolidation of socialism. Thus, after the building of the Berlin wall in August 1961, the East German press and youth officials focused heavily on converting the

---

110. Hannsgerd Prötsch, *So müssen unsere Soldaten sein: Eine Betrachtung über das politisch-moralische Antlitz der Nationalen Volksarmee der Deutschen Demokratischen Republik* (Berlin, 1957).

111. Stoph and Ulbricht, quoted in Lamprecht (n. 57 above), p. 87. See also Zentralinstitut für Lehrerweiterbildung, "Anleitung der Zirkelleiter zum Thema 'Jugendschutz in der DDR'", September 6, 1957, LAB (STA) (n. 44 above), Rep. 119, Nr. 22; "Bill Haley und die NATO," *Neues Deutschland* (Oct. 31, 1958); "Orgie der amerikanischen Unkultur," *Neues Deutschland* (Oct. 31, 1958); "Jugend wird systematisch vergiftet," *Neues Deutschland* (Nov. 2, 1958); "Strauß befahl: Jazz und rockt!" *Junge Welt*, no. 22 (Nov. 1958). See also Rauhut (n. 20 above).

112. See report from Leipzig in "Erfahrungsaustausch," 1960, JA-IzJ (n. 61 above), A6724; "Jugend zwischen 18 und 22 Uhr," *Junge Generation* 12, no. 1 (1958): 17–22; "Geständnis eines Rock 'n' Roll-Fans," *Junge Generation* 13, no. 10 (May 1959): 32; "Die Bluejeans-Boys und der Jugendklub," *Morgen* (March 7, 1961).

young men and women who had frequented bars and dance halls in West Berlin. Some concessions to faster-paced music were necessary, yet East German officials did not endorse rock 'n' roll. Within a week the East German press reported that state-run youth clubs had turned adolescent boys in blue jeans into respectable young men wearing suits and dancing with young women in fashionable dresses. An internal report, however, revealed these former *Grenzgänger*—transgressors of the border—as people who had transgressed more than the border between sectors in Berlin: they were young men and women who were hostile toward the state and who continued to cause riots and "striptease scenes" in some East Berlin youth clubs. Clearly, East German authorities perceived these gender transgressions as political expressions directed against their state. All attempts to accommodate these phenomena in 1956 and 1957 failed, as a conservative party elite opted for repression.[113] By 1959 the distance between the attitudes of East and West German government officials was clear: the West German youth magazine *Twen,* which—with a jazz trumpet as its symbol—treated premarital sex positively for both young men and young women after 1959, was attacked not by West German state authorities but by the Catholic church and the East German Party.[114]

In West Germany the ostensible "depoliticization" of consumer culture generally and of teenager styles specifically was a direct response to the ongoing politicization of these phenomena in East Germany. In fact, youthful expressiveness became part of the West German cold war liberal identity. In marked contrast to the statements of East German leaders, the chief of staff of the West German army, Adolf Heusinger, announced in 1959 that rock 'n' roll and juvenile delinquency were different things, and he warned against condemning "all signs of youthful frolicking." Revealing some ambivalence toward rock 'n' roll, Heusinger explained that such "excesses" were largely the fault of grown-ups and not a problem within the West German army. Yet he welcomed "modern forms of social life appropriate for adolescents, including the enjoyment of modern art."[115] West Germans had overcome their earlier contradictory stance of opting for Western integration while being openly hostile toward American culture. By 1959 another commentator called the youth rebellion a "rebellion against the unknown." And by the mid-1960s the notion of a youth rebellion had all but disappeared. This seems especially ironic given the fears that the adolescent constituencies of the West German student movement and counterculture would cause just a few years later.[116]

113. See "Am Tag darauf ohne Texashose," *Neues Deutschland* (August 22, 1961); "Heiße Rhythmen waren erster Schritt," *National-Zeitung* (August 27, 1961); "Bericht über Jugendklubs," November 11, 1962, LAB (STA), Rep. 121, Nr. 62.

114. See "In kleinen Dosen," *Twen* (October 1959), p. 20.

115. Adolf Heusinger, "Jugend und Bundeswehr" (January 1959), in his *Reden, 1956–1961* (Boppard am Rhein, 1961), pp. 74–78.

116. See Ruth Römstedt, "Blue-Jean-Boy und die Filmpoesie von heute," *Kurier* (January 16, 1959); Blücher (n. 21 above). It is important to investigate the relationship between the

West German authorities treated style as a nonpolitical category, yet they politicized that very attitude in the cold war context. Popular culture remained a cold war weapon. Now it enabled an attack on East German repression on different grounds: East German authorities did not properly respect the private sphere, overreacted to matters of style, and therefore oppressed their own citizens. Thus West German papers registered with some disdain the 1959 court conviction of East German fans who had publicly shouted their support for Presley and their disapproval of party leader Ulbricht. In 1962 a review of an East German dictionary mocked the entry that described rock 'n' roll as a political threat. For the West German authorities of the 1960s, leisure and pleasure were not what would destroy the West; in fact, enjoyed in good measure they would actually be a key weapon against the East, exposing its economic inferiority and lack of democratic choice. West Germans successfully countered East German attacks that had mobilized the ambivalence and even hostility toward America that existed on both sides of the wall.[117]

It was an "achievement" of West German cold war liberals in the late 1950s to push the issues of popular culture and sexuality into arenas defined as nonpolitical. This reconfiguration of culture and politics in the West had serious effects on how the 1950s have been remembered. It is largely due to a liberal vision of politics that defined popular culture and female sexuality as nonpolitical matters that the radicalism of the 1950s rebellion, and specifically the voices of women that participated in it, have been lost. This has affected popular memory as well as scholarship on 1950s East and West Germany. In both cases, young German women have been rendered "harmless" teenagers in petticoats who sometimes danced but were often confined within the walls of their rooms. Rather than investigating how this transformation came about, scholarship on the 1950s youth rebellion has simply accepted the notion that the social actions of young East and West German rebels consistently lacked political significance.

In retrospect, adolescents of the 1950s may have accepted this view of their own life stories. At the time they probably did not worry about whether their actions were political or not. Later, when they constructed their life stories, a narrow view of politics in West Germany may have prevented them from understanding as political their informal and public resistance to the very

---

1950s and 1960s rebellion. However I do not agree with Marina Fischer-Kowalski, "Halbstarke 1958, Studenten 1968: Eine Generation und zwei Rebellionen," in *Kriegskinder, Konsumkinder, Krisenkinder: Zur Sozialisationsgeschichte seit dem Zweiten Weltkrieg,* ed. Ulf Preuss-Lausitz et al. (Weinheim, 1983), pp. 53–70, that the *Halbstarke* of the 1950s themselves were the student rebels of the late 1960s in West Germany.

117. See "Zuchthaus für Presley-Fans," *Depesche* (November 3, 1959); "Presley-Fans hinter Gittern," *Spandauer Volksblatt* (November 3, 1959); "Zuchthaus für Elvis-Presley-Anhänger," *Westdeutsche Allgemeine* (November 3, 1959); "'Krieg' mit Rock 'n' Roll," *Abend* (August 16, 1962).

gender, racial, and sexual norms that in fact had been at the center of political reconstruction in both Germanies.

We cannot understand the upheaval of the late 1960s in West Germany without grasping the particular dynamics of containing the youth rebellion of the 1950s. Female rock 'n' roll fans of that decade participated in a revolt that can now be seen to have had clear political implications. Depoliticization did not diffuse the rebellion completely. As in the United States, the 1950s youth cultures raised expectations for individual expression and sexual openness among many young women, and some of them expressed these expectations in explicitly political terms in the 1960s. At the same time, "the politicization of private life" and a slogan like "The personal is political" could appear radical and new in an emerging West German women's movement in the late 1960s only after the dramatic reformulation of the relation between politics and culture in the late 1950s and early 1960s.[118]

This exploration of East and West German encounters with rock 'n' roll shows how closely intertwined hostilities toward black culture and the rejection of female sexual expressiveness were in the culturally conservative visions that dominated East and West Germany. Indeed, reactions to American popular culture afford us some insight into German racialist concepts after World War II. These ideas were not just leftovers from fascist times: in both states—as West Germany underwent a liberal transformation and as East Germany reasserted Stalinism—gender conservatism continued to set limits on tolerance toward racial and ethnic differences.[119]

Cultural debates, and more specifically the debates over American popular culture, were major sites for the construction of national identities in the two German states. Authorities in both states made their citizens' cultural consumption central to their political reconstruction efforts. In the East and West German conflicts over American influences such as rock 'n' roll, we can see how the two states tried to lay claim to a German identity in the aftermath of National Socialism and in the face of the cold war. Moreover, we can trace in these debates how the two states crystallized as separate entities. Most important, debates over American influences and rock 'n' roll were located in everyday life and on the political stage, and it is in the intersections between the two—in particular as they affected young women—that we can trace the changing cultural politics of national reconstruction and the German cold war.

---

118. "The Politicization of Private Life" is the title of the chapter on the West German women's movement in Ute Frevert, *Women in German History: From Bourgeois Emancipation to Sexual Liberation* (New York, 1989), pp. 287–303. On the connections between 1950s youth cultures and 1960s feminism in the United States, see Breines (n. 4 above). For West Germany, see Katrin Pallowski, "Wohnen in halben Zimmern," in Delille and Grohn, eds. (n. 4 above), pp. 23–29.

119. Michael Geyer, "The Stigma of Violence, Nationalism, and War in Twentieth-Century Germany," *German Studies Review* 15 (Winter 1992): 75–110, has observed that the legacy of nationalism in postwar Germany "consisted in the destruction of alternative voices and multiple identities *as public voices*" (pp. 102–3).

Part 5.
"Conservative Modernization" in the Adenauer Era?

"Reconstruction" and "Modernization": West German Social History during the 1950s

Axel Schildt and Arnold Sywottek

Introduction

Exactly when "the fifties" took on the quality of a distinct era in public memory is not certain. The first retrospective assessments of the 1950s in the early 1970s, which sought to move beyond contemporary commentaries on the "end of the postwar period" or "the Adenauer era,"[1] still focused largely on national political events. "Germany was divisible," commented Thilo Koch in 1972, summarizing his multipart television series on "the 1950s in Germany."[2] Soon thereafter, however, nostalgia must have set in. As early as 1978 a title story in the weekly magazine *Der Spiegel*[3] described the "longing for the counterfeit fifties" ("Heimweh nach den falschen Fünfzigern"); the story expressed a critical political undertone, which had been part of virtually every portrayal of the Federal Republic as a "CDU-State" since the 1960s.[4] Cataloging the phenomena of the 1950s, the article in *Der Spiegel* named all the characteris-

This chapter emerged from a research project funded by the Volkswagen Foundation (Volkswagen Stiftung) at the University of Hamburg's Historical Seminar entitled: "'Modernity' and 'Modernization' in the Federal Republic of Germany in the 1950s." In addition to the authors, Thomas Südbeck (research focus: motorization, transportation infrastructure and policies) and Michael Wildt (research focus: nutrition and consumption) collaborated on this project. The chapter includes passages from the unpublished project proposal (1986) as well as several internal working papers. Because of space constraints, citations have been limited to supporting evidence and a few references to more recent literature. (The translation was prepared by the editor with the assistance of Corinne Antezana-Pernet and Rita B. Bashaw.)

1. For an example of a balanced assessment, see Karl Dietrich Bracher, ed., *Nach 25 Jahren: Eine Deutschlandbilanz* (Munich, 1970).

2. Thilo Koch, *Deutschland war teilbar: Die Fünfziger Jahre* (Stuttgart, 1972).

3. *Der Spiegel*, no. 14 (1978).

4. See Gert Schäfer and Carl Nedelmann, eds., *Der CDU Staat: Analysen zur Verfas-*

tics that continued to lend a sense of fascination to the decade: fashion trends and architecture, the cinema and its stars, popular music, literature, and, last but not least, various philosophical tendencies.[5]

This fascination with the 1950s incorporates a mix of intellectual interest and the naive joy of discovery, as well as the calculations of those who seek to market the culture and lifestyle of the decade. In contrast, consideration of what motivated youth protest or later the *Null-Bock* (rejection of ambition) and "No-future" attitudes of the younger generation is eclipsed by an emphasis on the accomplishments of the generation, the grandparents of today, who rebuilt Germany, and by a focus on how things got better and better in the 1950s. The new women's movement has also been unable to find positive historical models in the 1950s.[6] For a moment, there was a provocative tendency to characterize the 1950s, politically and historically, as the "puberty of the republic," but this moment came and went.[7] Now, cultural history is "in," and to a certain extent aesthetic and anthropological approaches have pushed aside the methodologies of political scientists and sociologists. Only via a detour of discussions of "modernity" and "postmodernity," first in the history of aesthetics and style, have we once again begun to consider social and economic dimensions, stressing that the 1950s were a "period of modernity."

Traveling along different paths, historians have begun to arrive at the point where they are offering similar assessments of the period. In the 1970s, the thesis of "West German Restoration" was still widely held;[8] originating in the 1950s, this thesis made it possible for leftist intellectuals and politicians (from Walter Dirks to Kurt Schumacher) to understand the gap between their expectations and the reality of developments after the collapse in 1945.[9] In

---

sungswirklichkeit der Bundesrepublik (Munich, 1967).

5. Among the more recent overviews that offer a range of perspectives on cultural history, see Hermann Glaser, *Kulturgeschichte der Bundesrepublik Deutschland,* vol. 2, *Zwischen Grundgesetz und Großer Koalition 1949–1967* (Munich, 1986); Jost Hermand, *Kultur im Wieder-aufbau: Die Bundesrepublik Deutschland 1945–1965* (Munich, 1986); quite descriptive also is Dieter Bänsch, ed., *Die Fünfziger Jahre: Beiträge zu Politik und Kultur* (Tübingen, 1985); worth noting in the flood of publications about specific sectors of cultural development are, on fashion and design, Thomas Jasperson, *Produktwahrnehmung und stilistischer Wandel* (Frankfurt, 1985); on architecture, Werner Durth and Niels Gutschow, *Architektur und Städtebau der fünfziger Jahre* (Bonn, 1987); on literature, Ludwig Fischer, ed., *Literatur in der Bundesrepublik Deutschland bis 1967* (Munich, 1986).

6. See Anette Kuhn's preface in Doris Schubert, *Frauen in der deutschen Nachkriegszeit,* vol. 1, *Frauenarbeit 1945–1949: Quellen und Materialien* (Düsseldorf, 1984), 13–21.

7. See Nikolaus Jungwirth and Gerhard Kromschröder, *Die Pubertät der Republik: Die 50er Jahre der Deutschen* (Frankfurt, 1978); and Eckhard Siepmann, ed., *Bikini: Die Fünfziger Jahre: Kalter Krieg und Capri-Sonne* (Berlin, 1981).

8. See in particular Ernst-Ulrich Huster et al., *Determinanten der westdeutschen Restauration 1945–1949* (Frankfurt, 1972).

9. See Karl Prümm, "Entwürfe einer zweiten Republik: Zukunftsprogramme in den 'Frankfurter Heften' 1946–1949," in *Deutschland nach Hitler: Zukunftspläne im Exil und aus der*

1981 Hans-Peter Schwarz, the Adenauer biographer and historian of the Federal Republic, countered that what characterized the 1950s was not "restoration" but "modernization"; the 1950s, he argued, constituted an "era of dramatic modernization."[10] To be sure, Schwarz did not specify exactly what belonged under the umbrella of "modernization"; for him, the concept remained just as vague as it was for Ralf Dahrendorf and David Schoenbaum in their explanations of National Socialism's rise to dominance and the Weimar Republic's disintegration.[11]

"Modernization under a conservative guardianship"[12]—this formulation may ultimately best summarize the Adenauer era. However, we must first determine more precisely what constitutes "modernization." The "modernization theories" that circulated in the 1960s are of little use; like the "modernization" discussions among historians, they almost always were based on the analysis of the transition from agrarian to industrial society.[13] More recently, historians have convincingly labeled conditions in the Weimar Republic as "modern," using as a measure Weimar's social institutions and the development of the welfare state. The meaning of *modernity* in this instance is borrowed from contemporary sociologists (especially Max Weber).[14] From this perspective, the years after 1933 can be interpreted primarily as an unhealthy ("pathological") development of "modernity," though this framework offers no adequate explanation of the internal dynamics of specific aspects of social, political, and economic development.

Recent historical and sociological analyses have offered a convincing case for viewing the period from the end of World War I until the end of the 1960s as a unity,[15] identified as the "structural breakthrough of modernity" (*Strukturbruch der Moderne*);[16] this framework makes it impossible to exclude the years of the "Third Reich" from a social history of "modernity." Much his-

---

Besatzungszeit 1939–1949, edited by Thomas Koebner et al., (Opladen, 1987), 330–43.

10. Hans-Peter Schwarz, *Die Ära Adenauer: Gründerjahre der Republik 1949–1957* (Stuttgart, 1981), 382; also idem, "Modernisierung oder Restauration? Einige Vorfragen zur künftigen Sozialgeschichtsforschung über die Ära Adenauer," in *Rheinland-Westfalen im Industriezeitalter,* vol. 3, *Vom Ende der Weimarer Republik bis zum Land Nordrhein-Westfalen,* edited by Kurt Düwell and Wolfgang Köllmann (Wuppertal, 1984), 278–93.

11. Ralf Dahrendorf, *Gesellschaft und Demokratie in Deutschland* (Munich, 1965); David Schoenbaum, *Die braune Revolution: Eine Sozialgeschichte des Dritten Reiches* (Cologne, 1968).

12. Christoph Kleßmann, "Ein stolzes Schiff und krächzende Möwen: Die Geschichte der Bundesrepublik und ihre Kritiker," *Geschichte und Gesellschaft* 11 (1985): 485.

13. In particular, see Hans-Ulrich Wehler, *Modernisierungstheorie und Geschichte* (Göttingen, 1975).

14. Detlev J. Peukert, *Die Weimarer Republik* (Frankfurt, 1987).

15. This characterization also holds for the history of architecture, city planning, and housing. See, for example, Axel Schildt and Arnold Sywottek, eds., *"Massenwohnung" und "Eigenheim": Wohnungsbau und Wohnen in der Großstadt seit dem Ersten Weltkrieg* (Frankfurt, 1988).

16. Ulrich Beck, *Risikogesellschaft: Auf dem Weg in eine andere Moderne* (Frankfurt, 1987).

torical discussion has questioned whether 1933 should be seen as a political rupture, and recent research into the life histories of the postwar "reconstruction" generation (*"Wiederaufbau"-Generation*) has allowed us to conceive of the decades from 1930 to 1960 as a unity; this perspective has been particularly useful for the social historical understanding of the Adenauer era.[17]

For a German social history that spans political turning points, however, there are still many areas that have not been adequately studied. There are some breaks that cannot be glossed over so easily. World War II, the collapse, and the division of Germany tore apart the fabric of social and economic interrelationships. For example, we can point to the anticlimactic disappearance of the influential east Elbian Junkers, who had been such an anachronistic presence in the political culture of the Weimar Republic; this development has received virtually no scholarly attention. In addition, changes that register in economic data, though at first glance far less dramatic, have crucial implications for historical analysis. The west German economy of today is structured differently internally and is tied differently into the global economy than the pre-1945 regional and national economy from which it emerged; long-term statistical data for production and distribution make possible long-term comparisons over decades, and they can shed light on business management practices, but they do not illuminate economic history more broadly conceived.[18] How, for example, can we accurately assess the significance of state support for economic innovation in the 1950s if we do not locate it in the context of long-term developmental trends? The origins of the peaceful development of atomic energy in the 1950s is a case in point, one of the few areas of economic policy development that has been the subject of systematic analysis.[19]

In short, much remains to be done before we can start to offer an adequate picture of the "modernization" and "modernity" of West German society in the 1950s. In what follows, we offer an outline for future research that will make it possible to fill in this picture more completely:

We must first inquire about the relationship between "reconstruction" (*"Rekonstruktion"*) and "expansion (*"Ausbau"*) of West Germany society. In historical overviews, 1955 roughly marks the end of "reconstruction," that is, of "restoration," and the start of "expansion,"

---

17. See in particular the volumes of the project *Lebensgeschichte und Sozialkultur im Ruhrgebiet 1930–1960*, edited by Lutz Niethammer.

18. See the preface of Walther G. Hoffmann, *Das Wachstum der deutschen Wirtschaft seit der Mitte des 19. Jahrhunderts* (Berlin, 1965.)

19. Joachim Radkau, *Aufstieg und Krise der deutschen Atomwirtschaft 1945–1975: Verdrängte Alternativen in der Kerntechnik und der Ursprung der nuklearen Kontroverse* (Reinbek, 1983).

already characterized by contemporaries as the beginning of "modern-ization."[20] This two-phase model makes it possible to understand macroeconomic data, but it does not address the question of when exactly political, administrative, economic and social "planners" began to make use of the concept of "expansion." In addition, the relationship between "reconstruction" and "modernization" in the "restoration" process of the first half of the 1950s requires clarification.[21]

Second, the term reconstruction takes as a point of reference standards in place before 1945, underscoring the need to sort out the significance of long-term factors of continuity.[22] Despite all the myths about the unprecedented nature of postwar growth and prosperity, the level of technological development of industry in prewar German society was high (this was also true of certain sectors during wartime). In addition, the standard of living and level of social security in German society ranked at the top of industrial societies, despite the disruption caused by the world economic crisis and the "Third Reich." Indeed, from this perspective, the social development of the 1950s emerges as the resumption of trends that were interrupted by the destruction during World War II and the changes that took place in the postwar years. In addition, we also now know that under National Socialist rule, there were already elements of "modernity" experienced in daily life—from laundry detergent to Coca-Cola—that would intensify after the war.[23]

In the initial postwar years, the society of the Federal Republic was exposed to models of political culture and patterns of everyday life that

---

20. See, for example, Konrad Adenauer's opening address to the second legislative session of the West German parliament, October 20, 1953, in Hans Ulrich Behn, *Die Regierungserklärungen der Bundesrepublik Deutschland* (Munich, 1971).

21. State-subsidized housing development may serve as another example; here we can also find discussions of "modern" (i.e., rational) construction and housing. See the contributions in the richly illustrated catalog of Bernhard Schulz, ed., *Grauzonen, Farbwelten: Kunst und Zeitbilder 1945–1955* (Berlin, 1983); for a case study, Axel Schildt, *Die Grindelhochhaüser: Eine Sozialgeschichte der ersten deutschen Wohnhochhausanlage, Hamburg 1945–1956* (Hamburg, 1988); on the largely overlooked tradition of "modern" mass housing developments, Tilman Harlander and Gerhard Fehl, eds., *Hitler's sozialer Wohnungsbau 1940–1945: Wohnungspolitik, Baugestaltung und Siedlungsplanung* (Hamburg, 1986); on city planning and reconstruction in the 1940s, Werner Durth and Niels Gutschow, *Träume in Trümmern: Planungen zum Wiederaufbau zerstörter Städte in Westdeutschland 1940–1950* (Braunschweig, 1988); and Klaus von Beyme, *Der Wiederaufbau: Architektur und Städtebaupolitik in beiden deutschen Staaten* (Munich, 1987).

22. See the contributions in Ludolf Herbst, ed., *Westdeutschland 1945–1955: Unterwerfung, Kontrolle, Integration* (Munich, 1986); and more recently Martin Broszat, Klaus-Dieter Henke, Hans Woller, eds., *Von Stalingrad zur Währungsreform: Zur Sozialgeschichte des Umbruchs in Deutschland* (Munich, 1988).

23. See the somewhat overstated position of Hans-Dietrich Schäfer, *Das gespaltene Bewußtsein: Über deutsche Kultur und Lebenswirklichkeit 1933–1945* (Munich, 1981).

came from other Western industrial societies, particularly the United States. This took the form of the occupation forces' early attempts to bring about a "reeducation," then a "reorientation" to democracy. The opening of the West German economy to the world market, which soon followed, was another part of this process. Even at the time, many contemporaries labeled these developments "Americanization."[24] Thus, a third focus of research must be the assessment of the actual significance of these outside impulses for the development of the Federal Republic in the 1950s. To be sure, some individual aspects of economic and political relations have already been investigated.[25] However, studies of "Americanization" must also consider the extent to which postwar trends represented the resumption of patterns interrupted by the war; it is generally known that a first wave of "Americanization" took place in the 1920s.[26]

The two-phase model of development outlined here also offers a way in which to differentiate among different phases of "modernization." The contemporary characterization of the entire decade as "modern" is clearly an exaggeration; it appears that this label often meant little more than "new," "fashionable," or, in any case, "up-to-date"; it was a default category that could indicate many things. For example, a certain austerity in fashions and patterns of daily life might be interpreted as "modern"—the expression of a new style and aesthetic—in a society in which affluence was still measured on the yardstick of bourgeois excess, although this austerity was in fact an expression of thrift determined by scarcity. Particularly for those who lost all their possessions and often their social status through flight, expulsion, and bombing raids, the use of such labels was a way to facilitate their integration into new surroundings. The publicly subsidized housing projects that began to appear in many places in the 1950s offer another example that could be used to illustrate this point: Identifying these housing projects as representative of "modern times" was a way to displace traditional notions of taste, still the province of the more affluent classes, though it was precisely in these upper social classes that the "modern" had been "avant-garde." In addition, "modern" styles had

---

24. For a summary of the state of research, see Harald Guldin, "Außenwirtschaftspolitische und außenpolitische Einflußfaktoren im Prozeß der Staatswerdung der Bundesrepublik Deutschland (1947–1952)," *Aus Politik und Zeitgeschichte* B 32/87, 3–20.

25. See Werner Link, *Deutsche und amerikanische Gewerkschaften und Geschäftsleute 1945–1975: Eine Studie über transnationale Beziehungen* (Düsseldorf, 1978); and Hans Jürgen Grabbe, *Unionsparteien, Sozialdemokratie und Vereinigte Staaten von Amerika 1945–1966* (Düsseldorf, 1983).

26. On the economic and political linkages between Germany and America since 1918, see, for example, Manfred Knapp, *Die USA und Deutschland 1918–1975: Deutsch-amerikanische Beziehungen zwischen Rivalität und Partnerschaft* (Munich, 1978).

been officially taboo in the "Third Reich" as they were for many years in the German Democratic Republic; this, in turn, offered a political justification for favoring such "modern" styles in the West in the 1950s.

Patterns of Economic Development

Perhaps it is appropriate to begin a history of West German society's "modernization" in the 1950s with a consideration of particular patterns of economic development. The growth of the German economy in the 1950s was a source of fascination for contemporaries, and it has continued to fascinate those who have studied the decade.[27] Figures commonly used to measure the "singularity" of this "economic miracle"—for example, the tripling of the GNP between 1950 and 1960—can provide only a limited sense of the dynamism which set the Federal Republic at the forefront of Western European economies, surpassed in growth worldwide only by Japan. Perhaps a better sense of this dynamic development is possible if we recall the widespread concern about continued unemployment that existed at the beginning of the decade, replaced by the late 1950s by labor shortages: The number of those employed increased by 25 percent between 1950 and 1960, from twenty to twenty-five million. Even the majority of expellees and refugees, whose economic integration had initially been viewed as a burden, found employment. Newcomers from the GDR were soon welcome, and ultimately the East German state put a halt to this labor migration, enticed by the development of West Germany society, only by building the Berlin Wall (1961). Recruitment of guest workers from southern countries, which had already begun before the building of the wall, could only partially replace this influx of mostly skilled labor.[28]

27. See, for example, Elmar Altvater et al., *Vom Wirtschaftswunder zur Wirtschaftskrise: Ökonomie und Politik in der Bundesrepublik* (Berlin, 1979); Gerold Ambrosius, "Das Wirtschaftssystem," in *Die Bundesrepublik Deutschland*, vol. 2, edited by Wolfgang Benz (Frankfurt, 1983), 238–97; Knut Borchardt, "Die Bundesrepublik in den säkularen Trends der wirtschaftlichen Entwicklung," in *Sozialgeschichte der Bundesrepublik Deutschland: Beiträge zum Kontinuitätsproblem*, edited by Werner Conze and M. Rainer Lepsius (Stuttgart, 1983), 20–45; Werner Abelshauser, *Die Langen Fünfziger Jahre: Wirtschaft und Gesellschaft der Bundesrepublik Deutschland 1949–1966* (Düsseldorf, 1987); for international comparisons, see Herman van der Wee, *Der gebremste Wohlstand: Wiederaufbau, Wachstum, Strukturwandel 1945–1980* (Munich, 1984); and for a provocative global interpretation, Burkart Lutz, *Der kurze Traum immerwährender Prosperität: Eine Neuinterpretation der industriell-kapitalistischen Entwicklung im Europa des 20. Jahrhunderts* (Frankfurt, 1984).

28. Detailed figures are available in Siegfried Bethlehem, *Heimatvertreibung, DDR-Flucht, Gastarbeiterzuwanderung: Wanderungsströme und Wanderungspolitik in der Bundesrepublik Deutschland* (Stuttgart, 1982); see also Marion Frantzioch, *Die Vertriebenen: Hemmnisse und Wege ihrer Integration in der Bundesrepublik Deutschland* (Berlin, 1987); and Rainer Schulze, Doris von der Brelie-Lewien, and Helga Grebing, eds., *Flüchtlinge und Vertriebene in der westdeutschen Nachkriegsgeschichte: Bilanzierung der Forschung und Perspektiven für die künftige Forschungsarbeit* (Hildesheim, 1987).

The highly skilled nature of the German labor force, compared with other countries, was an important precondition for the German "economic miracle" in east and west, though this was not immediately recognized. Initially, the rapid economic development was seen as a more-or-less necessary consequence of the market economy that went into effect with currency reform in 1948. Subsequently, historians determined that the level of West German industrial capital stock was 10 percent higher than before the war, despite dismantling and the destruction experienced during the war.[29] They began to question whether American credit introduced by the Marshall Plan at the same time as currency reform in 1948 was necessary to jump-start West German economic development.[30] Apart from its positive psychological effect on the economy, there is little doubt that the Marshall Plan laid the groundwork for the West German capacity to enter strong foreign trade relationships. Once currency reform was in place and the fundamental administrative and political decisions of 1948 had been made, it was possible for the export of West German goods to become a significant pacesetter for economic development in the 1950s. Until the Korean War increased worldwide demand for German goods, particularly those of highly centralized sectors like iron and steel, the Allies maintained postwar restrictions on German industrial production; the suspension of these restrictions made possible the full exploitation of production capacity in these sectors. By 1952, the Federal Republic boasted a trade surplus. By 1960, the West German economy's exports represented 17 percent of the net national product; exports had reached approximately the pre–World War I levels of imperial Germany.[31] In the years that followed, the value of exports grew, reaching 25 percent of the net national product by 1970. The structure of exports was distinctive: In terms of value, finished industrial products in 1960 represented 82.4 percent of all exports (1950: 64.8 percent).[32] To an even greater extent than the Kaiserreich, the Federal Republic had become a country of finishing and processing industries.

The statistics mirror this "industrial miracle"[33] in many different ways: On average, between 1950 and 1960 the industrial and manufacturing ("secondary") sector of the economy grew 9.5 percent annually, while the agricultural ("primary") sector and the service ("tertiary") sector grew at aver-

---

29. See, for example, Werner Abelshauser, *Wirtschaft in Westdeutschland 1945–1948: Rekonstruktion und Wachstumbedingungen in der amerikanischen und britischen Zone* (Stuttgart, 1975).

30. This is the subject of an ongoing debate in the pages of the journal *Vierteljahrshefte für Zeitgeschichte*.

31. Among others, see Hoffmann, *Das Wachstum der deutschen Wirtschaft,* 151.

32. Statistisches Bundesamt, ed., *Bevölkerung und Wirtschaft 1872–1972* (Stuttgart, 1972), 196.

33. According to Dieter Mertens, *Die Wandlungen der industriellen Branchenstruktur in der Bundesrepublik 1950–1960* (Berlin, 1964), 23.

age yearly rates of 3.9 percent and 6.35 percent, respectively.[34] In 1960, industry contributed far more than 50 percent of the GNP, and measured along this scale, the Federal Republic stood at the top of Western European industrial societies.[35] This development is even more striking if we examine the distribution of the labor force: In the primary sector, the number of employed between 1950 and 1960 decreased by 1.4 million (a yearly average of 2.7 percent); in the secondary sector, employment increased by 3.4 million (a yearly average of 3.4 percent).[36] The tertiary sector grew by about the same amount as the secondary. Never before in German history had there been a comparable period of rapid change in the structure of employment. It has been calculated that in these years one-sixth of the increase in West Germany's economic productivity resulted from the transfer of employment from less productive sectors—such as agriculture—into sectors that already exhibited higher rates of productivity.[37]

Despite a decline in employment, mechanization and motorization were responsible for productivity gains in the agricultural sector as well, an indication that there was more than one way to stimulate the growth of the national economy. Despite Nazi propaganda, in the "Third Reich" agriculture received little significant support in comparison to industry; as a result, measured in terms of the extent of motorized machines, agriculture in the 1950s was a good twenty years behind the times and below the average of other comparable national economies. Friedrich Wilhelm Henning correctly identified the 1950s as the "beginning of the modern era for the agrarian sector."[38] In the industrial sector, the number of jobs that demanded highly skilled, better qualified workers also expanded, and the share of workers performing hard physical labor fell, triggering the earliest discussions of the "social consequences of automation".[39]

34. See Werner Glastetter, *Die wirtschaftliche Entwicklung der Bundesrepublik Deutschland im Zeitraum 1950–1975* (Berlin, 1977), 37f.

35. See Sachverständigenrat zur Begutachtung der gesamtwirtschaftlichen Entwicklung, *Mut zur Stabilisierung: Jahresgutachten 1973–74* (Stuttgart, 1973), 25.

36. For example, see the extensive statistical material available in Martin Osterland et al., *Materialien zur Lebens- und Arbeitssituation der Industriearbeiter in der BRD*, 3d ed. (Frankfurt, 1973).

37. See Peter Schwanse, *Beschäftigungsstruktur und Wirtschaftswachstum in der Bundesrepublik 1950–1963* (Berlin, 1965); also Karl-Heinrich Oppenländer, "Wirtschaftlicher und sozialer Wandel durch technischen Fortschritt: Überblick und Ausblick," in *Wirtschaftlicher und technischer Fortschritt: Bericht über den wissenschaftlichen Teil der 34. Mitgliederversammlung der Arbeitsgemeinschaft deutscher wirtschaftswissenschaftlicher Forschungsinstitute e.V.*, May 22, 1971 (supplement to *Konjunkturpolitik* [18]), 11–70.

38. Friedrich Wilhelm Henning, "Der Beginn der modernen Welt im agrarischen Bereich," in *Studien zum Beginn der modernen Gesellschaft*, edited by Reinhart Koselleck (Stuttgart, 1974), 114.

39. See Helmut Schelsky, *Die sozialen Folgen der Automatisierung* (Düsseldorf, 1957). Many of the studies by industrial sociologists are mentioned in Rene König, ed., *Handbuch der empirischen Sozialforschung*, vol. 8, 2d ed. (Stuttgart, 1977), 101–262; see also Johannes Weyer,

In the 1950s, the relative shares of industrial sectors shifted. Significant growth occurred primarily in industries of capital goods investment. The "growth industries" of this era were primarily oil refining, chemicals, production and processing of synthetics, the automotive industry, and (as it remains today) the electronics industry.[40] There is still no research into the extent to which domestic or foreign demand stimulated the growth of individual industrial sectors. The significance of domestic demand becomes apparent in the following sections that describe a society characterized by "mobility," "consumption," and "leisure."

The "Mobile" Society

When we speak of "mobility" or "mobilized society," we are referring both to spatial mobility—that is, migrations and changes of place of residence—and social mobility—that is, movement upward and downward in terms of social status. In the 1950s these processes were often inseparably intertwined. In the early postwar years, expellees, refugees, and returning POWs shaped contemporaries' picture of society. For Elisabeth Pfeil, writing in 1948, the refugee was the ideal-typical figure that embodied the spirit of the era.[41] And investigating the decline in social status of many refugees, Helmut Schelsky discerned a trend toward a "leveled-off middle class society" (*nivellierte Mittelstandsgesellschaft*), a view that served for many years as a popular framework for interpreting social development.[42] To be sure, geographic mobility quickly diminished. In the mid-1950s, statisticians began to speak of the tendency to "settle down" in the "new home" (*neue Heimat*), especially among refugees and expellees. The last great population shifts of expellees within the Federal Republic took place between 1953 and 1956. These occurred in response to targeted resettlement programs that offered solid prospects for jobs and housing in newly built apartments. Since 1956, there has been a resumption of a major trend of declining migration that could be traced back to World War I, interrupted only by World War II. In 1950, for every 1,000 inhabitants, there were 61.7 changes of residence; the number declined to 60.7 in 1960. One-third of these were moves between the various West German federal

---

Westdeutsche Soziologie 1945–1960: Deutsche Kontinuitäten und nordamerikanischer Einfluß (Berlin, 1984), 207ff.

40. For the first half of the 1950s, see the detailed statistical data in Klaus Leist, *Investitionen und Sozialstruktur in Westdeutschland* (Zürich, 1956), 56ff.; and in general, Bernhard Schäfer, *Sozialstruktur und Wandel der Bundesrepublik Deutschland* (Stuttgart, 1976), 141ff.

41. Elisabeth Pfeil, *Der Flüchtling: Gestalt einer Zeitenwende* (Hamburg, 1948).

42. First mentioned in Helmut Schelsky, *Wandlungen der deutschen Familie in der Gegenwart: Darstellung und Deutung einer empirisch-soziologischen Tatbestandsaufnahme* (Dortmund, 1953).

states; two-thirds occurred within state boundaries.[43] However, there was a clear increase in a special category of spatial mobility, that of "work-related commuting" (*Berufspendlertum*). In 1961, more than 30 percent of those employed did not live and work in the same place. In the preceding decade, the number of commuting workers, more than six million, had almost doubled.[44] This trend held true for urban areas such as Hamburg and for larger states with fewer big cities such as Bavaria.[45]

Compared to figures for the prewar period, the increase in the number of workers commuting was great. However, in order to understand this development, it is necessary to distinguish among different phases in the 1950s. At the beginning of the decade, local housing shortages in areas with many employment opportunities may have been the main cause of "commuting." However, in the years that followed, the reasons for commuting changed. The increasingly urban character of the entire society was one of the most significant consequences of industrial growth.[46] This was reflected in housing construction, heavily supported by the state, particularly in small and middle-size cities with populations of five thousand to fifty thousand inhabitants. It registered as well in the spread of industry and manufacturing into rural areas, a development that left contemporaries in a state of "complete amazement."[47] These consequences of industrial expansion completely altered patterns of mobility. The commuter was the symbol of urbanization, and it was the commuter who was particularly prominent among the class of new home owners that was part and parcel of the process of urbanization. By 1960, half of all commuting households owned "their own four walls." This was also a result of the second housing law, passed in 1956, that introduced measures to facilitate home ownership.[48] After years of housing shortages, it was far easier to satisfy the strong desire for individual home ownership in rural areas and on the outskirts—rather than in the center—of cities.

43. See Karl Schwarz, *Analyse der räumlichen Bevölkerungsbewegung* (Hannover, 1969), 80.

44. *Wirtschaft und Statistik* (1964): 216f.

45. For Hamburg, see the analysis of the area within a radius of 40 kilometers of the city, *Hamburg in Zahlen*, Sonderheft 2 (1963), 12; for Bavaria, Kurt Horstmann, "Zur Soziologie der Wanderungen," in *Handbuch der empirischen Sozialforschung*, vol. 5, 2d ed., edited by Rene König (Stuttgart, 1976), 135.

46. For the first attempt at an overview of this still much-neglected aspect of social history, see Jürgen Reulecke, *Geschichte der Urbanisierung in Deutschland* (Frankfurt, 1985).

47. Kurt Pritzkoleit, *Das gebändigte Chaos: Die deutschen Wirtschaftslandschaften* (Vienna, 1965), 9; for a sophisticated contemporary anthropological perspective, see also Hermann Bausinger, *Volkskultur in der technischen Welt* (Stuttgart, 1971) (new edition Frankfurt, 1986).

48. See Günther Schulz, "Eigenheimpolitik und Eigenheimförderung im ersten Jahrzehnt nach dem Zweiten Weltkrieg," Schildt and Sywottek, *"Massenwohnung" und "Eigenheim,"* 409–39.

Greatly intensified automobile traffic and a notable increase in the number of automobiles were consequences of this trend toward "settling down" in areas removed from the center of cities; when contemporaries spoke of "mobility," they most often had in mind car travel. A particularly powerful indication of these changing forms of mobility is offered by a look at the shifting relationship between public and private modes of transport: Between 1950 and 1961, the number of passengers served by public transportation grew by 32 percent to 7.2 billion riders.[49] In 1961, streetcars and subways still served more passengers than any other form of transportation. However, between 1950 and 1961, the share of *all* riders carried by these modes of public transportation declined from 58 percent to 41 percent. Beginning in 1957, the number of persons served by railway decreased as well, from about 27 percent (1950) to 18.5 percent (1961). Buses alone showed an increase in ridership; in 1961, they transported two-and-one-half times more people than in 1950, reflecting the rapid development of the transportation infrastructure and a demand for new branchlines.

After 1957, the number of riders using public transportation continued to increase, but at diminishing rates, and individual use of automobiles began to take on a new quality. In that year, there were more registered automobiles than motorcycles on West German streets (excluding mopeds, which were beginning to replace bicycles) for the first time. New registrations for automobiles had outnumbered those for motorcycles for the first time three years earlier. At over 2 million in 1955, the number of motorcycles had more than doubled since 1950, but it then declined to 1.5 million by 1960. In contrast, the number of automobiles jumped eightfold in the decade of the 1950s, reaching over 4 million by 1960.[50] This translates into approximately 80 automobiles per 1,000 inhabitants. In 1960, car ownership per capita was greater in other comparable Western industrial countries, but the rate of increase in new car ownership in the Federal Republic was unsurpassed.[51]

This heightened mobility, including visibly new forms of increased street traffic (and "traffic going nowhere" [*ruhender Verkehr*] alongside the street curbs), reflected increased incomes in the majority of households, but it was also a by-product of the increase in the number of those commuting to work. Statistics underscore this point: In 1960, 27 percent of all workers living in rural communities and only 14 percent of workers in cities had a driver's li-

---

49. See *Statistische Jahrbücher für die Bundesrepublik Deutschland*, 1952ff.

50. See Verband der Automobilindustrie, ed., *Tatsachen und Zahlen aus der Kraftverkehrswirtschaft* (Frankfurt, 1954).

51. For a summary and overview, see Jochen Siebke, *Die Automobilnachfrage: Die Nachfrage nach Personenkraftwagen in der Bundesrepublik Deutschland mit einer Prognose bis zum Jahr 1970* (Cologne, 1963), esp. 79ff.

cense.[52] Only one in eight worker's households owned a car, compared with one in four households of civil servants and salaried white-collar workers. However, by 1960, wage earners were responsible for more than half of automobile purchases (in 1950, they had constituted a bare 9 percent, by 1955, a good 28 percent of buyers).[53] We can thus safely assume that the search for a way to get to work that was more comfortable and less dependent on weather conditions sparked the continued boom in automobile ownership in the 1960s.

The automotive industry certainly made it easier to fulfill this wish by offering reasonably priced small cars. The costs of operating an automobile fell as well, both as a result of a drop in gasoline prices in 1958 and new tax policy regulations in 1955 that permitted deduction of commuting expenses. The used-car market also contributed to the increased supply of automobiles, and prices for used cars declined after the middle of the decade. Between 1950 and 1960, the volume of private motorized transport had increased sixfold. During the same period, public transportation increased by only about 60 percent.

Finally, the transportation policies of the federal government, under pressure from the automobile industry, fostered the move to a "society of car owners" with measures that were to the disadvantage of public transportation, especially rail transportation. Costs of short-distance travel with public transportation doubled on average during the same decade in which the costs of private automobile ownership dropped,[54] though further investigation is necessary to establish the phases of this development. What is certain is that car ownership became the means to achieve mobility, not only widening the range of everyday activity for many people, but also helping to open up the world in many different directions, all without leaving the "realm of privacy" (*Privatbereich*). The automobile thus became the symbol of the individual's efforts to construct and extend his or her individual existence, correctly emphasized by F. H. Tenbruck as a central feature of the 1950s.[55]

The "Consumer" Society

By the end of the 1950s, the automobile had become a symbol of societal well-being and affluence; in the memory of many contemporaries, this trend began

---

52. See Wolfgang Hartensein and Klaus Liepelt, *Man auf der Straße: Eine verkehrssoziologische Untersuchung* (Frankfurt, 1961), 91f.

53. See *Wirtschaft und Statistik* (1952): 267f.

54. See, for example, Winfried Wolf, *Eisenbahn und Autobahn: Personen- und Gütertransport auf Schiene und Straße, Geschichte, Bilanz, Perspektiven* (Hamburg, 1987), 142ff.

55. Friedrich H. Tenbruck, "Alltagsnormen und Lebensgefühle in der Bundesrepublik," in *Die zweite Republik: 25 Jahre Bundesrepublik Deutschland. Eine Bilanz,* edited by Richard Löwenthal and Hans-Peter Schwarz (Stuttgart, 1974), 296f.

in 1948. A common metaphor for describing the move toward an affluent society was the image of a "wave-like motion." A series of waves had washed over West Germans with "better foodstuffs, clothing, housing, automobiles."[56] Helmut Schelsky, writing in the early 1950s, offered one interpretation; the increase in "the universal consumption of industrial . . . mass production" was the most significant factor contributing to "overcoming the class conditions of industrial society" and providing for a "relative levelling of the stratified structure of social relations that once prevailed." This was, according to Schelsky, "perhaps the most dominant development in the present transformation of German society."[57] Like Theodor W. Adorno, Schelsky also felt obliged as early as the mid-1950s to warn of the dangers of "consumption terror" (*"Konsumterror"*),[58] and by the end of the decade, the term *consumption terror* was widely used. According to the interpretative framework put in place by the contemporary "sociology of prosperity"[59] that emerged in the 1950s, West Germans no longer confronted struggles around the distribution of scarce goods. Rather, the most pressing social problem was to make the best use of the multitude of goods and services that were available.

It is essential that we redraw this picture of the origins of the Federal Republic as a "consumer society" in a more differentiated and nuanced fashion: First, we cannot accept the myth of the 1950s—recently revived in the 1980s—of a seamless development from the "winter of hunger" to a "culinary heaven" (*Vom Hungerwinter zum kulinarischen Schlaraffenland*);[60] second, we should interrogate the usefulness of the wave metaphor; and third, we should keep in mind the problematic nature of Schelsky's thesis of the leveling of differences in class status.

To be sure, an unprecedented, rapid increase in prosperity and living standards was the "central experience of the West German population from 1950s

---

56. Wolfgang Zapf, "Die Wohlfahrtsentwicklung in Deutschland seit der Mitte des 19. Jahrhunderts," in Conze and Lepsius, *Sozialgeschichte der Bundesrepublik,* 61.

57. Helmut Schelsky, "Die Bedeutung des Schichtungsbegriffes für die Analyse der gegenwärtigen deutschen Gesellschaft (1953)," in idem, *Auf der Suche nach der Wirklichkeit: Gesammelte Aufsätze* (Düsseldorf, 1965), 332f.

58. See Theodor W. Adorno, *Prismen: Kulturkritik und Gesellschaft* (Frankfurt, 1955); and Helmut Schelsky, "Beruf und Freizeit als Erziehungsziele in der modernen Gesellschaft," in idem, *Auf der Suche nach der Wirklichkeit,* 160–81.

59. See Ernest Zahn, *Soziologie der Prosperität: Wirtschaft und Gesellschaft im Zeichen des Wohlstandes* (Cologne, 1960).

60. [*Trans. note: Schlaraffenland* is difficult to capture in English; not the biblical "land of milk and honey," it is a magical land where garden fences are made of sugar, roasted baby pigs wander happily with fork and knife sticking out of their backs waiting to be consumed, sausages hang from trees, and flowers are made of colorful candy.] See Wolfgang Protzner, ed., *Vom Hungerwinter zum kulinarischen Schlaraffenland* (Wiesbaden, 1987); for a more recent regional

on."[61] As early as 1950, real wages were at a level that had been reached previously only in the "top years" of 1913 and 1928; wages continued to grow until the end of the decade at an average annual rate of 5 percent, though with pronounced differences among economic sectors. Thus, wages increased in the agricultural sector by a scant 4 percent, while workers in industry and skilled trades enjoyed wage increases of more than 11 percent.[62] During the years of the "Adenauer era," spanning the 1950s and ending in 1963-64, real wages approximately doubled.

Josef Mooser correctly interprets this development as signaling a "farewell to the 'existence of a proletariat' [*Proletarität*]";[63] West Germans had overcome the norm of a life of poverty and an endless round of worries about the reproduction of labor power and fears of sickness and scarcity in old age. Facilitating this transition were new political initiatives to regulate wages and pensions, including measures to raise benefits for sickness and disability close to normal wage levels. In addition, in 1957 pensions for retired workers were pegged to the increase in the cost of living and wage levels among employed workers.[64] These developments and in particular the "full employment" that continued from 1955 on did not lead to the dissolution of class society nor result in "deproletarianization," as prominent sociologists of the time either noted or predicted. However, improved social security, rising wages, and steady work did make possible a predictable standard of living for members of the lowest income groups at a level that had been achieved only in a few "good" times before the 1950s.

The current conception that West Germans frantically ate, then dressed, then sought housing in a series of "waves" obscures the fact that general conditions of prosperity and social security were achieved only in the last third of the 1950s. The image of waves of consumption washing rapidly over West Germans becomes problematic if we consider sales statistics, broken down by economic sector, for the years immediately following the currency reform.

study of early postwar conditions, Gabriele Stüber, *Der Kampf gegen den Hunger 1945–1950: Die Ernährungslage in der britischen Zone Deutschlands, insbesondere in Schleswig-Holstein und Hamburg* (Neumünster, 1984); and Michael Wildt, *Der Traum vom Sattwerden: Hunger und Protest. Schwarzmarkt und Selbsthilfe* (Hamburg, 1986).

61. Josef Mooser, *Arbeiterleben in Deutschland 1900–1970: Klassenlagen, Kultur und Politik* (Frankfurt, 1984), 73.

62. For example, Hoffmann, *Das Wachstum der deutschen Wirtschaft,* 95.

63. Josef Mooser, "Abschied von der 'Proletarität': Sozialstruktur und Lage der Arbeiterschaft in der Bundesrepublik in historischer Perspektive," in Conze and Lepsius, *Sozialgeschichte der Bundesrepublik,* 143–86.

64. See the fundamental work of Hans Günther Hockerts, *Sozialpolitische Entscheidungen im Nachkriegsdeutschland: Alliierte und deutsche Sozialversicherungspolitik 1945–1957* (Stuttgart, 1980).

Shortly after currency reform, retail sales of clothing, linens, and especially house and apartment furnishings increased more rapidly than did sales of foodstuffs and luxury items. The privation and general lack of essential commodities in the immediate postwar period and the start of new housing construction by the late 1940s combined to establish the priorities mirrored in these statistics.[65] Moreover, the consumption and expenditure statistics for working-class households indicate that workers typically reduced what they ate in order to scrimp and save for other things. It was not until 1958 that the consumption of meat, a traditional indicator of the standard of living, reached the level of 1935–38.[66]

At the same time, the savings rate of private households grew from a comparably high 3.1 percent in 1950 to an unprecedented level of 8.7 percent ten years later.[67] According to a representative survey conducted at the end of the 1950s, more than 80 percent of housewives and heads-of-households indicated they believed thriftiness was an essential part of "good character"; 69 percent of those housewives questioned in the survey responded that they would rather wait two hours for the next bus than take a taxi. According to the poll, only 21 percent of households had made purchases on credit, and more than two-thirds had no debt.[68] Thriftiness in one's private life seems to have been a part of the "striving for security" that was an understandable goal in the early 1950s. Money was saved primarily for such durable consumer items as cars and homes; memories that focus on outfitting the home with the latest technological innovations do not accurately capture the reality of most people's lives. According to surveys conducted in April 1958, only 11 percent of working-class and 28 percent of white-collar households had a refrigerator, the accepted symbol of the "economic miracle"; electric washing machines were present in only 20 percent of working-class and 26 percent of white-collar households.[69]

The current debate over the history of women's emancipation has largely neglected the fact that the material improvement in the standard of living at the end of the 1950s and the beginning of the 1960s, especially for the lower classes, was to a considerable extent attributable to married women's work outside the home. Although in public opinion surveys, men still insisted that

---

65. See *Statistisches Jahrbuch für die Bundesrepublik Deutschland 1952*, 230ff.

66. See Bundesministerium für Ernährung, Landwirtschaft und Forsten, ed., *Statistisches Jahrbuch über Ernährung, Landwirtschaft und Forsten der Bundesrepublik 1959* (Hamburg, 1960), 141f.

67. See Klaus Hesse, *Das diskretionäre Einkommen, seine Bestimmung und Verwendung* (Berlin, 1974), 26; and Reinhold Exo, *Die Entwicklung der sozialen und ökonomischen Struktur der Ersparnisbildung* (Berlin, 1967).

68. See, for example, Günther Schmölders, *Der Umgang mit Geld im privaten Haushalt* (Berlin, 1969), 61.

69. See DIVO Institut, ed., *Der westdeutsche Markt in Zahlen: Ein Handbuch für Forschung, Werbung und Verkauf* (Frankfurt, 1958).

women should take on wage employment only in emergency situations,[70] estimates reveal that in the early 1960s, only two-thirds of working-class families could maintain their standard of living from the husband's earnings alone in "complete families" (*Vollfamilien*).[71] Between 1957 and 1966, the number of wives of working-class men who worked climbed from one in four to one in three; the proportion was lower among white-collar workers. Working-class wives worked mainly at unskilled or semiskilled positions; their main motivation in working outside the home was to increase the income of the household.[72] Only with the income earned by working-class wives and with the assistance of men's overtime and supplementary income from other jobs was it possible for working-class families to satisfy their desire to participate in the growing prosperity.

These developments reflected a deliberate economic policy, summarized in 1953 by Economics Minister Ludwig Erhard: The "luxuries of today" could "only become the general consumer goods of tomorrow . . . , if we accept that in an initial phase, they will only be available to a small group with elevated incomes who will have the purchasing power to obtain these goods."[73] The agencies that designed and administered economic policy sought not to achieve social and economic equality in the distribution of goods, but rather to create an "elevator" (U. Beck) effect that would lift the entire society. A good example of this tendency is offered by the wage agreements reached in most cases quickly and without labor conflict, once IG Metall (the metalworkers' union) had pointed the way by winning its fight to narrow the gap between the status of wage workers and white-collar salaried employees in 1956.[74] Only at the close of the 1960s did accumulation of capital and the ongoing concentration of wealth, welcome developments in the 1950s, again become a controversial political issue.

Just how little the increase in prosperity *directly* brought about a leveling of differences in social class becomes apparent if we consider the distribution

---

70. See particularly the extensive empirical data in Elisabeth Pfeil, *Die Berufstätigkeit von Müttern* (Tübingen, 1961); an interpretive view of contemporary social research on this theme is provided in Ingrid N. Sommerkorn's "Die erwerbstätige Mutter in der Bundesrepublik: Einstellungs- und Problemänderungen," in *Wandel und Kontinuität der Familie in der Bundesrepublik Deutschland,* edited by Rosemarie Nave-Herz (Stuttgart, 1988), 115–44.

71. See for example, Osterland et al., *Industriearbiter in der BRD,* 132.

72. See Karl Schwarz, "Umfang der Frauenerwerbstätigkeit nach dem Zweiten Weltkrieg: Erwerbsbeteilung und Arbeitszeiten," *Zeitschrift für Bevölkerungswissenschaft* 11 (1985): 241–60.

73. Ludwig Erhard, "Einen Kühlschrank in jeden Haushalt," in *Deutsche Wirtschaftspolitik: Der Weg der Sozialen Marktwirtschaft,* idem (Düsseldorf, 1962), 221.

74. See most recently Irene Dittrich and Wilfried Kalk, "'Wir wollen nicht länger Menschen zweiter Klasse sein!' Der Metallarbeiterstreik in Schleswig-Holstein 1956/57," in *Demokratische Geschichte: Jahrbuch zur Arbeiterbewegung und Demokratie in Schleswig-Holstein,* vol. 2 (Kiel, 1987), 351–93.

of the "cultural capital" (Pierre Bordieu), acquired primarily through socialization in families and educational institutions. Consider some of the general characteristics of the West German educational system. After a number of experiments in West Germany at the beginning of the 1950s, there was a return to a tradition of a rigidly organized system of schools, offering a general education; throughout the 1950s the scheme for distributing students to individual schools was no different from that which had prevailed at the beginning of the century. In 1951, 80 percent of all students in grade five or higher were in *Volksschulen*; the figure was the same in 1926–27, and by 1960 it had declined by only 10 percent. The proportion of students at *Gymnasien* increased in the 1950s, from about 10 percent to 15 percent.[75] The distribution of students is reflected by the relative number of students who completed various sorts of degree certificates: 4.4 percent of those who left school in 1958 did so after finishing the advanced *Abitur*; 13.3 percent had completed the "middle" (*Mittlereife*) or "professional school" (*Fachschulreife*) certificate.[76] Examining the social origins of students, the sociologist Morris Janowitz observed that although the top and bottom parts of the lowest social class constituted more than half the population, these groups accounted for only 5 percent of university students.[77] In the 1960s, these circumstances provoked the movement to develop West Germany's untapped educational potential.

The results of public opinion polling make clear that the mobilization of the 1960s against the skewed distribution of educational opportunities was essential; until the beginning of that decade, the vast majority of the population completely accepted the status quo.[78] When asked in 1961 whether a good education was available to everyone or whether it was dependent upon the wealth

---

75. Statistisches Bundesamt, *Bevölkerung und Wirtschaft,* 127f.; Helmut Köhler, *Der relative Schul- und Hochschulbesuch in der Bundesrepublik Deutschland 1952 bis 1975: Ein Indikator für die Entwicklung des Bildungswesens* (Berlin, 1978), 169. [*Trans. note*: In the 1950s, all school-age children attended the *Volksschule* for primary school, grades 1–4. Depending on the results of tests administered at the end of the fourth year, students either continued in the *Volksschule,* finishing their schooling with an examination at the end of the eighth grade, often moving immediately into an apprenticeship or another form of vocational training, or they entered the *Oberschule* (secondary school), which consisted of the *Gymnasium.* If a student completed six years of schooling after the *Volksschule,* he or she obtained the *Mittlereife* ("middle certificate") and left school upon completion of grade 10. Elite students completed eight years of advanced instruction and achieved the prestigious *Abitur,* a comprehensive school-leaving examination, after completing grade 12. The *Abitur* was a prerequisite for university studies. Today this picture is more complex as a result of school reforms; various *Oberschulen* exist, and it is possible to attend the university without having received an *Abitur* from the *Gymnasium.*]

76. See Heiner Meulemann, "Bildungsexpansion und Wandel der Bildungsvorstellungen zwischen 1958 und 1979: Eine Kohortenanalyse," *Zeitschrift für Soziologie* 11 (1982): 227–53.

77. Morris Janowitz, "Soziale Schichtung und Mobilität in Westdeutschland," *Kölner Zeitschrift für Soziologie und Sozialpsychologie* 10 (1958): 1–38.

78. See Janpeter Kob, *Erziehung im Elternhaus und Schule* (Stuttgart, 1963), 53.

and social status of the student's father, only slightly more than half of the sample of youth questioned responded that socioeconomic circumstances determined an individual's educational opportunities.[79] It is important to keep in mind that youth in the 1950s were far more profoundly shaped by work and occupational experience than youth today. In 1953, almost 70 percent of all seventeen-year-olds and 85 percent of all eighteen-to-twenty-year-olds were already members of the workforce; the figures for 1984 are 19 percent and 56 percent, respectively.[80]

For many students formal schooling did not end with wage work, but we know little about the function and significance of vocational schools—along with on-the-job training, part of the "dual system" of apprenticeship training—that had been standard in Germany since the 1920s. In 1949, mandatory vocational education was introduced throughout Germany; eleven years later, two-thirds of all boys but only two-fifths of girls who were required to attend did in fact participate in vocational training. One reason for this low rate was the inadequate supply of school training programs. By 1952, all male youth who were required by law to attend vocational school were enrolled, but 20 percent of girls were "held back" or excused from attending because there were still not enough vocational schools to accommodate them.[81]

To be sure, the long-term trend toward more highly qualified vocational training continued. Of those *Volksschule* students born between 1887 and 1896, 60 percent did not complete an apprenticeship upon leaving school; for those born between 1927 and 1936, this figure was 37 percent; and for those born between 1937 and 1946, who finished school in the 1950s, the figure dropped to 24 percent.[82] Despite these undeniable improvements, the pace of change in education and training in the Federal Republic lagged behind the rapid rates of economic progress and structural change, measured both in absolute terms and relative to other national experiences. The discussion in the 1960s of the "German educational disaster" (Picht) underscored this situation.

If we consider all the characteristics of the development of a "consumer society" that we have discussed here, then on balance, for the second half of the decade it would still be more appropriate to speak of a "society of work," not a "society of consumption."

---

79. See Peter Kmieciak, *Wertstrukturen und Wertwandel in der Bundesrepublik Deutschland: Grundlagen einer interdisziplinären empirischen Wertforschung mit einer Sekundäranalyse von Umfragedaten* (Göttingen, 1977), Table III, 10a.

80. See Jürgen Zinnecker, *Jugendkultur 1940–1985* (Opladen, 1987), 313.

81. See "Die berufsbildenden Schulen in der Bundesrepublik Deutschland im Jahr 1952," *Wirtschaft und Statistik* 6 (1954):188–90.

82. See Horst Steiger and Heinrich Tegtmeyer, "Sozialstruktur im Wandel," in *Soziale Strukturen und individuelle Mobilität: Beiträge zur soziodemographischen Analyse der Bundesrepublik Deutschland,* edited by Heinrich Tegtmeyer (Wiesbaden, 1979), 104; see also the study by Wolfgang Lengsfeld, "Vergleich der Schulausbildung von Kindern mit der ihrer Eltern," in ibid.

The "Leisure" Society

If the image of West Germany in the 1950s as a "consumer society" should be interrogated, then the concept of the 1950s as a "leisure society" deserves even greater scrutiny. The characterization of the 1950s as an age of "leisure" had already assumed mythical status in the analyses of contemporaries; it had also triggered a wealth of sociological, anthropological, and pedagogical interpretations that saw "leisure" as a "problem."[83] Behind these critical reflections was the thesis that fashion and the media "externally managed" the consumer and that consumers expressed themselves most fully in the realm of leisure activities. However, for most West Germans in the 1950s, there were no indications that there was a rapid increase in available leisure time.

By the mid-1950s, the actual workweek in industry had again reached forty-nine hours, the level of the 1930s.[84] Contrary to popular opinion, when the five-day workweek became the norm for many sectors in 1956-57,[85] leisure time did not dramatically increase, because on those five days, workers were expected to put in longer hours. Thus, between 1957 and 1960, the workday for those employed in industry declined by only 0.9 hours.[86] The thesis of a rapid increase of leisure time is even less convincing if we consider that the hours of industrial workers in large firms, well-documented since 1957, were the shortest work hours of any workers;[87] in smaller firms, workers put in many hours of overtime that were not recorded in the statistics. In addition, there are definitional problems. From 1957 on, we can document the tendency of many workers to take on a "second job" (*Zweitjob*); in 1961, this was how 7 percent of all wage earners used their "leisure time."[88] We also need to consider the sig-

---

83. For extensive references to the contemporary literature, see Erich Weber, *Das Freizeitproblem: Anthropologisch-pädagogische Untersuchung* (Munich, 1963); and for a critical analysis, especially Kurt Hammerich, *Kritische Studien zur Freizeitpädagogik und Freizeitsoziologie,* 2d ed. (Kastellaun, 1978).

84. See, for example, Eike Ballerstedt, *Soziologischer Almanach* (Frankfurt, 1975), 264f.

85. See Karl-Heinz Kevelaer and Karl Hinrichs, "Arbeitszeit und 'Wirtschaftswunder': Rahmenbedingungen des Übergangs zur 40-Stunden Woche in der Bundesrepublik Deutschland," *Politische Vierteljahrsschrift* 25 (1985): 52–75; and Michael Schneider, *Streit um Arbeitszeit: Geschichte des Kampfes um Arbeitszeitverkürzung in Deutschland* (Cologne, 1984), 152ff.

86. See Osterland et al., *Industriearbiter in der BRD,* table 60; work hours "rendered" [*"geleistete" Arbeitsstunden*]—a statistical measurement first recorded in 1957—refers to hours spent at one's workplace less industry-mandated break periods.

87. For data on the mid-1960s, see the figures provided by the Statistisches Bundesamt in Jürgen Dern, "Die Ausgaben für Freizeitgüter von Selbständigen- und Arbeitnehmerhaushalten in der Bundesrepublik Deutschland," in *Die Familienhaushalte im wirschaftlichen und sozialen Wandel: Rationalverhalten, Technisierung, Funktionswandel der Privathaushalte und das Freizeitbudget der Frau,* edited by Rosemarie Schweitzer and Helga Pross (Göttingen, 1977), 291–318 (here, 294).

88. See Hermann Funke, "Freizeit in der Stadt," in *Freizeit,* edited by Reinhard Schmitz-Scherzer (Frankfurt, 1973), 187.

nificance of "work after quitting time" (*Feierabendarbeit*), which was done by workers to pursue individual goals, for example, by working on a small agricultural holding or by participating in the common practice of mutual cooperation with neighbors in the building of private residences. Finally, we must also consider the time spent commuting to the workplace, an area that has received inadequate attention. In addition, the increasing employment of housewives and automobile ownership altered established routines of everyday life. Rather than organizing consumption to meet household needs with daily purchases over the course of the workweek, these chores were increasingly done on Saturday, making it difficult to see this day as "leisure time." Admittedly, "long weekends" did offer opportunities to maintain ties to family members and others; there was, however, little time for such forms of sociability during the week.

Responses to rather imprecise annual public opinion surveys confirm the impression that there was little increase in leisure time in the 1950s; between 1957 and 1960, these surveys indicated a daily increase in "leisure" of only eleven minutes. This brought the total up to scarcely three hours a day; today, the figure is four-and-one-half hours daily.[89] In general, the available evidence adds up to a picture of a population that was extremely industrious and hardworking. A survey conducted in Baden-Württemburg in the mid-1950s doubtless described other regions as well; it revealed that 80 percent of the population was in bed at 10:30 at night and up again before 7:00 the next morning.[90] According to a survey conducted in 1955, about 40 percent of West Germans felt stressed and overworked, and these sentiments were even more pronounced among white-collar salaried employees, civil servants, and the self-employed than among the working class.[91]

For the years before 1960, we know little about how people used their leisure time.[92] On the one hand, contemporary accounts from the first half of the 1950s revealed pronounced trends toward "domesticity," which would be in keeping with the straitened household budgets of new homeowners. On the other hand, contemporary observers also noted a strong "pull from outside"

---

89. See Pavel Uttiz, "Gesellschaftliche Rahmenbedingungen für die Entwicklung des Freizeitverhaltens von 1953 bis 1980 in der Bundesrepublik Deutschland," in *Zentralarchiv für empirische Sozialforschung,* edited by University of Cologne, ZA-Information 15/1984, 31; it is important to remember that the concept of what exactly constituted "leisure-time activities" changed over time.

90. See Institut für Demoskopie Allensbach, ed., *Süddeutscher Rundfunk: Die Rundfunkhörer 1953/54* (Allensbach, 1954), 18.

91. *Die soziale Wirklichkeit: Aus einer Untersuchung des Instituts für Demoskopie. Mit einem Vorwort von Otto Lenz,* (Allensbach, 1956), 25.

92. Especially worthy of mention is Erich Reigrotzki, *Soziale Verflechtungen in der Bundesrepublik: Elemente der sozialen Teilnahme in Kirche, Politik, Organisationen und Freizeit* (Tübingen, 1956).

(*Sog von draußen*);[93] the twofold increase in visits to the movies between 1950 and 1960 to about 800 million is but one indication of this.[94] We have more precise data on the leisure activity of youth, because it was investigated far more thoroughly.[95] One important conclusion of this research is that young people differed little from the older generation in how they used their leisure time, hardly surprising given the large percentage of young people already in the labor force.

In the early 1950s, radio had already exerted an influence on patterns of everyday life—such as meal times—and by the last third of the decade, television began to play a greater role in structuring leisure time.[96] Contemporary observers who emphasized the significance of leisure and consumption also called attention to the ways in which society was increasingly dominated by the media[97] and increasingly informal in nature.[98] In the early 1950s, the number of radio stations already surpassed prewar levels, and it continued to increase until the end of the decade. The introduction of an ultra-shortwave network (UKW-Netze) represented a trend toward "modernization"; by the mid-1950s, 40-45 percent of all households—about half of the radio audience—listened to the new frequencies.[99] This development reflected two types of "modernization": first, the expanded number of radio stations represented a technological innovation; second, a greater number of stations made possible a greater variety in program offerings, targeted at specific regional audiences, in contrast to the single alternative, broadcast to the entire nation, that had previously been available.

Despite these innovations, the preferences and attitudes of radio listeners diverged little from the traditions of the 1930s. Survey data indicate that radio was seen as a form of entertainment, a distraction from other concerns. Traditions established in the 1930s were also reflected in the structure of pro-

---

93. See Margarethe Rudorff, "Die Schrumpfung des Begriffes 'Wohnung' und ihre Folgerungen," *Soziale Welt* 6 (1955): 47.

94. See the detailed statistical material in Hermann Busch, "Der Absatz in der Filmwirtschaft unter dem Einfluß des Fernsehens" (Wirtschaftswissenschaftliche diss., University of Mannheim, 1962).

95. For an assessment of the contemporary empirical social research data, in addition to Zinnecker, see Helmut Fend, *Sozialgeschichte des Aufwachsens: Lebensbedingungen, Erziehungsverhältnisse und Jugendgestalten in der Bundesrepublik Deutschland* (Frankfurt, 1987).

96. See the various surveys of the Institut für Demoskopie Allensbach on behalf of *Süddeutscher Rundfunk.*

97. See Günther Anders, *Die Antiquiertheit des Menschen* (Munich, 1956), a book that attracted considerable attention when it was published.

98. See, for example, Helmut Schelsky, *Soziologie der Sexualität* (Reinbek, 1955), 51ff.

99. For figures on the regional service of the Hessischer Rundfunk, see Sepp Groth, *Strukturen und Stimmen der Rundfunkhörer in Hessen: Forschungsbericht über die Ereignisse einer Feldstudie im Oktober 1956 mit den dazu grundlegenden soziographischen Bestandsaufnahmen* (Frankfurt, n.d.), 100. This was a survey conducted by the Soziographisches Instiut of the Johann-Wolfgang Goethe University.

gramming, which divided broadcasts evenly between talk shows and musical programs.[100]

For most West Germans, the "television age" only began at the end of the 1950s. In 1957, one million television sets were in place to receive the ARD (Arbeitsgemeinschaft der Rundfunkanstalten Deutschlands, or Working Group of German Radio Broadcasters) program that started broadcasting on November 1, 1954; by 1960 this number had increased to almost four million. In terms of social class, the ownership of television sets was distributed roughly equally across all social groups, but it was by no means evenly distributed across all regions. In 1960, 14 of every 100 Bavarian households owned a television set, whereas the figure for North Rhine Westphalia was 30 in every 100,[101] though in terms of social class, the owners of television sets were distributed roughly equally across all social groups. The earliest data on television audiences[102] revealed that in 90 percent of the households with televisions, viewers turned on their sets every day and typically watched TV for about eighty minutes daily; they spent significantly more time watching television on the weekends. Declining numbers in restaurants, dance halls, and movie theaters, on the one hand, and no decrease in the readership for illustrated magazines, on the other, were additional indications of the tendency toward spending more time at home. This trend toward domesticity was more pronounced among workers and the residents of smaller towns and villages than among white-collar workers and residents of large cities. A 1958 survey investigated the motivations for purchase of a television set:[103] (1) 29 percent enjoyed television as a source of entertainment and distraction; (2) 21 percent reported that television allowed them to stay at home, it kept the family together, and it contributed to a cozy atmosphere in the household; (3) and 16 percent had purchased a television as a source of information.

There were strong similarities in the programming desires of television viewers and radio listeners. For example, we can point to the early success of the television family "Schölermann," "our neighbor this evening,"[104] a format that influenced the style and content of other programs. Those responsible for television programming quickly understood that the public "demanded" "technically perfect, well-made" wholesome, family-oriented shows, as Clemens Münster, head of television programming for the Bavarian Broadcast

---

100. For a detailed survey of radio programming in the Weimar years, see Deutsches Rundfunkarchiv, Historisches Archiv der ARD, ed., *Projektgruppe Programmgeschichte: Zur Programmgeschichte des Weimarer Rundfunks* (Frankfurt, 1986).

101. See H.-A. Zieling, "Der Ton- und Fernsehrundfunk in Niedersachsen," *Statistische Monatshefte für Niedersachsen* (1961): 393f.

102. *Der Fernsehzuschauer 1954/55: Ein Jahresbericht. NWDR. Hörerforschung* (Hamburg, n.d. [1955]).

103. See Josef Bennemann, "Verbrauch und Verbrauchswandlungen" (Wirtschafts- und sozialwissenschaftliche Diss., Erlangen/Nuremburg, 1962).

104. See NWDR, ed., *Die Ansage*, no. 214 (February 2, 1955).

Corporation, observed.[105] Although some middle-class viewers hoped that television might offer something of greater educational value, they received no more consideration than the radio listeners who had expressed similar desires in the 1930s.

At the same time that West German society accepted the television and related forms of a "new domesticity," citizens of the Federal Republic began, particularly in the summer months, to participate in the phenomenon of mass tourism, another characteristic of the "leisure society." To be sure, the only definitive study of tourism in the late 1950s correctly identified tourism as a form of luxury for consumers (*Luxuskonsum*).[106] However, by this point approximately one West German in three had consumed this luxury. By the end of the 1950s and the beginning of the 1960s, a vacation trip had become an obtainable goal.[107] There is no question that travel, particularly with one's own automobile, contributed to a feeling of "modernity"; particularly for vacationers, though their numbers were still limited, travel was a form of private mobility that allowed for a brief illusion of release from social constraints. However, a large portion of the 20 percent of vacationers who traveled abroad remained in German-speaking areas.

A Balance Sheet

Erich Kästner once ironically characterized the mix of traditional values with West Germans' willingness to accept certain aspects of modernity as a "motorized Biedermeier" [the paradoxical image of a German driving his new automobile, still holding on to the conservative values, tastes, and attitudes of the nineteenth century]. Kästner's image evokes several associations, invites further exploration,[108] and, in particular, points to the need for a more detailed consideration of political culture. In the early 1950s, there were marked continuities in political norms and patterns of political behavior.[109]

For most West Germans, political socialization had taken place under authoritarian forms of rule, and their experience was limited to authoritarian

---

105. Clemens Münster at the Third Television Conference of the Protestant Church, "Tagungsbericht Nr. 16," in *Deutsches Rundfunkarchiv* (dra), ARD 0-73.

106. See Hans-Jürgen Knebel, *Soziologische Strukturwandlungen im modernen Tourismus* (Stuttgart, 1960), 4; and Han Magnus Enzensberger's critical essay, "Eine Theorie des Tourismus," in *Einzelheiten,* idem, vol. 1 (Frankfurt, 1962), 147–68, an essay that attracted much attention at the time of its publication.

107. For an overview of empirical surveys since the end of the 1950s, see Erwin K. Scheuch, "Soziologie der Freizeit," in *Handbuch der empirischen Sozialforschung,* vol. 11, 2d ed., edited by Rene König (Stuttgart, 1977), 123ff.

108. For a contemporary attempt, see Norbert Muhlen, "Das Land der großen Mitte: Notizen aus dem Neo-Biedermeier," *Der Monat* 6 (1953): 237–44.

109. See Jürgen Falter, "Kontinuität und Neubeginn: Die Bundestagswahl 1949 zwischen Weimar und Bonn," *Politische Vierteljahrsschrift* 22 (1981): 241.

forms of politics (for example, the structures within which political parties developed their programs); West Germans had been shaped by the *Kaiserreich*,[110] the presidential regimes at the end of the Weimar Republic (1930-33), the National Socialist dictatorship,[111] and the rule of the Allied forces of occupation. In comparison, the legacy of the few years of a functioning democracy in the Weimar Republic was far less significant. For this reason, it is not surprising that when West Germans were asked in 1952, "In general—are you interested in politics?" only 27 percent responded in the affirmative. By 1959, the number of those answering "yes" had increased by only 2 percent.[112] In the early 1950s, public opinion surveys still recorded strong sympathies for the monarchy and authoritarian forms of government. Only a decade later did a majority of the population offer a positive assessment of the existing political system.[113]

Public opinion surveys recorded a "monotonously unequivocal orientation toward the west"[114] in the 1950s, but this tendency should not be exaggerated; it reflected less a rejection of a chauvinistic German *Sonderweg* (peculiar path) and an endorsement of the "modern west" than an alignment with the West in the global struggle of the Cold War. Perhaps the most striking example of how divergent political attitudes could be brought together by the pressure of the international context was the rebuilding of the West German army with soldiers who had begun their careers in the battle against the "Bolshevik East" and who in certain respects thus needed no reeducation.

It is difficult to disentangle the means by which various strands of political culture asserted themselves, collided, and coalesced in the 1950s. For the first part of the decade, unmistakably conservative sentiments were dominant. Social Democrats and conservatives were unified in their anticommunism, but a conservative rhetoric of a "Christian West" (*christliches Abendland*) not only helped establish the Federal Republic as a bulwark against the Soviet Union, it also hindered the development of liberal, democratic attitudes.[115] For the

110. On the political elite, see Frank R. Pfetsch, "Die Gründergeneration der Bundesrepublik: Sozialprofil und politische Orientierung," *Politische Vierteljahrsschrift* 27 (1986): 237–51.

111. See, for example, Heinz Bude, *Deutsche Karrieren: Lebenskonstruktionen sozialer Aufsteiger aus der Flakhelfergeneration* (Frankfurt, 1987); and Gabriele Rosenthal, *"Wenn alles in Scherben fällt": Von Leben und Sinnwelt der Kriegsgeneration* (Opladen, 1987).

112. See, for example, Hans Braun, "Das Streben nach 'Sicherheit' in den 50er Jahren: Soziale und politische Ursachen und Erscheinungsweisen," *Archiv für Sozialgeschichte* 18 (1978): 290ff.

113. See Elisabeth Noelle-Neumann, "Der Staatsbürger und sein Staat," *Zwanzig jahre danach: Eine deutsche Bilanz 1945–1965,* edited by Helmut Hammerschmidt (Munich, 1965), 82.

114. Hans-Peter Schwarz, "Die Westdeutschen, die westliche Demokratie und die Westbindung im Licht von Meinungsumfragen," in *Die Bundesrepublik Deutschland und die Vereinigten Staaten von Amerika: Politische, soziale und wirtschaftliche Beziehungen im Wandel,* edited by James A. Cooney et al. (Stuttgart, 1985), 101.

115. See Harold Hurwitz, "Antikommunismus und amerikanische Demokratisierungsvorhaben im Nachkriegsdeutschland," *Aus Politik und Zeitgeschichte* B 29/78, 29–46.

postwar years, Jürgen Habermas identified a general tendency to "combine positive attitudes toward social modernity with a negative assessment of cultural modernity,"[116] though he failed to specify the characteristics of "cultural modernity."

The positive assessment of "social modernity" in contemporary commentaries reflected the belief that liberal principles—such as individual achievement, individual freedom, or equality before the law—could be combined with traditional values of the family and conceptions of morality grounded in religion. A measure of West Germans' acceptance of "social modernity," aptly described by Hans Maier, was the prevailing tendency in the Federal Republic to evaluate technological innovation and change in objective terms; technological change was robbed of its demonic and dramatic quality.[117] From the mid-1950s on, the increasing acceptance of a "pluralistic society" by Catholic intellectuals[118] and the pragmatic move of the Social Democratic "camp" to distance itself from the Marxist-inspired "socialist idea"[119] reflected the same tendency to evaluate technological and social change in objective, nonideological terms. Dire, pessimistic warnings of the "dangers of technology" that could be conjured up after the experience of Hiroshima and the war were quickly pushed aside by positive prognoses for the future, embodied in particular in the optimistic assessment of the "second industrial revolution."[120]

Writing in the late 1950s, Ralf Dahrendorf concluded that after the war, West Germans had experienced a "change in values," moving away from a "heroic past and an emphasis on community and hard work" to an emphasis on "guiding principles of behavior [that stressed] individual success and the pleasures of life."[121] Dahrendorf's assessment was not entirely accurate. Perhaps he could identify hedonistic tendencies among young people who were just coming of age. However, satisfaction in work and "success in life" should not be so readily seen as mutually exclusive alternatives. A more adequate description would focus on the tendency for all attitudes to be structured increasingly

---

116. Jürgen Habermas, *Der philosophische Diskurs der Moderne: Zwölf Vorlesungen* (Frankfurt, 1985), 90; see also Richard Saage, *Rückkehr zum starken Staat? Studien über Konservatismus, Faschismus und Demokratie* (Frankfurt, 1983).

117. Hans Maier, *Die Deutschen und die Freiheit: Perspketiven der Nachkriegszeit* (Stuttgart, 1985); and very similar in this context, Günther Gaus, *Die Welt der Westdeutschen: Kritische Betrachtungen* (Cologne, 1986), 80.

118. Oswald von Nell-Breuning, *Wirtschaft und Gesellschaft heute,* vol. 3 (Freiburg, 1960), 3.

119. Wolfgang Abendroth, "Bilanz der sozialistischen Idee in der Bundesrepublik Deutschland," in *Bestandsaufnahme: Eine deutsche Bilanz 1962,* edited by Hans Werner Richter (Munich, 1962), 233–63.

120. Leo Brandt, *Die zweite industrielle Revolution* (Munich, 1957).

121. Ralf Dahrendorf, "Die neue Gesellschaft: Soziale Strukturwandlungen der Nachkriegszeit," in Richter, *Bestandsaufnahme,* 215.

by economic values; from this perspective, we can understand the obsession with consumption, characteristic of the late 1950s and the early 1960s, deplored by contemporaries as an expression of "western materialism."[122]

"Americanization" was another shorthand for describing the changes in West German society in the 1950s. On the one hand, this label pointed to characteristics of a functioning civil society and conscious resistance against state intervention into the private sphere. On the other, "Americanization" functioned as a negative symbol of lost norms and traditions that had created a sense of community. From both perspectives, "America" was a "sociological barometer," the mirror of one's own "modern" future.[123] The data on attitudes toward "America" are muddled, and assessments of "America" are confusing and inconsistent. In general, positive attitudes toward "Americans" intensified in the late 1950s.[124] But in the first half of the decade, the prevailing view was that even if there was much to be learned from Americans about technological innovation, Americans could teach Germans nothing about culture.[125] Despite significant efforts by the United States, for example, in "Amerikahäuser" and in programs to advance cultural exchanges, this prejudice against American culture only intensified in the early 1950s. U.S. public opinion surveys revealed that 70 percent of the German population subscribed to this prejudice in 1956, up from 58 percent in 1950.[126] We still do not have adequate documentation of whether young West Germans came to have more positive attitudes toward "Americans" because of the influence of American music and youth culture.

Ultimately internal developments are more central than external factors for explaining the modernization of West Germany in the 1950s. Trends toward modernization, initiated and advanced in the 1950s, became dramatically apparent in the arena of political culture at the end of the 1960s. By then, there was no question that the Federal Republic was a "modern western"

---

122. See Klaus Mehnert, "Die weltpolitische Situation," *Wo stehen wir heute?*, edited by H. Walter Bähr (Gütersloh, 1960), 121–30.

123. See Fritz Sternberg, "Die Deutschen in der Weltgeschichte: Soziologische Bermerkungen," in Richter, *Bestandsaufnahme*, 71; this also explains the broad interest in the work of the American sociologist David Riesman in the 1950s and 1960s. See, for example, David Riesman, *Die einsame Masse: Eine Untersuchung der Wandlungen des amerikanischen Charakters. Mit einer Einführung in die deutsche Ausgabe von Helmut Schelsky* (Reinbek, 1958).

124. In response to the question posed by the Allensbach Institute: "Do you like the Americans or do you not particularly like them?", in 1957, 37 percent responded with "like them"; in 1961, the figure was 51 percent. See Andreas Kirschhofer, "Die Deutschen über sich selbst: Meinungsumfragen sind in Bewegung geraten. Eine demoskopische Standortbestimmung," *Moderne Welt* (1967): 188.

125. See Heinz Hartmann, *Amerikanische Firmen in Deutschland: Beobachtungen über Kontakte und Kontraste zwischen Industriegesellschaften* (Cologne, 1963), 71.

126. See Heinz H. Fischer, "Das Amerikabild in der deutschen Bevölkerung nach dem zweiten Weltkrieg: Eine Untersuchung auf der Basis der OMGUS- und HICOG-Berichte," *ZA Information*, No. 17/1985, 51–60; No. 18/1986, 57–66.

society, although in the context of the relaxation of tensions between east and west, it was also apparent that it was entirely possible to revitalize nationalistic sentiments. The 1950s were characterized by economic growth, technological modernization, changes in patterns of consumption and lifestyles, and even signs of "changes in values." However, unlike the experience of the Weimar Republic, where challenges were met with extreme responses that resulted in failure, the dramatic changes of the 1950s combined to create a climate of stability, capable of withstanding the socioeconomic, political, and cultural convulsions of the 1960s. Perhaps after the experiences of "total war" and "years of starvation," Germans needed to appear modest and outwardly rigid and strict in order to redefine traditional virtues and norms in accord with the demands of a new age.

Selective Bibliography of Works on the History of the Federal Republic in the 1950s (1990–95)

General Works

Broszat, Martin, ed. *Zäsuren nach 1945: Essays zur Periodisierung der deutschen Nachkriegsgeschichte.* Munich, 1990.

Bührer, Werner, ed. *Die Adenauer-Ära: Die Bundesrepublik Deutschland 1949–1963.* Munich, 1993.

Doering–Manteuffel, Anselm. "Deutsche Zeitgeschichte nach 1945." *Vierteljahrshefte für Zeitgeschichte* 41 (1993): 1–29.

Erker, Paul. "Zeitgeschichte als Sozialgeschichte." *Geschichte und Gesellschaft* 19 (1993): 202–38.

"Die Fünfziger Jahre in der Bundesrepublik." (Special issue of) *Politik und Unterricht* 17 (1991).

Kaelble, Hartmut, ed. *Der Boom 1948–1973: Gesellschaftliche und wirtschaftliche Folgen in der Bundesrepublik Deutschland und in Europa.* Opladen, 1992.

Pfister, Christian, ed. *Das 1950er Syndrom: Der Weg in die Konsumgesellschaft.* Bern, 1995.

Schildt, Axel. "Nachkriegszeit: Möglichkeiten und Probleme einer Periodisierung der westdeutschen Geschichte nach dem Zweiten Weltkrieg und ihrer Einordnung in die deutsche Geschichte des 20. Jahrhunderts." *Geschichte in Wissenschaft und Unterricht* 44 (1993): 567–84.

Schildt, Axel. *Moderne Zeiten: Freizeit, Massenmedien und "Zeitgeist" in der Bundesrepublik der 50er Jahre.* Hamburg, 1995.

Schildt, Axel, and Arnold Sywottek, eds. *Modernisierung im Wiederaufbau: Die westdeutsche Gesellschaft der 50er Jahre.* Bonn, 1993.

Voy, Klaus, et al., eds. *Gesellschaftliche Transformationsprozesse und materielle Lebensweise: Beiträge zur Wirtschafts- und Gesellschaftsgeschichte der Bundesrepublik Deutschland (1949–1989).* Vol. 2. Marburg, 1991.

Economics and Politics

Berghahn, Volker R., and Paul J. Friedrich. *Otto A. Friedrich, ein politischer Unternehmer: Sein Leben und seine Zeit 1902–1975.* Frankfurt, 1993.

Buchheim, Christoph. *Die Eingliederung Westdeutschlands in die Weltwirtschaft 1945–1958.* Munich, 1990.

Deutschland im Kalten Krieg 1945–1963: Eine Ausstellung des Deutschen Historischen Museums 28. August bis 24. November 1992 im Zeughaus Berlin. Berlin, 1992.

Herbst, Ludolf, et al., eds. *Vom Marshallplan zur EWG: Die Eingliederung der Bundesrepublik Deutschland in die westliche Welt.* Munich, 1990.

Maier, Charles S., and Günter Bischof, eds. *Deutschland und der Marshall–Plan.* Baden-Baden, 1992.

Recker, Marie-Luise. "'Bonn ist nicht Weimar': Zu Struktur und Charakter des politischen Systems der Bundesrepublik in der Ära Adenauer." *Geschichte in Wissenschaft und Unterricht* 44 (1993): 287–307.

Rupieper, Hermann-Josef. *Der besetzte Verbündete: Die amerikanische Deutschlandspolitik von 1949 bis 1955.* Opladen, 1991.

Schröder, Hans-Jürgen, ed. *Marshallplan und westdeutscher Wiederaufstieg: Positionen—Kontroversen.* Stuttgart, 1990.

Expellees and Refugees

Ackermann, Volker. *Der "echte" Flüchtling: Deutsche Vertriebene und Flüchtlinge aus der DDR.* Essen, 1994.

Heidemeyer, Helge. *Flucht und Zuwanderung aus der SBZ/DDR 1945/49–1961: Die Flüchtlingspolitik der Bundesrepublik Deutschland bis zum Bau der Berliner Mauer.* Düsseldorf, 1994.

Uliczka, Monika. *Berufsbiographie und Flüchtlingsschicksal: VW-Arbeiter in der Nachkriegszeit.* Hanover, 1993.

Housing, Urbanization, Transportation

Durth, Werner, and Niels Gutschow, eds. *Architektur und Städtebau der Fünfziger Jahre: Ergebnisse der Fachtagung des Nationalkomitees fur Denkmalschutz in Hannover, Februar 1990.* Bonn, 1990.

Beyme, Klaus von, et al., eds. *Neue Städte aus Ruinen: Deutscher Städtebau der Nachkriegszeit.* Munich, 1992.

Klenke, Dietmar. *Bundesdeutsche Verkehrspolitik und Motorisierung: Konfliktträchtige Weichenstellungen in den Jahren des Wiederaufbaus.* Wiesbaden, 1993.

Schulz, Günther. *Wiederaufbau in Deutschland: Die Wohnungspolitik in den Westzonen und der Bundesrepublik von 1945 bis 1957.* Düsseldorf, 1993.

Südbeck, Thomas. *Motorisierung, Verkehrsentwicklung und Verkehrspolitik in der Bundesrepublik der 1950er Jahre: Umrisse der allgemeinen Entwicklung und zwei Beispiele: Hamburg und das Emsland.* Stuttgart, 1994.

Family, Women, Consumption

Moeller, Robert G. *Protecting Motherhood: Women and the Family in the Politics of Postwar West Germany.* Berkeley, 1993.

Niehuss, Merith. "Verhinderte Frauenarbeit? Arbeitsschutzmassnahmen für Frauen in den 1950er Jahren." In *Von der Arbeiterbewegung zum modernen Sozialstaat: Festschrift für Gerhard A. Ritter zum 65. Geburtstag,* edited by Jürgen Kocka et al. Munich, 1994.

Ruhl, Klaus-Jörg. *Verordnete Unterordnung: Berufstätige Frauen zwischen Wirtschaftswachstum und konservativer Ideologie in der Nachkriegszeit (1945–1963).* Munich, 1994.

Wildt, Michael. *Am Beginn der "Konsumgesellschaft": Mangelerfahrung, Lebenshaltung, Wohlstandshoffnung in Westdeutschland in den fünfziger Jahren.* Hamburg, 1994.

Youth and Education

Drescher, Joachim. *"Wer mehr kann, kommt voran": Berufliche Fort- und Weiterbildung in den 50er Jahren am Beispiel Hamburg: Ein Beitrag zur westdeutschen Gesellschaftsgeschichte.* Frankfurt, 1995.

Grotum, Thomas. *Die Halbstarken: Zur Geschichte einer Jugendkultur der 50er Jahre.* Frankfurt, 1994.

Füssl, Karl-Heinz. *Die Umerziehung der Deutschen: Jugend und Schule unter den Siegermächten des Zweiten Weltkriegs 1945–1955.* Paderborn, 1994.

Maase, Kaspar. *BRAVO Amerika: Erkundungen zur Jugendkultur in der Bundesrepublik in den fünfziger Jahren.* Hamburg, 1992.

Schlüter, Harald. "Zur Lage der Arbeiterjugend in Hamburg 1950–1960." In *Arbeiter im 20. Jahrhundert,* edited by Klaus Tenfelde. Stuttgart, 1991.

Mass Media

Fritze, Ralf. *Der Südwestfunk in der Ära Adenauer: Die Entwicklung der Rundfunkanstalt von 1949–1965 unter politischem Aspekt.* Baden-Baden, 1992.

Kreuzer, Helmut, and Christian W. Thomsen. *Geschichte des Fernsehens in der Bundesrepublik Deutschland.* 5 vols. Munich, 1993–94.

Kriegeskorte, Michael. *Werbung in Deutschland 1945–1965: Die Nachkriegszeit im Spiegel ihrer Anzeigen.* Cologne, 1992.

Schneider, Irmela. *Amerikanische Einstellung: Deutsches Fernsehen und US-amerikanische Produktionen.* Heidelberg, 1992.

Culture and Intellectual Trends

Foschepoth, Josef. *Im Schatten der Vergangenheit: Die Anfänge der Gesellschaft für Christlich-Jüdische Zusammenarbeit.* Göttingen, 1993.

Kiefer, Markus. *Auf der Suche nach nationaler Identität und Wegen zur deutschen Einheit: Die deutsche Frage in der überregionalen Tages- und Wochenpresse der Bundesrepublik 1949–1955.* Frankfurt, 1992.

Kittel, Manfred. *Die Legende von der "zweiten Schuld": Vergangenheitsbewältigung in der Geistesgeschichte der frühen Bundesrepublik.* Berlin, 1993.

Laak, Dirk van. *Gespräche in der Sicherheit des Schweigens: Carl Schmitt in der Geistesgeschichte der frühen Bundesrepublik.* Berlin, 1993.

Schildt, Axel. "Reise zurück aus der Zukunft: Beiträge von intellektuellen USA-Remigranten zur atlantischen Allianz, zum westdeutschen Amerikabild und zur 'Amerikanisierung' in den 50er Jahren." *Exilforschung: Ein internationales Jahrbuch* 9 (1991): 23–43.

Schornstheimer, Michael. *Die leuchtenden Augen der Frontsoldaten: Nationalsozialismus und Krieg in den Illustriertenromanen der fünfziger Jahre.* Berlin, 1995.

Stern, Frank. *Im Anfang war Auschwitz: Antisemitismus und Philosemitismus im deutschen Nachkrieg.* Gerlingen, 1991.

Contributors

Erica Carter is Research Fellow in German Studies at the University of Warwick, Coventry, England. She is the author of *How German Is She? Postwar West German Reconstruction and the Consuming Woman* (1997).

James M. Diehl is Professor of History at Indiana University, Bloomington, Indiana. He is the author of *Paramilitary Politics in Weimar Germany* (1977) and *The Thanks of the Fatherland: German Veterans after the Second World War* (1993).

Heide Fehrenbach is Associate Professor of History at Colgate University and author of *Cinema in Democratizing Germany: Reconstructing National Identity After Hitler* (1995). She is currently working on a social and cultural history of race and reproduction in American-occupied Germany.

Josef Foschepoth is Director of the Volkshochschule in Münster. He has written extensively on Adenauer's foreign policy and is the author of *Im Schatten der Vergangenheit: Die Anfänge der Gesellschaft für Christlich-Jüdische Zusammenarbeit* (1993).

Curt Garner is Wissenschaftlicher Mitarbeiter in the history department of the Technische Universität zu Berlin. He is completing a study of the reform of the German civil service in the early postwar period, and he has published on German political, social, and labor history in the period after 1945.

Constantin Goschler is Wissenschaftlicher Assistent in the Historical Institute of the Humboldt University in Berlin. He is the author of *Wiedergutmachung: Westdeutschland und die Verfolgten des Nationalsozialismus, 1945–1954* (1992), and is currently working on a biographical study of Rudolf Virchow.

Atina Grossmann teaches modern German and European history at the Cooper Union in New York City. She is the author of *Reforming Sex: The German Movement for Birth Control and Abortion Reform, 1920–1950* (1995) and numerous articles on the "new woman" and modernity in twentieth-century Germany. She is currently working on "Victims, Victors, and Survivors: War's End and Postwar Reconstruction, Berlin 1945–1949."

445

Robert G. Moeller teaches modern European and comparative European women's history at the University of California, Irvine. He is the author of *Protecting Motherhood: Women and the Family in the Politics of Postwar West Germany* (1993). He is currently studying how West Germans remembered National Socialism and the Second World War in the 1950s.

Uta G. Poiger is Assistant Professor at the University of Washington, Seattle, where she teaches German history, cultural history and European gender history. She is finishing her book, *American Culture, German Identities: Cold War Battles over Gender, Race, and Nation.*

Mark Roseman is Senior Lecturer in Modern History at Keele University, United Kingdom. He is the author of *Recasting the Ruhr, 1945–1958: Manpower, Economic Recover and Labour Relations* (1992), and he has published widely on the history of postwar Germany and on the social impact of National Socialism.

Axel Schildt teaches modern history in the Historical Seminar of Hamburg University. He has published widely on the social history of the postwar period, and his most recent book is *Moderne Zeiten: Freizeit, Massenmedien und "Zeitgeist" in der Bundesrepublik der 50er Jahre* (1995).

Rainer Schulze is Lecturer in Modern European History at the University of Essex, Colchester, England. He has published on the economic and social development of entrepreneurs and refugees in Western Germany after the Second World War. He is a coeditor of *Flüchtlinge und Vertriebene in der westdeutschen Nachkriegsgeschichte* (1987) and editor of *Unruhige Zeiten: Erlebnisberichte aus dem Landkreis Celle 1945–9* (1989).

Frank Stern is Professor of Modern German history at Tel-Aviv University and Ben-Gurion University of the Negev. He is the author of *The Whitewashing of the Yellow Badge: Antisemitism and Philosemitism in Postwar Germany* (1992) and is completing a project on "Jews in the Minds of Germans: The Ambiguous Shadow of the Past in German Film and Literature since 1945."

Arnold Sywottek is Professor of Modern History at Hamburg University. He has published widely on the history of Weimar and the Federal Republic, and with Axel Schildt is coeditor of *Modernisierung im Wiederaufbau: Die westdeutsche Gesellschaft der 50er Jahre* (1993).

Index

Abortion, 12, 33, 259–60; Nazi policy and, 41–42, 46–49; and rape, 44–46

Adenauer, Konrad, 3, 6, 19, 23, 78, 116, 229, 353; on Allied occupation, 79, 82; on anti-Semitism, 224, 226–27; conservatism of, 398; and constitutionality of equal rights legislation, 261–62; on declining birthrate, 122; on disabled veterans, 106; on dismantling programs, 84–86, 88; family policy of, 123, 264; foreign policy of, 15, 17–18; and former Nazi Party members in government ministries, 152–56; and hiring of former Reich civil servants, 139, 145, 148–52; and human rights, 276, 277. *See also* Adenauer era

Adenauer era, 323, 324, 328, 344, 355, 413, 415, 416, 427; characteristics of, 24; literature on, 5

Adviser on Jewish Affairs to the Military Governor, 236

Agricultural sector, 420–21

Ahrens, Hanns D., 84

Allied Control Council, 68, 87, 213

Allied High Commission, 145, 146, 182

Americanization, 23, 24, 27–28, 381–82, 418, 439

American Zone, 80; anti-Semitism in, 211; civil service and laws prohibiting sex discrimination, 178–79; concept of collective guilt in, 77; Jews in, 55, 202,

231–33; war-disability pensions in, 100–106. *See also* United States Military Government

Amtsblatt der Landesverwaltung Baden, 211

Anders, Georg, 165, 166, 167

Anderson, Benedict, 21

Anfang war Auschwitz, Im (Stern), 19

Ankermüller, Willi, 241–42

Anti-communism, 29, 70, 221–22, 332, 400, 437. *See also* Communism

Anti-Semitism, 228, 234, 256; in American Zone, 231–33; anti-communism and, 221–22; in Bavaria, 241–44, 245–49; bureaucratic, 210–14; and development of German democracy, 219; free speech and, 225–26; lack of historical acknowledgement of, 205–9; and Law of Restitution, 224; mass emigration from Eastern Europe and, 237–38; postwar, 19, 20, 202; preferential treatment of Jews and, 239–41. *See also* Displaced persons, Jewish; Jews

Apprenticeship programs, 431; and creation of national identity, 21–22; integration of, 302–3; moral education in, 316–17; political function of, 297–301; recruitment for, 291, 292–95; strategy of, 287–90, 317–20. *See also* Hostels, apprentice; Mining industry, Ruhr